The Palgrave Handbook of Digital and Public Humanities

Anne Schwan · Tara Thomson
Editors

The Palgrave Handbook of Digital and Public Humanities

Editors
Anne Schwan
School of Arts and Creative Industries
Edinburgh Napier University
Edinburgh, UK

Tara Thomson
School of Arts and Creative Industries
Edinburgh Napier University
Edinburgh, UK

ISBN 978-3-031-11885-2   ISBN 978-3-031-11886-9 (eBook)
https://doi.org/10.1007/978-3-031-11886-9

© The Editor(s) (if applicable) and The Author(s), under exclusive license to Springer Nature Switzerland AG 2022, corrected publication 2023
Chapter "The Role of Digital and Public Humanities in Confronting the Past: Survivors' of Ireland's Magdalene Laundries Truth Telling" is licensed under the terms of the Creative Commons Attribution 4.0 International License (http://creativecommons.org/licenses/by/4.0/). For further details see license information in the chapter.

This work is subject to copyright. All rights are solely and exclusively licensed by the Publisher, whether the whole or part of the material is concerned, specifically the rights of translation, reprinting, reuse of illustrations, recitation, broadcasting, reproduction on microfilms or in any other physical way, and transmission or information storage and retrieval, electronic adaptation, computer software, or by similar or dissimilar methodology now known or hereafter developed. The use of general descriptive names, registered names, trademarks, service marks, etc. in this publication does not imply, even in the absence of a specific statement, that such names are exempt from the relevant protective laws and regulations and therefore free for general use.

The publisher, the authors, and the editors are safe to assume that the advice and information in this book are believed to be true and accurate at the date of publication. Neither the publisher nor the authors or the editors give a warranty, expressed or implied, with respect to the material contained herein or for any errors or omissions that may have been made. The publisher remains neutral with regard to jurisdictional claims in published maps and institutional affiliations.

Cover illustration: imageBROKER/Alamy Stock Photo

This Palgrave Macmillan imprint is published by the registered company Springer Nature Switzerland AG
The registered company address is: Gewerbestrasse 11, 6330 Cham, Switzerland

ACKNOWLEDGMENTS

The editors would like to thank everyone at Palgrave for their support as we developed this volume for publication, particularly Lina Aboujieb, Emily Wood, Liviyaa Sree and Uma Vinesh. We also appreciate the feedback and support from anonymous reviewers. Amy King's editorial assistance and background research for the project have been invaluable, as was Callum Harper's editorial support during the final preparation of the manuscript. We thankfully acknowledge the financial support for editorial assistance from the School of Arts and Creative Industries at Edinburgh Napier University.

Contents

1 Introduction: Palgrave Handbook of Digital and Public Humanities 1
Anne Schwan and Tara Thomson

Part I Scholarship, Creative Practice and Engaging with "Publics"

2 Digital Humanities and Hybrid Education: Higher Education in, with and for the Public 11
Rikke Toft Nørgård, Susan Schreibman, and Marianne Ping Huang

3 Experiential Education as Public Humanities Practice 31
Ashley Bender and Gretchen Busl

4 Open-Data, Open-Source, Open-Knowledge: Towards Open-Access Research in Media Studies 49
Giulia Taurino

5 Adventures in Digital and Public Humanities: Co-Producing Trans History Through Creative Collaboration 69
Jason Barker, Kate Fisher, Jana Funke, Zed Gregory, Jen Grove, Rebecca Langlands, Ina Linge, Catherine McNamara, Ester McGeeney, Bon O'Hara, Jay Stewart, and Kazuki Yamada

6 SémantiQueer: Making Linked Data Work for Public History 89
Constance Crompton

7	Working with Incarcerated Communities: Representing Women in Prison on Screen Paul Gray and Anne Schwan	105

Part II   Making Memory, Making Community

8	Publics, Memory, Affect (or, Rethinking Publicness with Peter Watkins and Hannah Arendt) Marco de Waard	131
9	The Role of Digital and Public Humanities in Confronting the Past: Survivors' of Ireland's Magdalene Laundries Truth Telling Jennifer O'Mahoney	149
10	The Precarious Digital Micropublics of #MeToo: An Ethnographic Account of Facebook Public Groups and Pages Christina Riley	171
11	Literature, Technology, Society: A Digital Reconstruction of Cultural Conflicts in Chinua Achebe's *Things Fall Apart* Tunde Ope-Davies	195
12	Multilingual Handwritten Text Recognition (MultiHTR) or Reading Your Grandma's Old Letters in German, Russian, Serbian, and Ottoman Turkish with Artificial Intelligence Aleksej Tikhonov, Lesley Loew, Milanka Matić-Chalkitis, Martin Meindl, and Achim Rabus	215

Part III   Mobilizing the Archive

13	Open Pedagogy and the Archives: Engaging Students in Public Digital Humanities Trey Conatser	237
14	Practices and Challenges of Popularizing Digital Public Humanities During the COVID-19 Pandemic in Japan Nobuhiko Kikuchi	257
15	Breaking the "Class" Ceiling: The Challenges and Opportunities of Creating a Digital Archive of Edwardian Working-Class Book Inscriptions Lauren Alex O'Hagan	275

16 Learning Seneca: A Case Study on Digital Presentations
of North American Indigenous Languages   297
Francisco Delgado

Part IV   Digital Cultural Heritage

17 Acting on the Cultural Object: Digital Representation
of Children's Writing Cultures in Museum Collections   317
Lois Burke and Kathryn Simpson

18 A Data-Driven Approach to Public-Focused Digital
Narratives for Cultural Heritage   337
Nicole Basaraba, Jennifer Edmond, Owen Conlan,
and Peter Arnds

19 "People Inside": Creating Digital Community Projects
on the *YARN* Platform   357
Simon Popple and Jenna Ng

20 3D Modelling of Heritage Objects: Representation,
Engagement and Performativity of the Virtual Realm   377
Visa Immonen

21 Making Museum Global Impacts Visible: Advancing
Digital Public Humanities from Data Aggregation to Data
Intelligence   397
Natalia Grincheva

Part V   Engaging Space and Place

22 Maps, Music, and Culture: Representing Historical
Soundscapes Through Digital Mapping   423
Sara Belotti and Angela Fiore

23 Civic Interaction, Urban Memory, and the Istanbul
International Film Festival   441
Sarah Jilani

24 *Look at the Graves!*: Cemeteries as Guided Tourism
Destinations in Latvia   459
Solvita Burr, Anna Elizabete Griķe, and Karīna Krieviņa

Part VI   Public Discourse, Public Art and Activism

25 Public Historians, Social Media, and Hate Speech: The
French Case   481
Deborah Paci

26 The Public Artist as a Fringe Agent for Sustainability: Practices of Environmentalist Driven Art-Activism and Their Digital Perspectives 501
Diego Mantoan

Correction to: The Role of Digital and Public Humanities in Confronting the Past: Survivors' of Ireland's Magdalene Laundries Truth Telling C1
Jennifer O'Mahoney

Index 523

Notes on Contributors

Arnds Peter is an Associate Professor, Fellow, and Director of the MPhil in Comparative Literature at Trinity College Dublin, Ireland. He specializes in the fields of Comparative Literature, post-1945 German Literature, Literary Translation, and Environmental Humanities. He is the author of nine books and a Member of PEN International. In 2018, Peter was also elected into Academia Europaea, the pan-European Academy of Humanities, Letters, Law, and Sciences.

Barker Jason is a writer and director. In addition to *Adventures in Time and Gender* (2020), he is also a writer and director of the feature documentaries *A Deal with the Universe* and the *Field Guide to the Pregnant Men of the UK*.

Basaraba Nicole is a Lecturer in Media and Communications at Coventry University, UK. Her research focuses on evaluating and finding best practices for creating location-based digital narratives in non-fiction genres. She examines how participatory digital culture impacts narrative practices in cultural heritage, dark tourism, and public history contexts, particularly within creative and digital place-making. Basaraba completed postdoctoral research at the University of Luxembourg and Maastricht University in the Netherlands. She has a Ph.D. in digital media narratives and digital humanities from Trinity College Dublin, Ireland.

Belotti Sara (D.Phil. in Geography 2013 University of Naples "L'Orientale" and University of Bergamo, Italy) is Visiting Professor of Geography of Cooperation and Sustainable Development at the University of Bergamo. Between 2018 and 2020 she was a Research Fellow at the University of Modena-Reggio Emilia, with a project about the study of the ancient maps preserved at the Biblioteca Estense through digital humanities tools. She taught Geographical Information Systems at the University of Milan and Cultural Geography at the University of Modena. Her research has focused on territorial analysis connected with cultural heritage, environment preservation, and touristic promotion. This has included the collection of data through fieldwork and the implementation of participatory processes, and a reflection on the cartographic representation of phenomena through GIS.

Bender Ashley, Ph.D. is an Assistant Professor of English at Texas Woman's University, where she also serves as BA Program Coordinator for the English program. In collaboration with her co-author Dr. Gretchen Busl, she co-led "Building Global Perspectives in the Humanities," a National Endowment for the Humanities-funded project designed to enhance the TWU curriculum by training teachers to develop global perspectives courses with experiential education components. Her essays have appeared in *Eighteenth-Century Life*, *Restoration: Studies in Eighteenth-Century Literary Culture, 1660–1700*, and *Papers on Language and Literature*, and a forthcoming essay on professional development for undergraduate English majors will be published in the *ADE Bulletin*.

Burke Lois, Ph.D. is a Postdoctoral Researcher in the Digital Literature Consortium at Tilburg University in the Netherlands. She has interests in collections research, digital methods, the history of childhood, and nineteenth-century women writers. She is an editor of the bilingual journal *Jeunesse: Young People, Texts, Cultures*, and is an Early Career Member of the Royal Historical Society. Her first monograph, *Girlhood and Manuscript Culture in the Nineteenth Century*, is forthcoming with Edinburgh University Press.

Burr Solvita is a Senior Researcher at the Latvian Language Institute of the University of Latvia and a Visiting Lecturer at the University of Washington (Seattle, USA). Her research includes comprehensive studies of linguistic, semiotic, and cultural landscapes in terms of multilingualism, language policy, language management, multimodality, and language pedagogy. In 2020, she published a methodology book and a textbook (both in Latvian), both concerning how to include public texts in the language-learning process.

Busl Gretchen, Ph.D. is an Associate Professor and Graduate Program Coordinator for the MA in English and Ph.D. in Rhetoric at Texas Woman's University. She is the co-editor of *Antiheroines of Contemporary Media: Saints, Sinners, and Survivors* and has published in *Modern Language Review*, *Critique: Studies in Contemporary Fiction* and *English Studies*. After co-directing the "Building Global Perspectives in the Humanities" project funded by the National Endowment for the Humanities with her co-author Dr. Ashley Bender, she is currently co-directing a second NEH grant to support the "Quakertown Stories" project. She is a founding co-host of the International Society for the Study of Narrative's Narrative for Social Justice podcast.

Conatser Trey is an interim Director of the Center for the Enhancement of Learning and Teaching at the University of Kentucky, where he collaborates across disciplines and academic units to foster innovative, inclusive, and scholarly approaches to education. He has taught courses in digital humanities, writing, and college-level teaching, and published in venues such as *College Teaching* and the *Journal of Digital Humanities*. His research examines the value and uses of code and programming languages for humanities education with particular attention to markup in the writing class and student-driven text encoding projects in the archive.

Conlan Owen is a Professor in Computer Science at Trinity College Dublin, Ireland. He is the Director of Postgraduate Teaching and Learning (SCSS) and Co-director of the Trinity Centre for Digital Humanities. His research involves promoting new creative approaches to personalization including the multi-model, metadata-driven, cross-site personalization, four-phase for explorative personalization, and supporting metacognition and self-regulation approaches. He is one of the seven founding Principal Investigators of ADAPT, a Centre of Excellence for Digital Content Technology where he leads a multi-disciplinary team of researchers under the Personalizing the User Experience theme.

Crompton Constance is a Canada Research Chair in Digital Humanities at the University of Ottawa. She directs the Humanities Data Lab, and is a member of the Lesbian and Gay Liberation in Canada, Linked Infrastructure for Networked Cultural Scholarship, and Implementing New Knowledge Environments Partnership research teams. She serves as VP English of the Canadian Society for Digital Humanities/*Société canadienne des humanités numériques* and as an associate director of the Digital Humanities Summer Institute, North America's largest digital humanities training institute. She is the co-editor of *Doing Digital Humanities* and *Doing More Digital Humanities* (Routledge 2016, 2019). She lives and works on unceded Algonquin land.

de Waard Marco is a Senior Lecturer in literary studies and cultural analysis at Amsterdam University College (AUC) and a Research Fellow at the Amsterdam School for Cultural Analysis (ASCA). He teaches and writes at the intersection of cultural analysis, literary and film studies, and public sphere theory, in which he combines a special interest in questions of cultural memory and political imagination with a focus on contemporary cinema. Recent publications include an essay titled "Peter Greenaway's Artist-Entrepreneurs" in *Screening the Art World*, edited by Temenuga Trifonova (Amsterdam University Press, 2022).

Delgado Francisco is an Assistant Professor of English at Borough of Manhattan Community College (CUNY), where he teaches first-year writing courses and courses about multiethnic American literatures. In 2021, his proposal to add a class about Native American/Indigenous Literatures to the course catalogue was approved. His scholarship can be found, or is forthcoming, in *Teaching English in the Two-Year College*, *Transmotion*, and *Memory Studies*. He is also a published prose writer and poet with work in *Lost Balloon*, *JMWW*, and *Queensbound*, and elsewhere.

Edmond Jennifer is an Associate Professor of Digital Humanities at Trinity College Dublin, Ireland. She is also the co-director of the Trinity Centre for Digital Humanities, Director of the M.Phil. in Digital Humanities and Culture, and President of the Board of Directors of DARIAH-EU (the pan-European infrastructure for arts and humanities scholars). She holds a Ph.D. in Germanic Languages and Literatures from Yale University and applies her training as a scholar of language, narrative, and culture to the study and promotion of advanced methods.

Fiore Angela received her Ph.D. from the University of Fribourg, Switzerland, in 2015. She is now a researcher in Musicology and history of Music at the University of Messina. Her research fields include Neapolitan sacred music; the musical production of the House of Este-Modena; and historical soundscape of early modern cities. For her research she received grants from the Fondazione Pergolesi Spontini Jesi in 2007, Swiss National Science Found in 2011 and Pôle de recherche-University of Fribourg in 2014; Jacques-Handschin Prize 2016; and the American Musicological Society in 2017. She also has a diploma in violin and specialized in the baroque violin repertoire.

Fisher Kate is a Professor of Social and Cultural History at the University of Exeter. Books include *Birth Control, Sex and Marriage in Britain, 1918–60* (Oxford University Press, 2006), *Sex Before the Sexual Revolution*, with Simon Szreter (Cambridge University Press, 2010), and *Sex, Knowledge and Receptions of the Past*, co-edited with Rebecca Langlands (Oxford University Press, 2015). With Rebecca Langlands she co-directs the Sex and History Project which seeks to use historical objects and material to enhance sexuality education in a variety of settings. http://blogs.exeter.ac.uk/sexandhistory/.

Funke Jana is an Associate Professor of English and Sexuality Studies in the Department of English and Film at the University of Exeter. Books include *Sex, Gender and Time in Fiction and Culture* (2011, co-edited with Ben Davies), *The World and Other Unpublished Works by Radclyffe Hall* (2016), *Sculpture, Sexuality and History: Encounters in Literature, Culture and the Arts* (2018, co-edited with Jen Grove), *Sexological Modernism: Queer Feminism and Sexual Science* (forthcoming 2022), the first critical edition of Radclyffe Hall's *The Well of Loneliness* (forthcoming 2023, co-edited with Hannah Roche), and *Sexperts: A History of Sexology* (forthcoming 2024).

Gray Paul is an Associate Professor in film and Head of Subject for Screen & Performing Arts at Edinburgh Napier University. He has been involved in the visual arts and higher education for over twenty years. Gray is a writer, director, and producer, whose film practice informs his research, which focusses on the delineation between fiction and non-fiction narratives within film-making; film as a means of storytelling and introspective re-enactment; and the significance of anonymity in storytelling, when collaborating with vulnerable individuals and communities.

Gregory Zed is the Creative director of *They/Them Studio*. Their design work includes Duckie; Museum of Transology; Gendered Intelligence; Lady Malcolm's Servants' Ball, as well as Adventures in Time and Gender. See, https://www.theythemstudio.com/work.

Griķe Anna Elizabete is a Scientific Assistant at the Latvian Language Institute of the University of Latvia and a Lecturer at the University of Latvia and at the Art Academy of Latvia. With expertise in anthropology and folkloristics, her academic interests cover ethnology (traditions, rituals, Catholicism, and cultural encounters) and socio-onomastics (anthroponomy and toponymy).

Grincheva Natalia, Ph.D. is a Program Leader in Arts Management at LASALLE College of the Arts and an Honorary Senior Research Fellow in the Digital Studio at the University of Melbourne. She is an internationally recognized expert in innovative forms and global trends in contemporary museology, digital diplomacy, and international cultural relations. Her most recent publications are two monographs: *Museum Diplomacy in the Digital Age* (Routledge, 2020) and *Global Trends in Museum Diplomacy* (Routledge, 2019). Currently, she is working on a new co-authored monograph, *Geopolitics of Digital Heritage*, forthcoming in 2023 with Cambridge University Press. Dr. Grincheva's professional engagements include her dedicated work for the International Fund for Cultural Diversity at UNESCO (2011), International Federation of Coalitions for Cultural Diversity (2011–15) as well as service for the international Cultural Research Network (CRN) (2018–20).

Grove Jen is Programme Manager in Public Engagement at UKRI and Honorary Research Fellow at the University of Exeter. She is a co-founder of Sex & History http://blogs.exeter.ac.uk/sexandhistory/. Her academic publications include *Sculpture, Sexuality and History: Encounters in Literature, Culture and the Arts* (co-edited with Jana Funke, Palgrave 2018).

Huang Marianne Ping is an Associate Professor in the School for Communication and Culture, Aarhus University, Denmark. She works with cultural creative collaborations, creative industry partnerships, and digital cultures for CCSI ecosystems regionally and in Europe. She coordinates the Nordic Hub with DARIAH (ESFRI ERIC Digital Research Infrastructure for Arts and Humanities), co-heads DARIAH Research and Education Liaison and collaborates on the DARIAH Cultural Innovation Forum 2022. Her research is in open innovation, artistic research, and citizen inclusion in green, digital transition. Latest research and innovation projects are "City of Sounds, building creative capacity" and DiMPAH (Digital Methods Platform for Arts and Humanities).

Immonen Visa is an Associate Professor of Medieval Archaeology at the University of Bergen. He worked as a Professor of Archaeology at the University of Turku during 2018–22, and as an Assistant Professor of Cultural Heritage Studies at the University of Helsinki during 2016–17. Immonen was a postdoctoral fellow at the Getty Research Institute during 2015–16. Immonen's research focuses on medieval material culture, but he is also interested in heritage issues such as the use of digital media in heritage work. Presently he is directing a research project which explores the 3D digitalization of archaeological finds.

Jilani Sarah, Ph.D. is a Lecturer in English at City, University of London, teaching Anglophone postcolonial literatures and world film. Her first monograph, on subjectivity and decolonization in the post-independence film and novel, is forthcoming from Edinburgh University Press in 2023. She completed her Ph.D. at the University of Cambridge in 2021 and was selected as a BBC/AHRC New Generation Thinker the same year. She is a freelance culture journalist who regularly contributes to contemporary art, books, and world cinema to *The Economist, The Times Literary Supplement, BBC Radio 3,* and *ArtReview*. She was born and raised in Istanbul.

Kikuchi Nobuhiko is a Project Associate Professor at Kansai University. He earned his doctorate in European History from Kyoto University and published the book "19世紀スペインにおける連邦主義と歴史認識" (*Federalism and Historical Consciousness in 19th Century Spain*) in 2022. His research on digital public history in Japan has been published in *Journal of Historical Studies* (2021), *Japan Society of Information and Knowledge Journal* (2021), *Journal of the Japan Society for Digital Archive* (2021), and so on.

Krieviņa Karīna is a Ph.D. student in linguistics and a Researcher at the Kurzeme Humanities Institute of the University of Liepaja. Her research area and the topic of her doctoral dissertation are linguistic landscapes in cemeteries and the culture related to them.

Langlands Rebecca is a Professor of Classics at the University of Exeter. Books include *Sexual Morality in Ancient Rome* (Cambridge University Press, 2006), *Sex, Knowledge and Receptions of the Past* (edited with Kate Fisher, Oxford University Press, 2015), *Exemplary Ethics in Ancient Rome* (Cambridge University Press, 2018), and *Literature and Culture in the Roman Empire, 96–235: Cross-Cultural Interactions* (edited with Alice König and James Uden, 2020). With Kate Fisher, she co-directs the Sex and History Project which seeks to use historical objects and material to enhance sexuality education in a variety of settings. http://blogs.exeter.ac.uk/sexandhistory/.

Linge Ina is a Lecturer in German in the Department of Modern Languages and Cultures at the University of Exeter. She is the author of *Queer Livability: German Sexual Sciences and Life Writing* (University of Michigan Press, forthcoming 2023) and co-editor of a special issue on Sex and Nature for *Environmental Humanities* (forthcoming 2022).

Loew Lesley is a researcher working for the MultiHTR project. Her master's degree in Russian and English Literature and Translation at the University of Basel and her competencies in Russian, Yiddish, and different German scripts are valuable assets for the project. Loew is responsible for the development and training of specific models in Russian, as well as the preparation of manuscripts of German scripts for training. Along with other members, she is also in charge of the non-scientific communication aiming at the intended audience of the MultiHTR project.

Mantoan Diego is a tenure-track Assistant Professor in contemporary art history at the University of Palermo with a Ph.D. from FU Berlin. He is a founder of the Venice Centre for Digital and Public Humanities, Advisory Editor of Vernon Press Academic, and Associate Editor of *magazén|International Journal for Digital and Public Humanities*. His book *The Road to Parnassus* for Vernon Press (2015) was long-listed for the Berger Prize 2016. He recently edited *Paolozzi & Wittgenstein* for Palgrave (2019). He was a visiting fellow at NYU on public art and delivered speeches on related topics at Bibliotheca Hertziana, UCL London, Universität Bern, VU Amsterdam, UA Madrid, Sotheby's Institute of Art, Galerie Belvedere Vienna, and MAAT Lisboa.

Matić-Chalkitis Milanka is currently working as a researcher on the MultiHTR project, focusing on HTR model training for Ottoman-Turkish manuscripts. Together with other project members, she manages crowdsourcing on the social media channels of the project. Matić-Chalkitis studied Slavic Studies and Islamic Studies, and Economics at the Albert Ludwig University of Freiburg.

McGeeney Ester is a youth worker and researcher who specializes in conducting youth-centered research on relationships and sexualities and in using research to create innovative training and education materials. She is the author of *Great Relationships and Sex Education* (with Alice Hoyle, Routledge, 2019).

McNamara Catherine is Head of GSA (Guildford School of Acting) at the University of Surrey. She is a co-founder of Gendered Intelligence. She is a member of the Board for the New Theatre Royal, Portsmouth. Recent publications include "The TransActing project: why trans, non-binary and gender diverse people value spaces without cisgender people when engaging in creative practices," in *The Applied Theatre Reader (2nd Edition)* (Routledge, 2020) and "A Complex Matrix of Identities: Working Intergenerationally with LGBTQ people," in *Minding the Knowledge Gap* (Routledge, 2018).

Meindl Martin is a master's student of Slavic Philology at the Department for Slavic Studies at the University of Freiburg. Since 2018 he has been working at the department as a student assistant and has been participating in several of the department's research projects. Meindl has played a vital role in the creation of several Transkribus HTR models for Russian, Church Slavonic, German, and other languages.

Ng Jenna is a Senior Lecturer in Film and Interactive Media at the University of York, UK. She researches on digital culture, particularly in convergence with media, computational and visual culture. She is the editor of *Understanding Machinima: Essays on Filmmaking in Virtual Worlds* (Bloomsbury, 2013), and the author of *The Post-Screen Through Virtual Reality, Holograms and Light Projections: Where Screen Boundaries Lie* (Amsterdam University Press, 2021). She was a Co-Investigator on the *Pararchive* and *YARN* projects.

Nørgård Rikke Toft is an Associate Professor at the Danish School of Education, Aarhus University. She is on the steering committee of the Center for Higher Education Futures (CHEF), Aarhus University, elected board member of the international Philosophy and Theory of Higher Education Society (PaTHES), elected board member of the national Danish Network for Educational Development in Higher Education (DUN), and director of the Playful University Platform project (PUP). Nørgård researches the intersections of hybrid higher education, new formats for teaching and learning, and technology and design with a focus on the Arts and Humanities. Recent projects include STAK (Students' Academic Digital Competencies) and VASE (Teaching for Values in Design in Higher Education).

O'Hagan Lauren Alex, Ph.D. is a Postdoctoral Researcher in the School of Humanities, Education, and Social Science at Örebro University, Sweden, where she works on the project "Selling Healthy Lifestyles with Science: A Transhistorical Study of Food and Drink Marketing in the UK and Sweden (1880–1940)." She specializes in performances of social class and power mediation in the late nineteenth and early twentieth century through visual and material artifacts, using a methodology that blends social semiotic analysis with archival research. She has published extensively on the sociocultural forms and functions of book inscriptions, food advertisements, postcards, and music memorabilia.

O'Hara Bon is a teacher and youth worker, with expertise in supporting transgender and gender non-conforming young people in youth groups, via in person and online support, trips, overnight visits, and week-long camps. They are a founding member of the Transcend festival responsible for facilitating community building, conflict resolution and safeguarding. They are also a qualified Thrive practitioner, specializing in trauma recovery and healing.

O'Mahoney Jennifer, Ph.D. is a Lecturer in Psychology and a Chartered Member of the Psychological Society of Ireland. She is Co-Director of the Crime and Justice Research Group and a Senior Researcher at INSYTE (The Centre for INformation SYstems and TEchno-culture) at Waterford Institute of Technology. Her research focuses on how victimology and trauma are remembered and narrated; the relationship between memory and cultural heritage in digital humanities and activism and social change. She is the primary investigator of the Waterford Memories Project, which examines historical institutional abuse in Ireland.

Ope-Davies Tunde (Opeibi) is a Professor of English, Digital Discourse, and Digital Cultures at the University of Lagos, Nigeria. He has won a number of visiting positions such as the Commonwealth Professional Fellowship, University of Westminster, London; Alexander von Humboldt's Georg Forster Fellowship at Chemnitz University of Technology, Germany; DAAD Scholarship for Digital Humanities Institute, University of Leipzig, and Visiting Fellowship at the Institute for Advanced Studies in the Humanities, University of Edinburgh, United Kingdom. He is the convener of the Lagos Summer School in Digital Humanities (LSSDH); founder and Director, *Centre for Digital Humanities, University of Lagos (CEDHUL)*, and President, Digital Humanities Association of Nigeria (DHAN).

Paci Deborah, Ph.D. is currently a Research Fellow at the University of Corsica and an adjunct professor at the University of Bologna and the University of Modena and Reggio Emilia. She has previously held fellowships and taught at the University of Venice, the École française de Rome, the National and Kapodistrian University of Athens, and the University of Malta. Her main research interests focus on Public and Digital History, anti-Semitism, Island studies, Nationalism studies, Mediterranean and Baltic studies. She is also co-founder and director of *Diacronie. Studi di storia contemporanea* (http://www.diacronie.it) and co-director of *Public History Weekly* (https://public-history-weekly.degruyter.com/). See her profile on: https://www.sissco.it/soci/paci-deborah/.

Popple Simon is Senior Lecturer in Photography and Digital Culture in the School of Media and Communication at the University of Leeds. He has become increasingly focused on the co-production of digital tools which allow communities and organizations to develop independent access to cultural and historical resources as a means of communication, storytelling, campaigning, and social advocacy. His research is concerned with the relationships between individuals, communities, institutions, and concepts of democratic exchange, open space, and the digital sphere. He has worked with a range of community and arts organizations, charities, and SEND education providers, national institutions including the BBC, BFI, and the Science Museum Group and has led several AHRC/EPSRC funded projects in this area.

Rabus Achim holds the Chair of Slavic Linguistics at the Slavic Department of Freiburg University, Germany. Since 2018, he has been the president of the Special Commission on the Computer-Supported Processing of Mediæval Slavonic Manuscripts and Early Printed Books to the International Committee of Slavists. Rabus is the Principal Investigator of several national and international projects devoted to Handwritten Text Recognition funded by, among others, German Research Foundation and Humboldt Foundation, and the creator of a number of Handwritten Text Recognition models for Cyrillic and other scripts publicly available via the Transkribus platform.

Riley Christina is currently a Center for Humanities Research Fellow, Graduate Lecturer, and Cultural Studies doctoral candidate (ABD) at George Mason University. Her research focuses on the affective dynamics of group collectivity and ensuant sociopolitical relays unfolding both on/offline. Her interdisciplinary project incorporates insights and methods from Women's and Gender Studies, New Media and Network Studies, as well as Social Movement Studies. She has published in *The Second International Handbook of Internet Research*, *How to Do Things with Affect*, *Innovations and Implications in Persuasive Narrative*, and the *New Americanist* journal. She has a background in non-profit development, community-based education, and digital archival development.

Schreibman Susan is a Professor of Digital Arts and Culture at Maastricht University, The Netherlands. She works at the intersections of computationally based teaching and research in the interplay of the digital archive, cultural innovation, and participatory engagement design, processes, and projects. She is the series editor of the Topics in the Digital Humanities (University of Illinois Press). Her current research projects include: PURE3D, Contested Memories: The Battle of Mount Street Bridge, and #dariahTeach.

Schwan Anne is a Professor in literary and cultural studies and Director of the Centre for Arts, Media, and Culture at Edinburgh Napier University. Her research focuses on crime and imprisonment, with publications including *Convict Voices: Women, Class, and Writing about Prison in Nineteenth-Century England* (2014). She has worked with Scottish prisons for over ten years and has been involved in other outreach activities, such as an Arts and Humanities Research Council grant for impact and engagement (with Aston University) to raise awareness of First World War internment camps. She is the co-founder of the Scottish Universities-Prisons Network.

Simpson Kathryn, Ph.D. is a Lecturer in Digital Humanities in the Digital Humanities Institute at the University of Sheffield. Her research explores the use of digital tools to renegotiate the nineteenth-century archive, with a particular focus on counter-hegemonic readings of European narratives of travel across central and southern Africa and India. She also works on methods of digital creation and curation and its uses in the GLAM sector. She is a Trustee of the David Livingstone Birthplace Trust and an Associate Project Scholar and UK Outreach Director for Livingstone Online. Her current research—*Boundaries of gender: "petticoat governments" and secondary voices in nineteenth-century European travels in Africa*—mines digital content to foreground the many women, both European and African, who assisted and enabled David Livingstone (1813–73) in his journeys in Africa.

Stewart Jay is the CEO and co-founder of Gendered Intelligence (GI). He has published widely in the field of Trans Studies, focusing on transgender knowledge in popular culture, transforming museum and cultural spaces, and experiences of trans healthcare. He has published in *Trans Britain: Our*

Journey from the Shadows (edited by Christine Burns, Penguin, 2018) and *Genderqueer and Non-Binary Genders* (edited by Christina Richards and Meg-John Barker, Palgrave, 2017). His community-based arts and heritage work includes the Hacking into the Science Museum project, and the GI's Anatomy life-drawing workshops. He sits on the National Transgender Advisory Board for trans prisoners with the Ministry of Justice, is a founding member of the Trans Learning Partnership and gave oral evidence to the Trans Inquiry for the Women's and Equalities Select Committee.

Taurino Giulia is a Postdoctoral Fellow at The Institute for Experiential AI (Roux Institute—Khoury College of Computer Sciences, Northeastern University). Her research focuses on the forms of content organization on online platforms, digital archives and algorithmic technologies, AI, and the arts. Past and present affiliations include Brown University Virtual Humanities Lab, metaLAB (at) Harvard, MIT Data + Feminism Lab, NULab for Texts, Maps, and Networks. Giulia holds a Ph.D. in Media Studies and Visual Arts from the University of Bologna and University of Montreal. She served as Director of Research and Innovation at AI Impact Alliance, where she worked on AI ethics and sustainable development goals.

Thomson Tara is a Lecturer in cultural studies at Edinburgh Napier University. Her research in the digital humanities focuses on literary and geospatial data, data visualization, and digital engagement with cultural heritage. She was a Research Fellow on LitLong: Edinburgh (litlong.org), a large-scale text-mining and geolocation project that forged partnerships with cultural sector organizations including the UNESCO City of Literature Trust and the Edinburgh International Book Festival. She is a project partner on the Edinburgh Literature House with the UNESCO City of Literature Trust, researching and developing literary data, digital experiences, and engagement for Edinburgh's emerging new Literary Quarter.

Tikhonov Aleksej is a former member of MultiHTR and now a postdoc in a joint linguistics project between Humboldt University Berlin and the University of Oxford on "The History of Pronominal Subjects in the Languages of Northern Europe." Tikhonov defended his Ph.D. on semiautomated linguistic author and scribe attribution of historic Czech manuscripts in 2021. In MultiHTR, he was mainly responsible for the development and training of the HTR model for Russian, the acquisition of users, and the science communication of the project.

Yamada Kazuki is a Ph.D. candidate at the University of Exeter and the University of Queensland researching the history of later life sexuality in the mid-nineteenth to late-twentieth century Western sciences. He is also Technical Officer at the World Health Organization, supporting the implementation of the United Nations Decade of Healthy Ageing (2021–2030) through the development of its knowledge exchange platform.

List of Figures

Fig. 4.1	Data visualization of a crime TV series dataset extracted from Wikidata (distant reading with close-up). Made with Wikidata Visualization—Toolforge	57
Fig. 4.2	Data visualization of a crime TV series dataset extracted from Wikidata (distant reading). Made with Wikidata Timeline—Toolforge	58
Fig. 4.3	Data visualization of a crime TV series dataset extracted from Wikidata (sankey layout, distant reading with close-up). Made with Wikidata Metaphactory Demo	59
Fig. 6.1	A representation of the Thomson sibling relationship in RDF	91
Fig. 6.2	A page from volume 1 of Lesbian and Gay Liberation in Canada	94
Fig. 6.3	A network graph of connected entities from the lglc.ca database	96
Fig. 9.1	The College Street Campus of the South East Technological University	154
Fig. 9.2	The landing page and projects page of The Waterford Memories Project website	158
Fig. 9.3	Sample screenshot from the *Exploring Waterford's Magdalene Heritage: An activity and resource pack*	162
Fig. 11.1	*AntConc* frame showing the concordance lines highlighting Okonkwo as keyword in different contexts	203
Fig. 11.2	*AntConc* frame showing the concordance lines highlighting *Mr. Smith* as keyword in different contexts	204
Fig. 11.3	*SketchEngine* frame showing keywords and key terms on Okonkwo extracted from the web-based corpus	205
Fig. 11.4	Extracted keywords and key terms from web-based corpus on the text using *SketchEngine*	206
Fig. 12.1	Comparison of two pages from the VS using the "Compare Text Versions" function	222
Fig. 12.2	Manuscript written in Cyrillic and automatic transcription in Latin	226

xxiv LIST OF FIGURES

Fig. 12.3	OT manuscript (RTL) and the corresponding Latin transcription (LTR)	228
Fig. 13.1	Detail of a digital facsimile of a letter from the Frontier Nursing Service records, 1789–1985, courtesy of the University of Kentucky Libraries Special Collections Research Center	249
Fig. 14.1	Corona Archive @ Kansai University's homepage	259
Fig. 14.2	Tag cloud for the Corona Archive @ Kansai University. The largest tag 'コロナ対策 (measures against COVID-19)' indicates the most frequently used	266
Fig. 14.3	Co-occurrence network generated by the answers to the question "What do you think you should leave someone who might investigate the COVID-19 pandemic 30 years later?"	269
Fig. 15.1	A sample inscription for the Edwardian working-class digital archive (Image taken by O'Hagan [2015] and reproduced with the permission of Bookbarn International)	280
Fig. 15.2	A sample post from the "Prize Books and Politics" Instagram exhibition	290
Fig. 18.1	Seven-phase theoretical framework for interactive digital narrative (IDN) creation	345
Fig. 19.1	Discussions with the Isle of Bute Rothesay library community group	361
Fig. 19.2	Collage of post-it notes, workshops and sketches of discussion, planning and reiteration	361
Fig. 19.3	YARN's landing page	365
Fig. 20.1	Photogrammetry can be done with very simple equipment—here with two digital cameras on a tripod (*Photo* Annukka Debenjak-Ijäs)	382
Fig. 20.2	The Turku Goes 1812 virtual model produced by the Turku Museum Centre and launched in 2019 was highly popular (*Photo* Tanja Ratilainen)	389
Fig. 21.1	Melbourne Engagement Power layer	404
Fig. 21.2	Online Audience Engagement layer	409
Fig. 21.3	Local Engagement Power layer	412
Fig. 22.1	Este WebGis: comparison of the historical map of Domenico Vandelli, the nineteenth-century map of Modena, and the satellite image of modern Modena (Authors' elaboration. Use of historical maps by the courtesy of Ministero della Cultura—Gallerie Estensi, Biblioteca Estense Universitaria)	431
Fig. 22.2	Este WebGis: Teatro Fontanelli (Authors' elaboration. Use of historical maps by the courtesy of Ministero della Cultura—Gallerie Estensi, Biblioteca Estense Universitaria)	432
Fig. 22.3	Institution record: Teatro Fontanelli (Authors' elaboration)	433
Fig. 22.4	Este WebGis Screenshot: Events (Authors' elaboration. Use of historical maps by the courtesy of Ministero della Cultura—Gallerie Estensi, Biblioteca Estense Universitaria)	434
Fig. 26.1	Tega Brain, *Coin Operated Wetland* (2012), courtesy of the artist	507

Fig. 26.2	Tiziana Pers, *Vucciria* (2018), photograph by Isabelle Pers, courtesy of the artist	509
Fig. 26.3	Giovanni Scotti, Innobiliare Sud-Ovest (2020), courtesy of the artist	512
Fig. 26.4	Mary Miss, Stream/Lines (2015–2016), courtesy of the artist	514

List of Tables

Table 14.1	Examples of COVID-19 memories	265
Table 14.2	Classification results no. 1	270
Table 14.3	Classification results no. 2	270
Table 15.1	A sample entry for the Edwardian working-class digital archive	281

CHAPTER 1

Introduction: Palgrave Handbook of Digital and Public Humanities

Anne Schwan and Tara Thomson

This collection brings together some of the most recent international scholarship and developments in the interdisciplinary areas of digital and public humanities. Alongside a critical exploration of the production, distribution and scholarship of culture in relation to digital media and technologies, the collection examines the possibilities and challenges of publicly engaged scholarship in the digital humanities and beyond. Working with a broad definition of "public humanities," each chapter interrogates the multifaceted interface of arts and humanities scholarship and engagement with wider "publics" beyond academia, from literary and cultural heritage to creative arts. The volume explores key concepts, theories, practices and debates within both the digital and public humanities while also assessing how these two areas are increasingly intertwined.

Underlining the multiplicity of "publics," each of them contingent and "constitutive of a social imaginary" (Warner 2005, 12), key questions of access, ownership, authorship and representation run through the collection as a whole and link the individual sections and contributions. One of the volume's aims is to offer wide geographical range, and to present

A. Schwan · T. Thomson (✉)
School of Arts and Creative Industries,
Edinburgh Napier University, Edinburgh, UK
e-mail: T.Thomson2@napier.ac.uk

A. Schwan
e-mail: A.Schwan@napier.ac.uk

© The Author(s), under exclusive license to Springer Nature
Switzerland AG 2022
A. Schwan and T. Thomson (eds.), *The Palgrave Handbook of Digital and Public Humanities*, https://doi.org/10.1007/978-3-031-11886-9_1

scholarship and practice that engages with a multiplicity of historically underrepresented "publics"—in Nancy Fraser's (1992, 123) terms "alternative" or "*subaltern counterpublics*"—including LGBTQ+ communities (see chapters by Crompton, and Barker et al.), ethnic and linguistic minorities (see chapters by Delgado, and Tikhonov et al.), working-class communities (see O'Hagan's chapter), the incarcerated (see Gray and Schwan's chapter) or those affected by hate speech, personal or collective trauma (see chapters by Paci, O'Mahoney, and Riley).

Arts and humanities researchers today face growing expectations from higher education institutions and funding bodies to produce socially relevant work that demonstrates wider engagement, value for money and—in the UK academy—measurable "impact" in social, cultural or economic terms. While it is not the collection's primary objective to make a case for the "value" of arts and humanities or to conceive digital and public humanities as mere vehicles for achieving such recognition—we take the arts and humanities' right to exist for granted—it is essential to stay alert to such pressures for justification and to acknowledge that these concerns over value are inextricably linked to the emergence of "public humanities" as a concept (see Schroeder 2021).[1] At the heart of this volume lies the conviction that these demands can and must be addressed both critically and creatively; at their best, outward-facing scholarship and practice at the intersection of digital and public humanities have the potential to generate new insights that can invigorate both academic and public discourse and mobilize social justice agendas in the digital age, producing social, cultural and economic value almost inadvertently in the process. Conversely, unreflective practice and outreach activities risk reaffirming the often unequal power dynamics at play when so-called experts interact with publics. The collection seeks to assist scholars in arts and humanities, and practitioners in cultural institutions, in navigating these challenges with integrity while equipping them with new tools to contribute to critical agendas in provocative, ethical and meaningful ways.

1.1 Doing Digital and Public Humanities: Key Concepts and Debates

As Susan Smulyan (2021, 1) emphasizes in her Introduction to *Doing Public Humanities*, "[p]ublic humanities happens in collaboration," both within educational institutions and between universities and other communities. Similarly, in their Introduction to the most recent volume of *Debates in the Digital Humanities*, Matthew K. Gold and Lauren F. Klein (2019, n.p.) note, "digital humanities has always seen itself as a field that engages the world beyond the academy" and we are now in a moment to "usefully clarify our commitments to public scholarship, addressing our work not simply to 'the public' but also, as Sheila A. Brennan (2016, 386) has observed, to specific communities and the needs that they, and not we, identify as most pressing." Co-ownership, co-production or co-creation is thus a theme that runs through many chapters of our volume (e.g. Toft Nørgård, Schreibman and Ping Huang; Barker et al.; de Waard; Gray and Schwan; Popple and Ng), with contributors highlighting the new insights and experiences that emerge precisely in those spaces where academic and non-academic communities encounter each other; at its best, Matthew Frye Jacobson notes (2021, 167), such work results in "something wholly new in the social fabric," creating a circular flow of knowledge between academia, other organizations and communities. Rather than working with a one-directional model of "knowledge transfer," as it is sometimes referred to in the UK funding context—and what Robyn Schroeder (2021, 20), in relation to US-based public humanities, calls the "vertical" model that "maintains traditional expertise and endeavors to extend it 'downward'"—the volume as a whole promotes, to the extent possible, collaborative approaches where scholarly expertise and institutional resources help facilitate rather than dictate new project ideas. As some of the chapters demonstrate, though (e.g. Gray and Schwan), such work often involves careful balancing acts and a critical, self-reflexive pragmatism on the part of scholar-practitioners, who need to be aware of potentially conflicting agendas, and their own privilege and biases. Nobuhiko Kikuchi's contribution to this volume is also an important reminder that phrases such as "public humanities" are contingent and resonate differently (or perhaps not at all) in different national-geographical contexts.

The public—and similarly the digital—humanities may best be defined as a form of critical "praxis" (Schroeder 2021, 5), in other words, a "doing" (Jacobson 2021; Crompton et al. 2016) or practice that is grounded both in scholarship/theory and collective experience, rather than constituting a narrowly defined "field of study" (Schroeder 2021, 5). This conceptualization also aids in averting the risks associated with a fieldification or institutionalization of public humanities as a practice that scholars such as Mary Mullen (2014) have drawn attention to. Having said that, institutionalization does not necessarily bear negative consequences if it is achieved thoughtfully and, as the editors of the inaugural issue of *magazén: International Journal for Digital and Public Humanities*, a peer-reviewed journal associated with the relatively new Venice Centre for Digital and Public Humanities (VeDPH) at Ca' Foscari University put it, driven by an "urge towards openness and interdisciplinarity" (Fischer et al. 2020, 9).

In light of this debate, we choose not to capitalize digital and public humanities, concurring with Amy Earhart's (2016, n.p.) distinction of digital (and, we may add, public) humanities as a critical practice rather than a "monolithic and rigid, often exclusionary and uncritically dominant" field. This critical praxis of public and digital humanities is necessarily multi- and cross-disciplinary, reflected in the various disciplinary backgrounds represented by the volume's contributors, spanning the arts, humanities and social sciences.[2]

Although not every single chapter in the volume explicitly addresses the conjunction of the digital and public humanities, some contributors directly showcase what, with Sheila A. Brennan (2016, n.p.), we may call "digital public humanities" or "public digital humanities," defined "by the ways that it engages with communities outside of the academy as a means for doing digital humanities scholarship." Barbara Heinisch's (2020) discussion of "citizen humanities" as a "fusion" of digital and public humanities is also useful here. Heinisch (2020, 144) notes that "[w]hile the digital humanities provide the citizen humanities with data, tools, techniques and infrastructures that do not only facilitate humanistic inquiry but also communication and collaboration with different actors, the public humanities offer the means of communication and ways of engaging diverse publics in research activities." The collection as a whole articulates opportunities in this relatively recent juncture and offers new directions in scholarly research in the digital and public humanities. Readers with a particular interest in the digital humanities will gain awareness of how their work might be publicly engaged, while scholars primarily grounded in the public humanities will find inspiration for how their work might make use of the affordances of the digital.

The volume joins a body of recent publications in digital and public humanities theorizing and showcasing the opportunities and challenges brought by these modes of scholarship and practice. Publications focusing on the role of the public humanities tend to be dispersed in journal articles or collections on participatory culture and public engagement (see e.g. Mitchell 2008; Mitchell and Soria 2018; Mullen 2014; Sandy 2013). Kath Burton et al.'s White Paper (2021) specifically comments on the challenges related to the publication of publicly engaged scholarship, while Sommer (2014) showcases innovative collaborations between policymakers and creatives to tackle civic challenges through art projects. The *University of Toronto Quarterly*'s special issue (Gibbs 2016) offers a more sustained discussion of the shape and goals of public humanities; similarly, Smulyan's edited collection *Doing Public Humanities* (2021) provides a welcome addition to the literature, in its attempt to chart out the area's theoretical and practical parameters, as well as providing case studies, although its focus largely revolves around work coming out of Brown University's Center for Public Humanities and Cultural Heritage.

Publications on digital humanities have proliferated more visibly, with new priorities including decolonization (see e.g. Risam and Josephs 2021; Schweitzer and Henry 2019), gender democracy and intersectional feminism (see e.g. Losh and Wernimont 2018; D'Ignazio and Klein 2020), critical race studies (see e.g. Nakamura 2007; Gallon 2016; Noble 2018), ecology (see Cohen and LeMenager 2016), community archives (see Popple, Prescott, and Mutibwa 2020) and ethics and care in relation to the digital (see Gold and Klein 2019). Some scholars in digital humanities have begun to explicitly address the potential of digital and public humanities intersections (e.g. Christie et al. 2014; Stommel 2018), with Jordana Cox and Lauren Tilton (2019, n.p.) going as far as framing "the digital public humanities (DPH)" as "a relatively new subfield," defined as "those practices that facilitate reflection and collaboration with participants outside of the academy through digital theories and technologies." Yet, as Will Fenton (2018, n.p.) notes in *Inside Higher Ed*, "the public mindedness of the digital humanities, measurable in the public availability of work once relegated to subject-area specialists, is often left implicit." This present volume, then, also responds to Fenton's (2018, n.p.) call "that digital humanists own their role as public humanists" in its multifaceted forms.

This handbook builds on emerging trends in scholarship on the digital and public humanities, while offering the first extensive and truly international collection on the digital and public humanities as increasingly interconnected fields. Chapters typically offer specific case studies, embedded in wider theoretical reflections, thus serving as models for other scholars and practitioners, and facilitating future directions in scholarship and critically informed practice.

1.2 Overview of Thematic Sections and Chapters

The Palgrave Handbook of Digital and Public Humanities brings together 25 chapters and over 50 contributors based across four continents. The collection is divided into six thematic sections. The first one, "Scholarship, Creative Practice and Engaging with 'Publics'" explores new pedagogical approaches, questions of access and the co-production of historical knowledge and creative outputs in relation to historically marginalized communities. Section two, "Making Memory, Making Community," turns its attention to digital and public humanities' roles in recovering personal and collective trauma, in mobilizing affect and in forging new connections at a familial or community level. Section three, "Mobilizing the Archive," reflects on attempts to engage students and other publics through curation and digital editing, digital archives and public humanities during the Covid-19 pandemic, as well as digital archives' potential for giving voice to working-class and indigenous communities. Section four, "Digital Cultural Heritage," examines digital and public humanities in relation to museum collections and other innovative approaches to cultural heritage resources. Section five, "Engaging Space and Place," focuses on urban memory and community-making through investigations of digital mapping of historical soundscapes, film festivals and cemetery tourism. The final section, "Public Discourse, Public Art and Activism," considers the role of public historians and public artists in addressing hate speech and the climate crisis.

1.3 Coda

The US-based North Eastern Public Humanities Consortium (NEPH)'s White Paper (cited in Jacobson 2021, 169) sees the humanities as one necessary answer to the "crisis of atomization" affecting societies increasingly eroded by neoliberal politics. If the post-Crash economic climate of austerity made the humanities' ability to "generate counter-narratives to this atomization" (NEPH White Paper cited in Jacobson 2021, 169) particularly pertinent, the isolation and hardships experienced during the Covid-19 pandemic lend this promise a new urgency. At a moment when it is more than ever necessary to rebuild a sense of collectivity and community—and with renewed appreciation of the possibilities and limitations of the digital in underpinning human interaction—we hope that this handbook will offer a timely guide.

Notes

1. For more on this debate on "value" and "impact," see Bate (2011), Small (2013), and the special issue "Forum on the Public Value of Arts and Humanities Research" of *Arts and Humanities in Higher Education* edited by Paul Benneworth (2015).
2. For an in-depth consideration of interdisciplinarity in relation to digital humanities, see Klein (2015).

References

Bate, Jonathan. 2011. *The Public Value of the Humanities*. London: Bloomsbury.

Benneworth, Paul, ed. 2015. Special issue, *Arts and Humanities in Higher Education* 14 (1) (February).

Brennan, Sheila A. 2016. "Public, First." In *Debates in the Digital Humanities 2016*, edited by Matthew K. Gold and Lauren F. Klein. Minneapolis, MN: University of Minnesota Press. https://dhdebates.gc.cuny.edu/read/untitled/section/11b9805a-a8e0-42e3-9a1c-fad46e4b78e5#ch32.

Burton, Kath, Catherine Cocks, Darcy Cullen, Daniel Fisher, Barry M. Goldenberg, Janneken Smucker, Friederike Sundaram, Dave Tell, Anne Valks, and Rebecca Wingo. 2021. "Public Humanities and Publication: A Working Paper." Routledge, Taylor & Francis and National Humanities Alliance. https://hcommons.org/deposits/item/hc:37487/.

Christie, Alex, Jana Millar Usiskin, Jentery Sayers, and Kathryn Tanigawa. 2014. "Introduction: Digital Humanities, Public Humanities." *NANO: New American Notes Online* 5 (July). https://nanocrit.com/issues/issue5/introduction-digital-humanities-public-humanities.

Cohen, Jeffrey Jerome, and Stephanie LeMenager, eds. 2016. Special issue, *PMLA* 131 (2) (March).

Cox, Jordana, and Lauren Tilton. 2019. "The Digital Public Humanities: Giving New Arguments and New Ways to Argue." *Review of Communication* 19 (2): 127–46. https://doi.org/10.1080/15358593.2019.1598569.

Crompton, Constance, Richard J. Lane, and Ray Siemens, eds. 2016. *Doing Digital Humanities: Practice, Training, Research*. Abingdon, Oxon: Routledge.

D'Ignazio, Catherine, and Lauren F. Klein. 2020. *Data Feminism*. Cambridge, MA: MIT Press.

Earhart, Amy E. 2016. "Digital Humanities Futures: Conflict, Power, and Public Knowledge." *Digital Studies/le Champ Numérique* 6 (1). https://doi.org/10.16995/dscn.1.

Fenton, Will. 2018. "Literary Scholars Should Use Digital Humanities to Reach the Oft-Ignored 'Public' (Opinion)." *Inside Higher Ed*, January 29. https://www.insidehighered.com/print/views/2018/01/29/literary-scholars-should-use-digital-humanities-reach-oft-ignored-public-opinion.

Fischer, Franz, Diego Mantoan, and Barbara Tramelli. 2020. "A New Venture and a Commitment to Disciplinary Fusion in the Domain of Digital and Public Humanities." *magazén* 1 (1) (June): 7–16. https://doi.org/10.30687/mag//2020/01/000.

Fraser, Nancy. 1992. "Rethinking the Public Sphere: A Contribution to the Critique of Actually Existing Democracy." In *Habermas and the Public Sphere*, edited by Craig Calhoun, 109–42. Cambridge, MA: MIT Press.

Gallon, Kim. 2016. "Making a Case for the Black Digital Humanities." In *Debates in the Digital Humanities, 2016*, edited by Matthew K. Gold and Lauren F. Klein. Minneapolis, MN: University of Minnesota Press. https://dhdebates.gc.cuny.edu/read/untitled/section/fa10e2e1-0c3d-4519-a958-d823aac989eb#ch04.

Gibbs, Robert, ed. 2016. Special issue, *University of Toronto Quarterly* 85 (4) (Fall).

Gold, Matthew K., and Lauren F. Klein, eds. 2019. *Debates in the Digital Humanities*. Minneapolis, MN: University of Minnesota Press. https://doi.org/10.5749/9781452963785.

Heinisch, Barbara. 2020. "Citizen Humanities as a Fusion of Digital and Public Humanities?" *magazén* 1 (2) (December): 143–80. https://doi.org/10.30687/mag/2724-3923/2020/02/001.

Jacobson, Matthew Frye. 2021. "Afterword: The 'Doing' of Doing Public Humanities." In *Doing Public Humanities*, edited by Susan Smulyan, 165–173. New York, NY: Routledge.

Klein, Julie Thompson. 2015. *Interdisciplining Digital Humanities: Boundary Work in an Emerging Field*. Michigan: University of Michigan Press.

Losh, Elizabeth, and Jacqueline Wernimont, eds. 2018. *Bodies of Information: Intersectional Feminism and Digital Humanities*. Minneapolis, MN: University of Minnesota Press.

Mitchell, Katharyne, ed. 2008. *Practising Public Scholarship: Experience and Possibilities Beyond the Academy*. Malden, MA: Wiley-Blackwell.

Mitchell, Tania D., and Krista M. Soria, eds. 2018. *Educating for Citizenship and Social Justice: Practices for Community Engagement at Research Universities*. Cham: Springer.

Mullen, Mary L. 2014. "Public Humanities' (Victorian) Culture Problem." *Cultural Studies* 30 (2): 183–204. https://doi.org/10.1080/09502386.2014.978802.

Nakamura, Lisa. 2007. *Digitizing Race: Visual Cultures of the Internet*. Minneapolis, MN: University of Minnesota Press.

Noble, Safiya Umoja. 2018. *Algorithms of Oppression: How Search Engines Reinforce Racism*. New York, NY: New York University Press.

Popple, Simon, Andrew Prescott, and Daniel Mutibwa. 2020. *Communities, Archives and New Collaborative Practices*. Bristol: Policy Press.

Risam, Roopika, and Kelly Baker Josephs, eds. 2021. *The Digital Black Atlantic*. Minneapolis, MN: University of Minnesota Press.

Sandy, Marie. 2013. "Tracing the Liberal Arts Traditions in Support of Service-Learning and Public-engaged Scholarship in the Humanities." *Humanity & Society* 37 (4): 306–26. https://doi.org/10.1177/0160597613510704.

Schroeder, Robyn. 2021. "The Rise of the Public Humanists." In *Doing Public Humanities*, edited by Susan Smulyan, 5–27. New York, NY: Routledge.

Schweitzer, Ivy, and Gordon Henry, eds. 2019. *Afterlives of Indigenous Archives*. Hanover, NH: Dartmouth College Press.

Small, Helen. 2013. *The Value of the Humanities*. Oxford: Oxford University Press.

Smulyan, Susan. 2021. "Introduction." In *Doing Public Humanities*, edited by Susan Smulyan, 1–4. New York, NY: Routledge.

Sommer, Doris. 2014. *The Work of Art in the World: Civic Agency and Public Humanities*. Durham, NC: Duke University Press.

Stommel, Jesse. 2018. "The Public Digital Humanities." In *Disrupting the Digital Humanities*, edited by Dorothy Kim and Jesse Stommel, 79–90. Punctum Books. https://doi.org/10.2307/j.ctv19cwdqv.

Warner, Michael. 2005. *Publics and Counterpublics*. New York: Zone Books.

PART I

Scholarship, Creative Practice and Engaging with "Publics"

CHAPTER 2

Digital Humanities and Hybrid Education: Higher Education in, with and for the Public

Rikke Toft Nørgård, Susan Schreibman, and Marianne Ping Huang

2.1 Introduction

It is a running joke in digital humanities (DH) that digital humanists dread the question "but what exactly is digital humanities"? For most people, these two terms, *digital* and *humanities*, are not axiomatic: quite the contrary they feel, they could not be farther apart. And although much ink has been spilled in defining digital humanities (with even a random generator[1] providing definitions from the *Day of DH*[2]), perhaps another way to tackle the definitional conundrum is to think of digital humanities in terms of hybridity through its productive intermingling of disciplines, technological and cultural practices, with conceptualization and production reaching across diverse sectors such as arts, heritage and the creative industries. Rethinking DH pedagogic practices in terms of hybrid education could also extend, deepen and develop this hybridity. The field of hybrid education and hybrid learning environments—with its specific focus on higher education in, with and for the public[3]—provides a useful framework to expand the inherent productive intermingling of digital humanities with higher education research, educational design and pedagogical practice.

R. T. Nørgård (✉) · M. P. Huang
Aarhus University, Aarhus, Denmark
e-mail: rtoft@tdm.au.dk

S. Schreibman
Maastricht University, Maastricht, Netherlands

© The Author(s), under exclusive license to Springer Nature Switzerland AG 2022
A. Schwan and T. Thomson (eds.), *The Palgrave Handbook of Digital and Public Humanities*, https://doi.org/10.1007/978-3-031-11886-9_2

Hybrid education is a concept in the field of educational design and research into online, blended and other digitalized educational forms and learning spaces (see e.g. Doering 2006; Stommel and Rorabaugh 2012; Amaroso Leslie 2014; Rahm and Skågeby 2014; Köppe et al. 2017; Hilli et al. 2019; Cohen et al. 2020). These approaches to education have become commonplace, albeit frequently not carried out especially well, but in 2020–2021 during the pivot to online and blended education, schools and universities were forced into new learning and teaching modes during the Covid-19 lockdown. This 'new normal' characterized by challenging hybrid educational modalities, might also be seen as an opportunity to rethink our educational practices, focussing on the intersectionality and entanglement of higher education, inside and outside traditional classrooms, reaching out into public fora and upskilling for future work life.

Most digital humanists have experimented with and adopted—intentionally or unconsciously—elements of hybrid pedagogies out of necessity, in both formal and informal settings. These more intuitive practices, which are often part of research-led teaching, can foster digital citizenship, highlighting ways of bringing learning into the public domain or the public domain into education (Pedersen et al. 2018). What is too frequently looked on as simply adding workplace skills to humanities curricula, might more profitably be viewed as merging learning and work processes to facilitate knowledge integration and transition (Zitter and Hoeve 2012).

While higher education has largely abandoned a view of itself as monologic transmission of knowledge from ivory tower to society, new exigencies have emerged: higher education has increasingly found itself trapped by demands from policymakers and society in which higher education is seen as a "competence factory" being managed through a one-way transmission of demands for knowledge and competences from external stakeholders to the university (Nørgård et al. 2019). Within this factory mindset, the university must prove its socio-economic value by producing employable students to help secure economic growth. Nowhere is this pull towards imparting students with employable skills felt as strongly as in the humanities which consistently has to prove its ability to teach skills of value to the knowledge economy (Shumar 1997; Barnett 2011; Wright 2016). We offer a counter proposition for the humanities through a renewed practice of digital hybrid pedagogies. These new pedagogies embed into their design a revisioning of learning in, for and with the world, as opposed to an "upskilling" and competence factory approach to humanities students as seen through a neoliberal lens (Nørgård et al. 2019).

* * *

This chapter centres on hybrid education through a specific focus on one learning environment for the digital arts and humanities, #dariahTeach. #dariahTeach was designed by a European consortium with collaborators in Ireland,

Denmark, Austria, Switzerland and The Netherlands through an Erasmus+ grant to create a productive entanglement between formal learning, professional practice and societal engagement. Two of the authors of this article, Schreibman and Ping Huang, have been PI and Co-PI, respectively since its inception, with Nørgård active in its second phase, IGNITE (see below for more information on these phases). #dariahTeach was developed as a way to create new educational spaces, formats and processes to open up education in novel and experimental ways. It does this to reduce the gap between education, worklife and society by creating integrated and merged connections between higher education institutions, professional practice and the public sphere. As a platform that embeds hybrid entanglement, #dariahTeach has positioned itself in digital humanities education by:

- Opening up digital humanities education *for* the public by creating open educational resources, courses and learning materials that are open to all. Through its case studies and scenarios, it encourages students to create knowledge and/or products that are freely available to the public, either as stand-alone online products or via other public fora, such as social media.
- Practicing digital humanities education *with* the public by integrating external participants, practitioners and stakeholders in the learning environment and by offering opportunities for students to learn and collaborate with these stakeholders through authentic assignments.[4]
- Carrying out digital humanities education *in* the public by moving courses or teaching activities out into the public domain, having students set up exhibitions or events in the public realm as part of their education or conduct projects in workplace or public settings.

This chapter was accepted to this volume in what seems like a distant pre-Covid-19 past and has been authored under the shadow of our changed personal and professional existences during a pandemic. Within this strange new hybrid/online reality, #dariahTeach has taken on new significance, not only as a resource of open-source teaching and learning materials but perhaps as a model for higher education that exists beyond the confines of any one institution while belonging to many: an online and hybrid community-based site that both spans and gathers practitioners, professionals and students from across institutions, sectors, countries and continents to explore, to share and to experiment.

The authors of this chapter contend that hybrid learning spaces such as #dariahTeach can be considered a new model or mode for higher education—one that refracts relationships between learner and teacher, and between learners, teachers and society. In recent years, we have witnessed a growing demand for alternative conceptualizations of higher education, not only within higher education research but also in works addressing the notion of universities as an ontological structure (e.g. Peters and Besley 2013; Besley and Peters 2013; Barnett 2017; Wright 2016; Staley 2019).[5] These new ontological structures have been termed "the networking university" (Nørgård et al. 2019), "alternative universities" (Staley 2019), "the ecological university" (Barnett 2017), or "the creative university" (Peters and Besley 2013). Such new models aim for higher education and society "to co-create future knowledge and societal value that go beyond immediate use-value, present demand, or measurable output … focusing more on human societal value and citizenship … to create knowledge for an unknown and open future" (Nørgård et al. 2019, 74–75). This is exactly what the humanities are good at. However, to become central players in this new ontological positioning of the university, researchers, teachers, students and citizens, educational institutions, industry and public organizations need to enter into critical-creative partnerships that integrate and embed them into one another to the degree that they view each other as part of the same ecosystem and as co-creators of the same shared world (Barnett 2017; Nørgård and Bengtsen 2016). It is within these emerging new models for higher education, that we see digital humanities, framed as hybrid education and hybrid learning spaces, offering a new mode of education.

2.2   Unpacking the Notion of Hybridity and Hybrid Education

"Hybrid" originates from the Latin word "hybridia" meaning a mongrel or crossbreed in the form of offspring from separate parts or species fused into a new compound or species (Kapchan and Strong 1999, 240). Accordingly, a hybrid is decidedly composite and heterogeneous of origin, but simultaneously something new in its own right: A mule is neither a donkey–horse nor a horse–donkey, but something in and of itself, a mule. As such, hybrid formats and models fuse existing elements into new configurations (Stommel 2012). Here, hybridity becomes a way of intentionally and reflectively "overlapping and blending different concepts at the same time, such as online and offline, formal and informal" (Kohls et al. 2018) and a methodology for fostering new forms of participation, inclusion and engagement in learning and society (Köppe et al. 2017).

Within higher education, notions of hybrid, hybridization and hybridity in relation to learning have had a great increase in interest, searches and mentions in the last decade, especially since Covid-19 forced providers and institutions of learning to pivot to online. Here, hybrid education highlights the challenges and opportunities which transpire from the dissolution, entanglement or transgression of boundaries between contexts of learning, working and living, between online/offline and onsite/offsite synchronous/asynchronous education and between existing hybrid practices of thinking, doing and being in education and society. *Hybrid digital humanities pedagogies* are, then, digital humanities that intentionally and reflectively utilize the concept of hybridity to dissolve traditional dichotomies and engage in developing formats and models for hybrid learning inside and outside institutions. This is done through the intentional entanglement of normally separate dimensions such as participating in on-campus education (online) while simultaneously being in a workplace setting (onsite), bringing vocational practice and academic learning together in new ways, connecting students across different universities and areas of study to learn and work together, or by opening up formal education by bringing it to public spaces or institutions and by bringing citizens, practitioners and external stakeholders in as part of the teaching team (Zitter and Hoeve 2012; Kohls et al. 2017; Kohls et al. 2018; Hilli et al. 2019).

Following from this, hybrid digital humanities pedagogies may—through the bridging of hybrid education and digital humanities—become a new model for working intentionally with the in-betweenness of educational, vocational and public contexts, the fusion of traditional educational dichotomies and the amalgamation of educational and extra-educational formats, practices and ways of learning.

2.3 Digital Humanities Through Hybrid Higher Education

By connecting the fields of hybrid education and digital humanities, we see the opportunity for digital humanists to contribute to the formation of new hybrid learning cultures, environments and practices that open up deeper and more entwined societal engagement, beyond the boundaries of the institution (O'Byrne and Pytash 2015). According to Zitter and Hoeve (2012), a learning environment is considered hybrid if it incorporates both authentic and participation processes, that connects learning and working processes to benefit from the strengths of both formal learning and realistic experiences in the workplace. In short, "hybrid learning environments seek to *integrate and merge* learning and working" (Zitter and Hoeve 2012, 23).

By connecting the practices of digital humanities with the practices of hybrid education, concrete actionable "educational design patterns" for hybrid digital humanities become available (see e.g. Köppe et al. 2017; Kohls et al. 2017; Köppe et al. 2018; Kohls et al. 2018; Hilli et al. 2019) and will enable students to practice and explore digital humanities in, with and for the public while simultaneously submitting it to formal assessment systems (Leslie 2014). In this way, hybrid digital humanities pedagogies can, and in many instances already do, integrate and use already developed, tested and evaluated educational design patterns for hybrid education such as "open hybrid classroom," "integrating practitioners" or "street tasks" or "public exams" (Kohls et al. 2018). "Re-mediation" or "student shared resource space" (Köppe et al. 2018) are typically found in digital humanities classrooms, leading to "open development and open research" (Kohls et al. 2017). The maker culture ethos of DH typically emphasizes "real world contribution," "rapid prototyping,"

"DIY education" and "open hybrid classroom" (Köppe et al. 2017). And as face-to-face workshops have been pivoting to online offerings, "global online inter-university teaching" (Hilli et al. 2019) is becoming a norm.

As such, viewing digital humanities pedagogies as hybrid educational practices strengthens the pedagogical vocabulary of digital humanities and materializes its approaches to higher education in, with and for the public as concrete and reflective pedagogical practices. Moreover, this integration also highlights the shared effort of hybrid education and digital humanities in providing a shift in the structure and mandate of higher education towards connectivity, practitioner networks and collaborations through joint engagements in processes with one another and with society:

> In hybrid education people inside and outside the campus [or learning environment] meet and intermingle, academic life becomes mongrel as the personal, professional and academic merge. Even teacher, students and institutions cross-fertilize to construct new hybrid contexts and collectives across traditional boundaries ... On the grounds of such different hybrid constellations, the possibility for new higher education futures emerges. (Köppe, Nørgård, and Pedersen 2017, 2)

The aim of integrating hybrid education and digital humanities is, then, to take full advantage of the benefits and potentials of each field. As such, hybrid digital humanities pedagogies can promote a horizontal connectedness across spaces, activities and subjects inside and outside higher education institutions (Dumont and Istance 2010). And through such hybrid entanglements, students may engage in real-world contexts, professional development and authentic complex tasks and challenges that invoke active learning processes (Könings et al. 2005; Baartman and de Bruijn 2011), thus reducing the disconnect between higher education learning, professional development, societal engagement and the public sphere in ways that invite "people [to] connect and interact through a hybrid network of physical and technology-mediated encounters to co-construct knowledge and effectively engage in positioning practices necessary for their work" (Cook et al. 2015, 125).

Hybrid digital humanities pedagogies, then, concerns the integration and interweaving of formal and informal structures of learning, the synchronicity of onsite and online spaces, the combination of physical and digital tools mediating an individual's interaction with the world and society and the entanglement of roles that the individual occupies in the world across time, space, contexts and roles (Nørgård 2021). Generally, learning in and through hybrid digital humanities pedagogies for, with and in the public implies that learners will face and work through uncertainty, risk-taking, experimentation, open-endedness, dialogue and disruption—both in the public domain and within the hybrid learning environment itself (Köppe et al. 2017).

But how can we more specifically design for hybrid digital humanities in a way that scaffolds and promotes students'entangled practices? What concrete formats, activities, practices and cultures could we offer to support both teachers and students in initiating and engaging with hybrid digital humanities practices? Below we present two concrete examples of hybrid digital humanities. The first case is on the macro level and presents the #dariahTeach platform as an open educational resource that can help support and promote hybrid digital humanities that engage higher education for, with and in the public in different ways:

> #dariahTeach is a platform for Open Educational Resources (OER) for Digital Arts and Humanities educators and students, but also beyond this aiming at Higher Education across a spectrum of disciplines, at teachers and trainers engaged in the digital transformation of programme content and learning methods. #dariahTeach has two key objectives: sharing and reuse, thus developing a place for people to publish their teaching material and for others to use it in their own teaching. (from: https://teach.dariah.eu/local/staticpage/view.php?page=about)

The second case is on the meso level and presents the IGNITE project that is developing modules for the #dariahTeach platform. This project, in its ambition, is also a clear example of hybrid digital humanities:

> IGNITE draws together several disparate shifts in recent education policy and research: online education, digitally enhanced learning methods, innovation, entrepreneurship, and the turn in humanities education from theory to method.
>
> These shifts form the design axis in IGNITE, going beyond the provision of traditional academic competences by bridging knowledge, theories, and skills through a range of creative, problem solving techniques. A key impact of IGNITE is to meld design thinking methods through the ethos of Maker Culture. It does this through real-world case studies and scenarios from the cultural and creative sectors by integrating software, tools, and methods with analysis from the arts and humanities. (from: https://ignite.acdh.oeaw.ac.at/ignite-module/)

Taken together the two cases demonstrate different ways for institutions, teachers and students to engage in hybrid digital humanities in, with and for the public.

2.4 Case 1: #dariahTeach—A Platform for Hybrid Digital Humanities Education

#dariahTeach[6] is an example of hybrid digital arts and humanities pedagogies. As a platform and a project, it promotes education *with the public*, as opposed to *for the public*. Through a participatory and design thinking approach (Björgvinsson et al. 2012), content is co-created with partners across colleges, universities and research institutes, as well as with the creative and cultural industries through an interactive feedback loop with students in both formal and informal settings (Burdick and Willis 2011). Begun in 2013 with a grant from the European Union's Erasmus + programme (which focuses on education, training, sport and youth),[7] #dariahTeach was developed as a platform or model for the "ecological" (Barnett 2017), "networking" (Nørgård et al. 2019) or hybrid university in its performance of a collective: a way of "doing" the university in a more open and collaborative manner. In its first phase, eight courses were designed as open educational resources with partners in seven European countries to be used across institutions and sectors. These courses were designed for hybrid teaching and learning, to be taken/delivered synchronously and asynchronously, in more formal classroom settings, as well as in more informal workshops and summer schools. It has been used in face-to-face teaching, as well as online teaching, in flipped classroom settings as well as by individuals outside formal institutional teaching and learning situations (lone learners).

As engaged research, #dariahTeach has provided an ever-expanding cadre of content developers and designers with the opportunity of (re)thinking ways of materializing the values that drew many of us into Higher Education, focussing on occasions for co-creation, collaborative learning and knowledge sharing (Ratto 2011). Perhaps most importantly, the open educational resources created by or for #dariahTeach are developed "in the open," through an entanglement or ecosystem of people, places, contexts and institutions. With its second grant, IGNITE (April 2018–January 2021), this entanglement became intersectoral with partners in the creative and cultural industries and an interactive design cycle and feedback loop that involved students in Ireland, Denmark and The Netherlands, as well as colleagues from across Europe (see section 2.5 below for more details). As it has matured as a platform and as a pedagogic concept, #dariahTeach has in itself become and fostered a dialogue about who higher education is for, about collaborative co-creation that reaches beyond and across institutional and intersectoral boundaries, and the responsibility and possibilities we have as academic citizens.

While the content of #dariahTeach focuses on providing digital humanities skills, theories and methods to arts and humanities studies, it is delivered through a technology-enhanced learning platform (Wang and Hannafin 2005). It thus practices what it preaches (or teaches), taking a user-centred approach to developing both the content as well as the way that content is delivered (Burdick and Willis 2011; McKillgan et al. 2017). Courses are multimodal, catering to a wide range of learning styles, with moments for self-testing of knowledge through quizzes and more reflective assessments, typically attached to case studies.

From the outset, #dariahTeach was designed to include a plurality of voices. This is most visible in the course *Introduction to Digital Humanities*. Rather than introducing the field through a single narrative, short videos create an assemblage of perspectives, languages and individuals, each contributing a piece to the jigsaw of what is digital humanities: what it means to them as practitioners as well as how (and why) they perform it. Moreover, videos are a common multimodal element throughout all the other courses so as to cater to different learning styles of students. All videos are streamed through the #dariahTeach YouTube channel.[8] While utilizing YouTube alleviated a technical issue (the hosting partner did not need to have their own streaming server), equally as importantly it created an alternative space to distribute learning materials on a social media platform that increased the reach of our open learning resources. Since 2016, the videos on the channel have had over 115,000 views. YouTube provides #dariahTeach with a more public, less formal learning environment to distribute content. In a search on YouTube for *SGML* (Standard Generalized Markup Language), for example, the #dariahTeach video comes up second. Videos are created by the #dariahTeach team, particularly the *My Digital Humanities* series (in its own channel on YouTube) which features interviews in which a multiplicity of voices describe what digital humanities is/means to and for them. Each course also features its own channel. However, those outside #dariahTeach can and have contributed videos, particularly within the *Digital Humanities in Practice* channel. This public and participatory openness creates a win–win situation: #dariahTeach adds more diversity to its offerings, and individuals and projects are able to promote their research to a wider audience. Moreover, videos can be made in any language, with captions available in multiple languages. For the My Digital Humanities Part I video,[9] a crowdsourcing experiment took place in which the video was translated into eight languages.

The *Introduction to Digital Humanities* series is one type of clustering of educational content. Other clusterings include the suite of courses developed for the IGNITE grant (see below), and concepts and methods that resonate between courses; for example, three courses explore different editing strategies utilizing the Text Encoding Initiative: *Text Encoding and the TEI* (an introductory course], *Digitising Dictionaries*, and *Digital Scholarly Editions: Manuscripts, Texts and TEI Encoding*). Because of the ways in which these courses are formulated, the platform could easily host additional TEI-related material. Sound studies is another example where courses have been developed to expand and resonate with each other. In the first phase of #dariahTeach, *Sound Studies* was developed, and more recently a unit on audio narratives within the *Storytelling for Digital Narratives and Blended Spaces* was created which builds on the previous course and explores sound studies from a narrative perspective. The project's commitment to polyvocality encourages multiple perspectives and approaches in multiple languages. Not only are videos subtitled, but courses have also been translated from English into Spanish, French, Hungarian, Italian and Russian.

Pedagogically, #dariahTeach develops content by active and research-led teaching providing opportunities for students to collaborate on authentic assessments which typically embed three values: realism, contextualization and problematization:

Realism involves linking knowledge with everyday life and work, contextualisation characterises situations where knowledge can be applied in an analytical and thoughtful way, and problematisation invokes a sense that what is learned can be used to solve a problem or meet a need. (Villarroel et al. 2018, 841)

An example of this within the #dariahTeach context is the translation of three courses (*Text Encoding and the TEI, Introduction to Digital Humanities* and *Multimodal Literacies*) into Spanish by Amelia del Rosario Sanz Cabrerizo, her colleagues and her MA students in Digital Humanities at the Complutense University of Madrid in the Master en Letras Digitales programme. The focus of the MA is both translation and digital humanities, which made the translation of these courses an ideal authentic assessment (Villarroel et al. 2018; Tong et al. 2018). Not only did the students learn about digital humanities, but they also focussed on translating media-based content and learned project management skills through an iterative design cycle. At the end of the project, the translated courses were released on the #dariahTeach platform. MA students at Maynooth University (Ireland) and Maastricht University (Netherlands) also participated in course design by taking courses and then being asked for feedback through design thinking focus groups. The purpose of the focus groups was to not only get feedback for the #dariahTeach team but to teach students about how to use design thinking tools as a more active way to garner feedback beyond traditional ethnographic methods of interviews and surveys. This commitment to providing educational opportunities as both process and product provides individuals at varying stages of their careers with the opportunity to have agency in the pedagogic ecosystem being developed.

In this way, #dariahTeach is not only an open educational resource but in itself a collective laboratory or collaboratory about how to design open pedagogies, making education that is typically delivered in closed university settings open and connected to other formal and informal educational ecosystems. We are thus not simply engaging in DH educational development that is research-informed and research-based, but also research-producing (Carnell and Fung 2017).

#dariahTeach is radical in its openness: instructors can export from the #dariahTeach platform (a Moodle instance) and use it within their learning management systems or assign the content for their classes. Individuals can contribute content, translate it or enhance it. This is open pedagogies with an invitation to re/use content. As such, #dariahTeach has become an entanglement of materials for both teaching as well as for the international DH community to contribute their experience of the field, widening its boundaries beyond the academy, while reflecting on the community's methods and practices. The project and the platform have become a research collective for thinking about DH through the intersections of the platform, the courses and the content. #dariahTeach can be viewed as a model for an archiving and platform university: a laboratorium, collaboratorium, exploratorium and experimentarium for digital humanities pedagogies—the university as a participatory academic community and collective.

2.5 Case 2: IGNITE—Learning with Creative Ecosystems in Digital Transition

In 2017, the #dariahTeach community—with Maastricht University (NL), Aarhus University (DK), The Austrian Academy of Sciences and industrial partners, Filmby Aarhus (DK) and Cube Design Museum (NL)—responded to a call from the EU Commission and Creative Europe Media for master modules to connect the Arts and Sciences towards the Cultural and Creative Industries. This EU call complimented the START.eu[10] initiative, connecting science, technology and the arts and also an EIT (European Institute for Technology and Innovation) new Knowledge and Innovation Community (KICK) for the Cultural and Creative Industries by 2022.

The Cultural and Creative Industries (CCI) have been on the agenda with EU frameworks and programmes for more than a decade as an area for future growth, for which "cultural values, cultural diversity, individual and/or collective creativity, skills and talent" (European Parliament 2016) are the innovation drivers. Part of such programming for innovation with culture and creativity is the incubation, acceleration and scaling through digital transition and cluster economies. To a large degree this prospect for CCI builds on a late twentieth century paradigm for new knowledge production (Gibbons et al. 1994), arguing heterogeneity and transdisciplinarity in competency- and practice-orientation where academic insights are channelled to the public through "knowledge exchange." In the seminal Brighton Fuse-study (2010–2013), such new knowledge production was shown to be fuelled by culture and creativity, across cultural institutions, creative and media industries and new digital technologies. The implications are that the CCI innovation can be both incremental and radical, both soft and hard (Cooke and De Propris 2011), indications for which are found in labour market data, showing that CCI employs more people aged 15–29 than any other sector in Europe. The sector is considered "amongst the most entrepreneurial sectors, developing transferable skills such as creative thinking, problem solving teamwork and resourcefulness" (European Parliament 2016).

This overall traditional growth prospect for CCI may seem promising, but it is also nested in entanglements. First and foremost, the CCI cannot be considered *one* sector, but rather constitutes a diverse or hybrid horizon of industries in just as diverse a distribution across public and private sectors:

> they include the following sectors relying on cultural and creative inputs: architecture, archives and libraries, artistic crafts, audio-visual (including film, television, software and video games, and multimedia and recorded music), cultural heritage, design, creativity-driven high-end industries and fashion,

festivals, live music, performing arts, books and publishing (newspapers and magazines), radio and visual arts, and advertising. (European Parliament 2016)

Thus, building capacity across creativity and technology to the CCI at large calls for academic and educational interaction and feedback processes with multiple actors, audiences and publics. To IGNITE, this implied moving from an entrepreneurial and competence-oriented "upskilling" approach to an ecological, networking and hybrid innovation-model approach (Carayannis and Campbell 2012), based on new partnerships and experimental co-creation. From the outset, the IGNITE project would build on experiences from creating #dariahTeach DH courses in an academic, digital humanities collective, and from teaching HE Humanities and Digital Humanities programmes in collaboration with the GLAM sector and arts institutions, often building on trusted, long-term (public) partnerships.

While observing how new digital production technologies already accelerate incremental and linear innovation across some subsectors of the CCI, the guiding assumption for IGNITE was that humanities and the arts can contribute creative openings and critical insights towards more radical innovation in a more human-centred digital transition. IGNITE therefore responded to the EU "experimental pilot call" by going beyond a competence factory, linear innovation approach to immediate market tendencies and challenges, e.g. scaling design or creative industries production through a lean digital transition. Instead an experimental curricular frame was built (within the #dariahTeach framework) to revisit and empower creativity across humanities, arts and technology, arguing that this should be done on a diverse horizon of situated knowledges and practices matching the diversity of the CCI and in tandem with the present pervasiveness of design processes shaping our human, onsite and online environments.

The CCI innovation-drivers—"cultural values, cultural diversity, individual and/or collective creativity, skills and talent"—are (or have been) at the core of educating towards culture, arts and technology, but without recognizing to the full that although creativity is very diversely conceptualized within individual knowledge fields, this very diversity may contribute a productive, hybrid assemblage for a more holistic learning through creative or design processes. With IGNITE, the concept of critical creativity was framed with human-centred design thinking and maker culture (Ratto 2011), putting digital creative practices and cultural diversity at the centre while leveraging diversity through guided co-creation across disciplines. The IGNITE curriculum of five open online courses was developed to provide two mandatory courses on the theoretical foundations of and practice guides in human-centred design thinking and making, and from this to build capacity to bespoke areas with the Cultural and Creative Industries, such as 3D Modelling for Heritage, Digital Storytelling and Games Design. This approach to (re)learning creativity in cross-disciplinary environments involves applying and negotiating knowledge and practices towards complex challenges, while creating a socio-material and digital assemblage of situated design methods (Simonsen et al. 2014). As diversity in users, audiences and public is inherent to human-centred design thinking, no knowledge paradigm or method can be universal and no challenge can be viewed comprehensively from one position (Haraway 1988). Overall, this was a call for a learning environment representing diverse contexts, which also is the reason for deploying case studies as signature learning objects throughout the IGNITE curriculum, to grasp how real-life contexts impact knowledge, concepts, processes, practices, crafts and skills.

The IGNITE approach caters to humanities, arts and technology students with situated methods of co-creation or co-design, originating from both design-systems as, for example, various models of design thinking and from system-design as participatory design (Bjögvinsson et al. 2012), while integrating humanities and human-centred critical and speculative approaches. This hybridizing of knowledge paradigms—between, for instance, "pure" theoretical, situated and applied knowledge—which goes across disciplines, skill sets and understanding of talent is not easily contained or embedded within HE institutions and educational programs, though maybe recognizable on a strategic level. It calls for an active and value-based ecological, networking and hybridizing engagement in experimentation with public and stakeholders, and for academic citizenship as beyond campus "responsibility" (Haraway 2016) and agency towards real-life entanglements, complexities and challenges (Comunian and Gilmore 2015).

Addressing particularly humanities students and teaching professionals with the IGNITE curriculum is a call for the (digital) humanities to take part on this broader scale of academic citizenship, where disciplines steeped in knowledge of culture(s) and human creativity may rethink and re-invest themselves in a human-centred digital transition. When moving the humanities into the field of complex and real-life challenges, responding, for example, to the UN Sustainable Development Goals (SDGs), we immediately feel compelled that our competences for critical inquiry as well as the deep knowledge of the many domains will matter. But we also find—not least in the way these domains are taught, and henceforth how learning is provided and in what learning environments—that the humanities have been confronted with a not necessarily smooth transition from content to challenge-based learning. While many researchers in the humanities study critical societal challenges in domains such as decolonial studies, the post-human condition, gender and equality studies and in emerging and inherently transdisciplinary fields such as digital, environmental and medical humanities, the "traditional humanities" as well as the emerging fields, more than the sciences and the social sciences, have struggled to turn highly valuable practices and historically tested knowledge into critical and creative approaches towards real-life challenges.

Practicing digital humanities education *with* the public—by integrating external stakeholders, practitioners and professionals in the learning environment, as is done when inviting neighbourhood communities, municipalities or heritage institutions to take part, offering opportunities for students to learn and work with diverse audiences and user groups—is not new in the digital humanities, where public and open humanities have been prevalent for engaging digitally with the public. IGNITE has taken this a step further in engaging with ecological multi-stakeholder models, integrating public, private and citizens, through user- and stakeholder-centred design and co-creation processes as a foundation for designing the curricular framework, learning environment and course content. To establish feedback mechanisms for such a 360-degree approach, IGNITE offered master classes for teaching and heritage professionals in the last year of module development, and during the Covid-19 lockdown a further five online roundtable discussions, an online Summer School to Dutch junior researchers, and an online Autumn School for a global audience of 60+ students and professionals. Valuable feedback such as the outcomes of design thinking in online environments for the reach of both creative agency and the digital transition, for challenge-driven situated learning, and for the feasibility of co-creational sprints and various contexts for real-life cases, was integrated during the final development. Not least, running these activities during the pandemic, with the growing consciousness of its complexities across all audiences, proved productive for testing collaborative case-sprints as well as the mindset for participatory contributions to alternative future states.

In this broader and more hybrid engagement with the CCI's promises for innovating and building back better, IGNITE aims to build capacity within an experimental ecological and hybrid university model, with new partnerships for open innovation and in ecosystems of multiple stakeholders that integrate across learning communities, civic society and public and private actors (Schütz et al. 2019). Such partnerships—which are hybrid entities—are driven by global, collective and complex challenges. New partnerships have become a measure towards both human- and more-than-human-centred challenges such as those of the UN SDGs. Yet, the ecosystems of multi-stakeholder partnerships also fit the open hybridity of the CCI well.

2.6 Conclusion

Working towards conceptualizing, developing and offering hybrid digital humanities formats and practices such as #dariahTeach and IGNITE, carries with it the potential of new hybrid learning cultures, environments and practices that opens up deeper and more entwined societal engagement and development beyond the boundaries of the institution. In connecting the fields of hybrid education and digital humanities, we see an opportunity for digital humanities to move towards the hybridization of digital citizenship, public digital humanities and a deeper integration of higher education, society and the world into one another. The cases of #dariahTeach and IGNITE exemplify ways of working with opening up digital humanities education *for* the public, practicing digital humanities education *with* the public and carrying out digital humanities education *in* the public. This is achieved by creating open educational resources, courses and learning materials that are open to all,[11] integrating external participants or practitioners in the learning environment, offering opportunities for students to learn and work with the public during the course or through authentic assignments and by moving courses or teaching activities out into the public domain, having students set up exhibitions or events in the public as part of their education or conduct exams in workplace or public settings.

As a starting point, through the presented theoretical-pedagogical framework and our case studies, we have shown how integrating hybrid education and digital humanities might strengthen the pedagogical vocabulary of digital humanities pedagogies and materialize its approaches to hybrid higher education in, with and for the public as a concrete and reflective pedagogical practice. To develop the field of hybrid digital humanities pedagogies further, we propose (at least) three future steps:

1. *Developing closer and deeper connections between digital humanities and hybrid education:* Scholars, researchers, developers and practitioners from the fields of hybrid education and digital humanities should work together to conceptualize, develop and describe theoretically, methodologically and practically well-founded macro frameworks for hybrid digital humanities education.
2. *Creating new hybrid education formats, resources and platforms for digital humanities:* Based on proposed macro frameworks—such as the one presented in this chapter—developers and practitioners from the fields of hybrid education and digital humanities can work together to create and launch concrete "meso formats, resources and platforms" for the practice of hybrid digital humanities education.
3. *Developing a "pedagogical pattern language" for the practice of hybrid digital humanities education:* Based on the created macro and meso formats, resources and platforms—such as the #dariahTeach and IGNITE cases presented in this chapter—concrete "micro hybrid teaching and learning activities" can now be developed in the form of pedagogical design patterns and a shared pattern language for hybrid digital humanities teaching and learning.

The chapter has, in an exploratory way, approached the development of a practice for hybrid digital humanities education in, with and for the public. Combined, the chapter's sections constitute one step forward in the composition of a foundational theoretical framework, an intentional pedagogical practice and a reflective design materialization of hybrid digital humanities education. This chapter's contribution to digital humanities, hybrid education and public higher education calls for further research into hybrid digital humanities education—both in relation to the exploration of theoretical and methodological synergies, the experimentation with developing and trying out concrete meso formats and micro activities to develop the scholarship of teaching and learning (SOTL) as well as engaging the concrete teaching and learning experiences to better understand the potentials, benefits and challenges of such hybrid learning environments for digital humanities.

Notes

1. https://whatisdigitalhumanities.com/.
2. https://twitter.com/DayofDH.
3. #dariahTeach was designed for multiple publics. For the university students we teach, but also as a site where students who do not have digital arts and humanities expertise can learn DH skills and methods. For the most recent project completed, IGNITE, content was geared towards students and professionals in the heritage sector, and participants in #dariahTeach and IGNITE events have ranged from undergraduate students to university lecturers, to museum professionals.
4. Authentic assignments or assessments put an emphasis on the importance of contextualized tasks not being assessed in a summative way based on specific goal descriptions and criteria-based assessments as those will limit the authenticity. Instead, authentic assessment points to a "real-life practice" that is the focal point of view of the assessment activity, where students must present their ability to translate and integrate their knowledge in a variety of formats (as opposed to the more traditional tests, exams, and essays). The participation of stakeholders or people from an external community of practice constitutes an essential premise for conducting authentic assessment.
5. Practically, alternative conceptions have also emerged in recent decades such as the Connected Curriculum (Fung 2017; Carnell and Fung 2017; Tong et al. 2018).
6. https://teach.dariah.eu/.
7. https://ec.europa.eu/programmes/erasmus-plus/node_en.
8. https://www.youtube.com/channel/UCScSbG7XjiXbZVgilEp0Pkw.
9. https://youtu.be/I8aRtHW3b6g.
10. https://www.starts.eu/.
11. Since #dariahTeach is an open platform without the need to register, it is difficult to know the extent of its usage. Web stats provide some idea. Visits to the #dariahTeach Platform: c. 4700; YouTube followers: 678; Videos on #dariahTeach Youtube channel: 130; Youtube Views: 118.172.

References

Amoroso Leslie, C. 2014. Hybrid by Choice: Increasing Engagement in a High Enrollment Course. Hybrid Pedagogy. https://hybridpedagogy.org/hybrid-choice-increasing-engagement-high-enrollment-course/.

Baartman, Liesbeth K. J., and E. Elly de Bruijn. 2011. Integrating Knowledge, Skills and Attitudes: Conceptualising Learning Processes Towards Vocational Competence. *Educational Research Review* 6 (2): 125–134.

Barnett, Ronald. 2011. *Being a University*. Abingdon: Routledge.

Barnett, Ronald 2017. *The Ecological University: A Feasible Utopia*. London: Routledge.
Besley, Tina, and Michael A. Peters, eds. 2013. *Re-Imagining the Creative University for the 21st Century*. Rotterdam: Sense Publishers.
Bjögvinsson, Erling, Pelle Ehn, and Per-Anders Hillgren. 2012. Design Things and Design Thinking: Contemporary Participatory Design Challenges. *Design Issues* 28 (3): 101–116.
Brighton Fuse Final Report. 2013. Accessed August 31 2021. Available at http://www.brightonfuse.com/wp-content/uploads/2013/10/The-Brighton-Fuse-Final-Report.pdf.
Burdick, Anne, and Holly Willis. 2011. Digital Learning, Digital Scholarship and Design Thinking. *Design Studies* 32 (6): 546–556.
Carayannis, Elias G., and David F. J. Campbell. 2012. *Mode 3 Knowledge Production in Quadruple Helix Innovation systems*. New York: Springer.
Carnell, Brent, and Dilly Fung. 2017. *Developing the Higher Education Curriculum: Research-Based Education in Practice*. London: University College London Press.
Cohen, Anat, Rikke T. Nørgård, and Yishay Mor. 2020. Hybrid Learning Spaces: Design, Data, Didactics. *British Journal of Educational Technology* 51 (4): 1039–1044.
Comunian, Roberta, and Abigail Gilmore. 2015. *Beyond the Creative Campus: Reflections on the Evolving Relationship Between Higher Education and the Creative Economy*. London: King's College London.
Cook, John, Tobias Ley, Ronald Maier, Yishay Mor, Patricia Santos, Elisabeth Lex, Sebastian Dennerlein, Christoph Trattner, and Debbie Holley. 2015. "Using the Hybrid Social Learning Network to Explore Concepts, Practices, Designs and Smart Services for Networked Professional Learning." In *State-of-the-Art and Future Directions of Smart Learning, Proceedings of International Conference on Smart Learning Environments (ICSLE 2015), Sinaia, Romania. Lecture Notes in Educational Technology*, edited by Yanyan Li, Maiga Chang, Milos Kravcik, Elvira Popescu, Ronghuai Huang, and Kinshuk N.-S. Chen, 123–129. Heidelberg: Springer.
Cooke, Phil, and Lisa De Propris. 2011. A Policy Agenda for EU Smart Growth: The Role of Creative and Cultural Industries. *Policy Studies* 32 (4): 365–375.
Doering, Aaron. 2006. Adventure Learning. Transformative Hybrid Online Education. *Distance Education* 27 (2): 197–215.
Dumont, Hanna, and David Istance. 2010. "Analysing and Designing Learning Environments for the 21st Century." In *The Nature of Learning: Using Research to Inspire Practice*, edited by Dumont, Hanna, David Istance, and Francisco Benavides, 19–34. Paris: OECD.
European Parliament. 2016. Report on a Coherent EU Policy for Cultural and Creative Industries (2016/2072(INI)). Accessed 31 August 2021. Available at https://www.europarl.europa.eu/doceo/document/A-8-2016-0357_EN.pd.
Fung, Dilly. 2017. *Connected Curriculum for Higher Education*. London: University College London Press.
Gibbons, Michael, Camilla Limoges, Helga Nowotny, Simon Schwartzman, Peter Scott, and Martin Trow. 1994. *The New Production of Knowledge: The Dynamics of Science and Research in Contemporary Societies*. Los Angeles, CA: Sage.
Haraway, Donna J. 1988. Situated Knowledges: The Science Question in Feminism and the Privilege of Partial Perspective. *Feminist Studies* 14 (3): 575–599.

Haraway, Donna. 2016. *Staying with the Trouble*. Durham, NC: Duke University Press.
Hilli, Charlotta, Rikke T. Nørgård, and Janus H. Aaen. 2019. Designing Hybrid Learning Spaces in Higher Education. *Dansk Universitetspædagogisk Tidsskrift* 15 (27): 66–82.
Kapchan, Deborah A., and Pauline T. Strong. 1999. Theorizing the Hybrid. *The Journal of American Folklore* 112 (445): 239–253.
Kohls, Christian, Christian Köppe, Alex Y. Pedersen, and Christian Dalsgaard. 2018. "Outside in and Inside Out: New Hybrid Education Patterns." In *Proceedings of the 23rd European Conference on Pattern Languages of Programs*, 1–9. New York: Association for Computing Machinery.
Kohls, Christian, Rikke T. Nørgård, and Steven Warburton. 2017. "Sharing is Caring." In *EuroPLoP 2017: Proceedings of the 22nd European Conference on Pattern Languages of Programs*, 1–6. New York: Association for Computing Machinery.
Könings, Karen D., Saskia Brand-Gruwel, J.G. van Jeroen, and J.J.G. Merriënboer. 2005. Towards More Powerful Learning Environments Through Combining the Perspectives of Designers, Teachers, and Students. *British Journal of Educational Psychology* 75 (4): 645–660.
Köppe, Christian, Rikke T. Nørgård, and Alex Y. Pedersen. 2017. "Towards a Pattern Language for Hybrid Education." In *Proceedings of the VikingPLoP 2017 Conference on Pattern Languages of Program (VikingPLoP '17)*, 1–17. New York: Association for Computing Machinery. https://doi.org/10.1145/3158491.3158504.
Köppe, Christian, Christian Kohls, Alex Y. Pedersen, Rikke T. Nørgård, and Paul S. Inventado. 2018. "Hybrid Collaboration Patterns." *PLoP '18: Proceedings of the 25th Conference on Pattern Languages of Programs*, 1–14. New York: Association for Computing Machinery.
Leslie, Catherine A. 2014. "Hybrid by Choice: Increasing Engagement in a High Enrolment Course." *Hybrid Pedagogies*. Accessed 31 August 2021. Available at https://hybridpedagogy.org/hybrid-choice-increasing-engagement-high-enrollment-course/.
McKilligan, Seda, Nick Fila, Diane Rover, and Mani Mina. 2017. Design Thinking as a Catalyst for Changing Teaching and Learning Practices in Engineering. *IEEE Frontiers in Education Conference (FIE)* 2017: 1–5.
Nørgård, Rikke T. 2021. Theorising Hybrid Lifelong Learning. *British Journal of Educational Technology* 52 (4): 1709–1723.
Nørgård, Rikke T., and Søren. Bengtsen. 2016. Academic Citizenship Beyond the Campus: A Call for the Placeful University. *Higher Education Research & Development* 35 (1): 4–16.
Nørgård, Rikke T., and Kim H. Mathiesen. 2018. "Undervisningsbaserede forskningskollektiver. Fra Studenterundervisning til Akademiske Partnerskaber" [Teaching-Based Research Collectives: From Teaching Students to Academic Partnerships]. *Dansk Universitetspædagogisk Tidsskrift* 13 (24): 82–103.
Nørgård, Rikke T., Yishay Mor, and Søren. S. Bengtsen. 2019. Networked Learning in, for, and with the World. In *Networked Professional Learning: Emerging and Equitable Discourses for Professional Development*, edited by A. Littlejohn, J. Jaldemark, E. Vrieling-Teunter, and F. Nijland, 71–88. Cham: Springer.
O'Byrne, W. Ian., and Kristine E. Pytash. 2015. Hybrid and Blended Learning: Modifying Pedagogies Across Path, Pace, Time, and Place. *Journal of Adolescent & Adult Literacy* 59 (2): 137–140.

Pedersen, Alex Y., Rikke T. Nørgård, and Christian Köppe. 2018. Patterns of Inclusion: Fostering Digital Citizenship Through Hybrid Education. *Educational Technology & Society* 21 (1): 225–236.

Peters, Michael A., and Tina Besley. 2013. *The Creative University*. Rotterdam: Sense Publishers.

Rahm, Lina, and Jörgen Skågeby. 2014. "Making Change. Producing Hybrid Learning Products." *Hybrid Pedagogies*. Accessed 31 August 2021. Available at http://hybridpedagogies.org/making-change-produsing-hybrid-learning-products/.

Ratto, Matt. 2011. Critical Making: Conceptual and Material Studies in Technology and Social Life. *The Information Society: An International Journal* 27 (4): 252–260.

Schütz, Florian, Marie L. Heidingsfelder, and Martina Schraudner. 2019. Co-Shaping the Future in Quadruple Helix Innovation System: Uncovering Public Preferences Towards Participatory Research and Innovation. *The Journal of Design, Economics, and Innovation* 5 (2): 128–146.

Shumar, Wesley. 1997. *College for Sale: A Critique of the Commodification of Higher Education*. London and New York: Routledge.

Simonsen, Jesper, Connie Svabo, Sara M. Strandvad, Kristine Samson, Morten Hertzum, and Ole E. Hansen. 2014. *Situated Design Methods*. MIT Press.

Staley, David J. 2019. *Alternative Universities: Speculative Design for Innovation in Higher Education*. Baltimore, MD: Johns Hopkins University Press.

START.eu. Accessed 31 August 2021. Available at https://www.starts.eu/.

Stommel, Jesse. 2012. "Hybridity, pt. 2: What is Hybrid Pedagogies?" *Hybrid Pedagogies*. Accessed 31 August 2021. Available at https://hybridpedagogies.org/hybridity-pt-2-what-is-hybrid-pedagogies/.

Stommel, Jesse, and Pete Rorabaugh. 2012. "Hybridity, pt. 3: What Does Hybrid Pedagogies Do?" *Hybrid Pedagogies*. Accessed 31 August 2021. http://www.digitalpedagogieslab.com/hybridped/hybridity-pt-3-what-does-hybrid-pedagogies-do/.

Tong, Vincent C. H., Alex Standen, and Mina Sotiriou. 2018. *Shaping Higher Education with Students: Ways to Connect Research and Teaching*. London: University College London Press.

Villarroel, Veronica, Susan Bloxham, Daniela Bruna, Carola Bruna, and Constanza Herrera-Seda. 2018. Authentic Assessment: Creating a Blueprint for Course Design. *Assessment & Evaluation in Higher Education* 43 (5): 840–854.

Wang, Feng, and Michael J. Hannafin. 2005. Design-Based Research and Technology-Enhanced Learning Environments. *Educational Technology Research and Development* 53 (4): 5–23.

Wright, Susan. 2016. Universities in a Knowledge Economy or Ecology? Policy, Contestation and Abjection. *Critical Policy Studies* 10 (1): 59–78.

Zitter, Ilya, and Aimée Hoeve. 2012. "Hybrid Learning Environments: Merging Learning and Work Processes to Facilitate Knowledge Integration and Transitions." *OECD Education Working Papers* 81. OECD Publishing.

CHAPTER 3

Experiential Education as Public Humanities Practice

Ashley Bender and Gretchen Busl

3.1 Introduction

Historical practices in humanistic—and particularly literary—studies over the past century have tended to withdraw students from active participation in public life by focusing more on interpretation rather than application. Yet developing students as active participants in civic life is a core value of humanistic study. Furthermore, of the limited scholarship on experiential learning in the humanities, most only provides models for application, rather than offering theoretical foundations for that practice.[1] In this essay, we provide such a framework, arguing that experiential learning can be a public humanities practice that deepens the ways that students, especially undergraduates, engage with the ideas of their discipline and translate that knowledge into an enacted, embodied practice. We argue that moving toward a praxis of public scholarship shifts close reading from the end goal of literary study to the means by which students and their instructors can create and do public good. Moreover, when students engage in and with the multiple publics they encounter, those publics come to understand the value of the humanities in turn.

We begin by offering a brief history of English studies within the context of the changing nature of the humanities in the academy, primarily within a

A. Bender (✉) · G. Busl
Texas Woman's University, Denton, TX, USA
e-mail: abender@twu.edu

G. Busl
e-mail: GBusl@twu.edu

© The Author(s), under exclusive license to Springer Nature Switzerland AG 2022
A. Schwan and T. Thomson (eds.), *The Palgrave Handbook of Digital and Public Humanities*, https://doi.org/10.1007/978-3-031-11886-9_3

US context, providing a critical explanation of how close reading became the dominant modality. We contextualize this history within both the conversation of mind–body dualism and the ethical turn in critical theory. We then situate the notion of applied humanities within the framework of experiential learning pedagogies. In sum, this reevaluation of humanistic practices provides opportunities to address the university's role in civic education and the ways that public humanities can lessen an ever-increasing divide between the academy and its publics. Perhaps most importantly, such a reevaluation provides an opportunity for students to see themselves in new ways, as *student-scholars* equipped with the skills and dispositions they need to effectively engage with the publics that surround them.

3.2 Active Reading vs. Civic Action

Developing students as active participants in civic life is a core value of humanistic study that has long-standing tradition in the discipline. McComiskey (2006, 4) traces the origins of humanistic study to the academies of ancient Greece, when he says, "knowledge was treated as an integrated system, and academic inquiry drew from whatever arts and sciences were most useful in solving the problem at hand." Even with this interdisciplinary approach, rhetoric was still dominant because "it was at the center of political life, the deepest and most abiding concern of the democratic city-state," and "communal engagement was considered essential to attaining virtue, the individual's harmonious integration of knowledge, ethics, and aesthetics in daily activity" (Berlin 2003, xii). In other words, humanistic study in its most nascent state in the Western, European world had its focus not on the production and reproduction of textual analyses; rather, its power derived from its outward focus, from its applicability and purposefulness within a larger sociopolitical context and, significantly, within the individual's ability to deploy the skills of rhetoric (i.e., of humanistic study) to the stabilization, improvement, and perpetuation of the polis through engagement with others.

Although rhetoric would maintain a stronghold in European universities through the eighteenth century and in the US until the later nineteenth century (Berlin 2003), the institutionalization of rhetoric ultimately moved the aims of the discipline further away from public engagement. According to Berlin's history, rhetoric courses were once the primary focus of study, whereas "practical scientific training" was gained on the job (2003, 19). A confluence of social, economic, and political changes, among them a shift toward corporate capitalism and the establishment of land-grant universities in the US, refocused the college curriculum and contributed to the emergence of the research university (Berlin 2003, 19) and the beginning of rhetoric's decline. Although English departments remained important "to the idea of the university" in Britain and America, the predominant focus of these programs changed as rhetoric became less favored toward the middle of the nineteenth century in favor of philology (Gildea et al. 2015, 2).

Around this same time, the literary text emerged as the primary subject of English studies (Graff 1987; Cushman 2002; Berlin 2003), along with a bifurcation in the field between textual analysis and textual production, the coexisting and sometimes competing subdisciplines of literary studies and rhetoric-composition (Berlin 2003). Composition courses became a required course for all students, an effort to prepare them for the workforce, while textual analysis was increasingly seen as an ideal of the field, divorced from textual production and the preferred labor of professors over teaching composition. Even as early as the 1920s, English as a discipline was experiencing an identity crisis, with tensions building between those aspects of the field that focused especially on theoretical methodologies and those that focused on more "practical" studies, furthering the divide between false, Cartesian-inflected binaries: "theory was privileged over practice, knowledge over application, and mind over body" (McComiskey 2006, 11; Berlin 2003, xiv, 3), that is, a set of practices that sacralized the literary artifact at the cost of others, including rhetoric. Furthermore, while there was general consensus among English studies programs to focus on English/British literary texts (Berlin 2003), the approaches to study were a cause of tension.

The turn to New Criticism in the early twentieth century reinforced these divisions by making the literary object the central focus of the field's purpose (Yood 2003). On the one hand, both New Criticism, and the Practical Criticism of the UK that inspired it, were invested in practices that could address the needs of a quickly growing student body and allowed for a greater "democratization of literary study; since, unlike philological study, which required years of groundwork, training in the close analysis of textual particulars was available to undergraduate students of all backgrounds" (Hickman 2012, 13). On the other, the drive for a more empirical approach to literary study and the desire to legitimate the discipline led to the institutionalization of classroom practices—helped along by the publication of textbooks codifying such practices (Hickman 2012)—at both secondary and post-secondary levels that had a tendency to divorce the study of literature "from any relevance outside of the academy by locating meaning entirely within the confines of the text" (McComiskey 2006, 22).[2]

New Criticism's and formalism's claims to objectivity, the focus on the text alone, has long been the dominant practice in literature classrooms, even as new theoretical approaches led to a rise in critical discourses and theories—for example, Marxism, feminist criticism, and postcolonial criticism, among others—that had the ability to demonstrate the public relevance of English studies. These approaches, however, coincided with increasing fragmentation and specialization that further separated the field from "the nonacademic world" (McComiskey 2006, 32). Knights argues that the tensions among the plural disciplines of English departments in mid-century UK created a disciplinary divide between earlier approaches to literary scholarship focused on philology and historical-based readings and newer critical approaches grounded in theory, the result of which was "a classroom tradition [that] represent[ed] the polar opposite of a transmission model of education": producing knowledge that was "provisional, oblique, and only indirectly replicable" (2015, 18–19). Knights's argument points toward an isolated intellectual elitism, a claim still often hurled at academics, and not just those in English studies. And perhaps this is, to an extent, merited. A critical discourse divorced from public application reinforces an "us and them" dichotomy that underlies lingering myths about the lack of value of an English degree as a pathway to careers other than teaching.

We agree with McComiskey (2006) and Cushman (1999, 2002) that in order for English studies, and the humanities more broadly, to maintain—increase, even—its relevance in the twenty-first century, the applications of the field must reach beyond the walls of the academy: practitioners must demonstrate the value of the humanities to stakeholders within the academy (those who grant or deny financial support, especially) and to multiple publics that may have diminishing belief in the value of a liberal arts education. Indeed, we are seeing increasing mandates to make the humanities matter, both in the United States and in the UK: as Gildea et al. point out, "teachers and researchers are faced with mounting expectations that we contribute tangible benefits to society" (2015, 4).[3] However, classroom- and text-bound practices limit students' ability to put concepts they are learning into action, which contributes to the diminished importance of the humanities to public audiences (Veninga 1999). The study of arts and humanities should not only instill an appreciation for the subjects of study, but it should also establish their relevance to social action (Handley 2001). Instead, students all too often spend their time crafting essays that have little to do with their time outside of the classroom.

3.3 Rethinking the Mind–Body Divide

If, as Berlin argues, "a curriculum undertakes the creation of consciousness and behavior" (2003, 18), what consciousnesses and behaviors does prioritizing the act of reading literary texts create? Histories of English studies by Scholes (1985), Graff (1987), Berlin (2003), and McComiskey (2006) reveal an emphasis on division and hierarchization. This development stems primarily from the sustained influences of the Cartesian mind–body dualism that emphasizes rational thought as a product only of mental mechanisms, rather than as the product of an intertwined mind–body experience. Simply put, this dualism values *thinking* over *doing* and has long held sway in Western society. Its emphasis is far reaching and underscores other hierarchies within society, the academy, and humanistic study. Valuing analysis/thinking over production/doing creates related dualisms that hierarchize both the actions and objects of literary studies. The very nature of canon formation and the privileging of certain texts, primarily by dead white men, as ideal objects of study stems from nationalist impulses (Berlin 2003, 20), as well as from a sustained effort to class art in high and low categories, reinforcing social distinctions through cultural production. In Schaeffer's (2013) critique, literature is itself a construct that the discipline creates, reinforces, and perpetuates. The focus of literary studies is, supposedly, the literary object; the definition of what constitutes such an object remains narrowly defined. Thus the primary work of literary study *and* the object of that study are by their very nature exclusionary. Consequently, literary studies is often responsible for "reproducing and promoting the cultural values that society, or its dominant members ... thinks it necessary to promote," what Schaeffer calls a *"normative project"* (2013, 271).

The result of these simultaneous binary oppositions is an enclosure of literary studies at both the professional and pedagogical levels and the isolation of students and their learning to the classroom. As a result, the field of literary studies still overwhelmingly reproduces the status divisions and value systems its democratizing ethos purports to work against. The positioning of writing studies within the curriculum is a telling example: the "low" status of composition, taught primarily by underpaid, contingent instructors, reveals much about the discipline's devaluation of non-literary work and production. Yet, for students on a "traditional" literary track in English studies, composition is also the course with the strongest connections to non-academic audiences.[4] The persistent prioritization of literary tracks over those more engaged with "practical skills" also creates a wider wedge between "the task of teaching text production from that of teaching literary interpretation" (Berlin 2003, 20). Even as we see the emergence of undergraduate rhetoric and writing tracks in the US, they are still sometimes perceived by faculty as less valuable because they are associated with the practical arts of production.

Similarly, the increasing divide between the academy and wider publics isolates the literary scholar, reinforcing these divides and diminishing the ways that humanistic study contributes to a larger public good—and even public *goods*, including the cultural content so widely distributed and consumed. Thus we agree with Pileggi and Patton (2003), who cite Bourdieu's argument that "closure, autonomy, in effect isolates researchers in the 'ivory tower'" and "autonomy without engagement misses the point of human thought; the production of knowledge must be complemented by the diffusion of knowledge" (2003, 317). In other words, in an effort to maintain the social capital accorded through academic research, literary studies reinscribes the symbolic violence of larger social oppressions. In doing so, the academy is framed as a place of value, privilege, and elite status, while the publics beyond are framed as unworthy of such shared knowledge (see also Cushman 2002, 209).

Koritz suggests that the rewards system of US universities contributes to these effects and "makes it nearly impossible for faculty members to take initiative in addressing such a state of affairs beyond the context of their own teaching and writing" (2005, 84–85). The "publish or perish" model prioritizes the individual and their scholarly output over the dissemination and application of that work to wider, non-specialized publics where their ideas could be *enacted* for public good. The result, she suggests, leads to "disturbing consequences" (Koritz 2005, 85), among them a dissociation of learning from students' lived experiences. At its core, Koritz's argument asks that we reconnect the work of students' academic lives to the vast networks in which they participate beyond the university.

As a field, English studies (and the humanities more broadly) are uniquely positioned to address the injustices of society, yet the democratizing potential of the field was, until recent decades, curtailed by curricula that reinforced and replicated the social divisions of public/private, high/low, Literature/literature, poetic/rhetoric, analysis/application (Berlin 2003). Furthermore, the hierarchies foundational to the university's reward system often still shape what we ask our students to create: primarily, single authored essays for circulation between the student and instructor. For those faculty who do engage in public humanities, the reward system has been slow to respond (Schroeder 2020); even institutions that value public engagement still expect traditional scholarly output. The combined effect of these pressures has led to two intersecting consequences which, while diminishing, still persist. The first is a failure to make the literary work culturally relevant (Berlin 2003) and connect the work of literature classrooms to larger, outside communities. The second is the lingering prestige accorded to the written research paper/literary analysis, which allowed it to dominate as the primary mode of assessment for most of the last century.[5] Both practices and assessments denied students opportunities to apply their learning in more public ways, so they may practice and learn how to effectively intervene in extra-academic discourses and communities.

Berlin sums with damning accuracy the effects of a literary/rhetoric divide that has prioritized high literature and insular reading over more fully integrated and outward-looking practices in English curricula. Such a divide, he says,

> serves the interests of a privileged managerial class while discriminating against those outside this class. ... It also works to exclude from the ranks of the privileged managerial class those students not socialized from birth in the ways of the aesthetic response, doing so by its influence on the materials and methods of reading and writing required for success in secondary schools, college admission tests, and the colleges themselves. (2003, 15)

To be fair, much has changed since Berlin's book was originally published in 1996. Especially within the context of the civil rights movements of the past two decades (e.g., the #MeToo and Black Lives Matter movements), we have seen a turn in English studies to embrace "texts" other than those we define as traditionally literary. We have also seen an increasing growth in the range of critical approaches to literary study, with queer theory and disability studies informing critical approaches and calls for decolonizing syllabi informing pedagogical (and critical) practice. And yet we still see *within classroom practices* a tendency to keep classroom learning confined to that space. Increasingly, we embrace the study of texts within their social context, but students remain disconnected from those same social contexts.

So how do "curricula ... take account of the world for which their students (subjects) are being prepared" (McComiskey 2006, 43)? McComiskey's (2006) integrated model that emphasizes three mutual activities of analysis, critique, and production *theorizes* one way in. He suggests that the focus of study should include "social discourse" writ more broadly. Such a move is a step toward the goal of developing active, engaged citizens who connect regularly with publics during and beyond their programs. However, just replacing one object of study, the "text," with social discourse is not enough; students must also *engage* in social discourse and social practice. Shifting assessment practices beyond classroom-bound rhetorical situations provides a grounded, specific approach to achieving McComiskey's model (2006, 43). Authentic assessment, a practice very closely aligned with the experiential education movement, is an approachable way to encourage students to move beyond the literary page and apply the wide range of skills they gain in a literature classroom.[6] The same is true for experiential education, which, at its core, is the creation of learning opportunities that encourage students to apply concepts, theories, and skills developed in the classroom to situations outside it.

A simple definition of experiential education is complicated by what are often seen as competing theoretical approaches. In his analysis of "experience" in outdoor, place-based, and adventure learning, Roberts identifies three approaches: "interactive experience, drawn from pragmatist [Dewey] philosophy; embodied experience, drawn from Romanticism and phenomenology; and experience as praxis, drawn from critical theory" (2008, 21). Furthermore, we suggest that experiential learning can be a public humanities practice, one that both deepens the ways that students engage with the ideas of their discipline and translates that knowledge into an embodied practice. The goal is not to *simulate* these experiences; rather, it is to *enact* them, for students to be full participants in an authentic process, be it an observer participant at a cultural dance program, a team member pitching a marketing plan to a local firm, or a blogger drawing on in-class discussions to participate in a wider public discourse about a social topic. In defining experiential education in the literature classroom as public humanities practice, we believe all three approaches are important and intertwined, as experience not only points toward pragmatic applications but is also an embodied interaction that allows the learner to put critical theory into practice. Such a holistic understanding of experience enables students to recognize their relationship to and within the sociopolitical, economic, and educational institutions that affect the development of their identities and behaviors. Such an approach also encourages a recognition that the knowledge and artifacts they create as part of their education occur through the work of bodies engaged in particular spaces and in relation to other bodies (Fenwick 2007, 534). Disaggregating these facets of experience from each other diminishes the comprehensive nature of learning in/through action so embedded in existing experiential learning models, especially Kolb's

(1984) foundational experiential learning cycle that moves through concrete experience, to reflective observation, to abstract conceptualization, to active experimentation.

3.4 Limited Points of View

The phrase "experiential education" remains far more slippery than current discussions often reveal. Too often, "experiential education"—what it is and what it means—is taken as a given. Even the National Society for Experiential Education (NSEE), a leading organization for experiential education in the US, uses the phrase throughout their website without providing a clear definition. The closest they come is in their "8 Principles of Good Practice for All Experiential Learning Activities," which implies a complex set of relations among a series of actions that constitute the process of an experiential learning opportunity (see, e.g., Kolb 1984). They also offer insight toward a definition when they state that "both experience and learning are fundamental" to any experiential learning activity and that "between the learner and any facilitator(s) of learning, there is a mutual responsibility." These statements point to two key features of effective experiential learning: that neither the learning nor the experience (be it an extended internship, a single volunteer shift, or a few hours observing a public event) takes precedence—rather, they inform each other; and that the learner is a co-creator with their audience in knowledge and equally responsible for their own learning.

Perhaps unsurprisingly, much of the focus in experiential education is on STEM fields, where students' ability to work in labs or in the field is easier; English majors are too often left out of these conversations (Nikitina 2009; VanDette 2010). Training that addresses the specific needs of humanities curricula, while increasing, remains scarce. Because experiential education seems to have entered the English discipline through composition studies, much of what is available relates to these courses rather than literature courses. Even arguments in favor of experiential education in the literature classroom tend to focus primarily on service learning (see, e.g., Cushman 1999, 2002; Schutz and Gere 1998; Grobman 2005; Koritz 2005; VanDette 2010). To be sure, service learning—a pedagogical practice that includes volunteer or community service-oriented experiences as part of a course's curriculum—is a valuable pedagogical practice, one that we have both brought into our classrooms. Yet it is often disconnected from the mastery of the disciplinary concepts in the courses that employ these methods; furthermore, it is rarely a mode of discovery and more often conceived as "a highly asymmetrical relation in which students learn by serving the less fortunate" (Wiltse 2011). Unlike other forms of experiential education, such as internships, independent research, and the type of public humanities assignments we suggest, it is more likely to create unidirectional knowledge production (Kajner 2013), as programs often position students as the givers, not co-creators of knowledge.

And while some authors, such as Cushman (1999, 2002), theorize service learning, few extend theoretical approaches to these other forms of experiential education. One such approach is that of Grobman and Kinkead, who call for a refiguring of classroom practices that prioritizes an explanation of "our methodolog[ies]" and "ask[s] for authentic scholarship" (2010, x). While they do not explicitly refer to it as *experiential education,* they argue that "undergraduate research [is] one of the few certifiable high-impact educational practices (see xiii). Their emphasis, however, is on research with an academic audience; we argue that providing students an opportunity to engage in "authentic scholarship" also means opening ways for them to create with multiple publics in mind and to co-create with their communities. Similarly, Cushman (1999, 329) argues that instructors should position themselves as "public intellectuals," and in doing so "combine their research, teaching, and service efforts to address social issues important to community members in under-served neighborhoods."

Nikitina's arguments in favor of *applied humanities* come closest to offering broadly applicable models of learning that may begin with close reading practices but push students to put those theories into practice with the projects they produce. Such an approach, she suggests, helps instructors avoid the "overly self-referential" (2009, 36) practices currently limiting the scope of classroom activity and instead "[fosters students'] ability to own (enact and embody) a literary or philosophical insight" by making "concepts tangible … through media and the arts, through activism, through co-creation, through contemporization, and through cross-pollination" (2009, 38). As we will discuss, approaching experiential education as an embodied, enacted practice creates increased opportunities to engage students with public issues, both local and global. As a result, this "embodied and enacted humanism is," as Nikitina argues, "more powerful than its theoretical counterpart, and it results in better conceptual learning as well" (2009, 38). This holds true for experiential learning, which in its various forms can function *as* applied humanities, encouraging the shift from concept to application.

3.5 Benefits of Experiential Education to Students

Experiential education has a number of benefits for students and instructors. Imagined as a form of applied humanities, it creates what Eyler argues is a "deeper understanding of subject matter than is possible through classroom study alone." It also enhances "critical thinking and application of knowledge in complex or ambiguous situations"—problem solving—and instills an "ability to engage in lifelong learning" (2009, 26). Thus knowledge transfer is a fundamental facet of experiential education and one that can help demonstrate the discipline's relevance to social action. It gives the study of literature what Berlin calls "contemporary relevance" (2003, 18), a clear connection to what happens beyond the university's walls. This occurs, in part, because experiential education places students in a position where they can see their learning in action.

By applying their knowledge, students engaged in experiential learning can cultivate the critical literacy they need to effectively engage in and with their society (Berlin, 2003). Close reading alone does not improve this critical literacy. Rather, focusing only on close reading (and all too often, essay writing), encourages isolated acts of learning that remain classroom-bound. Further, it can often turn the practice and product of study into a kind of automated production about which students remain uncritical. Berlin argues, "literacy ought not be treated as merely an instrumental 'skill' ... a useful tool in the mastery of more significant and substantial academic subjects" (2003, 105). Drawing on Freire, he argues, "to learn to read and write is to learn to name the world, and in this naming is a program for understanding the conditions of our experience and, more important, for acting in and on them" (2003, 105–6). The larger goal of experiential education should be developing critical literacy and civic responsibility.

Well-conducted experiential education also helps students cultivate the metacognitive practices necessary for self-reflection. Students are consequently better able to articulate what these skills are and the ways that they can apply these skills to the improvement of society, thereby creating better engagement with the potential publics as advocates for the humanities. This is especially true for a discipline such as English studies, in which both students and the public often struggle to imagine how skills gained in a literature class have value beyond the university. The divide between popular perceptions and employer hiring practices is telling. At the same time that recent trends in employer data suggest humanistic study provides the very skills that employers seek in job candidates (Hart 2018), popular and state-sanctioned narratives surrounding the humanities and liberal arts continue to devalue these degrees.

This gap suggests a failure of articulation—not only about the skills students acquire but also (perhaps especially) about the actual content, that is, the literary knowledge itself. The public's inability to recognize the value of such knowledge, even as they consume the goods that result from continued literary critique and production—is another consequence of the increasing divide between the university and world beyond it. This divide suggests something about the ways students view their education. Laff's argument that "many students see their learning in each course as self-contained and almost discrete from their other coursework" (1998, 71) points toward curricular deficits and our failure to help students develop the vocabulary to effectively explain the value of their degrees. Experiential education is one important intervention, as it serves as a means of reinforcing and enhancing students' learning regarding content matter and application at the same time it creates opportunities for students to understand the "real-world" value of their degrees in action. Experiential learning can help establish new dispositions for students, enabling them to more effectively apply their mastery and engage in lifelong learning after completing their degrees.

Koritz calls for a "strengthen[ing of] the connections among the purposes of the classroom, the public mission of the university, and the skills of engaged citizenship. The walls that currently separate these realms," she claims, "must be breached" (2005, 82). Like Koritz, we argue that classroom practices that move beyond institutional boundaries and into public spaces can help us achieve this goal; however, we take a broader approach to experiential learning that encompasses any educational component that asks the student to engage with one, if not more, potential publics—from internships, to service learning, to client-based projects, to field observations, to performances, among other approaches. As Kajner notes, the idea of "engagement moves higher education beyond the idea of outreach … to engagement, whereby scholars and communities both contribute through mutually beneficial and reciprocal partnerships" (2013, 10–11). By engaging with these publics—that is, by creating knowledge with and not just for publics—students necessarily engage in democratized acts of knowledge making.

3.6 MAKING PUBLIC CONNECTIONS

The US-based National Endowment for the Humanities (NEH) defines the public humanities as projects that "enable … [people] to explore significant humanities works, ideas, and events. They offer new insights into familiar subjects and invite reflection upon important questions about human life." Similarly, Fisher (2020) defines public humanities as practices that "[extend] the benefits of the humanities beyond the classroom by engaging diverse communities in their work." He identifies five goals of the projects collected in the *Humanities for All* database, each of which provides a potential approach for experiential education in the literature classroom:

1. Informing contemporary debates;
2. Amplifying community voices and histories;
3. Helping individuals and communities navigate difficult experiences;
4. Expanding educational access; and
5. Preserving culture in times of crisis and exchange.

Envisioning public humanities praxis as experiential education involves a series of reconfigurations, the first being a repositioning of close reading and analytical writing as skill-building tools, rather than as the final outputs of student learning. Close reading is important, promoting skills in critical and analytical thinking; likewise, it fosters important skills in communication and argumentation. But to rely on a ten-page interpretive essay as the major assignment through which we assess these skills replicates the failures of the faculty to extend knowledge beyond a small audience and diminishes opportunities to help students learn modes of transferring these skills to situations they will encounter in their daily lives. Even the relatively simple move to incorporate public scholarship assignments can dramatically impact students' understanding of literature's role in society as well as their ability to imagine themselves as agents of change. For example, in Busl's course on Black, Indigenous, and People of Color (BIPOC) speculative fiction, assessing students' mastery of key historical and theoretical concepts by asking them to craft essays for popular websites like Electric Literature also functioned to reinforce their understanding of the role that literature—and its criticism—plays in challenging dominant narratives.

We do not suggest doing away with traditional classroom and assessment practices altogether; rather we see them as foundations for more expansive applications of student learning. Through careful scaffolding, a close reading of literature becomes practice for close reading of other artifacts; it also leads to critical analysis, problem solving, and the generation of new cultural content. For example, an assignment sequence might begin with classroom discussions of a text, followed by written close reading, a reflection that connects classroom conversations to extra-academic discourses, and then a critical analysis of those very discourses. Students can apply knowledge gained through this process to an array of experiential learning activities that require them to engage directly in these public conversations. Put another way, close reading becomes an essential part of the "preparedness and planning" (NSEE) so essential to effective experiential education practices. For example, in Bender's course on eighteenth-century female playwrights, close reading practices laid the foundation for two experiential projects. The first was a group project in which students created MTV *Decoded*-style videos that drew from the literature to explore important cultural concepts, such as rape culture and toxic masculinity. The second was a readers' theater that brought under-performed plays to a public audience. In both instances, students created opportunities for public audiences to engage with literary content and experience the ways that the humanities help society address pressing social issues.

Furthermore, reframing experiential learning as public humanities practice helps reveal the ways these practices align in compelling but often overlooked ways (see Schroeder 2020, 6). An expanded understanding of public humanities has the potential to reframe and reorient the work we do in classrooms to create more opportunities that focus on public engagement. While on the one hand, experiential education acknowledges its benefits to stakeholders outside of academic institutions, theoretical discussions still prioritize the pedagogical, that is, the learning-centered aspects of the practice. Even arguments like Koritz's (2005), which strongly advocate for service learning as a means of developing engaged citizens, focus on the ways that the practices support student growth, intellect, and maturity. Rather than focus solely on the gains to individual students, we advocate recalibrating the value system of literary studies to emphasize the reciprocity between the student and discourse communities developed during the learning experience.

The very nature of experiential education as a practice that moves students, physically and/or intellectually, outside of institutional spaces makes it a public humanities practice, that is, a practice of humanistic scholarship that engages with a range of public audiences. Hutchison and Bosacki (2000) argue that holistic education philosophy could benefit experiential education because of its focus on transformation, specifically its emphasis on interconnected networks. Framing experiential education as public humanities practice helps students to *see* these connections, to better analyze and understand their own situatedness. Schroeder offers examples of public humanities in practice, including

> translational scholarship; cultural organizing; production of programs, plays, performances, tours, festivals, exhibits or other audience-oriented humanistic activities. ... maker activities, particularly making art, music, writing, typically with an orientation toward an evidentiary basis and/or some form of expertise; and generally all ways of making meaning socially, or making personal meaning in public space. (2020, 6)

While Schroeder's list is by no means exhaustive, her examples provide a sense of what it means to do public humanities. The phrase "audience-oriented humanistic activity" is essential to this definition. Defining public humanities in these terms helps us understand that experiential education can turn the classroom into a laboratory of public humanities practice by emphasizing the intellectual positioning of the student-scholar as someone always already engaged with publics.

At their core, then, these two suggestions—reframing traditional classroom practices as a means, not an end, and redefining experiential education as public humanities practice—are as much about the language we use as about the *dispositions* we enact and reinforce in our own work as scholars. Boyer's scholarship of engagement model, which calls for the academy to "become a more vigorous partner in the search for answers to our most pressing social, civic, economic, and moral problems" (1996, 15), applies as much to *our own work* as it does to the work we ask our students to complete. The scholarship of application, or "making knowledge useful" (Boyer 1996, 23), should not matter just for faculty; by developing experiential education practices that emphasize the public application of humanistic study, we also teach students how to "make useful" what they acquire in our classrooms.

The growth of public humanities programs over the past decade and a half or so points toward the vitality and importance of praxis. However, their primary focus on graduate education and on scholars/researchers as the primary practitioners misses an opportunity to engage with the far larger constituency of undergraduate students studying humanities. According to the American Academy of Arts & Sciences, in 2015 212,512 students earned four-year humanities degrees. Hundreds of thousands more students enroll in humanities courses as part of their core curriculum or minors. Invigorating undergraduate courses across the humanities, not just in English studies, with the democratic ethic of public humanities practice would ensure that we heed

Boyer's call to "[connect] the rich resources of the university to our most pressing social, civic, and ethical problems." In doing so, "campuses would be viewed by both students and professors not as isolated islands but as staging grounds for action" (1996, 27), and students would also be better able to recognize their own role as important participants in this action.

Such a disposition would go a long way toward addressing the "disjunction between literary study and society" (Schaeffer 2013, 269) that too often limits the subject of study in literature classrooms; it would likewise address concerns of "deep paternalism" (Schroeder 2020, 15) and the "missionary ideology" (Cushman 1999, 332; see also Schutz and Gere 1998; Grobman 2005) that often manifests in service-learning models. Focusing on a public humanities practice that helps students develop an audience awareness at all stages of a project is one such approach. To engage an audience does not necessarily require a call and response. Rather, we can engage the publics in our work by teaching students to conceive of an audience beyond the instructor and their classmates with whom they can share their work and to whom they can respond as they craft their projects. Such a reframing encourages students to think about the multiple publics with whom they may create knowledge and the multiple goods that such collaborations could produce.

3.7 Conclusion

This reevaluation of humanistic practices provides opportunities to address the university's role in civic education and the ways that public scholarship can lessen the divide between the academy and a wide range of potential publics, in part by helping students to identify those publics with whom they can create knowledge. Universities' missions have long been tied to the development of civically minded, publicly engaged individuals who recognize their place as agents in an integrated network of people, institutions, and histories and who can effect positive change in their societies. Yet too often, this aspect of university missions—so closely allied to the goals of humanistic study—is lost in the actual practices of classroom spaces. Nowhere is this gap more resonant than in the literature classroom, so long encumbered by the weight of literary canons and limited approaches to assessment that we often fail to actually teach the dispositions that our discipline purports to defend (see also Koritz 2005, 83). Our own practices as scholars and the work we ask of our students must model the behaviors we hope they will engage in when they leave our institutions. We must teach them how to extend themselves across the academic-public divide; to develop, in other words, a kind of public literacy in and of itself.

Perhaps, then, our emphasis on "public humanities practice" misses the mark after all: rather, we should reconceive public humanities as a disposition unto itself—ways of being and thinking that shape all levels of engagement. Drawing on Knights, Eaglestone (2015) hints at the ways that disciplinary practices shape not just the subject of English studies but also the subjects who study English. The kind of work we ask students to do, regardless of their level of education, contributes to who they are, how they define themselves, and the behaviors and practices they carry with them when they leave academia. By adopting the practices described here, we more effectively answer Boyer's call for a scholarship of engagement. We work toward "creating a special climate in which the academic and civic cultures communicate more continuously and more creatively with each other" (1996, 27). An experiential education model grounded in public humanities practices allows us to train our students to more effectively participate in their many-layered discourse communities, enriching their own lives and those of others.

When framed as public humanities practice, experiential education has the potential to connect students and their learning beyond the classroom and, in turn, to help the public understand the value of the humanities (Schroeder 2020). This includes those within (administrations) and outside (governments) the academy in charge of controlling (and in recent years, slashing) humanities budgets. Humanities programs have increasingly been pressed to explain the benefits of their existence not only to people outside of the humanities but to their own administrations. Like Quay and Veninga (1990), we resist the forced opposition that pits "scholarship" against "public humanities" and delegitimates a scholarly practice that still struggles to find a foothold in the value systems of universities' tenure and promotion (Schroeder 2020, 19). By legitimating the work of public humanists within the academy, we create more opportunity for these practices to become an essential part of humanistic study and to develop student-scholars. Put another way, experiential education as public humanities practice fosters students' confidence in their own abilities and their own intelligence; it encourages them to find their voices, to know that their voices matter and are powerful enough to shape the public discourses that surround them.

Notes

1. For examples of theoretical framing connected to service learning in the humanities, see Cushman (1999, 2002) and Grobman (2005). The most extensive theoretical exploration of experiential learning in the humanities is Grobman and Kinkead's (2010) introduction to the volume *Undergraduate Research in English Studies*, which examines experiential learning within efforts to find a place for undergraduate research in humanities fields that undervalue collaborative work.
2. Some scholars push back against such simplistic accounts of New Criticism; for example, Hickman and McIntyre's (2012) collection suggests that New Criticism's focus on the text alone was not always fully divorced from the world beyond the text, though the editors acknowledge that the New Critics' "methods were in fact often intended to register and encourage certain attitudes toward art and culture, as well as certain ethical and epistemological stances" (Hickman 2012, 14).
3. Our research suggests this trend holds outside of an Anglo-American context, particularly in the areas of Africa, Asia, and Europe where research is tied to

public funding. See, e.g., Altbach (2008), Africa Humanities Program (2014), and Mittelstrass (2015).
4. This is likely why composition is also the course most likely to include experiential learning components (primarily "service learning" related—that is, courses that include a volunteer or community service-oriented component, e.g., tutoring elementary students in an afterschool program).
5. In the U.S., this may also be due, in part, to the fact that the doctorate, a research-focused degree, has remained the standard credential for college and university teaching; and while pedagogical training is standard in Rhetoric and Composition Ph.D. programs, it is overlooked in English and Literature programs in favor of focus on scholarly publication and dissertations of proto-book quality.
6. Authentic assessment measures are most commonly traced back to Wiggins (1993), who defined authentic assessment as "engaging and worthy problems or questions of importance, in which students must use knowledge to fashion performances effectively and creatively. The tasks are either replicas of or analogous to the kinds of problems faced by adult citizens and consumers or professionals in the field" (229).

References

Africa Humanities Program. 2014. "Recommendations for Reinvigorating Humanities in Africa." https://www.acls.org/uploadedFiles/Publications/Programs/Reinvigorating_the_Humanities_in_Africa.pdf.

Altbach, Philip G. 2008. "The Humanities and Social Sciences in Asia: Endangered Species?" *International Higher Education* 52: 4–6.

American Academy of Arts & Sciences. n.d. "Bachelor's Degrees in the Humanities." Accessed August 15, 2020. https://www.amacad.org/humanities-indicators/higher-education/bachelors-degrees-humanities.

Berlin, James. 2003. *Rhetorics, Poetics, and Cultures: Refiguring College English Studies*, 2nd ed. West Lafayette, IN: Parlor Press.

Boyer, Ernest. 1996. "The Scholarship of Engagement." *Journal of Public Service and Outreach* 1 (1): 11–20.

Cushman, Ellen. 1999. "The Public Intellectual, Service Learning, and Activist Research." *College English* 61 (3): 329–36. doi:https://doi.org/10.2307/379072.

Cushman, Ellen. 2002. "Service Learning as the New English Studies." In *Beyond English Inc.: Curricular Reform in a Global Economy*, edited by David B. Downing, Claude Mark Hurlbert, and Paula Mathieu, 204–18. Portsmouth, NH: Heinemann.

Eaglestone, Robert. 2015. "The Future of English and Institutional Consciousness: Threads and Disengagement." In *English Studies: The State of the Discipline, Past, Present, and Future*, edited by Niall Gildea, Helena Goodwyn, Megan Kitching, and Helen Tyson, 100–13. Basingstoke: Palgrave Macmillan. doi:https://doi.org/10.1057/9781137478054.0014.

Eyler, Janet. 2009. "The Power of Experiential Education." *Liberal Education* 95 (4): 24–31.

Fenwick, Tara. 2007. "Experiential Learning." In *The Praeger Handbook of Education and Psychology*, edited by Joe L. Kincheloe and Raymond A. Horn, 530–39. London: Praeger.

Fisher, Daniel. n.d. "Goals of the Publicly Engaged Humanities." *Humanities for All: Explore the Publicly Engaged Humanities*. Accessed October 16, 2020. https://humanitiesforall.org/essays/goals-of-the-publicly-engaged-humanities.
Gildea, Niall, Helena Goodwyn, Megan Kitching, and Helen Tyson, eds. 2015. *English Studies: The State of the Discipline, Past, Present, and Future*. Basingstoke: Palgrave Macmillan. doi:https://doi.org/10.1057/9781137478054.0001.
Graff, Gerald. 1987. *Professing Literature: An Institutional History*. Chicago: University of Chicago Press.
Grobman, Laurie. 2005. "Is There a Place for Service Learning in Literary Studies." *Profession*: 129–40.
Grobman, Laurie, and Joyce Kinkead. 2010. "Introduction: Illuminating Undergraduate Research in English." In *Undergraduate Research in English*, edited by Laurie Grobman and Joyce Kinkead, ix–xxxii. Urbana, IL: National Council of Teachers of English.
Handley, George B. 2001. "The Humanities and Citizenship: A Challenge for Service Learning." *Michigan Journal of Community Service Learning* 8 (1): 52–61.
Hart Research Associates. 2018. *Fulfilling the American Dream: Liberal Education and the Future of Work*. Accessed August 15, 2020. https://www.aacu.org/sites/default/files/files/LEAP/2018EmployerResearchReport.pdf.
Hickman, Miranda B. 2012. "Rereading the New Criticism." In *Rereading the New Criticism*, edited by Miranda B. Hickman, and John D. McIntyre, 1–18. Columbus, OH: Ohio State University Press.
Hickman, Miranda B., and John D. McIntyre, eds. 2012. *Rereading the New Criticism*. Columbus, OH: Ohio State University Press.
Hutchison, David, and Sandra Bosacki. 2000. "Over the Edge: Can Holistic Education Contribute to Education?" *Journal of Experiential Education* 23 (3): 177–82.
Kajner, Tania. 2013. "Beyond the Binary: Scholarship, Engagement, and Social Transformation." In *Engaged Scholarship: The Politics of Engagement and Disengagement*, edited by Lynette Shultz and Tania Kajner, 9–20. Rotterdam: Sense Publishers.
Knights, Ben. 2015. "English on Its Borders." In *English Studies: The State of the Discipline, Past, Present, and Future*, edited by Niall Gildea, Helena Goodwyn, Megan Kitching, and Helen Tyson, 15–24. Basingstoke: Palgrave Macmillan. doi:https://doi.org/10.1057/9781137478054.0006.
Kolb, David A. 1984. *Experiential Learning: Experience as the Source of Learning and Development*. Upper Saddle River, NJ: Prentice Hall.
Koritz, Amy. 2005. "Beyond Teaching Tolerance: Literary Studies in a Democracy." *Profession* 80–91.
Kress, Gunther. 1995. "Representational Resources and the Production of Subjectivity: Questions for the Theoretical Development of Critical Discourse Analysis in a Multicultural Society." In *Texts and Practices: Readings in Critical Discourse Analysis*, edited by Carmen Rosa Caldas-Coulthard and Malcolm Coulthard, 15–31. London: Routledge.
Laff, Ned Scott. 1998. "Seeking the Elusive/Illusive English Major." *CEA Critic* 61 (1): 6–17.
McComiskey, Bruce. 2006. *English Studies: An Introduction to the Disciplines*. Urbana, IL: National Council of Teachers of English.
Mittelstrass, Jürgen. 2015. "Humanities under Pressure." *Humanities* 4 (1): 80–86. doi:https://doi.org/10.3390/h4010080.

National Endowment for the Humanities. n.d. "Public Humanities Projects." Accessed July 13, 2020. https://www.neh.gov/grants/public/public-humanities-projects.

National Society for Experiential Education (NSEE). n.d. "Eight Principles of Good Practice for All Experiential Learning Activities." Last updated December 9, 2013. https://www.nsee.org/8-principles.

Nikitina, S. 2009. "Applied Humanities: Bridging the Gap Between Building Theory and Fostering Citizenship." *Liberal Education* 95 (1): 36–43. https://files.eric.ed.gov/fulltext/EJ861150.pdf.

Pileggi, Mary, and Cindy Patton. 2003. "Introduction: Bourdieu and Cultural Studies." *Cultural Studies* 17 (3–4): 313–25. doi:https://doi.org/10.1080/0950238032000083836.

Quay, James, and James Veninga. 1990. *Making Connections: The Humanities, Culture, and Community*. American Council of Learned Societies. Accessed on August 15, 2020. http://archives.acls.org/op/op11quay.htm.

Riddell, Jessica, Shannon Murray, and Lisa Dickson. 2020. "From Sherbrooke to Stratford and Back Again: Team Teaching and Experiential Learning through 'Shakesperience.'" *Arts and Humanities in Higher Education* 20 (2): 172–86.

Roberts, Jay. 2008. "From Experience to Neo-Experiential Education: Variations on a Theme." *Journal of Experiential Education* 31 (1): 19–35. doi:https://doi.org/10.1177/105382590803100104.

Schaeffer, J. M. 2013. "Literary Studies and Literary Experience." Translated by Kathleen Antonioli. *New Literary History* 44 (2): 267–83. http://www.jstor.org/stable/24542595.

Scholes, Robert. 1985. *Textual Power: Literary Theory and the Teaching of English*. New Haven, CT: Yale University Press.

Schroeder, Robyn. 2020. "The Rise of the Public Humanists." In *Doing Public Humanities*, edited by Susan Smulyna, 5–27. New York: Routledge.

Schutz, Aaron, and Anne Ruggles Gere. 1998. "Service Learning and English Studies: Rethinking 'Public' Service." *College English* 60 (2): 129–49.

VanDette, Emily. 2010. "Engaging American Literature: Connecting Students and Communities." *Teaching American Literature: A Journal of Theory and Practice* 4 (1): 73–101.

Veninga, James. 1999. *The Humanities and the Civic Imagination: Collected Addresses and Essays, 1978–1998*. Denton: University of North Texas Press.

Wiggins, Grant. 1993. *Assessing Student Performance*. San Francisco: Jossey-Bass Publishers.

Wiltse, E. 2011. "Doing Time in College: Student-Prisoner Reading Groups and the Object(s) of Literary Study." *Critical Survey* 23 (3): 6–22.

Yood, Jessica. 2003. "Writing the Discipline: A Generic History of English Studies." *College English* 65 (5): 526–40. doi:https://doi.org/10.2307/3594251.

CHAPTER 4

Open-Data, Open-Source, Open-Knowledge: Towards Open-Access Research in Media Studies

Giulia Taurino

4.1 Introduction: The Issue with Open-Access in Media Studies

Following the Declaration of the Budapest Open-Access Initiative, the ECHO Charter and the Bethesda Statement on Open Access Publishing, the 2003 Berlin Declaration officially acknowledged the pivotal role of open-access for academic research: "The Internet has fundamentally changed the practical and economic realities of distributing scientific knowledge and cultural heritage. For the first time ever, the Internet now offers the chance to constitute a global and interactive representation of human knowledge, including cultural heritage and the guarantee of worldwide access."[1] As a broad term, open-access defines free access to data, knowledge, and culture at large, and it is most commonly associated with digital archives, libraries, or journals as providers of information. In practice, this open framework translates into the implementation of copyright standards like the Creative Commons Attribution license (CC-BY) and its variants, which allow for the citing, sharing, and reusing of content available online. As much as the discussion on open-access and digital commons has now reached a global relevance, Tennant et al. (2016) lament a general lack of consensus as to the academic, economic, and societal potentials of open-access research literature, which still counts

G. Taurino (✉)
Northeastern University, Boston, MA, USA
e-mail: g.taurino@northeastern.edu

© The Author(s), under exclusive license to Springer Nature Switzerland AG 2022
A. Schwan and T. Thomson (eds.), *The Palgrave Handbook of Digital and Public Humanities*, https://doi.org/10.1007/978-3-031-11886-9_4

as universally accessible only 25% of all scholarly documents archived on the web (Khabsa and Giles 2014).

The topic appears even more complex when we observe trends in selected geographic or disciplinary areas. In Europe, for instance, field-based initiatives like Open Access in Media Studies[2] or MediArXiv[3] solicited the need to explore open-access and its impacts on scholarly communication in relation to disciplinary specificities and constraints. Since the rise of digital media, scholars have been seeking a constant upgrading and open-sourcing of the discipline (Merrin 2009) able to account for the rapid changes in the techno-cultural landscape. The concepts of open-research, open scholarship, and humanities commons in media studies have indeed shown to be much more complex, and often entangled with issues of accessibility to data sources, as well as to structured databases that would grant a more effective use of data processing and visualization softwares.

For the purpose of this research, I looked at the evolution of open-access in academic publishing between 2009 and 2018, as per data collected by the European Commission. At first glance, the transition of European-based scholarly publishing towards open-access[4] appears to be following a path towards homogenization and stabilization across scientific domains, with some exceptions in the medical and health-related research fields showing much higher OA uptakes. However, when we observe open-access at a more granular level and tackle it in its many declinations—open-access to data, tools, outputs—increasing differences emerge between scientific and humanities-oriented domains. In a recent article, "Discipline-specific open access publishing practices and barriers to change: an evidence-based review," Severin et al. (2020) show that even by focusing exclusively on open-access academic publishing, significant discipline-specific barriers and potentials exist. The article also highlights challenges in the definition of bibliometrical parameters for assessing OA uptakes, and thus encourages further research as to how open-access unravels in specific sub-disciplines.

Taking up this and other calls to investigate the uses of Wikidata for research (Mietchen et al. 2015) and to map them by field (Farda-Sarbas and Müller-Birn 2019), the research presented here focuses on openness in media research and on its contextual issues with accessing open-source data, softwares, tools, and with ultimately making digital humanities projects in media studies available to both academic and non-academic communities. Considering knowledge as a public resource (Hess and Ostrom 2007), this chapter discusses a possible application of an *open-access research* methodology for accessing, visualizing, and understanding large corpora in media studies. It does so by presenting a case study based on the extraction of a sample database of television series from Wikidata. The article will outline the steps required—data extraction, discovery, visualization—to make open-data not only freely available, but also understandable and readable with the support of open-source tools in order to generate what we might call "open knowledge."

Relying entirely on online resources, the project outlined here will help us frame the distinct traits of an open-access work-flow, where each step in the research can be retraced online, thus guaranteeing transparency and participatory practices. Similarly, it will contribute to evaluating both opportunities and challenges of creating an open-access environment for media research. Overall, I will discuss how open-access research can be implemented in the study of media history and culture by combining digital and public humanities. I will do so by showing how freely available online toolkits and resources can be deployed for enhancing co-design practices at different stages of project development, with different levels of digital literacy and competences. In particular, co-design is intended here as a participatory, collaborative practice that can serve as a way to *engage* (Sanders and Stappers 2014) the academic community in the creation of, discussion on, and interaction with open datasets for media research.

Much like the OA movement, contemporary media studies are intrinsically tied to the development of the world wide web and the effects of platformization (Helmond 2015; Nieborg and Poell 2018) on communication and public research initiatives. As Jeff Pooley (2019, 6148) argues "the topics that we write about are inescapably multimedia, so our publishing platforms should be capable—at the very least—of embedding the objects that we study." More than in other disciplines, in digital humanities and media studies the question of "openness" intersects with a variety of internet-based resources that go beyond the traditional association between open-access and academic writing, to include alternative audiovisual formats. Important scholarly networks like MediaCommons (2006–present) have been promoting initiatives in media and communication studies that explore new forms of electronic publishing, which resulted in projects experimenting with media of various length, as well as with emerging formats such as multi-modal digital essayism or videographic criticism and other deformative methods (Samuel and McGann 1999; Sample 2012).[5] By considering new experiments with open-access in media studies, in the following paragraphs I will propose an open-research methodology aimed at facilitating the creation of a green route of self-archiving (Harnad et al. 2008) for media-based research projects.

4.2 The Importance of Wikidata as an Open-Data Source

One of the main challenges in media studies, especially in sub-disciplines related to broadcasting media, is finding and accessing reliable open-source data and structured databases. Beginning with the definition of research questions, media scholars are often limited by the availability of data as well as open-access resources necessary for the problematization of the research topic (Bron et al. 2016). In all three phases of a media research project— exploration, design, and execution—researchers are likely to encounter major obstacles related to the lack of open-access resources. Given the recent history of audiovisual media like cinema and television, it is still relatively rare to find film and television archives providing comprehensive structured databases, and it is even more difficult to gain access to reliable data or datasets coming from the media industry and the private sector. If social media have offered new opportunities for research, they also came with several limitations concerning messy or noisy data and the overall access to databases infrastructures. While with digital platforms the collection of data became ubiquitous, along with the need to index content based on a solid structure of metadata, media researchers are now struggling to extrapolate such data and work effectively with the enormous amount of seemingly chaotic information that is being produced on the internet.

Challenges in introducing digital methods in media studies range from issues related to where to find the data, to issues concerning the type of data needed—e.g. textual, numeric, audiovisual data, metadata, and so on. Some open-access repositories offer interesting solutions for media scholars working with metadata related to film, television, or video games production—one of them being the Internet Movie Database. As the most popular user-generated database covering audiovisual media production, since 1998 IMDb has been owned by IMDb.com, Inc., a subsidiary of Amazon. As part of a private company, the access to IMDb datasets must comply with rigid conditions of use[6] and raises concerns about its transparency. To avoid copyright infringement, IMDb data can be downloaded only from a limited set of sources, such as the IMDb file transfer protocol interface,[7] or IMDb public API and other sources (e.g. OMBb API, TMDb API).

Evaluating the alternatives to profit-based corporate hosts similar to IMDb, the scholar Mayo Fuster Morell (2011) stressed the importance of mission-based infrastructure providers like the Wikimedia Foundation. In a context where most participatory platforms hosting Online Creation Communities (OCCs) are private and profit-driven, Wikipedia plays a fundamental role in ensuring a safe and inclusive environment for sharing knowledge, fostering collaboration, and guaranteeing openness and transparency, against the rising corporate economy of information access and sharing. To this point, a concept that emerged in relation to the academic discourse on open-access, open-science, and open-data is that of FAIR data (Wilkinson et al. 2016), an acronym standing for four main principles that should guide the creation of a sustainable and reliable dataset for academic research: Findable, Accessible, Interoperable, Re-usable.

Acknowledging the need for a FAIR data environment, digital humanities scholars have insisted on the unique value of Wikipedia and Wikidata as the world's largest structured humanities data sources (Crompton et al. 2020), with potential applications across universities, libraries, and other cultural institutions (Lemus-Rojas and Odell 2018; Allison-Cassin and Scott 2018; Ferriter 2019; Kapsalis 2019). For the purpose of the argument in favor of an open-access research work-flow, this article suggests the use of Wikidata as an open-source alternative to IMDb for media scholars interested in working with community-based, non-for profit, open-access data, and resources. Launched in 2012, Wikidata is "a free and open knowledge base that can be read and edited by both humans and machines."[8] It serves as a central repository for the structured free-licensed data of all publicly available Wikis that are part of the Wikimedia Foundation—that is to say, for Wikipedia and its sister projects (e.g. Commons, Wikiversity, MediaWiki). With Wikidata, Wikimedia projects have entered the so-called web of data or semantic web, an information framework that allows for data over the internet to be linked as well as machine-readable (Bizer et al. 2009).

By giving a centralized, formal reference to sparse data fragmented across multiple, multi-lingual entries of the popular online encyclopedia, Wikidata models information following an RDF triple structure. This makes it not only accessible to human users, but also manageable by computers. Such a process has outcomes on many levels: it provides an easy-to-query open-source knowledge base for third-party initiatives; it helps simplifying computational analysis and automated interventions on wiki entries across different languages via computers; it avoids the creation of duplicates and contradicting information; it stores facts and references over time. Indeed, one of the most impactful changes brought by Wikidata is the creation of a network structure of items, properties, and values, linked within statements (i.e. a property-value pairing; RDF graph format: Subject-Predicate-Object), which facilitates the interaction with the non-uniform mass of user-generated data and metadata. Furthermore, Wikidata can be easily explored by using the Wikidata Query Service,[9] an experimental tool that helps users filter and export selected linked open-data without having prior knowledge of query languages (e.g. SPARQL) or any other expertise in coding for data retrieval, analysis, and visualization.

Overall, while IMDb remains the largest repository of metadata relative to film and television content, it is safe to say that a user-friendly environment for SPARQL querying opens up to a more fluid distant reading and observation of media databases based on a shared, community-defined vocabulary built on a directed, labeled graph. When looking at the applications of Wikidata in academic research, Erxleben et al. (2014, 51) pointed out that "the relevance of Wikidata for researchers in semantic technologies, linked open data, and Web science ... hardly needs to be argued for." Similarly, in media studies, a linked open-data work-flow[10] would likely result in a simplified digital methodology process and in significant improvements for upscaling e-research in terms of openness, provenance, sustainability, and scalability. Some of the most common applications of knowledge bases in the humanities have been found in natural language processing (NLP) and generation (e.g. topic modeling), data validation and knowledge integration, as well as information retrieval and data visualization (Mora-Cantallops et al. 2019). In this article, I present a possible use of a sample database of television series extracted from Wikidata for information retrieval and data visualization. If integrated with other data sources (e.g. IMDb, TVDB, Movie Database), this application can also aid data validation and knowledge integration.

4.3 Wikidata for Media Research: A State of the Art

While Wikipedia's applications have been widely explored and systematically reviewed (Okoli et al. 2014) in a number of disciplines, the potentials of using Wikidata for open-access-based research still remain for the most part undocumented. This study intends to provide an overview of Wikidata uses for media research, guided by the following questions:

1. What subdomains of media research can benefit from adopting Wikidata as the main data source?
2. Which publications contribute to define a state of the art of existing media studies projects based on Wikidata?
3. Which applications of Wikidata are yet to be covered by existing research?
4. What opportunities and challenges can we outline from a case-specific analysis in television studies?

In the remaining sections, I will describe in more detail how the research was conducted, by outlining the keywords isolated to identify related literature, along with the methodology used for evaluating potential applications.

A list of the principal subdomains in media studies can be broken down as follows: film studies and history, radio studies, television studies, visual arts, digital culture, game studies, popular culture studies, and communication studies. While it is far from being exhaustive, this list gives us a broad indication of the subjects tackled in media studies: radio, film, television, visual media, new media, video and analog games, and online and mass media. The following overview serves the purpose of guiding us in the evaluation of possible uses of Wikidata for media studies and in helping us find more efficient keywords for querying existing scholarship and publications at the intersection between media research and linked open-data repositories. In this instance, I used Google Scholar as a general reference, paired with searches on the MediArXiv and in the e-journals listed under OA on the Media Studies website.[11]

A first generic search for the string *"wikidata" AND "media studies"* on Google Scholar shows an interesting prospectus. Publications indexed as relevant in both Wikidata and media studies are still limited, and span through very different applications. Results range from studies of the activity of editors and online creation communities on Wikidata (Steiner 2014; Kanke 2018), to the analysis of the connection between Wikidata and Wikipedia (Piscopo et al. 2017) and other comparative studies of free knowledge bases (Färber et al. 2015; Pellissier et al. 2016), to more applied projects, such as the creation of a search engine for new articles that leverages on Wikidata to create semantic annotations (Rudnik et al. 2019), or the evaluation of statistically relevant correlation between Twitter hashtags and Wikidata revisions

(Dooley and Božić 2019). Moreover, the search reveals much broader applications often overlapping with computer science, like projects focused on defining alternatives to property-suggesting systems currently employed by Wikidata (Zangerle et al. 2016) or on mapping Wikidata entities for evaluating disambiguation and linking systems (Bhargava et al. 2019).

The outputs appear more understandable when we insert in the search string specific subdomains previously mentioned and when we include searches on field-specific search engines on media networks and journals. It emerges a landscape where Wikidata is slowly finding its own role in contributing to media research by bridging existing gaps and challenges in the retrieval of information from media archives and industrial players. Evidently, applications of Wikidata are building a solid history in relation to visual arts, art heritage management, digital history, and preservation thanks to portals like Wikidata for Digital Preservation portal (Thornton et al. 2017). However, we also find projects that have been developed using Wikidata for film, television, games studies and, to a lesser extent, radio studies.

In film and archival studies, linked open-data is becoming a widespread and relevant topic among international audiovisual archives and networks, which are now considering the use of ontologies and identifiers for film from sources like Wikidata (Heftberger et al. 2019). Heftberger and Duchesne (2020) also noticed that, although at a slower pace, film archives are increasingly open to consider the benefits of Wikidata as a unique identifier mapping process for the audiovisual heritage sector. The FIAF Cataloguing and Documentation Commission (CDC)[12]

> had had the idea of mapping entities to the EN 15907 schema since 2015, and pioneering work had already been carried out by Nicola Mazzanti and Bram Biesbrouck at the Cinémathèque royale de Belgique. Raymond Drewy presented the invaluable work he had been undertaking at MovieLabs. Some film archives were also forerunners in this field: the Library of Congress (L°C) provided a linked data service on its website, while Sarah Blankfort Clothier presented the new American Film Institute (AFI) project, "Women They Talk About," funded by an National Endowment for the Humanities (NEH) grant, using LOD for gathering data on female film pioneers. (Heftberger 2019, 65)

Moreover, among other publications, a case study at the Netherlands Institute for Sound & Vision (Brooks 2018; de Boer et al. 2018) suggests to use metadata from Wikidata to enrich audiovisual archives like the Common Thesaurus for AudioVisual Archives (GTAA).

Wikidata as a resource and authority for arching and cataloguing media material through semantic annotation emerges as perhaps one of the main applications of linked open-data for media research, from film studies, as we showed in the paragraph above, to television studies for the implementation of linked open-data frameworks—i.e. Entertainment Identifier Registry IDs (EIDR IDs), European Broadcasting Union Linked Data model

(EBUCore)—in television collections,[13] but also games studies, in projects focusing on the creation of metadata for video games catalogs (Fukuda 2020). As an interdisciplinary dialogue in media studies, however, applications of Wikidata are not only limited to archival research. Examples of Wikidata's uses for media analysis can be found both in distant and close reading approaches. For instance, Agt-Rickauer et al. (2018) have presented a practical output of exploiting Wikidata, in synergy with another linked open-data knowledge base—namely, DBpedia, Schema.org, and Linked Movie Database—for the annotation and exploration of audiovisual patterns in film-analytical studies. The result is the AdA Annotation Explorer v1.0.1, freely accessible online.[14] At a more granular level, in television studies we observe some examples of uses of Wikidata datasets for data visualization of television production and distribution (Taurino 2019) as well as for the qualitative analysis of specific phenomena in popular culture (Dutta 2020). As media scholars attempt to move towards the use of Wikidata as a FAIR data source for their research, here we will consider a case study that might help us evaluate how effectively Wikidata datasets can replace other data sources like IMDb.

4.4 Case Study

In the previous paragraphs, I showed how open-access is not exclusively tied to the notion of open-publishing; instead, it can be applied to the broader context of open-science (Vicente-Saez and Martinez-Fuentes 2018), by embracing open-data frameworks and open-source tools in addition to complying with open-access scholarly publishing. The state of the art helped us examine how Wikidata is currently used among sub-disciplines in media research. A large part of the publications found focus on archival practices, and yet some experimental projects based on Wikidata resources are starting to consolidate in an emerging methodology for data analysis and visualization based on an open work-flow. In order to assess the actual advantages and disadvantages of Wikidata, I will examine more closely a case study conducted for a research project at the University of Bologna, and based on previous research carried out at the University of Montreal. The project was designed in collaboration with the DETECt Project Research Group[15] to aid the creation of a comprehensive database of crime television series. For the reasons stated above and in compliance with a FAIR data framework, I supported the DETECt team by identifying Wikidata as a data source and by using the Wikidata Query Service to make the query easily reproducible by other members of the research group, as well as scholars in the television networks who might be interested in having access to the dataset.

This open-research process can be tracked down to four main phases: data extraction, data discovery, and data visualization. This section walks us through these phases in order to highlight both gains and losses of adopting this methodology. By running a query[16] of all instances of television series on Wikidata, the object-count amounts to 62,069 results as of December 2020,

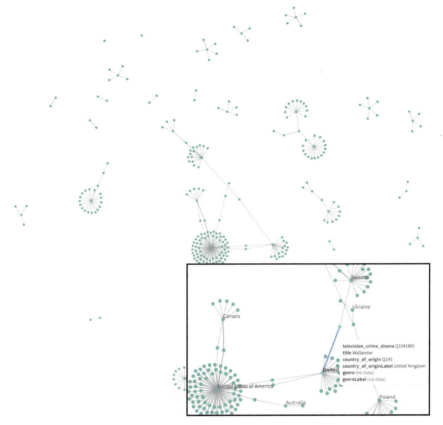

Fig. 4.1 Data visualization of a crime TV series dataset extracted from Wikidata (distant reading with close-up). Made with Wikidata Visualization—Toolforge

versus 196,972 TV series found on IMDb.[17] At this stage, we filtered all instances of television series classified as genre = crime serial and we extracted the property "title" and "genre."[18] The tabular form on the Wikidata Query Service interface shows a first limitation in the dataset: around 40% of the crime television series listed are from the United States of America, another 30% are equally partitioned among series from Canada, Czech Republic, Germany, Norway, Poland, Sweden, and the UK, and the remaining 30% of the database can be divided between Argentina, Australia, Austria, Balearic Islands, Belgium, Canada, Denmark, Finland, France, Hong Kong, Hungary, Iceland, India, Ireland, Israel, Italy, Japan, Malaysia, Mexico, Russia, Serbia, Slovakia, South Africa, South Korea, Spain, Turkey and Ukraine. While the percentages are not evenly distributed, the variety of countries that emerge in this small sample is proportionally higher than the number of countries found in other data sources. Of course, this is not enough to motivate the use of Wikidata as a good alternative to IMDb. By running a similar search on

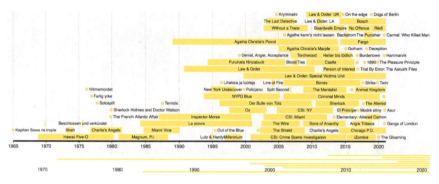

Fig. 4.2 Data visualization of a crime TV series dataset extracted from Wikidata (distant reading). Made with Wikidata Timeline—Toolforge[23]

IMDb,[19] it is clear that in terms of variety of countries represented and the amount of information relative to each item, IMDb remains by far the most comprehensive source of information on audiovisual media.

Nevertheless, Wikidata offers two important advantages: the query can be customized, run and accessed in a tabular form instantly[20]; data can be immediately extracted and visualized on open-source visualization tools directly connected to Wikidata. Here, we present three options for data discovery and visualization using the following open-access tools: Wikidata Visualization (https://dataviz.toolforge.org/), Wikidata Timeline (https://wikidata-timeline.toolforge.org/), and Wikidata Metaphactory Demo (https://wikidata.metaphacts.com/). On the one hand, the first two tools are available on Toolforge,[21] a cloud-based infrastructure developed by the Wikimedia Foundation that serves as hosting environment for community developers. Toolforge makes available tools that help users maintain and interact with wikis. The third tool is developed by a German software company with the goal of delivering "a generic platform with extensible, easy-to-use components and services for interacting with and leveraging the Wikidata knowledge graph query service."[22] What follows is a series of screenshots of visualizations generated using these open-source tools from the dataset extracted. In particular Fig. 4.1 shows the distribution of crime television series in the dataset extracted as divided per country of production. By zooming in (cf. Fig. 4.1), we notice that each node indicates a different country, and that some links correspond to television series that connect several countries, such as *Wallander* (2008–2016), a UK (production companies: Left Bank Pictures, TKBC) and Sweden (production company: Yellow Bird) co-production.

While the visualization in Fig. 4.1 focuses on the geographical location of each object contained in the dataset, Fig. 4.2 shows a timeline created from the same corpus that points at the duration of each television series. This timeline can help media scholars find historical connections among overlapping television content produced and broadcasted locally or internationally.

Fig. 4.3 Data visualization of a crime TV series dataset extracted from Wikidata (sankey layout, distant reading with close-up). Made with Wikidata Metaphactory Demo

It also gives an overview on the predominance of certain productions, spanning throughout several years, over others, with a more limited time presence. Although it does not report information on the programming schedules and repeated broadcastings, it does offer a valid visual reference for more fine grain studies of the cross-historical media contaminations that defined the evolution of television crime as a genre in itself.

Visualizations based on geographical and historical pollinations are certainly useful to conduct media research. However, media scholars are often interested in understanding subtle intra- and inter-cultural references that might be difficult to graph when focusing solely on information about the countries and years of production. Since the dataset extracted via Wikidata includes data related to the type of relation among entities, I opted for creating a third visual model that highlights the intertextual reference between television crime serials. As we can see in the close-up in Fig. 4.3, most television series appear to be interconnected simply because they are "based on," "followed by," "spin-off of" other story material. In most cases, this connection can hardly be detected through rendering production information on a network or timeline visualization, which would only be able to define relations at a larger scale. On the contrary, the visualization generated using Wikidata Metaphactory Demo, as seen in Fig. 4.3, is effective in isolating sub-clusters of media franchises, such as *Law & Order*.

Wikidata-based tools for visualizing Wikidata datasets let us explore the data and evidence the properties, structure, and composition of the information we are accessing. Other Wikidata visualization tools, like Histropedia, give the possibility of merging multiple queries in a single timeline visualization. Moreover, open-source data visualization frameworks like RAW Graphs can be used to generate a variety of visual models and easily represent data extracted from Wikidata as well as other sources. Overall, these interactive features allow us to navigate, manipulate and ultimately better understand the dataset we extracted in the very process of creating the dataset itself, without the need for more technical skills in computer programming. This enables non-expert users to observe and analyze large-scale datasets through a variety of visual lenses useful for both close and distant reading.

4.5 Conclusion

While Wikidata has been presented as a free, collaborative knowledge base (Vrandecic and Krötzsch 2014), the case study shows that it is still far from being a truly diverse source in terms of multilingualism and multiculturalism (cf. Wikidata 2017; 2020). Even though Wikidata is one of the most edited knowledge bases, it still risks to reinforce existing biases. This point explicitly emerges in most research projects using Wikipedia or Wikidata as a resource. Although easy-to-aggregate, the data found shows that most of the contributions come from anglophone countries. As Farda-Sarbas and Müller-Birn (2019, *online*) rightfully state "Wikidata is still predominantly used and studied from a Western perspective. This affects, for example, multilingualism and knowledge diversity in Wikidata. Although, data in Wikidata is available in various languages simultaneously, this applies only for a selected number of languages." Of course, "the quality of taxonomic structures is key to properly capturing knowledge in Wikidata" (Brasileiro et al. 2016, *online*), but researchers and experts across different countries can contribute to improve the quality of the information and data provided. For instance, part of the research agenda in a given research project could be devoted not only to collecting existing datasets, but also to the creation of new datasets by adding instances to Wikidata about content non included in the Wikipedia database or by adding data to poorly documented instances. As I suggested as a solution for data implementation for DETECt,[24] initiatives like collective Wikipedia and Wikidata edit-a-thon can be considered as useful calls for action to create a participatory culture around data creation and collection.

Despite the obvious language bias found in the extracted sample datasets of crime television serial, Wikidata might still represent the best option for media researcher to access information, knowing that, as Wikidata scales up, more controls will be needed to ensure that the linked data contained in the knowledge base are trustworthy, up-to-date, and adhering to principles of fairness and inclusivity (Mora-Cantallops et al. 2019). When running a comparative quality assessment of DBpedia and Wikidata, Thakkar et al. (2016) found that "the quality of Wikidata with regard to the majority of relevant metrics is higher than that of DBpedia." Undoubtedly, databases extracted from Wikidata are missing important data and the Wikidata Query Service still presents errors when running multiple queries. Nevertheless, integrated with participatory practices in the form of collaborative editing, combined with other archival resources in media studies and/or merged with other data sources (e.g. IMDb), Wikidata can be a useful tool to explore the epistemological biases of information found online on a given topic. It is also a unique pathway for media studies to cross into digital and public humanities and incorporate computational methods, in that it offers a way to easily access information and visualize narratives (Metilli et al. 2019) using linked open data. The original hypothesis and expectation for the case study presented here was that Wikidata would have allowed improvements on four levels: openness, provenance, sustainability, and scalability.

Openness is to be intended not only as a copyright terminology for open-access, but also as a techno-cultural concept with broader implications related to cyber-transparency, digital accessibility, and methodological commons. As the case study demonstrated, it is possible for film and television scholarships to create a more inclusive, open-research work-flow by relying less on hard-to-access corporate data and more on community-led databases, bypassing the biases and silos of media industry filtered information. Additionally, using the dataset extracted from Wikidata, we were able to solve the problem of discrepancies in classification labels, by relying on a data model that supports multiple definitions for the same item (e.g. crime television series and detective television series are identified as part of the same category). Another benefit of using Wikidata is that it is maintained by the Wikimedia Foundation as a public data source, and the risks of privatization or decay of the database are overall avoided. *Sustainability* was therefore another trait we found in the evolution of the project presented here, together with *scalability*, which allows us to scale our project up and expand preliminary data extractions and visualizations. We also found that the use of Wikidata promoted *inclusion* and communication in the very research process, by facilitating the accessibility of non-digital humanists to digital resources and lowering the barriers of technological divide and difference in digital competence. This was perhaps the most evident difference with other projects carried out on IMDb data,[25] where some programming knowledge and skills were required even when using open-source tools for visualizations.

Despite Wikidata's challenges, limitations and margins for improvement, we find that the case study presented in this chapter was successful in showing how a model for practicing "openness" within the entire research cycle is nevertheless possible. By relying entirely on online resources, the project proposed an argument in favor of an open-access work-flow, where each step in the research can be retraced online. I define this methodological framework as "open-research," aiming towards both transparency and engagement in academic research. Supporting a research perspective that embraces co-design, co-creation, and participatory action, this case study can be used as a model for rendering the entire research process replicable, rather than focusing only on its final open-access outputs. Furthermore, this switch towards open-research in the complex coexistence of making and spreading knowledge might have positive impacts for promoting digital pedagogy within media scholarship. Ultimately, open-knowledge is intended to represent the outcome of an open-process in research, where information is collected from open-data bases, discovered and analyzed through open-source software for data visualization, and presented to the community in the form of open-access publishing. Considering participation as an ecosystem (Morell 2011), as a concept profoundly grounded in space—be it physical, virtual or digital—this chapter points at Wikidata as a unique open-access environment for academic interaction. More than a fixed point of origin (data source) or output (research results), Wikidata proves to be a dynamic place for knowledge discovery and creation.

Notes

1. "Berlin Declaration." Max Planck Society. Archived from the original on 2015-10-27. Retrieved 2020-07-19.
2. "Open Access in Media Studies is maintained and curated by Jeroen Sondervan and Jeff Pooley, and in close collaboration with the European Network for Cinema and Media Studies (NECS). The site aims to inform about and promote open access publishing in the field of media studies."—https://oamediastudies.com/.
3. "MediArXiv is a free, community-led digital archive for media, film, and communication research (hosted on the Open Science Framework). We provide a non-profit platform for media, film, and communication scholars to upload their working papers, pre-prints, accepted manuscripts (post-prints), and published manuscripts."—https://mediarxiv.com/.
4. The European Commission defines Hybrid Open-Access as any "research outputs that are publications in a subscription journal that are open access with a clear license." Other definitions given to differentiate among the various ways to freely access research publications are the following:
   - "Gold Open Access: research outputs that are publications in an open access journal;".
   - "Green Open Access: research outputs that are publications in a journal that are also available in an open access repository;".
   - "Bronze Open Access: research outputs that are published in a subscription journal that are open access without a license." Source: https://ec.europa.eu/info/research-and-innovation/strategy/goals-research-and-innovation-policy/open-science/open-science-monitor/trends-open-access-publications_en.

5. Please consult the following list of web-based peer-reviewed academic resources for further reference on examples of alternative audiovisual formats in digital publishing: The Programming Historian (programminghistorian.org); The Digital Review (https://thedigitalreview.com/); Videographic Essay (http://videographicessay.org/works/videographic-essay/index); AUDIOVISUALCY: Videographic Film and Moving Image Studies and Video Essays (https://vimeo.com/groups/audiovisualcy).
6. https://www.imdb.com/conditions.
7. http://www.imdb.com/interfaces; https://datasets.imdbws.com/.
8. https://www.wikidata.org/wiki/Wikidata:Main_Page.
9. https://query.wikidata.org/.
10. https://www.wikidata.org/wiki/Wikidata:Linked_open_data_workflow.
11. https://oamediastudies.com/publish/journals/.
12. The full report on the proceedings of 2015 CDC meeting and FIAF workgroups may be found online on the following website: https://www.fiafnet.org/pages/E-Resources/LoD-Task-ForceWorkshop-2019.html.
13. An application of LOD in National Educational Television (NET) can be found in Pierce (2020).
14. Developed by the Semantic Technologies Group of HPI Potsdam, the film studies department of FU Berlin, and Joscha Jäger, the author of FrameTrail, the results of the AdA-project can be found at: http://ada.filmontology.org/explorer/.
15. DETECt—Detecting Transcultural Identity in European Popular Crime Narratives (2018–2021) is a cross-institutional research project coordinated by the University of Bologna as part of the Horizon 2020 grant scheme "Understanding Europe—Promoting the European public and cultural space." Website: https://www.detect-project.eu/.
16. Run the SPARQL query.
17. Data provided by IMDb via https://www.imdb.com/pressroom/stats/.
18. Please note that by extracting only the property "title," the number of entities lowers to less than 250 items.
19. To run search on IMDb please go to the following link: https://www.imdb.com/search/title/?title_type=tv_series&genres=crime&explore=title_type,genres&view=advanced.
20. This is not always true when we run queries with a high number of entities. In these cases, the Wikidata Query Service system might run into a timeout query error. If this happens, the issue might be solved by breaking down the query into multiple queries.
21. https://meta.wikimedia.org/wiki/Toolforge.
22. https://metaphacts.com/wikidata.
23. https://wikidata-timeline.toolforge.org/#/timeline?title=Crime%20Television%20Serial&wdq=claim%5B136:9335577%5D&languages=en,fr&defaultEndTime=now&sitelink=Wikipedia&sitelinkFallback.
24. https://www.detect-project.eu/edit-a-thon/.
25. Taurino and Boni (2018).

References

Agt-Rickauer, Henning, Christian Hentschel, and Harald Sack. 2018. "Semantic Annotation and Automated Extraction of Audio-Visual Staging Patterns in Large-Scale Empirical Film Studies." In *Proceedings of the Posters and Demos Track of the 14th International Conference on Semantic Systems (SEMANTiCS 2018)*, Vienna, Austria.

Allison-Cassin, Stacy, and Dan Scott. 2018. "Wikidata: A Platform for Your Library's Linked Open Data." *The Code4Lib Journal* 40. https://journal.code4lib.org/articles/13424.

Bhargava, Preeti, Nemanja Spasojevic, Sarah Ellinger, Adithya Rao, Abhinand Menon, Saul Fuhrmann, and Guoning Hu. 2019. "Learning to Map Wikidata Entities to Predefined Topics." In *Companion Proceedings of The 2019 World Wide Web Conference (WWW 2019)*. New York, NY: Association for Computing Machinery, 1194–202. https://doi.org/10.1145/3308560.3316749.

Bizer, Christian, Tom Heath, and Tim Berners-Lee. 2009. "Linked Data—The Story So Far." *International Journal on Semantic Web and Information Systems* 5 (3): 1–22. https://doi.org/10.4018/jswis.2009081901.

Brasileiro, Freddy, João Paulo A. Almeida, Victorio A. Carvalho, and Giancarlo Guizzardi. 2016. "Applying a Multi-Level Modeling Theory to Assess Taxonomic Hierarchies in Wikidata." In *Proceedings of the 25th International Conference Companion on World Wide Web*: 975–80.

Bron, Marc, Jasmijn Van Gorp, and Maarten de Rijke. 2016. "Media Studies Research in the Data-Driven Age: How Research Questions Evolve." *Journal of the Association for Information Science and Technology* 67 (7): 1535–54.

Brooks, John. 2018. "Researching Wikidata's Added Value in Accommodating Audio-Visual Researchers' Information Needs." https://www.semanticscholar.org/paper/Researching-Wikidata%E2%80%99s-added-value-in-accommodating-Brooks/0aefdbc432c4a44b4c8af8603608237e8f8b6ae3.

Crompton, Constance, Lori Antranikian, Ruth Truong, and Paige Maskell. 2020. "Familiar Wikidata: The Case for Building a Data Source We Can Trust." *Pop! Public. Open. Participatory* 2. https://popjournal.ca/issue02/crompton.

de Boer, Victor, Tim de Bruyn, John Brooks, and Jesse de Vos. 2018. *The Benefits of Linking Metadata for Internal and External Users of an Audiovisual Archive*. Cham: Springer International Publishing.

Dooley, Paula, and Bojan Božić. 2019. "Towards Linked Data for Wikidata Revisions and Twitter Trending Hashtags." In *Proceedings of the 21st International Conference on Information Integration and Web-based Applications & Services (iiWAS2019)*, 166–75. New York, NY: Association for Computing Machinery. https://doi.org/10.1145/3366030.3366048.

Dutta, Nandita. 2020. "The Networked Fictional Narrative: Seriality and Adaptations in Popular Television and New Media." PhD dissertation, University of Western Ontario. Electronic Thesis and Dissertation Repository. https://ir.lib.uwo.ca/etd/7287.

Erxleben, Fredo, Michael Günther, Markus Krötzsch, Julian Mendez, and Denny Vrandečić. 2014. "Introducing Wikidata to the Linked Data Web." In *Proceedings of International Semantic Web Conference*, 50–65. Cham: Springer.

Färber, Michael, Basil Ell, Carsten Menne, and Achim Rettinger. 2015. "A Comparative Survey of DBpedia, Freebase, OpenCyc, Wikidata, and YAGO." *Semantic Web Journal* 1, 1–5.

Farda-Sarbas, Mariam, and Claudia Müller-Birn. 2019. "Wikidata from a Research Perspective—A Systematic Mapping Study of Wikidata." *ArXiv* 1908 (11153).

Ferriter, Meghan. 2019. "Integrating Wikidata at the Library of Congress." https://blogs.loc.gov/thesignal/2019/05/integrating-wikidata-at-the-library-of-congress/.

Fukuda, Kazufumi. 2020. "Using Wikidata as Work Authority for Video Games." *International Conference on Dublin Core and Metadata Applications*, 80–87. https://dcpapers.dublincore.org/pubs/article/view/4245.

Harnad, Stevan, Tim Brody, François Vallières, Les Carr, Steve Hitchcock, Yves Gingras, Charles Oppenheim, Chawki Hajjem, and Eberhard R. Hilf. 2008. "The Access/Impact Problem and the Green and Gold Roads to Open Access: An Update." *Serials Review* 34 (1): 36–40. https://doi.org/10.1080/00987913.2008.10765150.

Heftberger, Adelheid. 2019. "Building Resources Together—Linked Open Data for Filmarchives." *Journal of Film Preservation* 101: 65–73.

Heftberger, Adelheid, and Paul Duchesne. 2020. "Cataloguing Practices in the Age of Linked Open Data: Wikidata and Wikibase for Film Archives." In *International Federation of Film Archives*, Brussels, Belgium. https://www.fiafnet.org/pages/E-Resources/Cataloguing-Practices-Linked-Open-Data.html.

Heftberger, Adelheid, Jakob Höper, Claudia Müller-Birn, and Niels-Oliver Walkowski. 2019. "Opening up Research Data in Film Studies by Using the Structured Knowledge Base Wikidata." In *Digital Cultural Heritage*, edited by Horst Kremers. Cham: Springer. https://doi.org/10.1007/978-3-030-15200-0_27.

Helmond, Anne. 2015. "The Platformization of the Web: Making Web Data Platform Ready." *Social Media + Society* 1 (2). https://doi.org/10.1177/2056305115603080.

Hess, Charlotte, and Elinor Ostrom. 2007. *Understanding Knowledge as a Commons: From Theory to Practice*. Cambridge, MA: The MIT Press.

Kanke, Timothy. 2018. "Exploring the Knowledge Curation Work of Wikidata." In *Proceedings of Joint Conference on Digital Libraries (JCDL 2018)*. New York, NY: Association for Computing Machinery.

Kapsalis, Effie. 2019. "Wikidata: Recruiting the Crowd to Power Access to Digital Archives." *Journal of Radio & Audio Media* 26 (1): 134–42. https://doi.org/10.1080/19376529.2019.1559520.

Khabsa, Madian, and C. Lee Giles. 2014. "The Number of Scholarly Documents on the Public Web." *PLoS ONE* 9 (5): e93949.

Lemus-Rojas, Mairelys, and Jere D. Odell. 2018. "Creating Structured Linked Data to Generate Scholarly Profiles: A Pilot Project Using Wikidata and Scholia." *Journal of Librarianship and Scholarly Communication* 6 (1). https://doi.org/10.7710/2162-3309.2272.

Merrin, William. 2009. "Media Studies 2.0: Upgrading and Open-Sourcing the Discipline." *Interactions: Studies in Communication and Culture* 1 (1): 17–34. https://doi.org/10.1386/iscc.1.1.17_1.

Metilli, Daniele, Valentina Bartalesi, and Carlo Meghini. 2019. "A Wikidata-Based Tool for Building and Visualising Narratives." *International Journal of Digital on Digital Libraries* 20: 417–32. https://doi.org/10.1007/s00799-019-00266-3.

Mietchen, Daniel, Gregor Hagedorn, Egon Willighagen, Mariano Rico, Asunción Gómez-Pérez, Eduard Aibar, and Karima Rafes. 2015. "Enabling Open Science: Wikidata for Research (Wiki4R)." *Research Ideas and Outcomes* 1. https://doi.org/10.3897/rio.1.e7573

Mora-Cantallops, Marçal, Salvador Sánchez-Alonso, and Elena García-Barriocanal. 2019. "A Systematic Literature Review on Wikidata." *Data Technologies and Applications* 53 (3): 250–68. https://doi.org/10.1108/DTA-12-2018-0110.

Morell, Mayo Fuster. 2011. "The Unethics of Sharing: Wikiwashing." *The International Review of Information Ethics* 15: 9–16. https://doi.org/10.29173/irie219.

Nieborg, David B, and Thomas Poell. 2018. "The Platformization of Cultural Production: Theorizing the Contingent Cultural Commodity." *New Media & Society* 20 (11): 4275–92. https://doi.org/10.1177/1461444818769694.

Okoli, Chitu, Mohamad Mehdi, Mostafa Mesgari, Finn Årup Nielsen, and Arto Lanamäki. 2014. "Wikipedia in the Eyes of its Beholders: A Systematic Review of Scholarly Research on Wikipedia Readers and Readership." *Journal of the Association for Information Science and Technology*. https://doi.org/10.2139/ssrn.2021326.

Pellissier, Tanon, Thomas Denny Vrandecic, Sebastian Schaffert, Thomas Steiner, and Lydia Pintscher. 2016. "From Freebase to Wikidata: The Great Migration." In *Proceedings of the 25th International Conference on World Wide Web, (WWW 2016)*, 1419–28. Montreal, Canada.

Pierce, Chris. 2020. "Unique Challenges Facing Linked Data Implementation for National Educational Television." *International Journal of Metadata, Semantics and Ontologies* 14 (2). https://doi.org/10.1504/IJMSO.2020.108323.

Piscopo, Alessandro, Christopher Phethean, and Elena Simperl. 2017a. "Wikidatians are Born: Paths to Full Participation in a Collaborative Structured Knowledge Base." In *50th Hawaii International Conference on System Sciences, HICSS 2017a*, Hilton Waikoloa Village, Hawaii, USA.

Piscopo, Alessandro, Pavlos Vougiouklis, Lucie-Aimée Kaffee, Christopher Phethean, Jonathon Hare, and Elena Simperl. 2017b. "What Do Wikidata and Wikipedia Have in Common? An Analysis of their Use of External References." In *Proceedings of the 13th International Symposium on Open Collaboration (OpenSym 2017b)*, 1–10. New York: Association for Computing Machinery. https://doi.org/10.1145/3125433.3125445.

Pooley, Jefferson. 2019. Open Media Scholarship: The Case for Open Access in Media Studies. MediArXiv. June 20. https://doi.org/10.33767/osf.io/te9as

Piscopo, Vougiouklis et al. 2017. What do Wikidata and Wikipedia have in common? An Analysis of their Use of External References. https://doi.org/10.1145/3125433.3125445

Rudnik, Charlotte, Thibault Ehrhart, Olivier Ferret, Denis Teyssou, Raphael Troncy, and Xavier Tannier. 2019. "Searching News Articles Using an Event Knowledge Graph Leveraged by Wikidata." In *Companion Proceedings of The 2019 World Wide Web Conference (WWW 2019)*, 1232–39. New York: Association for Computing Machinery. https://doi.org/10.1145/3308560.3316761.

Sample, Mark. 2012. "Notes Towards a Deformed Humanities." *@samplereality*. http://www.samplereality.com/2012/05/02/notes-towards-a-deformedhumanities/.

Samuels, Lisa, and Jerome McGann. 1999. "Deformance and Interpretation." *New Literary History* 30 (1): 25–56. http://www.jstor.org/stable/20057521.

Sanders, Elizabeth B.-N., and Stappers, Pieter Jan. 2014. "Probes, Toolkits and Prototypes: Three Approaches to Making in Codesigning." *CoDesign: International Journal of CoCreation in Design and the Arts* 10 (1): 5–14.

Severin, Anna, Matthias Egger, Martin Paul Eve, and Daniel Hürlimann. 2020. "Discipline-Specific Open Access Publishing Practices and Barriers to Change: An Evidence-based Review." *F1000Research* 7 (1925). https://doi.org/10.12688/f1000research.17328.2.

Steiner, Thomas. 2014. "Bots vs. Wikipedians, Anons vs. Logged-Ins (Redux): A Global Study of Edit Activity on Wikipedia and Wikidata." In *Proceedings of The International Symposium on Open Collaboration (OpenSym 2014)*, 27–29. Berlin, Germany.

Taurino, Giulia. 2019. "An Introduction to Network Visualization for Television Studies: Models and Practical Applications." *Series—International Journal of TV Serial Narratives* 5 (1): 45–57. https://doi.org/10.6092/issn.2421-454X/8975.

Taurino, Giulia, and Marta Boni. 2018. "Maps, Distant Reading and the Internet Movie Database: New Approaches for the Analysis of Large-Scale Datasets in Television Studies." *VIEW Journal of European Television History and Culture* 7 (14): 24–37. https://doi.org/10.18146/2213-0969.2018.jethc151.

Tennant, Jonathan P., François Waldner, Damien C. Jacques, Paola Masuzzo, Lauren B. Collister, and Chris. H. J. Hartgerink. 2016. "The Academic, Economic and Societal Impacts of Open Access: An Evidence-based Review." *F1000Research* 5: 632. https://doi.org/10.12688/f1000research.8460.3.

Thakkar, Harsh, Kemele M. Endris, Jose M. Gimenez-Garcia, Jeremy Debattista, Christoph Lange, and Sören Auer. 2016. "Are Linked Datasets Fit for Open-domain Question Answering? A Quality Assessment." In *Proceedings of the 6th International Conference on Web Intelligence, Mining and Semantics (WIMS '16)*. New York: Association for Computing Machinery. https://doi.org/10.1145/2912845.2912857.

Thornton, Katherine, Euan Cochrane, Thomas Ledoux, Bertrand Caron, and Carl Wilson. 2017. "Modeling the Domain of Digital Preservation in Wikidata." *iPRES*. https://wikidp.org/about.

Vicente-Saez, Ruben, and Clara Martinez-Fuentes. 2018. "Open Science Now: A Systematic Literature Review for an Integrated Definition." *Journal of Business Research* 88: 428–36. https://doi.org/10.1016/j.jbusres.2017.12.043.

Vrandecic Denny, and Markus Krötzsch. 2014. "Wikidata: A Free Collaborative Knowledgebase." Communications of the Association for Computing Machinery 57 (10): 78–85.

Wikidata. 2017. *Wikidata:Sources—Wikidata, The Free Knowledge Base*. https://www.wikidata.org/wiki/Help:Sources.

Wikidata. 2020. *Wikidata:Statistics—Wikidata, The Free Knowledge Base*. https://www.wikidata.org/wiki/Wikidata:Statistics.

Wilkinson, Mark D., Michel Dumontier, IJsbrand Jan Aalbersberg, Gabrielle Appleton, Myles Axton, Arie Baak, Niklas Blomberg et al. 2016. "The FAIR Guiding Principles for Scientific Data Management and Stewardship." *Scientific Data* 3. https://doi.org/10.1038/sdata.2016.18.

Zangerle, Eva Wolfgang Gassler, Martin Pichl, Stefan Steinhauser, and Günther Specht. 2016. "An Empirical Evaluation of Property Recommender Systems for

Wikidata and Collaborative Knowledge Bases." In *Proceedings of the 12th International Symposium on Open Collaboration (OpenSym '16)*, 1–8. New York, NY: Association for Computing Machinery. https://doi.org/10.1145/2957792.2957804.

CHAPTER 5

Adventures in Digital and Public Humanities: Co-Producing Trans History Through Creative Collaboration

Jason Barker, Kate Fisher, Jana Funke, Zed Gregory, Jen Grove, Rebecca Langlands, Ina Linge, Catherine McNamara, Ester McGeeney, Bon O'Hara, Jay Stewart, and Kazuki Yamada

5.1 Introduction

Engaging with non-academic partners and audiences, including inviting them to contribute to historical knowledge production, is much championed both inside and outside higher education.[1] Working with non-academic communities to produce historical knowledge is, however, not new. Public history has long recognized that authority to speak about the past is not limited to professional historians (Kean and Martin 2013). In particular, the history from below movements that emerged in the 1960s, the History Workshop movement, and oral history, all sought to collapse the divide between professional historical writing and lay knowledge. Many were committed to producing democratic histories and were embedded in community storytelling and radical politics.[2] The goal, in Raphael Samuel's much-quoted encapsulation, was for

---

J. Barker · Z. Gregory · E. McGeeney · B. O'Hara · J. Stewart
Exeter, UK

K. Fisher (✉) · J. Funke · J. Grove · R. Langlands · I. Linge · K. Yamada
University of Exeter, Exeter, UK
e-mail: k.fisher@exeter.ac.uk

J. Funke
e-mail: J.Funke@exeter.ac.uk

© The Author(s), under exclusive license to Springer Nature Switzerland AG 2022
A. Schwan and T. Thomson (eds.), *The Palgrave Handbook of Digital and Public Humanities*, https://doi.org/10.1007/978-3-031-11886-9_5

history to recognize and embrace its value as a "social form of knowledge; the work in any given instance of a thousand different hands" (1999, 15).

Recently, universities have been promoted as places of "engaged research," committed to public engagement in all aspects of their work (research, knowledge exchange, teaching and social responsibility) (Hinchliffe et al. 2018; Holliman 2017; Jay 2010, 14). Engaged researchers are envisaged as sharing their knowledge, resources and skills, and incorporating the expertise and insight of others. The principles are outlined in the UK by the National Co-ordinating Centre for Public Engagement (NCCPE).[3]

Collaborative initiatives inviting wider publics to take part in the production of history are increasingly mainstream. No longer associated with a radical critique of the anti-democratic structures of intellectual expertise, they are embedded in the business structures of universities, incorporated into university management, assessment and discipline, and tied to funding (both public and private).[4] Indeed, some critics have charged universities with co-opting the language of democratization to shore up systemic inequalities and add marketable value to attempts to tackle social problems, be they racism, elitism, injustice, or sexism (Ahmed 2012, 53–4). At the same time, the institutional promotion of engaged research provides opportunities, funding, and time for researchers to reflect critically upon the production, circulation and consumption of historical knowledge and engage in forms of democratization.

Many practitioners of public history promote co-production as a mechanism for ensuring democratic practices that counteract unidirectional approaches to public engagement that envisage knowledge as produced by the academy and subsequently shared, disseminated or otherwise imposed on publics (King and Rivett 2015). Yet what is meant by co-production varies significantly. It has not coalesced into a clear methodology or set of governing principles, and the ubiquity of the term masks the challenges involved (Davies 2010; Filipe et al. 2017; Williams et al. 2020). Nonetheless, use of the term demonstrates a belief in the value of multi-directional learning and represents an attempt to collapse, or at the very least interrogate and expand, the boundaries that regulate knowledge production in pursuit of shared authority (Pente et al. 2015; Butler 2017).

Digital modes of engagement and communication have in the past twenty years revolutionized possibilities of public history (King et al. 2016; Bishop 2017). Blogs, digital exhibits, social media posts, podcasts and websites now

---

J. Grove
e-mail: J.E.Grove@exeter.ac.uk

R. Langlands
e-mail: R.Langlands@exeter.ac.uk

C. McNamara
University of Surrey, Surrey, UK

provide a range of opportunities for history to be written, published and shared, and online data collections can (despite expensive paywalls) help democratize access to historical evidence.[5] The use of digital mapping and imaging provides new ways of making historical material accessible, or meaningful. Digital spaces can change the relationship between museums, archives, universities, curators and visitors. Digital spaces can disrupt the power structures determining what is made visible; content is more easily diversified or crowd-sourced, and, as some have argued, the use of the digital domain to present historical objects, material or analysis can have a restructuring effect that works to encourage a more democratic engagement with history or reallocation of authority (King et al. 77; Rosenzweig 2006; Gauld 2017).

Co-production is additionally seen as a productive way to rectify the systematic exclusion from historical knowledge production that marginalized communities experience. Trans studies have only relatively recently emerged as academic fields of study as signalled by the field-defining publication of the *Transgender Studies Reader* (2006), co-edited by Susan Stryker and Stephen Whittle, followed by the publication of Stryker's *Trans History* (2008). The last decades have also witnessed pioneering scholarship on trans history produced outside of academic networks, such as Morgan M. Page's podcast *One From the Vaults* (2015–present), Duckie's *Queer History Club*, or E. J. Scott's *Museum of Transology* (Scott 2014–). Yet, interest in trans history is anything but new. In the modern Western world, attempts to document trans experiences were often carried out by scientific professionals within pathologizing and colonially shaped frameworks.[6] The archive of trans and queer sources collected by German-Jewish sexologist Magnus Hirschfeld in the early twentieth century and largely destroyed by the Nazis in 1933 offers one important example. Importantly, there were other initiatives to record trans and queer history by and for trans and queer people, although these were also affected by historical erasure. Early journals like *Urania* (1916–40) in the UK, and *Frauenliebe/Garçonne* (1926–30) and *Die Freundin* (1924–33) in Germany, for instance, had a limited circulation and are difficult to access in archives today.[7] From the 1960s onwards, *Transvestia* magazine (1960–86), founded by Virginia Prince in the US, provided a forum for trans people to write about and share their experiences and histories, although this knowledge rarely reached broader audiences. As a result, trans history has, for a long time, remained relatively inaccessible. As Leslie Feinberg wrote in the pioneering *Transgender Warriors* (1996): "I couldn't find *myself* in history. No one like me seemed to have ever existed" (11). Although no form of co-production or public engagement can undo these forms of historical erasure, collaborative projects can offer one mechanism to interrogate and expand how knowledge is produced, by whom and for what purpose. As Kayte McSweeney and Jay Stewart note, support for and interest in co-production has been fuelled by "[c]oncerns for inclusion, diversity, representation, social justice and a broader understanding of what knowledge can be," not least because of the demands made by those who have "felt excluded, overlooked or unfairly represented" for "access, dialogue, debate and advocacy" (2017, 137). Digital platforms and online communications provide a particularly valuable, vibrant and accessible (if sometimes) fraught location for trans communities to support each other. As the literature drawing on the notion of "counter publics" demonstrates, social media technologies aid community building that challenges powerful narratives and protects oppressed communities.[8] As Lauren Malone shows, strategies for creative anti-oppressive culture and learning environments have much to learn from the often playful ways in which digital spaces have been used by trans people to build community, support each other, disrupt heteronormativity and respond to discrimination (2020).

In this chapter, we present our experiences of collaborating on a trans history project—*Transformations*—funded by a grant from the Wellcome Trust and linked to a project on the history of Western sexual science. *Transformations* led to a podcast and website: *Adventures in Time and Gender*. It involved academic researchers (in History, Classics, English and Modern Languages) working with young trans and non-binary people, writers and artists, youth workers, performers, directors and producers.[9] The production was not a conventional piece of history writing, but a set of new artistic works, including a drama podcast and website with creative visual and narrative responses to historical stimuli, a body of work that has the potential to contribute to cultural memory-making, as much as a piece of public history.

In this sense, *Transformations* did not seek to make academic knowledge accessible (De Groot 2016). The use of historians and other academics as fact-checking consultants has been the focus of recent critical reflections on the changing significance and meaning of authenticity and accuracy.[10] Increasingly championed are creative, stylized, knowingly anachronistic or playful representations of the past (Fogu 2009; Harris 2017). *Transformations* focused on developing inventive and creative responses to historical material that fed both the project production and our understanding of the past, a creative approach which has informed other recent projects.[11] The project team worked collaboratively to use historical evidence as a springboard for thinking and exploring multiple perspectives on contemporary issues, concerns or social needs.

In this chapter, we will explore the processes, challenges and achievements of this project, including its impact on a wide range of collaborators and different audiences. Through a discussion of the decision-making processes and activities, as well as the impact of the outputs, we show the value of co-produced, creative and innovative modes of digital public history on all participants. Our account is informed by an in-depth evaluation of the project, conducted by independent researcher, Ester McGeeney. The evaluation used a qualitatively driven, mixed methods approach to explore the experiences, outcomes and impact of *Transformations* for project participants and collaborators. It also tracked the reach of the project production, *Adventures in Time and Gender*, in order to understand its impact on key audience groups.

Creative and participatory methodologies ensured the safe, ethical and inclusive collection of research materials, including online focus groups, interviews and research diaries. Data has been anonymized. Further information about the evaluation research ethics and design, as well as details of the research findings, can be found in the evaluation report (McGeeney 2021).

5.2 Background of the Project

Transformations was funded by the Wellcome Trust, a UK-based funding body that has long seen public engagement as part of their mission to improve global health.[12] The relationship between project leads at the University of Exeter, charity Gendered Intelligence (GI), and lead artist and writer Jason Barker drew on previous collaborations. These included *Transvengers,* part of Wellcome Collection's *Institute of Sexology* (2014–15) and shared research interests in the politics of knowledge around sexuality and gender, explored in workshops, conferences and seminars.[13] A workshop on medical authority and knowledge organized in London in 2015 featured GI staff, artists, academics and GIC professionals, and the themes raised also shaped a major Wellcome Trust Grant (https://rethinkingsexology.exeter.ac.uk). GI (founded in 2008) is a trans-led and trans-involving grassroots charity that works to increase understanding of gender diversity and improve the lives of trans people. One element of GI's mission is to make the world more intelligent about gender by sharing knowledge, expertise and insights by trans and non-binary people. For this reason, GI is committed to engaging with the wider general public through educative opportunities across a variety of sectors. This work is vital since, as GI has identified, the educational sector (including universities, museums and heritage centres) rarely explores the diversity of gender or features stories by trans and non-binary people (McSweeney and Stewart 2017).

5.3 "…Look at All This Evidence. It's Really Mind Blowing."

A key aim of the project was to provide a rare space for young people to demonstrate their own insights into histories of gender, sexuality and science. As Jay Stewart, CEO of GI, writes, (referencing Halberstam 2011) young trans people often lack opportunities to share their expertise and knowledge:

> Experiencing the world as a person who does not conform to gender norms requires great thought. Trans people are intelligent about gender because they need to be. In many ways, the need of young trans people to know about gender in ways that are perhaps more rich and nuanced challenges the notions of the "expert" who can deem gender in more simple and albeit normative ways. GI as an organisation places centrally a calling to apply an intelligence when it comes to thinking about gender. Intelligence is about an aptitude; it demands a labour around processing and thinking. Moreover, when it comes to gender,

intelligence can be a process of learning, but it can also be an un-learning of the norms that are so deeply embedded.

Small groups of trans people (aged 16–24) took part in four historical workshops in Bristol. Youth worker Bon O'Hara facilitated to ensure a safe, inclusive environment. The academic researchers, who were all cisgender, worked with Jason Barker and Bon O'Hara to present a variety of historical materials in creative ways involving games, drama and storytelling, and scrapbooking. Activities were designed to be creative, varied and engaging. For instance, researchers told stories and performed as historical figures, discussions and games took place alongside collaging and scrapbooking. As one young participant responded: "I expected it to be like a lesson in school before I went there, but the atmosphere and the way people delivered information was just great" (McGeeney 2021, 19). The historical material explored three strands:

1. Exploring the History of Sexology: The scientific study of sexuality (sexology) emerged in the nineteenth century and shaped modern understandings of gender and sexual identity, including the "medicalization" of trans bodies. Early sexologists also drew upon historical and literary perspectives and sought input from trans and queer people when developing diagnostic categories and treatments. This complex material provided a springboard to discuss questions such as: Which forms of knowledge are seen as scientific/medical? What evidence is seen as authoritative when it comes to defining gender and sexuality? Which voices are heard—or ignored?
2. Exploring Past Trans Lives: We also looked at the lives of individuals who lived gender non-conforming lives outside or in tension with modern Western medical categories. We explored the origins and impact of the various names and labels, pronouns and categories used to make sense of gender and sexuality at various periods in the past. We asked what labels we need to gain recognition or obtain treatment, what roles labels play in identity formation and community building, and how labels can also close down alternative forms of fluidity or openness, including in non-Western cultures.
3. Exploring Stories of Transformations: We picked out stories that demonstrated the significance of gender diversity and fluidity in the imaginations of people in many past cultures. These included narratives from Classical and European Medieval as well as modern traditions in which characters spontaneously or miraculously transformed "from male to female" or vice versa. We discussed the possible functions of these stories: as reflections of reality, or as having fantastical, religious or educational purposes.

An oral history project, for which a group of young trans participants conducted twelve in-depth life histories with older trans people, provided additional material. This comprises a valuable new archive, including remarkable accounts of coming out, social and medical transitions and hostility, as well as empowering and life-affirming examples of support from family and friends, inspiring insights into personal strength and resilience, and powerful evidence of changing cultures and attitudes. Interviews also provided an opportunity for young and older trans people to compare experiences and reflect on historical shifts.

The historical material had a powerful impact on the young people involved. The project evaluation showed that young participants experienced an increase in confidence, validity, pride, and connection. They developed new skills and gained professional experience in research, creative writing and teamwork. Some joined local trans community groups and some made life-changing decisions with regards to work, education, family and healthcare support (McGeeney 2021). As these quotes from the two young participants below indicate, the historical learning was novel, exciting, and inspirational:

> I've never looked at anything like this before… it was amazing to see people like me in history… we don't really have a history in the media/general public, … so seeing that we have existed is really validating and special! … I'm really grateful for the opportunity and how much it inspired me. (McGeeney 2021, 8)

> It is very validating to be connected with our history and to have the chance to contribute creatively. (McGeeney 2021, 8)

In an interview Bon O'Hara commented that they were surprised "how transformative it would be for young people" to have access to powerful historical counter narratives to a hostile public discourse:

> If you imagine being part of an oppressed minority group and you walk into a space and you are suddenly given a huge amount of information that you never knew existed… When [the whole system] has been telling you that you are some sort of weird new trend… to walk into a room to have it suddenly spread out in front of you, like, look at all this evidence. It's really mind blowing. (McGeeney 2021, 8)

Contributing to history was meaningful for oral history interviewees too:

> I felt seen, heard and accepted during the interview and all of this helped me further value my own individual trans journey, … as well as feeling I had contributed to an invaluable archive of trans social history. (McGeeney 2021, 10)

The rhetoric of engaged research champions the role that external stakeholders and participants can play in producing effective articulations of new knowledge. The project amounted to a shared and collaborative interpretative process through which new analysis was produced that informed the resulting original creative works (podcasts and web pages) (Goldenberg 2019). In addition, all of the academic researchers involved documented the impact of the project on their own research in their research diaries, noting that participants' insightful interpretations of historical material was shaping new research questions, new ideas for teaching, and new (ethical) approaches to their roles as scholars:

> ...I was struck by the way in which the young participants and the trans facilitators were able to read into the text an empowering story of an intersex or gender-diverse person, whereas I tend to see it as evidence of the misogynistic, heteronormative binaries in Greek society ... they were able to focus on the survival of the gender-diverse person at the centre, who thrives, despite the way society treats them. (Grove quoted in McGeeney 2021, 38)

> The participants... picked up on elements of the story that I almost left out ... Participants latched onto the idea that the story could be interpreted as showing divine support for a trans relationship. I hadn't seen this coming; but it is an excellent and insightful reading. (Fisher quoted in McGeeney 2021, 38)

> The afternoon session on [literary writer] Bryher and also Campbell X's talk confirmed that I need to work more on the intersections between cisgender lesbian and trans history...I should stop labelling my literary scholarship as being about "women writers" and find other ways of describing it, e.g. it can be about feminist/queer writers, which is not a gendered description and allows for trans readings of these authors. Related to this, I feel inspired to use my position as a cis lesbian woman to say that writers that are conventionally read as belonging to lesbian history [like Radclyffe Hall or Bryher] also need to be read as part of trans history. I have acknowledged this before, but can do much more... (Funke quoted in McGeeney, 39)

Researchers were struck by the affirmative readings of historical materials offered by young people and facilitators and reflected on the importance of involving trans communities in the interpretation and analysis of texts:

> In preparation for this workshop ...I wanted to recoup a more affirmative version of trans history from our ancient sources...I found thought-provoking a blog written by a trans MA student about the text... that I had chosen (Lucian)...[that] made the point that this passage is systematically presented in scholarship ...and textbooks as being about lesbian women, obscuring the possibility of seeing Megilla/os as a trans man, and as part of trans history... I re-translated the Greek original in order to emphasize Megillos's own self-identification, and to avoid the misgendering that happens in all English translations I have seen.[14]

The responses of trans participants inspired researchers to form new reflections on the power and limitations of identity categories and debates about the use of anachronistic terms and categories to understand the past (Gailey 2016; Beemyn 2013). Several researchers reported their plans to explore plural and dialogical approaches to reading historical texts in ongoing research:

> The workshop has made me reflect on the issue of what to do with seemingly conflicting historical methodologies which challenge the labelling of historical people or challenge how far we can identify the "true identity" of people in the past. I feel that in this project we have to make room for both approaches to sit side by side. (Grove quoted in McGeeney 2021, 39)

> The workshops have also made me reflect on how important it is to remain flexible about how we categorise people in the past, and how we [therefore] allow people today to identify in beneficial ways with historical characters or categories. If we are too definitive about deciding that x person "was" e.g. a trans man rather than a lesbian woman, or vice versa, then we may shut off other possibilities that might be helpful to some people (as well as not being responsive to the nuances of the historical materials). It is better to acknowledge the possibility of a variety of different frames that bring different possibilities into focus, and offer different "possibility models." (Langlands quoted in McGeeney 2021, 39)

The political importance of this approach provided an additional challenge to the view that history can ever be a neutral or impersonal encounter with the past (Reis 2004).

> The first workshop brought home to me something that I had been aware of before but hadn't really had at the forefront of my thinking: the real and urgent importance of making trans history visible…Historians continually grapple with the questions of how far it is appropriate to use modern concepts to understand materials and events from the past, and how far we can universalize human experience across time. So for instance there have been recent debates about whether we can categorise women who had sexual/romantic relationships with other women as "lesbians" in our terms, if they were living in cultures and periods when the category as we understand it today did not exist (e.g. the work of Traub). In ancient Greece, it was expected that adult men would be attracted by younger teenage men and have sex with them; to what extent can we call these men "gay"? …The workshop helped me recognize such discussions as pressing and real…these discussions have implications that are more than just abstract and methodological. It made me reflect on my moral and political responsibilities as a historian of sexuality and gender. As a result, I have decided to update some of my teaching materials/practices, and also to undertake some new research addressing these issues, bringing contemporary trans issues and ancient history together in the hope that both can be enhanced.[15]

The history workshops underscored the urgency of making trans history visible and highlighted researchers' moral responsibility of using their platforms to engage in this work.

5.4 "THE MAGIC HAPPENED... IN THOSE CONVERSATIONS"

The insights developed through these historically based activities were fed into the creative stages of the project. A series of writers' rooms saw young participants collaborate with professional artists, writers and academic researchers to discuss themes and develop creative ideas.

Central to this process was an openness to creative possibilities. At the outset of the project no form of production was pitched; artworks, exhibitions, installations, curated objects, performances and musicals were all mooted. As the project took shape, ideas began to coalesce around the idea of a touring theatre performance, accompanied by a curated programme of audience activities and exhibits. Artist and writer Jason Barker drafted these ideas into an outline and explored dramaturgy and scenography with theatre and performance academic, Catherine McNamara.

Once the possibilities of live theatre disappeared following the outbreak of Covid-19 in early 2020, writer Jason Barker, producer Catherine McNamara, and director Krishna Istha considered various options, and in consultation with young participants, re-oriented the project into a digital format. Working online with young people created new challenges, for example, in ensuring engagement took place in a safe and nurturing space, and benefits, such as helping combat the isolation many experienced (Malone 2020, Lauren 2020). We now sought to work internationally, to reach audiences worldwide, and were able to recruit a rich pool of talented trans and non-binary writers, actors, artists and designers whose commitments altered as "lockdowns" were imposed on communities around the globe. A second round of (now online) writers' rooms re-worked the material into a 3-part drama podcast written by Jason Barker. The programme of events turned into a website, designed by Zed from They Them Studio, featuring "wormholes" of curated historical material and a varied portfolio of artistic responses to it, including e.g. photographic portraits, films, essays, poems, performances and artworks.

Co-production and the literature on participatory youth work stimulated by Roger A. Hart's "Ladder of Participation" informed the process (2008). At every juncture, each participant brought knowledge and authority to the room, and structures and activities recognized shared expertise. In the case of the academic researchers, this required adopting different roles and registers at different stages. When researchers introduced documents and material for exploration, their role as perceived experts was important. It differentiated these workshops from the kinds of youth group work many young people were familiar with. The researchers' presence gave the material validity and legitimized the study of trans history. As Bon O'Hara observed:

> I think there's definitely a difference between me delivering something in a youth group and someone who has got a doctorate in it and has spent years with it being their passion delivering it, you know?[16]

Nonetheless, it was critical that the interpretative skills of all participants were valued and activities emphasized the idea that everyone had a valuable contribution to make. Jason Barker drew particular attention to the role of the academics in walking a "tightrope" in which they displayed passion, knowledge and expertise, while simultaneously validating the authority of trans voices:

> There was also something about having people who were professors, who were historians ... that gave it authenticity, so I think that was really important. For me, there was something about it [trans history] being treated seriously... - this is history, this is things that historians talk...about.

For Barker, this was enhanced by researchers' presentation of the historical evidence as "completely open to interpretation - it was open to people talking about the story, asking about the story, saying their own take on it." This helped young people to access the stories, make their own interpretations and engage with the "strangeness" of some of the sources.[17] In the workshops and in the oral history stage, the authority of the researchers was also constructed as just one voice among many (Frisch 1990; Roque Ramírez 2012).

Later stages of the project saw researchers' roles adapt and change. The historical information was handled differently during the second phase (writers' room) and researchers developed new skills and perspectives. As Jana Funke recalled, not only was there less emphasis on providing information or material, but:

> I learned to change how I talk about these figures and their lives ... When we came back to [the early twentieth-century literary author] Bryher to flesh out their character, I shifted the way I talked about them, e.g. instead of saying "Bryher's father was a shipping magnate and probably the richest man in England," I would say "I see Bryher on a boat and as someone who loves to travel and can never sit still." This ... allowed the young people ... to build on my contribution by saying "yes, and I see Bryher doing x, y and z." It was really eye-opening and fascinating to see what Jason [Barker] was doing with the historical materials and to change and adjust the way I talk about my research quite radically. (Funke quoted in McGeeney 2021, 22)

The production stage saw creatives take up the central role, asking the researchers for advice or additional information when they saw fit. A core team of five—writer Jason Barker, who worked on the project from the outset, Krishna Istha who directed the podcasts, sound designer and editor Jo Jackson, web designer Zed and social media consultant and digital strategist Campbell X—led the production stage. The podcast was performed by an all-trans cast (and featured both well-established professional artists and young people for whom this project was their first professional job). The production was supported by sound artists, a foley mixer, foley artist, re-recording mixer and two musicians who created original music and sound. A range of writers, performers, photographers and graphic artists were commissioned to create work for the website "wormholes."

The final stage of the project allowed cis academics to step back and the project followed an approach to co-curation which allowed for a redistribution of authority/power and attention to the different skills of all participants. In this case, it ensured the final product is a showcase of trans creativity led by trans creatives. The collaborations with the academic team remained important, however. Designer Zed commented on the *"infectious"* enthusiasm of the research team and how productive it was to have conversations that involved collaborations between creatives and academics.

> One of the really interesting things about creating the wormholes was the conversations between a creative person and an academic person. It did work really well you know and it was a little kind of tennis match, it was like and then there's this and there's this and this is how you make that real. And this ...that's where the magic happened in this, in those conversations. (Gregory quoted in McGeeney 2021, 28)

For many, making trans voices central to the production stage was unusual and exciting. As one of the actors commented in an interview:

> I think most [of the cast] were really excited by the project because, one, there were so many trans people involved. It wasn't like there were three trans people on the stage - there were over 20 of them and they were all doing different things and the sound is done by a trans person, the website is done by a trans person. I think it is the kind of project that trans people always want to work on so I think for that reason I think everyone was very excited... I remember...people being like, that's amazing, I've never seen so many trans people in one place doing this and it's about us and it's by us.[18]

The production stage showcased the creative interpretations developed by participants in collaboration with professional audiences to ensure the final piece emphasized participants' histories, experiences, and ways of seeing.

5.5 "A GENTLE WAY OF INVOLVING EVERYBODY"

The workshops identified young trans and queer people as the key target audience and sought to market *Adventures in Time and Gender* as a product created by and for the trans community as a community resource. Project participants reflected on the transformative power of the project for themselves as participants and for future unknown audiences and website users.

> I am so incredibly proud of this project…I think this project is quite life-changing for people. I do think that if I had seen this as a young trans person I would have been so delighted, it would have changed my life…
>
> I hope that this will be shared widely once it's out and will help educate people on trans history and open their minds to all the different trans experiences it explores. And I hope, for any trans or questioning listeners, that it will make them feel seen, and that they can relate to some part of it. (Actor quoted in McGeeney 2021, 29)

The *Adventures in Time and Gender* podcasts and website were launched in October 2020, and released weekly during October and November 2020 with new web content also added during this time. Between 1st October and 31st December 2020, the podcast reached more than 21,481 listeners across Europe, Australia, North and South America and the website was accessed 12,461 times by 3692 users.

The audience feedback survey captured responses from thirteen people who identified as trans or non-binary who ranged in age from under eighteen to over fifty. E.g.:

> I love the wormholes on the website. It's such a wonderful place of exploration for trans people to learn about our vast and varied history – and present! The website design is also beautiful, which makes the experience of being on the website really nice.
>
> It's such a good learning resource and you don't get that from a lot of LGBT history. Most of it is quite hard to find and you need to look quite deep and they might not be good, and this is really, really good. It's really accessible, it's really informative and it's also funny.
>
> A resource like this is so incredibly important! There are not many podcasts by and for trans and non-binary people, and even less focused on our history – might this even be the only one?! I want to learn everything, and to hear trans people sharing it – it gives me a sense of belonging, of solidity, of knowing how the path before me has been shaped. (Survey respondents quoted in McGeeney 2021, 44–6)

Participants of the project also hoped to contribute to a change in the tone, dynamics and relationships commonly experienced between trans people and clinical or therapeutic organizations. As previous trans-led engagement projects have also found, trans people are often "silenced or excluded from the official narrative of science and medicine," and even when included, their voices are token, marginalized and not used to initiate lasting change (McSweeney and Stewart 2017, 149). However, we chose not to involve medical or clinical audiences directly since previous experiences of e.g. stakeholder engagement workshops showed that it was difficult to move beyond the power dynamics of a hierarchical doctor/patient relationship. In such environments many trans people do not feel they are seen as experts and end up exhausted by the labour of self-explanation and perceived scrutinization (Oborn and Dawson 2010; Vincent 2018). However, groups of practitioners who work on trans healthcare or deliver education on gender diversity reported during audience focus groups that they were profoundly affected by the podcast, despite not being its main intended audience. In disrupting the context and mode in which cis clinicians engage with trans voices, clinicians saw the podcast as helping improve the often tense and antagonistic relationships between health services and trans communities.

Six clinical practitioners took part in focus groups. Five worked at a Gender Identity Clinic (GIC) and one worked at a young people's sexual health clinic. They described *Adventures in Time and Gender* as "funny," "engaging," "beautiful," "interesting," "playful," "sweet" and "enticing." They welcomed the podcast as a playful "gentle and kind way of involving everybody" that explored gender identity from "different angles." Some of the GIC practitioners admitted that they had been fearful that they might be positioned as the "bad guys," but were relieved that instead "there was balance and the opportunity to see so many possibilities."

> I have to admit when I first started listening I was nervous because it mentions Gender Identity Clinics and how it's been modelled through history ... Initially I thought, we are going to be seen, dare I say, as the enemy ... but actually I think the podcast opens those dialogues and sees it from so many angles. (GIC practitioner quoted in McGeeney 2021, 47)

Clinical practitioners commented that the podcasts offer a "different narrative" driven by curiosity and play, rather than by fear. They felt that the podcast modelled the kind of open dialogue that they would like to be having with both clients and colleagues, and that they would like to see more widely "in society at large."

> What I quite liked is that there was an open dialogue and conversation in the podcast around conflicting thoughts and feelings around the importance of labels and not the importance of labels, and wanting boundaries and not wanting boundaries, and I thought that was quite reassuring from a clinic perspective, that actually there isn't one way of looking at this and we feel that too. (GIC practitioner quoted in McGeeney 2021, 48)

Adventures in Time and Gender is encouraging those clinical practitioners who engage with it to rethink aspects of their practice. Clinical practitioners reported feeling "better equipped" to understand "how difficult and problematic" it is for trans and non-binary young people in clinical settings, who face "labels and intrusive questions." These clinicians welcomed the podcast as providing a sympathetic and inclusive way for the "conversation" about gender and gender identity to "move on" and make "relationships [with clients] better" (GIC practitioner quoted in McGeeney 2021, 50).

5.6 Conclusion

Transformations and the resulting podcast and website, *Adventures in Time and Gender,* provided a critical and innovative examination of histories of Western sexual science and medicine by harnessing trans and non-binary people's knowledge, skills and creativity. This was made possible through the innovative collaborations at the heart of the project, which involved academic researchers, young people, artists and creatives, youth workers and designers. Key to the success of the project was the ongoing effort to manage and balance various forms of expertise and knowledge and to create a productive dialogue between historical research and creative approaches. Young trans participants were empowered and validated, learnt new skills and developed confidence in their knowledge. The historical researchers found new angles on their research and developed new lines of enquiry and plans for teaching. By embedding invention into the process, and encouraging distinctive, funny and imaginative work, in which trans voices were central, the project has the additional potential to contribute to changing the conversation around trans history and politics. Overall, it highlights the value of digital public humanities in facilitating novel and exciting modes of communication.

Notes

1. Much of this effort is fuelled in the UK (and beyond, e.g. in Australia) by the "Impact Agenda," which links some forms of university funding to an institution's track record in producing research that has a direct benefit to the non-academic world.
2. See Duggan (1986), Frisch (1990), Gentry (2015), Gwinn (2017), Scott-Brown (2017), Porter Benson et al. (1986).
3. "Manifesto for Public Engagement"; "Connected Communities".
4. See Ramos Pinto and Taithe (2015), Mandler (2015), Collini (2012), especially Chapter 9, "Impact".
5. See Cohen and Rosenzweig (2006), Butler (2017), Leon (2017), Taylor and Gibson (2017), Purkis (2017).
6. See e.g. Snorton (2017).
7. See e.g. Warner (2002), Murphy et al. (2017).
8. See Jackson et al. (2018), L. Malone (2020, Malone 2020).
9. The project was a collaboration between Jason Barker, the *Rethinking Sexology* and *Transformations* team at the University of Exeter and the University of Portsmouth, and Gendered Intelligence (GI). GI's involvement in the project was led by CEO and co-founder Dr. Jay Stewart and youth worker Bon O'Hara, who worked alongside the academic researchers from the outset. The research team included Professor Kate Fisher, Professor Jana Funke, Dr. Jen Grove, Dr. Sarah Jones, Professor Rebecca Langlands, Dr. Ina Linge, Dr. Catherine McNamara, and Kazuki Yamada. The project was evaluated by Dr. Ester McGeeney. The oral history workshops were also supported by Dr. Ruth Pearce.
10. On "authenticity," "accuracy," and public history see e.g. White (2005), Fisher and Langlands (2015), Greig (2015).

11. See Harvey (2015), Eisenstadt and McLellan (2020), "SPAN–a hands-on history project" (2021).
12. See TNS BMRB (2015). All major UK funding councils now prioritize public engagement, especially following the 2008 "Beacons for Public Engagement" initiative which sought to "inspire a culture change in how universities engage with the public," https://www.publicengagement.ac.uk/nccpe-projects-and-services/completed-projects/beacons-public-engagement. All the main funders of research in the UK have signed up to the 2013 "Concordat for Engaging the Public with Research," https://re.ukri.org/documents/hefce-documents/concordat-for-engaging-the-public-with-research/.
13. *Transvengers* empowered young trans and non-binary adults to interrogate historical sexological understandings through comic–making, https://wellcomecollection.org/exhibitions/XFximBAAAPkAioWv. Further ideas were exchanged at a workshop on medical authority and knowledge organized in London in 2015, which featured GI staff, artists, academics and GIC professionals. See also Fisher and Langlands (2015), and the *Rethinking Sexology: The Cross-Disciplinary Invention of Sexuality: Sexual Science Beyond the Medical, 1890–1940* project, funded by a major Wellcome Trust grant: https://rethinkingsexology.exeter.ac.uk.
14. Langlands, reflective diary. As part of the evaluation, researchers and workshop facilitators kept a diary to reflect on the process including responses to key questions posed by the independent evaluator.
15. Langlands, reflective diary.
16. O'Hara, reflective diary.
17. Barker, reflective diary. See also, McGeeney (2021, 21).
18. Krishna Isthna, interview. As part of the evaluation, participants were interviewed by the independent evaluator. See also McGeeney (2021, 30).

References

Ahmed, Sara. 2012. *On Being Included: Racism and Diversity in Institutional Life*. Durham, NC: Duke University Press.

Beemyn, Genny. 2013. "A Presence in the Past: A Transgender Historiography." *Journal of Women's History* 25 (4): 113–21.

Bishop, Catherine. 2017. "The Serendipity of Connectivity: Piecing Together Women's Lives in the Digital Archive." *Women's History Review* 26 (5): 766–80. https://doi.org/10.1080/09612025.2016.1166883.

Butler, Toby. 2017. "History 2.0.: History, Publics and New Technologies." In *The Oxford Handbook of Public History*, edited by James B. Gardner and Paula Hamilton, 34–45. Oxford: Oxford University Press.

Cohen, Daniel J., and Roy Rosenzweig. 2006. *Digital History: A Guide to Gathering, Preserving, and Presenting the Past on the Web*. Philadelphia: University of Pennsylvania Press.

Collini, Stefan. 2012. *What are Universities For?* London: Penguin.

"Connected Communities." Accessed November, 2021. https://ahrc.ukri.org/research/fundedthemesandprogrammes/crosscouncilprogrammes/connectedcommunities.

Davies, Sue M. 2010. "The Co-Production of Temporary Museum Exhibitions." *Museum Management and Curatorship* 25 (3): 305–21.
De Groot, Jerome. 2016. *Consuming History Historians and Heritage in Contemporary Popular Culture*. New York: Routledge.
Duggan, Lisa. 1986. "History's Gay Ghetto: The Contradictions of Growth in Lesbian and Gay History." In *Presenting the Past: Essays on History and the Public*, edited by Susan Porter Benson et al., 281–92. Philadelphia: Temple University Press.
Eisenstadt, Nathan, and Josie McLellan. 2020. "Foregrounding Co-Production: Building Research Relationships in University-Community Collaborative Research." *Research for All* 4 (2): 242–56. https://doi.org/10.14324/RFA.04.2.08.
Feinberg, Leslie. 1996. *Transgender Warriors: Making History from Joan of Arc to Dennis Rodman*. Boston, Mass: Beacon Press.
Filipe, Angela, Alicia Renedo, and Cicely Marston. 2017. "The Co-Production of What? Knowledge, Values, and Social Relations in Health Care." *PLoS Biology* 15 (5): e2001403.
Fisher, Kate, and Rebecca Langlands. 2015. "Introduction." In *Sex, Knowledge, and Receptions of the Past*, edited by Fisher and Langlands, 1–24. Oxford: Oxford University Press.
Fogu, Claudio. 2009. "Digitalizing Historical Consciousness." *History and Theory* 48 (2): 103–2. http://www.jstor.org/stable/25478839.
Frisch, Michael. 1990. *A Shared Authority: Essays on the Craft and Meaning of Oral and Public History*. Albany: State University Press.
Gailey, Nerissa. 2016. "Strange Bedfellows: Anachronisms, Identity Politics, and the Queer Case of Trans*." *Journal of Homosexuality* 64 (12): 1713–30. https://doi.org/10.1080/00918369.2016.1265355.
Gauld, Craig. 2017. "Democratising or Privileging: The Democratisation of Knowledge and the Role of the Archivist." *Archival Science* 17 (3): 227–45. https://doi.org/10.1007/s10502-015-9262-4.
Gentry, Kynan. 2015. "'The Pathos of Conservation': Raphael Samuel and the Politics of Heritage." *International Journal of Heritage Studies* 21 (6): 561–76.
Goldenberg, Barry M. L. 2019. "Rethinking Historical Practice and Community Engagement: Researching Together with 'Youth Historians.'" *Rethinking History* 23 (1): 52–77. https://doi.org/10.1080/1342529.2018.1494934.
Greig, Hannah. 2015. "As Seen on the Screen: Material Culture, Historical Accuracy and the Costume Drama." In *Writing Material Culture History*, edited by Anne Gerritsen, and Giorgio Riello, 303–19. London: Bloomsbury.
Gwinn, Ian. 2017. "'History Should Become Common Property': Raphael Samuel, History Workshop, and the Practice of Socialist History, 1966–1980." *Socialist History* 51: 96–117.
Halberstam, Jack. 2011. *The Queer Art of Failure*. Durham, NC and London: Duke University Press.
Harris, Katherine. 2017. "'Part of the Project of That Book Was Not to Be Authentic:' Neo-Historical Authenticity and Its Anachronisms in Contemporary Historical Fiction." *Rethinking History* 21 (2): 193–212. https://doi.org/10.1080/13642529.2017.1315968.
Hart, Roger A. 2008. "Stepping Back from 'the Ladder': Reflections on a Model of Participatory Work with Children." In *Participation and Learning*, edited by Alan Reid, Bjarne Bruun Jensen, Jutta Nikel, and Venka Simovska, 19–31. Dordrecht: Springer.

Harvey, Karen. 2015. "Envisioning the Past: Art, Historiography and Public History." *Cultural and Social History* 12 (4): 527–43. https://doi.org/10.1080/14780038.2015.1088257.

Hinchliffe, Stephen, Mark A. Jackson, Katrina Wyatt et al. 2018. "Healthy Publics: Enabling Cultures and Environments for Health." *Palgrave Communications* 4 (57).

Holliman, Richard. 2017. "Supporting Excellence in Engaged Research." *Journal of Science Communication* 16 (5): 1–10.

Jackson, Sarah J., Moya Bailey, and Brooke Foucault Welles. 2018. "#GirlsLikeUs: Trans Advocacy and Community Building Online." *New Media & Society* 20 (5): 1868–88.

Jay, Gregory. 2010. "The Engaged Humanities: Principles and Practices for Public Scholarship and Teaching." *Journal of Community Engagement and Scholarship* 3 (1): Article 14.

Kean, Hilda, and Paul Martin, eds. 2013. *The Public History Reader*. London and New York: Routledge.

King, Laura, and Gary Rivett. 2015. "Engaging People in Making History: Impact, Public Engagement and the World Beyond the Campus." *History Workshop Journal* 80: 218–33.

King, Laura, James F. Stark, and Paul Cooke. 2016. "Experiencing the Digital World: The Cultural Value of Digital Engagement with Heritage." *Heritage & Society* 9 (1): 76–80. https://doi.org/10.1080/09612025.2016.1166883.

Lauren, Malone. 2020. *Intersectional Digital Rhetoric Pedagogy: Queer & Trans People of Color and Digital Platform Engagement*. Ames, Iowa: Iowa State University. Accessed November 30, 2021. https://www.proquest.com/docview/2424090039?pq-origsite=gscholar&fromopenview=true.

Leon, Sharon M. 2017. "Complexity and Collaboration: Doing Public History in Digital Environments." In *The Oxford Handbook of Public History*, edited by James B. Gardner, and Paula Hamilton, 44–68. Oxford: Oxford University Press.

Malone, Eloise. 2020. Effervescent. "Top Tips: Facilitating Digital Co-Creation and Arts Activities During Lockdown." Accessed November 30, 2021. https://eff.org.uk/content/uploads/2020a/04/Effervescent-lockdown-top-tips-article-2.pdf.

Mandler, Peter. 2015. "The Impact of the State." In *The Impact of History? Histories at the Beginning of the Twenty-First Century*, edited by Pedro Ramos Pinto and Bertrand Taithe, 169–81. London and New York: Routledge.

"Manifesto for Public Engagement." NCCPE. Accessed November 30, 2021. https://www.publicengagement.ac.uk/support-engagement/strategy-and-planning/manifesto-public-engagement/about-manifesto.

McGeeney, Ester. 2021. "'It Changes How You Feel About Yourself to Have this History' Transformations Impact Evaluation: Summary Report." *Gendered Intelligence*, May. Accessed November 30, 2021. https://genderedintelligence.co.uk/AdventuresTimeGender.html.

McSweeney, Kayte, and Jay Stewart. 2017. "Hacking Into the Science Museum: Young Trans People Disrupt the Power Balance of Gender 'Norms' in the Museums 'Who Am I?' Gallery." In *The Impact of Co-Production: From Community Engagement to Social Justice*, edited by Aksel Ersoy, 137–54. Policy Press Online.

Murphy, Kevin, Jennifer Pierce, and Alex T. Urquhart. 2017. "Sexuality and the Cities: Interdisciplinarity and the Politics of Queer Public History." In *The Oxford Handbook of Public History*, edited by James B Gardner and Paula Hamilton, 178–89. Oxford: Oxford University Press.

Oborn, Eivor, and Sandra Dawson. 2010. "Knowledge and Practice in Multidisciplinary Teams: Struggle, Accommodation and Privilege." *Human Relations* 63 (12): 1835–57. https://doi.org/10.1177/0018726710371237.

Page, Morgan M. 2015–. *One From the Vaults*. Produced by Morgan M. Page. Podcast, MP3 audio. https://soundcloud.com/onefromthevaultspodcast.

Pente, Elizabeth, et al. 2015. "The Co-Production of Historical Knowledge: Implications for the History of Identities." *Identity Papers: A Journal of British and Irish Studies* 1 (1): 32–53.

Porter Benson, Susan et al., eds. 1986. *Presenting the Past: Essays on History and the Public*. Philadelphia: Temple University Press.

Purkis, Harriet. 2017. "Making Digital Heritage About People's Life Stories." *International Journal of Heritage Studies* 23 (5): 434–44. https://doi.org/10.1080/13527258.2016.1190392.

Ramos Pinto, Pedro, and Bertrand Taithe. 2015. "Doing History in Public? Historians in the Age of Impact." In *The Impact of History? Histories at the Beginning of the Twenty-First Century*, edited by Pedro Ramos Pinto and Bertrand Taithe, 1–20. London and New York: Routledge.

Reis, Elizabeth. 2004. "Teaching Transgender History, Identity, and Politics." *Radical History Review* 88 (1): 166–77.

Roque Ramírez, Horacio N. 2012. "Sharing Queer Authorities: Collaborating for Transgender Latina and Gay Latino Historical Meanings." In *Bodies of Evidence: The Practice of Queer Oral History*, edited by by Nan Alamilla Boyd and Horacio N. Roque Ramírez, 184–201. Oxford: Oxford University Press.

Rosenzweig, Roy. 2006. "Can History Be Open Source? Wikipedia and the Future of the Past." *The Journal of American History* 93 (1): 117–46. https://doi.org/10.2307/4486062.

Samuel, Raphael. 1999. *Theatres of Memory*. Volume 1. London and New York: Verso.

Scott-Brown, Sophie. 2017. "Re-Reading Raphael Samuel: Politics, Personality and Performance." *Life Writing* 14 (1): 19–36.

Scott, E. J. 2014–. *Museum of Transology*. Accessed November 20, 2021. https://www.museumoftransology.com/e-j.

Snorton, C. Riley. 2017. *Black on Both Sides: A Racial History of Trans Identity*. Minneapolis: University of Minnesota.

"SPAN–a Hands-on History Project." 2021. *Evaluation Report*. Accessed November 30, 2021. https://cpb-eu-w2.wpmucdn.com/blogs.bristol.ac.uk/dist/7/542/files/2019/06/SPAN-Full-Evaluation-Report-June-2021-.pdf.

Stryker, Susan. 2008. *Transgender History*. Berkeley, CA: Seal Press.

Stryker, Susan, and Stephen Whittle, eds. 2006. *The Transgender Studies Reader*. New York and London: Routledge.

Taylor, Joel, and Laura Kate Gibson. 2017. "Digitisation, Digital Interaction and Social Media: Embedded Barriers to Democratic Heritage." *International Journal of Heritage Studies* 23 (5): 408–20. https://doi.org/10.1080/13527258.2016.1171245.

TNS BMRB. 2015. "Factors Affecting Public Engagement by Researchers: A Study on Behalf of a Consortium of UK Public Research Funders." Accessed November 20, 2021. https://wellcome.ac.uk/news/what-are-barriers-uk-researchers-engaging-public.

Vincent, Benjamin William. 2018. "Studying Trans: Recommendations for Ethical Recruitment and Collaboration with Transgender Participants in Academic

Research." *Psychology & Sexuality* 9 (2): 102–16. https://doi.org/10.1080/19419899.2018.1434558.

Warner, Michael. 2002. "Publics and Counterpublics." *Public Culture* 14 (1): 49–90.

White, Hayden. 2005. "Introduction: Historical Fiction, Fictional History, and Historical Reality." *Rethinking History* 9 (2–3): 147–57. https://doi.org/10.1080/13642520500149061.

Williams, Oli, et al. 2020. "Lost in the Shadows: Reflections on the Dark Side of Co-Production." *Health Research Policy and Systems* 18 (43).

CHAPTER 6

SémantiQueer: Making Linked Data Work for Public History

Constance Crompton

6.1 Introduction

There is a tension at the heart of digital projects that bring together large amounts of Humanities data: Humanities scholarship often focuses on events, people, and trends that push back against dominant narratives, but preparing data to be computationally legible often collapses difference and removes nuance. This chapter explores this tension in the creation of linked data for the Semantic Web, drawing on the Lesbian and Gay Liberation in Canada (LGLC) project as a case study. While representing the events and people of the Canadian gay liberation movement in a standardized digital format does set up artificial boundaries about what constitutes a historical event or what may be recorded about a person, this chapter argues that since digital projects do not constitute all that can be said about historical circumstances, public-facing digital projects can use standards and shared data exchange formats to facilitate public understanding of the past to support more nuanced historical research.

This is not to say that the digital representation of history has to reify dominant historical narratives. While popular histories of gay liberation in Canada tend to focus on the activism of gay, white, urban, anglophone men, the analysis of the data from the first six years of the Lesbian and Gay Liberation in Canada project has shown that gay liberation was not solely driven by

---

C. Crompton (✉)
University of Ottawa, Ottawa, Canada
e-mail: ccrompto@uottawa.ca

this demographic. The SémantiQueer phase of the project introduced here combines archival research and linked data creation to develop techniques to represent the diversity and span of Canadian gay liberation organizing, intersectional personhood, and activist knowledge exchange, with a particular focus on LGBTQ+[1] women's[2] and francophone activism from 1960 to 1985. By engaging in collaborative linked data ontology development the LGLC team will also create computational systems that expect and deliver historical nuance and diversity and that recognize linguistic, cultural, and gendered difference.

6.2 What Is Linked Data, and What Is it Doing in Public History Projects?

Linked data is a network of data points connected by a common vocabulary, or ontology, that describes relationships between those data points. When that linked data is available online, it constitutes the Semantic Web. The commercial Semantic Web is already here and is shaping how members of the public access information online: any user who has seen a pop-up box on the right-hand side of a Google Search result with snippets of information about the subject at hand has interacted with the Semantic Web (Chah 2018; Noble 2018; Pouyllau 2012). Whether authoritative Humanities knowledge will be part of what Web users can get back from the Semantic Web depends on whether Humanities knowledge is made available in a Semantic Web format (Pouyllau 2013). The time is right for scholars to create Semantic Web data that shares the knowledge contained in Humanities projects. Linked data is *the* format for adding source citations, meaning, and context to the Web, and is part of the Web's original design (Berners-Lee 1997). The growth of the Semantic Web has been slow. The dearth of linked data in the early 2010s led Dean Allemang and James Hendler to note that "the Web often feels like it is 'a mile wide but an inch deep,'" and motivated them to ask: "how can we build a more integrated, consistent, deep Web experience" for knowledge seekers (2011, 2)? In 2014, linked data only made up 1% of the content of the Web (Simpson and Brown 2014). The quantity and quality of linked data has grown steadily in the intervening years. Much of the recent growth has been commercial (the Semantic Web is being used to find you cheap flights and hotel deals). That said, the growth is not solely commercial; the development of the Semantic Web has attracted the research efforts of scholars across the disciplines (Ciotti and Tomasi 2016; Pattuelli et al. 2013; Leon 2017; Watson 2019).

An outline of the format and working of the Semantic Web is an important underpinning to any critique of the Web. The Semantic Web is an extension of the World Wide Web that makes the meaning of Web data machine readable. Semantic Web data, or linked data, takes the form of uniform resource identifiers (URIs) that represent entities (real-world people, places, events, concepts, etc.) connected to one another through relationships defined by an ontology (a set of computational rules that govern the type of relationships URIs can have to one another). Linked data are also called *triples* which consist of subjects, predicates, and objects. Triples take their name from the three-part structure of linked data statements, for example (1) René Highway (subject), (2) was a (predicate), (3) dancer (object). (1) René Highway, (2) died in, (3) 1990. (1) René Highway, (2) cause of death, (3) AIDS. (1) René Highway, (2) has sibling, (3) Thomson Highway. In linked data the human-legible terms such as "René Highway" (subject entity) and "has sibling" (predicate or relationship) are accompanied by computer-legible URIs. These URIs let the computers differentiate, for example, between all the people who may share names with the Highway brothers and, through ontological rules, clarify what the "has sibling" relationship between entities means (Fig. 6.1).[3]

Ontologies are the computer-legible logic systems that provide the entity categories (called *classes*), pieces of information about an entity (e.g. a birthdate for a person, called *properties*), and relationships between entities. Ontologies communicate ideas, explain and facilitate predictions, and mediate between conflicting viewpoints. Most commercial ontologies do not offer the nuanced classes, properties, and relationships that historians and other Humanities scholars need. For example, the commercial Schema.org ontology, developed by Google, Yahoo, and Yandex to give the power of the Semantic Web to their search engines, only has 50 properties that are specifically used to define a person. Many of these properties have commercial value but little historical value, such as *tax identifier, British value-added tax identifier*, and *The North American Industry Classification System number*. Humanities and Information Science scholars would argue that people's lives are shaped by denser networks of context and circumstance than Schema.org's ontology permits. Ontology development and linked data creation offer an opportunity for Humanities scholars to intervene in the Semantic Web and for projects like the LGLC to queer online spaces at the level of code.

René Highway **has sibling** **Thomson Highway**
subject predicate object

```
<rdf:Description rdf:about="http://www.wikidata.org/entity/Q3933104">
    <schema:sibling rdf:about="http://viaf.org/viaf/92396428">
        <rdfs:label>Thomson Highway</ rdfs:label>
    </schema:sibling>
</rdf:Description>
```

Fig. 6.1 A representation of the Thomson sibling relationship in RDF

6.3 The Case for Linked Data

In the face of these shortcomings of commercial linked data, historians and Humanities scholars in general may be tempted to eschew the digital all together. For the sake of public history, we must not give in to this temptation. For members of the public who are casually interested in history and other Humanities topics, the open Web might be the first and last place to look for information. This is, therefore, where public Humanities scholars should be to meet them. What remains to be considered is how best to balance engagement with rather impoverished ontologies, like Schema.org, which flatten data but are widely adopted, with more nuanced ontologies that have a smaller user base, but which express information about entities with more nuance and care.

Humanities scholarship continues to lead to new insights and the integration of data extracted from large digital projects has the potential to change the nature and scale of evidence available to scholars and the public. The work of Humanities, Computer Science, and Information Science scholars to solve this problem couples the quantitative power of computers with the heightened subjectivity that underpins critical scholarship in the analysis of large data sets (Ramsay 2011, x; Drucker 2009). In partnership with libraries and librarians, many Humanities scholars have mastered techniques for analyzing the content of human-scale data and metadata (i.e., content that could reasonably be read by a single person, for example the content of a monograph or a small database); however, they have only just in the last decade started to create and exploit large linked data sets.

There is reason for optimism about the growth of the Semantic Web: the same data can be represented using different ontologies to encourage both discoverability and nuance. Furthermore, ontology development is not only a tool to represent diversity, but to train computational systems to expect diversity. Humanities scholars who are creating public linked data are proceeding with a caution borne of archival findings and knowledge of the silences new data environments can reveal and perpetuate. While archival research may reveal how people understood their historical situation and the identities available to or forged by them, the archival record is not neutral (Roberto 2008; Drabinski 2013). It is best to take a cue from Lauren Klein and Catherine D'Ignazio's call to preserve diverse (i.e., messy) data as a way to push back against statistical analysis' eugenicist roots, roots that have historically shaped cultural attitudes toward queer and other marginalized people (Subramanian 2014; Maxwell 2019; Sedgwick 1990).

6.4 Case Study: The Lesbian and Gay Liberation in Canada Project

In practical terms, how can public scholars use linked data, and why should they? The section that follows introduces the Lesbian and Gay Liberation in Canada project and its motivations for and moves to represent Canadian queer history in a way that exceeds Allemang and Hendler's vision of a Web that is more than "an inch deep." The Lesbian and Gay Liberation in Canada project, which I run with my research partner, Michelle Schwartz, combines archival research and database development in an attempt to tell the story of Canadian gay liberation organizing.[4] The first phase of the project, which was completed in 2020, lists information about events, people, places, and periodicals from the start of the homophile association at the University of Toronto in 1964 to the start of the AIDS crisis in 1981. The LGLC project started as a pair of self-published chronologies compiled by our collaborator Donald McLeod, *Lesbian and Gay Liberation in Canada: A Selected Annotated Chronology, 1964–1975* and *Lesbian and Gay Liberation in Canada: A Selected Annotated Chronology, 1976–1981* (McLeod 1996, 2017). McLeod is the Head of Book and Serials Acquisitions at the University of Toronto Libraries, and a long-time volunteer at the ArQuives: Canada's LGBTQ2S+ Archives, formerly the Canadian Lesbian and Gay Archives (CLGA). McLeod undertook the chronologies in response to his experience helping researchers at the CLGA: in the early 1990s he was unsettled by the number of people accessing the archives who did not know about the gay liberation organizing of the previous two decades.

In print form the *Lesbian and Gay Liberation in Canada* chronologies are remarkable books. Each volume is organized by year, and is comprised of lists of events that include a date and location, followed by a prose description and series of citations. To create the events, McLeod read though gay and lesbian periodicals at the CLGA, as well as the British Columbia Gay and Lesbian Archives, the Canadian Women's Movement Archives, the Glenbow Museum Archives, the Toronto Reference Library, Robarts Library, and beyond (McLeod 2017). In addition to chronicling the events of gay liberation in Canada, the chronologies now serve as important finding aids for researchers, pointing them to further resources about 3100 specific events in Canada (Fig. 6.2).

In 2013 Michelle Schwartz and I approached Donald McLeod to ask if we could digitize his text. The highly structured book was full of entities: people, places, events, periodicals, that even in print form had a database-like structure. McLeod had retained the copyright to his text and gave us permission. In 2013, with the help of research assistants, we encoded McLeod's text in TEI-XML, the leading encoding format of the digital Humanities. The TEI-XML encoding itself represents an intellectual intervention into the text, as encoding choices constitute an argument about what matters in a text and how entities are connected. Since the text base is in TEI-XML, a non-proprietary format that is meant to be customized to meet the theoretical and editorial principles of a research team, the LGLC project is safeguarded against the fate of many digital projects that have been lost when proprietary companies stop supporting the software, code, or systems that underpin projects, leaving team members unable to share, open, visualize, or analyze their data. Furthermore XML is a flat format which makes it archivable in data repositories, in a way

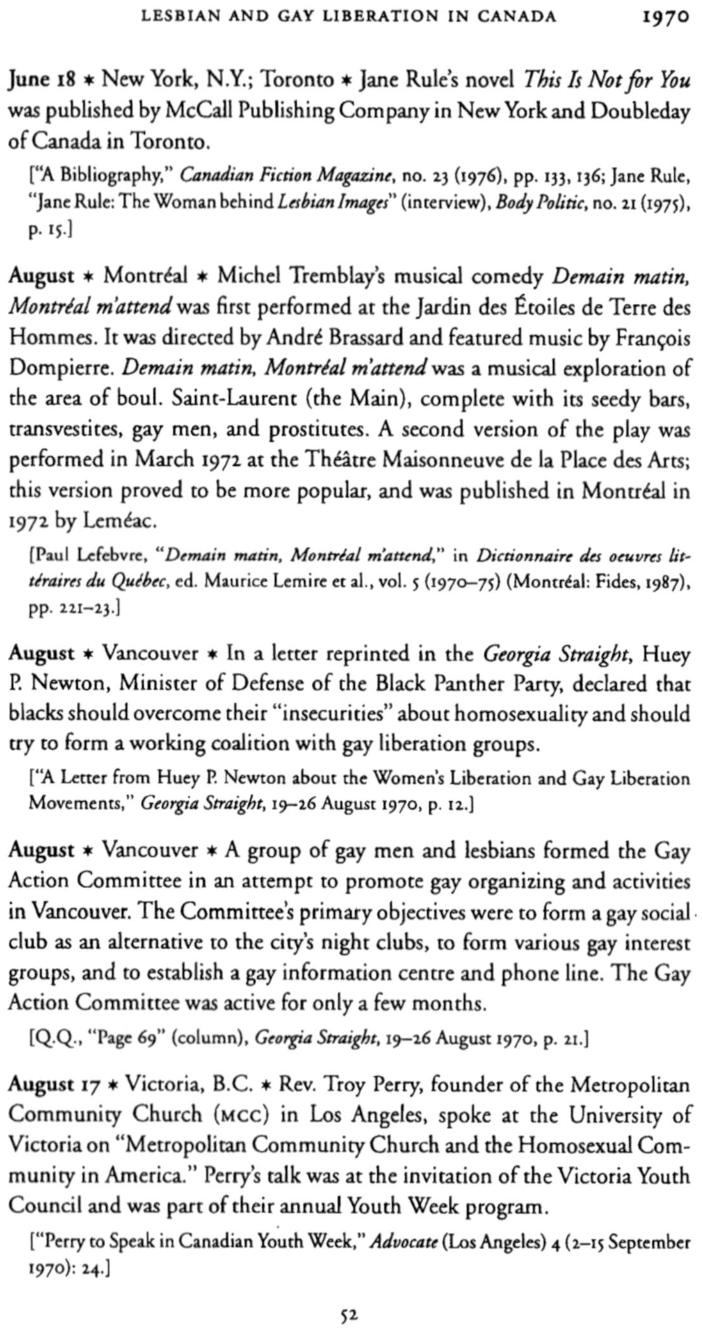

LESBIAN AND GAY LIBERATION IN CANADA   1970

June 18 * New York, N.Y.; Toronto * Jane Rule's novel *This Is Not for You* was published by McCall Publishing Company in New York and Doubleday of Canada in Toronto.

["A Bibliography," *Canadian Fiction Magazine*, no. 23 (1976), pp. 133, 136; Jane Rule, "Jane Rule: The Woman behind *Lesbian Images*" (interview), *Body Politic*, no. 21 (1975), p. 15.]

August * Montréal * Michel Tremblay's musical comedy *Demain matin, Montréal m'attend* was first performed at the Jardin des Étoiles de Terre des Hommes. It was directed by André Brassard and featured music by François Dompierre. *Demain matin, Montréal m'attend* was a musical exploration of the area of boul. Saint-Laurent (the Main), complete with its seedy bars, transvestites, gay men, and prostitutes. A second version of the play was performed in March 1972 at the Théâtre Maisonneuve de la Place des Arts; this version proved to be more popular, and was published in Montréal in 1972 by Leméac.

[Paul Lefebvre, "*Demain matin, Montréal m'attend*," in *Dictionnaire des oeuvres littéraires du Québec*, ed. Maurice Lemire et al., vol. 5 (1970–75) (Montréal: Fides, 1987), pp. 221–23.]

August * Vancouver * In a letter reprinted in the *Georgia Straight*, Huey P. Newton, Minister of Defense of the Black Panther Party, declared that blacks should overcome their "insecurities" about homosexuality and should try to form a working coalition with gay liberation groups.

["A Letter from Huey P. Newton about the Women's Liberation and Gay Liberation Movements," *Georgia Straight*, 19–26 August 1970, p. 12.]

August * Vancouver * A group of gay men and lesbians formed the Gay Action Committee in an attempt to promote gay organizing and activities in Vancouver. The Committee's primary objectives were to form a gay social club as an alternative to the city's night clubs, to form various gay interest groups, and to establish a gay information centre and phone line. The Gay Action Committee was active for only a few months.

[Q.Q., "Page 69" (column), *Georgia Straight*, 19–26 August 1970, p. 21.]

August 17 * Victoria, B.C. * Rev. Troy Perry, founder of the Metropolitan Community Church (MCC) in Los Angeles, spoke at the University of Victoria on "Metropolitan Community Church and the Homosexual Community in America." Perry's talk was at the invitation of the Victoria Youth Council and was part of their annual Youth Week program.

["Perry to Speak in Canadian Youth Week," *Advocate* (Los Angeles) 4 (2–15 September 1970): 24.]

52

Fig. 6.2 A page from volume 1 of Lesbian and Gay Liberation in Canada

that database-backed online projects are not (Goddard and Seeman 2019). The LGLC project has an existing data preparation workflow. As each research assistant encodes an event, they create ancillary TEI-XML records for entities that appear in the text. Using this method, the LGLC team has encoded the 3100 events originally written by McLeod and created 32,200 ancillary records about the entities listed in the events.

The TEI-XML is an excellent data preservation format, but it does not, on its own, lend itself to exploration by non-technical researchers. To serve the public history goals of the project we created the lglc.ca web app that lets Web users search through chronology text and ancillary records in a way that the print volumes do not permit. Visitors to the site can, for example, pull together all the events in a particular location, or all of the events that feature the work of a particular activist, or all of the events that share citations from a particular periodical. They can also aggregate content in a non-linear way, clicking on a location in an event, to find out more events at that location or selecting an organization to find out more about that particular organization's work over time. To create the web app we converted the TEI-XML into cypher, the language of Neo4j database, and then created the node.js app with pages generated by jade.js/pug.js templates that render the data as pages on the Web. The database features 68,700 interconnected relationships that let web app users both search and browse from entity to entity (Fig. 6.3).[5]

Like many database-backed websites, lglc.ca is a standalone project. It is not connected to other projects and their data in a computer- or human-legible way. However, our Neo4j graph database has a triple-like format, with each entity connected to another through a relationship. This prompted us to explore how we might convert our data to linked data for inclusion on the Semantic Web in a way that connected our data to that generated by others. This new phase of the LGLC project, SémantiQueer, is led by the following question: how can the LGLC team harness representational strategies and structures of the Semantic Web to represent and share the queer cultural diversity that tends to be flattened by commercial Semantic Web technologies?

6.4.1 Expanding the Project Scope Through Archival Research and Linked Data

The SémantiQueer phase of the LGLC project has two goals: first, to expand the project's coverage of LGBTQ+ women's and francophone Canadians' gay liberation activism from 1960 to 1985 on our public history website and in the more detailed datasets that the LGLC team uses for analysis, and second, to intervene in how information about people is recorded as linked data, adding the nuance, context, and authority of Humanities research on the Semantic Web. While our hope is that our linked data will be of good use to scholars and the general public, we specifically hope that the human-readable site and the linked data it houses will be useful to high school and university-aged

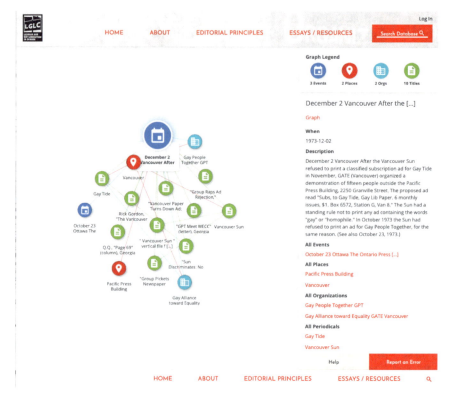

Fig. 6.3 A network graph of connected entities from the lglc.ca database

students living outside of urban centers. While much cultural-historical transmission can happen intergenerationally, this is not always an option available to queer youth through their biological families. By making Canada's unique multilingual and multigendered history available online through lglc.ca, we hope to expand on McLeod's original motivation for creating the chronologies, to show youth that this is their history and that Canadian gay liberation happened everywhere. While, as a matter of ethics, we do not use cookies or other user tracking on our website, public interest gives us some sense of our reach: for example the site has been used by Health Canada as part of their employee diversity and equity training, we have been interviewed by Radio Canada, and have been consulted for *The Village* podcast.

The original LGLC events skewed toward both anglophone activities and toward white men's activism. The anglophone men involved in the gay liberation movement tended to be more numerous and wealthier than women and francophones, with more print media, services, and spaces available to them. As a consequence, the evidence of their activism resulted in readily archivable material (Warner 2002; Crompton and Schwartz 2018; Alexander 2002; Caswell et al. 2017). As Ann Cvetkovich (2003) has argued, however, the work of gay liberation activists cannot be understood solely by focussing on the work of white, anglophone, urban, gay men. The LGLC team is now turning to other established and emerging archives to recover information about events beyond the protests, bar openings, raids, elections, and other events that end up in English-language newspapers and periodicals, to record information from and about French-language periodicals, consciousness-raising groups, dry dances, bookmobile tours, hotlines, and other francophone- and women-organized interventions and events (Dangoisse et al. 2022; Lang 2017; Cifor et al. 2018). Our initial pilot micro-project to test the French-language workflow proved to be a success: the LGLC database now includes a number of events in English and French drawn from *La vie en rose*, a French-language women's journal from Montréal. Our initial research into LGBTQ+ women's and francophone Canadian's experience has uncovered further events that serve the intersectional goals of the project. For example, our early research into trans women's activism in Québec appears to undermine the popular notion that Canada inherited American trans intellectual history in the 1990s (Ware 2017; Enriquez 2013; Mirha-Soleil Ross fonds 1972). The expansion of trans activism in the 1960s and of lesbian and bisexual mothers' activism in the early 1980s has led us to extend the LGLC coverage from 1964–1981 to 1960–1985.

Creating and publishing linked data will make our project's expanded data interoperable with the data for other projects. Linked data is distributed: no one project has to keep all records, but instead aggregator sites can bring together data from diverse projects. For example, author Margaret Atwood spoke at a number of protests following police raids on men's bath houses in Toronto in 1981. If our data is in linked data format Semantic Web users who are searching for Margaret Atwood could find out about her publications, awards, *and* liberation activism. The LGLC would have to not maintain records of Atwood's novels or prizes. Data from multiple projects could be brought together through a Semantic Web-facilitated search, featuring more information about Atwood's life's work maintained by other research projects. We are motivated in this work by Donald McLeod's original vision and his concern that stories of gay liberation that are not easily accessible may be forgotten in the span of a generation.[6]

In exploring how to convert our TEI-XML into linked data, we were confronted by the problems of impoverished commercial ontologies outlined above. Collaboration on ontology development and sharing that common ontology and URIs with other projects is the solution. The LGLC is now part of two national initiatives, both led by Susan Brown at University of Guelph: the Canadian Writing Research Collaboratory/Le Collaboratoire des Écrits du Canada (CWRC/CSEC cwrc.ca) and Linked Infrastructure for Networked Cultural Scholarship (LINCS lincsproject.ca). CWRC and LINCS design tools, including ontologies, and bring historical context and nuance online in ways that human readers and machine readers can understand, as part of ongoing work to build a responsible, Humanities-informed Semantic

Web. Collaboration within CWRC and LINCS is set to amplify the impact and the reach of both our historical research and digital scholarship. The chance to record the diversity we find in archives, and to translate that diversity into the CWRC/LINCS ontologies extends the utility of the LGLC beyond simply analyzing and sharing patterns in the history of gay liberation. Instead we will be creating computational systems that both expect historical nuance and diversity and that recognize linguistic, cultural, and gendered difference. Furthermore CWRC/LINCS linked data connects our data with the data from a wide range of projects with shared theoretical and historical interests, including *The People and The Text* (PI Deanna Reder), *Réseaux Littéraires Franco-Canadiens* (PI Lucie Hotte), *Rural Canadian Diaries* (PI Catherine Wilson), *Canadian Women Playwrights Online* (PI Anne Wilson), and *French and English Canadian Middlebrow Magazines* (PI Faye Hammill). These projects do not have to individually maintain duplicate information about any person, place, or organization, but can instead maintain project-specific information about each entity and still contribute to a LINCS-wide aggregation that offers users, and the Semantic Web in general, more complete and historically nuanced information about each entity. Through the shared use of the CWRC/LINCS ontology and shared authority records, LINCS' aggregate data is worth more than the sum of the contributing parts.

Now that the LGLC is creating linked data, the challenge of which ontologies to use is no longer only a theoretical challenge, it is also a practical problem: we have to weigh the relative merits of a number of ontologies. We are testing linked data using our beta prosopography, or collective biography, site (https://prosopography.lglc.ca/) to express to computers which entities are on the site (people, places, organizations, dates) and what the relationships are between them. Prosopography, or collective biography, is analysis of aggregate data about a population to find trends in that population's life course. Methodologically, prosopography comes from the study of the ancient world. While scholars may have very few records about the lives of individual people enslaved by the Romans, or women living in ancient Greece, they may have fragmentary data from census records, chronologies, and histories. Traditional prosopography amasses these data points to form a picture of, for example, an average enslaved person or woman in the ancient world. Traditional prosopographical researchers recover the probable patterns in lives of people who were not considered important enough to merit complete records at the time that they lived. In this way, prosopography is a welcome addition, and indeed correction, to the *great man* studies of history.[7]

Many digital Humanities projects have taken up prosopographical techniques (Hedley and Kooistra 2019; Brown et al., n.d.). These digital Humanities projects are not always faced by the paucity of data that the prosopography was originally developed to overcome, but instead, because digital Humanities projects often use databases and other aggregating tools, project team members can see patterns that would be invisible to text-only projects (Pasin and Bradley 2013). The activists represented in the LGLC project were active in the 1960s and 1970s, and so we often, but not always, know quite a lot about many of these activists' lives. Still, we find prosopographical analysis useful to the project. Prosopography lets us ask questions of the project's data, such as "what is the likelihood that gay men were arrested but not charged in a certain time period, relative to lesbians who were charged?" or "who is more likely to join urban activist organizations—people who move from small towns to cities before the age of 30, or people who have lived in cities all their lives?" The answers to these questions not only show us who shaped gay liberation in Canada, but also give us insight into the life conditions that make activism and social change possible. Contemporary digital Humanities prosopography may not be interested in creating a picture of an average life, but rather in using atomized data points to trace the spread of ideas or to understand the genesis of organizations in a way that can aid the development of future social justice activism.

We have chosen to use two ontologies to represent our data: Schema.org and the CWRC/LINCS ontology. Schema.org does not let us represent the nuance in our data—we only use it to represent names, dates, and locations and the relationship between people and those names, dates, and locations (for example, death date or birth location). Schema.org does not, for example, provide any means to express information about historically contingent identities. Schema.org does have the merit of broad uptake, which means that our data is legible to a large number of Semantic Web users in a way that fulfill McLeod's vision.

Perhaps more importantly, however, we are contributing to and using the CWRC/LINCS ontology. We have contributed information about historically specific identities which will permit CWRC/LINCS ontology users to model their data in more nuanced ways than commercial ontologies permit. The CWRC/LINCS ontology not only lets us connect our project to others through a shared computer-legible vocabulary and worldview, but also forces us to think critically about historically contingent patterns in queer lives. Furthermore, the integration of diverse and historically specific queer identities into the CWRC/LINCS ontology will let members of the public, for example, retrieve information about the cultural conditions of women's marriage traditions in a way that is sensitive to both historical and contemporary identities. For example, searchers will be able to pull up Katharine Peabody Loring and Alice James' Boston Marriage (a companionate and often sexual relationship between two often white, educated, wealthy women in late nineteenth-century New England), rather than simply return a statement that they were lesbians (an anachronistic term unavailable to Loring and James as anything but a slur). The ontology will also keep from flattening the classification of their relationship to a simple generic marriage, and will keep the context of place and time period, while still directing readers to other place- and time- specific instances of marriage, such as, for example the one between munition workers André Antoinette Arsenault and Eugenie Ouellette in Québec in 1942. The CWRC/LINCS ontology will preserve the nuance, ambiguity, and even conflict that is central to Humanities interpretation: the Arsenault-Ouellette marriage has not only been interpreted as a marriage between two lesbians, but also as a marriage between a trans man and a straight woman (Brown 2020; Kronk and Dexheimer 2020; Gagné 2009).

By using the CWRC/LINCS ontology, LGLC-linked data will always let researchers trace the assertions in our triples back to their source, so that, unlike the disinformation data that is characteristic of late 2010s online environments, our data will not circulate without the context and sources of its creation. The project's collaborative approach which brings the SémantiQueer PIs, collaborators, archival consultants, and students into the broader conversation about digital representation of Humanities data lets us "embrac[e] pluralism [as] a feminist strategy for mitigating th[e] risk" of "what Gayatri Spivak has termed *epistemic violence*, particularly when the people doing the work are strangers in the dataset" (D'Ignazio and Klein 2020, 147). The CWRC/LINCS ontological innovation of making sure that linked data assertions do not circulate without the context of their creation will further help mitigate against the risk of epistemic violence.

6.5 Conclusion

Public digital Humanities projects on the Web can appear to be all alike. Most online public history projects offer readers an attractive home page, and some contextualizing remarks by project directors. Readers can generally peruse digitized primary source material, or secondary digital scholarship that arises from that material. Sites may feature digital analysis tools and visualizations that could not exist in print-only form, including network graphs, interactive maps, and charts. It is, however, challenging for readers to understand just how large each project is. In traditional Humanities projects that produce books, it is easy for readers to use the size of a book as a proxy for project size: readers certainly know how much of a book they have engaged with by weighting the weight of the section of the book in their left hand relative to the weight of their right. Most database-backed digital projects do not offer readers such a visceral means of determining how much of the project they have engaged with. A database-backed project may have tens of thousands of records, or a few hundred, and in judging a site only by its search page it can be hard to gather any digital project's size and scope. It may not at first glance be clear how the data is represented beyond its expression in a browser for human readers, and yet the data's format and that format's archivability shape what Humanities knowledge will be available to current Web users and what can be preserved for future generations.

Even if human readers do not always know what is going on under the hood, there is so much that digital Humanities projects can do for diverse publics by taking up linked data production as part of the project workflow. In the case of the Lesbian and Gay Liberation in Canada project, the archival record gives us and the broader research community evidence of how people lived and understood their identities; ontology development gives us the power to represent that evidence about identity, activism, and social change with more nuance than the options offered by commercial linked data; and the linked data we create using various ontologies will let us represent and find patterns in tens of thousands of records to see how liberation ideas spread across Canada and how this expansion was shaped by activists' and organizations' local linguistic and gendered conditions.

Notes

1. I am using the terms *LGBTQ+* and *queer* to serve as a convenient, if anachronistic, shorthand in this chapter. That said, I guard against letting presentist terms like these predetermine the way that we represent historical identities both textually and digitally in the project (Bailey and Miller; Whisman).
2. I am using the term *women* rather than *lesbians* here to signal an interest in the experience of bisexual women, straight trans women, women-identified-women for whom relationships with women had primacy over those with men, and others who do not fall into the category of lesbian, but whose activism has shaped gay liberation in Canada.
3. In order to be machine readable, these human readable triples have to be *serialized*, that is to say published online in one of a number of linked data formats. Just as one can write phrases in Russian using the Cyrillic or Latin alphabet, one can create machine-readable linked data triples using one of three serializations: RDF-XML, turtle or JSON-LD. The http protocols signal to a site whether a human is accessing the site through a browser (in which case it is appropriate to return an HTML page for display in a browser) or whether a linked-data sensitive bot, search engine crawler, or related technology is requesting the page (in which case it is appropriate to return RDF-XML, turtle, or JSON-LD for the machine reader to engage with—including further URIs for the machine to follow on to more information about entities and their relationships). I highly recommend that readers who are interested in learning more about creating or querying linked data take Jonathan Blaney's excellent tutorial, Introduction to the Principles of Linked Open Data, published by *The Programming Historian* (https://doi.org/10.46430/phen0068, accessed October 20, 2020).
4. The project has been supported by two Social Science and Humanities Research Council of Canada Insight Grants (2014–2020, 2021–2025) and by the Ministry of Canadian Heritage's Canada History Fund (2021–2023). Grant partners include Susan Brown, Director of the Canadian Writing Research Collaboratory (CWRC University of Guelph), Don McLeod (University of Toronto Libraries), El Chenier, Director of the Archives of Lesbian Oral Testimony (ALOT Simon Fraser University), Fabien Galipeau (Archives gaies du Québec), Fangmin Wang and M.J. Suhonos (Toronto Metropolitan University Library & Archives). The project has been built with the support of 16 paid research assistants since 2014. Their scholarship has included archival research, encoding, UX, TEI conversion, conference participation, frontend design and implementation. We are also grateful for the support of the Toronto Metropolitan University Library Collaboratory, Toronto Metropolitan University's Centre for Digital Humanities, the University of Ottawa's Labo de données en sciences humaines/Humanities Data

Lab, the Canadian Foundation for Innovation, and Compute Canada (for more please see https://lglc.ca/about).
5. We have guided research assistants through every step of the project. They encoded the text, wrote the xslt scripts to convert it to cypher, designed the front end, created the app and its templates. In 2018 we had the front end redeveloped by a commercial company, Iversoft, to increase the app's security.
6. For more on the LGLC and privacy see the "Editorial Principles" section of the LGLC website. We have instructions for how to request data take down, and mechanisms for anonymizing nodes in the database and entitles in the linked data to remove identifying and identifiable information and connections, without erasing the fact that something happened as recorded in the archival materials used in the project. As of 2022, we have only had one takedown request (from a man who shares a name with his grandfather, a former Member of Parliament).
7. If, as a human reader, you would like to see what the beta LGLC prosopography linked data looks like, head to https://prosopography.lglc.ca/ and select your browser's developer tools > View page source. You will find the linked data at the bottom of the page in a <script type = "application/ld + json"> tag.

References

Alexander, Jonathan. 2002. "Introduction to the Special Issue: Queer Webs: Representations of LGBT People and Communities on the World Wide Web." *International Journal of Sexuality and Gender Studies* 7 (2): 77–84. Accessed October 10, 2020. https://doi.org/10.1023/A:1015821431188.

Allemang, Dean, and James A. Hendler. 2011. *Semantic Web for the Working Ontologist: Modeling in RDF, RDFS and OWL*. 2nd ed. Boston: Elsevier.

Berners-Lee, Tim. 1997. "Realising the Full Potential of the Web." Accessed August 23, 2020. https://www.w3.org/1998/02/Potential.html.

Brown, Susan. 2020. "Categorically Provisional." *PMLA* 135 (1): 165–74. Accessed August 23, 2020. https://doi.org/10.1632/pmla.2020.135.1.165.

Brown, Susan, Isobel Grundy, and Patricia Clemens, eds. n.d. *Orlando: Women's Writing in the British Isles from the Beginnings to the Present*. Cambridge: Cambridge University Press.

Caswell, Michelle, Alda Allina Migoni, Noah Geraci, and Marika Cifor. 2017. "'To Be Able to Imagine Otherwise': Community Archives and the Importance of Representation." *Archives and Records* 38 (1): 5–26. Accessed October 10, 2020. https://doi.org/10.1080/23257962.2016.1260445.

Chah, Niel. 2018. "OK Google, What Is Your Ontology? Or: Exploring Freebase Classification to Understand Google's Knowledge Graph." *ArXiv:1805.03885 [Cs]*, May. Accessed August 23, 2020. http://arxiv.org/abs/1805.03885.

Cifor, Marika, Michelle Caswell, Alda Allina Migoni, and Noah Geraci. 2018. "'What We Do Crosses over to Activism': The Politics and Practice of Community Archives." *The Public Historian* 40 (2): 69–95. Accessed January 9, 2022. https://doi.org/10.1525/tph.2018.40.2.69.

Ciotti, Fabio, and Francesca Tomasi. 2016. "Formal Ontologies, Linked Data, and TEI Semantics." *Journal of the Text Encoding Initiative* 24 (9) (September 2016–December 2017). Accessed November 8, 2018. https://doi.org/10.4000/jtei.1480.

Crompton, Constance, and Michelle Schwartz. 2018. "Remaking History: Lesbian Feminist Methods and the Digital Humanities." In *Bodies of Information: Intersectional Feminism and the Digital Humanities*, edited by Jacqueline Wernimont and Elizabeth Losh, 131–56. Minneapolis: University of Minnesota Press.

Cvetkovich, Ann. 2003. *An Archive of Feelings: Trauma, Sexuality, and Lesbian Public Cultures*. Durham, NC: Duke University Press.

Dangoisse, Pascale, Constance Crompton, and Michelle Schwartz. 2022 (forthcoming). "Wages Due Both Then and Now." In *Digital Humanities in Canada*, edited by Sarah Roger and Paul Barrett. Ottawa: University of Ottawa Press.

D'Ignazio, Catherine, and Lauren F. Klein. 2020. *Data Feminism*. Cambridge, MA: MIT Press.

Drabinski, Emily. 2013. "Queering the Catalog: Queer Theory and the Politics of Correction." *The Library Quarterly: Information, Community, Policy* 83 (2): 94–111. https://doi.org/10.1086/669547.

Drucker, Johanna. 2009. *Graphic Design History: A Critical Guide*. Upper Saddle River, NJ: Pearson Prentice Hall.

Enriquez, Mickael. 2013. "La contestation des politiques de changement d'identité de genre par les militantes et militants trans québécois." *Lien social et Politiques* 69: 181–96. Accessed August 11, 2020. https://doi.org/10.7202/1016491ar.

Gagné, Martin. 2009. "Histoires de Nos Vies." *Archivaria* 69: 335–38. Accessed August 11, 2020.

Goddard, Lisa, and Dean Seeman. 2019. "Negotiating Sustainability: Building Digital Humanities Projects That Last." In *Doing More Digital Humanities: Open Approaches to Creation, Growth, and Development*, edited by Constance Crompton, Ray Siemens, and Richard Lane, 38–57. New York: Routledge.

Hedley, Alison, and Lorraine Janzen Kooistra. 2019. "Prototyping Personography for The Yellow Nineties Online." In *Bodies of Information: Intersectional Feminism and the Digital Humanities*, edited by Elizabeth Losh and Jacqueline Wernimont, 157–72. Minneapolis: University of Minnesota Press.

Kronk, Clair A., and Judith W. Dexheimer. 2020. "Development of the Gender, Sex, and Sexual Orientation Ontology: Evaluation and Workflow." *Journal of the American Medical Informatics Association* 27 (7): 1110–15. Accessed October 11, 2020. https://doi.org/10.1093/jamia/ocaa061.

Lang, Tamara de Szeghero. 2017. "Democratizing LGBTQ History Online: Digitizing Public History in 'U.S. Homophile Internationalism.'" *Journal of Homosexuality* 64 (7): 850–69. https://doi.org/10.1080/00918369.2017.1280987.

Leon, Sharon. 2017. "Complexity and Collaboration: Doing Public History in Digital Environments." In *The Oxford Handbook of Public History*, edited by James B. Gardner and Paula Hamilton, 44–68. New York: Oxford University Press. Accessed October 10, 2020.

Maxwell, John. 2019. "Text Processing Techniques and Traditions (or: Why the History of Computing Matters to DH)." In *Doing More Digital Humanities: Open Approaches to Creation, Growth, and Development*, edited by Constance Crompton, Ray Siemens, and Richard Lane. London: Routledge. https://doi.org/10.4324/9780429353048.

McLeod, Donald W. 1996. *Lesbian and Gay Liberation in Canada: A Selected Annotated Chronology, 1964–1975*. Toronto: ECW Press/Homewood Books.

McLeod, Donald W. 2017. *Lesbian and Gay Liberation in Canada: A Selected Annotated Chronology, 1976–1981*. Toronto: ECW Press/Homewood Books.

Mirha-Soleil Ross fonds. 1972. "TS/TG General." F0033-05-12 Arquives. Accessed August 11, 2020.

Noble, Safiya. 2018. *Algorithms of Oppression: How Search Engines Reinforce Racism*. New York: New York University Press.

Pasin, Michele, and John Bradley. 2013. Factoid-based Prosopography and Computer Ontologies: Towards an Integrated Approach. *Digital Scholarship in the Humanities* 30 (1). Accessed August 3, 2022. https://doi.org/10.1093/llc/fqt037.

Pattuelli, M. Cristina, Matt Miller, Leanora Lange, Sean Fitzell, and Carolyn Li-Madeo. 2013. "Crafting Linked Open Data for Cultural Heritage: Mapping and Curation Tools for the Linked Jazz Project." *The Code4Lib Journal* 17 (21) (July). Accessed August 11, 2020. http://journal.code4lib.org/articles/8670.

Pouyllau, Stéphane. 2012. "Les moteurs de recherche profitent aussi de la sémantique." *Documentaliste – Sciences de l'Information* 48 (4): 36–37. Accessed August 23, 2020. https://doi.org/10.3917/docsi.484.0022.

Pouyllau, Stéphane. 2013. "Web de Données, Big Data, Open Data, Quels Rôles Pour Les Documentalistes?" *Documentaliste – Sciences de l'Information* 50: 32–33. Accessed August 23, 2020.

Ramsay, Stephen. 2011. *Reading Machines: Toward an Algorithmic Criticism*. Chicago: University of Illinois Press.

Roberto, K. R., ed. 2008. *Radical Cataloging: Essays at the Front*. Jefferson, NC: McFarland.

Sedgwick, Eve Kosofsky. 1990. *The Epistemology of the Closet*. Berkeley, CA: University of California Press

Simpson, John, and Susan Brown. 2014. "Inference and Linking of the Humanist's Semantic Web." In *INKE: Implementing New Knowledge Environments*. https://mcri.inke.ca/index.html%3Fp=1403.html.

Subramanian, Banu. 2014. *Ghost Stories for Darwin: The Science of Variation and the Politics of Diversity*. Champaign, IL: University of Illinois Press.

Ware, Syrus Marcus. 2017. "All Power to All People? Black LGBTTI2QQ Activism, Remembrance, and Archiving in Toronto." *TSQ: Transgender Studies Quarterly* 4 (2): 170–80. Accessed August 23, 2020. https://doi.org/10.1215/23289252-3814961.

Warner, Tom. 2002. *Never Going Back: A History of Queer Activism in Canada*. Toronto: University of Toronto Press.

Watson, Bri. 2019. "Queer as Data: Linked Data and Minoritized Digital Archives." September. Accessed August 23, 2020. https://scholarworks.iu.edu/dspace/handle/2022/23729.

CHAPTER 7

Working with Incarcerated Communities: Representing Women in Prison on Screen

Paul Gray and Anne Schwan

7.1 INTRODUCTION

This chapter considers public arts and humanities scholarship and practice in relation to penal settings, with a particular focus on film-making. University-prison partnerships have long been acting as one of the channels through which scholar-activists and creative practitioners have exercised their public humanities practice. Well established in the United States—and sometimes conceptualized as "service learning"—such arrangements have also begun to flourish in the United Kingdom, ranging from individual scholar-led projects and reading groups to arts and performance workshops involving participants from both sides of the prison wall.[1] There is a rich body of scholarship critically reflecting on the aims, politics and ethics of university-prison collaboration (see for example Davis and Roswell 2013; Karpowitz 2017; Wiltse 2011). In the US context specifically, such reflections often assess the extent to which collaboration with carceral environments can be reconciled with an abolitionist agenda (see Jacobi 2011). The latter, dedicated to ideals of social justice that call for the radical reconstruction of social relations and redistribution of resources to stamp out racial, class and gender inequalities typically at

---

P. Gray · A. Schwan (✉)
Edinburgh Napier University, Edinburgh, UK
e-mail: A.Schwan@napier.ac.uk

P. Gray
e-mail: P.Gray@napier.ac.uk

the root of criminal(ized) behaviour (Davis 2003), potentially sits uncomfortably alongside prison arts projects that require a certain degree of institutional collaboration with the penal apparatus.

The authors, who have been involved in university-prison partnerships and worked with people in prison, take a critical, yet pragmatic, approach to this conundrum, reflecting on what Nicole Fleetwood calls the "complex and messy" dynamics and politics of such collaborations that are inevitably shaped by "disparities" (Fleetwood 2020, 155, 157).[2] We recognize the challenge that officially sanctioned educational initiatives—because they focus on individual "rehabilitation" rather than systemic social transformation—risk becoming "a tool of the prison to manage and control populations" while acting as "a distraction from the whole social order itself" (Fleetwood 2020, 155).[3] Nevertheless, we concur with Tobi Jacobi's belief that the social justice ideals of prison abolitionism and the aims of educational-creative projects with prisons are not mutually exclusive, maintaining that such programs can enable "a more critical understanding of language and power" and "make space for more radical growth by individuals and [writing] groups that will contribute to a larger social movement" (Jacobi 2011, 46, 48). Our chapter joins the conversation on the value and the challenges of academic partnerships with prisons by combining these considerations with a critical analysis of participatory film-making practice as a potential tool for giving voice to women in prison, offering a case study of *On the Outside* (dir. Gray), a film co-developed with women serving sentences at HM Prison and Young Offenders Institution (YOI) Polmont, Scotland. The chapter thus brings together two strands—university-prison partnerships on the one hand, and a critique of representations of incarcerated women in film and popular culture on the other hand—to suggest new directions for the ethics and aesthetics of carceral film-making practices and prison-based public humanities.

7.2 Between Sympathy and Spectacle: Mediating the Voices of Imprisoned Women

First, we will establish a context to explore the challenges involved in "giving voice" to women in prison and the power dynamics at work in the mediation of these perspectives, paying particular attention to questions of genre, narrative voice, content and the role of the film-makers, with reference to some recent examples of depicting imprisoned women's lives. Attempts to "give voice" to women convicted of crimes date back centuries, ranging from early modern pamphlets and broadsides (Martin 2017) to nineteenth-century fiction and early forms of prison autobiography, further extended in contemporary historical fiction that re-imagines women's experiences of imprisonment in the past (Schwan 2014). Although the authenticity of historical women's perspectives is often doubtful, considering that past accounts frequently rely on the mediation of (typically male) writers or other figures of authority, there is clear evidence of a long tradition of "giving voice" to incarcerated women (Schwan 2014).

Contemporary criminology similarly recognizes the significance of "prisoner life stories" (Crewe 2013). New technologies such as podcasts, and other multimedia methods, have created innovative platforms for these expressions (Cecil 2020; Thomas 2020). Feminist criminologist Pat Carlen's pioneering edition *Criminal Women: Autobiographical Accounts* (1985) was an early attempt to create a space for (formerly) imprisoned women's viewpoints, including publication credit. On-screen, the tradition of conveying incarcerated women's lives finds its most vivid expression in the women-in-prison genre. With precursors in 1920s' Hollywood cinema (Zalcock 1998, 19–20), this genre encompasses a spectrum from serious social problem drama to more or less lurid "babes-behind-bars" films and television series (Mayne 2000, 119; Rafter 2000, 120), featuring typical elements such as the "new fish" (an innocent first-timer being initiated into the penal environment), a contrast between kindly and sadistic matrons, violence, lesbianism, riots and shower scenes (Walters 2001, 108; Morton 1986). While films and television shows about prison can be powerful tools for raising public awareness (Schwan 2016), eliciting empathy for those inside and contributing, from the early days of cinema, to debates about prison reform (Griffiths 2016), they can also reinforce damaging misconceptions and stereotypes about the incarcerated (Cecil 2007; Wächter 2020).

Women's imprisonment has long held a special appeal, to be explained by the shock and interest provoked by women's "double deviance," in other words the fact that female criminality is seen to transgress legal boundaries alongside normative expectations of gendered conduct in ways that male criminality does not (Heidensohn and Silvestri 2012). As a consequence, women's deviance is prone to sensationalist representations which are likely to "sell" and attract wider public attention, disincentivizing more critical or nuanced portrayals. In the contextualizing analysis that follows, we discuss some recent depictions of women's incarceration on screen—limited to British film-makers for reasons of space—assessing how they negotiate the delicate balancing act between, on the one hand, an existing repertoire of tropes and stereotypes to serve public expectations, and, on the other hand, an effort to create platforms for a more complex investigation of the life journeys of women in prison.

Films and television series on prison life take the form of documentary or fictional(ized) narratives, with some of the latter based on "true crime." Writing about prison documentary, Yvonne Jewkes suggests that this is "a genre that has a more explicit agenda in bringing to public attention the social contexts of crime and the realities of the experience of imprisonment" and that it "may be one of the few types of prison film that can claim to have made any difference at all to perceptions of prisons and prisoners" (Jewkes 2011, 193, 195). Nevertheless, Jewkes cautions that some variants of the genre "are simply voyeuristic and pander to stereotypes" and that "it is of course within the power of the director to control, manipulate or exploit the medium" (Jewkes 2011, 194, 195,). Prison life is usually represented through "a set of rehearsed images," an iconography which in turn "normalizes prisons" (Fleetwood 2020, 15). As our later case study will show, *On the Outside*'s aesthetic choices seek to defamiliarize and de-normalize the prison experience by transplanting the women and their stories into a different setting.

Set in the US, the BBC's *Girls Behind Bars*, part of the *Stacey Dooley in the USA* series (2012) follows the usual pattern of Dooley's action-fuelled, investigative journalism to shed light on the experiences of young women doing "Shock," a military boot camp-style Correctional Facility at Lakeview, New York State, that they have been sent to as an alternative to more conventional imprisonment, and others serving time at (now defunct) Bayview Correctional Facility in the heart of Manhattan. The beginning of the episode serves the clichés of carceral iconography, showing women processing into the military camp in shackles, with Dooley's voice-over announcing that "These girls are all facing up to three years in prison." Drawing on tropes of the women-in-prison genre, the documentary, for example, shows women in tears while having their heads shaved and depicts shower scenes in both facilities.

While Dooley's interactions offer some incarcerated women momentary opportunities, as speaking agents, to present their own perspectives, the futility of the show's attempt to provide an authentic insight into imprisonment is strikingly exposed. One woman rejects Dooley's plea to help her understand what life inside is like, maintaining "You cannot learn from my time here. You cannot understand nothing about what goes on in the penitentiary," and "You will not understand what my life is like. … No, I don't wanna try to explain. You're wasting my time. … You have to experience for yourself."

A further tension between the documentary's ability to create a platform for incarcerated women's voices and a tendency towards reaffirming carceral structures is evident in Dooley's role as interlocutor with both the women themselves and penal employees. Dooley is positioned ambivalently, as the incarcerated women's *confidante* whose presence enables them to open up so that the film crew becomes a catalyst on some of the women's rehabilitative journey. Most strikingly, newcomer Sharmeek Brown, who is struggling to adjust to the boot camp routine, says to Dooley that "you make me feel so good being here" and that she can talk to Dooley about anything; in a key scene that is deeply uncomfortable to watch, Brown is forced to take the hot seat in a group session, with others venting their grievances against her. The group facilitators pressure her into revealing traumatic details from her past—that she was sexually "violated" aged twelve—a disclosure that is seen as crucial to Brown's journey towards personal improvement.

Although Dooley subsequently discusses the situation with the therapist, contending that she felt Brown's treatment was "too harsh," the film team's decision to screen this humiliating scenario risks exploiting traumatic experiences for dramatic effect. Aylwyn Walsh, writing on theater performances in prisons, similarly argues that "the tendency to victimize participants by insisting on revelations of trauma might in fact fetishize the traumatic" (2019,

104). Dooley additionally becomes complicit in the penal apparatus's logic and attempts to classify when she analyzes one of the women's "vacant" facial expressions and comportment. This quasi-phrenological rhetoric is counterbalanced, though, by giving the woman, Nicole Hartman-McMurray, a space to speak about her life history, with Dooley concluding, "To hear her background, where she is from, you understand a lot more." The documentary employs a dialogical principle, allowing Hartman-McMurray to respond to the institution and Dooley's assessment of her as "a bit scary," first expressed by Dooley in conversation with the therapist. Dooley here stands in for the viewer, who, by implication, is also encouraged to see Hartman-McMurray as a person with a history, beyond the "scary" façade. The show thus partially encourages a critical viewing practice.

Two more recent documentaries broadcast on British television, ITV's *Inside Prison: Britain Behind Bars* and Channel 4's *Prison*, signal an ongoing fascination with (women's) imprisonment on screen, a trend which arguably received a significant boost by the international success of *Orange is the New Black* (2013–2019). Although not exclusively focussed on women, *Inside Prison: Britain Behind Bars* (2019), lures the viewer with the promise of "unprecedented access," interspersing footage from a men's prison, HMP Bullingdon, with scenes from women's lives at HMP Downview. While the show offers some back stories and context, it is primarily constructed as entertainment, signalled by its action-packed narrative that uses dramatic story arcs to create suspense. For instance, the voice-over by English actress Gina McKee announces that Gemma James, first introduced as a woman who convinces correspondents—her "sugar daddies"—to send money to pay off spice dealers on the wing, is "months away from release, but in prison, keeping away from trouble is easier said than done" (*Inside Prison* 2019, S1 E1). Emphasis is also placed on the tribulations of new officers—a twist on the women-in-prison genre's "new fish" trope—and soundtrack is used to evoke emotional responses.

Channel 4's *Prison*, season 2 (2020), produced and directed by multi-award-winning Paddy Wivell, is solely dedicated to the women at HMP Foston Hall which, Wivell's voice-over advises, "offers a progressive regime" (*Prison* 2020, S2 E1). The three-part series, consisting of themed episodes titled "Arrival," "Trauma" and "Family," presents itself as intellectually more demanding fare, announced by Channel 4's slogan introducing the show: "Challenge your thinking with documentaries on 4." Like *Inside Prison*, *Prison* uses music for emotional effect, framing season 2's first episode with the upbeat diegetic sound of a communal choir singing under the leadership of officer "Ms. Campion," beginning with Petula Clark's "Downtown" and ending with Amy Winehouse's defiant "Rehab." The series' title sequence and bluesy soundtrack additionally convey a sense of cool, renegade glamour echoing that of the self-conscious, ironic women-in-prison classic *Caged Heat* (1974) before ending abruptly with a banging door to remind the viewer of prison's harsher realities, an editing technique similarly employed in *Orange is the New Black*'s inaugural episode. Such disjunctive effects suggest a deliberate gesture to challenge viewer expectations, teasing the audience with generic features while subtly undermining these conventions.

Wivell's self-declared purpose with the show is to "gain a nuanced sense of what kind of work is being done within our prisons and what the experience of being in prison is like"—the latter, for him, equally involving the experiences of prison staff whom he sees as "heroic" and "underappreciated" in their hard work to prevent violence and deaths in custody (Ministry of Justice). Although the film-maker's intentions are honourable, his approach also risks being instrumentalized by government agendas that seek to downplay severe problems in the country's social structure and criminal justice system—England and Wales have the third-highest prison population rate in Europe, after Russia and Turkey, and the highest in Western Europe (World Prison Brief). Wivell's interview with the Ministry of Justice allows the Ministry to showcase its supposedly progressive approach as the interview appears next to the Ministry's tagline announcing its commitment to "a more effective, transparent and responsive criminal justice system" (Ministry of Justice). Such political entanglements demonstrate the potentially problematic role of creative practitioners co-operating with penal institutions and other agents of the state who have a vested interest in obscuring systemic inequalities and failures. The documentary exposes that most of the women at Foston Hall "serve short sentences of less than six months, for non-violent crimes" and that many of them return after release, making officer Ms. Campion "wonder if there's another way round things" (*Prison* 2020, S2 E1). Despite such revelations and subtle suggestions that the current prison system is not working, the film stops short of a more overt critique, merely having Ms. Campion conclude with the "sad truth [that], for many of them, life's harder on the outside than it is in prison" (*Prison* 2020, S2 E1).

Wivell's voice-over is key to the framing of the narrative overall, as he contextualizes the setting and the women's experiences, including some information on the residents' backgrounds ("Many women come in from a background of poverty and extreme homelessness. Drug addiction is often the root cause of female offending," *Prison* 2020, S2 E1). It is evident that Wivell has built trust with the residents of Foston Hall, most of whom interact with him with apparent ease and at times treat him as co-conspirator who sees what the viewer cannot (for example, the crew follows one of the women doing prohibited things, requesting "I need to get off the camera," *Prison* 2020, S2 E1). Wivell cannot resist drawing attention to women's romantic involvements—another trope that viewers of the women-in-prison genre have come to expect—turning the spotlight on the ten-year relationship between Laura Campbell and Katie, imprisoned at Foston Hall at the same time. The director probes into the practicalities of their physical relationship while also asking a female officer why such relationships are frowned upon. Even though Wivell here works within the generic frameworks of the women-in-prison genre to some extent, the overall approach brings some depth to the portrayal of prison romance and its challenges for the women involved. Such illuminations are paired with an earnest attempt to shed light on the women's life journeys, often characterized by experiences of sexual abuse, mental illness and domestic violence.

Wivell's didactic aims transpire when he asks a male officer if this makes him think that he might have ended up in a similar situation, had he had a similar background. Echoing Dooley's insight that knowledge of the women's backgrounds aids in understanding, officer "Mr. E" reflects: "You can understand to a certain degree why they are the way they are from what they've been through. Because I'm sure if I'd been through that, er, I wouldn't be the same as I am now" (*Prison* 2020, S2 E1). Mr. E, like Dooley in *Girls Behind Bars*, here acts as a mediator between the world of the prison and the wider public, eliciting sympathy for imprisoned women, even though it is still problematic that a figure of authority is needed to declare the women worthy of compassion. Despite such limitations, the scene demonstrates how films about imprisonment have at least the potential to contribute to the formation of what Fleetwood, in the context of prison art, calls "a provisional public, a space of engagement facilitated through and against how prisons have shaped the public sphere and relations among people differently positioned across carceral geographies" (Fleetwood 2020, 25). Like prison art, film-making can play an important role in creating "proximity" to those who are locked away, facilitating new connections (Fleetwood 2020, 184). In some cases, such shows even lead to advocacy by audience members; following the final episode of *Prison*'s season 2, some viewers called for the early release of Lexi Heckles who had killed her partner in what the show presents as self-defence (Fogarty, n.d.).

Similar to Dooley, Wivell focuses on trauma (the title heading of the second episode) as one of the forces shaping the women's journeys—another theme likely to provoke sympathetic understanding. Space is given to some of the women as they reflect on their emotions, their participation in therapeutic offerings or their refusal to engage with such schemes. The series walks a thin line between the desire for authentic representation of the women's struggles and problematic voyeurism, for example when the viewer is shown Janine covered in blood after self-harming, with cutting marks on both sides of her neck and both arms (*Prison* 2020, S2 E2). Viewers witness Janine talking to peer mentor Sonia about her difficulties in opening up about her traumatic experiences, some of which are eventually divulged in conversation with Wivell after he switches the camera off. Significantly, the director here reveals the process behind the scenes and Janine's decision to share some details: "With the camera off, Janine discloses some of her past experiences, and she decides to share the details of one of them" (*Prison* 2020, S2 E2). Despite Wivell's sensitivity in giving Janine some control of the situation—to the extent that an incarcerated person can ever be in control at all—an uncomfortable sense of coercion is palpable when the director responds to the woman's disturbing and evidently painful story of kidnapping by probing "What else did you have to endure?" Janine forecloses such curiosity by stating: "Loads. We'd be here all fucking week if I started talking about it. We really would" (*Prison* 2020, S2 E2). As these moments illustrate, the series places a strong emphasis on the women's own voices and their perception of their situation, but it also partially respects the women's right to silence. In addition, the documentary provides an insight into the value of community, friendship and peer mentoring. Such efforts are counterbalanced by scenes verging on voyeurism, the presence of figures of authority evaluating the women's behavior, and Wivell's voice-over which, at times, mirrors the analytical language of the penal regime, assessing the women's conduct.

In its overall approach, Wivell's series compares positively to Michelle Friel and Julien Kean's *Girls Behind Bars* (2008–2011), filmed at Scotland's only all-female prison HMP YOI Cornton Vale. The multi-award-winning show allows the women to tell their stories to some extent, but *Girls Behind Bars* arguably studies its subjects in an almost anthropological fashion. Some of the women are exposed as either aggressive troublemakers or deeply troubled, in disturbing scenes displaying extreme forms of vulnerability. Paula Gilligan, who discusses this "well-meaning (but in fact voyeuristic)" series alongside other examples of reality television that, in her view, promote the agenda of "Austerity Britain," suggests that the show "downplays the reality of the prison conditions" (which were notoriously bad at Cornton Vale), and that officers function as "our guides as to which prisoners deserve our sympathy and which do not" (2012, 247, 250). As Gilligan notes (2012, 250), the series unhelpfully focuses on women imprisoned for violent crimes, distorting statistical truths (most women are convicted of minor offences). The male voice-over could also be seen as problematic since it functions as a distancing device between the viewer and the women; even though the voice-over is by Scottish actor Steven Wren, the contrast between his Received Pronunciation and the obvious Scottishness of the women is striking, bolstering the women's "Otherness."

In analyzing these examples, we do not mean to dismiss the film-makers' earnest desire to raise awareness about prison conditions and related issues, but we are inviting ongoing critical reflection on the contradictory effects such representations can produce, and the ethics involved in screening imprisonment, especially when commercial demands are present. Such a critical-reflective practice can help counteract what Allison Page and Laurie Ouellette (2020) call the "prison-televisual complex." As the following section demonstrates, *On the Outside* takes a different approach to conveying the stories of imprisoned women, even if it cannot entirely escape the challenges involved in prison collaborations and representations of incarcerated women on screen. The preceding analysis has shown how the use of voice-over, music and narrative content can direct viewers' sympathies and understanding as well as usefully contextualize, or, conversely, evaluate and obscure the women's stories to more or less problematic effects. Our discussion of the process behind *On the Outside*, as well as its reception, highlights the project's attempt to give centre stage to the voices of imprisoned women by employing a participatory method in the creation of the film, to the extent possible in a carceral setting. Moreover, in the following section, we include reflections by some of the women involved in the project to underline this participatory approach.

7.3 Participatory Storytelling and the Limitations of Co-Authorship Within Carceral Contexts: A Case Study of *On the Outside*

On the Outside (dir. Gray), is a 42-minute film that is the outcome of a participatory film project involving incarcerated women at HM Prison and Young Offenders Institution Polmont, Scotland. Gray held seminars and discussions inside the prison that explored storytelling through the medium of film.[4] The resulting conversations were recorded, transcribed and used as the basis for the development of screenplays that give an account of four women's stories. Their individual narratives, edited from the recorded conversations, were restaged and dramatized within a car journey by four actors, who each represented one of the participants.

In this chapter, we use participatory film-making practice as a synonym for the term participatory video, which is a general catch all phrase for a myriad of participatory approaches (see High et al. 2012; White 2003) where "practices and histories of engagement are so varied that trying to reify them into a single orthodoxy risks obscuring the important lessons in their development" and where the "freedom to innovate and develop one's own ideas about participatory video is an important part of the tradition" (High et al. 2012, 45). In the context of adult education, Yang highlights the importance of collectivity and defines a "process in which a group of people creates a video about themselves or their concerns as a way of inquiring into and seeking solutions to challenges in their lives" (Yang 2016, 2). Takeda discusses the links between participatory video and participatory action research with an agenda for social change, which "aims not to study *on* people, but *with* people" (Takeda 2021, 4; emphasis in original). Takeda argues "that participatory video approaches in educational research can be broadly categorized into … three types," the second being most relevant to *On the Outside* where "story-oriented approaches … prioritize participants to tell their stories, and video recordings and editing are done by the researcher(s)" (Takeda 2021, 6).

On the Outside was completed in two stages, with part one undertaken within the education centre at HMYOI Polmont; the transcribed and edited conversations were used to create the final screenplays and subsequent film, which were created external to the prison environment. The conversations are presented anonymously within the film, where pseudonymized "characters" speak the exact words from the transcribed conversations, in effect circumventing the spectacle of the "authentic criminal" as the object of the film-maker's and consequently the audience's gaze. Conversely, it can be argued that disembodying the women's voices through re-enactment, as well as detaching specific statements from the women's identities, diminishes the agency of the individual participants. The premise of the project was to "empower participants as authors of their own representation" (Gray and Morgan 2017); however, the processes and creative outcome were largely defined by the incarcerating institution's rehabilitative learning agenda—and other considerations regarding risk management for the prison service, the imprisoned women and those who had been impacted by their crimes—that stipulated anonymity as a parameter of the collaborative brief.

In an attempt to redress this contradiction, commentaries from two participants, Alana and Dani, are included in this case study.[5] At the time of writing, they comment from a position of having been released for a period of approximately three years. Alana reflects on re-watching the film: "in a way, I actually felt quite proud; I actually forgot how difficult a time it was. It just took me back to remembering how far I've come as a person, like three years ago, I was speaking to you in a jail uniform and now I'm speaking to you about this project in between doing my two jobs." Similarly, Dani offers an introspective reflection on re-watching the film, stating "it took me right back to that place! I was able to identify and notice how much I had grown. Watching the character Abigail I could see my child self. It's mad when you're young and you think you're all grown up. It made me laugh. I was a character and a half when I was younger. I've really grown and matured and my opinions and perceptions have changed for sure … When watching Abigail you can feel the pain, the ownership, the guilt, the low confidence & self-esteem and I also feel like I was just too hard on myself back then. I feel like now I would be a completely different character." These insights remind us that representations of imprisoned women on screen are temporary snapshots that, at best, can only convey a fleeting sense of the person's experiences and state of mind, but which typically do not portray the individual's journey beyond incarceration.

On the Outside's existence depends on the cultural capital and material means associated with state-sponsored institutions, and therefore, the project arguably falls short of a vision for an initiative that is truly led by incarcerated people with a view to "resist[ing] the carceral rehabilitative ideology and the censoring and administrative approval that are part of state-endorsed programs" (Fleetwood 2020, 185). This ambivalence highlights the tensions in collaborating with prisons and the limitations of co-authorship opportunities between incarcerated individuals and external arts organizations or universities. However, opportunity can exist within such restrictions, as is evidenced in two separately authored works that are embedded within the film narrative of *On the Outside*. The purpose of the officially sanctioned seminar series was to inspire the participants to produce their own creative outputs, and this was successful for both Dani and Alana, who wrote a song and poem, respectively. Their writing activity was undertaken outside the scheduled sessions, as Alana reflects on writing her poem "My Freedom Has Gone" while locked in her cell in the evening that followed an afternoon seminar:

"When I was sitting there, once I started writing, it just kind of all came together. I have no explanation of how I even put it together, because it literally just flowed out and I don't even know where it came from. And it just felt like all this anger and all that just came out as well. I felt good after I wrote it." While this may reflect positive engagement within the context of what Fleetwood calls a "carceral rehabilitative ideology" (2020, 185), it also suggests an element of initiative by imprisoned people, albeit on an individual rather than collective basis. Yet, such individual work can produce a potential ripple effect, with both Dani and Alana willingly returning to subsequent sessions to present work to their peers. Alana read her poem both informally to other women in their cells and formally when she was invited to read at an Education Celebration Event at HMYOI Polmont, resulting in an impactful intervention within the prison community:

> With the first opening verse, I was trying to say we're in a world with so many different types of people. There's one hundred and sixty eight closed doors and one hundred and sixty eight different people with different mindsets, different problems and different personalities. You just don't know what anyone is going through in their individual cells. When I wrote it, I didn't think many people would understand it, so I was just more shocked how many people related to it. I just didn't really think anything of it; I was like, it's just a bunch of words. I'll never forget this girl Helen,[6] who was crying when I first read it to her, and I was like, oh, you're moved. I was pretty touched; I was pretty shocked.

Aside from shared understanding, Alana also highlights the personal significance of this validation and recognition, stating "I really love writing and all this has given me massive confidence. This is something I would like to pursue in the future. I have applied for college to study English and I start in September."

As these examples show, both Alana's and Dani's work took initial inspiration from the formal academically structured program, but was then created in a separate space outside external authorial interference by penal or educational staff. Although their words were retold through re-enactment by actors in the film, the content remains true to the original. Alana's poem is recited without change, but Dani's song underwent some interpretation by Sarah Dingwall (who plays Abigail) and a musician, who reworked and shortened the arrangement for the purposes of the film format. Dani's authorial intent remains intact—at least to some extent—as her reflection shows:

> Yes, I wish I could have sang and played at that part [in the film]; it would have meant more to me because I have the emotion and it was my experience. My songs are usually about my life and experiences; I write them like short stories … but it could be hard for another musician to portray "Mistake" because they may not have experienced that exact place (being in jail) but could definitely relate to making a mistake they regret. It was the first time hearing someone

else sing my song ... they made it their own but it still sounded like my song – they done a pretty good job! I just wish it was my voice cos it's my story but I'm glad it's in there and that's the main point.

This assessment again highlights a tension between the project's desire to give voice to imprisoned women's experiences and the institutional constraints that stipulate that the individual women are not to be identifiable in the film by voice or appearance.

Despite such limitations, it is important to note that creating the film through an educational collaboration rather than a commercial broadcast agenda—which shaped the other television shows discussed earlier—offered a freedom in form that allowed the film-makers to stray from narrative conventions more easily. The directorial agenda for *On the Outside* was based on a premise of "shaping existing narratives rather than creating them, with the purpose of relinquishing influence over the stories communicated" (Gray 2020, 194). Nevertheless, this does not necessarily negate "the power of the director to control, manipulate or exploit the medium" (Jewkes 2011, 194, 195), as is evidenced through the creation of an episodic narrative that plays out across the course of a day. Through discussion with the participants, a consensus was reached to create an emotional arc ending on a generally optimistic note, and conversations established the setting would include a car journey, bridges and the sea; however, it was ultimately the director's interpretation to stage the four women's final interaction outside of the confines of the car interior, and to position the women standing freely in front of a metaphorical background where bridges cross a body of water.[7] It is here that the women share their hopes, fears and aspirations for when they are released, discussing topics ranging from the everyday ("goin tae [going to] McDonald's, getting like a breakfast wrap") or family-oriented plans ("being with my son and daughter and being quite, the three of us, quite relaxed"), to the more profound ("it makes me mair [more] motivated tae [to], like, ... get everybody's happiness back, and, be a big, a strong unit"). The vernacular nature of these spoken words underscores a direct connection between participant and performance, and Dani confirms this when she reflects: "The way my personality and life was captured is just incredible. I really felt like I was watching and listening to myself and I feel like you got the cast down to a T." Alana offers a more critical assessment when she suggests "I feel like [actor] Kirsty represents me really well but the only one thing is it doesn't sound like me when she says the word 'fae.' It's just because I don't use that; I would say 'from.' It's not even a problem; it's just when you hear it, that's not what people from the West Coast are like." Although Dani identifies directly with the representation, she does so while also highlighting the absence of complete authenticity, and her lack of involvement in the casting, stating "you" got the cast down to a T, rather than "we." The evident error in pronunciation of the word "from" curtails Alana's ability to connect with and completely recognize herself in Abigail.

Both Alana's and Dani's comments underline that whatever the directorial intention of relinquishing influence over the stories communicated (Gray 2020), whether deliberately or accidentally, a consistently authentic depiction is not possible. Through its topic, *On the Outside* is inevitably bound by the representational tropes of the women-in-prison genre, but there are some principal differences when compared to the other films discussed here. The *mise-en-scène* consists solely of the view from the inside of a moving vehicle, eschewing the typical tropes associated with carceral visuality. By removing the women from a penal setting, while maintaining a sense of entrapment in an enclosed space, the staging reflects the participants' desire for mobility and creates agency by focusing the aesthetic strategies of the film on the content of the conversation. This atypical staging augments defamiliarization from carceral topoi that can reinforce what Michelle Brown (2009, 12) calls "a distanced mode of penal spectatorship."

While the film-makers make use of multiple techniques that creatively manipulate an audience's interpretation—the overall staging, intimate use of framing, measured narrative pacing—*On the Outside*, in contrast to other films discussed here, only uses natural, diegetic sound, focussing on the content of the women's stories rather than creating artificial suspense, or manipulating the viewer's emotional response through a soundtrack.[8] Similarly, throughout the duration of *On the Outside*, no analysis of the women's stories is offered. While the film-makers undertook an editing process to construct a narrative integrity for the film, the only available optic for each of the stories is via the interactions between the women. The dialogue flows freely, uninterrupted by voice-over or by contextualization from figures of authority, consequently offering further agency, via the "subjective conversations [that are] already pre-edited by the participants, in that they only shared the [parts of their] stories they wanted to tell. In effect, they remained the first and most significant authors of their representation and editors of the film" (Gray 2020, 195).

The film-makers' edit from transcription to screen has undoubtedly affected the dynamics of the conversation but it is not coercive, and attempts to reflect the supportive, social nature of the project. Alana highlights the importance of the female community that the film seeks to convey, suggesting that in prison, sometimes you can "sit and have deep heart to hearts, ... with the girls ..., with your close circle. I would say I was one of the lucky ones when I was in there, I just feel like I got along with everybody." Alana notes that this differs from the more stereotypical combative women-in-prison tropes and she stresses the discrepancies between most representations of imprisonment on screen and her own experiences:

> So many people come up and they're like "is prison just like *Orange is the New Black* or was it just like *Wentworth*"? And I was like, it's nothing like that at all. I do like *Wentworth*; I find it more realistic to what actually happens in prison, not with the [storylines], more about the conversations, like the division in the

groups but I thought *Wentworth* was more relatable. You're not battling with each other in there; you're actually just battling with yourself and just trying to get through. You don't have a top dog, you don't have like queen of the prison, you know, you don't have that in there. Nobody wants to be a top dog there because nobody wants to be there.

Every single real documentary, about real life prisons that I've watched, I just think they show all the bad things about the girls going mental, their fighting, their drug use. I don't think they represent the good things in prison. I think they're made out to be bad people. They're being asked questions – it's like "How long have you been addicted to drugs?" just showing you all the bad things. Instead of maybe looking for the positives instead of the negatives.

Alana's comment highlights the problematic implications of representations of imprisoned women on screen, as they potentially reinforce negative self-images as well as public misconceptions, focussing on the women's individual shortcomings, often detached from a wider structural analysis of these struggles.

The fetishization of (sexual) violence or other traumatic experiences is another problematic aspect of the women-in-prison genre, as discussed in our earlier analysis of prison documentaries. The participants of *On the Outside* voluntarily discuss personally traumatic topics; while the film-makers do have the final cut of the film and decide to include such topics, *On the Outside* attempts to avoid fetishizing the traumatic (Walsh 2019, 104) by limiting any manipulative use of soundtrack and minimizing any presence of the film-maker as the viewer's proxy. What remains is the subjective account of the participants' stories, albeit not devoid of institutional influence. In the film, we hear the character Sandy reassuring Abigail "Aw, don't talk about it if you don't want to," following Abigail's recounting of her experience of sexual assault. The line is delivered by Sandy; however, this was originally said by a tutor from the education centre who was briefly present in the room during the conversation between Gray and Abigail. The decision to have the line expressed by one of the participants was made for the narrative integrity of the film— there are only four characters to recount the conversations—but this could be interpreted as contradictory to the film's overall conceit, and the film-makers' assertion that "no words were added to the dialogue, other than to anonymise names and places" (Gray 2020, 195). The decision to attribute words spoken by one individual to another raises potential questions of misappropriation or narrative coercion. Despite such tensions, the circumstance and delivery of the line in the film remain true to the original supportive context and were "done within the parameters of the participants' intentions" (Gray 2020, 195).

Alana highlights another contradiction in the project, referring to the supposedly voluntary context within which such collaborative projects are situated, and the awkward complicity between nonincarcerated professionals and the incarcerating institutions, where "they push you to go to classes, they push you to educate yourself and learn your lessons and stuff like that. They used to drill into your head all the time, you're not here to be punished, being here is the punishment." Alana continues by emphasizing that "you're in a different mindset when you're in there, … some people if they were having bad days, were just left in their cell." However, both Dani and Alana confirm direct personal benefit, where both express a desire to effect positive change. Dani "appreciate[s] the voice you have gave me and these other three women" while Alana was "just so glad this all came together because it's helped push me more to what I want to do. The biggest part of it for me was turning my negative experience into a positive. So at least I can turn around and say I've managed to achieve this. As long as it helps other people. My aim isn't to become a massive writer—I would love that—but my aim is just to change people's views and change their perspective about people in prison because [the film] shows that not all people are just born to go to prison. Some people just need a bit of help rather than to be judged." These reflections gesture towards both personal and wider social transformations that can be stimulated by creative prison projects—in spite of, and to some extent because of, the constraining institutional collaborations underpinning this work.

7.4 Conclusion: Towards a Decarcerated Public Humanities?

The preceding discussion suggests that projects involving representations of incarcerated women on screen have the potential to align themselves with some of the principles of a critical public humanities committed to co-creation and social justice (see the volume's Introduction), but such work also makes visible the tensions and limitations inherent in this practice. The prison work the authors have been involved in, like many similar initiatives, largely remains caught in the rehabilitative logic that makes these partnerships possible in the first place—a logic which places responsibility on the shoulders of the criminalized individuals rather than providing a systemic critique of the root causes of crime and imprisonment. Nevertheless, it is our hope that by offering new insights and ways of connecting—on both sides of and across the prison wall—and by making wider audiences aware of such work, these projects can be the starting point for wider transformations on individual and communal levels that will incrementally contribute to social change, serving as a step towards "new imaginary horizons" (Fleetwood 2020, 189) and a "decarcerated social structure" (Jacobi 2011, 52).

Reactions to the film confirm this potential for wider transformation. While the initial anticipated audience for the project was the participants, the film has found larger viewership within academia and the film industry; within a non-commercial context the film is freely available to be used for educational purposes, where Alana's desire to "change people's views" was put into practice through workshops in secondary schools in Scotland. Senior school pupils (aged 16–18) concluded that the film allowed "the audience to look at the women as human being[s] who got lost and did some mistakes instead of looking at the crime they committed," with one pupil stating that "it made me realise that there is always more to the story and that I shouldn't be judgemental."

Despite such positive effects on public perceptions of imprisoned women, it is typically the nonincarcerated collaborators that "tend to be the biggest beneficiaries" (Fleetwood 2020, 160) of prison projects, because of the inevitable power hierarchies involved. Professional and academic benefits to the institutions and nonincarcerated individuals are easily identifiable, which for *On the Outside* have included academic research outputs, film festival screenings and awards.[9] However, the incarcerated co-authors are also the subject of the film, which raises questions as to whether co-authorship can truly be claimed on behalf of a project where (formerly) imprisoned people—for a host of reasons—cannot be equal agents in the final outcome. It is also worth noting that those in Scottish prisons cannot view the film through Amazon, like other audiences, because even controlled internet use remains prohibited, highlighting ongoing challenges of digital access for incarcerated communities. Nevertheless, there are moves to make the film available on the in-cell media and through prison screenings.

Acknowledging privilege while recognizing that benefits can be complex and more or less tangible for the different groups involved is key to a critical humanities practice. In the British context, where the "impact" agenda has become institutionally embedded in higher education through the Research Excellence Framework (REF)—which ranks universities based on their research achievements and transformational effects beyond academia—we need to be particularly careful to ensure that the underlying principles of a prison-based critical humanities practice are not co-opted. An ongoing examination of our own role and motivation remains paramount in this context. Although we may participate in exercises such as REF as part of our employment—resulting in professional rewards—we need to push against an instrumentalization of university-prison engagement and the persistence of one-directional concepts of "impact": true transformation can only ever happen in conversation.[10] It is in this spirit that we end the chapter with Dani's song and Alana's poem, allowing their words to speak for themselves.

"Mistake" (by Dani Gracie)

Winter, Spring and Summer,
I count my days cos I got numbers
I'm a prisoner, got locked up
The price I pay, mistakes I made
Reminded every day, I made mistakes

See the bars on the window
I don't want to be here no more
As I look out the window

Wondering where will my life go?
I got in to some trouble
Cause my past just won't leave me alone
I don't want to be here
I don't want to be here no more

I couldn't find any hope
But I read the bible
Pray to God every day
I don't want it to be this way
I want it to change
Cause I miss my family
It was just a mistake
It was just a mistake

Christmas, New Year and my Birthday
It has to be this way, sadly
I'm stuck here, I lost my freedom
Because all the alcohol
Yeah, it got me in trouble
It's not my fault, wish I could change it all
I made a mistake, it was just a mistake

It was a stupid mistake
I really regret that day
How my life has changed
Have to learn the hard way
See the bars on the window
I just want to go home

"My Freedom is Gone" (by Alana)

When you hear them keys rattle
you know it's the start of a hard battle
When I had my own keys
locked my door as I pleased
it put my mind at ease

But now my freedom is gone

The people down stairs fight their own battle
with a different type of rattle
Not knowing if it's day or night or night or day

Screaming and crying cos they don't know what to say

Their freedom is gone

I'm out a walk with my dog
Sun's in the sky
Gliding over them mountains
and they seem so high
There's a gentle breeze
I can feel the goosebumps
on my arms and knees
The grass so soft beneath my feet
I could stand here all day
and watch the people walk down the street
But I start work soon and I love my job
it's good pay and I don't care if I work 12 hours a day
When you work in a hospital, you have a duty of care
so if it's 12 hours or 24 I really don't care
I worked hard for this job, the training, the study, and a whole lot more
I never failed to smile walking in and out that hospital door

A year has gone by, I'm still the same person
but I feel rather shy
Because I'm now good friends with a really horrible guy
I feel all doom and gloom
when I used to feel like a rose that was starting to bloom
I have left my job and left my home
I live miles away with a guy that makes me cry all day
He says you can't do this and you can't do that
I wish I had the courage to call him a rat
Times gone by it's got to the stage
where my money is lower than my self esteem,
I just wish I could wake up
and this would be a horrible dream
So I run out the house and I hide in the pub
I ask for a job and get myself some grub
A guy over heard me
he was a stranger
he says I'll pay you loads if you carry this
You won't be in danger
At that moment in time with all my stress
I couldn't help but stupidly say yes
So the next day I got my suitcase
and ran to the train to start this crime race

It was all going well for a month or two

I could collect packages from strange public places
just like outside the zoo
They say do it under the public's noses and you won't get caught
But the shit I was carrying would make people rot
I always felt sad
cos I knew what I was doing was bad,
But this guy, who cannot be named
was honestly like a lion that cannot be tamed
And I'm that little mouse that just feels ashamed

I got to the stage where I would sit on the train and realise
I'm not this disguise
that could hide behind all the eyes
that stared at me all day
Did they know what I was doing and did not want to say?
I always told myself I won't get caught that won't happen to me
Until I walked off that train, into the arms of C.I.D.

I got bail, I got a wake up call
so I moved back home and changed my life
I got rid of that guy that wasn't nice
he was more annoying than a bunch of head lice
I got a new full time job,
and a new loving boyfriend
got me a house and a dog
I'm happy, I'm free from all that shite
that made me cry all night
I now have a great life
I'm happy
When I told my boss, he wasn't even cross
even though I committed a crime
and knew I had to serve time.

8 months later, court day
I have so much support from my friends and family
but I can no longer pretend that this day I go away
to the concrete crime school some might say
Bang goes the judge's stick
two years I got in the nick
My mind just feels like a bulb that has blown
in complete darkness
don't know whether I'm coming or going

My freedom is gone

> But I will walk out of here with my head held high
> I can't wait to feel the raindrops falling from the sky
> And when I walk I will scream and shout
> Fuck you jail and fuck your snout
> And when I hear them keys rattle
> I'll say well done
> You defeated the battle
>
> My freedom is back

Acknowledgements Anne Schwan would like to thank Jenny Hartley, Sarah Turvey, Tobi Jacobi and Ed Wiltse for providing inspiration for university-prison engagement. She is also grateful to Lori Pompa and colleagues at the Inside-Out Prison Exchange Program, including members of the Graterford Think Tank who helped facilitate the training in July 2014. Sarah Armstrong and other members of the Scottish Universities-Prisons Network continue to provide a much welcome source of conversation and support. Paul Gray would like to thank the cast and crew of *On the Outside* for the extensive creative talents they contributed to the film. He is particularly grateful to Nas Saraei, who produced the film and who played a significant role at every stage of the project. We are appreciative of Lindsay Morgan's efforts in helping facilitate Edinburgh Napier's prison work over the years, as well as Jim King's support in his former role as Head of Education at the Scottish Prison Service. Finally, warm thanks to everybody who has been involved in our prison projects, particularly the participants at HMYOI Polmont whose enthusiasm has made *On the Outside* possible.

Notes

1. Wiltse (2011, 8) notes the problematic implications of the concept of "service learning," which "implies a highly asymmetrical relation in which students learn by servicing the less fortunate, rather than the reciprocal collaboration of individuals from different communities and backgrounds, with different needs and resources."
2. Schwan set up a placement program between Edinburgh Napier University, HMP Edinburgh and Fife College, the Scottish Prison Service's education provider, in 2011, involving university students in literary and creative activities at the prison. The project won the *Herald Higher Education Partnership Award* in 2016; the arrangement has since been extended to other prisons and subject areas, including Gray's film-related work at HMYOI Polmont and HMP Shotts.
3. We purposefully use quotation marks for "rehabilitation" to problematize the term. For a critique of the term and its implications, see Carlen (2013).
4. Seminars were held weekly over a period of three months and included screenings of short films and scenes from feature films. The films were generally examples of a more unconventional narrative form that explored the human condition and human relations. Seminars were followed up with 1:1 meetings

between Gray and the participants. Most seminars were attended by producer Nasreen Saraei, and the initial seminars and 1:1 meetings were also attended by an education tutor who helped facilitate the project. The majority of the seminars and 1:1 meetings were only attended by the participants, Gray and producer Saraei. The intention was for participants to develop script ideas, under a working title of *A Visual Letter*, that would be used as the basis for the production of short films. See Gray (2020) for further detail on the impact of the films on the participants' work.

5. All four participants were given pseudonyms in the film and were credited in the film under their character names; however, at their request, both Dani and Alana will be referred to by their first names in this chapter. Alana is represented by the character Gemma and is played by actor Kirsty Finlay. Dani is represented by the character Abigail and is played by actor Sarah Dingwall.
6. This name has been changed to maintain anonymity.
7. The original intention was to have the participants more involved in the final production and edit of the film; however, due to the complexities of working within a prison environment, the initial seminar activities progressed more slowly than anticipated and overall time constraints resulted in Gray having to interpret more of the participants' intentions at the production stage than initially planned.
8. We refer to the film-makers in the collective, rather than specific roles within the process, for the following reasons: the film is created through a co-authoring of the screenplay by director Paul Gray and the four participants; Gray collaborated closely with producer Nasreen Saraei who had significant input into the narrative construction, having been present for the majority of the group sessions at Polmont and having produced the film throughout the production process; cinematographer Alkistis Terzi and editor Olivia Middleton also played significant roles in the final narrative outcome of the film. While the directorial voice was male, all other main head of department roles were female—the small cast and crew of the film numbered twenty-five, of whom twenty were female.
9. The film-makers and the director in particular have benefited with clearly identifiable outcomes. *On the Outside* won best International Film at *Alexandria Film Festival* (Virginia, 2019), and was shortlisted in both the *Outstanding Contribution to the Local Community* category of the *Times Higher Education Awards 2019* and the *Partnership Award* category of *The Herald Higher Education Awards 2019*. Further academic benefits resulted from screenings by advocacy groups: Howard League Scotland, the country's leading penal reform organization, screened the film, followed by a panel Q&A in January 2019; the Koestler Trust, the UK's best-known prison arts charity, presented the film as part of a wider expression of prisoner creativity during *Voices from Prison, London Literature Festival 2018*, and at the Scottish Parliament in December 2018, as part of an exhibition titled "*100 Years On – An Art Trail by Women in Prison.*"
10. See also Popple and Ng in Chapter 19 of this volume.

REFERENCES

Brown, Michelle. 2009. *The Culture of Punishment: Prison, Society, and Spectacle*. New York: New York University Press.

Caged Heat. 1974. Film. Directed by Jonathan Demme. New World Pictures.

Carlen, Pat. 2013. "Against Rehabilitation: For Reparative Justice." *Criminal Justice Matters* 91 (1): 32–33. https://doi.org/10.1080/09627251.2013.778760.

Carlen, Pat, Jenny Hicks, Josie O'Dwyer, Diana Christina, and Chris Tchaikovsky. 1985. *Criminal Women: Autobiographical Accounts*. Edited by Pat Carlen. Cambridge: Polity.

Cecil, Dawn K. 2007. "Looking Beyond *Caged Heat*: Media Images of Women in Prison." *Feminist Criminology* 2 (4) (October): 304–26.

Cecil, Dawn, K. 2020. "Ear Hustling: Lessons from a Prison Podcast." In *The Palgrave Handbook of Incarceration in Popular Culture*, edited by Marcus Harmes, Meredith Harmes, and Barbara Harmes. Palgrave Macmillan. https://doi-org.ezproxy.napier.ac.uk/10.1007/978-3-030-36059-7_4.

Crewe, Ben. 2013. "Writing and Reading a Prison: Making Use of Prisoner Life Stories." *Criminal Justice Matters* 91 (1): 20. https://doi.org/10.1080/09627251.2013.778750.

Davis, Angela Y. 2003. *Are Prisons Obsolete?* New York: Seven Stories Press.

Davis, Simone Weil, and Barbara Sherr Roswell, eds. 2013. *Turning Teaching Inside Out: A Pedagogy of Transformation for Community-Based Education*. New York: Palgrave Macmillan.

Fleetwood, Nicole R. 2020. *Marking Time: Art in the Age of Mass Incarceration*. Cambridge, MA: Harvard University Press.

Fogarty, Paul. n.d. "Prison: Channel 4 Fans Call for Lexi Heckles' Release after Documentary Reveals Tragic Story." https://www.hitc.com/en-gb/2020/03/03/prison-channel-4-lexi-heckles-fans-call-for-release-tv/.

Gilligan, Paula. 2012. "'Harsh Realism': Gender, Reality Television, and the Politics of the 'Sink' Housing Estate in Austerity Britain." *Television & New Media* 14 (3): 244–60.

Girls Behind Bars. 2008–2011. Documentary Series. Directed Michelle Friel and Julien Kean. Aired 2008–2011. Friel Kean Films for BBC One.

Girls Behind Bars. 2012. Documentary. Directed by Xavier Alford. Aired October 22, 2012. BBC Three.

Gray, Paul. 2020. "*On the Outside*: Film-Making as Story-Telling Through Introspective Re-Enactment, and the Significance of Anonymity in the Spoken Word." *Media Practice and Education* 21 (3): 185–99.

Gray, Paul, and Lindsay Morgan. 2017. Visual Letters Education Partnership Agreement Between Edinburgh Napier University, Fife College and Scottish Prison Service. Unpublished.

Griffiths, Alison. 2016. *Carceral Fantasies: Cinema and Prison in Early Twentieth-Century America*. New York: Columbia University Press.

Heidensohn, Frances, and Marisa Silvestri. 2012. "Gender and Crime." In *Oxford Handbook of Criminology*, 5th ed., edited by Mike Maguire, Rod Morgan, and Robert Reiner, 336–69. Oxford: Oxford University Press.

High, Chris, Namita Singh, Lisa Petheram, and Gusztáv Nemes. 2012. "Defining Participatory Video from Practice." In *Handbook of Participatory Video*, edited by

E.-J. Milne, Claudia Mitchell, and Naydene de Lange, 35–48. Lanham: AltaMira Press.
Inside Prison: Britain Behind Bars. 2019. Documentary Series. Directed by Jamie Batten. Aired September–October 2019. Chalkboard TV for ITV.
Jacobi, Tobi. 2011. "Speaking Out for Social Justice: The Problems and Possibilities of US Women's Prison and Jail Writing Workshops." In *Reading and Writing in Prison*, edited by Anne Schwan. Special issue, *Critical Survey* 23 (3): 40–54. https://doi.org/10.3167/cs.2011.230304.
Jewkes, Yvonne. 2011. *Media & Crime*, 2nd ed. London: Sage.
Karpowitz, Daniel. 2017. *College in Prison: Reading in an Age of Mass Incarceration*. New Brunswick, NJ: Rutgers University Press.
Martin, Randall. 2017. *Women and Murder in Early Modern News Pamphlets and Broadside Ballads, 1573–1697*. Essential Works for the Study of Early Modern Women, Series III, Part One, Volume 7. N.p: Taylor & Francis.
Mayne, Judith. 2000. *Framed: Lesbians, Feminists, and Media Culture*. Minneapolis: University of Minnesota Press.
Ministry of Justice. "Paddy Wivell, Director of Documentary 'Prison,' On What Prison Life is Really Like," January 14, 2019. https://medium.com/@MoJGovUK/paddy-wivell-director-of-documentary-prison-on-what-prison-life-is-really-like-f7aba3f81977.
Morton, Jim. 1986. "Women in Prison Films." In *Incredibly Strange Films*, edited by V. Vale and Andrea Juno, 151–52. London: Plexus.
On the Outside. 2019. Film. Directed by Paul Gray. Good Well Films. https://vimeo.com/paulgray/ontheoutside or https://www.amazon.co.uk/dp/B09KSXBQJT.
Orange is the New Black. 2013–2019. Television Series. Created by Jenji Kohan. Lionsgate Television for Netflix.
Page, Allison, and Laurie Ouellette. 2020. "The Prison-Televisual Complex." *International Journal of Cultural Studies* 23 (1): 121–37.
Prison. 2020. Documentary Series. Series 2. Directed by Paddy Wivell. Aired February–March 2020. Spring Films for Channel 4.
Rafter, Nicole Hahn. 2000. *Shots in the Mirror: Crime Films and Society*. Oxford: Oxford University Press.
Schwan, Anne. 2014. *Convict Voices: Women, Class, and Writing about Prison in Nineteenth-Century England*. Durham, NH: University of New Hampshire Press. Open Access. https://scholars.unh.edu/unh_press/2.
Schwan, Anne. 2016. "Postfeminism Meets the Women in Prison Genre: Privilege and Spectatorship in *Orange Is the New Black*." *Television & New Media* 17 (6): 473–90. https://doi.org/10.1177/1527476416647497.
Takeda, Yuya. 2021. "Toward 'More Participatory' Participatory Video: A Thematic Review of Literature." *Learning, Media and Technology*. https://doi.org/10.1080/17439884.2021.1945089.
Thomas, Jennifer C. 2020. "Women Behind Bars: Dissecting Social Constructs Mediated by News and Reality TV." In *The Palgrave Handbook of Incarceration in Popular Culture*, edited by Marcus Harmes, Meredith Harmes, and Barbara Harmes. Palgrave Macmillan. https://doi-org.ezproxy.napier.ac.uk/10.1007/978-3-030-36059-7_26.
Wächter, Cornelia. 2020. "*Wentworth* and the Politics and Aesthetics of Representing Female Embodiment in Prison." In *The Palgrave Handbook of Incarceration in Popular Culture*, edited by Marcus Harmes, Meredith Harmes,

and Barbara Harmes. Palgrave Macmillan. https://doi-org.ezproxy.napier.ac.uk/ https://doi.org/10.1007/978-3-030-36059-7_40.

Walsh, Aylwyn. 2019. *Prison Cultures: Performance, Resistance, Desire*. Bristol: Intellect.

Walters, Suzanna Danuta. 2001. "Caged Heat: The (R)evolution of Women-in-Prison Films." In *Reel Knockouts: Violent Women in the Movies*, edited by Martha McCaughey and Neal King, 106–23. Austin: University of Texas Press.

White, Shirley A. 2003. *Participatory Video: Images that Transform and Empower*. Thousand Oaks: Sage.

Wiltse, Ed. 2011. "Doing Time in College: Student-Prisoner Reading Groups and the Object(s) of Literary Study." In *Reading and Writing in Prison*, edited by Anne Schwan. Special issue, *Critical Survey* 23 (3): 6–22. https://doi.org/10.3167/cs.2011.230302.

World Prison Brief Database. Accessed July 1, 2021. https://www.prisonstudies.org/highest-to-lowest/prison-population-total.

Yang, Kyung-Hwa. 2016. *Participatory Video in Adult Education: Cultivating Participatory Culture in Communities*. Singapore: Springer.

Zalcock, Beverley. 1998. *Renegade Girls: Girl Gangs on Film*. London and San Francisco: Creation Books International.

PART II

Making Memory, Making Community

CHAPTER 8

Publics, Memory, Affect (or, Rethinking Publicness with Peter Watkins and Hannah Arendt)

Marco de Waard

8.1 Introduction

No inquiry into the public humanities would seem complete without consideration of the experiential modalities through which members of the public—or, better, of publics in the plural (cf. Warner 2002)—orientate themselves toward the public domain, developing and sustaining a sense of themselves as potential political actors. Those experiential modalities range from the deliberative and the participatory to the imaginative and the affective, and the latter may productively be approached, or so it will be argued, by attending to cultural evocations of historically specific public life environments—which is to say that some form of cultural memory is involved. The point of departure here will be the ongoing revival of interest, across the humanities, in the work of Hannah Arendt, whose account of political action as the exercise and experience of public freedom offers a unique starting point for exploring those modalities and for interrogating the conditions in which a sense of publicness may be nourished—and thrive—in the first place. As we will see, "action," in Arendt, is an essentially fragile category, on account of the facts of human plurality and interdependence to which she relates it in her thought. And yet Arendt wrote powerfully about the role of memory (or remembrance) and narrative (or what she simply called "stories") in constituting a "common world" where the relationships created by action and speech might be consolidated and prolonged

M. de Waard (✉)
Amsterdam University College, Amsterdam, Netherlands
e-mail: J.M.deWaard@uva.nl

© The Author(s), under exclusive license to Springer Nature Switzerland AG 2022
A. Schwan and T. Thomson (eds.), *The Palgrave Handbook of Digital and Public Humanities*, https://doi.org/10.1007/978-3-031-11886-9_8

(1998, 175–207). In what follows, I will first consider how recent Arendtian public sphere theory has taken up this relationship between (political) action and the (public) world that sustains it, leading to a new attentiveness to memory, affect, and more broadly dynamics of transmission. Next, I will turn for a case study to the collaborative method of film-maker Peter Watkins, whose work with a mnemonic counter-public of actor-participants resonates with Arendtian thought in ways that illuminate both. I will end by proposing a concept of "imaginaries of publicness" to further bring into focus the nexus of experiential qualities which are at stake here, and which include something like attachment to publicness itself and the relationships it permits in society and culture. At heart, the imaginaries whose concept I want to advance are about keeping the idea of publics imaginatively available as both a cultural and a political form, and about maintaining a sense of the possibility of collective world-making that is held out by it across moments in time.

8.2 Acting in Public: Arendtian Departures

The impact of the Covid-19 pandemic has underscored, in dramatic form, the extent to which the shrinking or closing down of public spheres—certainly in their physical dimensions—is a phenomenon that may affect publics viscerally and emotively in a way that is about more than the loss of access in a purely formal sense. As much of public life was put on hold, the desire to appear as members of a (political) public paradoxically intensified: something that might help explain the intense momentum and special affective charge of the Black Lives Matter (BLM) protests that exploded internationally in the late spring of 2020, occasioned by the violent death of George Floyd in Minneapolis in May, and coming in the immediate aftermath of a tentative relaxation of lockdown measures stringently implemented in countries around the globe. Not only Arendt's account of the human faculty for "action," but also her conception of the public realm as a "space of appearances," has the capacity to speak to this situation. Action, in Arendt, is a fragile domain of activity in that it is unpredictable and transient. In this regard it contrasts with the activity of "work," which results in products that are durable and testify to a degree of control, even mastery, on the part of their maker. As she puts it, we "always act into a web of relationships," and therefore "the consequences of each deed are boundless, every action touches off not only a reaction but a chain reaction, [and] every process is the cause of unpredictable new processes" (Arendt 2018, 306). What nonetheless makes action a privileged domain for her, and indeed, what makes it political in a broad and egalitarian sense, is that it is the one domain of activity where we disclose who we are to others: "In acting and speaking, men show who they are, reveal actively their unique personal identities and thus make their appearance in the human world" (Arendt 1998, 179). The BLM protests arguably generated just such "spaces of appearance." As examples of the human capacity to "act in concert" (Arendt 1998, 179), they permitted people to disclose themselves as political agents while affirming the condition of plurality as one that at the same time separates *and* unites.

In the context of public humanities research, I am interested in how Arendt's action concept—which for a long time was read as strictly demarcated from non-political domains of activity, to the point of seeming overly formal or restrictive (or both)—has recently been (re)inscribed into a rich continuum of cultural practices that include public and political art as well as forms of mnemonic and affective transmission. Indeed, if an earlier moment of reappraisal of Arendt was largely internal to the field of political and democratic theory (e.g., Honig 1993, 1995), the current revival assumes a wider radius of application for Arendtian thought, adding a distinctly novel coloring that reflects political experiences specific to the current juncture. As new dynamics of politicization arose in global protest cultures from the 2010s onwards—often centered on preserving the very publicness of public space as such—new political and social ontologies have emerged in which Arendt would seem to resonate rather more easily than before (cf. Mitchell 2012; Butler 2015). Crucially, they have invited new attention for the role of theatricality, embodiment, and staging in contemporary public spheres, discovering in Arendt a productive interlocutor insofar as her account of action as inherently theatrical anticipates current trends to approach theatre and theatricality in an "expanded"—aesthetico-political—sense (Schmidt 2017, 124; cf. Arendt 2006, 152). I would add that Arendt's theorization of politics and action speaks with equal eloquence to the new attention in humanities scholarship for the relations between memory work and activism—as in recent calls that more attention is paid to "the mechanisms by which positive attachments are transmitted" in public culture (Rigney 2018, 370). My premise here is that the public humanities might function productively as a site of encounter to host this kind of interdisciplinary conversation and inquiry, while an Arendtian orientation might also give guidance to calls within this emergent field "to take seriously publicness as a form of authority in and of itself" (Mullen 2016, 197).

For my purpose in what follows, two recent inquiries will be of special pertinence; both are daring Arendtian theorizations of the experiential texture of modern publicness. In a lecture series published as *Public Things: Democracy in Disrepair*, Bonnie Honig has put forward "a lexicon for a political theory of public things" in which Arendt, surprisingly, is read together with the object-relations theory of child psychologist D.W. Winnicott (Honig 2017, 37). The idea is that precisely because Arendtian "acting in concert" is fragile and transient, it needs the support of stabilizing forces that help bestow a measure of longevity and reliability on the "common world" that is constituted by human "words and deeds." Such forces might be found in the infrastructural world of "public things": just as in Winnicott one becomes attached to so-called transitional objects that mediate one's relationship with the world—even or especially when they suffer damage, and they "respond" by demonstrating their object permanence—so the public in Arendt's account of action may cultivate attachment, in Honig's reading, to the public libraries and bridges that thereby come to function as a "democratic holding environment" (54). Appropriately, this line of reading makes a lot of room for a notion of Arendtian "care." Honig's reorientation converges with Patchen Markell's, who, in a series of articles on Arendt (Markell 2006, 2011, 2014), has similarly sought to expand received understandings of Arendtian action in a way that takes it "away from the thematics of the moment" to affirm its interdependence with domains of activity whose politicality is not always easily discerned (Markell 2014, 115). However, while Honig uses Arendt to rethink how "public things" "mediate our relations with others and with ourselves as subjects and citizens" in public space (Honig 2017, 38), Markell attends to the temporalities involved in bolstering our sense of ourselves as participants in public action. Against a longstanding reading of *The Human Condition* and *On Revolution* which understands the revolutionary "beginnings" to which Arendt attended in terms of exceptional (and exceptionally fragile) "moments," Markell draws attention to the retrospective framing through which Arendt prolongs those "beginnings" to make their aftermaths a vital part of the action context itself. Simply put, what this means is that the time of action thickens as well as lengthens: for Markell, it includes what he dubs "power-after" (2014, 126), a temporality that includes acts of augmentation and more broadly cultural transmission to keep the political energy of "founding deeds" alive. As I see it, one exciting result of this thickening of Arendtian action time is that it folds subjects' inner "attunement" to publicness, as Markell calls it, into the category of "action" itself, and that it makes room, in doing so, for the role of the arts and cultural practices in giving political action length of duration—and, indeed, a path or a course (Markell 2006). It is not coincidental that in both Honig and Markell, Arendt's "work" appears as a more important and valued domain of activity than in readings that take *The Human Condition* to privilege the capacity for "action" at the expense of what she calls "work" and "labor." While forms of "work" like storytelling (and other acts of remembrance) would not commonly qualify as integral to Arendtian action, they can now be seen to be right at the crossing point where political and artistic or creative forms of agency might meet.

My aim here is not to add another reading of Arendt to these stimulating reworkings. Rather, in the spirit of contributing to public humanities debates, I aim to show how these perspectives on the relationship between political action and dimensions of cultural production and transmission open up new possibilities for analysis and interpretation. The case of Peter Watkins's film-making and participatory method will be used here to show how a reconstructed Arendtian framework which includes the notions of "attachment" and "attunement" helps us analyze, and better understand, some of the imaginative and affective forms through which cultural production may resituate us vis-à-vis today's public spheres—whose publicness is not only affirmed, but may be reinvented, in the process. I will preface the consideration of this case with some brief remarks on the notion of publics, seen as a cultural form.

8.3 Peter Watkins's Imaginary of Publicness

Before clarifying the concept of "imaginaries of publicness" and developing a working definition (as I attempt to do in the final section of this essay), and before attending to my case study (the aim of the present section), let me specify the stakes by demarcating this concept from other social and cultural imaginaries, most typically national ones, that have a specific and more easily delineable chronotope. I take my cue here from Michael Warner's proposition, in his seminal *Publics and Counterpublics*, that we see publics as "a cultural form, a kind of practical fiction" that is marked by qualities of fundamental openness (Warner 2002, 8). In contrast to imagined communities like the nation, which put down firm coordinates in time and space, regulating membership through the assumption of an "outside" (cf. Anderson 1991), publics *qua* cultural form include us through their discourse by addressing us as "strangers" who might be nonidentical with the object of address that is projected by the discourse itself (Warner 2002, 74–76). Effectively, we are teased into membership of these publics by "mere attention" alone (87), in awareness of the commonality this creates with people who might be different. This emphasis on openness, voluntary participation, and "stranger-relationality" (75) is not meant to idealize publics—Warner recognizes all too well that there are "damaged forms of publicness" whose world-making is shaped by "conflict with the norms and contexts of their cultural environment" (63)—but it is to define them through contrast with forms of community-making that are more forcefully interpellative or even impositional, and where a clearly contoured identity is held out as a putative social ground. For Warner, the experience of being part of a public leaves much greater room for the transformative or, as he calls it, "world-making" capacity that is involved in this reflexive form of self-organization. Insofar as public world-making is orientated to a place, it is through what I would call a kind of contingent belonging: it works by attaching not so much to a place as such, as to the public life forms and possibilities of co-creation which are enabled by that place, in a way that need not rely on fictions of origin, self-identity, authenticity, or immediacy.

In contrast with national imaginaries, then, an imaginary of publicness may accommodate a rather more horizontal, pluralistic, and indeed more democratic vision of the form of collectivity to which it addresses itself and of which it holds out an image. Certainly, the case of Peter Watkins might help us see how it is precisely by keeping the idea of a public open that such a vision would be able to emerge and find, as it were, a place to settle. Right from the start of his career in film-making, in the late 1950s, Watkins's central ambition has been "to break down the artificiality of conventional cinema and to lower the barriers that usually exist between subject and viewer—in order to engage members of the audience as individuals who must also participate in the film experience" (Gomez 1979, 138). It is thus consistent that in his writings as a media theorist and critic, the term "publics" always carries an aspirational and strong normative thrust.[1] In a self-interview from 2005, for instance, he reflects on his method, working with non-professional actors, as follows: "I believe that the process by which the 'actors' in my films participate in the creative act shows that political action can be linked to creative action. It is a process by which the public take charge of the way that history is presented"—more so than "is usually allowed by the media" (Watkins 2007, 60). In the early BBC film *Culloden* (1964), he used historical re-enactment scenes within an eighteenth-century setting that was anachronistically penetrated by modern media techniques (e.g., live interviewing); the result was a self-consciously artificial documentary film which countered viewers' alienation or estrangement with a strong sense of immediacy as it lent its images a strong affective charge. The following decade, his work with a Norwegian public to produce *Edvard Munch* (1974) marked a new point in the development of his collaborative method, which he intensified in subsequent films. Although he later recognized that "the level of participation by the public" in it "is nowhere near as extended" as in his later work, he saw the film as a co-creative form that offered an alternative to the hegemonic media's "hierarchical control" (Watkins 2007, 60). It is his final film, *La Commune (Paris, 1871)* (1999), that insists most forcefully to be discussed, not in terms of the film as "product," but in terms of collaborative making as process and event: as we shall see, it called into being a mnemonic counter-public of co-creators who, as they exercised their historical imagination on individual terms, took distance from the forms of cultural authority involved in more official forms of transmitting the (national) past. In the process it reinvented relationships between medium, film-maker, participants (Watkins only ever calls them "actors" between scare quotes), and the real and imagined social spaces of their joint creative work. It arguably took to the furthest extreme, within Watkins's trajectory, what is needed to recover the *publicness* of public television.

The early amateur film *The Forgotten Faces* (1961) helps us trace this imaginary back to its beginnings in a nexus of concerns around historical experience, news images, the influence of public media, and revolutionary action. A film about the Hungarian Uprising of 1956, it proceeds by restaging Budapest street scenes documented in *Paris Match* and *Life* magazines, in gripping photojournalism by John Sadovy among others. *The Forgotten Faces* is thus an act of visual recall that reconstructs, realistically, testimony of inner-city conflict and its in-the-moment "feel" (Gomez 1979, 25; cf. Poggi 2015). In the process it actively participates, through the form of its remediation, in the energies it retrieves from the moments it revisits. The climactic high point comes some eight minutes into the 18-minute film, when a young revolutionary called Margit Zeke is persuaded to come on stage to read her latest article for a revolutionary gazette. Having overcome her initial reluctance, she reads her text with passion, whipping herself into a state of spirited political emotion as the assembled students and workers at her feet respond with visceral enthusiasm. We do not hear Zeke's text (the narrator is commenting in voiceover) but the camera cuts from close-ups of her face, shouting out her words, to individual audience members, who listen attentively and then shout in encouragement or repeat the woman's words. Arendt has spoken of the "pathos of novelty" that attends revolutionary beginnings (Arendt 1963, 27). The sequence conveys a sense of joy at the event of being together in action; in what is overall a film in a tragic mode, it affirms the dream of a revolutionary public (briefly) identical with itself, as a body of citizens freely expressing ideas in an atmosphere of passion around the act of public participation. Indeed, coming just prior to the counterrevolutionary invasion and crackdown by the Soviets, it holds out a positive image of a space of appearance in Arendt's substantive sense as a space "where freedom can unfold its charms and become a visible, tangible reality" (1963, 26).

In the only existing monograph on Watkins's work to date, the sequence is criticized for its proximity to Eisenstein's *October* (1928) on account of its overly dramatic rendering, underscored by "stirring Hungarian music" (Gomez 1979, 25). The contrast with the scenes of violence that straddle it, grimly realistic, is stark indeed—and yet the public life sequence adds something essential. From the perspective of our inquiry, it permits us to ask what happens when filmic remediation transmits the "pathos of novelty" in an encounter with other media, re-encoding the language of visual testimony to modulate its affective energy and special political charge. In this regard, I would argue that Watkins, far from idealizing the memory of revolutionary pathos in an Eisensteinian manner, actually understands it as ambivalent—as a closer consideration of the contrast with *October* might help to see. First, pace Gomez, what disables a positive comparison with Eisenstein's film—specifically its depiction of crowds and masses—is that *The Forgotten Faces* demonstrates aliveness to what Arendt calls the "condition of plurality" (Arendt 2005, 20). Rather than defining the Hungarian people in national or class terms, as a film on the model of *October* might have done, it presents them as internally variegated, as the voiceover text insists: "these are their faces," it comments on a montage of close-up portrait shots, "highly individual, with conflicting beliefs." Watkins's imaginary of publicness comes into being in such moments of disarticulation from either a national or a class-based narrative, or a combination of both. The second and still more pertinent point is that, in the context of the film as a whole, the public life sequence recognizes the limits of "pathos" as an experiential mode, in contrast with Eisenstein's affirmation of it within his famous "montage of attractions." It has recently been suggested that Watkins holds a place in a modernist tradition of the critique of pathos that includes Walter Benjamin, Herbert Marcuse—both likely influences on his media theory—and, I would add, Arendt (Duarte 2018, 26–33). Just like Benjamin, with whose critical assessment of the impoverishment of modern experience she was likely to be familiar, Arendt associated the ephemerality of pathos with a problem of modern sensibility: indeed, what may sometimes look like an idealization of the "pathos of novelty" on her part (Arendt 1963, 27) is qualified by her concern with the decline and dissipation of the political energy which she associated with foundational beginnings and with the struggle to keep it alive beyond a generation of "founders." The question how to sustain such energies and give them longevity is one of *On Revolution*'s most original themes. Watkins's cinema, I argue, inscribes itself within this problematic on account of its interest not so much in intensifying "pathos" to draw viewers in, as in modulating it in order to free up affective currents that make viewers more actively attuned to the social conditions of their own lives. This is where his aesthetic of remediation might be seen to work to political effect: *The Forgotten Faces* ends by remediating a radio announcement about the Soviet invasion of Budapest to a montage of photographs of revolutionaries, many of whom lost their lives. The friction between these different layers of remediation holds out an appeal notably different from that of pathos. The effect of Watkins's montage is to intensify involvement with the tragedy of Budapest's freedom fighters on the one hand, while not suspending a critical stance vis-à-vis our news media on the other—working against a standardized form of reporting that would simply numb or alienate, threatening to translate the squashed revolution into spectacle. The radio broadcast is given an affective undercurrent that is politicizing insofar as it keeps a sense of involvement open: we become differently attuned, indeed.

In bringing together a thematic of revolutionary beginnings and popular-democratic energy with an aesthetic of remediation that has critical potential vis-à-vis contemporary media landscapes, *The Forgotten Faces* has many of the hallmarks of Watkins's later work. What became increasingly prominent, after his early amateur films and subsequent short-lived career at the BBC (he fell out with them in 1965), is that his critique of the mass media, and the way they close down discussion about their own political function in society, became ever more integral to his creative practice and collaborative method. *La Commune (Paris, 1871)* is the culmination of his approach to working with publics and of the unique historical and media pedagogy which he brought to bear on many of his projects. It follows through on his words that his work is driven by a "desire to add a dimension and a process to television…: that of the public directly, seriously and in depth participating in the expressive use of the medium to examine history—past, present and future" (qtd. in Cook 2010, 231). The mostly non-professional actors were cast according to type—i.e., possible sympathizers with the Commune were cast as *communards*, more critical participants as *bourgeois*—but, importantly, not to simply confirm them in a given political identification. The burden of research and on-set improvisation—the more than 200 participants all developed their own characters and wrote or improvised their lines—pushed them through an experience in which they could come into their own as political subjects. There are two points to make about this process. First, it is intriguing how the formation of a mnemonic counter-public on the set worked together with what happens in the film's diegesis, simultaneously mirroring it and lending it affective resonance, in a way not uncommon to the embodied, performative practices of bringing the past "alive" that go by the name of historical re-enactment (cf. Agnew 2007). In narrative terms, the film traces the story of the Paris Commune from its hopeful beginning in March 1871 to its tragic ending two months later, when the experiment in municipal self-government was brought to a halt by a violent crackdown on the part of the national government under Adolphe Thiers. The creation of a counter-public is explicitly thematized since, anachronistically, the narrative folds the foundation of a *communard* news channel into its historical exploration of the dynamics of political action and constituent power inside the Commune context.[2] The effect equals that of the mixed temporalities in *Culloden*: pitting the foundation of a rival channel, "TV Communale," against the government's "TV Nationale," broadcast from Versailles, Watkins's attention to the role of media in forming publics—in calling them into being and imaginatively sustaining them—prevents the conceit of an objective world of representation with its illusions of immediacy and historical veracity. This is enhanced by the use of a "vox pop" mode of reporting, with the actor-participants speaking directly into the camera, breaking with the fourth wall and making contact with the viewer. Watkins's "communal" public life imaginary would thus seem to have been realized on a formal level.

But the second point concerns the way that this representational structure, experimental and innovative as it is, is ruptured and further transformed by developments that unfolded unexpectedly on the set. The "mass audiovisual media," Watkins has written, "have gone to immense lengths to deny people any meaningful participation in the creation of TV as a truly public medium" (Watkins 2007, 60). At a certain point, participants started to relate in this very spirit to the project underway, "criticiz[ing] Watkins's employment of [the vox pop] reporting style" insofar as it homogenized their voices and put constraints on self-representation; it was even objected that it might work "as a new version of the monoform"—Watkins's term of denunciation for the standardized audiovisual formats that dominate most television making (Ramos-Martínez 2016, 213; cf. Cook 2010). We see this friction enter into the diegesis where the "vox pop" mode breaks down and gives way to direct, indeed unmediated debate among the re-enactors—still in costume, but stepping out of character—about the meaning of the Commune today and about the modern media landscape and how it manipulates historical knowledge and understanding. As a thorough-going interruption of the field of representation that takes Watkins's "communal" imaginary further than he had foreseen, it is a high point of the film—which, in its original version, is much the longer for it at close to six hours. The group discussions make for highly touching, affectively charged scenes. They include a discussion among female re-enactors who chose to separate themselves out as a group to debate their involvement. One of them turns to the question of the distribution of the film, for which she feels a sense of responsibility or care: "What about the distribution of a work like this? ... This experience is full of hope, and in that sense, extremely positive. We should distribute not only the film, but also the life that took place around it." It is an interesting comment on the fragility of this kind of creative process precisely as an action context whose energy is realized to have significance beyond the film as product: it is understood to hold out the promise of a truly democratic public world, inhabitable on more inclusive terms.

My interest is in the role of mnemonic and affective resonances within this experiential reorientation. Speaking with Lauren Berlant, we might call the special counter-public sphere that took shape on the set an "affect world," defined by attachment to public life as much as by public argument and debate (Berlant 2011, 226). In terms of the precise emotional and affective qualities attending the experience, we might also approach the film by way of historian Enzo Traverso's notion of "left-wing melancholy": a term delineating an emotional and temporal structure that is essentially ambivalent, as it links political mourning, or an elegiac sense of public loss, to a prolongation—no matter how weakened—of utopian aspiration (Traverso 2016). As the spirit of the Commune itself suffuses or runs through the discussion scenes within the film, the latter aspect is especially pertinent. Kristin Ross, in a recent book on the Commune, speaks of the event's own "expanded temporality" as projected from within the initial experience, resulting in "a kind of afterlife that does not exactly *come after* but … is part and parcel of the event itself"; indeed, in her words, its "*prolongation*" is "every bit as vital to the event's logic as the initial acts of insurrection in the streets of the city" (Ross 2015, 6; italics in the original).

Considering the complex emotional, affective, and temporal structures of *La Commune*, it is all the more appropriate that Geoff Bowie's documentary film about its making, *The Universal Clock: The Resistance of Peter Watkins* (Bowie, 2001), should pay ample attention to the experiences and subjectivities of the re-enactors. Some five of them are interviewed at length, against a background of moving images of them pre-shot in their domestic surroundings. A central theme is that of the unique experience of being included in a form of public television making that would otherwise seem to them to be marked by exclusivity. One interviewee, a social worker, recounts her surprise at being included despite "being fat"; her excitement at taking part resonates with that of others, who all comment on the element of "*prise de parole*"— literally, the capture of speech—afforded by the project. Kamel, a *sans papier* from a Parisian *banlieu* who features among the Algerian (Kabyle) community depicted in the film, eloquently relates the story of how his involvement, most especially the experience of researching his lines, made available to him a chance "to reinhabit [him]self": the fight to retain an inner life, to (re)gain a positive experience of his own subjectivity, being at the heart of the predicament of statelessness as he narrates it. Footage of Watkins talking to other participant-actors—instructing them, consulting with them—resonates with this undocumented man's reflections: the director's insistence is that the participants speak as and on behalf of themselves ("*c'est vous!*"), not through an approach of their role as belonging to a character somehow outside or other than themselves. The adoption of a historical persona here functions, I propose, in the spirit of Arendt's retrieval of the theatrical origins of the word "persona," which originally, in ancient drama, referred to the use of masks to "make it possible for the voice to sound through," offering a mode of appearance which, while hiding the actor's countenance, at the same time makes individuation possible (Arendt 1963, 102). The perspective on the relationship between theatricality and political action that we find here helps gauge the special experience and mode of inhabiting publicness that Watkins's method made available.

For contrast, let us recall that the dominant critical paradigm that has informed the discussion of his film so far is Brechtian, emphasizing *La Commune*'s political significance in terms of its didacticism and the way it offered participants "a lesson in collectivity" (Koutsourakis 2018, 181).[3] The Arendtian discussion that has been attempted here, while not at odds with the Brechtian paradigm, might go further in highlighting the potential of Watkins's method to stimulate forms or modalities of political individuation insofar as it offers spaces of experience that are radically open. In this perspective, Watkins is not so much a "community filmmaker" (Cook 2010, 227) as, to borrow Stuart Hall's words about the artist Jeremy Deller—another experimenter with historical re-enactment techniques, whose affinity with Watkins is stark—a "*metteur-en-scène*" who "constructs environments" as well as films or artworks (Hall 2012, 82). For Watkins, not film but the public itself is the medium of his art.

8.4 Imaginaries of Publicness: Notes Toward a Concept

One of the larger aims of this discussion has been to explore the value of notions of "attachment" and "attunement" in understanding how a sense of publicness—a strong sense of inhabiting a "common public world" (Arendt 1998, 257)—might be sustained and transmitted over time. I have not primarily been concerned here with recruiting Watkins's method as a model for "doing" public humanities; nor has it been my aim to simply establish the applicability of an Arendtian framework to the director's practice. Producing models seems less appropriate than interrogating the case to obtain a larger sense of possibility, and to bolster a self-critical stance that might help public humanities projects keep their distance from the impulse, observed in some institutional contexts, to assimilate them to "civic education" or "service learning" paradigms that would seem to take inherited notions of cultural authority and indeed of publicness itself all too easily for granted (as when they reproduce these notions through their practices while failing to contest, or even be concerned with, the dynamics of inclusion and exclusion they may tacitly entail; cf. Mullen 2016). Indeed, if there is one thing the public humanities might learn from Watkins's work, it is that there are forms and practices of aesthetico-political engagement and education that may unfold in public culture while keeping radically open the conception of publicness itself, as well as related notions of community, citizenship, and belonging. We recall that the modalities of experience that have been traced here are not, in my reading, prescribed or "scripted" in any way. Watkins's practice works by creating spaces in which they may emerge from the bottom up, allowing participants to find ways to (re)inhabit public space—and themselves as political subjects—on terms of their own making. If *La Commune (Paris, 1871)*, qua artistic process, offered a space for participants to "appear," it did so by using historical imagination as a medium for performative co-creation.

With the above proviso in mind, and insisting that no logic of exemplarity is intended, let me attempt to theorize a concept of "imaginaries of publicness" which, while building on the discussion of Watkins's film, might have wider resonance in the current juncture—one in which public spheres are shrinking or being eviscerated under pressures of various kinds, whether we understand these as neoliberal, illiberal and authoritarian, post-political, or as a mix of all of these. A first attempt to develop the concept of public life imaginaries, as distinct from national and other imaginaries that typically foreclose their notions of community, would need to include at least the following three points. To begin with, it seems vital to associate them with an idea of publics as essentially, irreducibly plural and heterogeneous in character. Watkins's work, as we have seen, pushes against a homogenizing treatment of publics, assemblies, and crowds that would unite them around a figure other (or larger) than itself. There is a dynamic at work that shows human groupings break into stubborn particularities, into individual parts that may relate across sometimes ineradicable differences within the same political or social space. Insofar as there are moments of totalization, they are overcome or suspended—reconfigured on account of the dynamics of publics' self-constitution as an open-ended and reflexive process. Second, no conceptualization of public life imaginaries would seem complete without the notion that they affirm the "world-making" capacity of publics, understood in terms of their potential for transformation of the spaces of encounter in which they appear. Following Warner, but extending his approach to publics as a "cultural form" in a political direction, the point would seem open to exploration in meta-pragmatic terms, for not only is a new experience of public life made available, an understanding of publics' world-making powers is transmitted to audiences and viewers in ways that might be traced through the modes of address that are being used (cf. Warner 2002, 16). In Arendtian terms, additionally, we might also (re)describe this "world-making" power in terms of an expanded sense of political action, with creative and artistic practice folded into it; the idea is that action contexts are strengthened and prolonged by the poietic powers which are brought to bear as (counter-)publics come together to act in concert. Third, to the extent that imaginaries of the kind under discussion are invested in a pluralistic understanding of human uniqueness and diversity, they are theatrical in an elemental sense; more precisely, they acknowledge the aspect of theatricality that is integral to every mode of appearing in public. This applies not only on the representational level of the films I have discussed here; in Watkins's case the point is equally pertinent to the method deployed in enabling participants' *prise de parole* as political subjects—using historical imagination and re-enactment in the fashioning of a "persona" that permits "the voice to sound through" (Arendt 1963, 102).

What emerges, then, is a view of publics as essentially plural, as "world-making" in an enlarged and capacious sense, and as making their appearance through forms of staging and self-staging (*mise-en-scène*) that must be seen as constitutive of political life, with theatricality understood not just as an expressive mode but as a medium of publicness in its own right: in each of these regards, the public life imaginaries whose concept I aim to delineate work under the signs of openness, fluidity, and *autopoiesis* or self-making. But this is to say that there is an underlying ontological orientation that renders publics the sign or figure of their own putative "ground." After all, what do these different characteristics point to, if not to the groundlessness of the political itself—the fact that no "ground" of authority is naturally "given" but that it needs to be asserted, indeed re-grounded, time and again, in an incessant movement of grounding and ungrounding (cf. Marchart 2007)? This necessitates a further three points which are complex and thus deserve to be developed at more length. The first of them is that it seems essential that imaginaries of publicness attend to the *constitutive* role of publics in founding the political, and that in doing so, they confirm it. In Arendtian terms, publics' capacity for action is associated with constituent, not constituted power. On the representational level, we may see this at work whenever publics, crowds, audiences, or assemblies can be seen to exercise power or collective agency of some elemental kind—typically seized in the moment, no matter how episodic or fleeting,—in a way that pits this power or agency against formal or symbolic structures of rule. In *La Commune*, we see this most typically in moments of contestation where the people take control of "public things," such as the cannons of Montmartre or the *Hôtel de ville de Paris*. As members of the public they do not, however, lose their individuality: even the "vox pop" reporting mode in Watkins's film does not homogenize the public into a crowd or mob or into a collective protagonist of some kind. As the film's crowds and publics are entered by a hand-held camera—a "participant" camera, indeed (Gomez 1979, 23)—the dynamic of breaking the public up into individual elements continues even in the action scenes (cf. Ramos-Martínez 2016).

Second, it is important to specify the kinds of collective identification which public life imaginaries might encourage or enable. I would argue that in an ideal sense, imaginaries of publicness have the capacity to make publics identify, not so much with a putative "ground" of the community—e.g., an idea of the nation or the ethnos—as with the very processes of debate and politico-historical contestation through which a community perpetually (re)constitutes itself. Such identification is ultimately focused on the never-ending movement of (de)constitution itself—a movement in which history is grasped in its contingency, in which a sense of agency is expanded, and in which conflict and dissensus might be given a place. The point is not as abstract or remote from practical concerns as it may sound. Agonistic political theory has long recognized the importance of democratic forms of imagination in staving off "political closure," and in keeping spaces of discussion open in ways that recognize conflictuality as integral to democratic life (Keenan 2003). In the study of public memory, too, the possibility is well understood that such cultural and imaginative forms have the capacity to strengthen a democratic ethos, insofar as they help create "environment[s] in which competing claims can be channeled away from the possibility of violence and into democratic structures robust and flexible enough to accommodate ineliminable political contestation" (Bell 2008, 159). What a democratic culture requires are forms of identification that are resolutely non- or anti-identitarian and have the capacity to focus the imagination on the democratic process itself.

The third and final point is that such forms of identification go together with forms and dynamics of transmission that have their own distinct temporal structures and modes of historical awareness. With regard to temporal structures, we might take our cue from Warner's observation that publics and counter-publics "act historically according to the temporality of their circulation" (2002, 96). They are temporalities that are shaped by the media, yet in ways that are open to creative intervention and change. The distance that Watkins keeps from the rhythms and standardized formats of the "monoform" illustrates how there might be a time of and for counter-publics that is shaped around their own needs of participation and expression; we have seen how his final film opened itself up—also time-wise—to debate. The issue of historical awareness is a broader one, and I want to link it to the question that was raised earlier about the dynamics of transmission of "positive attachments." Ann Rigney writes that "[r]emembering the past, shaping the future remembrance of the present, and struggles for a better future feed into each other in ways that still need unpacking along with the distinctive cultural forms and practices that are used in the transmission of civic commitment" (2018, 372). The public humanities, like the field of memory studies, would do well to pay heed to such a call, and I suggest that attending to imaginaries of publicness might be integral to this pursuit. Watkins himself seemed aware that the historical sense associated with the experience of publicness is multi-directional when he wrote in 1977: "I believe that we are all history, past, present, future, all participating in a common sharing and sensing of experiences which flow about us, forwards and backwards, sometimes simultaneously, without limitations from time or space" (qtd. in Gomez 1979, 125). His work holds out a form in which such flows of experience might be felt the more intensely.

Notes

1. Watkins's most important publication as media critic is an often reworked treatise called *Media Crisis*. The latest English version is available from his website (http://pwatkins.mnsi.net/). In book form it is available in a French translation by Patrick Watkins, maintaining the same (English) title (Watkins 2015).
2. I use the term "counter-public" here in Warner's sense as when "a dominated group aspires to re-create itself as a public and in doing so finds itself in conflict not only with the dominant social group but with the norms that constitute the dominant culture as a public" (Warner 2002, 112).
3. Assessments of Watkins's (qualified) Brechtianism are many and diverse. Some scholars have argued, in classic Brechtian terms, that *La Commune* approximates a didactic "*Lehrstück*" in cinema (Jovanovic 2017, 155–66; Koutsourakis 2018, 178–82); others assimilate the film, again through Brecht, to postcolonial "Third Cinema" with its organization of the narrative around a collective protagonist in its fight against an oppressive, typically colonial power (Wayne 2002; Cook 2010).

References

Agnew, Vanessa. 2007. "History's Affective Turn: Historical Reenactment and Its Work in the Present." *Rethinking History* 11 (3): 299–312.

Anderson, Benedict. 1991. *Imagined Communities: Reflections on the Origin and Spread of Nationalism*. Revised ed. London and New York: Verso.

Arendt, Hannah. 1963. *On Revolution*. London: Faber & Faber.

Arendt, Hannah. 1998. *The Human Condition*. 2nd ed. Chicago and London: The University of Chicago Press.

Arendt, Hannah. 2005. *The Promise of Politics*. Edited by Jerome Kohn. New York: Schocken Books.

Arendt, Hannah. 2006. "What is Freedom?" In *Between Past and Future: Eight Exercises in Political Thought*, 142–69. London: Penguin.

Arendt, Hannah. 2018. "Labor, Work, Action." In *Thinking Without a Banister: Essays in Understanding, 1953–1975*, edited by Jerome Kohn, 291–307. New York: Schocken Books.

Bell, Duncan. 2008. "Agonistic Democracy and the Politics of Memory." *Constellations* 15 (1): 148–66.

Berlant, Lauren. 2011. *Cruel Optimism*. Durham, NC: Duke University Press.

Bowie, Geoff, dir. 2001. *The Universal Clock: The Resistance of Peter Watkins*. Montreal: National Film Board of Canada. https://www.nfb.ca/film/universal_clock_resistance_peter_watkins/.

Butler, Judith. 2015. *Notes Toward a Performative Theory of Assembly*. Cambridge, MA: Harvard University Press.

Cook, John R. 2010. "'Don't Forget to Look Into the Camera!': Peter Watkins' Approach to Acting With Facts." *Studies in Documentary Film* 4 (3): 227–40.

Duarte, German A. 2018. "From Pathos to Pathology: Peter Watkins and the Monoform in Contemporary Media." In *Future Revolutions: New Perspectives on Peter Watkins*, 26–33. Berlin: PoGoBooks.

Eisenstein, Sergei, dir. 1928. *October*. Tartan Video, 2007. DVD.

Gomez, Joseph A. 1979. *Peter Watkins*. Boston: Twayne Publishers.
Hall, Stuart. 2012. "Jeremy Deller's Political Imaginary." In *Jeremy Deller: Joy in People*, 81–89. London: Hayward Publishing.
Honig, Bonnie. 1993. *Political Theory and the Displacement of Politics*. Ithaca and London: Cornell University Press.
Honig, Bonnie, ed. 1995. *Feminist Interpretations of Hannah Arendt*. University Park, PA: The Pennsylvania State University Press.
Honig, Bonnie. 2017. *Public Things: Democracy in Disrepair*. New York: Fordham University Press.
Jovanovic, Nenad. 2017. *Brechtian Cinemas: Montage and Theatricality in Jean-Marie Straub and Danièle Huillet, Peter Watkins, and Lars Von Trier*. Albany, NY: State University of New York Press.
Keenan, Alan. 2003. *Democracy in Question: Democratic Openness in a Time of Political Closure*. Stanford, CA: Stanford University Press.
Koutsourakis, Angelos. 2018. *Rethinking Brechtian Film Theory and Cinema*. Edinburgh: Edinburgh University Press.
Marchart, Oliver. 2007. *Post-Foundational Political Thought: Political Difference in Nancy, Lefort, Badiou and Laclau*. Edinburgh: Edinburgh University Press.
Markell, Patchen. 2006. "The Rule of the People: Arendt, *Archê*, and Democracy." *American Political Science Review* 100 (1): 1–14.
Markell, Patchen. 2011. "Arendt's Work: On the Architecture of *The Human Condition*." *College Literature* 38 (1): 15–44.
Markell, Patchen. 2014. "The Moment Has Passed: Power After Arendt." In *Radical Futures Past: Untimely Political Theory*, edited by Romand Coles, Mark Reinhardt, and George Shulman, 113–43. Lexington: University Press of Kentucky.
Mitchell, W. J. T. 2012. "Image, Space, Revolution: The Arts of Occupation." *Critical Inquiry* 39 (1): 8–32.
Mullen, Mary L. 2016. "Public Humanities' (Victorian) Culture Problem." *Cultural Studies* 30 (2): 183–204.
Poggi, Isotta. 2015. "The Photographic Memory and Impact of the Hungarian 1956 Uprising During the Cold War Era." *Getty Research Journal* 7 (1): 197–206.
Ramos-Martínez, Manuel. 2016. "People Fever: On the Popular Passions of Peter Watkins's *La Commune (Paris, 1871)*." *Screen* 57 (2): 197–217.
Rigney, Ann. 2018. "Remembering Hope: Transnational Activism Beyond the Traumatic." *Memory Studies* 11 (3): 368–80.
Ross, Kristin. 2015. *Communal Luxury: The Political Imaginary of the Paris Commune*. London and New York: Verso.
Schmidt, Theron. 2017. "Is This What Democracy Looks Like? The Politics of Representation and the Representation of Politics." In *Performing Antagonism: Theatre, Performance & Radical Democracy*, edited by Tony Fisher and Eve Katsouraki, 101–30. London: Palgrave Macmillan.
Traverso, Enzo. 2016. *Left-Wing Melancholia: Marxism, History, and Memory*. New York: Columbia University Press.
Warner, Michael. 2002. *Publics and Counterpublics*. New York: Zone Books.
Watkins, Peter, dir. 1961. *The Forgotten Faces*. Included as a special feature on *Privilege: A Film by Peter Watkins*. London: BFI, 2016. DVD.
Watkins, Peter, dir. 1964 and 1965. *Culloden* and *The War Game*. London: BFI, 2016. DVD.
Watkins, Peter, dir. 1974. *Edvard Munch*. London: Eureka, 2007/2011. DVD.

Watkins, Peter, dir. 1999. *La Commune (Paris, 1871)*. Paris: Doriane Films, 2000. DVD.

Watkins, Peter. 2007. "Edvard Munch: A Self-Interview." DVD booklet. *Edvard Munch: A Film by Peter Watkins*, 46–67. The Masters of Cinema Series.

Watkins, Peter. 2015. *Media Crisis*. Translated by Patrick Watkins. Paris: Éditions L'Échappée.

Wayne, Michael. 2002. "The Tragedy of History: Peter Watkins's *La Commune*." *Third Text* 16 (1): 57–69.

CHAPTER 9

The Role of Digital and Public Humanities in Confronting the Past: Survivors' of Ireland's Magdalene Laundries Truth Telling

Jennifer O'Mahoney

9.1 Introduction

The Magdalene Laundries[1] are a prominent part of Irish social history, which operated as philanthropic, lay institutions in the 1700s. The Religious Orders took ownership of the institutions in the mid-1800s until the last Laundry closed in 1996. Over time, the running of the institutions became increasingly punitive, ensuring psychological and physical control of the "penitents" through strict regimes to encourage compliance. The Magdalene Laundries were used by the Irish State and Religious Orders to incarcerate girls and women who were deemed to be immoral, including unmarried mothers, victims of sexual assault, and girls referred through the criminal justice system. The Irish State and Religious Orders are gatekeepers of the "official" archives related to the Magdalene Laundries, restricting all access to the data, which has contributed to an ongoing silencing and marginalization of the women's experiences (O'Mahoney-Yeager and Culleton 2016).

Magdalene institutions were initially established in the mid-eighteenth century in Ireland (and across Europe, the US, Canada, and Australia) as asylums for poor and destitute women, primarily run by religious orders to

---

The original version of this chapter was revised: The chapter has been changed from non-open access to open access and the copyright holder has been updated. The correction to this chapter is available at https://doi.org/10.1007/978-3-031-11886-9_27

J. O'Mahoney (✉)
South East Technological University, Waterford, Ireland
e-mail: Jennifer.OMahoney@setu.ie

provide opportunities and training to the women (Luddy 2007; Smith 2007). The symbolism of a repentant Mary Magdalene was adopted by the institutions, emphasizing the role of work and penance in the forgiveness of sins. British rule ended in Ireland in 1921, after which the ten remaining Magdalene institutions in the new independent Ireland were afforded a role in contributing to the identity of the new national Irish discourse, which emphasized the moral and puritanical supremacy of Ireland in contrast to her former colonizers (Howell 2003; O'Rourke et al. 2021). The complicity of State and Church in Ireland was established from the 1920s, when the newly constituted Irish State formed its national identity based on a strong Gaelic and Catholic ethos; this complicity was formalized by the Irish State granting the control and daily operations of education, health, welfare entitlements, and religious life to the Catholic Church (O'Mahony and Delanty 2001). The complicity of Church and State in Ireland was further sanctioned by documents such as the Carrigan Report (1931), which established a state-sanctioned precedent criminalizing sex outside marriage, thus establishing a clear State attitude towards sexual immorality which targeted young women while exculpating young men (Smith 2007). Magdalene Laundries, then, provided a powerful mechanism for patriarchal control by the Irish State and Religious Orders, which deemed sexuality the primary cause of immorality in society. After 1922, the Magdalene Laundries were run solely by Catholic orders in Ireland, with the final Laundry closing in 1996.

Testimony collected by The Magdalene Oral History project (O'Donnell 2012) and the Waterford Memories Project[2] (O'Mahoney 2015) demonstrates that girls and women incarcerated in the Laundries were frequently victims of incest and sexual violence, and only a minority had given birth outside wedlock. This testimony is in stark contrast to the national narrative, which maintained that the Laundries existed to rehabilitate "fallen" women. Some had intellectual disabilities, while others had committed minor crimes or were destitute, sent to the Laundries via the criminal justice system, religious orders, or their families (O'Donnell 2012; O'Mahoney 2015; O'Rourke et al. 2021). The McAleese Report (Department of Justice 2013) confirms that the youngest to enter the Magdalene Laundries was nine years old, the oldest 89, with a median age of 20.[3]

Within the Laundries, the regime and living conditions were harsh and punitive; the girls and women were locked in, forced into hard labour (typically Laundry work) without pay, and returned by police if they escaped. The girls had their given names changed, wore a uniform, and spent the day in silence, often only permitted to vocalize in prayer. They slept in cold dormitories with no privacy, poor sanitation, and meagre food rations. Visitors were strictly discouraged and friendships forbidden, and inmates were frequently disappeared (to another Laundry, psychiatric institution, or affiliated Catholic institution) with no warning (O'Donnell 2012).

In response to lobbying the government of Ireland for two years for an investigation into Ireland's Magdalene Laundries, advocacy group Justice for Magdalenes took the case to the United Nations Committee Against Torture (UNCAT), arguing that the exploitation of the girls and women amounted to violations of their human rights. In 2011 the UNCAT requested that the Irish State investigate the allegations. The Irish Government ratified a committee, chaired by Senator Martin McAleese, to establish the facts of the Irish State's involvement with the Magdalene Laundries. The committee's report was published in 2013, and found significant State involvement in the running of the Laundries between 1922 and 1996.

The McAleese report places little import on survivors' testimony, stating that "the Committee did not make specific findings in relation to [the living and working conditions in the Magdalene Laundries], in light of the small sample of women available" (Department of Justice 2013, 50). This finding was made in the final 2013 report, despite a submission made to the McAleese Committee in August 2012 by the Justice for Magdalenes Research group consisting of a 145-page document collating evidence of State complicity, supported by 796 pages of survivor testimony (JFMR 2012). Furthermore, the archive created by the Committee for the purposes of this investigation is embargoed and not available to the general public or scholars. The Religious Orders which ran the institutions similarly refuse to release their records. This heavy restricting of the archives "points to the role of the Irish state and religious orders as gatekeepers of information and key participants in gendered violence toward survivors" (O'Mahoney-Yeager and Culleton 2016, 134–35). The archival restriction ensures that our knowledge of the Laundries continues to be fractured, as we lack a comprehensive narrative which encapsulates the interconnected cultural, social, and economic trends, which allowed the Laundries to exist in Irish society until 1996.

9.2 The Waterford Memories Project

The Waterford Memories Project (WMP) began in 2013, after the release of the "Report of the Inter-Departmental Committee to establish the facts of State involvement with the Magdalen Laundries" by the Department of Justice and Equality (the "McAleese Report"). The report was heavily criticized for being too narrow in scope, as it focused solely on establishing the facts surrounding the extent of the State's involvement with the Laundries. WMP is an oral history driven study in digital humanities, publicly documenting survivor narratives of the Magdalene Laundries in the South-East of Ireland. The project initially aimed to capture and examine the oral histories of those who lived and worked within the Magdalene Laundries and Industrial Schools located in the South-East of Ireland to address the continuing silencing of the Magdalene women and the lacuna of their experiences available to the public (O'Mahoney 2018; O'Mahoney-Yeager and Culleton 2016). The College Street Campus of the South East Technological University (my employer) was purchased in 1994, and is the former site of a convent of the Congregation of Our Lady of Charity of the Good Shepherd of Angers (commonly known as the Good Shepherd Sisters), as well as the St. Mary's Good Shepherd Laundry and St. Dominick's Industrial School.

Two events occurred around the same time in 2013, which led to the development and launch of the WMP. Firstly, I was engaged in research examining the longitudinal impact of sexual violence and met two women who described their experiences in the Magdalene Laundries. Both had been "penitents" in the Waterford Laundry, in the very building I was now working in. While I knew an Industrial School existed on the premises I never realized that the Laundry also existed on the campus. At the time, news of the the release of the McAleese Report was dominating the media. I felt compelled to understand more about the Laundries and to contribute to shining a light on what these women had experienced in these buildings where I work, which was not memorialized in any way in Waterford. I began by interviewing one of the women I met in my previous research journey. From there, participants reached out to me through word of mouth or in response to hearing me speak about the project. The project's development has been organic, in response to what survivors highlight as important. As a result, there has never been a traditional call for participants, and the recording of the women's stories is ongoing.

The project began as a minimal computing digital humanities project. I am a psychologist by training with no background in technology. I began the project with the relatively simple aim of creating a platform to amplify the women's voices and stories according to their wishes. Chen (2019) suggests that when a novice user is confronted with needing technology for a purpose they should limit to what they need to achieve, use as little infrastructure as possible, and focus on establishing the minimum viable product so that the product can be progressed quickly. Minimal computing strategies made introducing the women's stories to the public simpler. At this stage, there was no financial support for the project and I needed to record and publicly disseminate the stories of survivors. I had to displace my reliance on expertise and learn how to produce, disseminate, and preserve scholarship digitally. Over time, this minimal computing approach to the project has provided the groundwork to apply for financial support for various project outputs.

At its core, the WMP is about aiding the survivors to advance social change; as a result, digital humanities projects like the WMP are contributing to a larger discussion about how technology alters our social and cultural existences (O'Mahoney, 2022). The project brings together both the digital and public humanities to understand the Magdalene Laundries and their relevance to Irish heritage. The humanities broadly consider how we understand and document the human experience, while digital humanities considers this investigation through a digital lens. This chapter will consider the role of the WMP in contributing to affording agency to the Magdalene survivors by providing a public platform for their truth-telling efforts. The methodology of oral history narratives will be critically considered in the context of a digital humanities project. The survivors' narratives demonstrate how the oral histories have a dual purpose of providing both a way for the women to understand the meaning of their experiences, while simultaneously creating a permanent and public record of these first-hand accounts. Oral histories demonstrate a clear aim to bring history to the public which is of considerable import in addressing the absence of survivor testimony in official histories of the Laundries (Ritchie 2015, 28).

Derrida (1995) has argued that archives can be locations of violence, existing as manifestations of state power which perpetuate the silencing of marginalized voices. In this way, the inaccessibility of both the State and Religious Orders' archives act to perpetuate gendered violence against the survivors, while motivating public forgetting of the Magdalene Laundries. Developed at the intersection of oral history and digital humanities theory and practice, the WMP aims to address this gendered violence, silencing of the women's narratives, and motivated forgetting. In conjunction with other oral history work on documenting Ireland's institutions, this project will contribute to what Stuart Hall has called a "living archive of the diaspora" (Hall 2001, 89). The concept of a living archive for the WMP is one that recognizes that the project exists in perpetuity and will not reach a completion date. A living archive further encourages continued interaction and new ways of thinking about and analysing the digitized project data (as well as the rich information stored within the data itself), while protecting the data against destruction.

The concept of a living archive is not restricted to the continued use of the data in textual analyses, but also in its potential to inform arts and advocacy work. For instance, in 2016 the survivor oral histories were used as a basis for a one-day, multidisciplinary event recognizing the history and memory of the Laundries and Industrial Schools in the South-East of Ireland titled "When Silence Falls: Exploring bodily and literary memory in the Waterford Laundry." This event incorporated a live art durational performance and audio/visual installations in the former Laundry buildings, contextualized by academic talks about the Laundries. Performing arts students and professionals used the oral history testimony as a basis to design individual live performances based on themes identified in the narratives (such as incarceration, silence, etc.), focusing on how site-specific performance can be used to interpret the history of the Magdalene Laundries, revealing the social constructions of that history (O'Mahoney et al. 2021) (Fig. 9.1).

Oral histories can act to "fill in" the historical record, and the events can be recounted decades after they occur, or immediately after an event, to facilitate people's understanding of experiences of events or periods of time (Leavy 2011). But oral histories offer a lot more to scholars. Having worked in the field of Narrative Psychology for many years, I am drawing on this perspective since it affords rich opportunities to examine how people construct stories and meanings of their experiences. As a method, oral history similarly emphasizes the process of meaning-making, and is particularly appropriate for examining "subjective experiences of shifting historical periods" (Leavy 2011, 23). Survivor oral histories therefore provide powerful challenges to the official silencing of the Magdalene story. Oral histories also provide a method for considering how survivors make sense of their past by making both micro-

Fig. 9.1 The College Street Campus of the South East Technological University

and macrolevel connections between their individual memories and collective experiences of the other survivors, and to the mechanisms of the state and religious orders (O'Mahoney-Yeager and Culleton 2016). As Paul Thompson (2000, 6–7) maintains, "Once the life experience of people of all kinds can be used as its raw material, a new dimension is given to history."

However, it is what an oral history methodology offered the women who tell their stories which was of highest import to the WMP. The Magdalene women have experienced a range of physical, psychological, and financial sequelae as a result of their incarceration in the Laundries. Telling their stories publicly is "a subversive act, especially in light of powerful…forces working against it" (Sloan 2014, 273), as the women resist the collective forgetting and continued silencing of their experiences. The oral histories reflect an organized collaboration between the WMP and survivors to address the omission of survivor testimony in the official histories of the Irish State, and are maintained to bring these testimonials to the public. Gathering and analysing these oral histories was essential to documenting Ireland's cultural heritage, which is better achieved by locating the women's stories within a larger social and historical narrative.

9.3 Digital Humanities and Oral Histories in the WMP

From the outset, the Waterford Memories Project was conceptualized and contextualized as a digital humanities (DH) project, "interven[ing] in the way knowledge is produced and constituted at the particular sites where a localized power-discourse prevails" (Harvey 1989, 46). The WMP is a DH project in social justice activism. Rather than using the internet to disseminate essays, petitions, blogs, etc. regarding the experiences of the survivors of the Magdalene Laundries, the project was designed to marry scholarly investigation with activism, to "build advocacy work into the ordinary work of the humanities" (Liu 2012, 497). The project is premised on the belief that academic scholarship exists for public use and consumption. It becomes the responsibility of DH to translate the academic jargon and abstractions into intuitive, rich, and compelling projects demonstrating the public relevance and value of the humanities and DH. In emphasizing the communication (and import) of the public, the WMP has used multiple digital formats and approaches to bring the academic findings to the public, such as survivor testimony, public performances, academic articles, and educational packs for use in schools. In developing these materials, the WMP emphasizes the co-production of all materials with survivors and other stakeholders. For instance, the educational pack was launched in 2020. The first step of this project involved bringing together stakeholders to deliberate about the format and content of these multi-media resources. The group was comprised of survivors of the Magdalene Laundry; academic experts in education, psychology, culture, and media; student body representatives; a Deputy Principal/secondary school history teacher; a founding member of Justice for Magdalenes; a Librarian/archival expert; Vice-Chair of the Waterford Archaeological and Historical Society; and local artist/theatre-maker. Co-production and co-design with survivors and other stakeholders are at the heart of the project's work.

DH's emphasis on public scholarship and dissemination of digitized data afforded a framework which directly correlates with my own work in survivor advocacy and activism. It was always essential that the project was (and is) survivor-centred, ensuring that the survivors' voices inform the research project, with the centrality of ethics at all stages of the project. As Eichmann-Kalwara et al. (2018, 75) have argued, "By centering marginalized voices, scholarly institutions have the ability to send messages about who belongs in academia. The same applies to the digital humanities community." My role as Principal Investigator of the project is best perceived as platforming the women's stories and voices and promoting what Boyer (1996) calls the scholarship of engagement, where scholarship is measured by its service to the community and nation. The project website and digitization of the women's stories is a direct action towards social change, challenging the void of archival data restricted by the Irish State and Religious Orders (O'Mahoney 2018).

An extensive amount of literature has debated the meaning and parameters of digital humanities. The broad, comprehensive description of digital humanities by Hughes et al. (2020, 556) explains that digital humanities encapsulates approaches by humanities, arts, and social science scholars and a recognition that engagement with digital tools, techniques, and media can impact and alter how we produce, analyse, and disseminate research and knowledge, all of which is essential in digital humanities scholarship. While this definition emphasizes that digitization has changed how we interact with data, the role of the cultural critique embedded in digital humanities work must also be considered at all stages of a research project. Culture can be understood "as a unique meaning and information system, shared by a group and transmitted across generations, that allows the group to meet basic needs of survival, pursue happiness and well-being, and derive meaning from life" (Matsumoto and Juang 2013, 15).

Culture surrounds us, informing and framing all aspects of our lives. By extension, digital humanities work must consider the cultural context of a project (and its data) in all stages of a project. The oral history interviews of the WMP, for instance, cannot be appreciated without being framed by the culture which surrounds the stories; the economic, political, and social context of life in Ireland. Technocultures are, by extension, "the various identities, practices, values, rituals, hierarchies, and other sources and structures of meanings that are influenced, created by, or expressed through technology consumption" (Kozinets 2019, 621). The study of technocultures, then, examines the nexus of technology and culture, and the expression of that nexus in the patterns of economic and social life.

Since the 2000s, digital humanities has emerged alongside significant cultural changes and advances in technological infrastructure, which facilitated these cultural shifts. Jones (2013, 16) explains that "In this sense, the digital humanities is the humanities everted," the humanities turned inside out, where "the institutional and disciplinary changes are part of a larger cultural shift, a rapid cycle of emergence and convergence in technology and culture" (Jones 2013, 31). In other words, the digital humanities and culture are inseparable, both in theory and practice. The core potential of digitizing the humanities, then, is in the way that "the digital reshapes the representation, sharing, and discussion of knowledge" (Sample 2014, 256). The digital humanities offer a powerful method through which a wide array of data can be both represented and disseminated in a multitude of ways. Mullen (2014, 237) takes this point further, arguing that all scholars exist at some point of a digital humanities spectrum, using digital practices and concepts to some degree, where moving into the digital humanities is a "difference of degree, not kind…we're all digital humanists now."

It is clear that the development of DH is heavily interconnected with cultural, social, and economic trends, the significance of which should be considered as part of any DH project. An emphasis on culture as part of the design (and subsequent analysis and dissemination) offers the most salient framing of digital humanities for work with survivors of Ireland's Magdalene Laundries. The remainder of this chapter will consider the role of digitization in public humanities in confronting a difficult and contested past, namely, that of Ireland's Magdalene Laundries, through the survivors' own oral history testimonies. As Tam (2019, v) explains, "the advent of digital technologies has greatly impacted the way society functions and how culture is (re/)mediated, (re/)produced, consumed, interpreted, and manipulated." This chapter will therefore consider how knowledge of the Laundries is (re/)produced and disseminated in the digital age, and the relevance of this digital dissemination for confronting a difficult past through (digital) truth-telling.

9.3.1 The Benefits of a Digital Humanities Approach for the WMP

The benefits of a digital humanities approach to the project are threefold (Hughes et al. 2020): it enhances existing knowledge about the Laundries through digital tools; it enables new research which would not have been possible without digital methods; and it galvanizes new research questions and possibilities which are only possible through digital methodologies. The following will discuss each of these benefits in turn.

Firstly, a digital humanities approach to the project enhances existing knowledge about the Laundries through digital tools. In the case of the WMP, enhancing existing knowledge primarily focuses on promoting user interaction via different platforms (i.e. audiorecordings of testimony, a visual photographic tour of the former buildings, links to academic analysis, etc.). Put simply, scholars want the public to access recorded oral histories. In the majority of contexts, the participants want their stories heard. It is, therefore, essential for scholars to continue to respond to problems and adapt to new technologies which facilitate user access. Access to digitized data has become greatly facilitated by free (or low cost) programmes, website builders, and the Internet. "The Internet has, quite frankly, blown the hinges from doors of the archive, and *access* has come to have a completely different meaning" (Boyd and Larson 2014, 4). The core data of the WMP focuses on audio-visual recordings of interviews with survivors, visitors, and scholars of the Magdalene Laundries, which can be accessed publicly via the project website. Potential interviewees are given the option to have their oral histories recorded in audio-visual (.mp4) or audio format (.wav), or only in transcribed format (PDF). In my experience, participants have chosen overwhelmingly an audio-visual format. Fourteen years ago, Frisch (2006, 102) commented that scholars universally recognize that due to the data's inaccessibility, the audio-visual components of oral history data are underutilized, "unlistened to and unwatched" due primarily to issues of accessibility of the data. Fourteen years later, scholars can disseminate and make available data at the click of a button. There is a distinct advantage to seeing a person's expressions and hearing their voice, encouraging engagement from listeners. Reading a transcript does not provide us with the plethora of context associated with seeing and hearing the speaker. The richness of the audio-visual interview is a clear example of what Boyd (2014, 79) has called "the digital empowerment of the audio and video in the oral history user experience." As a method for capturing people's stories, oral histories have changed depending on what tools and technology have been available to the scholar to collect, preserve, and retell these stories (Boyd and Larson 2014). These digitization methods have helped to emphasize the importance of the role of voice in considering history and culture and, more importantly, provided a way to preserve survivor stories in times of contested histories (Fig. 9.2).

Since the WMP interviews are recorded as video files the dissemination of the oral histories via the website acts to both preserve the recording,

158   J. O'MAHONEY

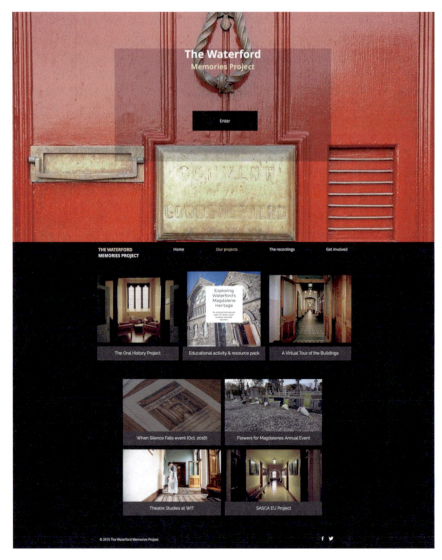

Fig. 9.2 The landing page and projects page of The Waterford Memories Project website

while maintaining the integrity of the video interview as a primary source. Respecting the integrity of the videos as a primary source has additional and essential relevance to scholars' examination of the work, as we share equal access to the same data and format. This is often not the case in disseminated interview scholarship, which typically provides brief excerpts without access to the full interview conducted. Open access to the full remit of data analysed by a scholar will allow for increased public visibility of data and analysis, increased opportunity for scholarly debate, and (ideally) increased reliability of results and findings as a result. The question of which form of recording has primacy has merit (e.g. the original audio-visual format, audio format, or transcript generated from the recording), but potentially misses the essential need for context when considering a participant's story. In the case of the WMP, it is the survivor who chooses whether the story should be audio-visual, audio, and/or text format, and not the scholar. The survivor also chooses whether to release the data immediately or to hold the interview for a predetermined amount of time, as well as whether they will use their name or a pseudonym. These are important distinctions and contribute to the preservation of the project metadata as it provides context information.

In June 2018, a two-day event in Dublin called "Dublin Honours Magdalenes" brought together 230 survivors of the Laundries. As part of this event, a formal listening exercise was held to gather views from survivors on how the Laundries should be remembered by future generations. The summary report from the exercise clearly demonstrated the women's desire to have their stories heard, so that we might learn from the past and ensure the coercive confinement they endured does not happen again (O'Donnell and McGettrick 2020, 21). Similarly, the centering of the survivors in all aspects of the WMP is essential to respecting the wishes of the survivors, and the advocacy and activism agenda of the project. Survivors have told the WMP:

> It'll take more than me to speak out because I think it's too hidden. Since I've come back, I've realised now bout us Irish, we love to think that we're loved around the world. We give a false impression about ourselves, we can't accept that we're corrupt, we're immoral…so wrong about human rights, right across the board, and then on top of it women and children's human rights. (Elizabeth)

> Well, I'd like the public to know what happened, and to know the truth, and hopefully it will never happen to any of them, or their children. Because with knowing what went on you don't know if it's still going on, because it's hidden. And that's what I think. They still kept doing it until the 70s and the 80s because it was all hidden. So when it comes out in the open, hopefully, hopefully it will never, never, never happen again. (Kathleen)

> Well, I love that it's highlighted… It's them people out there, highlighting, giving out to people out there, there is that side to it that we're grateful to, that we're thankful for. (Maureen)

It is in responding to this desire expressed by the survivors that the WMP focuses strongly on public scholarship. Today, access and usability of various interview recording formats is primarily a matter of preference rather than effort. However, recording and preserving the context of why a particular format is used contributes to preserving information which is related to interpreting the survivor narratives into the future. The project's informed consent documentation asks survivors which format they prefer (audio-visual, audio; and/or written transcript), as well as how they wish to be identified (real name versus pseudonym). Survivors are encouraged to take time to think through these options carefully as once an interview is disseminated online we cannot guarantee that someone unknown has not saved or made a copy of the recording. For this reason, the project currently has a small number of recordings which are being held (but not yet publicly released) as per survivors' wishes. Careful, protected storage of this data is essential but is also an added lens through which to understand the lifetime effects of coercive confinement, and the perpetuation of feelings of shame associated with these institutions. Thus, the benefits of a digital humanities approach to the project is clearly demonstrated in its use of digital tools to enhance stakeholder interaction with the project outputs.

The second and third benefits of a digital humanities approach to the project highlighted earlier by Hughes et al. (2020) enable new research which would not have been possible without digital methods and galvanize new research questions and possibilities which are only possible through digital methodologies. These two benefits are highly interrelated in the WMP, which has involved continued collaboration with other humanities disciplines, as well as computational and information technology fields. Two examples of project strands (an educational resource pack and an interactive map of the Waterford Laundry) to demonstrate these benefits will be considered.

A secondary aim of the WMP is to create useful educational material in order to facilitate the primary aim of recording and disseminating the survivors' narratives. The focus on the development of inclusive educational tools, which should be openly and freely available, has formed how dissemination is viewed by the project. Simply recording the narratives and placing them online does not meet the survivors' desire for "Public education, and in particular the education of school children," which was a consistent theme in the Dublin Honours Magdalenes Listening Exercise (O'Donnell and McGettrick 2020, 33). A focus on the life-long impact of a lack of education is consistent across the women who have told their stories to the WMP:

> Well I left and I didn't, I couldn't read. I used to copy like someone would be in front of me and look over but I never received an education. I was too frightened. Frightened the whole time I was there. No, I couldn't do nothing, nothing. (Martha)

> They deprived us of an education. We worked the Laundries instead of getting an education… it's very humiliating when you're sitting there with your child and they're trying to do homework and you can't do it. You cannot do it. (Deirdre)

> I wanted to be a nurse, but God help me, I thought I was a nobody, I had no confidence at all. 'Cos the nuns used to say you were a nobody, and you'll never be anything at all. They used to say it to the other poor girls, like we

were orphans, like, they used to say that to the poor girls, you know what I mean? You'll never be anything, your mother was a prostitute. (Marina)

Returning to the concept of a living archive, much digitized dissemination of the work of the WMP is about creating a repository for cultural resource materials on the study of institutional abuse, but it is also the goal of the WMP that these resources are proactively used as educational pedagogical tools. Many of the strands of the project have been publicly funded and should be openly publicly accessible, as a method of honouring the survivors' experience of being excluded from education and their emphasis on its importance.

While all aspects of the project could be deemed to have educational value, a specifically developed educational activity and resource pack designed for 16–18-year-old students and their teachers was launched in March this year[4] (O'Mahoney and McCarthy 2020). This pack uses the former Magdalene Laundry in Waterford as a case study for students and the public to explore local culture and heritage through a set of research-informed, multi-media resources. The activities in each section are designed for students to discuss, consider, question, reflect on and respond to the experiences of women in the Waterford Laundry. The pack was developed based on discussions with 13 stakeholders representing academic experts in education, psychology, culture, and media; student body representatives; a Deputy Principal/secondary school history teacher; expert in Magdalene Laundry history/member of Justice for Magdalenes; survivors of the Magdalene Laundry; a Librarian/archival expert; Vice-Chair of the Waterford Archaeological and Historical Society; and local artist/live art facilitator. The stakeholders considered the format and inclusion of primary sources (oral history interviews with survivors, podcasts with experts, etc.); secondary sources (historical records, Justice for Magdalenes Research archive, local and national library and museum archives, media coverage, etc.); and academic analysis (peer-reviewed journal articles and books, media content, etc.). The final 60-page resource pack launched on the project website in March 2020 incorporates best practice across multiple domains in education, history, psychology, and humanities and addresses many important themes such as human rights and social change via the case study of Waterford's Magdalene Laundry. The pack incorporates a range of resources from academic texts, exercises, video links, survivor testimony, music, poetry, etc., as well as appendices containing tasks for teachers to facilitate their role in engaging with the materials.

The format and design of the pack would not have been possible without new, low-cost digital methods. The pack is available in HTML5 "Flipbook" form (which can be downloaded in PDF form). A flipbook is an interactive, online publication that is designed to "look and feel" like a physical book or magazine (complete with page-turning sound effects, page shadows, etc.). The benefit for the user is the book is free and available to download from the website. Media and embedded items are clickable right from the Flipbook, which allows for a more interactive (and linked) user experience. For example, in Fig. 9.3, the user has activities to complete on the left page (where live links will take them to the assigned task material) before listening to a clip from a survivor's oral history on the right (which will play when clicked) (Fig. 9.3).

The stakeholders were involved in the process of co-creating the educational resource pack; after all, "digital Humanities = Co-creation" (Presner and Schnapp 2009, para. 23). A shared goal of oral historians and digital humanists (and, indeed, the Magdalene women themselves) is recognizing that data and information is a social asset, which should be shared and consumed by the public. Digital humanities and oral histories demonstrate a clear aim to provide public access to historical information, which is of considerable import in addressing the dearth of survivor testimony in official histories of the Laundries. In doing so, the project contributes to making visible the content of the project and a cultural heritage collection which has been hidden and inaccessible, and which continues to be contested.

A third and final example of Hughes et al.'s (2020) benefit of a digital humanities approach to the project galvanizes new research questions and possibilities which are only possible through digital methodologies. I have recently joined the Centre for INformation SYstems and TEchno-culture (INSYTE) research group at the South East Technological University as a Senior Researcher. At my initial meeting with the group I presented the work I have been doing with the Waterford Memories Project and a discussion developed about a number of architectural master plan schematics I had recently come across, mapping out the planned building changes when the Waterford

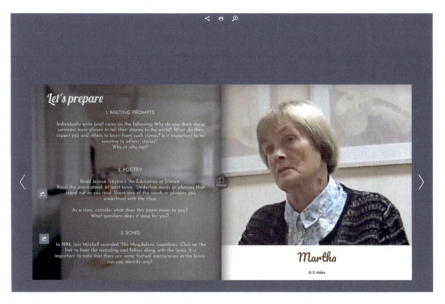

Fig. 9.3 Sample screenshot from the *Exploring Waterford's Magdalene Heritage: An activity and resource pack*

Laundry was purchased by the Waterford Institute of Technology (currently the South East Technological University) in the mid-90s. This initial discussion has now developed into a piece of research (which has been funded by the Irish Research Council), which will use Interactive Mapping to explore what Smith (2007) has called "the architecture of containment" in Waterford's Magdalene Laundry. The project brings together expertise in digital humanities (Cultural Studies, Psychology, and Information Technology), in order to develop an educational tool for learning about Waterford's former Magdalene Laundry, highlighting the import of our social history, cultural and built heritage in an interdisciplinary STEAM project. The project involves creating high definition scans of three architectural images of the footprint of the complex in Waterford. These scans will be further programmed to allow the user to interact by "clicking" on various rooms and locations on the map. This will open various resources (ranging from textual data to audio clips) for the user, providing historical information and data about the building and people who lived there. The digital map will be free and publicly available from the Waterford Memories Project website in 2021. Before engaging with IT expertise via INSYTE I would have been unable, as a solo scholar, to generate the methodology and procedure to achieve the goal of digitizing the images and encoding them into an interactive map. Digital humanities can address the intersections between society and culture with technology at multiple points, offering exciting innovations through the galvanizing of new research questions and possibilities in humanities, which are only possible through digital methodologies.

In both educational project strands discussed here, the emphasis on collaboration and interdisciplinarity in the WMP is paramount in delivering on the ethos of public scholarship and offers new and innovative methodologies for how we are to answer the survivors' calls to "protect younger generations from a similar fate" through education (O'Donnell and McGettrick 2020, 33). "It should be under social history…It should be compulsory…I'd like them to read the whole history of the Magdalene Laundries" commented one of the survivors (ibid.). However, Boyd (2014) warns us that if we do not create an enhanced user experience and adapt to accommodate changing user demands and expectations our digitized audio-visual will not be used, echoing the benefit of a digital humanities approach to the WMP, which considers the user experience offered by the interface itself. Even today, despite the availability of digitized audio-visual material, scholars prefer a transcript as the ability to seek and find specific information is expedited (Boyd 2014). An enhanced user experience is reinforced by connecting listeners to the voice (and, ideally, image) of the speaker where possible. However, rather than an "either or" situation, transcripts of the interviews, alongside the audio-visual interview, can further facilitate text-based analysis to complement other forms of scholarship.

A word of warning is required about the creation of a set of digital data for educational purposes; ease of access to digital information should not equate to an unconditional acceptance of the validity or reliability of the information. Archiving the silenced testimony of the Magdalene women is important. However, this archive is not final and complete, and does not purport to ever be complete. In this way, the WMP replicates at least some of the hierarchies and exclusions exemplified in the controlled State archives. We select and prioritize information as "experts" in order to maintain some logic on the project website and rely on our academic training and expertise, as well as financial support from funders in order to do so. The contrast of this, however, is an archive where there are no selection processes for materials uploaded and deposited, no commitment to preserve the materials, and no process to ensure validity or reliability of materials or data. As a core aim of the WMP is to make the invisible or hidden visible, the project works to ensure that the content can be shared and used in a variety of contexts, but we must remain cognizant that scholars involved in the storage of data and creation of archives will shape those archives. It is acknowledging that my role as Principal Investigator is inextricable from the project, which led to conceptualizing the WMP as a living archive. Recognizing the ongoing and open-ended nature of the work means that the project (and its metadata) is available to scholars in the future who may challenge the shaping of data and analyses, presenting alternative interpretations. As Hall (2001, 90) maintains, "it is this ongoing dispute that is the stuff of a discursive tradition." In order to meet these living archive (future) goals, the significance of recording the metadata of an archive as essential contextual information for interpretation of stored data becomes clearer.

The WMP has recently turned its attention to the value of the project's metadata, both as an avenue for additional analysis, as well as to future-proof the project data. In the context of a research project, metadata is typically created at project level and data level. The project level metadata contains the "who, what, where, when, why," providing context to understand why the data was collected and how it was utilized, while the data level includes more granular information such as the data type and acquisition details (Lorente and Castillo 2021). The WMP is in the process of working with South East Technological University Libraries to archive the WMP with the Digital Repository of Ireland (DRI). We intend to maintain the ethos and objectives of the WMP in a new digital environment, while taking advantage of the DRI's ability to disseminate its digital collections to international repositories (specifically Europeana). These steps ensure that the WMP is safely preserved and made available to a wider international community.

Clearly, metadata is an essential indicator of people's behaviour and engagement with the project's educational resources going forward. For instance, website data from April 2021 demonstrates that visitors to the site spend the most time on the recordings page, with a large rise in traffic to the activity and resource pack (very likely the result of a talk on the resource hosted by Waterford Libraries held in the same month). Almost half of the site visitors were direct referral to the website, followed by 17% from Google. Furthermore, the academic publications from the project are beginning to receive citations in academic publications, demonstrating research engagement with the materials.

Metadata is becoming increasingly important in human rights advocacy, particularly when documentation, images, and video contribute to a bank of "evidence" and access to official data is restricted. For instance, metadata about how the interviews are being used (and by who, when, and where) adds value to the original recording, and informs about how people are engaging with the project website. With this in mind, we are in the process of identifying new ways to capture and query the project metadata. For example, project student volunteers are being asked to document their experiences of working with the data and project to contribute to the overall picture of the research and archival process for future generations to consider. While the primary focus of the WMP is to safely store and provide access to the survivor testimony, metadata provides us with a guide for how to further disseminate and highlight the project and outputs, and, importantly, how to more completely capture and store the processes of the project.

9.4 Concluding Comments

The WMP was developed in response to the release of the 2013 McAleese report as a direct challenge to many of the assumptions on which Governmental digital archives are built and communicated. However, the digital and digitization of cultural phenomena have raised many complex questions about memory, knowledge production, and dissemination where "technologies offer new futures for our pasts; [and] the past and present are increasingly thought through in terms of future access and preservation" (Taylor 2010, 2). What is clear is that digital culture and digitization of the humanities have revolutionized how we produce, present, interpret, and research (Tam 2019). Some cultural texts, forms, and practices are transformed through this process, while other new cultural forms and interactions are created.

However, as Taylor (2010, 3) reminds us, "we have always lived in a 'mixed' reality' [where] the embodied, the archival, and the digital overlap and work together and mutually construct each other." Highlighting the (often neglected) central role of cultural criticism in the digital humanities is premised on interdisciplinary scholarship "so as to extend reflection on core instrumental technologies in cultural and historical directions," which at least partially involves facilitating research outside and beyond the academy in advocacy work, especially when the arts and humanities are at risk of continued systematic defunding. Examining sociocultural meaning-making is essential to the analysis of the Laundries and the digitized data of the WMP. The culture of the WMP is embedded within the wider local and national Irish culture, and understanding these various levels of embedded cultural context allows for a more informed engagement with internationally relevant issues such as institutionalization and human rights violations.

There is a time sensitive demand to record narratives of the Magdalene survivors, as the women are elderly. Our "anxiety about loss and forgetting," as Taylor (2010, 15) calls it, might explain "our current obsession with archives and the nostalgia both for embodiment and for the object…— the need to preserve not just *things* (documents, bones, fossils) but ways of *thinking* and *knowing*—sociability, affect, emotions, gestures, memories, etc., and *processes*— i.e. the ways in which we work, select, transmit, access, and preserve." Hall (2001, 92) maintains that the activity of archiving is always critical, historically located, contested, open to future challenges, and disruptive as we "re-open the closed structures into which they have ossified." The opening of any archive to continue contributions or analysis involves bearing witness to the experiences documented therein. As such, individuals visiting the digitized collection of the WMP "become part of the collective discourse of the Magdalene story" as they bear witness to the historical trauma documented in the archive (O'Mahoney 2018, 13).[5] This is essential both to challenge and grow the data in the archive, the subsequent analyses by scholars, and to ensure the women's stories do not remain "unlistened to and unwatched" (Frisch 2006, 102).

A continued analysis of the project metadata will increase our understanding of the reach and impact of the archive. These oral histories demonstrate a clear aim to bring "meaningful history to a public audience" (Ritchie 2015, 28), where the digital feeds back into the traditional textual scholarship of research and dissemination. In documenting survivor narratives, the WMP challenges the withheld archives of the Irish Government and Religious Orders and lacuna of survivor testimony, countering the continued silencing of the Magdalene women in a direct action towards social change.

Notes

1. The institutions referred to as "Magdalene Laundries" take their name from St. Mary Magdalene, whose name is associated with both contrasting histories (i.e. a reformed prostitute versus a companion of Jesus) as well as different spellings (i.e. Magdalene versus Magdalen). The image of Mary Magdalene as a "fallen" woman inspired the institutions which were initially named "Magdalen Asylums." The additional "e" in the name has dominated contemporary references to the saint and is the preferred spelling used by Justice for Magdalenes Research, a leading survivor advocacy group. This chapter has therefore adopted the spelling of "Magdalene."
2. The Waterford Memories Project site can be accessed from www.waterfordmemories.com.
3. The McAleese Report data is based on "8,852 girls and women for whom this data is available" where the largest concentration of girls and women were aged between 15 and 21 (16.5% of entrants were aged 15–16; 20.1% aged 17–18; and 19% aged 19–21) (Department of Justice 2013).

4. *Exploring Waterford's Magdalene Heritage: An activity and resource pack* is available from https://www.waterfordmemories.com/activity-and-resource-pack.
5. Naturally, this process of bearing witness has ethical implications. There is a complex debate about whether "trigger warnings" are necessary or helpful, but the WMP errs on the side of caution. We provide a content warning on the webpage for the recordings, including a link to a list of international supports.

References

Boyd, Douglas. 2014. "'I Just Want to Click on It to Listen': Oral History Archives, Orality, and Usability." In *Oral History and Digital Humanities: Voice, Access, and Engagement*, edited by Douglas Boyd and Mary Larson, 77–98. New York: Palgrave Macmillan.

Boyd, Douglas, and Mary Larson. 2014. "Introduction." In *Oral History and Digital Humanities: Voice, Access, and Engagement*, edited by Douglas Boyd and Mary Larson, 1–18. New York: Palgrave Macmillan.

Boyer, Ernest L. 1996. "The Scholarship of Engagement." *Bulletin of the American Academy of Arts and Sciences* 49 (7): 18. https://doi.org/10.2307/3824459.

Chen, Amy. 2019. "Use Minimal Computing Principles to Facilitate GBL." Minimal Computing: A Working Group of GO::DH. Accessed May 3, 2021. https://go-dh.github.io/mincomp/thoughts/2019/10/10/gbl/.

Department of Justice and Equality. 20 October 2011. *Inter-Departmental Committee to Establish the Facts of State Involvement with the Magdalen Laundries, Interim Progress Report*. Dublin: Department of Justice and Equality. Accessed June 25, 2020. http://www.justice.ie/en/JELR/Appendix%201.pdf/Files/Appendix%201.pdf.

Derrida, Jacques. 1995. *Archive Fever: A Freudian Impression*. Chicago: University of Chicago Press.

Eichmann-Kalwara, Nickoal, J. Jorgensen, and S. Weingart. 2018. "Representation at Digital Humanities Conferences (2000–2015)." In *Bodies of Information: Intersectional Feminism and Digital Humanities*, edited by Elizabeth Losh and Jacqueline Wernimont, 72–92. Minneapolis, MN: University of Minnesota Press.

Frisch, Michael. 2006. "Oral History and the Digital Revolution: Toward a Post-Documentary Sensibility." In *The Oral History Reader*, edited by Robert Perks and Alistair Thomson, 2nd ed., 102–114. London: Routledge.

Hall, Stuart. 2001. "Constituting an Archive." *Third Text* 15 (54): 89–92. https://doi.org/10.1080/09528820108576903.

Harvey, David. 1989. *The Condition of Postmodernity: An Enquiry into the Origins of Cultural Change*. Oxford: Wiley.

Howell, Philip. 2003. "Venereal Disease and the Politics of Prostitution in the Irish Free State." *Irish Historical Studies* 33 (131): 320–341.

Hughes, Lorna, Agniatus Benardou, and Ann Gow. 2020. "English Language and Digital Cultural Heritage." In *The Routledge Handbook of English Language and Digital Humanities*, edited by Svenja Adolphs and Dawn Knight, 555–67. London: Routledge.

JFMR, Justice for Magdalenes Research. 2012. *State Involvement in the Magdalene Laundries: JFM's Principal Submissions to the Inter-Departmental Committee to Establish the Facts of State Involvement with the Magdalene Laundries*. Dublin:

JFMR. Accessed July 29, 2020. http://jfmresearch.com/wp-content/uploads/2017/03/State_Involvement_in_the_Magdalene_Laundries_public.pdf.

Jones, Steven. 2013. *The Emergence of the Digital Humanities*. New York: Routledge.

Kozinets, Robert V. 2019. "Consuming Technocultures: An Extended JCR Curation." Edited by J. Jeffrey Inman, Margaret C. Campbell, Amna Kirmani, and Linda L. Price. *Journal of Consumer Research* 46 (3): 620–27. https://doi.org/10.1093/jcr/ucz034.

Leavy, P. 2011. *Oral History*. Oxford: Oxford University Press.

Liu, Alan. 2012. "Where Is Cultural Criticism in the Digital Humanities?" In *Debates in the Digital Humanities*, edited by Matthew Gold, 490–510. Minneapolis, MN: University of Minnesota Press.

Lorente, Clara Llebot, and Diana Castillo. 2021. *Research Data Services: Metadata/Documentation*. Oregon State University. Accessed May 5, 2021. https://guides.library.oregonstate.edu/research-data-services/data-management-metadata.

Luddy, M. 2007. *Prostitution and Irish Society: 1800–1940*. Cambridge: Cambridge University Press.

Matsumoto, David Ricky, and Linda P. Juang. 2013. *Culture and Psychology*. 5th ed. Belmont, CA: Wadsworth Cengage Learning.

Mullen, Lincoln. 2014. "Digital Humanities Is a Spectrum, or 'We're All Digital Humanists Now'." In *Defining Digital Humanities: A Reader*, edited by Melissa Terras, Juliannae Nyhan, and Edward Vanhoutte, 237–38. Surrey, UK: Ashgate Publishing.

O'Donnell, Katherine. 2012. *Magdalene Institutions: Recording an Oral and Archival History*. Dublin: Government of Ireland Collaborative Research Project funded by the Irish Research Council. Accessed July 3, 2020. http://www.magdaleneoralhistory.com.

O'Donnell, Katherine, and Clare McGettrick. 2020. *Dublin Honours Magdelenes Listening Exercise Report Vol 1: Report on Key Findings*. Dublin: Justice for Magdalenes Research. Accessed August 20, 2020. http://jfmresearch.com/wp-content/uploads/2020/04/DHM-Listening-Exercise-Report_Vol-1.pdf.

O'Mahoney, Jennifer. 2015. *The Waterford Memories Project*. Waterford, Ireland. Accessed August 3, 2020. https://www.waterfordmemories.com.

O'Mahoney, Jennifer. 2018. "Advocacy and the Magdalene Laundries: Towards a Psychology of Social Change." *Qualitative Research in Psychology*. https://doi.org/10.1080/14780887.2017.1416803.

O'Mahoney, Jennifer. 2022. "The Role of Born Digital Data in Confronting a Difficult and Contested Past Through Digital Storytelling: The Waterford Memories Project." *AI & Society*, February. https://doi.org/10.1007/s00146-021-01372-0

O'Mahoney, Jennifer, and Kate McCarthy. 2020. *Exploring Waterford's Magdalene Heritage: An Activity and Resource Pack*. Waterford, Ireland: The Waterford Memories Project. Accessed August 1, 2020. https://www.waterfordmemories.com/activity-and-resource-pack.

O'Mahoney, Jennifer, Kate McCarthy, and Jonathan Culleton. 2021. "Public Performance and Reclaiming Space: Waterford's Magdalene Laundry." In *Legacies of the Magdalen Laundries: Commemoration, Gender and Systems of Abuse*, edited by Miriam Haughton, Emilie Pine, and Mary McAuliffe, 31–51. Manchester: Manchester University Press.

O'Mahoney-Yeager, Jennifer, and Jonathan Culleton. 2016. "Gendered Violence and Cultural Forgetting: The Case of the Irish Magdalenes." *Radical History Review* 126: 134–46.

O'Mahony, Patrick, and Gerard Delanty. 2001. *Rethinking Irish History: Nationalism, Identity and Ideology*, 66–67. London: Palgrave Macmillan.

O'Rourke, Maeve, Jennifer O'Mahoney, and Katherine O'Donnell. 2021. "Institutional Abuse in Ireland: Lessons from Survivors and Legal Professionals." In *Nothing About Us Without Us: Giving Voice to Diversity in Criminological Research*, edited by Orla Lynch, James Windle, and Yasmine Ahmed, 67–88. Bristol, UK: Bristol University Press.

Presner, Todd, and Jeffrey Schnapp. 2009. *The Digital Humanities Manifesto 2.0*. Accessed August 2, 2020. http://manifesto.humanities.ucla.edu/2009/05/29/the-digital-humanities-manifesto-20/.

Ritchie, Donald. 2015. *Doing Oral History*. 3rd ed. Oxford: Oxford University Press.

Sample, Mark. 2014. "The Digital Humanities Is Not About Building, It's About Sharing." In *Defining Digital Humanities: A Reader*, edited by Melissa Terras, Juliannae Nyhan, and Edward Vanhoutte, 255–58. Surrey, UK: Ashgate Publishing, 2014.

Sloan, Stephen. 2014. "The Fabric of Crisis: Approaching the Heart of Oral History." In *Listening on the Edge: Oral History in the Aftermath of Crisis*, edited by Mark Cave and Stephen Sloan, 262–74. London: Oxford University Press.

Smith, J. 2007. *Ireland's Magdalen Laundries and the Nation's Architecture of Containment*. South Bend, IN: Notre Dame University Press.

Tam, Kwok-kan. 2019. "Preface." In *Digital Humanities and New Ways of Teaching*, edited by Anna Wing-bo Tso, v–vi. Singapore: Springer.

Taylor, Diana. 2010. "Save As... Knowledge and Transmission in the Age of Digital Technologies." *Imagining America*, 7. Accessed July 2, 2020. https://surface.syr.edu/ia/7.

Thompson, Paul. 2000. *Voice of the Past: Oral History*. 3rd ed. Oxford: Oxford University Press.

UNCAT (United Nations Committee Against Torture). June 2011. "Forty-Sixth Session May–3 June 2011: Consideration of Reports Submitted by States Parties Under Article 19 of the Convention." Accessed August 15, 2020. http://www2.ohchr.org/english/bodies/cat/docs/CAT.C.IRL.CO.1.doc.

Open Access This chapter is licensed under the terms of the Creative Commons Attribution 4.0 International License (http://creativecommons.org/licenses/by/4.0/), which permits use, sharing, adaptation, distribution and reproduction in any medium or format, as long as you give appropriate credit to the original author(s) and the source, provide a link to the Creative Commons license and indicate if changes were made.

The images or other third party material in this chapter are included in the chapter's Creative Commons license, unless indicated otherwise in a credit line to the material. If material is not included in the chapter's Creative Commons license and your intended use is not permitted by statutory regulation or exceeds the permitted use, you will need to obtain permission directly from the copyright holder.

CHAPTER 10

The Precarious Digital Micropublics of #MeToo: An Ethnographic Account of Facebook Public Groups and Pages

Christina Riley

10.1 INTRODUCTION

Digital public humanities is an emergent discipline seeking to reframe digital humanities scholarship as a *publicly accessible* field of inquiry. But what does this mean? Promoting inclusion and accessibility in digital public humanities projects does not simply promote open-access scholarship; it centers the role of the community from the project's onset. This becomes crucial when we consider investigations into digitally-based social movements, or social collectives that are conceived and shaped within the digital public sphere. Today's Social Movement Studies scholars are progressing closer to digital public humanities practitioners; this should surprise no one. In today's technoscape, social movements inevitably straddle both online and offline worlds; the two spheres symbiotically define and progress a people's politics. This chapter seeks to provide a model of what such a project might entail.

As a digital public humanities project, I offer a critical investigation that explores how historical social movements influence digital social movements, and, in turn, how digital movements deviate from their historical predecessors. For this examination, I will be considering how the feminist practice of consciousness-raising (C-R) has shaped the feminist digital collective, #MeToo. But first, I must differentiate MeToo the movement from #MeToo the digital collective. In 2006, grassroots activist Tarana Burke first used

---

C. Riley (✉)
George Mason University, Fairfax, VA, USA
e-mail: criley11@gmu.edu

MeToo to generate solidarity for sexual assault survivors, developing her vision of "empowerment through empathy" to explicitly support survivors of color. In 2017, #MeToo as a hashtag re-emerged in response to a Tweet by actress Alyssa Milano, quickly culminating into a massive global viral event that documented the prevalence of sexual violence. Undoubtedly, #MeToo the feminist digital collective would not exist had it not been for the vital efforts of Burke and others in their establishment of MeToo healing networks. Burke's "empowerment through empathy" modality has crucially influenced the tenor and content of this digital collective. To best distinguish Burke's organizing from the #Metoo feminist digital collective of 2017, I will be incorporating the representative hashtag to differentiate the two eras of MeToo activism. Further, I must note that I am using the phrase "feminist digital collective" to designate a digital group that has coalesced around women-centric concerns like sexual harassment in the workplace and sexual assault or rape. The phrase does not directly imply that all individuals connected through using the #MeToo hashtag are feminists, per se.

In this chapter, I argue that #MeToo's digital virality enabled Tarana Burke's grassroots movement to become a feminist activism. Yet, critical analysis of digital virality often centers the organizational processes of networked coordination while more qualitative assessments considering localized impacts are often left behind. While it is true that big data assessments of #MeToo have proven invaluable when charting the hashtag's geographic accretion, associated trending topics and hashtags, and sentiment analysis, it is also the case that big data researchers all too often lose the human through such explorations. Emphasis is instead placed on aggregates—sizeable chunks of a digital audience that can be dissected, defined, analyzed, and "engaged" with. When considering the already-precariat group of sexual assault survivors, such macro-analyses threaten to overlook digitally induced perils that jeopardize these human actors. I want to briefly consider my own "unsuccessful" digital ethnography to emphasize how its "failure" underscores the need for more critically compatible investigations to safeguard the interests and health of the digital participants involved, particularly those from precarious and/or underserved groups. I argue that though my investigation was ultimately botched in completing my objective, there is still valuable knowledge unearthed through the process. *Data Feminism*'s (2020) Catherine D'Ignazio and Lauren F. Klein call for an intersectional feminist approach to data research that emphasizes theories of data justice which include critical reflexivity (60). The foundation for reflexivity is *transparency* which is the "new objectivity," a phrase coined by AI researcher and technologist, David Weinberger. Data transparency is a process that begins by "… activating the value of multiple perspectives to acknowledge the partiality of your own. This means disclosing your project's methods, your decisions, and… your own positionalities" (D'Ignazio and Klein 2020, 136). In line with a data feminist framework, it is my hope that by sharing my research process as well as the dangers I encountered, I may prevent others from combatting such obstacles.

In the critical investigation that follows, I will demonstrate how a digital social movement, the feminist digital collective #MeToo, benefits from a digital public humanities approach. I intend to produce key insights that may be directly employed by and for the broader #MeToo community's benefit, understanding that this macro-community is ultimately composed of smaller, on-the-ground, localized groups, or what I have termed *micropublics*. Methodologically, I am invested in progressing a publicly accessible, "little-data" or folk data position. I study the largest feminist digital collective, #MeToo, by closely examining Facebook Public Groups and Pages through a digital ethnographic approach that will maintain anonymity for those involved, prioritizing data justice over data collection. I analyze these groups' histories, online interactions, emotional and affective atmospheres, and threats/dangers. My previous research on earlier feminist digital collectives like #YesAllWomen demonstrate how past feminist strategies, particularly C-R, afforded feminist groups an advantage in gaining visibility and membership through social media channels. For this analysis, I wish to consider the precarity of #MeToo's unfolding in more enclosed, intimate digital community spaces (or micropublics) like Facebook Groups and Pages. Ultimately, I find these online spaces as disrupting fundamental feminist work like C-R building by greatly imperiling their members' material, psychological, and even physical well-being.

I will initially outline applicable historical feminist theories, strategies, and tensions to contextualize #MeToo's place within the broader feminist movement. I then provide a brief overview of W. Lance Bennett and Alexandra Segerberg's concept of digitally connective action (2013) as well as Zizi Papacharissi's work on digitally-based social movements and affect (2014), situating #MeToo within the broader sphere of online activisms to reveal its form and structure. Finally, cycling through various #MeToo-focused Facebook public Groups and Pages, my investigation uncovers a world fraught with precarity, exposing victims of sexual trauma to harassment, misinformation, and isolation while concurrently exploiting Group and Page moderators through their digital and emotional labor. Rather than creating a feminist-inspired space akin to second-wave feminist-era C-R sessions, these digital micropublics greatly endanger sexual assault survivors who are seeking community, refuge, and valid information sharing.

Currently, there are fewer than 100 public #MeToo-focused or associated Facebook Groups and Pages. One may find these digital micropublics also on listservs, chatgroups, Twitter hashtag communities (like #BlackTwitter), and Reddit Threads; these digital micro-communities differ from broader digital publics in both magnitude and rhetoric. Twitter coheres millions instantly through the utilization of a hashtag. Digital micropublics mimic on-the-ground local communities not only because they are smaller in scale, but they further offer the promise of understanding, familiarity, and trust among members expected in more confined communities. Unfortunately, my analysis of these spaces shows them as more deceptive and/or volatile than their offline counterparts. In the face of such instabilities, we may ask ourselves, how does the digital terrain itself not only build-on, but challenge and disrupt past feminist efforts? And equally pressing—can something even resembling a feminist or group solidarity be achieved in these technocapitalist, neoliberalized environments? Answers to these questions unearth what loyalties feminist approaches prioritize, and how these reverberations move in and among our networked worlds.

10.2 Feminist Collectives, Consciousness-Raising, and the Promise of Solidarity

Women's Studies scholars and feminist activists alike have persistently grappled with the dynamic complexities of collectivity since the movement's inception. Debates over how to form a feminist collective have often been framed in terms of achieving a feminist "solidarity;" yet the application of this term has proven so polarizing that it has been understood as both a boon and blasphemy for the movement. In 1851, Sojourner Truth's "Ain't I A Woman?" speech at the Women's Rights Convention famously elucidated the interlocking nature of oppression by vocalizing, sharing through narration, how her own embodied, lived experience of womanhood was vastly dissimilar to her white female peers. By doing so, not only did she deny her erasure from the burgeoning feminist movement, but she further bucked the conventions that ensured her silence. And perhaps most importantly, the emboldening power of Truth's words found resonance among other women's experiences, igniting a collective feminist spirit that soon became the hallmark of what many refer to now as the "first-wave" of feminism. This early twentieth-century movement became localized in specific causes (right to vote), organizations (American Equal Rights Association), and strategies (petitions, marches), concretizing such collective dynamism.

Not long after achieving the right to vote, many women were soon forced to occupy economic positions traditionally held by men who were now in short supply due to First and Second World War drafts. As soldiers returned to their abandoned economic roles, women were forced back into the domestic sphere. Feminism's "second-wave" slowly began to foment as many women felt unsatisfied in these traditional roles of wife and mother. Feminist groups began to coalesce again, but this time greater attention was allotted to the development of grassroots strategies beyond marches and protests. 1960s feminist "rap" groups engaged in C-R sessions which took inspiration from previous radical left social movements like Mao Tse-Tung's efforts to elevate Chinese women's political consciousness to encourage their membership in the National Revolutionary Army (Striegel 1975, 17) as well as the civil rights movement which included "…Southern revival-style mass meetings at which Blacks got up and 'testified' about their own experiences of oppression" (Brownmiller, para. 14). According to socialist feminist Juliet Mitchell, feminist C-R was "…the process of transforming the hidden, individual fears of a woman into a shared awareness of the meaning of them as social problems, the release of anger, anxiety, the struggle of proclaiming the painful and transforming into the political (2015, 67)." The second-wave feminist's mantra of the "personalization of the political" underscored this transformation of women's private pain from social isolation and subjugation into a point of political activation. This sharing of feelings and experiences surrounding patriarchic oppression kickstarted the politicization of many women across the country, uniting and organizing into a revamped Western feminist social movement.

By the late 1960s, many feminist C-R groups resembled what social movement scholars may term a "collective": these are leaderless groups where all members are on level footing and share equivalent workloads. Soon, C-R feminist collectives became a key element in feminist grassroots mobilization, offering a non-hierarchical way of organizing group members which not only challenged established patriarchal hierarchies, but also created a communal space for more women's voices to be heard. Despite a seeming lack of structure, C-R collectives still had broad-spectrum rules: (1) an individual must speak personally, (2) One should not interrupt a person and listen closely, (3) One should not judge, criticize or give advice to a member concerning her experiences, thoughts or feelings, and (4) There must be absolute confidentiality among the group members (Striegel 1975, 47). C-R feminist collectives tended to be leaderless, smaller, localized groups of women from the same neighborhood, community, or background. Generally speaking, new members were discouraged as these spaces sought to encourage trust and intimacy among members.

Feminist C-R collectives brought many women together in local, communal storytelling networks where members joined to share their histories and experiences. These meetings underscored the importance of emotional exchanges and candid dialogues among members. The credo of the "personal is political" politicized these affective, narrative-sharing sessions, turning "political therapy" sessions into feminist action. National feminist groups like National Organization of Women sought to consolidate these more intimate local groups into a larger feminist "sisterhood" network, often striving to erase boundaries among members in hopes to initiate a group coalescence around "central" feminist aims. Instead, a deficit narrative developed, silencing the perspectives of many marginalized women's groups within the movement itself. To reclaim a voice and space in feminism, intersectionality emerged as a feminist practice necessarily complicating the notion of feminist solidarity, striving to progress feminism into a global, transnational movement with increasingly diverse participation. Intersectionality understands social justice problems (like gender inequality) as overlapping with other injustices (such as racial inequality), creating intersecting, interrelating levels of oppression.

As Black and lesbian groups like the Combahee River Collective and The Furies continued utilizing C-R strategies to mobilize disenfranchised groups, their meetings often lacked participation from White, Western, middle-class women; the reverse was often true for predominately middle-class, White feminist rap groups. It seemed as if solidarity only came in certain forms, reserved for certain groups. For many intersectional, transnational, and postcolonial feminists, the term had become a dangerous abstraction, promoting essentializing strictures and preserving Western hegemonic entrenchment. Despite this, C-R approaches continued to play a foundational role in validating women's oppression through expression, making visible patriarchic violences like sexual harassment, and offering the possibility of connection through communication.

It is this feminist struggle over the often mythologized "sisterhood of solidarity" that has engendered a productive instability in today's network society. Rather than such precarity thwarting feminist work, digital environments have proven fertile ground for reinvigorating and reworking feminism's battles against the essentializing erasures of historical feminisms. To be certain, feminist digital collectives do not quite resemble the C-R feminist groups which gathered in living-rooms and rec centers throughout the 1960s. Rather, these groups are global networks of individuals who cohere around affectively-induced, spontaneous appeals that center women-centric issues in the digital public sphere. Some of these digital participants consider themselves feminists while others do not; some members value group "unity" over diversity while others understand intersectional emphasis as the foundation for solidarity. Rather than these differences within the collective threatening the end of the digital campaign or movement, the instantaneous, broad-sweeping, exponentializing nature of online interactions facilitates future feminist openings; just as one collective ends, another may begin.

10.3 What Is a Digital Collective?

In 1995, less than 1% of the world's population had dial-up internet connectivity with half of this population residing in the United States. By the first decade of the twenty-first century, faster broadband technologies brought personal computers into many Western homes; in 2020, nearly half of the world's population had internet access.[1] Digital connectivity has revolutionized the way that we communicate, both at an inter/personal and group level. On-the-ground social struggles began to expand into digital terrain, enabling new forms of activism(s) with a broader, accelerated outreach potential. Termed digital activism, this includes any activist effort that occurs in or is enabled by new media technologies. Digital activism relies on new media for information dissemination, networking, airing of grievances, and group construction as well as its organization and mobilization. Instantiations of digital activism include hashtag activism, GoFundMe appeals, listserv groups, sharing of online video footage (as a means of citizen surveillance or information dispersal), or hacking attacks/information leaks.

Digital activism also includes "crowd" events termed "collectives" by W.L. Bennett and Alexandra Segerberg (2013); these are coherent, defined online groups that are not managed by a particular leader or organization. They often sprout spontaneously around expressive appeals and interconnected, chained narration. Bennett and Segerberg found that the coherence of digital collectives was enabled by "connective actions," coordinated via information sharing practices among peers. These exchanges are often linked to material social struggles, political institutions, and discourses; however, initial participation in digital collectives does not revolve around tactical initiatives unlike most on-the-ground activist collectives. The semiotic association utilized by digital collectives is expressed by URLs and/or hashtags which maintain the coherence of the digital discourse. Bonilla and Rosa (2015, 5) further describe the usage of hashtags like #MeToo as not merely performing a search function, but as a mechanism to categorize a mentality or state of being. They describe this process of linking oneself to others as "indexing." #MeToo the feminist digital collective was formed through digitally connective actions induced by the sharing of experiences of sexual harassment or assault to both support those that suffered and to garner visibility around the issue.

Indisputably, the last decade has produced ample scholarship regarding digitally-based social movement formation. Much of this research emphasizes how digital networks improve communication practices, quickly and broadly mobilizing and coordinating individuals as well as efficiently assembling movement resources. Others, such as the originator of the term "slacktivism," media scholar Ethan Zuckerman (2013), maintain that forms of digital activism are lazy modes of participation which forgo emphasis on more pressing offline activities like street canvassing or community volunteering. Lisa Blackman's *Immaterial Bodies* (2012) contends that a new sort of hyper-responsive collectivity becomes possible with digital activism: "What we witness in the twenty first century is the transformation of 'the crowd' into a series of more flexible, adaptable and mobile entities" (26). When discussing the role of crowd communication, Blackman writes of the blurred boundaries between self and other, where action is often propelled in ways of feeling or affect rather than explicit expression or directives (27). Earlier crowd psychology theorists would have termed such behavior as an almost telepathic exchange, the riotous contagion that makes animals of wo/men. Instead, when employing an affective framework, the bodily transmission of information becomes more "mimetic" (32), an almost neurocognitive impulse to align with others. To put Blackman in conversation with #MeToo's growth, this theory suggests that many of those who shared #MeToo messages may have done so via an affective triggering which located feelings like anger or anxiety in particular moments in time, in people or events. Thus, it would be incorrect to assume that everyone who shared #MeToo messages explicitly wished to take part in coordinated feminist action. Rather, many may have been prompted to share #MeToo due to the surfacing of heightened affective states or feelings of emotional similitude which associated them with #MeToo-centered social networks or content.

Like Blackman, Zizi Papacharissi's *A Private Sphere* (2010) understands digital media as a tool for expression that can elicit narratives of liberation and agency (14). Utilizing the Habermasian concept of the "public sphere," Papacharissi claims that digital media has drastically altered the nature of our political worlds. She writes, "Mobile tech allows for a new private/public sphere – I argue that in this private sphere citizens feel more secure in preserving their individual autonomy and the integrity of their civic identity, and in control of their civic fate" (22). She understands digital media as convergent technology that grants autonomy via digital medias' expanding platforms for social expression, interaction, and control on individualized levels (111). Convergence is a term utilized in media ecology, adopted by theorists such as Henry Jenkins (2008) to describe the ways in which media consumers become media producers. Social medias create a certain hybridity of public and private space. Thus, the digital citizen is perhaps less political (for they are not completely engaging in the public sphere as a political subject), but more individualized, or "autonomously defined" (Blackman 2012, 162).

Papacharissi's *Affective Publics* (2014) studies affect and emotion and their role in social media; specifically, she is interested in how these responses direct social media transformations which can then be utilized to better recognize technological and sociopolitical changes. Papacharissi describes affect as "…the energy that drives, neutralizes, or entraps networked publics" (2014, 7), or prediscursive intensities which abound in digital communication. Papacharissi then defines affective publics as "networked public formations that are mobilized and connected or disconnected through expressions of sentiment" (125). Her methodology includes both deep (rhetorical, linguistic) and network analysis; through this mixed-methods approach, Papacharissi seeks to discern how affect creates politics on social media. Through her case studies, social media-generated movements like the Arab Spring enable politics by generating emergent subjectivities that align to form new "networked," interrelated social worlds. Her research material includes a collection of tweets created during the Egyptian uprising of 2008 (280,000 tweets) as well as the Occupy movement (150,000 tweets), and other digital rhetoric created for what she terms "storytellings of the self" (or apolitical Twitter trends). Papacharissi utilizes a historical materialist framework, connecting these digital media artifacts to their historical context to better understand how these points of connection emerge.

Yet, convergent technologies are not wholly democratizing and empowering. Papacharissi (2014, 43) is not ignorant that, "Information communication technologies further augment these tendencies by enabling locational surveillance of private behaviors through mobile phones, digital video recording systems and other household devices, and challenging the meaning of private property within regulatory frameworks that do not legally address privacy in its entirety." Despite the stripping of user privacy and discreet data collection emboldened by engagement in this new private/public sphere, the new digital subject understands digital technology as recasting citizenship as that which can be better realized. Thus, digital citizens are more emboldened to question authority and revolt. She writes, "The citizen of new media associates citizenship primarily with autonomy, control and the ability to question authority, and secondarily with the ability to do so collectively" (163). Papacharissi understands the collective as still within the purview of the digital citizen; furthermore, networked involvement emphasizes connections rather than struggles which reconsiders traditional Marxist approaches to interrogating history and social change. As we shall see in #MeToo Facebook Groups, many members have joined in hopes to instigate social change with little attention paid to surveillance or privacy concerns that such digital participation often propagates.

As this brief survey illustrates, Social Movement and New Media scholars alike found promise in digital terrain as an opportunity to establish more effectual, widespread social change. Considering #MeToo specifically, the promise of digitality offered possibility for a feminist political agenda that could overcome the confines of corporeality. Women could now evade the restrictions placed on them in their material existence by operating online, taking advantage of the anonymous, open-source configuration of digital networks. Additionally, single-issue as well as multimodal activist efforts could operate across an array of women's concerns creating potential for greater networked collectivity among diverse feminist efforts. It is this intertwining and networking of individuals, associations, and campaigns that characterize a vital, flexible, and diverse feminist digital collective. It positions women as a robust threat to patriarchal control via networked power diffusion. The potential for freedom found in escaping sexualization and objectification—materially and historically imposed—allows feminists to reaffirm control over their own spaces and bodies that had been historically usurped by patriarchic (hegemonic, colonial, racist) regimes.

10.4 #MeToo as a Feminist Movement?

But perhaps here we must pause. Online crowd events which engender group coalescence around an affective appeal—such as a provocative hashtag like #MeToo—are constituent of but cannot fully characterize the larger social movement that they may support. Rather, a digital event like #MeToo operates alongside the broader feminist movement, actively constructing a climate and a rhetoric around sprouting feminist appeals. Tarana Burke initially created the MeToo hashtag to publicize her grassroots feminist organization; utilizing #MeToo to draw support for an on-the-ground black feminist group exemplifies localized action that bolsters the larger black/feminist movement. But what of the millions of individuals who are not actively working to further feminist causes in their day-to-day lives, but did Tweet #MeToo? Are they members of the feminist movement? Motivations matter in expressions seeking social change; undoubtedly, some Tweeted #MeToo ironically, antagonistically, or apathetically. Some #MeToo Tweeters may not identify as feminists.

Such complexities of digital collectives cause many critics to charge digital activism as armchair activism or "slacktivism." But these assaults understand digital activism as somehow divorced from its material effects, forgetting that what happens online cannot be decoupled from what happens offline.

Digital activism and/or digital collectives can manifest material change in a myriad of ways. I previously demonstrated how #YesAllWomen was a therapeutic tool for many victims of sexual violence. #MeToo-inspired activisms, both on and offline, in the US and abroad, have successfully motivated visible feminist dissent around workplace sexual harassment, producing state and corporate legislation enhancing workers' rights.[2] Both #YesAllWomen and #MeToo digital collectives engendered constructive conversations across cultural and geographic boundaries, shaping our collective understandings of not only patriarchy and sexual violence while connecting #MeToo participants through digital discourse. Many argue that #MeToo has laid the groundwork for a tidal wave of new women politicians as seen in the U.S. congressional elections of 2019 and 2020. There are more women in the U.S. Senate and House of Representatives than there have ever been; many female elected politicians have attributed their entrance into the political arena as directly inspired by feminist digital collectives like the Women's March of 2017. A day after the Women's March, Emily's List conducted a training session in Washington, DC, to help women learn the logistics of entering into various types of political office. Over 500 women attended while an additional 500 crammed the waitlist. This notable peak in participation "speaks to the fact that this march was not just a day of action, but the start of months or years of action."[3]

Further measurable effects of #MeToo include the development of state legislation banning non-disclosure agreements that include sexual harassment, increased efforts to actively test and update rape kits, and improved worker protections for sexual harassment claims. Such concrete political and legislative change is not only unfolding in the U.S., but #MeToo's reach arguably has had the greatest global impact of all previous instances of feminist digital activisms. Iran is currently undergoing a parliamentary vote on a bill that criminalizes violence and sexual abuse against women.[4] Marlène Schiappa, inspired by #BalanceTonPorc ("Expose Your Pig") wrote a comprehensive bill on sexual harassment which was passed by French parliament in August of 2018; this bill protracted the statute of limitations for sex crimes, creating new sanctions for cyberstalking and street harassment.[5] In Morocco, #MeToo reportedly reinvigorated support for new legislation on violence against women, criminalizing sexual harassment as well as forced marriage and domestic violence.[6] Countries spanning the world over, from Mexico, Colombia, China, Japan, South Korea, Poland, India to Australia have witnessed notable on/offline protests directly connected to the #MeToo hashtag.

10.5 C-R Work Online

To assert that such political participation influenced by #MeToo can be decoupled from #MeToo's digital conversations overlooks the compelling impact of the feminist practice of C-R. I would further assert that the very qualities of feminist C-R work readily blend with the nature and scale of digital communication. Social media platforms like Facebook and Twitter encourage the production of identity communicated through short expressive appeals seen via Tweets, comments, shares, hashtags, or various other messaging formats. This construction of identity is intentionally cast forth into the digital polis, spawning ever-expansive connective actions. In his 2015 work, *Thumbelina*, sociologist Michel Serres asserts that connective action is primarily characterized by the personalization of all matters and topics, open to all by the multiplicity of entry points afforded by digital technologies. Thus, we may consider digitally connective action and the construction of a networked collective as not only expansive in nature but continually in-process, evolving.

Intriguingly, digitally connective actions featuring the *expression* and *sharing of* the self are also the fundamental features of C-R. As previously discussed, C-R sharing sessions were considered political therapy by feminists of the 1960s and 70s. The political aim of C-R meetings was to connect the personal to the political; this was achieved through the sharing of personal stories, feelings, and experiences, and then the connection of these states and experiences as influenced by patriarchal institutions. Women's Liberation Movement founding member, Pam Allen (1970), outlines the C-R group process as undertaking personal narrative-sharing to illustrate to members how interwoven women's histories were, underscoring the shared sociological root of women's oppression. Once the structural nature of women's oppression became elucidated, the analysis of this oppression was then meant to stimulate women into political action, aided by "abstractions" which sought to then universalize woman's experience. What is extraordinary about the C-R process is that it is only by a group member's self-expression that they are then determined a political agent and simultaneously connected to the larger group. The C-R "self" may then be considered as an expressive force radiating outward, only gaining form and definition through its communication.

This is not unlike the process of Tweeting, or sharing a Facebook status with your community. As previously discussed, #MeToo Tweets are characterized by individuals sharing stories of sexual assault, discrimination, and other patriarchic violence in social media environments. The rhetorical practice of including #MeToo instantly connects one's message to all past and even future #MeToo shares. If one were to think of the #MeToo online community as only defined after the second #MeToo message was shared, then this must also mean that as one expresses oneself with the tag #MeToo, one simultaneously enters into a distinct digital group solely through the process of expressing and sharing of the personal.

#MeToo and C-R groups engender the formation of the subject through its expression, but integral distinctions must also be made between these two collectives. We know that C-R strategies adopted by second-wave feminists composed only one aspect of the social movement's organization, albeit a vital one. But while C-R efforts worked to construct not simply a collective, but a politicized, *feminist* collective, the same cannot be said for #MeToo. There are countless examples of cyber trolls who have used #MeToo with the intention to hurt, criticize, or ridicule the #MeToo community while others may have Tweeted #MeToo but do not identify as feminist. As stated earlier: to say that everyone who Tweeted #MeToo is a feminist would be woefully inaccurate. But, it also cannot be ignored that #MeToo Tweets galvanized and centered feminist concerns in the public sphere.

One approach to making sense of this discrepancy between C-R work and the #MeToo digital collective would be to chart the ways these two group dynamics differ, and then compare the potential effects of these variances. To do this, we must first go back to the late 60s' living room C-R session. These rather informal meetings were often attended by neighbors and local community members, implying a certain homogeneity among members. Though you might not necessarily know everyone in the group, you most likely knew "of" everyone in the group. Such communal proximity generates a certain level of accountability among members.

As outlined before, further C-R rules include: you do not interrupt when others are speaking; you do not judge what members share. Much C-R literature suggests staying away from advice and orienting others towards self-help. Perhaps most important to note—C-R groups were not one-off meetings which then ushered members into the feminist movement directly. Rather, they were considered *working groups* which met weekly or monthly, but consistently, allowing members to develop familiarity and trust among each other.

This is certainly not the case with #MeToo hashtag users. This digital collective, unlike past feminist C-R collectives, requires no commitment, shared community, or aligned political ethos. Utilizing #MeToo to share a story of patriarchic oppression may collectively produce an opening for a feminist politics to emerge, but this is not always the case. In fact, I have found evidence of the contrary. Collection and analysis of more intimate #MeToo-centric online groups suggest that these spaces may engage in narrative sharing as a means to connect individuals to one another and perhaps feminism, but cannot provide the security of previous local C-R feminist collectives. As I hope to illuminate, though C-R tendencies may behoove a feminist politics to emerge online, #MeToo's digital sharing sessions can significantly imperil those involved. The future of feminism requires us to educate ourselves on how our histories resurface online as well as how our online worlds destabilize our future(s).

10.6 THIS IS NOT YOUR LIVING ROOM, OR THE DANGERS OF #MeToo FACEBOOK GROUPS

Integrating a data justice framework as well as recognizing the fruit of affective dissonance I encountered as a researcher, I would like to briefly describe my abandoned digital ethnography of Facebook's public Groups and Pages centered on #MeToo.[7] The Facebook Group is a digital space meant for users with common interests where they can share information or knowledge, generate content, and communicate with members. Any person can create a group about any topic, cause, or event. Facebook Groups are categorized by topic and level of privacy (public, private, secret). They are distinguished from Pages because the latter is geared towards increasing follower count, often utilized by businesses to drum up new customers. Currently, Facebook's algorithm prioritizes publishing from Facebook Groups as these publications are displayed on the user's main feed while Page posts are relegated to the "Community" section.[8] Thus, the more you interact with a Group, the more the Group's content is displayed in your general feed. Some have posited that this algorithmic change is in response to Facebook's "fake news" controversies of 2016; people are less inclined to trust and engage with businesses or brands, preferring more "localized" content from friends, family, and groups.[9] Facebook's Groups have been constructed to represent ways of interacting with others that one may encounter in the material world, something akin to community groups.

However, as a recent *Wired* headline warned Americans, "Facebook Groups Are Destroying America."[10] Facebook Groups have come under fire as the circulation of misinformation continues to exponentially swell in the digital sphere; currently, I am writing in Washington, DC, where only a year ago, QAnon conspiracy-driven rioters took the Capitol building under siege. To be blunt, the circulation of misinformation is no longer taken lightly. Facebook's platform has arguably felt the sting of public backlash since 2018's congressional hearings which investigated Facebook's data privacy leaks and the 2016 Russian election interference scandal. Facebook's response to the bad press? Let's go private. In a 2019 blogpost, Zuckerberg wrote, "Many people prefer the intimacy of communicating one-on-one or with just a few friends."[11] For many, it would seem as if Facebook was investing in the appeal and safety of digital micropublics to quell the proliferation of misinformation. Seemingly, a digital micropublic would produce a similar environment proffering the sense of community and intimacy that feminist C-R spaces required.

But as the Facebook congressional hearings demonstrated, online privacy is a deceptive term, particularly when this privacy occurs through the largest social networking platform in history. Instead of security, Facebook's pivot to privacy and community ethics also endangers users, particularly those drawn to the platform seeking to develop a *trusted* community of friends and peers. What is more, as Facebook's first director of monetization, Tim Kendall, testified to Congress in 2018, the platform's business model has been driven principally by increasing users' levels of *engagement*, the highly sought after special formula enabling the platform to accrue profitable user data. Heightened social media engagement can prove a very powerful tool, attracting public opinion to instantaneous appeals, sensational headlines, or something more sinister. Engagement proves particularly perilous when individuals are sharing misinformation which is false with the intention that it not only deceives, but engenders action grounded on inaccurate evidence. Misinformation shares a common linguistic root with disinformation which also translates to false information shared to deceive or counter public opinion. Disinformation is not limited to the digital age; many may recall the Soviet claim in 1985 that the US invented AIDS. It is Facebook's fixation on engagement that so precisely illustrates what Marxist feminist Jodi Dean (2009) had described as communicative capitalism, or new media's tendency to perpetuate capitalist exploitation rather than proliferate democratic values.

So, how do you generate increased engagement on a social media platform? It turns out that it is not so different than real life. Consider an impetuous child who wants to catch someone's attention, say a person who is actively ignoring them—the child will most likely escalate their attempts at engagement to stimulate a response. They may start insulting the person, or perhaps say something controversial or provocative. Facebook's psychologists suggested similar ploys to increase content responsiveness. In an investigative report from May of 2020, *WSJ* obtained internal documentation from the corporation which acknowledged how, "...Our algorithms exploit the human brain's attraction to divisiveness... If left unchecked [Facebook's algorithms would serve] more and more divisive content in an effort to gain user attention and increase time on the platform" (Horwitz and Seetharaman 2020). Thus, divisive messaging was algorithmically prioritized on Facebook, ensuring that disruptive content fully saturated the platform's communication channels. Of course, regulation of communication on Facebook is only considered acceptable in the most extreme instances of violence; generally, free speech rules the scene.

While most user sharing and messaging occurs among one's chosen contacts, Facebook is currently pivoting to increasing user participation through the Facebook Public Groups feature. If one were to share a status publicly, their status would be mostly viewable to one's established network as well as accounts that have been algorithmically prioritized as potentially engaged parties. But Facebook Public Groups broaden the level of participation from users without seemingly forcing unfamiliar content on users. It provides a sense of belonging for users because they chose to take part in a particular Public Group. Again, the term micropublic captures this sense of *chosen publicity*, more intimate than the general public sphere while concurrently maintaining shared publicity. Thus, Facebook Public Groups appear reassuring through the users' elected membership. According to Facebook, "Our goal is to grow diverse perspectives and increase authentic conversations across Public Groups, while giving admins the tools they need to keep their groups safe and the quality of conversations high."[12] Objectively, this sounds like an ideal venue for a feminist C-R setting; undoubtedly, many activist groups have comparable verbiage in their mission statements or embedded in grant applications. But what this statement more concretely acknowledges is that Facebook's content regulation is the responsibility of admins who are not required to undergo training, nor are they required to be discipline experts or elected representatives. Rather, anyone who starts a group, public or private, is an admin of the group.

Again, what separates Public Groups from Private or even Secret Facebook groups is the "open" membership access; Public Groups are *so* accessible that they can even be accessed *outside* of Facebook's platform. Currently, Facebook is updating Public Groups to let non-group members comment or post in the group without even joining the group. Facebook asserts that such developments ensure that Public Groups are as "inclusive" as possible; in this way, they stand distinct from Facebook's Private Groups. Group admins do have the ability to manage who posts or comments in groups with Facebook recently unveiling a "post approval" option which can then be algorithmically managed by an "Admin Assist" feature which will flag certain types of content for the Admins' closer inspection.

Facebook Pages are positioned as oppositional to Facebook profiles though you do need a Facebook profile to create a Page. Facebook Pages are intended for public-facing individuals, businesses, causes, or organizations. Pages are meant to engage customers and fans; when someone likes or follows a Page, they will start seeing updates from that Page in their News Feed; this is in contrast to Profiles where friends must be accepted. Pages have a slightly different layout and capabilities; for example, they do not have chat features though individuals can send messages to Pages. Facebook Pages are often used for public figures like politicians; President Joe Biden has a Facebook Page which can be integrated with further features like Events, Live Broadcasts, Groups, etc. Facebook Pages are envisaged as a civic resource and may be then conceptualized as more public-facing spaces than Facebook Public Groups though, functionally, both features generate content that is user-elected and publicly accessible. Of course, current digital privacy legislation permits the mining of all publicly-facing social media data by data analytics companies. This data can then be used for everything from marketing purposes, to the shaping of public infrastructure projects to determining who may receive bank loans or secure healthcare policies.

Publicly available social media engagement also provides fodder for cyberbullying and trolling, cyber hacking, and the emboldening of reactionary digital cultures. Particularly since the election of former President Donald Trump, many American women have felt anxiety regarding the quickly evolving incel movement composed of men's rights activists spurred on by the popularity of the *NYTimes* dubbed "Custodian of the Patriarchy," Jordan Peterson, as well as the rise of the manosphere represented by the misogynist mythos of Reddit's "red pill" community. Incels may be defined as online communities of men who show hostility towards women due to their inability to attract them; incels understand men as either occupying the alpha or beta role with alphas best exemplified by Donald Trump. Elliot Rodger, the UC-Santa Barbara killer, was an avowed incel, spurring the #YesAllWomen feminist digital collective only two years earlier. Trump's rise prompted the growth of several highly-visible Southern Poverty Law Center identified male terrorist organizations, the Proud Boys, a far-right neo-fascist organization established by *Vice* magazine cofounder Gavin McInnes, as well as QAnon, a far-right male majority conspiracy theory community credited for galvanizing other far-right groups to lay siege on the U.S. Capitol on January 6, 2021.

These male supremacist groups perform much of their intimidation work online, producing notable threat to women in social media environments. Many women who took part in the #MeToo movement became the objects of misogynistic online attacks with some estimates projecting that nearly a quarter of those who shared #MeToo messages experienced various instances of cyberbullying and trolling (McNabb 2021). #MeToo's digital trolling was primarily comprised of women-specific insults, victim-blaming, slut-shaming, and violent language including rape and death threats. More extreme cases of cyberbullying occurred on Twitter where those who shared #MeToo posts were "doxxed," meaning their private identifying information was maliciously shared online. Gender-based trolling under the #MeToo hashtag was further intensified by bot accounts, or software programmed to create simplified online messages; many #MeToo users noted how bots often responded to their tweets with abusive, vicious language.

10.7 Facebook Groups as Folk Data

Within the confines of Facebook Public Groups and Pages, I began my digital ethnography to determine if these digital spaces were capable of cultivating an intimate, community space for #MeToo collectives, something akin to 60s and 70s-era feminist C-R sessions. At the time I started this review in mid-2019, there were over 100 #MeToo-associated Groups and over 40 #MeToo Pages.[13] After hand-coding every Public Group and Page, I found them to be overwhelmingly toxic and dangerous places, particularly for already precarious groups like sexual assault survivors. Further, this investigation showed little resemblance to the intended objectives and benefits of second-wave feminist CR-raising sessions.

With membership numbers ranging from over 10,000 to three, I discovered that, despite the overall member number, I encountered few signs of digital listening, a core tenant of the C-R process. I measured "listening" as directly responding to a message posted. Rather, most group members shared content such as popular feminist memes, peddled #MeToo merchandise, and distributed news stories often featuring sexual harassment and/or assault accusations against public figures. Notably, during the summer of 2020, I encountered the same news story chronicling details regarding Canadian fashion designer and alleged sex trafficker, Peter Nygard. A #MeToo group moderator disclosed that this story was being shared by bot accounts to #MeToo-related groups, causing not only additional labor by group moderators forced to weed out bot-generated spam, but many of these stories included unsubstantiated misinformation geared towards initiating responses of outrage and horror.

Those that do share intimate stories of sexual violence in these public forums are particularly vulnerable, often subjected to cyberbullying, harassment, and/or extended unsafe advice. For example, a member described having flashbacks and nightmares that resulted in emotional outbursts, and this is exacerbated when they are alone in their home and hear noises. The initial advice proffered is to, "…try not to eat bleached flour or potatoes for a month… I lost 100 lbs in 4 months; it works." Here, we see an individual seeking psychological advice and instead receiving diet tips provided by what is most likely a bot. Rather than receiving community support or a mental health hotline, the offered counsel is so incongruous that it feels akin to mockery. The post's creator had already confessed to feeling psychologically unsound; the post's engagement demonstrates such a lack of concern or empathy that such a response could easily push the unstable into a heightening state of crises. They are left with little support despite joining a digital space purportedly offering discussion, secure disclosure, sharing and healing for victims of sexual violence.

Beyond a dearth of listening and member endangerment, Facebook #MeToo Public Groups and Pages also deviated from C-R practices by lacking a trained group facilitator. C-R sessions do not discourage confrontation; however, for fruitful confrontation to occur, groups require a trained leader. As we know, digital environments produce heightened affective and emotional atmospheres; feelings will get hurt. However, there is frequently no trained group facilitator to work with the members to achieve group mediation. Additionally, group admins have little recourse in dealing with cybertrolling; they may force members to leave a group and delete their posts, but beyond reporting issues to Facebook's security team, they have no alternatives to ensure the safety of the group's space. And, in many cases, once trolling occurs, the damage has already been done as personal information can be effortlessly garnered through compromising screenshots or the seizure of profile information.

As discussed, Facebook Groups can bruise egos and enflame emotional and psychological states, but are there further risks that #MeToo Facebook Public Groups and Pages pose? A more serious example of potential endangerment is shown via a posting which describes a member's suicidal ideation. The first commenter suggests that, rather than immediately seeking professional help with links to suicide prevention hotlines and organizations, they should get to know Jesus Christ. Their comment is then "loved" showing further group consensus. After receiving proselytizing feedback, a potentially suicidal member of a #MeToo Public Facebook Group might experience further alienation, upset, or desperation. One might further imagine that suicidal individuals seeking support on Facebook Public Groups might also lack the resources to secure outside, valid treatment options. Unfortunately, this was not the only concerning exchange regarding suicidal ideation that I encountered throughout my survey. But what these discursive sketches highlight are the great precarity that publicization of trauma narratives pose in public social media spaces.

Of course, it is no secret that such digital micropublics are often homes to potentially vulnerable individuals; thus, cyberbullying and doxxing can be intensely fueled in such spaces. In addition to Facebook's expectation that individuals use their legal names for their profile name, a [public] group I surveyed featured filmed sexual assault disclosures which endanger the narrator who becomes more easily identified and targeted by potential perpetrators or cyberbullies.[14] Additionally, moderators lack the resources to ensure that cyberbully accounts are not granted access to public #MeToo groups. When one member of the largest #MeToo group, #MeToo [OFFICIAL] Public Group, asks what to do when they are being sexually harassed in the workplace, a masculine-presenting profile trolls the question with, "I gave in and let her have me." Again, an inquiry seeking suggestions on how to best address workplace sexual harassment is ridiculed rather than earnestly engaged with. On this same post, another responder suggested that the victim approach the man and ask to be left alone, otherwise the man may begin to harbor anger towards women and become "…hostile or psychologically ill and criminal like serial killers of women."[15] The poster's inquiry is therefore met with mockery and masculinist scare tactics.

Fiscal extortion is also directed towards members of these groups; again, the largest #MeToo Public Group's rules included in the "About" section contain a passage reminding members to not give money to Group admins or members—"NOTE: please take care when joining other groups as we are having reports of admins and moderators acting inappropriately and asking for money from members. Please report anything you see and do not feel comfortable with."[16] The fact that this warning was included in the Group's dictums suggests that such member extortion was not a one-time occurrence; rather, it must have occurred with such regularity that other moderators felt the need to warn of its potentiality. In this vein, I further encountered multiple consumer-seeking #MeToo Facebook Groups and Pages which were poised as places to share sexual assault stories, but instead were selling self-help books or publicizing films on rape and sexual assault.[17]

Group moderators have also come forward describing the time and emotional toll required to manage these spaces, from combatting increasing numbers of fake news postings during the COVID-19 pandemic to the emotional labor required to supervise the onslaught of incoming posts and member concerns. These moderators are not qualified to respond to sexual violence crises, and oftentimes, are sexual violence survivors themselves. They are performing unpaid digital labor for Facebook while opening themselves up to potential triggering of traumatic events through their desire to build a supportive digital community for survivors. I came across multiple posts where moderators described having to "take a personal leave of absence," or apologized for their absence from the Group or Page due to the need for self-care. Of course, while these moderators take their much needed respite, other Group members are left on hold, wondering why their posts have not yet been approved, or perhaps falling prey to varying degrees of digital exploitation.

I recognize the Facebook Group moderator dilemma as emblematic of critiques regarding digital labor as conceptualized by Marxist network theorists as well as feminist theorists' notion of emotional labor; both labor theories enhance our understanding of how technocapitalist profiteering is actually felt and seen by these sexual violence survivors. In digital forms of labor, anyone who accesses Facebook, Twitter, Instagram, or Google both consumes data as well as produces data; Christian Fuchs and Marisol Sandoval (2014, 57) describe this role as the "prosumer." Today's digital participation creates a prosumer who relies on affective labor to produce and circulate communication that establishes social meaning and norms, or what Marx (1972) may term "use-values." Yet, under communicative capitalism, all digital communication is collected and sold to advertisers and big data companies for a profit, also creating an exchange value for such messaging. Prosumers often are not aware of their appropriation under digital labor and are therefore unwittingly thwarted from selling their labor power. They do not own the digital platforms, tools, or code which renders a present-day form of worker alienation. Thus, Facebook Group moderators are forced to labor during their personal time with little recognition or compensation. Often sexual assault survivors themselves, they are positioned to experience heightened precarity through Facebook's exploitative brand of digital labor.

This collapsing of the personal and private in contemporary labor practices was also tackled back in 1983 in Arlie Hochschild's investigation into emotional labor. Her renowned ethnography, *The Managed Heart*, examined how various employers place expectations on workers to produce and/or manage their emotion(s) to optimally influence customers' emotional and psychological states. Hochschild notes that privately individuals engage in emotion work frequently such as calming themselves down when anxious. But when this regulation of emotions happens not for the self, but for others, this work then becomes emotional labor. Hochschild (1983, 11) describes how women's role as domestic laborer reproduces a gendered discrepancy in today's labor market: "As traditionally more accomplished managers of feeling in private life, women more than men have put emotional labor on the market, and they know more about its personal costs." In later works such as *The Commercialization of Intimate Life* (2003), Hochschild expands on this idea, arguing that it was feminism's failure which allowed women's emotional labor to be required both inside and outside of the home, so that women are granted no respite while occupying either space. As we see with the Facebook group moderators, they are performing digital labor for Facebook's benefit but, oftentimes, to their personal detriment. They are not compensated; their only recompense for performing their emotional labor is the hope that they are building a better community for sexual violence survivors.

10.8 Conclusion: The Facebook Micropublics of Precarity and Exploitation

Though I have found examples of #MeToo online communities as experiencing heightened precarity due to their enclosure within and reliance on digital platforms, it would be misrepresentative to argue that this effect erases any promise of support and empowerment that is facilitated through these spaces. The closest resemblance to feminist CR-work occurring in these spaces occurred when members responded to sexual assault statements with affirmative, supportive responses like, "I hear you, you are loved," or, "You are not alone in this." And much akin to transnational examples of #MeToo like China's #RiceBunny, I found that many of the Facebook Groups and Pages localized the #MeToo movement within their own particular community's concerns. I came across multiple "interest" Public Groups that applied #MeToo's dominant features, notably making visible the prevalence of sexual violence in the workplace, to their own contexts; there was a Dance #MeToo group and a Yoga #MeToo group. I found location-specific groups, such as #MeTooFrederick, #MeToo Afghanistan, and #MeTooMongolia хөдөлгөөн. There were issue-driven #MeToo groups, like Free Xueqin which supported the release of a "leading Chinese #MeToo activist and independent journalist Sophia Huang Xueqin [who] has been arrested by Chinese authorities for 'picking quarrels and provoking trouble.'"[18] There were also local activism groups like The SCSU Healing Project #MeToo Quilt which showcased how #MeToo inspires material, on-the-ground activism. The Group describes the project's motivation instigated by, "Recent world, national and local events, including the hate-filled flier that was posted outside of the Women's Studies Office, have brought up painful memories for some members of our community and underscore the disparities and inequities that many members of our community experience in their personal, work and school lives... We have asked ourselves how we can represent and honor the resilience and strength of survivors in our community and contribute to our community's healing. Our response is to create a healing quilt. We are calling it The SCSU Healing Project #MeToo Quilt."[19] Notice, too, how the quilting project's language centers survivors, activating local networks to create a safe, healing space for those that have been most disenfranchised.

To mitigate the endangerment individuals face in #MeToo Public Groups and Pages on Facebook, the platform must radically increase transparency around the interworking of these spaces. Group moderators must be better equipped with the necessary training and tools to mitigate the dangers that may befall an-already precarious population such as sexual assault survivors. Another improvement includes better scrutinization for moderators before being assigned moderation privileges. And, when considering the exploitative properties of digital and emotional labor, Facebook should consider paying moderators for effectively performing their role. Facebook Public Group members must be made more knowledgeable regarding the spectrum of risks they take on when sharing information, testimonials, confessions, images, videos, etc. Ultimately, the platform must go further in protecting the micropublics that participate in their Public Groups and Pages features. I would further assert that rather than Facebook suggesting various Groups or Pages based on algorithmically determined criteria, users should more actively seek out spaces relevant to their own interests and motivations.

Though #MeToo the feminist digital collective may feature some foundational characteristics of past feminist C-R practices such as narrative sharing, the personalization of the political, and emotion work, this investigation argues that the digital setting of Facebook Public Groups and Pages provides an unstable space for such work to flourish. What my "failed" digital ethnography of these digital micropublics suggests is that they are ripe for members' manipulation, exploitation, harassment, and bodily/psychological/emotional endangerment. Though there are some instances of seemingly fruitful solidarity-building and localized activisms developing through these channels, most instances of #MeToo-centric Facebook Groups and Pages suggest they are spaces that make more precarious the precariat. While I do not deny that productive, healing feminist C-R can occur online, I do find that the exploitative properties of communicative capitalism continue to plague the digital public sphere, even among more cozy, communal nodes like the Facebook micropublics I have examined. Until social media users become more savvy regarding the potential pitfalls of intimate sharing in the digital polis, individuals will continue to place themselves at the mercy of callous digital platforms, algorithms, data miners, and cybertrolls. Though #MeToo may have heralded the onset of an emergent digitally-induced feminist wave, the great facility of digital exploitation maintains the fetters of patriarchal tyranny and subjugation.

Notes

1. Statistics derived from https://www.statista.com/statistics/617136/digital-population-worldwide, Accessed on 12/2/2020.
2. See https://www.americanbar.org/groups/litigation/publications/litigation-news/featured-articles/2020/new-state-laws-expand-workplace-protections-sexual-harassment-victims/.
3. https://www.csmonitor.com/USA/Politics/2017/0202/Surge-in-young-women-planning-to-run-for-office.
4. https://www.nytimes.com/2021/01/05/world/middleeast/iran-sexual-violence-metoo-women.html.
5. https://foreignpolicy.com/2019/03/07/metooglobalimpactinternationalwomens-day/.

6. https://www.washingtonpost.com/world/middle_east/morocco-debates-a-law-to-protect-women-passing-it-is-another-matter/2017/11/05/8aa859d8-ba7e-11e7-be94-fabb0f1e9ffb_story.html?utm_term=.a9a266fbd7cf.
7. Institutional Review Board (IRB) approval required that all groups and pages in the ethnography must have a "public" privacy setting.
8. https://metricool.com/facebook-groups/.
9. https://www.falcon.io/insights-hub/industry-updates/social-media-updates/facebook-algorithm-change/.
10. https://www.wired.com/story/facebook-groups-are-destroying-america/.
11. https://www.facebook.com/notes/mark-zuckerberg/a-privacy-focused-vision-for-social-networking/10156700570096634/.
12. https://www.facebook.com/community/whats-new/new-public-groups-experience/.
13. These numbers do not count Facebook groups and pages that only used the name #MeToo for attention-grabbing purposes but, upon closer inspection, had no connection to the movement.
14. On December 15, 2015, Facebook announced in a press release that it would be providing a compromise to its real name policy after protests from groups such as the gay/lesbian community and abuse victims. The site is developing a protocol that will allow members to provide specifics as to their "special circumstance" or "unique situation" with a request to use pseudonyms, subject to verification of their true identities.
15. https://www.facebook.com/groups/yesmetoo/posts/439942970064579/?comment_id=440816323310577&__cft__[0]=AZVCVTbYUMhBJOqTp-eLMgY5GGcInAo3eo91J91qEkITN_WSzb0CIMhtRQhl-WJX-NZaMyeXzIzx5nD5m0GskDqQGlGePbI7cnWCGCgVl0qa0hg35LqH6_oxombTjNasYBo&__tn__=R]-R.
16. https://www.facebook.com/groups/yesmetoo/about.
17. Examples of such groups include #MeToo the Book, #MeToo It's time to Tell and Share Our Stories, and MeToo Reality.
18. https://www.facebook.com/groups/FreeXueqin/.
19. https://www.facebook.com/groups/601433523645702/posts/601433536979034/?comment_id=601436600312061&__cft__[0]=AZWQ42ZaIEJzysMM3h1U5Ms2Ws2c4ff6ZwtLofi2rsY5T1MGuJqYHGgTLxJZTVDScB5ra7Fdxvi2NP5dlVprE26zYPkwQGTVbFD2XWAk2uYpbjkteDLalt50xmOHadyL5gK4xOgWqC7T1FKBKS_V3XZn6BH67CHH4wdsABrCx3X80AKE1WuO1OZdUeezf9G-guE&__tn__=R]-R.

References

Allen, Pam. 1970. *Free Space: A Perspective on the Small Group in Women's Liberation.* Albany, CA: Women's Liberation Basement Press.

Bennett, W. Lance, and Alexandra Segerberg. 2013. *The Logic of Connective Action Digital Media and the Personalization of Contentious Politics.* Cambridge: Cambridge University Press.

Blackman, Lisa. 2012. *Immaterial Bodies: Affect, Embodiment, Mediation.* London: SAGE. https://dx.doi.org/https://doi.org/10.4135/9781446288153.

Bonilla, Yarimar, and Jonathan Rosa. 2015. "#Ferguson: Digital Protest, Hashtag Ethnography, and the Racial Politics of Social Media in the United States." *American Ethnologist* 42 (1): 4–17. https://doi.org/10.1111/amet.12112.

Brownmiller, Susan. 1970. "Sisterhood Is Powerful." *The New York Times*, March 15. https://www.nytimes.com/1970/03/15/archives/sisterhood-is-powerful-a-member-of-the-womens-liberation-movement.html.

Dean, Jodi. 2009. *Democracy and Other Neoliberal Fantasies: Communicative Capitalism & Left Politics*. Durham, NC: Duke University Press.

D'Ignazio, Catherine, and Lauren F. Klein. 2020. *Data Feminism*. Cambridge, MA: MIT Press.

Fuchs, Christian, and Marisol Sandoval. 2014. *Critique, Social Media and the Information Society*. New York: Routledge.

Hochschild, Arlie Russell. 1983. *The Managed Heart: Commercialization of Human Feeling*. Berkley, CA: University of California Press.

Hochschild, Arlie Russell. 2003. *The Commercialization of Intimate Life: Notes from Home and Work*. Berkeley, CA: University of California Press.

Horwitz, Jeff, and Deepa Seetharaman. 2020. "Facebook Executives Shut Down Efforts to Make the Site Less Divisive." *Wall Street Journal*, May 26. https://www.wsj.com/articles/facebook-knows-it-encourages-division-top-executives-nixed-solutions-11590507499.

Jenkins, Henry. 2008. *Convergence Culture: Where Old and New Media Collide*. New York: New York University Press.

Marx, Karl. (1858) 1972. *Grundrisse*. Edited by David C. McLellan. London: Macmillan.

McNabb, Danielle. 2021. "#MeToo in 2021: Global Activists Continue to Build on the Movement Against Sexual Violence." *The Conversation*, February 3. https://theconversation.com/metoo-in-2021-global-activists-continue-to-build-on-the-movement-against-sexual-violence-152205.

Mitchell, Juliet. 2015. *Woman's Estate*. London: Verso.

Papacharissi, Zizi. 2010. *A Private Sphere: Democracy in a Digital Age*. Cambridge: Polity.

Papacharissi, Zizi. 2014. *Affective Publics: Sentiment, Technology, and Politics*. Oxford Scholarship Online. https://doi.org/10.1093/acprof:oso/9780199999736.001.0001.

Serres, Michel. 2015. *Thumbelina: The Culture and Technology of Millennials*. Translated by Daniel W. Smith. London: Rowman & Littlefield International.

Striegel, Quincalee Brown. 1975. "Self Reported Behavioral and Attitudinal Changes Influenced by Participation in Women's Consciousness-Raising Groups." PhD diss., University of Kansas.

Zuckerman, Ethan. 2013. *Rewire: Digital Cosmopolitans in the Age of Connection*. New York: W. W. Norton & Company.

CHAPTER 11

Literature, Technology, Society: A Digital Reconstruction of Cultural Conflicts in Chinua Achebe's *Things Fall Apart*

Tunde Ope-Davies

11.1 INTRODUCTION

Chinua Achebe's *Things Fall Apart* (1958) has remained one of the most widely circulated and read African novels all over the world. This iconic literary work earns its global reputation through its fine artistic reconstruction of a typical Igbo traditional community in South East Nigeria struggling to contend with the invasion of Western civilization and foreign cultures in its native territory during the colonial occupation in Nigeria. The author remains one of the most celebrated Nigerian writers that have successfully used their literary works to mirror African precolonial societies, counter Eurocentric stereotypes of the African cultures and sociopolitical and cultural institutions. Among all the novels written by Achebe, *Things Fall Apart* (*TFA*) has continued to attract global appeal due to its simple narratology and near-accurate representation of the Igbo cosmogony and sociohistorical and cultural worldviews predating the invasion by the colonialists. The narrative is a literary illustration of the actual real-life dilemma and conflicts that confronted most African communities during the precolonial and colonial periods. Some scholars, for example, Aziz (2015) and Vuletic (2018) would suggest that some of the thematic thrusts in Achebe's text reflect the outworkings of multiculturalism which was initially designed to manage linguistic diversity before being mainstreamed into literary criticism. Aziz (2015, 157), for instance,

T. Ope-Davies (✉)
University of Lagos, Lagos, Nigeria
e-mail: bopeibi@unilag.edu.ng

© The Author(s), under exclusive license to Springer Nature Switzerland AG 2022
A. Schwan and T. Thomson (eds.), *The Palgrave Handbook of Digital and Public Humanities*, https://doi.org/10.1007/978-3-031-11886-9_11

observes that "...[m]ulticulturalism causes to raise chaos in societies because it leads to cultural assimilation and racial segregation." While multilingualism was not successful in Europe because it does not lead to citizenship, it was forcefully exploited by the British colonialists to promote their indirect rule policy in the territories. The colonial rule provided the hub for cultural conflicts further fuelled by linguistic and communication gaps as shown in the novel.

The application of digital tools to explore popular literary texts like *TFA* provides a scholarly platform to demonstrate the potential of digital humanities "to play a vastly expanded creative role in public life" (Burdick et al. 2012, n.p.). These scholars argue that the era of digital humanities is now representing and reframing scholarship and knowledge production in the traditional disciplines of the humanities: "...values and knowledge of the humanities are seen as crucial for shaping every domain of culture and society" (2012, n.p.). It is believed that digital technologies are inspiring the massive transformation of knowledge, society, and culture that is unfolding, which has a lot of implications for research and scholarship in the humanities. One such benefit or transformation is the availability of computational approaches and digital tools that we can deploy to present traditional and pristine epistemologies hidden behind the print in a more visually compelling quantitative and qualitative way. This present study aligns with these new perspectives and orientation in deploying new tools to answer old questions and unearth new information in literary and creative scholarship. For instance, computational methodologies now assist contemporary audiences to be immersed in the visual and emotional experiences in the texts even beyond the original conception of literary writers. Vast amount of literary data can now be transformed into digital formats for immediate consumption of the audience and transmitted through multiple media and digital platforms to audiences across the world. Literary critics that add value to the content, context, and nuances of meaning in these literary works are now provided technology-mediated tools to weaponize their interpretations and criticisms of the works.

11.2 The Context of the Study

The novel is set in South-East Nigeria, located in Sub-Saharan Africa, to fictionalize the experience of the Igbo during the period. It is important to keep in mind that early twentieth-century Nigeria was significantly different from the present twenty-first-century political entity with 36 states and Federal Capital territories. The country was colonized by the British between 1884 and 1960.

The novel narrates the gripping story of the character, achievements, and tragic end of Okonkwo, an Igbo ("Ibo" in the novel) leader and local wrestling champion in the village of Umuofia. The narratives in the novel follow the unfolding tragic stories of the main character Okonkwo, and the Igbo society. The book reveals how the presence of the British colonial rule and Christian missionaries disrupted the traditional life and practices of the Igbo community. The consequential impact of the cultural conflicts from these cultural impositions on the local traditional cultural systems and values of the Igbo people throw up the social, cultural, and political lessons the author wishes to communicate to his readers.

Published in 1958, it is unquestionably the world's most widely read African novel, having sold more than eight million copies in English and having been translated into fifty languages. To further highlight the key role of the hero, the German version is titled: "Okonkwo." Most of the narratives occur in the village of Umuofia, located west of the actual city of Onitsha (present-day Anambra State), on the east bank of the Niger River in Nigeria. The events of the novel unfold in the 1890s.

To gain a better understanding of the novel, it is important to put in perspective the traditional Igbo cultural setting. A close reading of the text reveals that (i) the novel's world is typically patriarchal; (ii) its beliefs and submission to local cultures, African Traditional Religion (ATR), supersede rationality and individual choices. Loyalty to the traditions and oracles is total and non-negotiable (iii) citizens and residents are controlled by a collective allegiance to these traditions and cultures; and (iv) success in life is measured by masculinity, agricultural wealth, number of wives, fearlessness, victory in local wrestling contests among other well-established and entrenched sociocultural values that are alien to European cultures.

In portraying the main character, readers are often left to choose between his portrayal as a tragic hero or a protagonist. It is, however, obvious that Achebe focuses on the story of Okonkwo to ventilate his own disapproval of cultural impositions by the colonial imperialists on traditional African communities. As the protagonist, Okonkwo dominates the entire narrative and represents the author's mouthpiece. He is depicted as the locus of the layers of tension and conflicts between the two major cultures/civilizations depicted in the novel. The novel unveils the cultural politics of the white man in Nigeria. It describes very vividly Okonkwo's fierce attempt to resist the systematic control of the Igbo community by the British colonialists.

It has been observed that *TFA* remains largely popular among the older generations of readers and public audiences around the world based on the number of hard copies sold (about 20 million copies) in the last five decades. It may be argued, however, that the twenty-first-century digital age now presents a fresh opportunity to engage with the contents of the narrative and retell the stories in ways that will create a fresh appeal to the public. The availability of digital analytics, visualization tools, virtual reality, and embedded reality technologies now enable online readers and virtual audiences to engage with the thrills, frills, and emotions that are captured in the original world of the author and natural context of the hard copy. Since it was first published in the late 1950s, numerous writers and critics and countless critical works around the world have examined, interpreted, and reassessed the stories of *TFA* from different academic, literary, and sociocultural traditions (e.g., Aziz

2015; Vuletic 2018). However, there still exist some yawning gaps in adopting new digital methodology to reconstruct the narratives in ways that capture new modes and new audiences. This present study thus adds to the growing body of literature that will be adopting digital and public humanities approaches based on new technology-driven techniques to engage with the content of this creative work.

11.3 Theoretical Issues

Critics have argued that Achebe appears to grapple with a number of objectives in this novel. One, he attempts to [re-]dress the Igbo cultures with dignity against the backdrop of the often-denigrating view projected by the colonialists and Western writers. Rhoads (1993, 61), quoting Achebe, shows that "…he sets out to illustrate that before the European colonial powers entered Africa, the Igbos 'had a philosophy of great depth and value and beauty, they had poetry and, above all, they had dignity'." For instance, Achebe creatively projects the Igbo society's sophisticated democratic systems, acceptance of other cultures, means of redistributing wealth, a viable system of morality, reward for industry and hard work, a traditional capitalist system that recognizes social welfare, an effective system of justice, though patriarchal yet gender-sensitive, rich cultural heritage and art. Two, he portrays the elements of common humanity that often play out in most democratic societies the world over. Three, the author demonstrates the interplay of human frailties and foibles and the sense of communal life moderated by general principles of fairness and justice. Four, the work shows the danger of imposing the way of life and system of government of one people on another. He paints the fatal mistake of the British colonialists in expecting the same British monarchical and parliamentary systems to operate in Mbata or Igbo communities, whereas the Igbos had developed their own democratic system of government through the *ndichie* or council of elders, clan rules that mediate and determine systems of justice in the villages. Achebe also intends to present the Igbo system of religion at parity with the Europeans' Christian faith.

While different scholars, for example Banypriya & Sujatha (2017), have explored different aspects and themes of this novel, very little has been done on how digital tools can help to amplify some of the preoccupations of the author. This study thus addresses this gap by focusing on the use of digital humanities tools to:

(i) discuss the dominant figure of Okonkwo, his character and key actions, and how all these contribute towards the clash of cultures in the novel; (ii) establish the grounds for and different manifestations of the clash of cultures; (iii) explore how new technologies help to plot and explain the manifestations and dimensions of the cultural conflicts in the novel; (iv) highlight the significance of the application of digital tools in literary studies, and (v) amplify the cultural conflicts in the novel with more visual impact.

11.4 Digital Literary Discourse as Public Humanities

Digital literary discourse may be viewed as the systematic application of digital tools in the exploration, description, and analysis of the contents of creative writing, literature, and orature. As digital humanities (DH) and the use of digital technologies spread across different disciplines in the human sciences, scholars are increasingly becoming aware and fascinated by the amazing power and possibilities offered by computational methodologies in humanistic research and studies. Since the 1990s and 2000s, the use of digital tools has increased in the fields of humanities and social sciences leading to the emergence of DH as a discipline or an approach. Whether DH is considered as a full-fledged discipline or as an approach, most scholars agree that digital technologies have become critically useful in helping scholars in the humanities to objectify, simplify, and amplify the interpretation and analysis of language and/or literary text. The ability to supply quantitative information to complement qualitative interpretation contributes toward a more rigorous analysis of themes and meaning in a text. The capacity for recreation and reconstruction of cultural objects and literary works for new local and global audiences across the world makes a compelling case for technology-driven public humanities. With the application of digital tools, literary scholars are now able to present their works in a more creatively visual and convincing manner:

> Digital tools, techniques, and media have expanded traditional concepts of knowledge in the arts, humanities and social sciences, but Digital Humanities is not solely "about" the digital (in the sense of limiting its scope to the study of digital culture). Nor is Digital Humanities only "about" the humanities as traditionally understood since it argues for a remapping of traditional practices. Rather, Digital Humanities is defined by the opportunities and challenges that arise from the conjunction of the term digital with the term humanities to form a new collective singular. The opportunities include redrawing the boundary lines among the humanities, the social sciences, the arts, and the natural sciences; expanding the audience and social impact of scholarship in the humanities; developing new forms of inquiry and knowledge production and reinvigorating ones that have fallen by the wayside; training future generations of humanists through hands-on, project-based learning as a complement to classroom-based learning; and developing practices that expand the scope, enhance the quality and increase the visibility of humanistic research. (Schnapp 2013, 2)

Similarly, Eve (2019, n.p.) argues that the use of computational methods is not new to English studies. The field "has long been accustomed to using quantitative evidence in its reasoning." However, the advent of digital technologies has reduced the previous laborious manual counting of words to denote linguistic significance in a text. According to Eve (2019, n.p.), "the methods are claimed to permit us, at a distance, to ingest, process, and perhaps understand texts within grand perspectives." Close reading of literary text with computers now allows processes such as iteration, repetition, and quantitative analysis that yield power of amplification of minute details and meanings of textual elements presented by authors. It is these new possibilities through new technologies that inspired Fenton (2018, n.p.) to argue that "The digital humanities provide literary scholars with a platform for various levels of public engagement, from access to inclusion to reinterpretation."

Brennan (2016, cited in Fenton, n.p.) sees public digital humanities as a scholarly effort that goes beyond making creative works available online. It may then be argued that digital literary discourse will involve not only digitalizing or digitizing the literary objects but also creating the works in a way that local communities can relate with them, own them, engage with them, and allow these works to tell their own stories in media formats that can appeal to younger generations all over the world. According to Brennan (2016, cited in Fenton, n.p.), "Doing any type of public digital humanities work requires an intentional decision from the beginning of the project that identifies, invites in, and addresses audience needs in the design, as well as the approach and content, long before the outreach for a finished project begins." On one hand, scholarship in this field thus requires researchers to focus on how the project can be of benefit to the larger community that owns the cultural data and on the other hand, how the global community can receive a fresh understanding of the social and cultural information encoded in the works by their authors. It is that conviction that made Resnik Planinc et al. (2020) assert that "Digital Humanities has enabled humanities scholars to research, experiment and interact with source materials in a way that leads to new insights."

Literary works are deliberately created to encode and preserve rich local, social, and communal practices. Writers use these narratives as channels to communicate to the outside world, the cultural practices, histories, epistemologies, and traditional practices of the people. In most precolonial and colonial narratives, African writers attempt to retell the stories and pristine cultural ecosystems of their people and the negative impact of slavery, colonialism, and Western civilization. It is no surprise to observe how Achebe brilliantly captures and balances his background in Igbo cultural practices and his training in Western civilization. The application of digital technologies to explore these preoccupations as presented in this chapter amplifies the tenor of the narrative and may appeal to more contemporary audiences across the world (Risam 2018).

11.5 Computational Stylometry: Unveiling Fresh Understanding of Text

Rybicki et al. (2016) observe that computational stylistics may involve simple text searches, concordances, and textual manipulation and selection to some kind of statistical analysis, ranging from t-tests to Principal Components analysis and cluster analysis, to Delta analysis, data mining of various kinds, support vector machines, topic modeling, and even neural networks. Basically, from whatever orientation the analysis is conducted, this approach tends to achieve one key objective of improving our understanding of texts. Style itself as an attempt to unveil and interpret property of texts has a lot of implications for opening up the literary works to limitless possibilities of interpretation. Herrmann et al.'s (2015, 16) description of style frames the focus of the analytical framework pursued in this study. They see style as "a property of texts constituted by an ensemble of formal features which can be observed quantitatively or qualitatively." Boukhaled (2016, 22) asserts that:

> Computational stylistics is a subdomain of computational linguistics located at the intersection between several research areas such as natural language processing, literary analysis, stylistics and data mining. The goal of computational stylistics is to extract style patterns characterising a particular type of text using computational and automatic methods. In other words, it aims to investigate texts from the standpoint of individual style (style related specifically to a certain author) or functional style (style related to more complex concerns or subjects such as genres or registers) in order to find patterns in language that are not or very hardly demonstrable without computational methods and linked to the processes of writing style in its wider sense. (Craig 2004)

Some critics have argued that reducing any text, or any collection of texts to an abstract quantitative and numerical form cannot preserve the totality of its meaning and individual traits that makes it unique and different from others. Thus, the question of the quantitative representation and the frequency interpretation must be taken carefully (Boukhaled 2016, 26). The counterbalancing effect of qualitative interpretation to complement the quantitative methods obviates the weakness in the use of the only statistical method.

Mahlberg (2013, cited in Boukhaled, 24) argues that computational stylistics possesses the

> potential to add systematicity and objectivity to the process of analysis by providing quantitative data in a systematic and objective way for a given phenomenon under investigation. The author gives the simple yet illustrative example of a concordance analysis tool that can, for instance, help tracing linguistic features exhaustively throughout a whole text. Another aspect that can be considered as a valuable contribution of computational stylistics to the literary analysis studies is the algorithmic aspect. In fact, from the computational point of view, computational stylistic methods are framed as algorithms that are able to extract, count and rank linguistic features in a given text based on measures of *interestingness*.

Mahlberg's submission speaks directly to the focus of this study that espouses the validity and appropriateness of the use of technology in exploring literary and cultural data. This conflates with the emerging preoccupations in digital humanities and public humanities that seek to objectify and globalize information in literary and creative works for the benefit of larger society. The argument however lies in the complementary role that technology-driven quantitative methods can play in further enhancing the primary role of traditional qualitative approaches in humanities-related researches and analyses of discourses. Essentially, quantitative methods thus need to be complemented by qualitative data and interpretation.

11.6 Methodology

The dataset used in this study was extracted from a self-collected corpus from an ongoing project titled *Corpus of Nigerian Literary Discourse (CNLD)*. It involved transforming the electronic copy of *TFA* into a txt file. A close reading of the text was done to gain additional insight for qualitative analysis. The webscraping method was used to build a self-developed temporary web-corpus created with the use of a data harvesting tool on *SketchEngine*. The next step involved using aspects of stylometric analysis: the study used a range of digital and computer software packages to digitally explore the major thematic concerns, especially clash of cultures. The tool kits of computational stylistics were used to explore the character of Okonkwo and instances of clash of cultures via a number of mentions, word clouds, concordancing, and *Key Word In Context (KWIC)* analyzes. The methodological and analytical procedures involved a critical and systematic reading and analysis of the novel. The digital version of the novel was processed in txt file. The digital analysis was done with the aid of some software packages such as Voyant *Tools*, *AntConc*, *Tagcrowd*, and *SketchEngine* for concordancing and *KWIC* analysis.

The application of digital tools helps the study to electronically provide quantitative empirical evidence and instances of words and expressions that throw more light on the thematic preoccupations in the novel and clash of cultures that occurs at both the individual and societal levels.

11.7 Data Analysis and Discussion

Using *easyweb extract*, a more streamlined web scraping tool, the online popularity of *TFA* is confirmed with 125,000 results while *Google search* on the general web yielded 812,000 results on the novel and all the mentions connected with the novel. The data was downloaded on the desktop as a self-collected corpus with the aid of *SketchEngine* application. The use of this simple digital approach merely confirms and throws some light on the popularity of the novel across the globe. Several critics and readers across the world have commended Achebe's bold and courageous attempt to document the true-to-life stories of the Igbo people in contact with the British colonialists [e.g., Whittaker and Msiska (2007); Caroll (1990)]. Although the novel's author has consistently argued, for example Achebe (1994), that the book may not be described as a model of cultural conflicts, most critics see the narratives in *TFA* as a cluster of cultural conflicts.

As mentioned earlier, *SketchEngine* was deployed to harvest relevant online information and build a small corpus. The web search yielded some interesting and quick overview of the content of the narrative. The quantitative analysis based on frequency counts, keyword in context, and concordance list of the keywords throws more light on the thematic preoccupations as shown in Figs. 11.1, 11.2, 11.3 and 11.4.

In the first instance, it should be pointed out here that the figures demonstrate the usefulness of digital tools to provide relevant information on the novel. Exploring the motif of this study is based on the following elements that provide the premise for the conflicts of cultures identified in the novel: (i) Differences in value systems (ii) Differences in socioeconomic and political systems (iii) Differences in religious beliefs (iv) Fallout of/Reaction to Slave trade history and experience, and (v) Resistance/Protest to the imposition of foreign value systems on pristine traditional cultures. It is these cultural gaps among others that created the tension in the novel with Okonkwo as the hub of the conflicts. In the same breath, some key characters in the novel (especially, Africans and Europeans) symbolize or act out the various manifestations of clash of cultures in *TFA* with Okonkwo as the leading figure. Conflicts in *TFA* manifest at the following levels: (i) Internal conflicts within Okonkwo (ii) External Conflicts—Okonkwo vs. community/Western values (iii) Communal Conflicts—The villagers vs. white colonialists/missionaries and (iv) National Conflicts—Foreign system of governance vs. traditional chiefdom system.

Some key characters spotlighted in the figures such as Okonkwo, Mr. Smith, egwugwu, the goddess, are catalytic objects that trigger a range of conflicts of culture in the novel. As some scholars have observed (e.g. Ashcroft

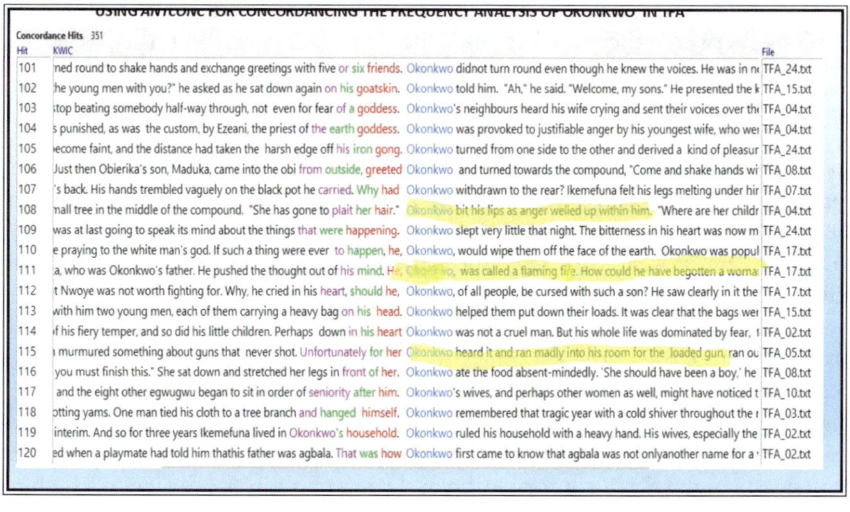

USING ANTCONC FOR CONCORDANCING THE FREQUENCY ANALYSIS OF OKONKWO IN TFA

Concordance Hits 351

Hit	KWIC		File
101	ned round to shake hands and exchange greetings with five or six friends.	Okonkwo didnot turn round even though he knew the voices. He was in n	TFA_24.txt
102	he young men with you?" he asked as he sat down again on his goatskin.	Okonkwo told him. "Ah," he said. "Welcome, my sons." He presented the k	TFA_15.txt
103	top beating somebody half-way through, not even for fear of a goddess.	Okonkwo's neighbours heard his wife crying and sent their voices over th	TFA_04.txt
104	s punished, as was the custom, by Ezeani, the priest of the earth goddess.	Okonkwo was provoked to justifiable anger by his youngest wife, who we	TFA_04.txt
105	ecome faint, and the distance had taken the harsh edge off his iron gong.	Okonkwo turned from one side to the other and derived a kind of pleasur	TFA_24.txt
106	Just then Obierika's son, Maduka, came into the obi from outside, greeted	Okonkwo and turned towards the compound, "Come and shake hands wi	TFA_08.txt
107	's back. His hands trembled vaguely on the black pot he carried. Why had	Okonkwo withdrawn to the rear? Ikemefuna felt his legs melting under hi	TFA_07.txt
108	nall tree in the middle of the compound. "She has gone to plait her hair."	Okonkwo bit his lips as anger welled up within him. "Where are her childr	TFA_04.txt
109	was at last going to speak its mind about the things that were happening.	Okonkwo slept very little that night. The bitterness in his heart was now m	TFA_24.txt
110	e praying to the white man's god. If such a thing were ever to happen, he,	Okonkwo, would wipe them off the face of the earth. Okonkwo was popul	TFA_17.txt
111	a, who was Okonkwo's father. He pushed the thought out of his mind. He,	Okonkwo, was called a flaming fire. How could he have begotten a woma	TFA_17.txt
112	t Nwoye was not worth fighting for. Why, he cried in his heart, should he,	Okonkwo, of all people, be cursed with such a son? He saw clearly in it the	TFA_17.txt
113	with him two young men, each of them carrying a heavy bag on his head.	Okonkwo helped them put down their loads. It was clear that the bags we	TFA_15.txt
114	f his fiery temper, and so did his little children. Perhaps down in his heart	Okonkwo was not a cruel man. But his whole life was dominated by fear, t	TFA_02.txt
115	murmured something about guns that never shot. Unfortunately for her	Okonkwo heard it and ran madly into his room for the loaded gun, ran ou	TFA_05.txt
116	you must finish this." She sat down and stretched her legs in front of her.	Okonkwo ate the food absent-mindedly. 'She should have been a boy,' he	TFA_08.txt
117	and the eight other egwugwu began to sit in order of seniority after him.	Okonkwo's wives, and perhaps other women as well, might have noticed t	TFA_10.txt
118	otting yams. One man tied his cloth to a tree branch and hanged himself.	Okonkwo remembered that tragic year with a cold shiver throughout the	TFA_03.txt
119	interim. And so for three years Ikemefuna lived in Okonkwo's household.	Okonkwo ruled his household with a heavy hand. His wives, especially the	TFA_02.txt
120	ed when a playmate had told him thathis father was agbala. That was how	Okonkwo first came to know that agbala was not onlyanother name for a	TFA_02.txt

Fig. 11.1 *AntConc* frame showing the concordance lines highlighting Okonkwo as keyword in different contexts

Hit	KWIC	File
1	cessor was the Reverend James Smith, and he was a different ki	THINGS FALL APART _chinua Achebe.txt 0 1
2	aying the prophets of Baal. Mr. Smith was greatly distressed by	THINGS FALL APART _chinua Achebe.txt 0 2
3	ks of his arrival in Umuofia Mr. Smith suspended a young wom	THINGS FALL APART _chinua Achebe.txt 0 3
4	scourage it from returning. Mr. Smith was filled with wrath whe	THINGS FALL APART _chinua Achebe.txt 0 4
5	rums were beaten for him. Mr. Smith danced a furious step and	THINGS FALL APART _chinua Achebe.txt 0 5
6	istians had met together at Mr. Smith's parsonage on the previ	THINGS FALL APART _chinua Achebe.txt 0 6
7	The chilling sound affected Mr. Smith, and for the first time he s	THINGS FALL APART _chinua Achebe.txt 0 7
8	ad never happened before. Mr. Smith would have sent for the D	THINGS FALL APART _chinua Achebe.txt 0 8
9	y. "One thing is clear," said Mr. Smith. "We cannot offer physica	THINGS FALL APART _chinua Achebe.txt 0 9
10	ord, save Thy people," cried Mr. Smith. "And bless Thine inherit:	THINGS FALL APART _chinua Achebe.txt 0 10
11	toxicated with destruction. Mr. Smith was in his church when h	THINGS FALL APART _chinua Achebe.txt 0 11
12	l of dust and weird sounds. Mr. Smith heard a sound of footste	THINGS FALL APART _chinua Achebe.txt 0 12
13	th of the clan on the pastor. Mr. Smith had rebuked him in very	THINGS FALL APART _chinua Achebe.txt 0 13
14	onfronting the angry spirits, Mr. Smith looked at him and smile	THINGS FALL APART _chinua Achebe.txt 0 14
15	spirits. He then addressed Mr. Smith, and as he spoke clouds c	THINGS FALL APART _chinua Achebe.txt 0 15
16	o you know me?" he asked. Mr. Smith looked at his interpreter,	THINGS FALL APART _chinua Achebe.txt 0 16
17	so that we can talk to you." Mr. Smith said to his interpreter: "Te	THINGS FALL APART _chinua Achebe.txt 0 17
18	how his. Let him go away." Mr. Smith stood his ground. But he	THINGS FALL APART _chinua Achebe.txt 0 18
19	oner returned from his tour. Mr. Smith went immediately to him	THINGS FALL APART _chinua Achebe.txt 0 19

Fig. 11.2 *AntConc* frame showing the concordance lines highlighting *Mr. Smith* as keyword in different contexts

et al. 2003), usually, cultural dynamics often give room for context reconstruction. As shown in the novel, the typical Igbo traditional settings rudely encroached upon by the colonialists create tensions between the cultures as well as different interpretive voices and actions. The failure to acknowledge the dynamics and fundamental differences in the sociocultural configuration and ecosystem of the two interacting worldviews creates room for the simmering tensions between the cultures and the key characters and the emotional undercurrent that runs through the text.

The use of *AntConc*, and *SketchEngine* in this study has enabled us to throw fresh perspectives on the thematic thrust in *TFA*. These digital text-mining tools improve our understanding of the novel that cannot be easily acquired through manual close-reading. *Voyant* tools help to analyze relative frequencies of some keywords that provide significant meaning and implication to the themes in the novels. Although the author (Achebe 1994) may have argued about some Eurocentric interpretations that were being applied to the narrative, critics agreed that clash of cultures stands out as a major theme in the novel. With the use of these digital corpus analytical methods, the study identifies layers of clash of cultures that manifest in the novel. As pointed out earlier, the study uses digital tools to present visual and quantitative information that supports textual explanation and qualitative interpretation of the theme. The screencasts highlight key information and present a bird's eye view of the high points of key storylines in the novel.

Essentially, if we were to apply the use of Voyant tools it would be shown that the focus of the text and the cultural context revolves around Okonkwo,

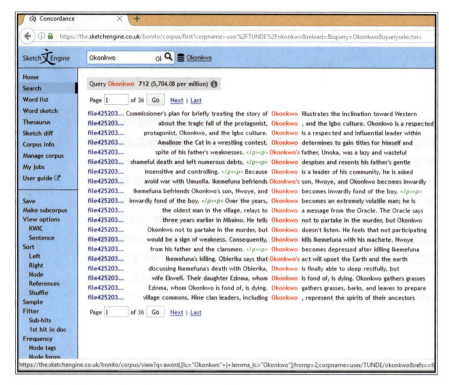

Fig. 11.3 *SketchEngine* frame showing keywords and key terms on Okonkwo extracted from the web-based corpus

the protagonist, as it earns 297 mentions in the novel. By the same token, some keywords associated with the gender and status of Okonkwo such as "man" "men" occur 258 and 208, respectively, some of the most frequently mentioned words in the text. This may confirm that the Igbo society in *TFA* is predominantly male-dominant and patriarchal. It is common knowledge that Achebe's novel is an honest portrayal of any typical African traditional society.

The *SketchEngine* screencast in Figure 11.4 drawn from the general web search provides another interesting picture of the dominance of the character of "Okonkwo" in the narrative. The *keyness score* in the single-word column returns 4, 148.45 far above the score for "Achebe," the author. It has a frequency score of 1498 with relative frequency of 1395. It simply suggests that the available global information on the novel seems to project "Okonkwo" as a more popular keyword associated with the novel than the name of the writer. While this argument is drawn from extratextual information, the point being made here points to how technology-generated information on a literary text can support internal evidence in the text. The web-based search equally confirms that the most critical works written and

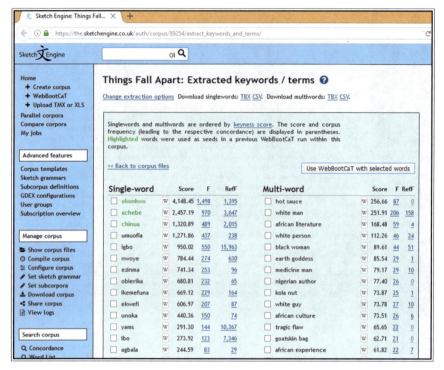

Fig. 11.4 Extracted keywords and key terms from web-based corpus on the text using *SketchEngine*

produced on the novel since it was published have discussed Okonkwo as the central figure that triggers the clash of cultures in the text. The web search was based largely on the contents shared in critical works that are now available online, harvested with the aid of digital tools. The quantum of such extra-textual information drawn from different scholars from different parts of the world that enriches our understanding of the novel would have been impossible without technology.

Quantitative data on keywords in the text represent the stereotypical precolonial male-dominated African society where masculinity is viewed as the greatest virtue. It was the lack of that virtue that made Okonkwo to hate Unoka, his father. Beyond the focus on the dominant male characters, the action verbs "said," "came," and "asked" support the notion that most of the actions in the novel are, to a large extent, associated with male characters. They further support the argument on the patriarchal nature of the setting of the novel and the fast-paced action-loaded events in the narrative that ultimately lead to the tragic end of Okonkwo, the protagonist. The use of the action verbs spotlighted in the screencasts may also help the reader to be engaged by the narrative technique that the author deploys to achieve his thematic preoccupations. Clashes can only be amplified in the environment of actions projected through such concrete dynamic verbs, and literary writers use them deftly to achieve their narrative goals.

Having highlighted the complementary role that computational methodologies can provide in interpreting some hidden information in the novel as shown through technology-generated keyword in context, concordance lines, frequency counts, readers, and audiences may come to better understand and appreciate the themes of *TFA*. It may be useful to summarize the different shades and levels of cultural conflicts in the text as follows:

　i. Civilizations: Modern vs. Ancient: At the general sociopolitical and institutional levels, the novel displays a constant tension between the perceived imposition of the modern Western cultural outlook and practices into the fabric of the existing traditional cultural practices rooted in the daily lives and routines of the communities presented in the novel. For instance, the British colonialists believe in the use of monarchical and parliamentary systems of government to engage the citizens while the Igbo communities rely on the established line of authority structured through the elders, chiefs, family heads, clan heads.
　ii. Education: Native Intelligence, Local Wisdom, Home Schooling vs. Western Education.
　iii. Political cultures: Chiefdom system vs. Colonial British Empire System.
　iv. Economic Cultures: Farming vs. Colonial Government/White Collar Office Job.
　v. Religious Cultures: Traditional Religion vs. Christianity.

Sometimes both the religious and economic cultures are intertwined with the actions and activities of some of the characters influencing the socio-economic realities of the community as a result of religious decisions.

Wa Thiong'o and Mirii (1982, 56–57) capture this well in "I'll Marry When I want":

> All the missionaries of all the churches
> Held the Bible in the left hand,
> And the gun in the right hand.
> The white man wanted us
> To be drunk with religion
> While he,
> In the meantime,
> Was mapping and grabbing our land,
> And starting factories and businesses
> On our sweat.

This perspective based on the qualitative interpretation of the content of the novel based on keyword in context demonstrates how Okonkwo, as a typical advocate for the preservation of traditional values fights to prevent the white men from taking over the land and disrupting the traditional social, cultural, and economic ways of life of his people. The concordance lines in Figs. 11.1, 11.2, and 11.3 show the various contexts that set up the clash of cultures highlighted above. When analyzed closely, readers are able to catch a glimpse of the various contexts in the novel where Okonkwo attempts to defend the Igbo traditional practices. This submission is further demonstrated in the section that follows.

11.8 CONCORDANCING KEYWORDS AS DISCOURSE

The highlight on the concordance lines visually and objectively presents keywords that have contextual significance. The screenshots from *AntConc* and *SketchEngine* applications (Figs. 11.1, 11.3, and 11.4) show some keywords in their natural contexts and how they enable easy interpretation of their meanings and implications through the focus on the concordance lines. In Fig. 11.1, for instance, the analysis of the keyword in context throws some light on the character and actions of Okonkwo who sees himself as the champion of the local cultures.

  i. Okonkwo bit his lips as anger welled up within him....
  ii. Okonkwo was called a flaming fire. How could he have begotten a woman....
  iii. Okonkwo heard it and ran madly into his room for the loaded gun...

These lines provide some interesting facts about the conflict in the character of the hero who struggles throughout the narrative to come to terms with his definition of the demands of tradition and his complex view of the ideal Igbo society. They show Okonkwo's exaggerated view of his strength and natural weakness in every human being, his struggles to suppress the naturalness of human emotions, his humanity against the communal humanity, and his failure to accept and embrace the reality of a changing society facing the "invasion" of a new civilization. By the same breath, these confirm his struggles with his internal conflicts and tension between the determination to demonstrate his manliness against the failures of his father. He hates Christianity with an unbridled passion and considers the converts of the new religion including his Nwoye as cowards, traitors, and enemies of the community. At another level, he equates Western cultures/Christianity with femininity and weakness while for him the Igbo cultures represent masculinity and courage. Having a daughter therefore will be a sign of weakness. A man like him must not breed girls nor have boys that behave like women. He sets up the clash between Western cultures and Igbo local cultures, and a clash between Christianity and the African Traditional Religion, which he attempts to vigorously and angrily defend by murdering the white man and ending up in suicide.

Before drawing the curtain on the key discussions, it is important to once again highlight the key argument that underpins the fulcrum of the study. The major thrust has been to demonstrate the increasing usefulness and relevance of digital technologies in enhancing our exploration of hidden information and meaning in literary texts. Using Achebe's *TFA*, the study has demonstrated how the deployment of computational methodologies and some software can provide more objective reading of the novel. For instance, one can attempt to expand the discussion further by using *AntConc3.4* to analyze other keywords in context that illustrate clash of cultures in the novel. Such words may include "Christians," "Church," "White men," and "goddess." A closer reading of the novel reveals that these words are the catalysts for the two major religious cultures that are in conflict. The use of *AntConc 3.4* to generate the concordance lists helps readers to focus more specifically on the contextual information that objectifies and validates several instances of clash of cultures. For instance, one can quickly access the details of the conflicts when the keywords are explored further in the contexts of the novel as shown in the synopses below. By utilizing information extracted from the concordance, readers can have quick and easy access to the content and context of the conflicts. These examples include: (i) Clash between Western values and African traditional values, Achebe (1958, 108) (ii) Clash between the church (New God) and the [old] gods and goddesses of Igboland; (iii) Clash between white men and black men (98); (iv) Clash between foreigners and indigenous people (98; ch. 20, 124); (v) Clash between British monarchical system, full compliments of democratic government and traditional cultural /political system-chiefdoms (ch. 17, 105; ch. 18, 110; ch. 20, 123) (vi) Clash between community wish and preservation of personal/social status (ch. 7, 43); (vii) Clash between local Christian converts and traditional religion adherents (101), Nwoye, Okonkwo's son was converted into new Western religion (viii) Clash of cultural perspectives (ch. 17, 106); (ix) Clash of modes of worship (church vs. shrine, sacrifices vs. Christian songs and prayers); (x) Clash of the [g]ods (Christian church built in the evil forest, 106); (xi) Clash between change and status quo, bravery and cowardice; (xii) Clash between Igbo language and English language (Led to the murder of the first white man in Abame, ch. 15, 98); (xiii) Clash between modern technologies and local intelligence (ch. 15, 98); (xiv) Clash between Western education and traditional system of education (making chalk on the wall) (ch. 17, 107); (xv) Clash between one's *chi(fate)* and the notion of personal responsibility (Okonkwo) (92, 108); (xvi) Clash based on slave trade history (99); and (xvii) Physical conflict between *egwugwu* and Mr. Smith's church in Umofia over Enoch's desecration of one *egwugwu* (ch. 22, 133–35). The church was destroyed by the *egwugwu*.

The manifestation of different types of cultural conflicts also includes (i) Social Cultures: Kinship system vs. Nuclear Family system (ii) Global vs. National/Local Igbo cultures (iii) Private vs. Public cultures (individualism vs. communal/collectivism) (iv) Foreign vs. Local cultures and (vi) Tradition vs. Modernity—Mysticism (oracle) vs. Empiricism/Rationality. The story of Okonkwo in *TFA* thus shows the struggle between the inevitability of change and preservation of tradition as the two major cultures are in contact. It is this contact that serves as the locus for the pervading tensions depicted in the novel. Rhoads (1993, 69) puts this in a perspective that reinforces how the conflict is represented by two key figures in the novel:

> Both Igbo and the British cultures are for Achebe a mixture of types of human beings. Okonkwo and Mr. Smith are warrior types who will not compromise when their own cultures are threatened…Likewise, the Reverend James Smith is against compromise: "He saw the world as a battlefield in which children of light were locked in mortal conflict with the sons of darkness." (p. 169)

Significantly, it may be safely argued that the digital exploration of the novel (i) provides easy access to hidden information in the novel (ii) enables a systematic unveiling of social meaning and sociocultural interpretation beyond the intuitive level (iii) helps to give a more objective, unbiased and scientific analysis of the text (iv) brings together a wider perspective of critical writings on the text to confirm its global audience and international appeal and (v) demonstrates how discourses emanate and crystalize around key characters, key events and the main preoccupations in the novel. In addition, the *Key Word In Context* analysis (*KWIC*) highlights key factors, helping to focus the attention of readers on critical issues that are central in the novel. It equally helps to throw more light on some keywords and key terms that may unlock some of the nuances of meaning that the author wishes the readers will extrapolate on their own, based on the contextual information highlighted through the digital tools. They also help to provide visual contexts to the events as they unfold in the text. One can put the right construction to the narratives as technologies guide the readers through the gripping stories in the novel. The wordcloud analysis brings to the fore the key themes in the novel revealing the thematic thrust which illuminates the notion of cultural conflicts. The application of digital tools to explore the text demonstrates the significance of technology-driven approaches to redefine and repackage humanities scholarship. The visualization of the text not only communicates instantiation of deeper meanings, but it also provides both visual and textual impact for the message that the author wishes to communicate. It enlarges the scope of the interpretation for the global audience to harvest new meanings. From the quantitative information supplied through *SketchEngine* in Figure 11.4, the global popularity and acceptance of the novel are further reinforced. Google search also yielded 246,000 mentions of the novel on the internet. It is also observed that the major characters such as "Okonkwo" and the "white men," the key figures that represent the two cultures in conflict, receive significant mentions online through the web search.

The study shows that a closer reading of the text may show some evidence of the emerging theory of multiculturalism and its implication for personal and group or communal identities and freedom. Essentially, this speaks to the struggles between tradition and modernity against the backdrop of the expectation of pristine societies which form the focus of most African novels published around the same period.

It may be useful to add that a digital exploration of literary works can aid the teaching of postcolonial literatures in international English classrooms. The visualization and quantitative techniques may help the generation z ("the digital natives") to engage more intensely with literary works. The tools provide quick access to some key information in the texts while reducing the laborious efforts of having to read the texts manually. The close reading of the text may help to enlarge the contextual information and minute details that might have escaped the digital tools because those details were never used as keywords by the software deployed for that purpose.

Within the framework of this study, one may argue that the application of these digital tools tells us something more about Okonkwo and cultural conflicts in the novel which would have been difficult to detect manually. It becomes easier, more objective, and scientific to track conversation, analyze key events and monitor other characters as well as issues that are receiving more attention in the text. It is equally possible to observe how the quantitative information about the thematic thrust is highlighted through the prominence and intensity of discursive issues and interactions around the major thematic thrust and author's preoccupations. The digital exploration shows the significance of these issues and themes in the novel within the local and global contexts. When explored further within the context of the tool, it guides readers to another link that provides additional information presented within the windows/screencasts. The digital exploration of the keywords also shows their social relevance and wider cultural implications conveying fresh and vivid information to the public.

11.9 Conclusion

In this study, I have made some efforts to discuss how the use of digital technologies can unveil new possibilities in the ways literary works can reconnect with the primary audience and engage with new public audiences. Reconnecting with the primary audience resonates with what McLean (2020, 91) describes in relation to how digital technologies can be used by Indigenous peoples and groups from the Global South. By helping to throw fresh perspectives on the content of postcolonial literature, digital tools can help the works to make more compelling and convincing appeals in generating fresh public debates on the perspective shared by the authors. This study has utilized some digital tools to highlight conflicts of cultures and retell the story of Okonkwo in Achebe's *TFA* by focusing more on how the author portrays the indigenous Igbo society, attempting to accommodate and at the same time reject Western culture and its associated new religious and sociopolitical systems. Achebe attempts to highlight the discursive violence of colonial practices. By highlighting the benefit of embracing the use of technologies in disciplines across the humanities and social sciences, the study has shown that digital humanities can indeed offer tremendous potential for democratizing scholarly knowledge by creating platforms through which indigenous creative works and knowledge production can be [re-]processed, [re-]purposed and republished for new audiences around the world.

The analysis of the web corpus also reveals that coloniality is generally portrayed from a negative standpoint as a disruptive factor in the transition of traditional African communities from their precolonial days to the modern era. But it may be argued that though Western civilization may be accused of impacting negatively on the traditional ways of life of the African communities as portrayed in *TFA*, it has provided the postcolonial writers such as Achebe, Wole Soyinka, and Ngũgĩ Wa Thiong'o with tools and platforms to broadcast the practices and epistemologies of their cultural heritage and histories to the global community. Essentially therefore, while Achebe presents the culture of conflicts in the text, highlighting the negatives in both cultures, he unwittingly harps on the strengths and virtues in both cultures suggesting the need for mutual respect for cultures that are in contact. That for me remains a vital lesson that the novel presents to the global community. Generally, this study thus further reinforces research on close reading in literary texts but reveals through DH patterns, techniques, nuances, and tools. In all, it connects, through the reconstruction of social and historical realities, computational methods with literary data.

References

Achebe, Chinua. 1958. *Things Fall Apart*. Ibadan: Heinemann.
Achebe, Chinua. 1994. "The Art of Fiction No. 139." Interview by Jerome Brooks. *Paris Review* 133 (Winter): 142–67.
Ashcroft, Bill, Gareth Griffiths, and Helen Tiffin. 2003. *The Post-Colonial Studies Reader*. London: Taylor & Francis.
Aziz, Sawza. 2015. "Multiculturalism in Chinua Achebe's Novels *Things Fall Apart* and *No Longer at Ease*." *Journal of Literature, Languages and Linguistics* 13: 142–57.
Banypriya, A., and B. Sujatha. 2017. "Cultural Conflict in Chinua Achebe's *Things Fall Apart*." *International Journal of English Language, Literature and Translational Studies (IJELR)* 4 (3) (July–September): n.p. Accessed December 13, 2020. http://www.ijelr.in.
Boukhaled, Mohamed Amine. 2016. "On Computational Stylistics: Mining Literary Texts for the Extraction of Characterizing Stylistic Patterns." PhD diss., Université Pierre et Marie Curie—Paris VI. NNT: 2016PA066517. https://tel.archives-ouvertes.fr/tel-01493312v2/document.
Burdick, Anne, Johanna Drucker, Peter Lunenfeld, Todd Presner, and Jeffrey Schnapp. 2012. *Digital Humanities*. Cambridge, MA: MIT Press.
Caroll, David. 1990. *Chinua Achebe: Novelist, Poet, Critic*. London: Macmillan.

Craig, Hugh 2004. Stylistic Analysis and Authorship Studies. In *A Companion to Digital Humanities* edited by S. Schreibman, R. Siemens, and J. Unsworth, London: Blackwell Publishing Ltd. https://doi.org/10.1002/9780470999875.

Eve, Paul Martin. 2019. *Close Reading with Computers: Textual Scholarship, Computational Formalism and David Mitchell's Cloud Atlas.* Stanford: Stanford University Press. Accessed December 21, 2021. https://www.sup.org/openebook/9781503609372/.

Fenton, Will. 2018. "The Digital Humanities as Public Humanities." https://www.insidehighered.com/views/2018/01/29/literary-scholars-should-use-digital-humanities-reach-oft-ignored-public-opinion.

Herrmann, J. Berenike, Karina van Dalen-Oskam, and Christof Schöch. 2015. "Revisiting Style, a Key Concept in Literary Studies." *Journal of Literary Theory* 9 (1): 25–52. http://dx.doi.org/10.1515/jlt-2015-0003.

McLean, Jessica. 2020. "Decolonising Digital Technologies? Digital Geographies and Indigenous Peoples." In *Changing Digital Geographies*. Cham: Palgrave Macmillan. https://doi.org/10.1007/978-3-030-28307-0_5.

Rhoads, Diana Akers. 1993. "Culture in Chinua Achebe's *Things Fall Apart*." *African Studies Review* 36 (2): 61–72.

Resnik Planinc, Tatjana, Marko Krevs, Lea Rebernik, Karl Donert, Linda Helene Sillat, and Manisha Khulbe. 2020. *The Role of Digital Humanities in Higher Education: Understanding the Challenge of Integration Handbook.* https://doi.org/10.13140/RG.2.2.28294.19524.

Risam, Roopika. 2018. "Decolonizing the Digital Humanities in Theory and Practice." Accessed January 22, 2021. https://digitalcommons.salemstate.edu/english_facpub/7.

Rybicki, Jan, Maciej Eder, and David L. Hoover. 2016. "Computational Stylistics and Text Analysis." In *Doing Digital Humanities: Training, Practice, Research*, edited by Constance Crompton, Richard J. Lane, and Ray Siemens, 123–44. London: Routledge. Accessed January 23, 2021. http://www.infotext.unisi.it/upload/rybickihoovereder_with_figures.pdf.

Schnapp, Jeffrey. 2013. "A Short Guide to the Digital Humanities." Accessed November 12, 2020. https://jeffreyschnapp.com/wpcontent/uploads/2013/01/D_H_ShortGuide.pdf.

Vuletic, Snezana. 2018. "From Colonial Disruptions to Diasporic Entanglements: Narrations of Igbo Identities in the Novels of Chinua Achebe, Chimamanda Ngozi Adichie and Chris Abani." PhD diss., Stockholm University. Accessed December 18, 2021. https://su.diva-portal.org.

Wa Thiong'o, Ngũgĩ, and Ngũgĩ Wa Mirii. 1982. *I Will Marry When I Want.* Oxford: Heinemann.

Whittaker, David, and Mpalive-Hangson Msiska. 2007. *Chinua Achebe's Things Fall Apart.* Abingdon: Routledge.

Wikipedia. n.d. "Things Fall Apart." https://en.wikipedia.org/wiki/Things_Fall_Apart.

CHAPTER 12

Multilingual Handwritten Text Recognition (MultiHTR) or Reading Your Grandma's Old Letters in German, Russian, Serbian, and Ottoman Turkish with Artificial Intelligence

Aleksej Tikhonov, Lesley Loew, Milanka Matić-Chalkitis, Martin Meindl, and Achim Rabus

12.1 Introduction

Imagine finding old letters from your grandmother in the attic, and you are burning with curiosity and excitement to read them. But it turns out that you are not able to do so because you do not recognize the letters used. They are not written in the same alphabet you use. This frustration is experienced by speakers of different languages: people with a migrant background whose ancestors used a different script, people who use a script that has changed through time, or people whose ancestors used a script that is no longer in use.

The MultiHTR project[1] tries to circumvent this impasse with the help of artificial intelligence. This paper presents the one-year work (mid-2020 to mid-2021) of the project in the field of handwritten text recognition using neural networks and machine learning. In this paper, we proceed as follows: First, we introduce HTR (Handwritten Text Recognition) and the main migrational languages in Baden-Württemberg, a federal state in the southwest of Germany where the project team is based; next we break down the four main languages we are working with, German, Russian, Serbian, and Ottoman

A. Tikhonov · L. Loew · M. Matić-Chalkitis · M. Meindl · A. Rabus (✉)
University of Freiburg, Freiburg, Germany
e-mail: achim.rabus@slavistik.uni-freiburg.de

A. Tikhonov
e-mail: multihtr@slavistik.uni-freiburg.de

© The Author(s), under exclusive license to Springer Nature Switzerland AG 2022
A. Schwan and T. Thomson (eds.), *The Palgrave Handbook of Digital and Public Humanities*, https://doi.org/10.1007/978-3-031-11886-9_12

Turkish, and outline our approach to multilingual model training, and our current findings. We examine more general issues related to multilingual HTR, and more language-specific challenges, for example, the right-to-left direction of reading and writing in Arabic-Persian script for Ottoman Turkish. Finally, we conclude this paper with a discussion of our findings as well as the project's public interaction and network building.

12.2 Handwritten Text Recognition

Today, Artificial Intelligence (AI) is considered indispensable, in marketing, or in applications at home such as Amazon's Alexa, but also in police work or the criminal justice system. In addition to the generalized fear of the relegation of human labor to the fringe (see Aust 2021, 77 and 93), complications arise, when using data for AI training, which lead to discrimination on a racial, gender, and sexual level (see Aust 2021). Biases in data used to train AI are biases turning up in the application of AI (see Kurpicz-Briki and Leoni 2021).[2]

With this in mind, there are great benefits gained by the application of AI in assisting human work (see Aust 2021, 98). The MultiHTR project makes use of Transkribus (see "Transkribus," READ-COOP, and TRANSKRIBUS Team at University of Innsbruck 2021), a web and server-based tool that allows for training models for Handwritten Text Recognition (HTR). This tool, which uses AI and machine learning, serves not only to support and simplify processes of manuscript transcription, but it makes AI training accessible to the layperson, giving an insight into how AI can be employed. Within the MultiHTR project, our goal is not only to train HTR models for different languages and script styles, but also to introduce the tool and its capabilities to anyone who is interested and willing to learn its use, so anyone will quintessentially be able to scan and transcribe their family archives or diaries written in scripts that are no longer in use or in handwritings that are hard to read. This has the fringe benefit that the black box AI might be brought closer to the general public, thus illuminating its advantages and not only its detriment.

As opposed to the traditional Optical Character Recognition (OCR) technology, HTR recognizes not individual characters, but uses a line-based approach, thus utilizing contextualized data to decode its content (see Rabus 2019). The Handwritten Text Recognition (HTR) engines implemented in Transkribus (HTR+ and PyLaia) allow users to train their own models. The neural networks learn to recognize any character in context in real-life manuscripts and create the corresponding digital output. While there are other HTR tools available, Transkribus is arguably the most advanced both with respect to existing, publicly available models, the ease of use, and the size of the community using it.

In order to train an HTR model, it is first necessary to create Ground Truth (GT) which serves as the basis of the training. GT consists of typed transcriptions that correspond as closely as possible to the handwriting of the scanned manuscript. The larger and more accurate the data of the GT, the better the performance of the HTR algorithm. The Character Error Rate (CER) is low in this case, and the algorithm accordingly makes fewer errors when recognizing new text.[3] The transcription is fed into Transkribus line by line in correspondence with the layout of the manuscript. The training of a model consists of comparing the image of the original manuscript to the corresponding lines, words, and characters in the transcription. The repetition thereof is called an epoch, and the number of epochs (the standard is set to 50 epochs for HTR+) needs to be adapted to the size of the training data. The more repetitions the model does going over the data, the better it learns the handwritten text and its corresponding digital transcription. The accuracy of the model is seen in the CER and is tested by using a Validation Set (VS) that has been put aside from the GT at the beginning of the training. The CER is computed by comparing the machine-generated transcriptions to the ones created manually.

12.3 Focus Languages and Public Interaction

Many written languages have undergone reforms over the last two centuries. After some of these reforms, older handwritten texts have become inaccessible to the majority of people that learned to read and write after these reforms. The longer the distance to the period the text was created, the more difficult it is to read and understand the text. This problem affects researchers and people outside academia if we think of old letters, recipes, postcards, diaries, certificates, and similar manuscripts in private family archives or in local parishes. Examples of this include *Kurrent* or *Sütterlin* script in German or the Russian alphabet before the October Revolution 1917/1918. Our project covers the four largest language groups present in Baden-Württemberg—German, Russian, Serbian (as well as Bosnian, Croatian, and Montenegrin), and Turkish. These languages with the exception of German are the main migrational languages in Baden-Württemberg, which is why they have been chosen for this project. The state counted almost 3.37 million people with a migration background in 2017. This makes up around 31% of the state's total population (see "Baden-Württemberg in Zahlen: Bevölkerung"). The diverse reasons for migration include fleeing political unrest, such as the communist revolts in the 1910s and 20s in Russia or the Yugoslav wars of the 1990s (see Schroer-Hippel 2016) as well as seeking opportunities of employment.

Part of the data used within the MultiHTR project is collected using the principle of crowdsourcing and a win–win relationship with our partners and partner institutions inside and outside academia. We chose the most straightforward way of interaction with a diverse non-academic target audience. Crowdsourcing is mainly realized via social media, namely Instagram and Facebook. Both platforms have the possibility of public and private interactions. Most users have one to five pages that can be transferred easily and quickly via private messages. The possible reduction of quality when receiving data over social media proved to be insignificant for the machine learning and only in a few cases did the quality prove to be too poor. The problem usually lay in an initially low quality of photos or scans.

In story highlights on Instagram, postings on Facebook, and the project's website, we inform users that the data is processed following the data protection regulation of the European Union. The users are also made aware that the social media platforms have their own data protection guidelines, for which we do not take responsibility (MultiHTR 2020).

Besides our outreach on social media, several reports in newspapers and online news portals made it possible to reach a wider audience. The people interested in the project used e-mail as the main source of contact. E-mail was also used for data transfer when the user provided over five pages of script, and in the case of larger documents (25 Mb or more) we resorted to free sharing services such as WeTransfer.

Generally, the project's audience includes German citizens with a migrant background in the second or third generation, whose heritage language is Russian, Serbian, or Turkish. Nevertheless, German speakers without migrant backgrounds are also inspired by the project to look back on their German-speaking/-writing family history. Russian handwriting can be realized differently according to the target audience; the Russian script experienced a spelling reform in the twentieth century, reducing the number of characters used. Both factors often make it difficult to read letters and recipes, diaries and birth certificates, and other documents from family archives. Serbian experienced a more profound change in the late twentieth century when the Latin alphabet started to replace the Cyrillic. However, the Cyrillic alphabet never ceased to be in use and exists today alongside the Latin alphabet. It is common for the first generation of Serbian migrants living in Germany to read and write Cyrillic, while the second and third generations can no longer read or write it. Turkish is probably the language that has undergone the most significant change. The Latin alphabet of modern Turkish replaced the Arabic-Persian alphabet of Ottoman Turkish during the language reforms of 1928.

In many cases, all these aspects make reading and understanding family, community, or other documents difficult or even impossible for multicultural families in Germany today. Families who own historical manuscripts in German, often written in *Kurrent*, or *Sütterlin* face problems. With HTR technologies, the project helps people decipher their old documents and offers them an opportunity to participate in the algorithm training process themselves. The team members show how data can be entered, trained, and validated directly in Transkribus without any programming knowledge. This creates the added benefit of reducing prejudices held towards artificial intelligence, neural networks, and machine learning.

12.4 Visual Conditions of the Manuscripts

During model development, we encountered some peculiarities regarding the writing tools. Texts written with pencil often show a lower contrast between the handwriting and the writing surface. Training HTR models with these texts required more data and time than the training process with texts written in ink. Because of that, we experimented with grouping texts according to language, period, and according to the writing tool for model training.

In the optical preprocessing of texts written with pencil, two methods were tried to create a more efficient training basis. Using commercial image editing programs, we increased the contrast, corrected the tonal values, and balanced the gray tones. The editing resulted in grayscale digital copies that were more legible to human readers. However, from the point of view of the training algorithm and the layout analysis tools from Transkribus, the texts were less suitable for training—lines were divided into several sections; the beginnings and endings of lines were often not recognized, individual words were defined as lines and much more. An attempt to enhance AI readability of a pencil manuscript was made with Contrast Limited Adaptive Histogram Equalization (CLAHE), a computer image processing technique, transforming, or rather redistributing, pixels with a transformation function correlating to their neighborhood. The AI performed worse than when shown the original. Further tests with different images are needed to resolve this issue in the future.

While the digitization process does not play a significant role for the resulting HTR models, the color setting does. Grayscale digital copies often require more effort and data to develop a functioning model. The subsequent standardization through the color conversion to grayscale creates a visual unity from a subjective human perspective. Some trial runs have shown that it might be helpful to separate the training data according to grayscale and color copies. The more different the data, the more data the training will require.

The image quality itself is an aspect that should not be underestimated. While smartphone cameras mostly take pictures in an adequate resolution, the photos might still be blurry or shaky. For many of the photos in our project, we could not control the creation process—users sent us the photos of the manuscripts. Model training with an AI-transcription of blurred photos is possible, but the CER value only slowly decreases.

12.5 German

German underwent a significant change in its writing during the early twentieth century. The *Kurrent* script was the prevalent handwriting. It originated in the sixteenth century and continued to play an important role in the formation of later scripts (see Schneider 2009, 84–86). In 1917, the *Sütterlin* script, a simplified version of the earlier *Kurrent*, gained popularity, to then be abolished in 1941 in Nazi Germany. It was replaced by the handwriting based on the Latin script still used today (see Braun 2015, 8). The two older scripts,

Kurrent and *Sütterlin*, differ profoundly from modern handwriting, leaving the majority of the general population unable to read them unless an effort is made to learn the scripts.

During our crowdsourcing part of the project, German has expectedly received by far the strongest reaction among the population, peaking after a local newspaper published a report on our project.[4] The material we were presented with is very heterogeneous not only in terms of writing style but also in content. Numerous letters were sent to us, both of official and private character, recipes, diaries, amateur poetry, and even military records. The variety of material was as intriguing as it was challenging from an AI perspective.

The majority of people gave positive feedback on the automated transcriptions, even if the text produced by the AI was often unintelligible. The overall interest in our project as well as the technology behind the transcription process led to multiple dialogues between the team and the public.

Besides these individual smaller documents, there were also some small-scale organizations, most of which used volunteer workers to digitize their documents, who reached out to us. Working mostly with archival materials, the institutions showed interest in collaborating with our research project in order to aid the transcription process of their manuscripts. So far, we have only begun testing with these materials and trained first, small models. These models already perform quite well despite their rather small size. Still, a lot of people are interested in and willing to engage with AI technology and are curious to try it out themselves.

Since some of the texts we received were from the early nineteenth century and the latest one from the early to mid-twentieth century, the material was not only diverse in content but also in writing styles and scripts. When confronted with a new document we are presented with the option to use an already existing, public model in Transkribus or one of our own models to produce a transcription. For the more historical texts, the first option usually gave solid results. The two largest public German models in Transkribus have a historical bias toward the nineteenth century as well as toward Swiss German dialects. This second circumstance can lead to problems with language recognition when confronted with a German manuscript. Transkribus does not only learn to decipher individual characters but also acquires vocabulary or, more specifically, a set of typical language features. This may lead to problems when transcribing texts that are not written in that specific variety or language.

Due to their bias, the publicly available models are able to transcribe more historic texts, i.e., from the nineteenth century, somewhat accurately, but later texts, which are in the process of changing to modern handwriting, could not be transcribed as easily. Here, our models came into play. Our German models are mainly based on sources from the Deutsches Tagebucharchiv Emmendingen (The German Diary Archive, see "Deutsches Tagebucharchiv Emmendingen") with which we have entered productive cooperation. The archive supplies us with various sources of already transcribed documents and in return, we facilitate the transcription process of their documents by (pre)transcribing the manuscripts using our Transkribus models. We generally use the data recycling method when creating our own models, i.e. reusing already transcribed and mostly publicly available data, to efficiently train models for new scripts.

Our first German models were of a very small scope: roughly 5000–10,000 words. Generally speaking, these models gave mediocre results, especially for data that has not been seen during model training. The first bigger model was a combination of two diaries from one handwriting (1944, 12,000 words) and a series of 10 diaries from another hand (1914/1915, 75,000 words). The CER on the VS is 10.68%. Usually, models with a CER of 5% or lower produce transcriptions that are intelligible without any issue, if they are used on a text from the period they are based on. Models with a CER of 15% or above usually produce hardly intelligible text. The transcription capabilities of the model on the VS looked very promising. The VS consists of excerpts from both handwriting styles the model saw during training, while the quantitative difference in training data is reflected in the size of the excerpts in the VS. Additionally, when comparing the transcription results of the different handwriting styles, the quantitative bias is evident.

Figure 12.1 has been created with the tool "Compare Text Versions" of Transkribus, illustrating this bias. This function compares two versions of the transcription. For Fig. 12.1, the "Hypothesis" (the transcription the model produced, red) was compared to the GT (green). The left column shows a page taken from the 1944 handwriting, which is the smaller part of the training data, the right column a page taken from the larger part of the training data, the diaries from 1914/1915. The corrections are lower in number on the right page, the left shows entire lines transcribed incorrectly by the AI, while on the right page most errors are single letters or mistakes in punctuation. Besides the quantitative difference in training material, the quality of the scans might also be a deciding factor. The document from 1944 is also, in large part, of poor quality and the image contrast had to be enhanced to improve AI performance. Additionally, it is not a usual notebook format consisting only of lines of handwritten text, but is in the format of a pocket calendar, containing printed text such as numbers of days or names of the month, which posed an additional challenge for the AI. However, the 1914/1915 handwriting is mostly written with pencil and not in ink, resulting in a less clear and less distinct letter shape. As this discussion shows, there were still a lot of issues to be solved, most importantly the matter of model size. Even so, the first attempt to train a large model was promising.

To tackle the issue of size, we combined our data with data from existing larger models. The idea was to have a large-scale model as a general basis and then to specify the model with our data. As we still lacked enough data to create a general model for German ourselves, we used large models created in other projects as a starting point. Taking data from such models and combining it with ours resulted in a model with roughly 550,000 words (of which approximately 80,000 stems from our data) and a CER of 9.19%.

Fig. 12.1 Comparison of two pages from the VS using the "Compare Text Versions" function

At first glance, the CER might not look significantly better. But the advantage of large models is the possibility of using Language Models (LM). When choosing the options for the transcription process, one can select to use an LM generated from training data. Simply put, an LM is the system of words and n-grams of the transcribed language the model acquired during training. For example, the AI might incorrectly transcribe the word "friend" as "freind." It has very likely never seen the word "freind" during training, but it has seen "friend" multiple times. Using an LM, the falsely transcribed "freind" will consequently be replaced with the correct "friend." For big models, this significantly improves the transcription quality.

The author of the diaries from 1944 has written numerous diaries, spanning the time frame of several decades starting in her childhood. She worked as a secretary for high-ranking Nazi officials, which leaves her diaries of cultural and historical importance and of special interest for the German Diary Archive. In order to improve performance results for this specific handwriting, we transcribed more of her diaries to get additional training data. To facilitate the transcription process, we created an automatic pre-transcribed version using our HTR+ models which was then manually corrected. The transcription of two more diaries added another 40,000 words of training data to the model. The resulting model is just short of 600,000 words and has a CER of 9.05%, and again, the real-world performance with the LM option proved to be considerably better. Even fairly difficult handwriting was transcribed very well, resulting in mostly readable, albeit not perfect, transcriptions. Rare words were still incorrectly transcribed, most likely because the LM has not yet seen the words either, but the more common vocabulary is mostly correct, keeping in mind that Transkribus also counts punctuation and small mistakes which human readers would mostly overlook for the CER.

In conclusion, the strategy of adapting a large, generic model to a specific source by adding a small amount of training data from that specific source proved to be very effective. We also use models created through this method to transcribe more modern documents we receive on our social media accounts and the results are usually readable. Therefore, the model was not only specified toward the specific writing style of our data, but acquired the capability to transcribe more modern scripts. The model will be further improved and also combined with model data we have received from other sources to improve its general capabilities and general transcription quality.

12.6 Russian

Currently (mid-2021), there is one specialized public model for Russian for the modern period (late nineteenth to early twenty-first century, published by the members of the INEL project ["INEL"]), but—besides our model published in July 2021—no generic model publicly available on the Transkribus platform. In order to generate data for the creation of different models (including Russian models), we started crowdsourcing over social media, but also additional data acquisition scenarios were developed. We have considered using publicly available documents that are, for example, available without restrictions in the digital collections of European and non-European libraries. Another approach was to consider the manuscripts of famous personalities from the end of the nineteenth to the beginning of the twentieth century. In many cases, both the scans of the originals and the modernized transcriptions are available. The manuscripts are primarily letters, diaries, and poems. The modernized transcriptions can be converted by using the online open-source tool Slavenica (see "Slavenica") which creates transliterations out of transcriptions. The critical difference between transcriptions and transliterations is that during the orthographic reform 1918 the graphemes <i>, <ѣ>, <ѳ>, and <ѵ> were excluded from the Russian alphabet. Including these graphemes, one would get a transliteration. However, in 1918, the alphabet had increased by two graphemes <ё> and <й>. In addition, the grapheme <ъ> lost its function at the end of word forms that end with a hard consonant.

Right from the start, however, the project received requests for cooperation from private individuals, initiatives, and institutes. Early on, we were contacted by the initiative JewishGen from New York, USA (see "JewishGen. Ukraine Research Division"). The members of this initiative are trying to transcribe old Russian birth and death records from the nineteenth and twentieth centuries from their ancestors who were born in the Russian Empire. So far, they had been working manually by transcribing all the data themselves. The cooperation promised to facilitate their transcription process as well as give us access to new data. Admittedly, the data was difficult to work with as it consisted of large tables with partially repeating text.[5] The MultiHTR team was able to work on new models with the team members of JewishGen initiative directly in Transkribus. Another partner is the Prozhito Project, located at the European University of St. Petersburg in Russia (see "Prozhito"). Since 2015, Prozhito has been digitizing and transcribing diaries from Belarus, Russia, and Ukraine from the nineteenth to twenty-first centuries manually. To date, the project has around 6000 authors in its database who are both well-known individuals and ordinary people—teachers, workers, etc. In total, Prozhito has over 500,000 daily entries from these authors. The third partner for Russian is the National Archives of Estonia ("National Archives of Estonia"). The archives have numerous documents in Russian from the nineteenth and the first half of the twenty-first century, when Estonia was first occupied by Tsarist Russia and then by the Soviet Union in various historical periods. Using the data provided by our partners, we trained several specific and generic models and made the beta version of a generic model publicly available.

The data of all four institutional partners is in Russian and from around the same period. Nonetheless, we faced various issues during GT creation and model development.

12.6.1 Body Texts and Tables

Body texts and their transcriptions or transliterations are an efficient basis for forming the GT of a generic HTR model. A model developed on body texts can also work for the automatic transcription of tables as we could see working with the tables of our partners from Estonia and the USA. There is only the complication of the different layouts of the pages during the model training. The algorithm is based not only on individual characters and character combinations, but also on the course of the line, line length, and optical interruptions in the text. The training algorithm recognizes lines in tables as shorter than in the body texts because they are interrupted by the table columns. This difference may result in three possible solutions (i) The development of two separate HTR models, one for tables and one for body texts (ii) The optical processing of the tables before uploading to Transkribus, e.g., by saving individual columns as separate image files (iii) Processing so much data for the training that the high quantity will render the visual difference between the two types of documents insignificant. The number of manually transliterated words for case (iii) is at least 100,000 words. Large generic models can consist of considerably more words. Currently, the largest public model available (for German *Kurrent*) has been trained on 26 million words.

12.6.2 *Quantity Over Quality?*

The principle of "the more, the better" is not universal for all cases of HTR-algorithm training. The quality of the texts chosen for the training is important as well. If the transcripts or transliterations used for the training are maximally close to the original manuscript, fewer data will be needed for training. The proximity to the original text encompasses several aspects. How accurate is the rendering of characters? There are two purposes of an HTR algorithm—transcription or transliteration. In the case of an automated transcription, it would be sufficient to replace the prerevolutionary Russian grapheme <ѣ> with <e> or <ё>, i.e., use a modern transcription for training on an old text. The final model would then also replace <ѣ> with <e> and <ё>. On the other hand, transliterations are the second possibility. Here, each grapheme must correspond to a grapheme and consider its historical versions, so <ѣ> would be <ѣ>. Creating such transliterations takes longer, but afterward, training a new model is more straightforward.

Ultimately, it is possible to train specific models with a low CER with considerably less than 100,000 words. However, another aspect plays a role here. Manuscripts, photos or scans should be of good quality in terms of lighting, contrast, image resolution, and the plan view of the digitized manuscript page with an angle of about 90° when it comes to photos of manuscripts. The resolution of the camera of a conventional smartphone of around 8 megapixels is sufficient. The smartphone cameras manufactured after 2019, however, usually have even higher quality.

12.7 Serbian

Although Cyrillic is the official script in Serbia (partly also in Bosnia), many of the local population use Latin script. The use of both scripts is natural. For people living outside of Serbia, the Latin script is preferred in most cases. This leads to not only a great demand for transliterations, but also transcriptions of Cyrillic into Latin script; not only for historical manuscripts, but also for contemporary writings.

Through close cooperation with the University Library in Belgrade, a first model for Serbian was created. It is based on four Cyrillic manuscripts of famous Serbian academics, each containing approximately 80–100 pages, together amounting to approximately 27,000 words and resulting in a CER of 6.44%. This was one of our first models trained with some smart capabilities, i.e., the capability of a model to read Cyrillic and transcribe it into Latin. This capability can be seen in Fig. 12.2. The two lines in the manuscript are written in the Cyrillic script which the model transcribed (1–3 and 1–4) in Latin script. Overall, we have tested several ways to find the most efficient solution to convert the training data from one script to another, in this case from Cyrillic to Latin script. This continues to be useful for other languages

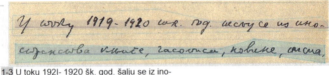

1-3 U toku 192l- 1920 šk. god. šalju se iz ino-
1-4 stranstva knjige, časopisi, novine, pisma.

Fig. 12.2 Manuscript written in Cyrillic and automatic transcription in Latin

and scripts as well as, for example, for Ottoman Turkish (see Sect. 12.8 on Ottoman Turkish in this chapter).

We were able to test the performance of this generic model on a document sent via social media, although the general response on social media was not as high as expected. The low level of public participation might be due to the parallel use of both scripts as well as the close connection of members of the Serbian communities in Germany to their home country and families/friends in Serbia. We have received a chemistry exercise book, which proved to be very challenging, especially for the layout analysis (LA). The text was written on squared paper, which had a significant negative impact on the automatic LA. As explained in Sect. 12.6, the training algorithm tends to recognize the vertical lines as boundary markers between individual text areas. Therefore, on squared paper, the text lines are usually cut off. Often, text lines are recognized where they do not exist at all, or text regions are marked that do not contain any text.

Additionally, the content of the text itself posed a problem. The HTR algorithm had tried to interpret the chemical formulas and element symbols, which were not seen during the training and thus could not have been learned to be transcribed correctly. This resulted in nonsensical automatic transcriptions. Also, the poor contrast of the scan diminished the HTR potential and led to an altogether rather disappointing result. Nevertheless, it is a good example that the HTR tools should be optimized for the recognition of symbols and characters used outside the humanities as well, for example, mathematical or chemical formulas.

12.8 Ottoman Turkish

Ottoman Turkish (OT) was the administrative language and lingua franca in the Ottoman Empire, used primarily by the educated upper class.[6] It was written in a modified version of the Arabic-Persian script. Today, modern Turkish uses the Latin script, which was introduced as a new writing system during the alphabet reform in 1928. The new script brought an additional challenge: the opposite direction of writing. While the Latin script is written from left-to-right (LTR), the Arabic-Persian script is written from right-to-left (RTL) (see Lewis 2002).

Together with the strong influence of the Arabic and Persian languages (both in lexis and grammar), the script and writing direction make OT largely inaccessible to the general Turkish-speaking public now. For most people with a Turkish migrant background living in Germany the access to their cultural or general historical heritage is almost impossible.

After starting with the crowdsourcing phase of the project, we quickly realized that private handwritten material from the general public for OT (not only in Germany) is very difficult to generate. The main reason could be the high illiteracy rate in the territory of the present Republic of Turkey at the time of the Turkish language reform in the late 1920s/early 1930s. OT was a privilege of the upper class not only as a spoken, but especially as a written language. Handwritten material is therefore not abundant. Writings that originated in the elite circles are usually stored in various archives and libraries, while private bequests are very rare.

As a result, we have not been able to obtain data for OT via crowdsourcing. Since the transcription of OT is indispensable for historical research and the interest in as well as the demand for transcriptions are increasing, the decision was made to choose a more traditional way of data acquisition. While plenty of manuscripts exist in high digital quality, only transcriptions of a few prominent historical documents are available in archives. Thus, we contacted various experts from the field of Ottoman studies in order to generate sufficient and, above all, usable material for creating different HTR models.

Depending on when the source to be transcribed was created and its physical quality, transcribing OT texts is a very time-consuming and laborious task. By using the recycling approach mentioned above, we were able to train the first OT models with a data set of about 200,000 words in a short time. This data set consists of various predominantly literary texts from the sixteenth and seventeenth centuries. A small amount (about 60,000 words) of printed newspaper text from the beginning of the twentieth century extends this data set for comparative and verifying experimental purposes. Working with OT in Transkribus imposes some requirements on both the source material and the transcriptions and is therefore very challenging. The main challenges relate to the text's directionality, the layout, and various transcription standards.

12.8.1 Text Directionality

The HTR algorithm is based on the correct mapping of transcriptions to the original text in the images, by default using the same writing and reading direction. In the case of the Arabic-Persian script used in OT, the RTL writing direction of the source text does not match the LTR writing direction of the corresponding Latin transcriptions, so that a correct assignment cannot be made easily. This challenge was addressed in two different ways. First, by reversing transcriptions, and second, by mirroring the source text, i.e., the images. The second solution was invented and successfully applied by our project team. In both cases, matching directionality was achieved, but with

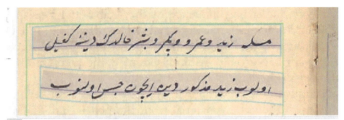

1-1 mesele Zeyd ve ʿAmr ve Pekir ve Beşir Ḫālid üñ deynine kefīl
1-2 olub Zeyd i meẕkūr deyn içün ḥabs olınub

Fig. 12.3 OT manuscript (RTL) and the corresponding Latin transcription (LTR)

different data preparation and data entry as well as different output. However, since March 2021 it is possible to train models with RTL scripts without any additional effort. For this purpose, upon our request (together with our partners), a new feature was integrated into Transkribus which allows users to work with source text images and transcriptions of different writing directions (see Fig. 12.3). During training, the transcriptions are automatically reversed to match the directionality of the original text.[7]

12.8.2 Layout

How well the automatic layout analysis performs depends largely on the structural complexity and the general quality of the source. In the case of OT data the project members work with, there are roughly two different layout types that differ significantly from each other. The first is the standardized layout of a printed newspaper without images. The second is a very free and variable layout of handwritten literary texts. While printed texts follow precise rules such as uniform font color and size, exact text orientation, etc., the handwritten texts (especially, literary writings) can contain an artistic note that manifests itself in many details. For example, single lines of text or passages can be written in a different (in this case usually red) text color. Each writing is characterized by a very individual style, whereby text size, text slant, and legibility vary greatly. Characteristic for the handwritten literature is ornamentation as well as a bow-like writing style of the verses. The particular verse arrangement indicates the reading direction and significantly determines the layout. In extreme cases, there is no single line of horizontal text written on an entire page. The automatic LA in Transkribus is mainly intended for the recognition of plain text and thus horizontally written text lines. Text lines that are aligned differently next to the main text body (such as diagonal or inverted margin notes) are usually not detected correctly and have to be corrected manually.

12.8.3 *Transcription Standards*

Transcription of OT texts into the Latin alphabet is not based on a unified transcription system, which greatly affects both model training and the AI-transcription process. Among Ottomanists, there is no consensus on the transcription rules. The basis for a successful and straightforward performance of the HTR algorithm, is the one-to-one correspondence of the individual characters and their transcribed counterpart. This correspondence is not given in OT. Like Arabic, OT is characterized by unwritten, but pronounced vowels. Omitted vowels are added in the transcription by the transcriber. Some of the vowels and consonants are ambiguous, i.e., they correspond to more than one sound in Modern Turkish. Furthermore, some orthographically similar letters cannot be kept apart easily in handwriting.[8]

For today's speakers of Modern Turkish and a non-academic audience, a pronunciation-based transcription is crucial for understanding texts written in OT. In the scientific field, on the other hand, a precise philological transcription scheme is followed. This scheme considers the specific transcription rules of all language elements occurring in the OT language: Arabic, Persian, and Turkish elements are transcribed according to different rules (see Buğday 1999, 11–16). Thus, pragmatic-everyday transcriptions and academic character-accurate transcriptions face each other.

Due to the challenges mentioned, HTR for Ottoman Turkish is still in its infancy and it will take some time until models perform well enough to be published. With this goal in mind, a small network has formed to share data, experiences, progress, and new ideas to develop models for OT.[9]

The project's goal concerning OT is to create at least one "smart" generic model that does not produce perfect, but workable transcriptions. "Smart" refers to the special capability of the model to deal with various linguistic peculiarities of OT besides the directionality issue, i.e., to complement vowels as well as to adjust vowel harmony, to resolve ligatures, and furthermore, to handle multiple individual handwritings as well as to cover different time periods. The demands on the automatically generated transcriptions can vary greatly depending on the user's needs. Thus, attention has to be paid to different user expectations regarding transcription quality and, most importantly, accuracy. Many non-academic users are interested in so-called "ad-hoc" transcriptions in order to be able to understand the source text in broad strokes. Historians, for example, need a better transcription enabling them to search for specific terms or phenomena.[10] Finally, for linguists and literary scholars, the most accurate transcription possible is of great advantage.

To serve all these needs, several models have been developed which are constantly supplemented with new data and qualitatively optimized. First, specific models were trained, mostly based on a single document available. These models are rather small (up to 10,000 words) and their CER ranges from about 15 to 30%, which is not yet adequate for a good model performance. Depending on the amount of data, consistency of transcriptions as well as the occurrence of various confounding factors (such as image quality, illegibility, subscripts, marginal notes, etc.), the CER turns out to be smaller or higher. In the next step, the above models were combined into larger, generic models. This mainly resulted in a combination of two or more handwritten models, a combination of printed and handwritten data, and big models containing all available data. The average CER of the combined, generic models is roughly in the range of about 14–20%.

Compared to the other languages relevant to the project, these CER values appear to be rather high. However, considering the complexity and peculiarities of the Ottoman language, the results are very promising. Although still in the early stages, it is apparent that the models have certain "smart" capabilities (such as vowel completion and vowel harmony adaptation), which makes the training of further models encouraging. By adding more data, the model's capabilities will be optimized and the quality of performance will be tested.

12.9 Conclusion

So far, MultiHTR has witnessed a very high demand for HTR technology, not only for historic and linguistic research but also for the general public. People have sent us over 1000 pages of manuscripts, reaching out over social media and e-mail. Despite high demand, there is still skepticism to participate in the AI and HTR model training, not only because of a potentially high personal effort but also because of general distrust toward AI.

These sentiments toward AI in general and HTR in particular are present inside and outside academia. Philologists, historians, and archivists have often acquired their reading and transcription skills of various historical and modern manuscripts over many years, thus producing hegemonic knowledge. In many cases, the automatically generated results do not meet the expectations of such experts, since the HTR results are usually worse than expert transcription. The lack of tolerance for less-than-perfect results is the biggest hurdle in the path of acknowledging the benefits of automatic transcriptions.

Sometimes, the skepticism toward HTR technology is also economically motivated. However, the machine is not intended to replace humans but to complement them. Firstly, the machine is not yet free of errors; most automatically generated transcriptions need to be manually corrected by humans to achieve the desired accuracy and quality. Secondly, the machine requires human input so that HTR models can be trained and used successfully. Thirdly, while the machine does the quantitative part of the work, the qualitative part is left to the humans. And lastly, besides mass accessibility, the HTR technology is above all time, and therefore, cost-saving. Those who previously did manual transliterations can edit more texts in less time now.

Overall, the overwhelming majority of HTR models are trained for Northern and West-European languages in Latin script and for earlier time periods. MultiHTR focuses on training and publishing models which not only cover languages such as Ottoman Turkish or Russian, but also models for the more modern time period of the nineteenth and twentieth centuries.

By working with several different scripts and languages, MultiHTR is able to help the lesser researched languages in Transkribus grow and join a large global network of researchers. An equally important part of our project is to reach out to the general public in order to not only gather data but to engage with their (family) history in manuscripts trying to make Transkribus accessible to everyone and thus reduce the prejudices against AI.

Notes

1. Multilingual Handwritten Text Recognition (MultiHTR) is a project in the Department of Slavic Languages and Literatures at the Albert Ludwig University of Freiburg, Germany, funded by the state of Baden-Württemberg. The project deals with the development of Handwritten Text Recognition (HTR) models using the Transkribus platform with regard to some of the migrational languages relevant in Germany, especially in Baden-Württemberg. The team consists of the principle investigator Prof. Dr. Achim Rabus, researchers Milanka Matić-Chalkitis (M.A.), Lesley Loew (M.A.), Aleksej Tikhonov (M.A.), as well as assistant researcher Martin Meindl (B.A.). We would like to thank our cooperation partners at the Albert Ludwig University of Freiburg Prof. Dr. Johanna Pink and Prof. Dr. Veronika Lipphardt.
2. This is what Aust colloquially coined as "Garbage in, garbage out" (2021, 78).
3. A model with a CER lower than 10% is considered to perform adequately and with a CER lower than 5% considered to perform well.
4. The article "Wie Künstliche Intelligenz dabei helfen kann, die Handschrift der Uroma zu entziffern" (How Artificial Intelligence can help decipher great-grandma's handwriting) was an interview conducted by René Zipperlen with the project PI Achim Rabus, published in the independent daily newspaper *Badische Zeitung* in April 2021 (Zipperlen, April 10, 2021).
5. The issue of table-based data will be discussed later.
6. Sievert describes in detail how complex Ottoman language is and what exactly is meant by it (see Sievert 2018).
7. OT has adopted the Arabic numerals, which generally have a left-to-right orientation and thus, oppose text directionality. In a model training, the LTR direction of the numbers can be maintained, although the text is reversed.
8. Suphan Kirmizialtin, who has pioneered model training for OT based on printed newspapers, describes in detail the linguistic peculiarities and also challenges of OT for the AI-transcription process (see Kirmizialtin and Wrisley 2020). Prof. Dr. Yavuz Köse and his team from the University of Vienna are also working on developing HTR models not only for handwritten material in OT but also in Armeno-Turkish. HTR Model training for Ottoman diplomacy sources is the subject of Merve Tekgürler's research at Stanford University.
9. The Ottoman Text Recognition Network (OTRN) was established to bring together researchers and all those interested in text recognition technologies for OT (see "The Ottoman Text Recognition Network").
10. Transkribus also offers a searching tool "Keyword Spotting" (KWS) to search for specific words in documents (see "Transkribus Glossary. Keyword Spotting [KWS]").

References

Aust, Holger. 2021. *Das Zeitalter der Daten: Was Sie über Grundlagen, Algorithmen und Anwendungen wissen sollten.* Berlin: Springer.

"Baden-Württemberg in Zahlen: Bevölkerung." Accessed June 29, 2021. https://www.baden-wuerttemberg.de/de/unser-land/land-und-leute/bevoelkerung/.

Braun, Manfred. 2015. *Deutsche Schreibschrift: Kurrent und Sütterlin lesen lernen. Handschriftliche Briefe, Urkunden, Rezepte mühelos entziffern.* München: Droemer Knaur.

Buğday, Korkut M. 1999. *Osmanisch: Einführung in die Grundlagen der Literatursprache.* Wiesbaden: Harrassowitz.

"Deutsches Tagebucharchiv Emmendingen." Accessed June 29, 2021. https://tagebucharchiv.de/stiftung/.

"INEL. Grammatiken, Korpora und Sprachtechnologie für indigene nordeurasische Sprachen." Accessed June 29, 2021. https://www.slm.uni-hamburg.de/inel.html.

"JewishGen. Ukraine Research Division." Accessed June 29, 2021. https://www.jewishgen.org/ukraine/.

Kirmizialtin, Suphan, and David Wrisley. 2020. "Automated Transcription of Non-Latin Script Periodicals: A Case Study in the Ottoman Turkish Print Archive." http://arxiv.org/pdf/2011.01139v1.

Kurpicz-Briki, Mascha, and Tomaso Leoni. 2021. "A World Full of Stereotypes? Further Investigation on Origin and Gender Bias in Multi-Lingual Word Embeddings." *Frontiers in Big Data* 4. https://doi.org/10.3389/fdata.2021.625290.

Lewis, Geoffrey L. 2002. *The Turkish Language Reform: A Catastrophic Success.* Repr. Oxford linguistics. Oxford: Oxford University Press.

MultiHTR. 2020. "Datenschutz." Accessed June 29, 2021. https://www.multihtr.uni-freiburg.de/?Datenschutz.

"National Archives of Estonia." Accessed June 29, 2021. https://www.ra.ee/en/.

"Prozhito." Accessed June 29, 2021. https://prozhito.org/.

Rabus, Achim. 2019. "Recognizing Handwritten Text in Slavic Manuscripts: A Neural-Network Approach Using Transkribus." *Scripta & e-Scripta* 19: 9–32.

READ-COOP. "Scantent." Accessed June 29, 2021. https://readcoop.eu/scantent/.

READ-COOP. "Transkribus." Accessed June 29, 2021. https://readcoop.eu/transkribus/.

Schneider, Karin. 2009. *Paläographie und Handschriftenkunde für Germanisten: Eine Einführung.* 2. überarbeitete Auflage. Sammlung kurzer Grammatiken Germanischer Dialekte 8. Tübingen: Max Niemeyer.

Schroer-Hippel, Miriam. 2016. "Die Zerfallskriege Jugoslawiens." In *Gewaltfreie Männlichkeitsideale: Psychologische Perspektiven auf zivilgesellschaftliche Friedensarbeit*, edited by Miriam Schroer-Hippel, 99–134. Politische Psychologie. Wiesbaden: Springer Fachmedien Wiesbaden.

Sievert, Henning. 2018. "Was ist eigentlich Osmanisch." In *Bulletin / SSMOCI*, edited by Schweizerische Gesellschaft Mittlerer Osten und Islamische Kulturen. Special issue 46: 20–25. Accessed June 12, 2021. https://www.uni-heidelberg.de/md/ori/islamwissenschaft/was_ist_eigentlich_osmanisch.pdf.

"Slavenica." Accessed June 29, 2021. http://slavenica.com/.

"The Ottoman Text Recognition Network." Accessed June 29, 2021. https://otrn.univie.ac.at/.

"Transkribus Glossary. Keyword Spotting (KWS)." Accessed June 29, 2021. https://readcoop.eu/glossary/keyword-spotting-kws/.

Zipperlen, René. 2021. "Wie Künstliche Intelligenz dabei helfen kann, die Handschrift der Uroma zu entziffern." *Badische Zeitung*, April 10. Accessed June 14, 2021. https://www.badische-zeitung.de/wie-kuenstliche-intelligenz-dabei-helfen-kann-die-handschrift-der-uroma-zu-entziffern--201144295.html.

PART III

Mobilizing the Archive

CHAPTER 13

Open Pedagogy and the Archives: Engaging Students in Public Digital Humanities

Trey Conatser

13.1 Introduction

With the release of the first edition of *Debates in the Digital Humanities*, Matthew K. Gold (2012) announced the arrival of "the digital humanities moment," an occasion long in the making but marked by a sudden visibility at mainstream scholarly venues such as the Modern Language Association's annual convention and in emergent discourse communities on the web and social media. For Gold, this moment signaled an irrevocable turn toward a future in which the digital humanities would be an object of public attention and debate. In the collection's opening chapter, Matthew Kirschenbaum (2012) speculates that "the digital humanities today is about a scholarship (and a pedagogy) that is publicly visible in ways to which we are generally unaccustomed, a scholarship and pedagogy that are bound up with infrastructure in ways that are deeper and more explicit than we are generally accustomed to, a scholarship and pedagogy that are collaborative and depend on networks of people and that live an active, 24–7 life online." Since then, scholars have critiqued the alleged arrival of digital humanities in the academic mainstream regarding the availability of educational and career opportunities, the diversity and inclusivity among practitioners, and the politics and representation of knowledge production (Underwood 2018; Risam 2019, 23–24). In a field rife with manifestos and proclamations, it is worth asking what we

T. Conatser (✉)
University of Kentucky, Lexington, KY, USA
e-mail: trey.conatser@uky.edu

© The Author(s), under exclusive license to Springer Nature Switzerland AG 2022
A. Schwan and T. Thomson (eds.), *The Palgrave Handbook of Digital and Public Humanities*, https://doi.org/10.1007/978-3-031-11886-9_13

are making visible and explicit, whom we are inviting into collaborative and networked relationships, and how our work engages different publics, online or otherwise.

This chapter investigates what Kirschenbaum initially encloses parenthetically; what does it mean for a digital humanities *pedagogy* to be publicly oriented? In this way, I broadly aim to contribute to the growing body of literature on teaching and learning in the digital humanities, especially following calls—themselves emerging from the digital humanities moment—to center pedagogy rather than "bracketing" it as an aside (Hirsch 2012, 5). I also intend to discuss digital humanities pedagogy with careful attention to scholarly context and interventions in addition to recounting particular activities and the use of digital tools (Ball 2013). As Amy Earhart (2012) writes, particularly about the production of digital scholarly editions, "we have much theoretical work to do in the selection of materials and application of digital tools to them." Applying her exhortation to teaching, I take as a focus one of the more ubiquitous cases for digital humanities work as public scholarship: digital exhibits or editions that make otherwise difficult-to-access archival materials available for public viewing and study via open access on the web. Early and large-scale projects such as the William Blake Archive, the Rossetti Archive, the Walt Whitman Archive, and the Women Writers Project frequently appear as milestones of public scholarship in historiographies of the digital humanities, but their scale presents a considerable barrier for pedagogical approaches that would involve students, especially undergraduates, as decision-making agents throughout the larger intellectual journey that such a project represents.

As a way of engaging students in public and digital humanities scholarship I turn to the local context of institutional archives and small-scale, curated, boutique projects that attend to the methods and meanings that go into producing, processing, and presenting qualitative sources and datasets that would otherwise be unknown and/or inaccessible as physical collections (Ball et al. 2013, 5; Crawford 2017, 9–11). These projects draw from Johanna Drucker's (2011) distinction between data and *capta*, an epistemological shift along an axis of scale that emphasizes the contingent and constructed nature of knowledge as opposed to encountering large datasets as an a priori representation for computational analysis. Pedagogically speaking, "tamed data" allows students to engage reflectively in "a trajectory from exploration to valid argument" while unwieldy "data in the wild" often present barriers for courses that intend for students to have coherent and intellectually rewarding experiences (Goldstone 2019). In pursuit of that goal, this chapter first reviews pedagogical engagements with the archive, particularly as practice with research methodologies, encounters with primary sources, and activities with curatorial goals. Relatively underdeveloped, however, are frameworks for student partnerships and project-based learning with the institutional archive. Drawing from precedents in rhetoric and composition, library collaborations, and digital humanities, I propose an open pedagogical approach for the creation of public-facing, publicly engaged digital resources. As a model for operationalizing this approach, I review a course that scaffolds student learning from the curation of archival materials to the publication of an open-access, digital documentary edition of historical correspondence.

13.2 Students and the Archive

"I believe pedagogical work should be honored as the best kind of research, and our scholarship should be pedagogical," Jesse Stommel writes in *Disrupting the Digital Humanities*. For Stommel, the disruptive (and public) potential of digital humanities lies in "mak[ing] the work legible" so that students, teaching-focused faculty and institutions, and broader audiences are invited into the process of knowledge production in "a more intimate, more provocative" way (2018, 84). Engaging students in open pedagogy and the archives certainly makes the work more legible and accessible for them, but it also invites them to make the work legible and accessible for others. In other words, students stand to do more than *use* archives; their greatest potential lies in partnering with archivists, instructors, and other stakeholders to participate in the ongoing project of refining, assessing, revising, and leveraging our historical imagination. While students themselves represent one "public" in this network, they also act as a conduit through which the archive and the academy at large can address audiences in other professional organizations and contexts as well as among the lay community.

There remains a significant opportunity to develop pedagogical frameworks and research on institutional archives and public digital humanities. Teacher-scholars have addressed the archive in a variety of ways, including how archival spaces and materials offer students an opportunity to practice research methodologies central to humanities disciplines. One example from rhetoric and writing—notably, a graduate-level course—offers a representative dyad of learning outcomes: "to expose students to the practical aspects of working in an archives facility" and "to provide them with opportunities to practice arguing with and about archived material" (Buehl et al. 2012, 281). Others have explored the use of digital archives to foreground information literacy and primary sources in undergraduate courses where students might otherwise encounter only secondary material in textbooks, modern editions, and other mediated/mediating resources. Jessica Enoch and Pamela VanHaitsma (2015) advocate for a focus on "archival literacy" in courses that ask students to make observations and arguments from digital or digitized materials. Emphasizing the "rhetorical characteristics of digital archives" leads students to consider "the archive's power, its promise, and, indeed, its problems," they write, lending more nuance and a critical mindset to student work with archival sources (218–19).

The nature of archives, of course, remains contested, and scholars have examined the "institutionalization" of the archive in terms of the actors, purposes, and interests involved in creating, maintaining, and providing access to archival collections housed in educational, museological, cultural heritage, and other institutions (Manoff 2004, 19). Digital humanities projects may describe the curation and exhibition of materials as the construction of an archive, but Kate Theimer (2012) reminds us that a less fungible sense of archival work implicates the acquisition, metadata, organization, access, storage, and sustainability of entire collections as opposed to the short-term exercise of curatorial agency. This latter pursuit represents a third branch of archival pedagogy that engages students in the assembly of small-scale collections or exhibits that convey messages or inquiries relevant to the course's learning goals. Supported by content management systems such as Wordpress, Omeka, or Scalar, students may construct open-access websites where they articulate their insights and organize what they have selected from archived materials (Tanaka et al. 2021, 42). Students may also collect or generate records from the field as "pop-up" endeavors with the goal of "enacting the work of archiving" and involving students in the networked relations and actions between archivists and subjects in situ (Rice and Rice 2015, 251). These efforts may be isolated to a single course or attached to the development of larger archival projects; for example, assignments involving the Digital Archive of Literacy Narratives have asked students to locate subjects and record interviews in their local communities (Comer and Harker 2015, 71).

To develop a pedagogical grounding for digital humanities in the institutional archive, I draw from Wendy Hayden's (2017) notion of "the archival turn's pedagogical turn" in courses across the disciplines that engage students in "inquiry-based model[s] of education" (135). The specific activities and goals of these courses are myriad, but Hayden finds common ground in an emphasis on "collaboration, invitation, locally-based research, and activism" with "outcomes of recovery, rereading the archives as a source of knowledge and public memory, and archival creation by students" (145). Owing to the central role that uncertainty plays in archival research, a pedagogy of the archives leads students to see their learning less as "knowledge accumulation" and more as the "inquiry and knowledge production" of scholar- and author-apprentices (145). We see these principles at work in faculty-student collaborations that treat the archive as "a site to experiment with new ideas, methodologies, projects, and pedagogies" such as the University of Southern Mississippi's Save Our Stories project, an open-ended call for essays based on items in the archival collections (Brannock et al. 2018, 168). With flexibility to the needs of individual courses and an openness to genre from the creative to the critical, Save Our Stories enacted a partnership with distributed authorship and agency for the stories told by and about the materials in an institutional archive.

When it comes to involving students in curating, encoding, and producing digital editions of archival materials, Clayton McCarl's (2018) "Editing the

Eartha M.M. White Collection" at the University of North Florida is particularly instructive. Designed "as a partial internship," the summer course engaged students in a typical classroom format as well as "workshop sessions" for individual or small group work with the end goal of launching "a prototype website" along with a campus presentation of students' experiences (528–29). While students found the work energizing, they also felt challenged by its "unpredictability" and "constantly evolving nature," which McCarl attributes to "the largely unstructured approach" of the course (533). The summer term's short time frame is not unusual for instruction in digital editing and encoding, which often takes place in workshops or modules ranging from a day to several weeks. Similar efforts have found that students need time and structure to reflect on their role as editors, to connect their work with an impact on stakeholders, and to understand how individual activities support larger course objectives (Duke and Stanley 2019, 65–68). With a more sustained academic term in mind, the following sections establish pedagogical orientations and lay out a scaffolding that attempts to balance structured learning and instructional guidance with student agency and the organic nature of research. Ultimately, through the lens of public scholarship, students encounter archives as "a crucible of activity" for the negotiation and creation of knowledge as opposed to the passive materiality of sealed-off, "static" collections (Decker 2020, 238).

13.3 Pedagogical Orientations

Given the complexity of the course project for undergraduate students who are likely unfamiliar with digital humanities as a scholarly area as well as its conceptual and technical methods—I first encountered such a course at the doctoral level—there is a temptation to devote a good amount of time at the outset of the course to covering content knowledge, i.e., the basic information, theories, and practices with which students ostensibly must be familiar to engage in the higher order thinking that the project demands. However, this approach delays the project-based and collaborative learning that should characterize the entirety of students' experiences in the course, which ideally works more like a research lab or team than a class per se. To spur team-building and engagement around the basic premises of digital humanities and text (en)coding, students may reflect on an approachable conversation piece such as Kirschenbaum's (2009) "Hello Worlds" during the first class meeting. But the larger pedagogical approach involves what researchers have described as "the flipped, flipped classroom" (Schneider et al. 2013) and the "flipped flip" or "co-creational" model (Uskoković 2018). While the traditional flipped approach (which has not been as novel for humanities pedagogy as it has been for STEM disciplines) begins a lesson with lectures, readings, and other materials that students study prior to application-based exercises during class meetings, a further "flip" of the format *first* engages students in activities for which they have not yet been systematically prepared. Other researchers have described this approach as designing for "productive failure" insofar as students "consolidat[e]" these uneven, exploratory experiences with later instruction and learning activities as the class hones in on more optimal solutions, strategies, decisions, and deliverables (Kapur 2016, 289–90).

Part of my rationale for a co-creational design is merely practical; a single academic term does not provide enough time for students to gain a repertoire of knowledge and skills *prior* to conducting the project itself from conception to (pre-)publication. Even given adequate time, however, designing for productive failure stands to foster curiosity and motivation as students exercise agency in the course by considering unknowns and challenges, areas that merit further study or deliberation, connections between new and previous experiences, and adjustments of plans and schedule to accommodate new issues and insights. As Karen Cangialosi (2018) has written, "[o]ur primary role as teacher can be simply to create the best culture chambers for students to flourish" in learning environments that center inquiry and agency for projects that always will exceed content knowledge and familiarity with the discipline. Similarly, for undergraduate digital humanities courses, Ryan Cordell (2016) found that the initial impulse to introduce students to the field of digital humanities through the (content)ious "what is DH?" genre ultimately failed because it did not draw from student interests, experiences, or prior knowledge. He recommends instead that we "start small" with experiential activities that scaffold toward larger objectives in ways that are sensitive to the range of students' digital literacies and backgrounds. Experimental studies in psychology education support Cordell's sense that "many texts and lectures presuppose a level of differentiated knowledge that is not available to novices," and that guided discovery via "contrasting cases" provides a basis for "a deep[er] level" of engagement and understanding with later explanations and activities (Schwartz and Bransford 1998, 477, 504).

At a macro-level, the pedagogy of archival work and digital scholarly editing follows in the spirit of authentic assessment, an approach to assignment design and evaluation that eschews the testing of decontextualized knowledge in favor of involving students in tasks that are critical or common in particular fields of work (Wiggins 1990). Authentic assessment involves realism, cognitive challenge, and frequent and formative feedback; notably, however, there seems to be less of a focus on decision-making processes, teamwork, and collaborative learning: a gap that project-based courses are poised to address (Villarroela et al. 2018, 844–46). One of the closest graduate-level cognates to the course I describe in this chapter, for example, asked students to work individually on different projects (Engel and Thain 2015). Beyond authenticity, ethical considerations frame the need to involve students in what Anne B. McGrail (2016) calls "the whole game" of digital humanities as opposed to merely "teaching them *about*" the field or treating them as "crowdsourced labor" that completes "microtasks" for projects in which they otherwise have no agency. Addressing the place of community colleges and their students in the digital humanities, McGrail warns that we undermine the democratic potential of digital and public humanities pedagogy if we "reinscrib[e] students into their place in a hierarchy that is all too familiar" in the academy. My commitment to students, for example, is that they will work and be credited as members of the editorial team; of course, this is easier said than done given our habituation to the gatekeeping culture of higher education and the delicate pedagogical balance of instructional presence and student agency.

Lastly, though certainly not least, my thinking takes a cue from open pedagogy, which Robin DeRosa and Rajiv Jhangiani (2017) summarize as "an access-oriented commitment to learner-driven education" and "a process of designing architectures and using tools for learning that enable students to shape the public knowledge commons of which they are a part." Merging constructivist and critical traditions with the open access and open education movements, open pedagogy most notably sees students *build* educational resources in addition to drawing on them for learning. Students quickly see that they are doing the same kind of work as researchers who publish digital editions, archives, and other resources; in terms of authenticity, the realism of the project is apparent. And, through the curricular scaffolding I describe in the following sections, students encounter cognitive challenges in ways that make space for exploration and productive failure, all the while building their capacity for evaluative (self-)judgment through the uniquely collaborative nature of the coursework. Overall, I suggest that undergraduate curricula in digital and public humanities via the curation, modeling, encoding, editing, and publication of archival materials should engage students in a "non-disposable" project whose three dimensions are time, space, and gravity: the persistence of student work beyond the timeframe of an activity or course, the reach for external audiences beyond an instructor and class, and the "value/impact" for those audiences and students themselves (Seraphin et al. 2019, 89–90).

13.4 Curation and Digitization

As a case study for how this pedagogical approach can be implemented as a scaffolded curriculum I turn to "Digital Editing and Publishing," a junior seminar I designed and taught in the Lewis Honors College at the University of Kentucky with critical support and partnership from the UK Libraries Special Collections Research Center. Prior to the first offering of the course, I consulted with the director of research services and education to identify collections that aligned with my course goals and would present a compelling connection for local contexts and audiences. Approaching the special collections faculty and staff without a firm decision beforehand was important for the open (and public) design of the course. As a best practice for course design, working "with collections staff early in the course development process" helps to identify the best choices for materials and also provides an opportunity to develop "scaffolded approaches to working with primary sources" (Tanaka et al. 2021, 51). With this advice, I selected the Frontier Nursing Service collection: specifically, the correspondence of its founder, Mary Breckinridge, during 1919 when she worked in rural France as a nurse and administrator of relief efforts for women and children reeling from the devastation of the first world war. Later bringing the first nurse-midwifery services to the United States, Breckinridge's life and work are significant for the history of nursing, public health, and Appalachian studies. Given our location at the doorstep of the Appalachian region where Breckinridge's nurses on horseback brought specialized medical care to isolated communities, her work resonates as part of our local history and evokes the affordances and flexibility of place-based education in the archives (Beam and Schwier 2018, 13–16). In fact, the UK Special Collections Breckinridge Research Room, where many of our class meetings were held, is named after her family.

I wanted to get students in the archive as quickly as possible, and after two introductory class meetings, we spent a month in Special Collections. In addition to drawing from the flipped-flip model, this approach follows Silvia Vong's (2016) sense of constructivist learning in the archive, which emphasizes "[c]onnection between prior knowledge and new knowledge; [s]ocial interaction between students or students and the instructor; [r]eal-life tasks or experiences that relate to new knowledge; and [a]ctivities that prompt reflection on one's own learning and experience(s)" (155–56). As Paul Fyfe (2011) suggests, this "unplugg[ed]" work in the archive positions students to "appreciate, by contrast, their active mediation of similar work in the digital field, which too frequently seems transparent, or so flattened that students fail to notice its own critical topologies." In other words, experiencing "the insistent materiality" of archival objects leads students to understand how their work *transforms* texts in digital editions (Engel and Thain 2015). Our time in Special Collections was devoted to studying the letters: piecing together their narrative, refining our sense of their significance (biographical, historical, literary), and curating a selection that students would transcribe, encode, and research for a digital documentary edition. Readings on archival theories and methods enriched the experiential learning while students also compared the letters with autobiographical and scholarly accounts of Breckinridge's life. Class meetings began and ended with group discussions of progress and goals while much of the time involved a balance of individual work and team deliberation. In the spirit of constructivism, student observations and insights drove our work: what did they notice? what was compelling or confusing? what were others' reactions to the same document(s)? Students concluded the month in Special Collections by using specialized scanners to create digital facsimiles of their selected letters (one or two per student depending on length and complexity). Before they began to transcribe and encode the letters in earnest, however, we turned our attention to how researchers model texts in digital environments to build a theoretical foundation for the detail-intensive work that would soon follow.

13.5 Modeling Text and Correspondence

Arguing for the value of teaching computer programming in/as humanities coursework, Kirschenbaum (2009) eschews learning outcomes concerned with coding skills per se—students can go elsewhere for that—as he recounts an activity that asks students to model snowballs in an object-oriented programming environment:

> What are a snowball's salient characteristics? What do you do with one? Well, you toss the snowball at someone else. But wait, before you do that, you first have to shape it, form it, pack the snow. Once you do toss it, do you still have it? No. So the program has to be able to distinguish between possession and nonpossession of the snowball. And maybe, if you hang onto it too long, it starts to melt. The exercise of thinking through what it takes to model a snowball in a believable fashion goes a long way toward capturing the appeal of what I mean by programming as world-making.

Modeling is a core activity of digital humanities scholarship often defined as an interpretive and transformative pursuit (e.g., as world-making). In the foundational monograph *Humanities Computing*, Willard McCarty (2005) describes modeling capaciously, as "a representation of something for purposes of study, or a design for realizing something new" (24). At the same time, the novel possibilities of modeling are always in tension with "the fundamental dependence of any computing system on an explicit, delimited conception of the world or 'model' of it" (21). Computer code thrives on "univocal, correct, 'activating' interpretations" and cannot work with the "ambiguity, context, and polysemy" that are a fundamental condition of human thought and language (Golumbia 2009, 84). In other words, nothing goes without saying when modeling phenomena for/with computers, but for humans, models will always leave something out and will not serve equally across every context or application. However, it is this very constraint that digital humanists find to be generative, especially for pedagogy; in deciding what to include, how to include it, and what to leave out when modeling concepts, actions, and other phenomena, students engage in a "mental discipline" that "self-reflexive[ly]" discovers, questions, and "make[s] explicit our understanding of the thing being modeled" along with "our assumptions and beliefs about it" (Sperberg-McQueen 2019, 287–88).

My goal for modeling exercises is that students practice a kind of thinking unique to text encoding, where instead of snowballs, scholars model documents, language, writing, and social and historical context. Our work focuses specifically on correspondence, which presents a unique test case given its complex nature as a document and mode of communication. Text encoding and digital editions are particularly adept at addressing the challenges of correspondence given that (1) letters are often held in multiple, "far flung" locations with an "equally dispersed" audience of archivists, scholars, commercial interests, and lay enthusiasts; (2) print editions cannot contain contextual and associated artifacts that defined the social networks in which letters operated; and (3) the study of letters in codex form "essentially reduces and thus misrepresents the relational aspect of correspondence" (Hankins 2015). In short, correspondence presents the challenge of modeling text that gestures outward or elsewhere, and students explore how the computational and representational capabilities of markup technologies address the nonlinearity, referentiality, and contextuality of correspondence. This work engages students with a kind of writing that they likely use regularly, however modernized their own media and conventions are by comparison.

As an initial exercise, I asked students to model correspondence using only a wall in the classroom and small sticky notes. The task was deceptively simple: create a model of correspondence that is as comprehensive and accurate as possible. As a heuristic, I provided a list of generative questions: who is involved in correspondence? how is it structured? what does it contain? how does it move across space and time? what are its physical aspects? what documents or objects are associated with it? what do letters tell us, and what would we want to do with them? Initially, students generated as many ideas as possible; each went on a sticky note. Next, students worked as a group to cluster their notes around common themes. Once an initial affinity map was complete, students reflected on what was represented most and least, what needed to be combined or better distinguished, and what still was absent from the model. At this point, the class attempted to categorize and build relational hierarchies with the goal of constructing a tree diagram of the correspondence model. Naturally, students disagreed on certain points and particular items seemed to fit in several places, or in no place at all. These moments served as useful reminders that the exercise seeks to engage students reflectively in the process and choices that go into modeling a text and document for different purposes.

For the next meeting, students studied an article recounting the Text Encoding Initiative's development of a model for encoding correspondence as part of the TEI Guidelines. Recalling their experiences in the same task, students considered the theories of correspondence that the authors review and model in extensible markup language (XML). Letters are at once object, text, and event, they conclude, each of which implicates people, dates, places, and sequences. The TEI task force ultimately arrived at a "communication-oriented concept of correspondence" with tags for action and context in an overall description wrapper (Stadler et al. 2016):

```
<correspDesc>
   <correspAction type="sent">
     <persName>Carl Maria von Weber</persName>
     <settlement>Dresden</settlement>
     <date when="1817-06-23">23 June 1817</date>
   </correspAction>
   <correspAction type="received">
     <persName>Caroline Brandt</persName>
     <settlement>Prague</settlement>
```

```xml
        </correspAction>
        <correspContext>
            <ref type="prev" target="http://www.weber-gesamtausgabe.de/A041209">
                Previous letter of <persName>Carl Maria von Weber</persName> to <persName>Caroline Brandt</persName>: <date from="1817-06-19" to="1817-06-20">June 19/20, 1817</date>
            </ref>
            <ref type="next" target="http://www.weber-gesamtausgabe.de/A041217">
                Next letter of <persName>Carl Maria von Weber</persName> to <persName>Caroline Brandt</persName>: <date when="1817-06-27">June 27, 1817</date>
            </ref>
        </correspContext>
</correspDesc>
```

With guiding questions, students arrived at the next meeting to compare the TEI model with their own, as well as with the precedents that the TEI task force considered. We discussed how and to what extent the <correspDesc> model is, as its developers write, "both theoretically justifiable and practically useful" in the overall context of the TEI Guidelines (Stadler et al. 2016). Why, for example, would it be desirable to minimize the creation of new elements to action- and context-oriented tags aside from the overall wrapper? How might modeling textual data in this way allow for interchange and interoperability with other researchers and projects? Beyond those, why do models and metadata like this matter for a public audience? Students may also consider alternative models such as Dumont et al.'s (2019) suggestion to include a unique witness identifier, editorial certainty, entities mentioned, and type of publication. The TEI's model should not present a foregone conclusion at which students must sooner or later arrive; instead, it offers students an opportunity to consider the needs of their own project and, in the spirit of open pedagogy, collectively decide if customization is needed. The activity concluded with students encoding their letters' metadata as <correspDesc> structures in the project corpus file either in person or as homework, connecting theoretical modeling to encoding practice as a scaffolded, experiential learning activity. Overall, as a result of this sequence, students were able to describe the importance of modeling for text encoding and digital scholarly editions, as well as evaluate the affordances and constraints of various models and modeling approaches. These skills were critical for a mid-term assignment that asked students to select, analyze, and evaluate a published digital scholarly edition of correspondence and present their insights to the class.

13.6 Transcriptional and Contextual Encoding

For the next two months, students transcribed, encoded, and edited their selected letters. As is standard for text encoding projects, we used the TEI P5 Guidelines, a flexible vocabulary for XML that facilitates metadata interchange and interoperability. At a basic level, XML specifies only a syntax and structure for encoded text, meaning that it requires a particular form and arrangement for the code but does not mandate the vocabulary that describes texts. Elements are the basic unit of XML; they may have any number of attributes, each with a range of possible values. Since the late 1980s the Text Encoding Initiative has refined a framework for modeling documents and texts in markup language—first, using a standard generalized markup language (SGML) and later, XML—with a controlled lexicon based on the document type. Prior to the TEI Guidelines, text encoding schemes "typically reflected the specialized interests of their originators and were, by and large, incompatible...a text encoded for one purpose or piece of software often required substantial editing to be used for another purpose or with other software, if it was reusable at all" (Ide and Sperberg-McQueen 1995, 5). Students understood the value and purpose of the TEI standards in terms of the ethos of public scholarship whereas requirements in other courses such as paper and citation formatting may strike them as arbitrary. As they gained experience and consulted the taxonomies and examples in the TEI Guidelines, they appreciated the "modularity, modifiability, [and] numerous alternative means of handling analogous phenomena" (Huitfeldt 2014, 176). In other words, the narrative of teaching and learning with text encoding involves the recentering of student agency among what at first glance may appear to leave little room for self-determination. As my students and I reflect, "[w]e dedicated much of our time to identifying and applying the elements and attributes that would best serve our project, especially given the theoretical possibility that almost everything in a letter can be encoded in some way" (Conatser et al. 2019, 30).

Text encoding was split into two phases: transcriptional markup and contextual markup. The class met twice per week with one meeting usually focusing on design and theory while the other provided time for work and problem-solving. Challenges may arise at the transcriptional stage based on the physical state of the documents as well as their compositional method. Our letters were relatively modern, mostly undamaged, and with few exceptions written with a typewriter; while we did not need to engage in paleography or extensive handwriting analysis, the documents nonetheless presented many challenges for transcription: overtyped characters or words (sometimes twice or even three times over), faint or missing characters, handwritten emendations, and small tears. Collaboration was key, and we spent a significant amount of time as a community determining the best reading or interpretation for ambiguous moments in the text. Once the transcriptional markup was mostly complete, students began contextual markup, which involved tagging, researching, and describing named or referenced entities such as people, places, events, and organizations. Unique identifiers linked the contextual markup in the body text to fully descriptive entries in the metadata header for the corpus file. At this stage, the markup itself took little time compared to the research and writing to flesh out Breckinridge's references, some of which veered into the obscure and led to spirited detective work on the students' part. Students added their own editorial notes following Matthias Bauer and Angelika Zirker's (2015) theory and best practices for literary annotation in digital

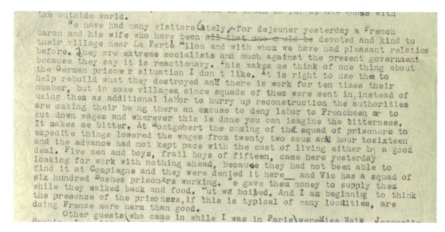

Fig. 13.1 Detail of a digital facsimile of a letter from the Frontier Nursing Service records, 1789–1985, courtesy of the University of Kentucky Libraries Special Collections Research Center

humanities. With this "reader-oriented approach" the class considered what merited further explanation for general comprehension as well as special interests, given the time constraints around what could be researched effectively before the end of the term. Throughout this process, students continued to collaborate on shared references and annotations that applied to multiple letters. The example markup for Fig. 13.1 shows transcriptional markup for deletions, additions, editorial regularizations, and line breaks as well as contextual markup for place references and editorial annotations.

```
Five men and boys, frail boys of fifteen, came here yesterday <lb/>
looking for work with nothing ahead, becau
     <del rend="overwritten">e</del>
     <add quantity="1" unit="chars" place="over" rend="handwritten">s</add>
e they had not been able to <lb/>
find it at <placeName xml:id="compiegne">Compiegne</placeName> and they were
denied it here
     <choice>
       <orig>_</orig>
       <reg resp="studentname"/>
     </choice>
and <placeName xml:id="vsa">Vic</placeName> has a squad of <lb/>
six     hundred     Boshes<ptr     type="annotation"     subtype="linguistic"
target="bosh-etymology"/> prison
     <add rend="handwritten" place="inline">e</add>
rs working. We gave them money to supply them <lb/>
while they walked back and food. But we boi
     <del rend="overtyped">p</del>
     <add quantity="1" unit="chars" place="over" rend="typed">l</add>
ed. And I am beginnin
     <add quantity="1" unit="chars" place="over" rend="typed">g</add>
     <choice>
       <orig><space quantity="2" unit="chars"/></orig>
       <reg resp="studentname"> </reg>
```

```
    </choice>
to think <lb/>
the presence of the prison
    <del rend="overtyped">rs</del>
    <add quantity="2" unit="chars" place="over" rend="typed">er</add>
s, if this is typical of many loca
    <add quantity="1" unit="chars" place="over" rend="typed">l</add>
ities, are <lb/>
doing France more harm than good. <ptr type="annotation" subtype="historical"
target="pow-labor"/>
```

"Textual encoding has never been as sexy as text analysis," writes Ryan Cordell (2014); yet, it involves a transparency and public accountability regarding "the relationships among preservation, presentation, access, and interpretation." Students indeed found text encoding to be demanding and detail-intensive but they also "found even the most granular acts of description to be profoundly interpretive," blurring the line between technical and intellectual labor (Conatser et al. 2019, 30). Periodically dedicating class time to brief case studies reinforced the modeling work that continues throughout the project and connects the minutiae of markup to significant ethical and scholarly questions. Two examples that serve well in this role concern the encoding of racialized eye dialect and personal pronouns. In the first case, editors of *Race and Children's Literature in the Gilded Age* sought to regularize eye dialect for machine readability without making claims regarding value or correctness in their handling of the markup (Gailey 2011). Authorial origin and cultural legacy add further complexity as the texts in question (the Uncle Remus stories of the late nineteenth century) were written by white folklorist Joel Chandler Harris and inspired the now-infamous Disney film *Song of the South* (1946). In the second case, a proposal initiated by Ashley M. Clark (2020) led to the formal adoption of markup for personal pronouns in the TEI Guidelines. Favoring the "queer solution" of combining computationally tractable attribute values with qualitative parsed character data (i.e., the text within XML tags), Clark also suggests a mechanism for recording the evidence on which editors base the pronouns they have indicated for the person at hand. Students may consider approaches to these and other issues and compare their ideas with the solutions advanced by scholar-editors for real projects.

13.7 Conclusion: Transformation and Sustainability

One of the fundamental concepts of digital scholarly editing is the distinction between encoding and presentation: "to record and document the physical, structural, and semantic data" on the one hand and "to determine and instruct how the registered data of the source material are to be processed with regard to selection, display, and format" on the other (Pichler and Bruvik 2014, 180–81). Students recognized this distinction as critical to the sustainability of our digital edition as they produced a platform-independent corpus file of descriptive markup that could be adapted for any number of venues (or research projects) through extensible stylesheet language transformations (XSLT). A single academic term did not provide time for students to learn other coding languages, i.e., not only the stylesheet language, but also the HTML, CSS, and JavaScript that are required to generate a browser-accessible edition. In place of coding, students addressed the production of digital editions from a conceptual and design standpoint. Midway through the term they presented and led discussions on published digital documentary editions with an eye toward our own. Students plotted out structure, content, and user experience given that digital documentary editions record "as many features of the original document as are considered meaningful by the editors, displayed in all the ways the editors consider useful for the readers, including all the tools necessary to achieve such a purpose" (Pierazzo 2011, 475). In addition to Elena Pierazzo's rationale for digital documentary editions, students consulted the Association for Documentary Editing's standards for electronic editions, the Modern Language Association's guidelines for editors of scholarly editions, and the University of Pittsburgh Visual Media Workshop's sociotechnical sustainability roadmap. The learning goals for this phase of the course focused more on understanding and appreciating considerations for future development; were the curriculum year-long, it could involve students directly in designing, transforming, and even preparing the edition for scholarly review.

A critical part of the course's public engagement and students' reflection on their learning was a group presentation for local stakeholders on campus and a collaboratively written essay for a specific venue and audience. We devoted class time during the final month of the semester to plan, develop, and finalize both of these assignments. I advertised the presentation across campus and particularly to audiences for whom our project would resonate because of a connection with the edition's subject matter or with our archival and digital methods. The pedagogy of assigning and leading students through a collaborative essay deserves its own chapter, but I will note here that it requires proactive and creative thinking on the instructor's part to secure an authentic venue for student work. For one instance of the course, for example, I explored a peer-reviewed medical humanities blog before turning to an archival organization's newsletter. Writing for a real audience, venue, and purpose fulfilled the course's promise that students would be taken seriously as editors, and that their work would matter as a form of public scholarship. It would, as we found, underscore the public stakes of our collective learning and clarify what it means, à la Kirschenbaum, for pedagogy to be open and visible, bound in infrastructures both archival and digital, and deeply committed to collaboration.

With crises of public health, climate change, social injustice, and political instability, the early 2020s strike teacher-scholars as a reckoning not only with the orthodoxies of higher education but also with how we have traditionally imagined innovation in teaching and learning. In one take on what this moment "means" for academics, Paul Hanstedt (2020) urges us to engage students in issues of public interest that "foreground [the] messy interactions" between disciplines and professions, such as "how data influences poetry and how poetry can shape our ability to give meaning to data." Moreover, Hanstedt argues, educators are called on to explore the "possibility of agency" for students in more intentional and systematic ways. Now a decade beyond the "digital humanities moment" that anticipated a more publicly engaged and publicly visible scholarly community, our current moment asks us to imagine our students as part of that community and to *re*imagine their learning through open pedagogy and public-facing work. The approach I have described in this chapter is one way to respond to that call, with students exploring how text encoding and digital scholarly editing influence our understanding of historical records and how those records grant palpable meaning and public stakes to digital humanities learning environments.

References

Ball, Cheryl. 2013. "Logging On." *Kairos: A Journal of Rhetoric, Technology, and Pedagogy* 17 (2) (Spring). https://kairos.technorhetoric.net/17.2/loggingon/index.html.

Ball, Cheryl, Tarez Samra Graban, and Michelle Sidler. 2013. "The Boutique Is Open: Data for Writing Studies." http://ceball.com/wp-content/uploads/2013/11/NHUK-chapter-rhetoric.io-PREPRINT.pdf.

Bauer, Matthias, and Angelika Zirker. 2015. "Whipping Boys Explained: Literary Annotation and Digital Humanities." In *Literary Studies in the Digital Age: An Evolving Anthology*, edited by Kenneth M. Price and Ray Siemens. New York: Modern Language Association. https://doi.org/10.1632/lsda.2015.12.

Beam, Carey, and Carrie Schwier. 2018. "Learning in Place: The Teaching Archivist and Place-Based Education." *Archival Issues: The Journal of the Midwest Archives Conference* 29 (1): 7–25.

Brannock, Jennifer, Craig Carey, and Joyce O. Inman. 2018. "Starting from the Archives: Digital Humanities Partnerships, Projects, and Pedagogies." In *Digital Humanities, Libraries, and Partnerships: A Critical Examination of Labor, Networks, and Community*, edited by Robin Kear and Kate Joranson, 163–76. Cambridge, MA: Chandos Publishing.

Buehl, Jonathan, Tamar Chute, and Anne Fields. 2012. "Training in the Archives: Archival Research as Professional Development." *College Composition and Communication* 64 (2) (December): 274–305.

Cangialosi, Karen. 2018. "But You Can't Do That in a STEM Course!" *Hybrid Pedagogy*, June 26. https://hybridpedagogy.org/do-in-a-stem-course/.

Clark, Ashley M. 2020. "Proposal: New Element <persPronouns> #2010." Text Encoding Initiative Repository (GitHub), June 29. https://github.com/TEIC/TEI/issues/2010.

Comer, Kathryn B., and Michael Harker. 2015. "The Pedagogy of the Digital Archive of Literacy Narratives: A Survey." *Computers and Composition* 35 (March): 65–85. https://doi.org/10.1016/j.compcom.2015.01.001.

Conatser, Trey, Jake Beavin, Cassie Bradley, Dylan Clark, and Brianna Gill. 2019. "Coding (and) the Archive: Texts, Markup, and Open Pedagogy." *Midwest Archives Conference Newsletter* 47 (1) (July): 29–31.

Cordell, Ryan. 2014. "On Ignoring Encoding," May 8. https://ryancordell.org/research/dh/on-ignoring-encoding/.

Cordell, Ryan. 2016. "How Not to Teach Digital Humanities." In *Debates in the Digital Humanities 2016*, edited by Matthew K. Gold and Lauren F. Klein. Minneapolis: University of Minnesota Press. https://dhdebates.gc.cuny.edu/projects/debates-in-the-digital-humanities-2016.

Crawford, Cole. 2017. "Respect the Gap: From Big to Boutique Data Through *Laboring-Class Poets Online*." MA thesis, Oregon State University.

Decker, Juilee. 2020. "No More 'Dusty Archive' Kitten Deaths: Discoverability, Incidental Learning, and Digital Humanities." In *Quick Hits for Teaching with Digital Humanities: Successful Strategies from Award-Winning Teachers*, edited by Christopher J. Young, Michael Morrone, Thomas C. Wilson, and Emma Annette Wilson, 232–40. Bloomington, IN: Indiana University Press.

DeRosa, Robin, and Rajiv Jhangiani. 2017. "Open Pedagogy." In *A Guide to Making Open Textbooks with Students*, edited by Elizabeth Mays. Montreal: Rebus Community. https://press.rebus.community/makingopentextbookswithstudents/chapter/open-pedagogy/.

Drucker, Johanna. 2011. "Humanities Approaches to Graphical Display." *Digital Humanities Quarterly* 5 (1). http://www.digitalhumanities.org/dhq/vol/5/1/000091/000091.html.

Duke, Rachel C. S., and Sarah Stanely. 2019. "'Decoding' with Encoding: Digital Tools in the Special Collections Classroom." In *Teaching Undergraduates with Archives*, edited by Nancy Bartlett, Elizabeth Gadelha, and Cinda Nofziger, 60–70. Ann Arbor: Maize Books. https://doi.org/10.3998/mpub.11499242.

Dumont, Stefan, Ingo Börner, Jonas Müller-Laackman, Dominik Leipold, and Gerlinde Schneider. 2019. "Correspondence Metadata Interchange Format (CMIF)." In *Encoding Correspondence: A Manual for Encoding Letters and Postcards in TEI-XML and DTABf*, edited by Stefan Dumont, Susanne Haaf, and Sabine Seifert. Berlin: Berlin-Brandenburg Academy of Sciences and Humanities. https://encoding-correspondence.bbaw.de/v1/CMIF.html.

Earhart, Amy E. 2012. "Can Information Be Unfettered? Race and the New Digital Humanities Canon." In *Debates in the Digital Humanities*, edited by Matthew K. Gold. Minneapolis: University of Minnesota Press. https://dhdebates.gc.cuny.edu/projects/debates-in-the-digital-humanities.

Engel, Deena, and Marion Thain. 2015. "Textual Artifacts and Their Digital Representations: Teaching Graduate Students to Build Online Archives." *Digital Humanities Quarterly* 9 (1). http://www.digitalhumanities.org/dhq/vol/9/1/000199/000199.html.

Enoch, Jessica, and Pamela VanHaitsma. 2015. "Archival Literacy: Reading the Rhetoric of Digital Archives in the Undergraduate Classroom." *College Composition and Communication* 67 (2) (December): 216–42.

Fyfe, Paul. 2011. "Digital Pedagogy Unplugged." *Digital Humanities Quarterly* 5 (3). http://digitalhumanities.org/dhq/vol/5/3/000106/000106.html.

Gailey, Amanda. 2011. "A Case for Heavy Editing: The Example of *Race and Children's Literature in the Gilded Age*." In *The American Literature Scholar in the*

Digital Age, edited by Amy E. Earhart and Andrew Jewell, 125–44. Ann Arbor: University of Michigan Press. https://doi.org/10.3998/etlc.9362034.0001.001.

Gold, Matthew K. 2012. "The Digital Humanities Moment." In *Debates in the Digital Humanities*, edited by Matthew K. Gold. Minneapolis: University of Minnesota Press. https://dhdebates.gc.cuny.edu/projects/debates-in-the-digital-humanities.

Goldstone, Andrew. 2019. "Teaching Quantitative Methods: What Makes It Hard (in Literary Studies)." In *Debates in the Digital Humanities 2019*, edited by Matthew K. Gold and Lauren F. Klein. Minneapolis: University of Minnesota Press. https://dhdebates.gc.cuny.edu/projects/debates-in-the-digital-humanities-2019.

Golumbia, David. 2009. *The Cultural Logic of Computation*. Cambridge, MA: Harvard University Press.

Hankins, Gabriel. 2015. "Correspondence: Theory, Practice, and Horizons." In *Literary Studies in the Digital Age: An Evolving Anthology*, edited by Kenneth M. Price and Ray Siemens. New York: Modern Language Association. https://doi.org/10.1632/lsda.2015.13.

Hanstedt, Paul. 2020. "Might This Be the Beginning of Education?" *Inside Higher Ed*, April 28. https://www.insidehighered.com/views/2020/04/28/how-pandemic-might-create-better-educational-opportunities-opinion.

Hayden, Wendy. 2017. "And Gladly Teach: The Archival Turn's Pedagogical Turn." *College English* 80 (2) (November): 133–58.

Hirsch, Brett D. 2012. "</Parenthesis>: Digital Humanities and the Place of Pedagogy." In *Digital Humanities Pedagogy: Practices, Principles and Politics*, edited by Brett D. Hirsch, 3–30. Cambridge, UK: Open Book Publishers.

Huitfeldt, Claus. 2014. "Markup Technology and Textual Scholarship." In *Digital Critical Editions*, edited by Daniel Apollon and Claire Belisle, 157–78. Urbana-Champaign: University of Illinois Press.

Ide, Nancy M., and C. M. Sperberg-McQueen. 1995. "The TEI: History, Goals, Future." *Computers and the Humanities* 29 (1): 5–15. https://doi.org/10.1007/BF01830313.

Kapur, Manu. 2016. "Examining Productive Failure, Productive Success, Unproductive Failure, and Unproductive Success in Learning." *Educational Psychologist* 51 (2): 289–99. https://doi.org/10.1080/00461520.2016.1155457.

Kirschenbaum, Matthew. 2009. "Hello Worlds: Why Humanities Students Should Learn to Program." *Chronicle of Higher Education*, January 23. https://www.chronicle.com/article/hello-worlds/.

Kirschenbaum, Matthew. 2012. "What Is Digital Humanities and What's It Doing in English Departments?" In *Debates in the Digital Humanities*, edited by Matthew K. Gold. Minneapolis: University of Minnesota Press. https://dhdebates.gc.cuny.edu/projects/debates-in-the-digital-humanities.

Manoff, Marlene. 2004. "Theories of the Archive Across the Disciplines." *Portal: Libraries and the Academy* 4 (1) (January): 9–25.

McCarl, Clayton. 2018. "Editing the Eartha M.M. White Collection: An Experiment in Engaging Students in Archival Research and Editorial Practice." *The Journal of Academic Librarianship* 44 (4) (July): 527–37. https://doi.org/10.1016/j.acalib.2018.02.011.

McCarty, Willard. 2005. *Humanities Computing*. Basingstoke and New York: Palgrave Macmillan.

McGrail, Anne B. 2016. "The 'Whole Game': Digital Humanities at Community Colleges." In *Debates in the Digital Humanities 2016*, edited by Matthew K. Gold and Lauren F. Klein. Minneapolis: University of Minnesota Press. https://dhdebates.gc.cuny.edu/projects/debates-in-the-digital-humanities-2016.

Pierazzo, Elena. 2011. "A Rationale of Digital Documentary Editions." *Literary and Linguistic Computing* 26 (4) (December): 463–77. https://doi.org/10.1093/llc/fqr033.

Pichler, Alois, and Tone Merete Bruvik. 2014. "Digital Critical Editing: Separating Encoding from Presentation." In *Digital Critical Editions*, edited by Daniel Apollon and Claire Belisle, 179–99. Urbana-Champaign: University of Illinois Press.

Rice, Jenny, and Jeff Rice. 2015. "Pop-Up Archives." In *Rhetoric and the Digital Humanities*, edited by Jim Ridolfo and William Hart-Davidson, 245–54. Chicago: University of Chicago Press.

Risam, Roopika. 2019. *New Digital Worlds: Postcolonial Digital Humanities in Theory, Praxis, and Pedagogy*. Evanston, IL: Northwestern University Press.

Schneider, Bertrand, Paulo Blikstein, and Roy Pea. 2013. "The Flipped, Flipped Classroom." *The Stanford Daily*, August 5. https://www.stanforddaily.com/2013/08/05/the-flipped-flipped-classroom/.

Schwartz, Daniel L., and John D. Bransford. 1998. "A Time for Telling." *Cognition and Instruction* 16 (4): 475–522. http://www.jstor.org/stable/3233709.

Seraphin, Sally B., J. Alex Grizzell, Anastasia KerrGerman, Marjorie A. Perkins, Patrick R. Grzanka, and Erin E. Hardin. 2019. "A Conceptual Framework for Non-Disposable Assignments: Inspiring Implementation, Innovation, and Research." *Psychology Learning and Teaching* 18 (1): 84–97. https://doi.org/10.1177/1475725718811711.

Sperberg-McQueen, C. M. 2019. "Playing for Keeps: The Role of Modeling in the Humanities." In *The Shape of Data in Digital Humanities: Modeling Texts and Text-Based Resources*, edited by Julia Flanders and Fortis Jannidis, 283–310. New York: Routledge.

Stadler, Peter, Marcel Illetschko, and Sabine Seifert. 2016. "Towards a Model for Encoding Correspondence in the TEI: Developing and Implementing <correspDesc>." *Journal of the Text Encoding Initiative* 9 (Sep. 2016–Dec. 2017). https://doi.org/10.4000/jtei.1433.

Stommel, Jesse. 2018. "The Public Digital Humanities." In *Disrupting the Digital Humanities*, edited by Dorothy Kim and Jesse Stommel, 79–90. Goleta, CA: Punctum Books.

Tanaka, Kurtis, Daniel Abosso, Krystal Appiah, Katie Atkins, Peter Barr, Arantza Barrutia-Wood, Shatha Baydoun, et al. 2021. *Teaching with Primary Sources: Looking at the Support Needs of Instructors*. New York: Ithaka S+R. https://doi.org/10.18665/sr.314912.

Theimer, Kate. 2012. "Archives in Context and as Context." *Journal of Digital Humanities* 1 (2) (Spring). http://journalofdigitalhumanities.org/1-2/archives-in-context-and-as-context-by-kate-theimer/.

Underwood, Ted. 2018. "A Broader Purpose." Accessed May 2, 2021. https://tedunderwood.com/2018/01/04/a-broader-purpose/.

Uskoković, Vuc. 2018. "Flipping the Flipped: The Co-Creational Classroom." *Research and Practice in Technology Enhanced Learning* 13. https://doi.org/10.1186/s41039-018-0077-9.

Villarroela, Verónica, Susan Bloxham, Daniela Bruna, Carola Bruna, and Constanza Herrera-Seda. 2018. "Authentic Assessment: Creating a Blueprint for Course

Design." *Assessment and Evaluation in Higher Education* 43 (5): 840–54. https://doi.org/10.1080/02602938.2017.1412396.

Vong, Silvia. 2016. "A Constructivist Approach for Introducing Undergraduate Students to Special Collections and Archival Research." *RBM: A Journal of Rare Books, Manuscripts, and Cultural Heritage* 17 (2): 148–71.

Wiggins, Grant. 1990. "The Case for Authentic Assessment." *Practical Assessment, Research, and Evaluation* 2 (2). https://doi.org/10.7275/ffb1-mm19.

CHAPTER 14

Practices and Challenges of Popularizing Digital Public Humanities During the COVID-19 Pandemic in Japan

Nobuhiko Kikuchi

14.1 Introduction: Japan, Where Public Humanities Is Still in Its Infancy

In Japan, the term "public humanities" has not yet taken hold. The reason for this is that each discipline has its own public humanities activities, and it is difficult to create a space for activities under the big umbrella of "humanities" that transcend the fields of sociology, archaeology, history, etc.[1]

It is difficult to keep track of the movements in the different disciplines of the humanities in Japan, but it is in the fields of archaeology and folklore that the public humanities have been addressed in their respective disciplines since the 2000s. According to the National Diet Library (NDL) Search, which provides access to a broad range of literature in Japan, terms such as "public archaeology" and "public folklore" started appearing around 2005–2006 (Kokusai Kogyo 2005; Yagi 2006). "Public history" was founded as a field after archaeology and in 2018, researchers in Japan formed the Public History Association of Japan (PHAJ, パブリックヒストリー研究会) (Kenmochi 2018; Suga and Hojo 2019). The PHAJ set off the expansion of the field of theorizing and practicing public history. I, as one of the founders of this association, have been active in these efforts.

The concept of public humanities was brought to Japan mainly by the activities of individual disciplines in Europe and the US. Of course, this does not

N. Kikuchi (✉)
National Institute of Japanese Literature, Tokyo, Japan
e-mail: kikuchi.nobuhiko@nijl.ac.jp

© The Author(s), under exclusive license to Springer Nature Switzerland AG 2022
A. Schwan and T. Thomson (eds.), *The Palgrave Handbook of Digital and Public Humanities*, https://doi.org/10.1007/978-3-031-11886-9_14

mean that there had been no research or practice related to "public archaeology," "public folklore," or "public history" prior to the arrival of these terms. In fact, the archaeological and historical communities, as well as institutions in libraries, archives, and museums (MLA) had been engaged in activities that would now be treated as public history or public archaeology (Okamoto 2018). However, the research and practice specific to public humanities, and its interface with the digital humanities, have only just begun to take form in our consciousness.[2] At present, we use the term "public humanities" to refer collectively to public archaeology, public folklore, and public history.

The spread of public humanities was just beginning in Japan when the COVID-19 global pandemic happened. We can say that collecting material related to this pandemic is an example of the essential work of public humanities, that is, to "mov[e] humanistic knowledges among individuals and groups of people" (Smulyan 2021). The digital public history project, titled "コロナアーカイブ@関西大学 (Corona Archive @ Kansai University)" (see Fig. 14.1), was created under this principle. This project is a community archive that collects material related to COVID-19 from the public.[3] However, as mentioned earlier, promoting the practice of public humanities, which has not yet taken root in Japan, has been met with various challenges.

This chapter mainly introduces the Corona Archive @ Kansai University and, using our experience in maintaining this project, answers the following questions: What are the challenges in engaging the public in public humanities activities in Japan? How can we ensure that the public humanities take root in Japan? How should we, as public humanities practitioners, communicate and disseminate our work? To answer these questions, the next section looks first at how the project can be placed in the context of the global and Japanese practice of digital archiving of COVID-19-related material.

14.2 The Corona Archive @ Kansai University as a Digital Public History Project: Its Position in Japan and the World

The Corona Archive @ Kansai University was launched on 17 April 2020 when the state of emergency in Japan was extended nationwide. Initially, I started the Corona Archive @ Kansai University voluntarily, as the motivation for it was personal. It was inspired by the changes in European cities caused by the outbreak of COVID-19 infections and other countries' efforts to collect material amid the pandemic (Kikuchi 2020; Kikuchi et al. 2020; Kikuchi et al. 2021). In this sense, European digital public humanities influenced this project, just as European countries and the US introduced public archaeology and public history to Japan.

Except for this project, efforts to collect and preserve COVID-19-related material in Japan have been made exclusively in museums. The Urahoro Town Museum (浦幌町立博物館) in Hokkaido and Suita City Museum in Osaka

14 PRACTICES AND CHALLENGES OF POPULARIZING … 259

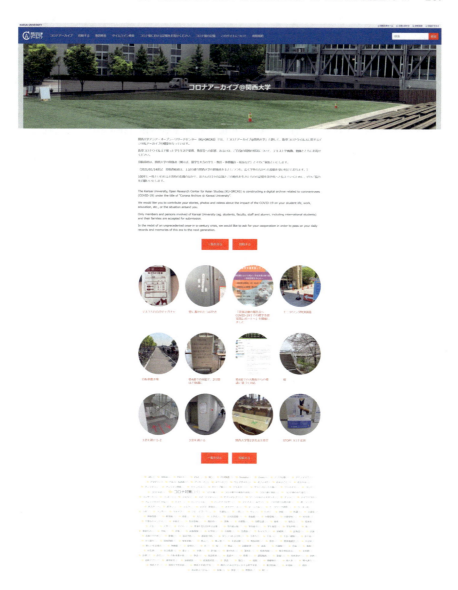

Fig. 14.1 Corona Archive @ Kansai University's homepage

Prefecture were among the first to start such initiatives (Saotome 2021). Both museums collect ephemera, such as posters and leaflets, and hold exhibitions on materials that represent life during the pandemic (Mochida 2021; Saotome 2021). The Tsubouchi Memorial Theatre Museum, Waseda University (早稲田大学坪内博士記念演劇博物館) is known for specializing in theatre. It employs a unique approach in that it has collected flyers and other material of theatrical performances that were canceled due to the pandemic. It presents this material to the public in the online exhibition "Lost Performances: The Coronavirus Crisis and the Recording/Memory of Theatres" (「失われた公演——コロナ禍と演劇の記録/記憶」) (The Tsubouchi Memorial Theatre Museum 2021). In Japan, those museums have been collecting and preserving materials related to the pandemic, but the approach of the Corona Archive @ Kansai University is different from such museums. The reasons are that the Corona Archive @ Kansai University is a digital archive, and it has adopted a crowdsourcing approach as digital public humanities.

The International Federation for Public History (IFPH) and Made by Us have compiled information on global efforts to collect and preserve COVID-19-related material. As of 31 May 2021, they have visualized 523 of these efforts on Google Maps (IFPH 2020) which presents a global map of digital archive initiatives and projects. It includes two digital archive projects that were particularly helpful in the development of the Corona Archive @ Kansai University. The first is the "coronarchiv," a joint project of the University of Hamburg and three other German universities. It was launched on 26 March 2020. Although it is a project of a German university, it is open to anyone interested in submitting material and memories from outside Germany. The second is the "COVID-19 memories" of the Luxembourg Center for Contemporary and Digital History (C^2DH), which was launched on 10 April 2020. The platform is open to anyone who lives or works in Luxembourg. The "memories" are displayed as polka-dot thumbnails on the top screen and visualized over time on an Open Street Map, equipped with designs. The metadata is simple; it consists only of a title, a description of the content, the file, and geoinformation. The digital archive has 328 items as of 31 May 2021.

Aside from these two projects, there are many digital archive projects in other countries and regions worldwide that are actively developed across organizational and national boundaries.[4] However, in Japan, there is no significant digital archive activity other than the Corona Archive @ Kansai University. Although many earthquake archives were constructed and community archives created after the Great East Japan Earthquake in 2011,[5] there has not been as much activity by citizens to document the COVID-19 pandemic. Before discussing the reasons for this, I would like to introduce the Corona Archive @ Kansai University and its features and initiatives first.

14.3 Features of the Corona Archive @ Kansai University

In constructing the Corona Archive @ Kansai University, four items were considered. By discussing these items, I hope to clarify the outline and characteristics of this project.

14.3.1 Adoption of User Participation and Eligibility for Contributions

In April 2020, when we started to think about collecting COVID-19-related material, a state of emergency had been declared. Although it was not legally enforceable like the lockdowns in Europe and the US, there were calls for people to stay at home ("#stayathome") and a consensus on voluntary restraint in going out. This situation made it difficult for me to collect material for the digital archive and I had no choice but to ask for user participation through the community archive.

How is eligibility for contributions set in a community archive approach? Both the German and Luxembourg case studies mentioned in the previous section made anyone eligible to contribute. However, at the beginning of the development of the Corona Archive @ Kansai University, it was difficult to predict how many submissions would be received because there had not been a similar system in Japan. As mentioned above, I manage this project voluntarily; there was a risk that if there were too many contributions, I would have difficulty verifying all of them. For this reason, initially, the eligibility of contributors was limited to only those affiliated with Kansai University (i.e., students, including international students, faculty members, alumni association members, members of affiliated schools, and their families), and later, we accepted the submissions from the general public. However, I believe that this restriction at the first stage has harmed the status of the project. I will discuss this later.

14.3.2 System Construction and Material to Be Collected

The Corona Archive @ Kansai University was developed when COVID-19 infections were already widespread in Japan, so I needed to construct it quickly and easily. Not having the skills to build a system from scratch, I chose to use the publishing platform Omeka Classic as it met the requirements of easy and fast. Both the coronarchiv and COVID-19 memories discussed in the previous section use Omeka S, which is part of the Omeka Classic series. The Corona Archive @ Kansai University was upgraded to Omeka S in October 2020.

The project was designed, as a necessary function, to support various file formats, such as texts, images, sounds, and videos. Providing the contributor with the ability to post information on the map was also considered a basic feature, so that users could easily locate the submitted material. These goals were achieved by implementing plugins for Omeka. A Folksonomy function was also added, so that users can add tags to the material themselves to enrich the search. The tags added by Folksonomy are CC0; that is, contributors are required to waive their copyrights.

14.3.3 Dealing with Copyright and Portrait Rights Issues

Dealing with copyright comes with collecting material voluntarily through submission by users. To address this problem, we developed a set of terms and conditions that require all contributors to agree to provide and publish their material under the terms of the Creative Commons License Attribution-NonCommercial 4.0 International (CC BY-NC 4.0). The data itself is published under these conditions and available in an International Image Interoperability Framework (IIIF) format; this means that users can use it freely and openly.

It is also necessary to consider the possibility that people may appear in the images, which may give rise to issues related to portrait and privacy rights. For this reason, the Terms of Use require contributors to confirm that they have permission from the person before posting it. It also states that any photo posted will be deemed to have that permission. In addition, we participated in the proving test of the "Portrait Rights Guidelines (Draft) (Version 3)" by the Legal System Committee of the Japan Society for Digital Archive (JSDA), and we approached issues regarding rights in accordance with the guidelines (JSDA 2021). Moreover, users themselves can express their intention to post their data privately.

14.3.4 Ensuring a Long-Term Preservation System

The Kansai University Open Research Center for Asian Studies (KU-ORCAS), with which I am associated, is the project implementer. However, it operated only for a specific period, which ended in FY2021. This means that the data and material collected by the Corona Archive @ Kansai University could have been lost once KU-ORCAS winded down. To avoid this and preserve the data for a long time, I cooperated with the Kansai University Museum and University Archival Office.

The Corona Archive @ Kansai University started accepting submissions on 17 April 2020. As face-to-face publicity was not allowed, I have promoted the project through the KU-ORCAS website and SNS. However, if I only open a digital archive to the public, they will not submit material voluntarily. Therefore, I had to perform several practical activities to collect material. In the next section, I will describe the three types of public humanities practices.

14.4 Public Humanities Practices for Collecting Material

As part of our digital public history or digital public humanities practice, we invited the public to help us collect COVID-19-related material. In this section, I will introduce these practices.

14.4.1 Archivathon

The first activity was called "Archivathon" (アーカイバソン), an online event where participants could submit documents together. This is a term coined from the words "archive" and "marathon," following Wikipedia's Editathon. Since meeting in person to collect material during the COVID-19 pandemic was difficult, we thought of collecting records from different parts of Japan by inviting participants online. The eligibility for submissions to the Corona Archive @ Kansai University was initially limited to those affiliated with Kansai University, but it was eventually extended to the wider public when the amount of material did not increase much after a certain period. Therefore, the Archivathon was opened to all MLA members in Japan, to increase the momentum for the collection of COVID-19-related material in MLA communities.

I held Archivathon events two times, one in October and another in November 2020. In both cases, the number of participants was only about 10, which is not a large number. Still, as we had hoped, we attracted participants from all over Japan. In the first Archivathon, Saotome who is a curator at Suita City Museum discussed how the material is collected at his museum, so that MLA members could learn about the concept of and criteria for collecting material (Saotome 2021). After his presentation, I gave a lecture on how to submit material to the Corona Archive @ Kansai University.

After the lecture, each participant spent the afternoon collecting material from around their homes and workplaces and registering them on the Corona Archive @ Kansai University. As a result, we were able to obtain twice as many materials as we had before the event began. One example is the photographs of Zenkoji Temple (善光寺) in Nagano Prefecture, which is one of the most important temples in Japan and is located far from Osaka Prefecture, where Kansai University is. The photographs of Zenkoji Temple show us the measures taken to prevent infection (アーカイバソン参加者 2021).[6]

14.4.2 The Discovery of Material on the Spanish Flu

The COVID-19 virus has often been compared to the Spanish flu that caused a global pandemic over 100 years ago. One of the aims of the Corona Archive @ Kansai University is to find material on the Spanish flu. To this end, I organized an event in which people were invited to provide their household

14.5.1 Overall Characteristics of Photographs

First, I would like to explore the photographs. As described in Section. 14.3.2, contributors can map the location of their material. Looking at the data on this map, users can see that most contributors are near Kansai University and are, therefore, concentrated in the Kansai area, which is in the middle of Japan. However, because of the two Archivathons, contributions from the Kanto area, where Tokyo is located, and other regions are also visible. In more detail, most of the contributions are concentrated around the Senriyama Campus of Kansai University (Suita City, Osaka Prefecture). Kansai University has campuses in Sakai City, Takatsuki City, and Suita City. There are very few contributions from these campuses, suggesting that even though this is a university project, there is no cooperation within the university.

In addition, users can add one or more tags to the material when submitting it. Based on this information, the Corona Archive @ Kansai University has 179 tags as of 31 May 2021 (see Fig. 14.2). The tags can be roughly divided into "measures against COVID-19," "Events," "Scenes on and around campus," and "Family."

The most frequently used tag is "コロナ対策 (measures against COVID-19, 19 cases)." Related tags include "マスク (mask)" (6), "ハンドジェル (hand gel)" (3), "ソーシャルディスタンス (social distance)" (2), and "フェイスシールド (face shield)" (2). The second most common tag,[7] "式典取りやめ (Cancellation of ceremonies)" (7), relates to Kansai University's 2019 graduation and 2020 entrance ceremonies, reflecting the time when COVID-19 was in full swing.

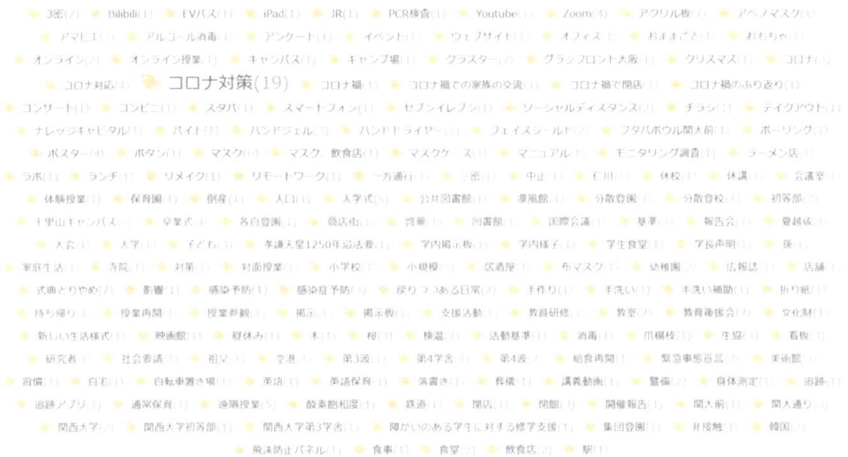

Fig. 14.2 Tag cloud for the Corona Archive @ Kansai University. The largest tag 'コロナ対策 (measures against COVID-19)' indicates the most frequently used

Previous examples of community archives in Japan have focused on the "local community" and collected "local cultural resources" and "information oriented to local residents and the local environment" (Sato et al. 2018; Manabe et al. 2020; Nakamura et al. 2020). The Corona Archive @ Kansai University has been initiated with a primary focus on "university community" and is therefore building a collection of material that is different in nature from the earlier community archives in Japan.

More importantly the Corona Archive @ Kansai University does not contain any photographs on COVID-19 patients or healthcare workers. The lack of photographs on patients could be attributed to the lack of medical schools and hospitals at Kansai University, whereas the lack of photographs on infected people could be because they may have been afraid of the possibility of discrimination. The simple fact that materials that the public in the present age don't want to preserve will not remain in the future indicates a major challenge for community archives as a practice of digital public history.

However, if we consider the various earthquake archives, for example, Great East Japan Earthquake Digital Archive (National Diet Library. https://kn.ndl.go.jp/) that were created as soon as the Great East Japan Earthquake occurred, it cannot be simply concluded that people do not leave behind painful memories and therefore they will not remain in the future. It can be said that the loss of a large number of lives and the instantaneous loss of a familiar city in the Great East Japan Earthquake provided a strong motivation to remember and record the disaster. On the other hand, although COVID-19 was a disaster of unprecedented scale, there was little change in the landscape, which made it easier to "become accustomed" to the disaster than the Great East Japan Earthquake, and information about the infection flowed continuously, which may have made it difficult for people to have the will to preserve it.

14.5.2 *Analyzing Memory Posts from a Public Humanities Perspective*

We received 151 memory submissions. Over 90% of the responses were from undergraduate and postgraduate students of Kansai University, making this a generally coherent collection of student memories. By analyzing these memories, I want to clarify the public, more precisely, students' consciousness in participation in making the COVID-19 history. This analysis will reveal the challenges in promoting public history.

In the memory-posts program, we set the following four questions: "Tell us about your life during the COVID-19 pandemic," "Tell us about your school life during the COVID-19 pandemic," "Tell us about the state of society during the COVID-19 pandemic from your point of view," and "What do you think you should leave someone who might investigate the COVID-19 pandemic 30 years later?" The first three questions, as required responses, asked how the respondents perceived their personal lives, school life, and the state of society from their perspective. In contrast, the last optional question asked what was necessary to examine the present from the future perspective. If, for example, a respondent posted his or her personal memories in the first three questions and then answered that he/she needed materials other than ego-documents in the last question, we can conclude that the respondent is not aware that he or she is participating in history-making through Memory Posts. This is because stating that what is needed to investigate the COVID-19 pandemic in the future is not personal memories but other materials means that the respondent is not aware of the meaning of his/her doing Memory Posts, i.e., the act of preserving historical records for future generations. On the other hand, if the respondent answered in the last question that the personal memories are necessary for future research on this period, it means that the respondent is aware that he or she was contributing ego-documents for the future. Therefore, analyzing the difference between the responses to the first three questions and the last question is necessary to investigate the consciousness of participation in making history.

Based on the above ideas, we first checked what topics were raised in the first three questions by using KH Coder, a text-mining tool, and found the following results. Regarding the respondents' personal lives, they talked about part-time jobs, whether they had coronavirus (including their friends and acquaintances), frequency of going out, and online classes. Looking at the details of whether they had COVID-19, most of them said that they and not many of their friends had been exposed to the virus. In addition, there were posts about not going out for fear of the virus and not being able to work because their part-time jobs had ended. Regarding questions about school life, many of the topics were about the evaluation of online and face-to-face classes. Regarding the state of society from the respondents' perspective, the following topics were described: changes in Japanese and international society, impact on the economy, society going online, and the appearance of society and people today. These topics tend to describe the scenes at present times and in the future. The discussion thus far had been predictable to a certain extent, because 90% of the responses came from students.

For the last question, Fig. 14.3 shows the co-occurrence network of extracted words. Topics that emerged include government policies and measures and their effects (orange), changes in personal life and their records (green), data on the number of infections and patients (blue), medical records (emerald green), and social and economic changes (red). A check of the top 150 extracted words shows that topics such as "response" (17 cases), "countermeasures" (16), and "policies" (11) indicate how society and governments confronted the pandemic. The words "record" (14), "data" (14), "photograph" (9), "material" (7), and "film" (5) refer to the form of the material. Topics related to individuals would include "people" (17), "person" (30), "life" (12), "memory" (6), and "experience" (6). Several words that describe society also appear: "government" (13), "society" (9), "country" (6), and "economy" (6). Still, there were many "no answers" (32). Based on the extracted words, it would be appropriate to classify them into the five clusters (or topics) depicted in the co-occurrence network.

Based on this analysis, we developed a coding rule around the extracted words to classify them into five topics. The results are shown in Table 14.2 (The total % exceeds 100% because of duplication in the data). As you can see, only 27% of the responses discussed memories and records relating to individuals.

I would like to supplement this result with a different perspective. After extracting the characteristic words from the first three answers and setting a coding rule to describe the answers to each question, we could classify the answers to the last question, as shown in Table 14.3 (the total % exceeds 100% because of duplication in the data). Again, as in Table 14.2, only about 25% of the responses could be classified as relating to personal and school life, that is, personal records and memories.

In the free text box provided in the Memory Posts, some participants wrote positive comments: "Through this questionnaire, I have been able to

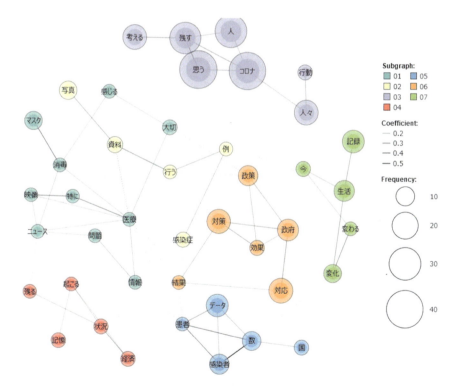

Fig. 14.3 Co-occurrence network generated by the answers to the question "What do you think you should leave someone who might investigate the COVID-19 pandemic 30 years later?"

Table 14.2 Classification results no. 1

Code	Number of documents	Percentage (%)
*No answer	32	13.39
*Memories and records relating to individuals	66	27.62
*The outcome of the government's response and its record	38	15.9
*Records of medical care and infectious diseases themselves	95	39.75
Material form	33	13.81
Records of Changes	14	5.86
No code	42	17.57
(Number of documents)	239	

Table 14.3 Classification results no. 2

Code	Number of documents	Percentage (%)
*Personal life	35	14.64
*School life	23	9.62
*Social context	87	36.4
*No answer	32	13.39
No code	96	40.17
(Number of documents)	239	

face COVID-19," and "I think it is an important project to preserve the archives." However, the analysis showed that only about 25% of the respondents answered that we need to preserve "personal records and memories" to investigate this pandemic for the future. This suggests that the "public's" sense of the historical value of ego-documents, such as those collected by the Corona Archive @ Kansai University, is not as high as that of social records and data. This is a result of the disparity between the act of submitting memories and the meaning of the memories as historical documents, or, in other words, the lack of a sense of participation in "making history" by submitting memories.

14.6 Conclusion: Challenges in and Suggestions for Popularizing (Digital) Public Humanities in Japan

In this chapter, I have clarified the practice of digital public humanities through the Corona Archive @ Kansai University and the public's awareness of participating in public humanities. I want to conclude by pointing out the above analysis and the necessary course of action so that public humanities take root in Japan.

Based on the actual situation of collecting COVID-19-related material in other countries, the JSDA formed the special interest group "Study Group on Digital Archives of Covid-19 Infections" and issued a statement calling for the collection of COVID-19 material (JSDA 2021). In addition to our project, the efforts of some museums such as the Urahoro Town Museum, Suita City Museum, Waseda University Theatre Museum have been introduced in the mass media many times. Therefore, the fact that we have to collect, and are currently collecting, COVID-19 materials is a matter of public knowledge.

However, it is difficult to say that activities to collect COVID-19-related material have become active in Japan. I have run the Corona Archive @ Kansai University for a year but have not been able to collect as much material as I would like to. In contrast to the various activities in other countries, I must admit that the Corona Archive @ Kansai University is a failure as a public humanities practice.

Why is that? One reason could be that there is a general lack of awareness of the value of ego-documents as historical sources. This can be seen from the analysis in the Memory Posts pointed out in the previous section. Therefore, it is necessary for public historians to communicate the importance of personal memories and ego-documents as cultural and historical material to the public in their public humanities or history practices. In other words, public humanists/historians must continue to repeatedly explain the significance of their activities to the public, especially to MLA staff who are not yet familiar with the new research field of public humanities in Japan. With this in mind, I have created a virtual reality (VR) exhibition of the Corona Archive @ Kansai University (Kikuchi 2021). This VR exhibition is a spin-off of the 2021 Spring Special Exhibition "Confronting the Plague: What is Taken, What is Born" (「疫病に立ち向かう―奪われしもの、生まれしもの―」) organized by the Kansai University Museum. The purpose of this exhibition is to show the use of the material collected by the Corona Archive @ Kansai University to the public, make them aware of the significance of ego-documents, and encourage them to contribute their own material.

Another reason why participation in public humanities practices is not thriving is that the public perhaps sees nothing to be gained by participating in such activities. For example, when I opened the Corona Archive @ Kansai University, I received almost no active contributions from people within the university. However, when I started paying JPY 1000 for each Memory Posts, more than 100 students who had not previously contributed joined in just a few days. The lesson of this fact is easy to understand. To get the public to actively participate in public humanities, we as public humanists need activities that affirm and make sense of the public's participation in the practice. Fortunately, there is currently a trend toward open science, which takes on a slightly different dimension to public humanities, as a way of valuing and affirming activities that engage with the public.

As data and material become more open, research to promote "citizen science" will be conducted. It is natural to expect similar activities to be conducted, even if the term "public humanities" is not used. In the future, public humanities in Japan may be given a place as an activity of the humanities in the realm of open science. Till that time, we, humanities scholars, must prepare in our own research fields to find value in the practical activities of engaging with the public and affirm these activities as achievements.

Notes

1. The only article that has been given a Japanese translation "公共人文学" ("Public Humanities") was published in 2011. It was translated by Yale University literary scholar Wai Chee Dimock. Titled "公共人文学としての文学" ("Literature as Public Humanities"), it introduces public humanities to Japan. However, it is difficult to conclude that the appearance of this article signifies the establishment of "Public Humanities in Japan" (ディモック 2011).
2. Among the most successful examples of digital public humanities in Japan is "Minna de Honkoku" (みんなで翻刻). This is a platform for crowdsourcing the transcription of pre-modern Japanese classics. However, this project does not use the phrase "public humanities" (みんなで翻刻 2021).
3. I initiated the Corona Archive @ Kansai University project as a personal project in April 2020. Then in July 2020, the research unit I belong to received a research grant from Kansai University and continued it as a joint research, the "Project for Collecting and Disseminating Records and Memories of the COVID-19 and Spanish Flu with the Corona Archive @ Kansai University" until March 2021. As of May 2021, I am continuing it again as a personal project.
4. For example, "A Journal of the Plague Year" collects a large number of COVID-19-related material worldwide, especially from the United States.
5. It is beyond the scope of this chapter to discuss disaster archives in Japan. As regards this topic, the following material may be helpful: the NDL's Great East Japan Earthquake Digital Archive (https://kn.ndl.go.jp/) and this book, 今村文彦, and 鈴木親彦, eds. 災害記録を未来に活かす. 1st ed. 東京: 勉誠出版, 2019.
6. アーカイバソン参加者. 善光寺（長野県長野市）. コロナアーカイブ@関西大学. https://www.annex.ku-orcas.kansai-u.ac.jp/s/covid19archive/item/289 (accessed May 31, 2021).
7. The next highest number of tags was seven for "Primary School," but this is thought to have been consciously tagged as representing something other than the university, as the initial qualification for submissions was that they were related to "Kansai University".

References

"A Journal of the Plague Year." Accessed May 31, 2021. https://covid-19archive.org/s/archive/page/welcome.

Anonymous. "大学入試をやっと終えて、モチ…." コロナアーカイブ@関西大学. Accessed May 31, 2021. https://www.annex.ku-orcas.kansai-u.ac.jp/s/covid19archive/item/658.

Coronarchiv. Accessed May 31, 2021. https://coronarchiv.geschichte.uni-hamburg.de/.

Corona Archive @ Kansai University. Accessed May 31, 2021. https://www.annex.ku-orcas.kansai-u.ac.jp/s/covid19archive/page/covidmemory.
"COVID-19 Memories." Luxembourg Centre for Contemporary and Digital History. Accessed May 31, 2021. https://covidmemory.lu/.
"Great East Japan Earthquake Digital Archive." National Diet Library. Accessed May 31, 2021. https://kn.ndl.go.jp/.
IFPH. "Mapping Public History Projects about COVID 19." International Federation for Public History (2020). Accessed March 24, 2021. https://ifph.hypotheses.org/3225.
KH Coder. Accessed May 31, 2021. https://khcoder.net/en/.
Kikuchi, Nobuhiko. "Corona Archive @ Kansai University VR Exhibition." Accessed May 31, 2021. https://hubs.mozilla.com/uChitEm/corona-archive-at-kansai-university-vr-exhibition.
Kikuchi, Nobuhiko, Uchida Keiichi, Okada Tadakatsu, Hayashi Takefumi, Fujita Takao, Ninomiya Satoshi, and Miyagawa So. 2020. "Digital Public History during the COVID-19 Pandemic: Discussion on the Corona Archive @ Kansai University." *Proceedings of the 10th Conference of the Japanese Association of Digital Humanities*: 46–49. https://jadh2020.lang.osaka-u.ac.jp/programme/jadh2020proceedings.pdf.
NDL Search. Accessed May 31, 2021. https://iss.ndl.go.jp/.
Okamoto, Michihiro. 2018. "Public History in Japan." *International Public History* 1, no. 1: 20180004. https://doi.org/10.1515/iph-2018-0004.
"Omeka Classic." Accessed May 31, 2021. https://omeka.org/classic/.
Omeka S. Accessed May 31, 2021. https://omeka.org/s/.
Saotome, Kenji. "Preserving the Tangible and Intangible for the Next Century – The Efforts of Suita City Museum During the COVID-19 Pandemic." *ICOM Japan*. Accessed May 31, 2021. https://icomjapan.org/en/updates/2021/03/30/p-2242/.
Smulyan, Susan, ed. 2021. *Doing Public Humanities*. New York: Routledge.
The History Harvest. Accessed May 31, 2021. https://historyharvest.unl.edu/.
The Tsubouchi Memorial Theatre Museum. 2021. 失われた公演――コロナ禍と演劇の記録/記憶. The Tsubouchi Memorial Theatre Museum, Waseda University (早稲田大学坪内博士記念演劇博物館). Accessed May 31, 2021. https://www.waseda.jp/prj-ushinawareta/.
アーカイバソン参加者. 2021. "善光寺 (長野県長野市)." コロナアーカイブ@関西大学. Accessed May 31, 2021. https://www.annex.ku-orcas.kansai-u.ac.jp/s/covid19archive/item/289.
今村文彦 and 鈴木親彦, eds., 災害記録を未来に活かす, 1st ed. (東京: 勉誠出版, 2019).
菊池信彦. "コロナアーカイブ@関西大学の開設経緯、特徴とその意図," カレントアウェアネス-E, no. 395 (2020): e2282. https://current.ndl.go.jp/e2282.
菊池信彦. "コロナ禍の歴史を作るための「コロナアーカイブ@関西大学」," in 新型コロナで世の中がエライことになったので関西大学がいろいろ考えた。 ed 関西大学, 1st ed. (大阪: 浪速社, 2021), 215–27.
菊池信彦, 内田慶市, 岡田忠克, 林武文, 藤田高夫, 二ノ宮聡, and 宮川創. "コロナ禍におけるデジタルパブリックヒストリー -「コロナアーカイブ@関西大学」の現状と歴史学上の可能性、あるいは課題について-," 歴史学研究. no. 1006 (2021): 23–31.

剣持久木, ed. 越境する歴史認識：ヨーロッパにおける「公共史」の試み, 1st ed. (東京: 岩波書店, 2018).

国際航業, ed., "発信する遺跡 (I) 英国のパブリック・アーケオロジーの潮流から," 文化遺産の世界, no. 17 (2005): 1–18. https://www.isan-no-sekai.jp/list/vol17.

五月女賢司. "吹田市立博物館における新型コロナ資料の収集と展示. デジタルアーカイブ学会誌," デジタルアーカイブ学会誌 5, no. 1 (2021): 53–5. https://doi.org/10.24506/jsda.5.1_53

佐藤知久, 甲斐賢治, and 北野央. "コミュニティ・アーカイブをつくろう！―せんだいメディアテーク「3がつ11にちをわすれないためにセンター」奮闘記," 1st ed. (東京: 晶文社, 2018).

ディモック ワイ チー. "公共人文学としての文学," 21世紀倫理創成研究, no. 4 (2011): 34–49.

デジタルアーカイブ学会. "COVID-19 に関するアーカイブ活動の呼びかけ." デジタルアーカイブ学会. Accessed May 31, 2021. http://digitalarchivejapan.org/bukai/sig/covid19/call.

デジタルアーカイブ学会. "肖像権ガイドライン." デジタルアーカイブ学会, April 2021. http://digitalarchivejapan.org/wp-content/uploads/2021/04/Shozokenguideline-20210419.pdf.

菅豊, and 北條勝貴, eds., "パブリック・ヒストリー入門: 開かれた歴史学への挑戦," 1st ed. (勉誠出版, 2019).

中村覚, 宮本隆史, and 片桐由希子. "コミュニティ・アーカイブの方法論の構築に向けて: 千代田区におけるデジタルアーカイブ・ワークショップの事例より," デジタルアーカイブ学会誌 4, no. 2 (2020): 109–12. https://doi.org/10.24506/jsda.4.2_109

真鍋陸太郎, 水越伸, 宮田雅子, 田中克明, 溝尻真也, and 栗原大介. "参加型コミュニティ・アーカイブのデザイン: デジタル・ストーリーテリングや参加型まちづくりの融合," デジタルアーカイブ学会誌 4, no. 2 (2020): 113–16. https://doi.org/10.24506/jsda.4.2_113

みんなで翻刻. Accessed May 31, 2021. https://honkoku.org/.

持田誠. "コロナ関係資料からみえてくるもの," デジタルアーカイブ学会誌 5, no. 1 (2021): 47–52. https://doi.org/10.24506/jsda.5.1_47.

八木康幸. "パブリック・フォークロアと「地域伝統芸能」," 関西学院史学, no. 33 (2006): 53–87.

CHAPTER 15

Breaking the "Class" Ceiling: The Challenges and Opportunities of Creating a Digital Archive of Edwardian Working-Class Book Inscriptions

Lauren Alex O'Hagan

15.1 Introduction

The Edwardian era (1901–1914) marked an important period in the history of the British working classes. More than twenty years of free and compulsory education had resulted in a highly literate population, while rapid changes in book production methods meant that book prices had decreased dramatically. As a result, book ownership became democratized and increasingly possible for both male and female members of the working classes (McKitterick 2009, 73–74). Access to literature sparked an awareness of the inequalities in British society, leading many working-class individuals to question the deeply rooted division between "those who served" and "those who were served" (Todd 2015, 28). These individuals became active participants in the labor movement, joining trade unions, signing up to the newly established Labour Party and enrolling their children in Socialist Sunday Schools. They formed mutual improvement societies, accessed Mechanics' Institutes and Miners' Libraries and attended Workers' Educational Association classes to exchange ideas and share experiences. This wave of self-education, community spirit, industrial militancy, and political mobilization meant that the working classes were no longer helpless bystanders with no say in the decisions made by Westminster; they were now a collective force with their own identity, goals, ambitions, and strategies (O'Hagan 2020b, 202).

L. A. O'Hagan (✉)
Örebro University, Örebro, Sweden
e-mail: lauren.ohagan@oru.se

© The Author(s), under exclusive license to Springer Nature Switzerland AG 2022
A. Schwan and T. Thomson (eds.), *The Palgrave Handbook of Digital and Public Humanities*, https://doi.org/10.1007/978-3-031-11886-9_15

One surprising way in which many of these working-class changes are captured is in the Edwardian book inscription. Inscriptions dominated books in this period, from simple hand-written declarations of possession and gift marks to prize stickers and bookplates. These traces of ownership provide unprecedented knowledge of working-class life and culture in early twentieth-century Britain, standing as important first-hand evidence of people's identities, social circles, jobs, hobbies, beliefs, hopes, and fears. While some provide the formative voices of future Labour MPs or trade union leaders, most capture the voices of men and women who passed their lives under the radar but made important contributions to Edwardian society in their own ways, whether through serving, mining, sewing, building, teaching, or soldiering. Thus, book inscriptions enable new understandings of everyday life in Edwardian Britain for men, but perhaps more significantly for women, who are too often relegated to the sidelines in working-class history (cf. Dunk 2003; Loveday 2014).

Many of these book inscriptions are rare, only exist in a single instance and are not protected in official archives or libraries. Without some form of intervention, they face endangerment and entire narratives of working-class culture and history risk being eradicated. A digital archive of Edwardian working-class book inscriptions offers a permanent way to safeguard these material artifacts and give their creators "pictorial enfranchisement" (Phillips 2004, 4), thus ensuring their survival for future generations. The archive would be of considerable use for academics (particularly in the fields of book history, social history, literacy studies, sociology, and sociolinguistics), as well as librarians and archivists. It also has high pedagogical value for teachers and would be an important resource for members of the general public with an interest in family history and local history. For several years, I have been trying to lay the groundwork for its creation, but I have faced numerous challenges along the way. In this chapter, I reflect on some of those challenges and how they might be overcome in order to give a permanent voice to the voiceless and break the "class" ceiling.

15.2 The Case for a Digital Archive of Edwardian Working-Class Book Inscriptions

Although the idea of giving a voice to the working classes may seem perfectly reasonable, it is, in fact, a historically radical view. This position had to be forged over time against the assumption that only the histories of high-status individuals merited academic study (O'Hagan 2020a, b, c, 14). The foundations for this change in mentality were largely laid in the 1960s by the work of E.P. Thompson and his pioneering "History from Below," which emphasized historical events from the perspective of common people rather than leaders. Through its focus on class relationships, political movements, and organized labor, History from Below fostered a new way of looking at the working classes that helped restore a sense of power and agency to them

(Thompson 1966, 279–80). However, in the 1980s, there was a shift back to focusing on the lived experiences of the middle and upper classes, which led to working-class history becoming "an increasingly disregarded fragment of historical studies" (Hitchcock 2004, 295). In 2004, Tim Hitchcock advocated for a "New" History from Below that based historical research on sources *from* ordinary people and not merely *about* them. Hitchcock received support from Martyn Lyons who argued that a "New" History from Below must recognize the autonomy of working-class writers and refuse to regard them as "passive receptacles for information and ideologies produced by someone else" (2010, 59.4). By bringing individual experiences to the forefront, the "New" History from Below aimed to foster a re-evaluation of how ordinary people navigate the emerging institutions of the modern state and how their behavior shapes such institutions. In short, it would make the working classes active agents in shaping their own lives and culture (O'Hagan 2020a, 16).

The "New" History from Below fits well with the new agendas of archives and libraries to provide a more diverse representation of society in their collections. Institutions began to recognize that they wielded great power in the shaping of public memory and, therefore, they had to act socially responsible and use this power in safe and inclusive ways (Seale 2013; Caswell 2017). Equality and diversity are now high on the collection policies of all institutions. The National Archives, for example, promotes an annual Diversity Week, where "hidden" histories from their records are shared with the general public. They have also produced specific research guides to help users find records relating to Black history, LGBTQ+ history and women's history. However, most institutions continue to pay little attention to the working classes, often viewing this group as falling into the remit of community and specialist archives that are typically driven by social or political movements [e.g., Working Class Movement Library in Manchester; South Wales Miners' Library in Swansea] (Flinn et al. 2009). This disregard leaves a burgeoning gap in the history of members of the working classes who were not politically mobilized (particularly women), a gap that book inscriptions can fill.

Equally, despite its claim to be built on openness and a sense of community, the field of digital humanities has also been criticized for failing to give sufficient voice to historically marginalized groups. Ezell (2010, 107) claims that a bias against manuscript evidence means that certain texts remain prioritized over others and push the work of minor and anonymous authors to the side. This view is supported by Risam (2015) who argues that a heavy focus on digitizing copyright-free material has privileged canonical texts and writers, who are predominantly white, middle-class men. Furthermore, research by Bordalejo (2018) on diversity in digital humanities has found that most digital humanists are binary, white, affluent, and anglophone, which has led to an overwhelming bias in the types of texts that are digitized and studied. In light of these criticisms, Earhart (2012) recognizes the need to "examine the canon that we, as digital humanists, are constructing" to ensure that the working classes, women, people of color, and LGBTQ+ communities are all represented. By not giving these minorities a digital presence, the field risks replicating historical practices that favor the dominant culture and relegate difference to its margins (Risam 2015). Higgin (2010) goes further, arguing that digital humanities as a whole downplays issues of cultural politics because of "a disposition that the battles of race, gender, class and ecology have already been won, their lessons have been learned and by espousing a rhetoric of equity, everything will fall into place." Potter (2013, 358) supports this notion, asserting that, although new digital technologies have their own history, they resonate with historical questions of race, class, gender, nationalism, and sexuality, and, consequently, must not be separated from them.

In the past five years, increasing attention has been paid to the need to diversify digital humanities and make it a more inclusive field of study. Gallon (2016, 43) has pushed for a "technology of recovery" to fill the aperture between Black Studies and digital humanities and "help unmask the racialized systems of power at work" in how we understand the field and use its associated techniques. Similarly, Ruberg et al. (2018) have emphasized the importance of a "queer digital humanities" to make visible histories of queer representation and issues affecting queer communities and, in doing so, to foreground social justice and value social criticism and people as much as computation and data. Important work has also been carried out by Risam (2018) to decolonize digital humanities and Losh and Wernimont (2018) to introduce a feminist perspective to the field. Mahony (2018) and Liu (2020) have focused instead on linguistic and cultural diversity, arguing that the digitization of non-English texts must be prioritized in order to strengthen and diversify our understanding of how we view and understand the world around us. However, despite these important breakthroughs in the field of digital humanities, inclusive representation and diversity in terms of social class remain largely ignored.

Although there is still much to be done, there are several pioneering digital humanities projects taking place in the United Kingdom that aim to give a platform to these historically "silent" groups. The Stray Voices project (SOAS University of London), for example, draws attention to the stories and images of homeless men and women in order to understand the social, administrative, and cultural history of vagrancy, while Writing Lives (a collaboration between Brunel, Liverpool John Moore, the Open University, and Sheffield Hallam) is an initiative to digitize "out-of-print, inaccessible, unexcavated and critically neglected" working-class autobiographies. The Edwardian Postcard Project (Lancaster University) is another important resource of 5,000 postcards that can be used to explore the writing practices, travel patterns, and social networks of (largely) working-class and lower-middle-class Edwardians. However, there is currently no existing digital archive of working-class book inscriptions.

On the whole, inscriptions held in formal institutions have either been disregarded as "mundane" and not deemed necessary of photographing or, when they have been photographed by researchers, this has been carried out solely for the purposes of fieldwork and the images have not been publicly shared. The creation of a digital archive of working-class book inscriptions would, thus, offer an innovative, interdisciplinary resource that "constitutes a rich chronicle of ordinary experience" (Edwards 2004, 29). This is because collected inscriptions would not just be safeguarded and made accessible to users, but would also be tagged with detailed metadata on the local context of the book, the inscription, the awarding institution (when relevant), the inscriber's personal life, and the broader context of Edwardian society. As the rate of literacy in Edwardian Britain was almost 100%, book inscriptions offer the unique opportunity to learn just as much about female experiences as male. In doing so, the archive would act as a critical and analytical space that challenges users to rethink their current understanding of working-class life and culture in early twentieth-century Britain.

A sample inscription can be seen in Fig. 15.1, with the type of information that would be tagged and made searchable for users in the accompanying Table 15.1. It comes from my own dataset of 4000 book inscriptions, collected as part of my doctoral and postdoctoral research (see Sect. 15.3.2 for further details). The first field indicates a basic transcription of the text provided in the inscription; the second field outlines the category and sub-categories of inscription, the writing implement used, the printing technique used, the surface material used, the date of inscription, and its position in the book; the third field details the title of the book, its author, publisher, place of publication, and date of publication; the fourth field specifies the various institutions or people involved in the awarding of the book (when relevant); the fifth field documents the name of the recipient/inscriber and their gender, age, location, and occupation; the sixth field enables biographical notes on the recipient/inscriber to be recorded; and the seventh field allows open text on any other pertinent information. The biographical information is obtained from census records and other official documents available on www.ancestry.com, while details on social institutions of the Edwardian period come from www.britishnewspaperarchive.co.uk. Together, these fields provide comprehensive information about the social life of the book inscription that emphasizes its function as a social object that is laden with culturally specific meanings and is part of the reproduction and performance of social values.

Overall, a digital archive of Edwardian working-class book inscriptions would be of considerable importance from both a conservation and research perspective. First, it would provide, for the first time, a permanent and freely accessible place to store examples of inscriptions that have been historically suppressed, ignored, or undervalued. This, in turn, would also offer a platform through which the stories of forgotten, "everyday" Edwardians can be shared with the general public. The archive would also facilitate a dialogue with national institutions of power regarding how to preserve and protect endangered memories and increase the presence of underrepresented people in archival and library collections. From a research perspective, the archive

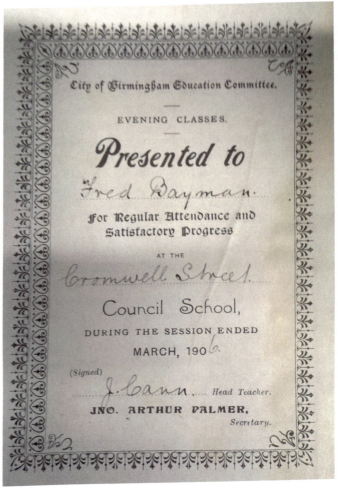

Fig. 15.1 A sample inscription for the Edwardian working-class digital archive (Image taken by O'Hagan [2015] and reproduced with the permission of Bookbarn International)

would enable the study of variation in working-class book ownership and inscriptive practices according to gender, age, occupation, and geographical location. It would also open up new ways of exploring and thinking about people's relationships with their books and broader social institutions, networks, values, and traditions, as well as foster a new recognition of the multiple social, communicative, and performative functions of the book inscription for working-class Edwardians. These insights have the potential to diversify current understandings of social class by questioning the transmission of culture as a unidirectional process from dominant to less dominant

Table 15.1 A sample entry for the Edwardian working-class digital archive

Transcription	City of Birmingham Education Committee. Evening Classes. Presented to Fred Bayman for regular attendance and satisfactory progress at the Cromwell Street Council School, during the session ended March, 1906 (Signed) J. Cann Head Teacher Jno Arthur Palmer, Secretary
Inscription	
Inscription Category	Prize sticker
Inscription Sub-Category(ies)	School
Writing implement	Evening Continuation Classes
Printing technique	Plain black ink pen
Surface material	Offset lithography
Date	Gummed paper
Position	1906
Bookseller's label	Centre of front endpaper
	None
Book	
Title	Pitman's Shorthand Dictionary
Author	Isaac Pitman
Publisher	Pitman
Place of publication	London
Date of publication	1902
Awarding Institution(s)	
	City of Birmingham Education Committee
	Cromwell Street Council School
	Evening Continuation Classes
	J. Cann, John Arthur Palmer
Recipient	
Gender	Fred Bayman
Age	Male
Location	17
Occupation	Birmingham
	Engine fitter

Biographical notes
Fred Bayman (1889–1923) left school in 1902 and worked as an engine fitter. However, in 1905, he decided to enrol in evening continuation classes at Cromwell Street Council School to improve his Commercial knowledge. During lessons, Fred learnt arithmetic, English, commerce and shorthand. His prize book—*Pitman's Shorthand Dictionary*—reflects his choice of subjects. Shortly after completing his course, Fred found work as a railway clerk—a position which shows that his hard work and perseverance paid off

(continued)

groups, as well as reshape existing knowledge on working-class life in Edwardian Britain and challenge historical perceptions of the working classes as "passive" and "mindless."

Table 15.1 (continued)

Other comments
Evening continuation schools were established in the late nineteenth century for children over fourteen and adults. Under the 1902 Education Act, most places at these schools were funded by local education authority grants. The City of Birmingham Education Committee was particularly committed to this type of teaching. Courses were divided into Commercial, Domestic, General, Industrial and Rural and classes were taught on average for six hours per week across three evenings

15.3 Diversifying the Digital Archive: Challenges and Opportunities

Although a digital archive of Edwardian working-class book inscriptions would provide an important and long-overdue resource for documenting the book ownership and readership practices of a historically marginalized group, there are three main challenges that hinder its development: the survival of working-class inscriptions in official institutions, the accessibility of working-class inscriptions in official institutions, and traditional attitudes to "ordinary writing," which make it challenging to obtain funding for establishing and sustaining such an archive on a permanent basis. Nonetheless, these challenges can be overcome by sourcing material from outside official institutions, collaborating with official institutions as an entry point to digital archiving, and arranging events to change perceptions of working-class literacy practices.

15.3.1 Challenge 1: The Survival of Working-Class Inscriptions in Official Institutions

Special collections and archives are generally considered to be impartial institutions "mandated to create, maintain, use and provide records of a shared national history" (Sutherland 2017, 10). It is, therefore, ironic that historical bias in their collection policies has tended to obscure the history of "ordinary people" (Zinn 1977, 21). Sinor (2002, 185) notes that working-class voices in such institutions largely "linger as shadows" in documents by higher authorities. These indirect sources often frame the working classes as helpless victims, whether as names in workhouse registries or Poor Law records, or "writing upwards" in letters to employers or politicians.

The statistics are even more concerning when dealing with books rather than documents. Interviews with archivists and librarians at the 36 institutions that are members of Research Libraries UK revealed that, historically, acquisitions have been weighted in favor of upper-class, wealthy, male individuals (O'Hagan 2020c). Not only did these individuals tend to be more educated, and therefore more literate, but they also had the necessary disposable income to afford books in the hand-press period. Although book ownership had been democratized by the Edwardian era, for much of the twentieth-century, institutions continued to prioritize the books of "prestigious" people and did not deem working-class books worthy of collection. Today, acquisition decisions are no longer influenced by an owner's social status. Nonetheless, this historical prejudice means that most books in institutional collections had socially elite or wealthy male owners.

For these reasons, Lyons (2013, 5) claims that most "ordinary writing" resides outside of traditional institutions and its survival often depends on the good conservation practices of personal collectors. This is supported by Caswell et al. (2017), who state that the most valuable collections documenting the lives of marginalized people are within community or specialist archives. As Hall and Gillen (2010, 170) note, ordinary writing represents an "elusive quarry" of information on working-class literacy and provides a rare opportunity to hear working-class voices directly.

15.3.2 Opportunity 1: Sourcing Material from Outside Official Institutions

According to Caswell et al. (2017), community and specialist archives present an excellent opportunity to access records from diverse communities that challenge mainstream representations of history. However, when dealing with working-class history, they have a tendency to reflect a certain type of working-class individual: a militant and politically active male campaigner who struggled against traditional authority and hierarchies of power (Flinn 2007, 29). While this was true for a certain stratum of working-class Edwardians, it was not the norm. Book inscriptions routinely reveal how male and female working-class individuals realized the potential of the spaces provided on endpapers to record things that mattered to them, such as births, deaths, marriages, new jobs, retirement, and illness ("my baby boy was born today 28th May at 6:15 pm"; "Alice Urie went to Canada June 8th 1911"; "In memory of dear brother David who died Feb 25th 1904"). Furthermore, they turned to their books to record world events, such as war or a change in government ("Today England declared war against Germany, August 4th 1914"; "May 31st 1902, Peace proclaimed in South Africa today"), challenging the myth that many members of the working classes were uneducated or ignorant about current affairs.

Interviews with the 36 members of Research Libraries UK confirmed that bookshops currently present the best opportunity to access working-class book inscriptions (O'Hagan 2020c). Unlike libraries and archives, bookshops are non-discriminate in the types of books that they sell (providing that they are in good condition) and, hence, non-discriminate in the social backgrounds or genders of their owners. In addition, as middle- and upper-class inscriptions have been typically filtered out into institutional collections, bookshops are statistically more likely to contain a higher number of working-class inscriptions. This is particularly the case for the Edwardian period because more than twenty years of free, compulsory education, coupled with the introduction of newspaper print methods to book production, had resulted in a highly literate working class with the financial means to purchase their own books. Choosing bookshops as a data-collection source, thus, directly challenges the failure of mainstream repositories to collect a more diverse representation of society. It also confronts digital humanities with a new way to avoid unintentionally propagating historical bias by looking outside of national institutions for data and resources.

In order to trial this initiative, I contacted two of the leaders in the second-hand book trade in Britain: Oxfam and Bookbarn International. Oxfam was the first charity shop to sell books secondhand and, since 2011, has successfully sold books online via its own website (www.oxfam.org.uk/shop). It is now the largest online retailer of second-hand books in Europe, selling roughly 12 million per year and making around £9.6 million annually from book sales (Oxfam 2020). Bookbarn International, on the other hand, is located in Hallatrow, Somerset, and is the largest "bricks and mortar" bookshop in the UK. It stocks over two million antiquarian books and generates sales of roughly £2 million annually (Cotton 2019). Both shops responded positively to my research and agreed to let me use their stock to collect inscriptions over a period of nine months.

As Oxfam and Bookbarn International only record information on bookplates or inscriptions by famous figures in their online database, I decided to collect the inscriptions through a simple random sampling method, which involved manually searching the shelves of the shops and identifying an Edwardian book inscription from its date or appearance, as well as the book's date of publication. This method also ensured that I did not collect a biased sample of inscriptions or that my sample was distorted by any preconceived ideas on the types of books or authors that were popular in Edwardian Britain. All signs of ownership were photographed (e.g. hand-written or printed ownership marks, booksellers' stamps, library stickers, university paste-ins) and basic information on the book, inscription, and owner were recorded. Then, I researched the inscriber using official records hosted on www.ancestry.com, including census returns, military registers, probate documents, and birth, marriage and death certificates. I used five main criteria to determine whether an inscriber was working class or not: occupation, father's occupation, size of family, number of infant mortalities in family, and address.

In total, I collected 4000 Edwardian book inscriptions, 2500 of which belonged to working-class Edwardians—a considerable amount that would provide a solid foundation for a digital archive. Of these 2500 inscriptions, there was almost an even 50:50 male/female split, ensuring that voices from a diverse range of Edwardians were captured.

15.3.3 Challenge 2: The Accessibility of Working-Class Inscriptions in Official Institutions

Although it is rare to find examples of books belonging to the working classes in official institutions, in some cases, copies may be present, but staff are unaware of their existence. This is because, until recently, copy-specific cataloguing was rarely attended to beyond easily identifiable provenances, such as armorial bookplates of institutionally significant or historically significant individuals. This means that if any examples of working-class book ownership exist, they are unlikely to have been recorded and, thus, are exceedingly difficult to find. This issue remains a challenge today because the DCRM(B) cataloguing guidelines that most libraries follow state that provenance should only be recorded "if considered important" and only for "individuals of interest." The librarians and archivists that I interviewed expressed concern that this practice risked "a skewed vision of book ownership" that turned cataloguing into a highly subjective procedure that is dependent on an individual's own discretion (O'Hagan 2020c).

Most librarians and archivists agreed that it would be very useful to highlight examples of working-class book ownership in their collections, but believed that they lacked the staff capacity to carry out, what they considered to be, such a time-consuming process. Some also emphasized the tensions between the expectations of librarians and researchers: "We are there to make the basic information available. It is up to the researcher to use that information in whichever way they see fit" (O'Hagan 2020c, 5). In other words, the librarian should record basic provenance information, but it is the role of the researcher to investigate the social history of the inscription. Another issue identified is the sheer quantity of books produced in the Edwardian era, which made it "near impossible," as one librarian claimed, to record provenance data for any books from the period, let alone working-class books (ibid.). Furthermore, there is much debate over whether an Edwardian book should be classed as "rare" or "modern," which has an impact on whether provenance is recorded.

Overall, while there is not necessarily an intentional class-based approach to cataloguing today, perpetuating traditional practices can lead to unintentional bias and unrepresentative collections that distort the history of book readership and ownership in Edwardian Britain. This lack of accessibility was the main reason why I used bookshops as an original way to collect working-class book inscriptions. However, when it came to applying for funding, I encountered problems because most investors were disinterested in data from non-institutional collections. Five of my applications were unsuccessful, with feedback describing my data-collection sources as "eccentric" and "unconventional." My arguments surrounding the importance of book inscriptions as evidence of working-class literacy and political mobilization were also disregarded as "improbable" and "inconsequential." This type of "intellectual snobbery" continues to put marginalized writing at a disadvantage and propagates a one-sided account of history told by the most privileged.

15.3.4 Opportunity 2: Collaboration with Official Institutions as an Entry Point to Digital Archiving

While the above issue is frustrating and discredits the rich data that can be found in bookshops, there are creative ways to lay the groundwork towards a digital archive of Edwardian working-class book inscriptions. As discovered from my interviews with libraries and archives, many institutions contain books that require retrospective cataloguing. These books may feature previously undocumented inscriptions that provide new evidence on working-class literacy. Collaborating with institutions when creating a digital archive offers a mutually beneficial way to pool together resources and obtain greater access to funding bids. As a researcher, I can improve the cataloguing of books by contributing knowledge beyond what is expected of a rare books librarian, while also adding new inscriptions to my own dataset that I can use in a future digital archive.

To this end, I decided to change tack and apply for funding to explore working-class literacy through the Edwardian book inscription rather than to develop a digital archive. In 2019, I successfully obtained a grant from the Economic and Social Research Council for a one-year project entitled "Reading, Writing and... Rebellion: Understanding Literacies and Class Conflict Through the Edwardian Book Inscription." As part of this project, I was able to allocate one day a week to work in a special collection to help increase representation of Edwardian working-class book inscriptions.

I decided to approach Cardiff University's Special Collections and Archives (SCOLAR) because in 2014, they received a donation of 800 Victorian and Edwardian working-class children's books, now known as the Janet Powney Collection, that have remained uncatalogued ever since. The Janet Powney Collection is unique because all the books were awarded as prizes by schools, Sunday schools, or clubs to working-class children. Therefore, they provide a rare insight into working-class literacy, schooling, religion, social life, and culture in late nineteenth/early twentieth-century Britain for both boys and girls.

Over a period of one year, I catalogued all 800 books in the Collection, with a specific emphasis on detailed information that I could reuse in a future digital archive. I organized all details according to the fields identified in Table 15.1. A sample record with full provenance details can be seen below:

In the Summer Holidays by Jennett Humphreys, Blackie & Son, London, 1892.

50p in pencil and prize sticker printed in offset chromolithography with decorative art nouveau border on front endpaper stating "High Town Primitive

Methodist Sunday School Presented to Ellen Foxen for good conduct and early attendance during the year 1890 J. Harding, Mnister, J. Giltrow, Supt".

Ellen Foxen (1880-1959) was born and died in Luton, Bedfordshire. Her father was a straw hat blocker and her mother was a straw hat sewer. She had three siblings. In 1900, she married Harry Wilding Bates, a railway van man. They had three sons together. During this time, Ellen worked as a straw hat finisher. Ellen was widowed in 1910. She remarried in 1912 to Ernest William Lundy, a straw hat stiffener. She was widowed yet again in June 1915 when Ernest commit suicide after throwing himself into a lake. According to local newspaper reports, the couple had been arguing and Ernest had been suffering from temporary insanity. Ellen remarried again in October 1915, this time to William F. Collins. After William passed away in 1935, Ellen remained a widow for the rest of her life.

High Town Primitive Methodist Church was established in Luton in 1852. By 1897, the congregation had expanded so rapidly that a new chapel was built and the old church was adjoined and became the Sunday school. The chapel cost £2,566 to build and accommodated 900 people. The High Town Methodist Church is still an active place of worship today.

As part of the project, I also created regular blog posts for SCOLAR that highlighted particular working-class inscriptions or individuals in the Collection (scolarcardiff.wordpress.com). The collaboration has been very successful for both parties: SCOLAR has benefitted from making their Collection discoverable to users, while I have added 800 new inscriptions to my own dataset (418 male; 382 female). We are now discussing the possibility of specific volunteer and intern schemes aimed at this type of research to help increase the presence of other working-class inscriptions in collections. Using a collection from a well-established institution offers a more appealing and sustainable way to start a digital archive for funding bodies, yet gives me the possibility to add my own bookshop dataset to the archive gradually. Dorothy Entwistle, an academic who collected 1,200 working-class inscriptions in the 1990s as part of her Ph.D. research, has already contacted me expressing interest in incorporating her own data into my digital archive. This would mean a total of 3,700 working-class inscriptions could be brought to light for the first time.

15.3.5 Challenge 3: Traditional Attitudes to "Ordinary Writing"

Strongly linked to the historical collection policies of official institutions is the greater value that has typically been placed on the writing of the elite when constructing official narratives of history (Lillis 2013, 5). "Ordinary" writing often does not conform to literary standards or expectations (Hall and Gillen 2010, 188): it is not normally produced with the reception of others in mind, nor is it aesthetically crafted. Consequently, it often lacks an obvious context or the embellishments that might be found in literary texts (O'Hagan 2020a,

7). Banal, mundane, discardable, unremarkable, invisible, irrelevant, boring, commonplace, and valueless are just some of the many words that have been used to describe ordinary writing (Sinor 2002, 5; Barton and Papen 2010, 10; Hall and Gillen 2010, 188). These unfair classifications have devalued its importance as one of the few opportunities to access the first-hand views of working-class people, which, in turn, has devalued the writers themselves.

Lyons (2013, 2) outlines two other mistaken assumptions that have hindered the study of ordinary writing: that the working classes left few written traces and that their life is too difficult to understand. Although it is true that, prior to the late nineteenth century, a strong percentage of working-class people were illiterate or semi-illiterate, they were still able to make their voices heard through scribes, images, or functionally literate texts (Richards 2019). Moreover, by the Edwardian era, almost 100% of Edwardians were literate and used writing in their daily lives, whether to write letters and postcards, diary entries, shopping lists, receipts, or memoirs. Book inscriptions are an important example of this literacy for men and women. To overlook these written traces and their writers is to miss valuable evidence of self-representation and identity construction that empowers the working classes, gives them agency, and recasts larger cultural narratives.

Estill (2019) notes that digital humanities continues to offer a skewed perspective on literacy because of its persisting preference for literature over ordinary writing. She cites the fact that certain authors such as Shakespeare are heavily overrepresented in this field to the detriment of ordinary writers. She warns that "biased sources can only lead to biased scholarship," which is a danger, particularly for students who may not be well-versed in identifying this prejudice. Bourg (2018, 460) claims that digital humanists must be prepared to "engage in conscious acts of resistance" by ensuring that digital tools do not reflect and perpetuate inequalities and that the limited binary that divides writing into high and low forms is removed. Doing so will enable a better understanding of what writers can do and how readers can respond, thus countering the negative and persisting stereotypes on ordinary writing.

15.3.6 *Opportunity 3: Arranging Events to Challenge Perceptions on the Value of "Ordinary Writing"*

A 2019 report from Research Libraries UK recognized the increasing importance of impact and engagement activities to provide local communities with opportunities to learn, explore, and interact, to raise the profile of institutions and collections, and to encourage openness in scholarship and culture. Another important aspect of impact and engagement is to challenge perceptions and encourage people to think in a new way. In order to stimulate interest and foster support for a digital archive of Edwardian working-class book inscriptions, I decided to share some of the collected examples through three key outreach events: workshops, a family history show, and a digital exhibition.

Jones (2018, 89) notes that book inscriptions have high pedagogical value and can be used to develop curricula and introduce students to new learning resources. With this in mind, in November 2019, I organized a pilot specialist workshop with students and staff in the School of English, Communication, and Philosophy at Cardiff University to showcase the value of working with working-class book inscriptions. I provided each participant with an image of a book inscription and asked them to think about what it might reveal about the owner's social status (e.g., choice of words, spelling mistakes or grammatical errors, handwriting, writing implement, content). Then, I demonstrated how www.ancestry.com can be used to ground these suppositions in primary evidence from official records. The students enjoyed the opportunity to engage with an unfamiliar text in an innovative way and were particularly excited about the potential of book inscriptions to reveal new information about working-class life, particularly for women who are often overlooked or underrepresented in research on the topic. They also generally agreed that a digital archive would provide an excellent pedagogical tool to interact with these inscriptions more personally and explore one specific feature that may be of interest (e.g. gift inscriptions from mothers to sons; books inscribed by miners; inscriptions written with indelible pencil). To commemorate International Women's Day 2020, I also delivered a presentation, drawing attention to female inscriptions and the stories behind them, which formed part of Cardiff University's Migration, Ethnicity, Race, and Diversity Research Conference. Given the positive feedback, these workshops have since been rolled out with history and sociology students (tailored to their specific interests).[1] I also plan to conduct similar sessions with students in creative writing, book history, and literature.[2]

The Family History Show is an annual event that brings together historians, genealogical organizations, and amateur genealogists to provide expert advice on family history research. I organized a stall at the February 2020 event that showed members of the public how to use inscriptions as an entry point into researching their family tree. I brought along physical examples of Edwardian books containing book inscriptions and demonstrated how the details (e.g., owner's name, date of birth, location) could be inserted into www.ancestry.com to find biographical information on the inscriber. The stall proved popular with visitors and the general feedback obtained was that it had made them "reconsider the value of book inscriptions." One respondent particularly acknowledged their worth at shedding light on events that may not be recorded in surviving official documents or provide new perspectives on national history (e.g., showcased examples included endpapers used to write first-hand accounts of Queen Victoria's funeral procession and King Edward VII's coronation and express support for female suffrage, the Labour Party, and Darwinism, to name but a few). These types of shows could offer an innovative way for academics and other professionals to engage with the public and assess general interest in their research.

On 5 March 2020, I launched a digital exhibition on Instagram entitled "Prize Books and Politics: Rethinking Working-Class Life in Edwardian Britain." Over a period of 6 weeks, I posted one inscription per day that encapsulated the life of the working classes in Edwardian Britain (ensuring a 50:50 gender balance). Each image was accompanied by a short written reflection exploring its main message, which aimed to encourage readers to rethink current perceptions of the working classes. A sample post can be seen in Fig. 15.2.

Thomas (2017, 22) warns against using social media to host digital exhibitions because it gives historical images the same value and identity as other images, which risks downplaying their importance. Nonetheless, Instagram offered an important way to experiment with a "transient" digital archive, in addition to attracting interest and obtaining feedback from a completely different audience to that of the Family History Show. Instagram also enabled me to engage directly with users through tagging and comments. Tagging served as an important means of democratizing inscriptions by using the "everyday words of the crowd" (ibid., 2017, 74) and emphasizing social language over descriptive language.

Feedback from the digital exhibition was overwhelmingly positive. Visitors from across Europe, America, and Australia all stated that it had changed their perception of the working classes and transformed the way they think

Fig. 15.2 A sample post from the "Prize Books and Politics" Instagram exhibition

about how working-class people are represented in the media today. While some visitors felt that the exhibition highlighted the injustices concerning the historical representation of working classes, others believed that it served to celebrate the working classes and their culture. Many also stated that the exhibition showcased how book inscriptions can be a powerful medium for expression and communication, even at a time when the working classes were oppressed or had a limited voice. They were also pleased that the exhibition moved arguments beyond simplistic categorizations of respectable/roughs, drinkers/thinkers, etc., and encouraged visitors to think about the working classes in new ways, with a particular emphasis on voices not often heard, such as women and children. When asked about future plans to create a digital archive of Edwardian working-class book inscriptions, most users expressed enthusiasm and agreed that it would be a beneficial resource to open up new platforms for debate and challenge others to reflect on a topic that they may not have considered in this way before.

Although these events are relatively small-scale, they have succeeded in their aim of challenging users to rethink their attitudes toward ordinary writing and recognize its worth as a resource for exploring working-class life in Edwardian Britain. They provide some indication of the power of impact and engagement and demonstrate that there is general support for a digital archive of Edwardian working-class book inscriptions. The supportive evidence provided by participant feedback may help build a convincing case for potential funders to subsidize the project.

15.4 Conclusion

For too long, the book inscription has been disregarded as a simple declaration of ownership. This has obscured the multifaceted functions that it performs and the broader cultural experiences and sociohistorical context that it encompasses. Book inscriptions are shaped by personal needs, traditions, and knowledge, yet each belongs to wider scale historical narratives. These pieces of material culture "operate at a junction between personal memory and social history, between public myth and personal unconsciousness" (Spence and Holland 1991, 13) and define who we are within broader social networks and our place in society.

Edwardian working-class book inscriptions, in particular, offer an important yet previously overlooked resource for exploring, rethinking, and reshaping our understanding of working-class life in early twentieth-century Britain. By bringing personal experiences to the forefront, these inscriptions can help us re-evaluate how working-class Edwardians organized their lives and made sense of their experiences, and how culture and knowledge is produced, reproduced, and performed. They can also open up perspectives on working-class life beyond the male-centered context of the labor movement and shed light on the everyday experiences of women who played an equally important role in "keeping the country going," albeit largely behind the scenes. In doing so, inscriptions can help foster fresh understandings of working-class life and culture that showcase how both men and women were able to use literacy to take control of their own lives.

A digital archive of Edwardian working-class book inscriptions would provide a permanent place to protect these "vulnerable" artifacts and construct a self-generated history of voices that are scarcely heard in official histories yet are intertwined with the events that made up the period. Furthermore, its digital search functions have the potential to drive new research into gender-, age-, and occupation-based patterns in working-class book ownership and inscriptive practices, as well as how semiotic and material choices were used by working-class individuals to assert identity, personal beliefs, and belonging. The archive, thus, provides an unprecedented opportunity to tap into working-class lives in ways that have not been done before and reveal a wealth of information on the multiple realities from which people constructed their self, their social circle, and the Edwardian era as a whole and how class was felt, read, passed on, and communicated.

Despite the growing recognition for open-mindedness in digital humanities research, there is still some reluctance to fund a project of this type. Although I received overwhelmingly positive feedback from the general public and fellow academics, feedback from funders considered a digital archive of Edwardian working-class book inscriptions to be "overly ambitious" and did not feel that there was much need for such a resource. A digital archive of this sort is not possible without important changes regarding the value of ordinary writing, as well as the survival and accessibility of working-class inscriptions in official institutions. In this chapter, I have suggested several ways to counter these challenges through bookshops as alternative data collection resources, collaborations with official institutions, and impact and engagement events. McGann (2005, 72) claims that, in the coming decades, "the entirety of our cultural inheritance will be transformed and reedited in digital forms." If this is the case, we must ensure that working-class people are at the forefront of this representation of culture. To lose their voices is to lose an important part of our cultural heritage.

Notes

1. History and sociology students used newspaper archives to conduct an investigation of one of the awarding institutions and build up a general picture of their history and how they were involved in the prize book movement.
2. Creative writing students could be shown a range of inscriptions and encouraged to think about how they can develop a story, poem, or play using the ownership mark as a starting point; literature students could explore how content analysis and corpus tools can be used to explore gender stereotypes in prize books and track historical bias; and book history students could be introduced to www.ancestry.com and given a specific book owner to track down using the records.

REFERENCES

Barton, David, and Uta Papen. 2010. *The Anthropology of Writing*. London: Continuum.

Bordalejo, Barbara. 2018. "Minority Report: The Myth of Equality in Digital Humanities." In *Bodies of Information: Intersectional Feminism and Digital Humanities*, edited by Elizabeth Losh and Jacqueline Wernimont, 320–43. Minneapolis, MN: University of Minnesota Press.

Bourg, Chris. 2018. "The Library Is Never Neutral." In *Disrupting the Digital Humanities*, edited by Dorothy Kim and Jesse Stommel, 455–72. Goleta CA: Punctum Books.

Caswell, Michelle. 2017. "Identifying and Dismantling White Supremacy in Archives." *The Library Quarterly: Information, Community, Policy* 87 (3): 222–35.

Caswell, Michelle, Christopher Harter, and Jules Bergis. 2017. "Diversifying the Digital Historical Record: Integrating Community Archives in National Strategies for Access to Digital Cultural Heritage." *D-Lib Magazine* 23: 5–6.

Cotton, B. 2019. Bookbarn grows sales of real books by extending global reach and local connections, Business Leader, https://www.businessleader.co.uk/bookbarn-grows-sales-of-real-books-by-extending-global-reach-andlocal-connections/. Accessed 2 August 2022.

Dunk, Thomas W. 2003. *It's a Working Man's Town: Male Working-Class Culture*. Montreal: McGill Queen's.

Earhart, Amy E. 2012. "Can Information Be Unfettered? Race and the New Digital Humanities Canon." In *Debates in the Digital Humanities*, edited by Matthew K. Gold. Available at https://dhdebates.gc.cuny.edu/read/untitled-88c11800-9446-469b-a3be-3fdb36bfbd1e/section/cf0af04d-73e3-4738-98d9-74c1ae3534e5#ch18. Accessed 8 July 2021.

Edwards, Elizabeth. 2004. "Little Theatres of Self: Thinking about the Social." In *We Are the People*, edited by Tom Phillips, 26–41. London: National Portrait Gallery.

Estill, Laura. 2019. "Digital Humanities' Shakespeare Problem." *Humanities* 8 (1). https://doi.org/https://doi.org/10.3390/h8010045. Accessed 8 July 2021.

Ezell, Margaret J. M. 2010. "Editing Early Modern Women's Manuscripts: Theory, Electronic Editions, and the Accidental Copy-Text." *Literature Compass* 7 (2): 102–9.

Flinn, Andrew. 2007. "Community Histories, Community Archives: Some Opportunities and Challenges." *Journal of the Society of Archivists* 28 (2): 151–76.

Flinn, Andrew, Mary Stevens, and Elizabeth Shepherd. 2009. "Whose Memories, Whose Archives? Independent Community Archives, Autonomy and the Mainstream." *Archival Science* 9 (1–2): 71–86.

Gallon, Kim. 2016. "Making a Case for the Black Digital Humanities." In *Debates in the Digital Humanities 2016*, edited by Matthew K. Gold and Lauren F. Klein, 42–49. Minneapolis, MN: University of Minnesota Press.

Hall, Nigel, and Julia Gillen. 2010. "Edwardian Postcards: Illuminating Ordinary Writing." In *The Anthropology of Writing*, edited by David Barton and Uta Papen, 169–89. London: Continuum.

Higgin, Tanner. 2010. *Cultural Politics, Critique and the Digital Humanities*. Blog Post, May 25. Available at https://www.tannerhiggin.com/2010/05/cultural-politics-critique-and-the-digital-humanities/. Accessed 8 July 2021.

Hitchcock, Tim. 2004. "A New History from Below." *History Workshop Journal* 57: 294–99.
Jones, Kiana. 2018. "The Pedagogical Value of Provenance Research in Rare Books and Cultural Heritage Collections." *Art Documentation: Journal of the Art Libraries Society of North America* 37: 82–89.
Lillis, Theresa. 2013. *The Sociolinguistics of Writing*. Edinburgh: Edinburgh University Press.
Liu, Alan. 2020. "Toward a Diversity Stack: Digital Humanities and Diversity as Technical Problem." *Publications of the Modern Language Association of America* 135 (1): 130–51.
Losh, Elizabeth, and Jacqueline Wernimont. 2018. *Bodies of Information: Intersectional Feminism and Digital Humanities*. Minneapolis, MN: University of Minnesota Press.
Loveday, Vic. 2014. "'Flat-Capping It': Memory, Nostalgia and Value in Retroactive Male Working-Class Identification." *European Journal of Cultural Studies* 17 (6): 721–35.
Lyons, Martyn. 2010. "A New History from Below? The Writing Culture of Ordinary People in Europe." *History Australia* 7 (3): 59.1–59.9.
Lyons, Martyn. 2013. *The Writing Culture of Ordinary People in Europe, c. 1860–1920*. Cambridge: Cambridge University Press.
Mahony, Simon. 2018. "Cultural Diversity and the Digital Humanities." *Fudan Journal of the Humanities and Social Sciences* 11: 371–88.
McGann, Jerome. 2005. "Culture and Technology: The Way we Live Now, What Is to Be Done?" *New Literary History* 36 (1): 71–82.
McKitterick, David. 2009. "Introduction." In *The Cambridge History of the Book in Britain: Volume 6, 1830–1914*, edited by David McKitterick, 1–75. Cambridge: Cambridge University Press.
O'Hagan, Lauren Alex. 2020a. "Introduction: Ordinary Writing and Rebellion." In *Rebellious Writing: Marginalised Edwardians and the Contestation of Power*, edited by Lauren Alex O'Hagan, 1–46. Bern: Peter Lang.
O'Hagan, Lauren Alex. 2020b. "Rethinking the Book Inscription as a Site of Class Struggle." In *Rebellious Writing: Marginalised Edwardians and the Contestation of Power*, edited by Lauren Alex O'Hagan, 201–37. Bern: Peter Lang.
O'Hagan, Lauren Alex. 2020c. "A Voice for the Voiceless: Improving Provenance Practice for Working-Class Books." *Journal of Librarianship and Information Science* 53 (1): 16–28.
Oxfam. 2020. *Oxfam Annual Reports and Accounts 2019/20*. Available at https://www.oxfam.org.uk/documents/264/Oxfam_GB_Annual_Report_2020.pdf. Accessed 8 July 2021.
Phillips, Tom. 2004. "Introduction." In *We Are the People*, edited by Tom Phillips, 14–26. London: National Portrait Gallery.
Potter, Claire Bond. 2013. "Thou Shalt Commit: The Internet, New Media, and the Future of Women's History." *Journal of Women's History* 25 (4): 350–62.
Richards, Jennifer. 2019. *Voices and Books in the English Renaissance: A New History of Reading*. Oxford: Oxford University Press.
Risam, Roopika. 2015. "Beyond the Margins: Intersectionality and the Digital Humanities." *English Faculty Publications*, Paper 4. http://digitalcommons.salemstate.edu/english_facpub/4. Accessed 8 July 2021.

Risam, Roopika. 2018. "Decolonizing the Digital Humanities in Theory and Practice." *English Faculty Publications*, Paper 7. http://digitalcommons.salemstate.edu/english_facpub/7. Accessed 8 July 2021.

Ruberg, Bonnie, Jason Boyd, and James Howe. 2018. "Toward a Queer Digital Humanities." In *Bodies of Information: Intersectional Feminism and Digital Humanities*, edited by Elizabeth Losh and Jacqueline Wernimont, 108–28. Minneapolis, MN: University of Minnesota Press.

Seale, Maura. 2013. "The Neoliberal Library." In *Information Literacy and Social Justice: Radical Professional Praxis*, edited by Shana Higgins and Lua Gregory, 39–61. Sacramento, CA: Library Juice Press.

Sinor, Jennifer. 2002. *The Extraordinary Work of Ordinary Writing: Annie Ray's Diary*. Iowa City: University of Iowa Press.

Spence, Jo, and Patricia Holland. 1991. *Family Snaps: The Meaning of Domestic Photography*. London: Virago Press.

Sutherland, Tonia. 2017. "Archival Amnesty: In Search of Black American Transitional and Restorative Justice." *Journal of Critical Library and Information Services* 1 (2): 1–23. https://doi.org/10.24242/jclis.v1i2.42. Accessed 8 July 2021.

Thomas, Julia. 2017. *Nineteenth-Century Illustration and the Digital: Studies in Word and Image*. London: Palgrave Macmillan.

Thompson, E. P. 1966. "History from Below." *Times Literary Supplement*, April 7, 279–80.

Todd, Selina. 2015. *The People: The Rise and Fall of the Working Class, 1910–1920*. London: John Murray.

Zinn, Howard. 1977. "Secrecy, Archives, and the Public Interest." *MidWestern Archivist* 2 (2): 14–26.

CHAPTER 16

Learning Seneca: A Case Study on Digital Presentations of North American Indigenous Languages

Francisco Delgado

16.1 Part I

As literature scholars, we recognize the immutable power of language. We understand, and communicate to others, the multitude of ways that language not only expresses our perceptions of the world but also shapes them. To lose a language, then, is to lose much more than just a mode of verbal expression. For many Indigenous peoples of the United States, losing their language was brought about through deliberate measures by Euro-American colonists. Targeting Indigenous languages, and cultures more generally, colonists attacked entire modes of knowing and interacting with the world. In this way, the loss of a language is not just personal in scope but steeped in the social, economic, and political histories of entire nations, which I will overview later in this chapter. To learn a Native American/Indigenous language, then, is an act of decolonization, one way in which we can connect with family across generations and, in the case of online learning, with one another across geography. Digital platforms can help us connect with others on their own language learning journeys who, due to the colonial histories of the United States and Canada,[1] find themselves removed from their family's home territories and unable to take advantage of the face-to-face language classes being offered there.

F. Delgado (✉)
Borough of Manhattan Community College, CUNY, New York, NY, USA
e-mail: fdelgado@bmcc.cuny.edu

© The Author(s), under exclusive license to Springer Nature Switzerland AG 2022
A. Schwan and T. Thomson (eds.), *The Palgrave Handbook of Digital and Public Humanities*, https://doi.org/10.1007/978-3-031-11886-9_16

The project I discuss in this chapter chronicles my learning of the traditional language of the Seneca (hereafter, the *Onöndowa'ga:'* or "People of the Great Hills"), one of the Six Nations of the Haudenosaunee Confederacy of upstate-New York. I am pleased to be included in the "Mobilising the Archive" section: to mobilize something is to compel it to move. It is a verb that connotes change, growth, and aliveness. At first glance, one might not associate aliveness with the archive. Public conceptions of archives, and of archival work, perhaps relegate it to museums and libraries. The archives, however, are inclined just as much to the future as they are toward the past. Ellen Cushman (2013, 27) writes that "digital archives are beginning to define the disciplinary work we do" in literary studies. Archival work taking digital formats is more than a trend in the profession. It delineates a clear shift about how knowledge is, and can be, developed and shared. Literary theorist Jean-Christophe Cloutier (2019, 3) notes in his own analysis of African American literary archives: "The archive is never an end in itself—otherwise we might as well call it a dumpster—but rather a speculative means to possible futures, including unknowable teleologies guided by unborn hands." Cloutier's characterization of the archive as a "speculative means to possible futures" illustrates how the archive, despite public perception, is geared more toward the future (or "futures") than it is toward the past. While the source material is rooted in the past, the archive is ultimately cultivated by the "unborn" hands of those yet-to-be, who are already implicated in the socio-political relations of history.

History, in fact, surrounds us in ways we often do not notice. For instance, my hometown, Canandaigua, New York, derives its name from the *Onöndowa'ga:'* word, *Tganödä:gwëh*, meaning "the chosen spot." It is believed to be the birthplace of the *Onöndowa'ga:'* people, who are said to have emerged from the Earth at the foot of the southernmost hills. However, despite growing up in a location so closely linked to *Onöndowa'ga:'* hi/story, I did not grow up, as Penelope Myrtle Kelsey (2014, xi) explains in her own articulation of her kinship/descent, "on-territory and within the ceremonial cycle of the year." My siblings and I knew we were *Onöndowa'ga:'* through our *akso:dgë'ö'*, or late grandmother. This matrilineal kinship qualified us for enrollment—meaning we qualified as members of the community based on the criteria set forth by the *Ta:nöwöde'*, or Tonawanda, community. But beyond the occasional road trip to the reservation at *Ta:nöwöde'* with my grandparents for cigarettes, we had minimal connection to *Onöndowa'ga:'* cultures and ceremonies—let alone the language at their roots. This would seem to result from my grandmother's own estrangement from her culture, as she admitted to me in a personal interview in 2017.

My grandmother, Alice Quinata Eastwood (née Pangborn), was born in 1936 to Gilbert Pangborn and Beaulah Jackson, who was born to the Wolf clan of the Tonawanda Band of Seneca as Clarinda Jemison. My grandmother's time with her parents, in particular her *Onöndowa'ga:'* mother, was brief: her earliest memories, she stated, are of a foster home in Jamestown, New York. She was around the age of ten when she and her siblings moved into a white foster home. As my grandmother explained (2017), this arrangement came about because "there were no Indian foster families at the time." My grandmother's experiences are common for Native children during this time period. Her time spent in a white foster home, as opposed to a home with a Native family, estranged her and her siblings from their culture, including the language. In the subsequent years of her adolescence, up until when she enlisted in the military and met my grandfather, Daniel Quinata, who was born and raised in the island of Guam, she attended a series of public schools in nearby towns like Burdett and Odessa in central New York. My grandmother describes these towns as predominantly white, as one would expect for the geographical region at the time, and she mentioned (without wanting to go into too much detail) the ridicule and discrimination she and her siblings faced "for being Indian" (Eastwood 2017).

She internalized the racism she faced to a degree that made her direct it toward other Native children. She spoke about the one time she remembers stepping foot on an Indian school, the well-known (and now infamous) Thomas Indian School near the Ga'dä:gësgë:ö', or Cattaraugus, reservation of the Seneca Nation of Indians. She remembers thinking that the kids there looked "mean" and "tough," not understanding at the time the harsh conditions these students endured at the hands of their so-called educators—conditions which I will elaborate on further in the following section of this chapter where I give some historical context. My grandmother, then, admitted to growing up thinking there were "good Indians" and "bad Indians," and she was always mindful of belonging to the former group in the eyes of white people. In this way, among others that I am sure she felt but never expressed, she was taught at a young age to feel ashamed of her Onöndowa'ga:' heritage.

I give the context of my grandmother's life, as she relayed it to me, because it is foundational to understanding my reasons for beginning the work on a language learning website in late 2015 that eventually became *Learning the Seneca Language* (https://www.learningthesenecalanguage.com/). At the time, I was finishing my doctoral studies at Stony Brook University and, more importantly, had recently become a father. These circumstances, particularly the latter, prompted me to think more deliberately about the nature and scope of my work. I had heard of the New York Council for the Humanities (now known as the Humanities New York) fellowship for graduate students and viewed it as an opportunity to create something that would transcend the traditional scope of academic work, i.e., specialized journals and conferences with limited, albeit passionate, audiences. I wanted to create something that would exist in the non-academic world that my son had just been born into.

Thus, I proposed creating a publicly-accessible website presenting conversational words and phrases[2] of the Seneca language—hereafter referred to as *Onöndowa'ga:' Gawë:no*, or "language of the People of the Great Hills." It was important for me that the project reached a wider audience than is often afforded to academic work because I proposed it with my grandmother, and my entire family, in mind. It was an added bonus that the online format, and public accessibility, might help other *Onöndowa'ga:'* unable to take advantage of the face-to-face language programs on the *Ohi:yo'* (or "Allegany"), *Ga'dä:gësgë:ö'* ("Cattaraugus"), and *Ta:nöwöde'* reservations. The only online resources I found in my searches at that time were available on the website native-languages.org. While a good introduction to vocabulary about colors, animals, and numbers, this website unfortunately did not (and, as of the time of this writing, does not) provide any further materials for learners who wished to continue their *Onöndowa'ga:' Gawë:no* studies. My aim was to create something slightly more expansive—its limitations mostly related to my own tenuous grasp of the language—that would help address the looming reality of linguistic genocide[3] of the *Onöndowa'ga:' Gawë:no*.

The number of fluent speakers has long been a source of concern. In 2015, Heather Rozler, an Education Consultant at the *Ganöhsesge:kha Hë:nödeyë:sta'*, or Faithkeeper's School, conjectured that the number could be as low as 40 persons (Murray 2015, para. 3). Native-languages.org provides a slightly more optimistic estimation of 100 speakers. So, how did the *Onöndowa'ga:' Gawë:no*, the traditional language of the Seneca Nation of Indians, with its 8000 enrolled members living on and off the reservation, and the Tonawanda Band of Seneca, with its own enrolled membership totaling almost another one thousand, become so threatened? In the next section, I will address this multi-faceted colonial phenomenon in greater detail, beginning with land displacement policies before moving on to the deleterious effects of boarding schools. Policies that drive cultural genocide are not in any way particular to the Seneca—or even the Haudenosaunee.[4] These policies have impacted Indigenous peoples throughout the Americas, as one can see with the implementation of the Native American Languages Act of 1990 in the United States, which finally advocated for Native peoples to use their own languages—nearly five-hundred years after the arrival of Columbus and two-hundred years after the Treaty of Canandaigua, which pledged peace and friendship between the Haudenosaunee Confederacy and the United States.

Following this historical overview, I describe the features of my own website, which I use as a platform to share my own growing knowledge of the *Onöndowa'ga:' Gawë:no*. I then describe my efforts to connect with other efforts to promote *Onöndowa'ga:' Gawë:no* usage in my role as a language student. Undoubtedly, this has been one of the most valuable learning lessons with this project: understanding that academia's emphasis on expertise and (single-author) authority does not translate to a public-facing endeavor, which tends to be more communal in scope and execution.[5] As digital humanities scholar Lisa Spiro (2016, 21–22) asserts, for digital projects, "information is not a commodity to be controlled but a social good to be shared and reused." I recognize that the work of chronicling my language learning journey comes from a place, not of specialization, but of genuine curiosity to learn and of an enthusiasm to share. It exists outside of the regular schedule of academic work, in that there is no strict termination date. The website, like the learning process it chronicles, is and should be open-ended. As Ricardo L. Ortiz (2019) concludes in his own analysis of public-facing projects, we must "devote our talents and our labor... in whatever way it makes the most sense for us, and in whatever way we each best understand our vocation as scholar, or critic, or teacher, or artist, or writer, or activist, or citizen" (para. 20). While I agree with Ortiz's list of identities, I would add to it the identity of learner. We must in some way understand our vocation as lifelong learners, reflecting on what knowledge we work to acquire, what knowledge we share with others, and what values that knowledge promotes. Each section of this chapter, then, foregrounds my role as a learner throughout my endeavor into the public-facing digital humanities.

16.2 Part II

As a doctoral student in English, I was feeling increasingly confident in my understanding of contemporary Native American literatures. However, at the start of this digital project, I still had plenty to learn about the history of the *Onöndowa'ga:'* people. I set out right away to learn this history because how could I help promote the *Onöndowa'ga:' Gawë:no* online if I could not chronicle the history of language loss in Seneca speaking communities? The impacts of land displacement policies of the eighteenth and nineteenth centuries and boarding schools on Haudenosaunee peoples have been rigorously studied. For instance, Melissa Borgia (2014), Professor at Thiel College in Pennsylvania and Language Instruction Consultant at *Ganöhsesge:kha:' Hë:nödeyë:stha*, as well as Laurence Hauptman (1999), Distinguished Professor of History at the SUNY New Paltz, trace these phenomena to the Seneca alliance with the British during the American Revolution. Prior to this war, the treaties between Natives and European settlers were based on coexistence and peace. In the context of New York state, examples of these treaties include the Two Row Wampum Belt from the seventeenth century, which pledged perpetual friendship between the Haudenosaunee and the Dutch settlers, and further down state, the William Penn Belt between the Lenape and William Penn (founder of the state of Pennsylvania), which "features a singular Native figure and European figure holding hands in friendship on a white background" (Kelsey 2014, 28). As Penelope Kelsey (2014, 59–60) points out, Haudenosaunee peoples, including the *Onöndowa'ga:'*, view wampum belts (visual representations of a particular agreement between parties) as lasting "for as long as the natural world continues its regular and observable processes (i.e. flowing water/grass growth moving in circles)." It is not a stretch, then, to assume that *Onöndowa'ga:'* peoples believed these pledges of friendship would continue to be upheld, even in light of settler desires to occupy and own the lands that were promised to the *Onöndowa'ga:'* in the Treaty of Canandaigua in 1794. Their conception of the treaties, particularly in relation to their duration, contrasts to the settler perspective of treaties as constantly up for revision or, when suitable to their own interests, blatant disregard.

The subsequent fallout of the American Revolution on Haudenosaunee-settler relations is evident right away. The Treaty of Paris (1783), which marks the official end of the war, was signed with no Native allies present. The only signees of this treaty are King George III of Great Britain and representatives of the United States—this, despite the fact that the Oneida and Tuscarora in fact sided with the American colonists. Kelsey (2014, 29) argues that this omission of Haudenosaunee presence in the signing of this treaty perhaps necessitated the signing of the Canandaigua Treaty (1794), "the first comprehensive treaty negotiated after the close of the Revolutionary War, the omission of Native allies in the Treaty of Paris (1783), and the genocidal campaign of generals Sullivan and Clinton into Iroquoia." The Clinton-Sullivan campaign during the Revolutionary War, in particular, served the purpose of "[taking] a large number of Indians prisoners, to be held as hostages to help ensure the "good behavior" of the Indians in the future" ("The Clinton-Sullivan Campaign of 1779," para. 2). "Good behavior" here refers to subservience, a tactic seemingly enacted through the exclusion of Natives in the signing of the Treaty of Paris, which indicated that Native allies were not equal parties to the British and the American colonists, who certainly valued them during the war in various capacities, including as scouts.

The Treaty of Canandaigua extends the friendship pledged in the Two Row Wampum Belt to the newly-formed United States of America. Particular articles of the treaty, for instance, recognize the existence of and parameters of reservation territories of the Haudenosaunee in upstate-New York and that these lands "shall remain theirs, until they choose to sell the same to the people of the United States" (Kelsey 2014, 30). While this treaty recognizes the land rights of Haudenosaunee peoples, it also explicitly makes possible the reality of land sales. Settler desires to displace (and replace) *Onöndowa'ga:'* peoples—as well as Haudenosaunee peoples, in general—would become more apparent in the early-1800s through a series of treaties signed at Buffalo Creek.

The Buffalo Creek treaties of 1826, 1838, and 1842 illustrate the displacement practices that the *Onöndowa'ga:'* people had to face and, to a certain extent, ultimately resulted in the fracture between the Seneca Nation of Indians and the Tonawanda Band of Seneca. The first of these treaties, the Treaty[6] of 1826, ceded Genesee Valley lands,

> including Big Tree, Canawaugus, and Squawky Hill reservations in Livingston County; the remaining two square miles at the Gardeau Reservation in Wyoming County; and the sixteen-square Caneadea Reservation in Allegany County... the sizes of the Buffalo Creek, Tonawanda, and Cattaraugus reservations were substantially reduced: Buffalo Creek by 36,638 acres; Tonawanda by 33,409 acres; and Cattaraugus by 5,120. (Hauptman 2011, 24)

This sizable land cession was perhaps not agreed to peacefully. Hauptman (2011, 24) conjectures that Red Jacket and other Seneca leaders may have only signed the treaty under the tangible threat of displacement (without monetary compensation) from the federal commissioner. In particular, Red Jacket, a Seneca chief renowned for his oratory and diplomatic skills, may have only signed the treaty because he knew he could successfully lobby against it afterward due to connections in the white world (Hauptman 2011, 25). Seizures of Native lands, even if not formally ratified by the U.S. Senate like the Buffalo Creek Treaty of 1826, were certainly part of the general milieu of the time period. Relocation, illustrated most vividly by the Indian Removal Act of 1830,[7] was favored as the preeminent method of dealing with Native communities seen as impeding the progress of the United States. The construction of the Erie Canal[8] in 1825 made traditional *Onöndowa'ga:'* lands, especially at Tonawanda and Buffalo, simply too valuable to be inhabited by non-Americans, according to American settlers. They thus figured that removal was a necessary growth measure for the United States to make room for the population increase of Euro-American settlers, which in New York state alone went from 340,000 after the American Revolution to 3.5 million people right before the Civil War (Hauptman 1999, 213).

The Treaty of Buffalo Creek of 1838 resulted in the cession of Allegany, Buffalo Creek, Cattaraugus, and Tonawanda to the Ogden Land Company in exchange for a 1,824,000-acres in Kansas, which the *Onöndowa'ga:'* had five years to occupy before they would cede this territory, as well. Because this treaty was brought about thanks to "bribery, forgery, the use of alcohol, and other nefarious methods," it is often seen by historians and activists as illegitimate (Hauptman 2011, 43). That, however, does not mean that the United States government did not attempt to swiftly bring it to fruition. Only activism on the part of the *Onöndowa'ga:'*, including advertisements in local newspapers, circulating petitions, and restricting access to outsider parties in pursuit of "statistical data that they thought could be harmful to their interests," prevented the outright execution and seizure of these territories (Hauptman 2011, 125). While the subsequent Treaty of Buffalo Creek of 1842 initiated the return of Allegany and Cattaraugus, it did not promise the return of the territories at Buffalo Creek and Tonawanda, which caused a split between the *Onöndowa'ga:'* at Allegany and Cattaraugus with those at Tonawanda who felt that their own territory rights had been sacrificed and that their decision-making process, which required unanimous agreement, had been disregarded.[9]

These legislative acts account for the messy, and sometimes contentious, nature of *Onöndowa'ga:'*-U.S. relations, and they provide a backdrop for boarding school policies that followed, which historian Keith Burich (2007, 107) describes as originating from a mixture of "coercion" on the part of the government and "desperation" on the part of Native parents. Burich (2007, 93), who also works as the Director of the American Indian Center at Canisius College, argues that boarding schools were "the most destructive agents of the heavy-handed and clumsy federal policy of forced assimilation that removed Indian children from their reservations, *their language*, and their culture" (emphasis added). These were not educational institutions; these schools were designed to remove children from their parents, thus weakening the modes of cultural transmission and appreciation in the name of assimilation into American culture, including western religion. Missionary presence was stronger at Cattaraugus and at Allegany than it was at Tonawanda. The Quakers, for instance, ran the Tunesassa Boarding School at Allegany. The *Onöndowa'ga:'* largely viewed the Quakers favorably for their benevolence—the Quakers, for instance, never asked for land payment for the resources they donated—but the Quakers nonetheless sought their assimilation, thereby placing a strong emphasis on learning English at the neglect of the traditional language. The Presbyterians created and ran the Thomas Indian School. The Thomas Indian School will serve as my primary focus in this analysis. Along with the Carlisle Indian Industrial School and the Mush Hole Indian Residential School, the Thomas Indian School helps illustrate the damaging impact of these institutional attempts at American assimilation. It also links to my own family history, in that it is the boarding school that my grandmother had visited as a young child. The Tonawanda Band of Seneca, in contrast, had far fewer western religious intrusions than the other Seneca reservations. Hauptman (2011, xxiv) points out that, at most, there was some Baptist influence[10] but that the Quaker and Presbyterian influence was nonexistent.

Founded as the Thomas Asylum for Orphan and Destitute Children, the Thomas Indian School was opened by Phillip Thomas, of the Quaker Society of Friends, and Asher Wright, a Presbyterian missionary in 1855. The state of New York took over the administration of the school in 1875 and not long after, in 1889, perhaps motivated by the ideology expressed most famously by Captain Richard H. Pratt as "Kill the Indian, Save the Man," outlawed the use of the *Onöndowa'ga:' Gawë:no'* on school property (Borgia 2014, 61). Thomas Donaldson, who worked for the US Census Bureau's bulletin on New York Indians, also speaks to the motivations behind this rule forbidding the use of the language when he describes the *Onöndowa'ga:'* students' inability to speak English as the "'greatest evil' affecting their advancement" (Borgia 2014, 61). The notion of "advancement" as it is expressed here is rooted in western-cultural ideals: to speak and write in the language of English, is more "advanced" and valuable than for the students to speak and write in their own languages. Students arrived at Thomas coming from poverty and found themselves in an environment only slightly less poverty-stricken. Quoting Hauptman, Borgia (2014, 56) explains that the Department of Social Services, known at the time as the State Board of Charities, "served many of the present functions of the contemporary departments of education, health, housing, and mental hygiene 'yet it was... plagued with racism.'" Despite this, *Onöndowa'ga:'* people from Cattaraugus and Allegany were eager to send their children to Thomas to live and to receive instruction that would presumably help them transition to life outside of the reservation. As Burich (2007, 103) writes, "Indians on the New York reservations had already been stripped of their traditional way of life by the pressure to assimilate, were all but forgotten by state authorities, and were deprived of the services available to other residents of the state." However, in contrast to the promise of a better education that Cattaraugus and Allegany parents believed their children would receive, students at the school received no differentiated instruction, thereby leading to many students' educational and personal needs being neglected, or had their difficulties acclimating to the rigid school culture attributed to their Indian-ness, i.e., that if they struggled in school, it was not because of the conditions but because they were Indian (Burich 2007, 100). Thus, generations of students ended up estranged from their families and their cultures while not any more suited for what administrators considered to be a successful transition into mainstream, white, American society. Many former students, to quote social worker Catherine Tidd, whose report precipitated the closing of the school, "drift[ed] back to the reservation and settled into the same relatively low standard of living from which they had originally come" (Burich 2007, 100). Borgia (2014, 94) similarly summarizes the school's legacy on its students: "At best, [students] returned to homes where they were neither comfortable nor welcome. At worst, they died alone in distant places, all in the name of the misguided and destructive policy of assimilation." Boarding schools, in other words, failed to deliver on their promise of assimilation: rather than acclimating their students to life outside of the reservation, these schools left them estranged from both the American and *Onöndowa'ga:'* cultures, resulting in generations of children with little to no knowledge of their own culture and language.

These experiences are often neglected in the more common narrative of American history, which tend to be far removed from the lived experiences and memories of *Onöndowa'ga:'* peoples. The Thomas Indian School, in fact, did not close until 1956—meaning, for instance, that my grandmother visited this institution in the last decade of its existence. The fact that her experiences at the Thomas Indian School was only as a visitor is a good thing—and something I told her she, and we, should be thankful for. Without having learned the *Onöndowa'ga:' Gawë:no'* growing up, the children at these boarding schools were not as fluent in their traditional language as their parents had been raised to be. This, in turn, prevented them from teaching their own children and grandchildren. The rise of boarding schools in the second-half of the nineteenth century, up until their closure a century later, in no small way explains how the *Onöndowa'ga:' Gawë:no'* became so threatened, necessitating the concerted efforts of language teachers and activists on the reservations, as well as the proliferation of online resources for language learners in the last few years. Online resources in particular are valuable: according to Emily Donellan (2017, 350), citing the 2010 census, only 22% of Native Americans live on tribal lands, meaning Native/Indigenous communities are increasingly both on and off reservation lands. Next, I provide an overview of my website's layout, explaining in greater detail what I had hoped to accomplish and what purpose the website serves to the general public that come to visit it on their own language learning journeys.

16.3 PART III

Learning the Seneca Language marked my first (and, so far, only) foray into website creation. In learning how to create a website, I ultimately had to learn how to be fine with experimenting, and with failing, and with trying again—in other words, the same type of learning process many of us emphasize for our students. My primary objective was to create a digital space that would be useful for visitors and be easily accessible because digital projects are not automatically accessible to the public. As academics, we are all too familiar with paywalled websites that, at most, perhaps offer only the first few paragraphs for free. Recently, I met with colleagues to prepare for a roundtable scheduled for the 2021 meeting of the Modern Language Association (MLA) in Toronto, Canada on the relationship between public humanities work and teaching at a community college. Ultimately, we arrived at a question that in many ways relates to the scope of this collection: if the emergence of the public humanities is in response to, by opposition, the private humanities, what in fact are the private humanities? As literature scholars, we do not want to think that the work we do is only marginally engaged with the public, but the reach of our work—from specialized conferences with registration fees to academic journals requiring annual subscriptions—unfortunately shows that the majority of our work is indeed "private" in nature and scope. Digital humanities scholar Matthew Kirschenbaum (2016, 9) writes:

> the digital humanities today is about a scholarship (and a pedagogy) that is publicly visible in ways to which we are generally unaccustomed, a scholarship and pedagogy that are bound up with infrastructure in ways that are deeper and more explicit than we are generally unaccustomed to, a scholarship and pedagogy that are collaborative and depend on networks of people and that live an active, 24-7 life online.

The "collaborative" spirit of digital humanities scholarship contrasts with the singularly-authored work that, for better or worse, often remains the most highly regarded in humanities fields and counts the most toward tenure.[11] Digital projects reveal our interests in ways that we are "unaccustomed" to them being. The reward, however, is that our work reaches a broader audience—what Kirschenbaum (2016, 9) refers to as "networks of people [living] an active, 24-7 life online."

Our work becomes accessible, and beholden to, the public in a way that a peer-reviewed journal on a paywalled website intentionally is not. As Julie Ellison (2013, 289) explains, quoting Timothy K. Eatman, public-facing work marks "a commitment to public practice and public consequence." *Learning the Seneca Language* primarily chronicles my learning of the *Onöndowa'ga:' Gawë:no'*. My public role as a student is in contrast with the values of a profession that historically regards, and continues to regard, expertise only. The public humanities and the digital humanities are relatively new fields to the profession of literary studies; the roles of practitioners have yet to be neatly defined—and this is perhaps for the best, as both fields prioritize adaptability and openness in a way that rigid project roles risk inhibiting. To me, we are at our best when we foreground our own identities as learners, which is noticeably absent in Ortiz's list of roles that I quoted at the end of the first section. By foregrounding our identities as learners, we show the general public, including our own students and colleagues, that learning is a lifelong commitment and not something that ends with the receipt of a degree. Furthermore, our continued assertion of our identities as learners shows students that lives devoted to educational pursuits, like ours are, do not make us into know-it-alls. Rather, a life devoted to educational pursuits has fueled our curiosity even further, our confidence to get something wrong and to learn from it.

Paraphrasing David Perkins, Anne B. McGrail (2016, 22) asserts the importance of the role of "expert amateurs"—or those "who are able to know enough about learning something new that they can continue to learn new skills and adapt themselves to a changing world." My mission with *Learning the Seneca Language* is expressed right on the homepage. I explain that the website "chronicles my own personal journey learning the Seneca language. Its limitations—and any of its mistakes are my own, and I happily welcome corrections" via email (Delgado "Home," para. 4). In this way, I attempt to be transparent about my own objective with the website and my own journey: in other words, I present myself not as someone fluent in the language but as a fellow learner. As my learning of the language progresses—and, truthfully, this is not nearly as linear and regular a process as I hoped and would have originally thought—I update the vocabulary presented on the website. My role as learner is further evident when I write that my objective "is to share conversational words of the Seneca language... as I learn them" (Delgado "Home," para. 4). My choice of verb here, "to share," is deliberate: while I hope that visitors learn from the website, I consciously refrained from stating that my objective was "to teach" because placing myself in the role of teacher, to put it bluntly, exceeds my comfort and skill levels. My emphasized role as learner certainly sets my website apart from other online resources: the Allegany Language Department, for instance, provides a much more expansive database of the language, including video and audio files, booklets on grammar, and an English-to-Seneca dictionary. Each of these resources is wonderful. The dictionary, in particular, helps visitors identify how to write, and say, a particular word or phrase in Seneca, and a grammar book by Wallace Chafe provides wonderful breakdowns of individual components of words and complete sentences.

The focus of *Learning the Seneca Language* on conversational words and phrases, though, stems from what my grandmother expressed she would find most useful. The website design therefore heeds the words of Sheila A. Brennan (2016, para. 7) who asserts that "Each public digital humanities project must begin by identifying audiences outside of the academy" ("Public First"). From the homepage, visitors will see a menu on the top of the screen that presents these conversational words and phrases in categories: "Hello/Goodbye," "Getting Around Town," "People/Family," "Kinship Clans," among others. These categories prioritize social interaction. For instance, the "Hello/Goodbye" page covers phrases that begin a conversation, including "*Nya:wëh sgë:nö'*" meaning "I am thankful you are well (a common conversation starter), "*Gi'shëh*" meaning "Excuse me," and "*Sadögweta?'*" meaning "How are you doing?" ("Hello/Goodbye"). These phrases are offered as tools to engage members of the *Onöndowa'ga:' Gawë:no'* speaking community in conversation.

As a second example, the "Asking Questions" page includes "*Dë'ëh ni:s šya:soh?*," meaning "What are you called?", and "*Ga:weh ni:s'ah?*," meaning "Where are you?" ("Asking Questions"). These phrases are valuable in an everyday social context, and as Kirschenbaum (2016, 5) writes, "digital humanities is also a social undertaking." The lifecycle of the materials we upload do not end at that moment. They are up for review and correction, as well as what Lisa Spiro (2016, 22) calls "remixing," to anyone who encounters them at all hours of the day. I opened my chapter with the claim that there is an immutable power to language—to express our perceptions, as well as to shape the perceptions of others—but that does not mean that languages themselves are immutable. They are constantly in flux, fluid in various directions, and these qualities make languages perfect for the types of "remixing" that Spiro describes here.

As languages change, so too do our understandings of them. To bolster my goal of learning publicly, I included a blog feature on the website designed to chronicle, albeit irregularly, my own learning of the *Onöndowa'ga:' Gawë:no'*. The blog, similar to the email information I provide on the homepage, is designed to foster the type of "openness and collaboration" that Lisa Spiro (2016, 16) positions as foundational to digital projects. The first of these blog posts explains my own family history, centering—as it did in the first section of this essay—on my maternal grandmother ("My Onöndowa'ga:' Family History"). This type of personal writing is not typical in academic essays, but it is a cornerstone to any worthwhile explanation of the *Learning the Seneca Language* website. The second blog post, composed a few months after my grandmother's passing, provides an overview of some of the changes I made in the vocabulary to the website, as well as accounts for how I have progressed with my own learning of the language ("For Akso:t (My Grandmother)"). It is important to me to be upfront about my role as learner—and, more specifically, the struggles that have arisen during my language learning journey.

Email exchanges, as well, speak to my commitment to openness with the website. A number of visitors have taken me up on my offer on the homepage soliciting "[q]uestions and/or corrections" (Delgado "Home," para. 10) for help on their own language learning.[12] Questions range from vocabulary inquiries (for words like "deer" and "grandmother," for instance) to broader questions about the linkages among Haudenosaunee languages (Seneca and Cayuga, in this case), as well as visitors simply wishing to share their own *Onöndowa'ga:'* family histories. For all the academic scholarship speaking to the importance of public "input" and "conversation" (Spiro 2016, 16) in regards to digital projects, I am ultimately just humbled and honored by people's willingness to share their own stories and link them, however briefly, to my own. I hope to use these email exchanges as opportunities to solicit guest posts by my fellow language learners. While the website originated as a way to chronicle my own language learning, as well as to connect with my grandmother, I believe the platform will get closer to realizing its public-facing potential if other voices are invited into this discussion. The website will thus become a more communally-created archive and less a chronicling of my own individual journey.

16.4 Part IV

The online landscape has drastically shifted since I first proposed and began working on *Learning the Seneca Language*. In 2015, online resources to learn the *Onöndowa'ga:' Gawë:no'* were scarce; now, at the time of this writing, online Seneca language resources include an expansive language database assembled and maintained by the Allegany Language Department, who also began offering classes to distant learners of the *Onöndowa'ga:' Gawë:no'* on Skype, and the Cattaraugus *Onöndowa'ga:' Gawë:no'* group on Facebook, a social media website where the group offers frequent tutorials that are subsequently uploaded onto their page. I take advantage of these learning opportunities whenever my schedule allows—which, is to say, not nearly as often as I would like. They have certainly increased my knowledge of the language, not just from a vocabulary standpoint but in giving me (and others) the chance to hear the language spoken in context. Perhaps more importantly, it has given me a small taste of the type of learning community many of us try to foster in our classrooms each semester.

By conscious design, the website shows my own growing pains as a language learner and as a member of the amorphous online learning community of the *Onöndowa'ga:' Gawë:no'*. It shows, as digital projects tend to do, my ongoing commitment to learn and share, and even to fail, publicly. For many of us, our academic training has conditioned us to *not* want to be wrong. But for me, with this particular project, I am less concerned with being wrong than I am about ever responding to a correction with defensiveness. Every interaction I have with a fellow language learner is an opportunity to grow— and while the prospect of doing so publicly can seem scary (and sometimes it is), handling my mistakes and the corrections they solicit shows the public that academic training, despite what some of them may think, does not automatically make people arrogant or standoffish. In fact, our handling of our mistakes and our commitment to grow can drum up support for humanistic studies, which are increasingly threatened in colleges and universities throughout the United States. David Shumway (2016, 41) explains, "The humanities must be public so that the public can come to understand them and thus be willing to lend them their support." I only hope that my project in some way contributes to the promotion of the humanities—and, more specifically, the *Onöndowa'ga:' Gawë:no'*. I also hope that the website becomes a space of community for other online learners, who can share their own learning journeys. Ultimately, I hope my grandmother is proud, wherever she is: *Dëjinyadade:gë'ae'*, We will see each other again.

Notes

1. These histories are by no means specific to the United States and Canada. However, the United States and Canada are most central to the project that I describe in this chapter.
2. In my subsequent studies, especially most recently, I realize that while learning individual words and phrases is important, the end-goal should be, and should have always been, on piecing together complete sentences. This has been the focus of my current studies, and I hope to update the website soon when I am more comfortable in this knowledge to share it. Throughout this essay, I will refer to my language learning as a journey (cliché as it may sound). Some journeys, like my own, are slow.
3. Linguistic genocide is a part of the larger processes of cultural genocide that the U.S. settler state has imposed on Native/Indigenous communities. As I will discuss in section II of this chapter, these genocidal policies are linked to other settler policies like land theft and assimilation tactics. I refrain from referring to the threat posed to the Onöndowa'ga:' Gawë:no' as "language loss" because "language loss" implies that the phenomenon is without a perpetrator. For more on how languages "die" or are "murdered," see James Crawford's "Seven Hypotheses on Language Loss Causes and Cures."
4. Multiple spelling variations exist for the name of the confederacy, including Haudenosaunee and Hodinōhsō:ni'. I will use the former throughout this essay for consistency. The Haudenosaunee Confederacy includes the Tuscarora, the Seneca, the Cayuga, the Onondaga, the Oneida, and the Mohawk people of upstate New York, southern Ontario, and parts of Wisconsin and Oklahoma. They are also known as the Iroquois, a name that originated with French settlers in the area.
5. Recently, there has been considerable discourse, and pushback, against this model, including on recent panels at conferences like the Modern Language Association. Moves away from the traditional dissertation have also been discussed by Kim Nehls in "Alternative Dissertation Formats: Preparing Scholars for the Academy and Beyond" in the book *Contemporary Approaches to Dissertation Development and Research Methods*, as well as in publications for wider audiences, such as Natalie Berkman's "Rethinking the Dissertation" on the MLA Humanities Commons website, as well as "Ph.Ds. Embrace Alternative Dissertations" by Vimal Patel on *The Chronicle*.
6. Laurence M. Hauptman refers to the 1826 Treaty of Buffalo Creek more accurately as the "Treaty" of Buffalo Creek, as it was never ratified by the

United States Senate and is thus not an official treaty by the United States' own procedural standards.
7. The Indian Relocation Act of 1830 was signed by President Andrew Jackson and facilitated the relocation of the "Five Civilized Tribes" of the American Southeast. These five tribes are the Choctaw, the Chickasaw, the Cherokee, the Seminole, and the Muscogee-Creek. They were relocated to the present-day state of Oklahoma in what is known as the "Trail of Tears."
8. Laurence Hauptman (1999, 3) writes that the Erie Canal helped make "Syracuse the primary salt city of the United States; Rochester, the primary flour and flower city of the United States; and Buffalo, the primary granary depot of the United States in the decades before the Civil War."
9. Hauptman (2011, 45–46) points out that this treaty is variously nicknamed the "Compromise Treaty" by the Seneca Nation of Indians, as it resulted in the return of two of their territories, while the Tonawanda Band of Seneca refer to it as the "Compromised Treaty." A later treaty in 1857 allowed the Tonawanda to buy back 7549 acres of land and also ensured the continued existence of the Tonawanda reservation.
10. My grandmother's own life experiences bear out this influence. She was a practicing Baptist her entire life, even raising her children—my mother (aknó'ëh), my aunt (age:hak), and my uncles (haknó'sëh)—in that faith. I was raised Catholic, however, due to other colonial influences in my family history.
11. For more information about how digital projects are being evaluated for tenure and promotion, please visit the MLA guidelines: https://www.mla.org/About-Us/Governance/Committees/Committee-Listings/Professional-Issues/Committee-on-Information-Technology/Guidelines-for-Evaluating-Work-in-Digital-Humanities-and-Digital-Media. See, as well, Todd Pressner's "How to Evaluate Digital Scholarship" for a list of specific questions that review committees should ask when evaluating digital work.
12. Recently, the number of visitors has ranged from 203 (February 2020) to 397 (March 2021), with a marked increase in visitors during the month of November (780 visitors), when Americans celebrate Thanksgiving. Users are evenly split by the device they are using (mostly desktop or mobile device, with a small number using a tablet) and arrive at the website by searching terms like "seneca language" or "seneca greeting."

REFERENCES

Berkman, Natalie. 2017. "Rethinking the Dissertation." *MLA Connected Academics*. https://connect.mla.hcommons.org/rethinking-the-dissertation/. Accessed 1 Aug 2021.

Borgia, Melissa. 2014. "Seneca Storytelling: Effect of the Kinzua Dam on Interpretations of Supernatural Stories." *Oral Tradition* 29 (1): 87–98.

Brennan, Sheila A. 2016. "Public, First." In *Debates in the Digital Humanities*, edited by Matthew K. Gold and Lauren F. Klein. Minneapolis: University of Minnesota Press. https://dhdebates.gc.cuny.edu/read/untitled/section/11b9805a-a8e0-42e3-9a1c-fad46e4b78e5#ch23. Accessed 29 Aug 2021.

Burich, Keith R. 2007. "'No Place to Go': The Thomas Indian School and the 'Forgotten' Indian Children of New York." *Wicazo Sa Review* 22 (2): 93–110.

Cloutier, Jean-Christophe. 2019. *Shadow Archives: The Lifecycles of African American Literature*. New York: Columbia University Press.
Crawford, James. 1995. "Seven Hypotheses on Language Loss Causes and Cures." Delivered at Northern Arizona University, May 4. https://files.eric.ed.gov/fulltext/ED395731.pdf. Accessed 22 Aug 2021.
Cushman, Ellen. 2013. "Wampum, Sequoyan, and Story: Decolonizing the Digital Archive." *College English* 76 (2): 115–35.
Delgado, Francisco. 2016. "Home." Last modified April 3, 2016. https://www.learningthesenecalanguage.com/.
Delgado, Francisco. 2017. "'My Onöndowa'ga:' Family History." Last modified Oct 7, 2017. https://www.learningthesenecalanguage.com/post/my-onondowa-ga-family-history.
Delgado, Francisco. 2020a. "Hello/Goodbye." Last modified Jan 3, 2020. https://www.learningthesenecalanguage.com/hello-goodbye.
Delgado, Francisco. 2020b. "Asking Questions." Last modified Jan 3, 2020. https://www.learningthesenecalanguage.com/asking-questions.
Delgado, Francisco. 2020c. "For Akso:t (My Grandmother)." Last modified Feb 20, 2020. https://www.learningthesenecalanguage.com/post/for-akso-t-my-grandmother.
Donellan, Emily. 2017. "No Connection: The Issue of Internet on the Reservation." *American Indian Law Journal* 5 (2). https://digitalcommons.law.seattleu.edu/ailj/vol5/iss2/2/?utm_source=digitalcommons.law.seattleu.edu%2Failj%2Fvol5%2Fiss2%2F2&utm_medium=PDF&utm_campaign=PDFCoverPages. Accessed on 20 Aug 2020.
Eastwood, Alice. 2017. "Personal Interview." March 24.
Ellison, Julie. 2013. "The New Public Humanists." *PMLA* 128 (2): 289–98.
Hauptman, Laurence M. 1999. *Conspiracy of Interests: Iroquois Dispossession and the Rise of New York State*. Syracuse: Syracuse University Press.
Hauptman, Laurence M. 2011. *The Tonawanda Senecas' Heroic Battle Against Removal: Conservative Activist Indians*. Syracuse: Syracuse University Press.
Kelsey, Penelope Myrtle. 2014. *Reading the Wampum: Essays on Hodinöhsö:ni' Visual Code and Epistemological Recovery*. Syracuse: Syracuse University Press.
Kirschenbaum, Matthew. 2016. "What Is Digital Humanities and What's It Doing in English Departments?" In *Debates in the Digital Humanities*, edited by Matthew K. Gold and Lauren F. Klein, 280–86. Minneapolis: University of Minnesota Press.
McGrail, Anne B. 2016. "The 'Whole Game': Digital Humanities at Community Colleges." In *Debates in the Digital Humanities*, edited by Matthew K. Gold and Lauren F. Klein, 16–31. Minneapolis: University of Minnesota Press.
Murray, Anne. 2015. "Reclaiming Traditional Seneca Culture." *The Allegheny Front*. http://archive.alleghenyfront.org/story/reclaiming-traditional-seneca-culture.html. Accessed 22 Aug 2020.
Nehls, Kimberly. 2016. "Alternative Dissertation Formats: Preparing Scholars for the Academy and Beyond." In *Contemporary Approaches to Dissertation Development and Research Methods*, edited by Doris L. Watson, 43–52. Hershey: Information Science Reference (an imprint of IGI Global).
Ortiz, Ricardo L. 2019. "Introduction: Public Humanities as/and Comparatist Practices." *Post45*. https://post45.org/2019/07/introduction-public-humanities-as-and-comparatist-practice/. Accessed 20 Aug 2020.

Patel, Vimal. 2016. "Ph.Ds. Embrace Alternative Dissertations: The Job Market May Not." *The Chronicle of Higher Education.* https://www.chronicle.com/article/ph-d-s-embrace-alternative-dissertations-the-job-market-may-not/. Accessed 20 Dec 2021.

Pressner, Todd. 2012. "How to Evaluate Digital Scholarship." *Journal of Digital Humanities* 1 (4). http://journalofdigitalhumanities.org/1-4/how-to-evaluate-digital-scholarship-by-todd-presner/. Accessed 29 Aug 2021.

Shumway, David R. 2016. "Why the Humanities Must Be Public." *University of Toronto Quarterly* 85 (4): 34–45.

Spiro, Lisa. 2016. "'This Is Why We Fight': Defining the Values of the Digital Humanities." In *Debates in the Digital Humanities*, edited by Matthew K. Gold and Lauren F. Klein, 16–35. Minneapolis: University of Minnesota Press.

The Clinton-Sullivan Campaign of 1779. *Fort Stanwix National Park Service.* https://www.nps.gov/fost/learn/historyculture/the-western-expedition-against-the-six-nations-1779.htm. Accessed 20 Aug 2020.

PART IV

Digital Cultural Heritage

CHAPTER 17

Acting on the Cultural Object: Digital Representation of Children's Writing Cultures in Museum Collections

Lois Burke and Kathryn Simpson

17.1 Introduction: The Museum's Potency

In this chapter we uncover the emancipatory potential in digitally interpreting children's writings in museum exhibition spaces. To do this we first examine how those exhibition spaces are becoming increasingly amalgamated with digital technologies. We then propose that the use of digital spaces can increase visitor access to children's histories and provide new understandings of child-made objects and children's textual cultures. Furthermore, we argue that digital exhibition techniques designed with ethical principles can actively facilitate child visitors' novel engagement with child-made objects.

Museum visitors' practice of "meaning-making" was studied at length in 1990s museology (Silverman 1995). This work showed that visitors construct their own personalized interpretations of exhibitions based on memory and perception, which are "inextricably linked" (Fraser 2004, 3). Although curators cannot take full responsibility for the message that visitors take from an exhibition, modern public museums are required to be transparent and ethical about their aims and responsibilities. Standards such as the Museum

---

L. Burke
Tilburg University, Tilburg, The Netherlands
e-mail: L.M.Burke@tilburguniversity.edu

K. Simpson (✉)
University of Sheffield, Sheffield, UK
e-mail: Kathryn.Simpson@sheffield.ac.uk

Association's Code of Ethics, first published in 1977, puts forward the standards of ethics that ought to be adhered to in museums. Point 2, concerning the "Stewardship of Collections" states that museums should aim to "Preserve collections as a tangible link between the past, present and future [and] Balance the museum's role in safeguarding items for the benefit of future audiences with its obligation to optimize access for present audiences" (Museums Association 2016). This demonstrates that stewardship should serve the historical representation of collections while simultaneously looking to the future and optimizing access to them.

Today, museums ideally seek to serve the interests of the public and respond to the contemporary socio-cultural environment. In this vein feminist and decolonizing critiques of museum spaces have challenged and given rise to significant changes in curatorial practices, encouraging museums to examine "Whose stories go untold and what are the implications of seeing this?" (Clover and Williamson 2019, 144). Tony Bennett (2017, ix) notes that these critiques "go far beyond the politics of what is put on display and how it is displayed to encompass new conceptions and relations of curatorial responsibility, new forms of custodianship, and more politically sensitive practices of conservation." Currently there exists an expectation that museums must use their social influence to not only provide information and education for all, but also promote a more just society (Fraser 2004, 1). But, it is important to note that the critical practices of collecting, public programming, object-labeling and interpretation, writing metadata, and so on, are bound up in subjective decision-making, institutional policy, bias, and economic restraints (Seebach 2018).

Unfortunately, the rich body of work which traces museums' adaptation of their practices in light of social and cultural justices has a gap where children's objects, histories, and child-visitor experiences are concerned. Yet this important ongoing work of redressing social injustices and widening participation is particularly germane to those institutions whose collections concern the history of childhood. Historically, children have been deprived of agency in a manner akin to other marginalized groups (Birch 2018). Furthermore, the collections and archives of children, comprising a variety of material and documentary evidence, are often difficult to locate for researchers and thus their obscurity further limits understanding of the child subjects.

In this chapter we will develop new possibilities for interpretations of childhood and the written object by critiquing the potential exhibition and interpretation opportunities brought about by digital methods. This chapter will consider the ethical concerns surrounding the exhibition of child-made objects, and both current and future practices of digital interpretation. It will examine how digital environments enable children's writings as cultural artefacts to be "read" in new ways, to behave in ways un-proscribed and malleable, and ultimately how the physical and digital form enables an exploration of both object and its "intangible human emotional archaeology" (Simpson 2020). This research is underpinned by an interview with a curator at the Museum of Childhood in Edinburgh who provided critical professional insights into the current obstacles faced by curators, and the curatorial interests and priorities in interpreting and exhibiting children's written cultures. The real-world implications of the research ideas presented can thus be explored.

17.2 Children's Cultures

A fundamental consideration for this study, then, is the nature of child-made objects and museums' understandings of youth culture. In the eighteenth century, when some of the earliest museums were founded, children were considered as being part of a group whose lack of civility could not appreciate the truth or beauty in a museum exhibition. As Steve Shapin (1994, 90) writes, "children, common people, women and the sick" were, as one contemporary put it, "most subject to being led by the ears." Today, the richness of children's contributions to culture is well documented. Although the relationship of children's cultures to adult authority is disputed (Gilderdale 2019), textual and material examples of these cultures provide new historical insights. This data can then help us to reconceptualize understandings of childhood and children's agency and feed into debates about the rights of children. Kate Douglas and Anna Poletti (2016, 5) acknowledge that there is a

> prevalent misconception that there is something new and unusual about a young person wanting to share his or her life story with a public. While technologies have made self-representation much more accessible, prevalent and popular, self-representation, through varied cultural modes, has been happening for as long as people have lived.

Children have always found ways to represent and express themselves; one of the areas that provides a unique insight into that agentic behavior is children's writing. Children's writings, which here we define loosely as diaries and journals, manuscript magazines, creative writings, and drawings, can offer abundant information on the individual's lived experience, interests, sociocultural environment and ambitions. In some instances, children present as active critical readers and offer value judgments on their own writing and the writings of others. These works are striking demonstrations of a child's unique literary culture in a certain time and place.

Yet, collections of children's writings are disparate and dissimilar: the writings might have been preserved and collected because the child who produced them became notable later in life (such as the writers Lewis Carroll and Virginia Woolf). During the nineteenth century especially, children's writings played an important part in the construction of the family archive and identity (Baggerman 2002), so they may have been kept by descendants. It should be noted that, as is the case in collections representing adult figures, children's archival collections often represent individuals from privileged and affluent backgrounds. Despite the fact that the representation of the child in collections of writing is limited, a renewed research interest in juvenilia and children's cultures has shone a light on its importance.

Recent work across several disciplines has identified the collaborative nature of nineteenth-century children's writings, children's organization and understanding of hierarchy, as well as notions of cultural capital (Gleadle 2016; Burke 2019). In regard to current children's cultures, Anne Haas Dyson has written on the ways in which children adapt and appropriate popular media and create new products from pre-existing "semiotic stuff" (2013, 13). The scholarly recognition of these group cultures of child writers, whether in the nineteenth or twenty-first century, is based on the agentic construction of narratives which "influence the context of children's social participation" (Scollan and Farini 2020, 38). In other words, within the child's interaction, there is a multi-modal engagement between object, environment, and creator. Given such an understanding of the creation and context of children's creative works, museums must actively look to understand their own practices of representation. To present children's creative works in a singular static way is to deny many of the aspects of this engagement.

The perspective of the child museum visitor is also an important part of this consideration. Various studies into how museum visitors engage with and learn from exhibitions have demonstrated that these interactions are not passive; "meaning-making" among museum visitors relies on both group and individual knowledge and experience and is thus deeply personal (Birch 2018; O'Connor et al. 2020; Eklund 2020). Using digital tools to interpret and exhibit children's cultures and engage child visitors can provide new avenues of meaning-making, especially if these tools facilitate young people's involvement in collaborative digital curation. As Angela Scollan and Frederico Farini (2020, 38) note

> Either pessimistic or optimistic about the intersection of digital technologies and generational relationships, research has been concerned about the use of digital technologies for children's learning rather than focusing on children's active role as authors of knowledge as they move between digitally enhanced experiences and non-digitally enhanced experiences.

Our own work engages with children's capacity to be "authors of knowledge" and how we can facilitate that within a museum setting both as creators of knowledge and exhibition audiences.

17.3 Museums and the Ethics of Child-Created Objects

As noted above, children and young people have always found ways to narrate their own socio-cultural experience. Yet, there is a perceived ontological binary between adults and children and the idea of their shared human experience. This can be seen in a museum setting, in the unnatural barrier that has been created between child and adult creation and engagement. Whether knowingly or not, adults control the boundaries of their dominion through ascribed behaviors, expectations, content, and label interpretation. The child-made object can often be seen as unusual or idiosyncratic and it could be said that children as creators and consumers are treated as "other" in the museum environment. We argue that similar to Magrit Shildrick's (1996, 1) explanation of the representation of women, children "are the non-subject other, the excluded, the embodied, the monstrous." Children are physically distant in the museum space, both as creators and visitors. Their physical embodiment by their very nature of being children is smaller and messier. They stand as representative of that which does not fit within the structured and organized museum space, what Donna Haraway would call "inappropriate/d others" (1992, 300). Therefore, it can seem an enormous challenge to facilitate interpretation and representation that adequately allows the "other" creator and visitor agency.

In engaging with the objects which are created by children there are three specific ethical aspects of which the adult curator must be aware:

- Firstly, that those who receive these objects acknowledge the ethical implications of their handling, curation, interpretation, and translation of the object.
- Secondly, curators must acknowledge that not all children have had the materials, time, or inclination to create, and those that do are not all privileged to do so.
- And thirdly, the adult curator needs to understand that these child-created objects are not imbued with the essence of childhood.

These three aspects (acknowledging a sensitivity towards the interpretation of the object, creator privilege, and avoiding an essentialist view of childhood) highlight how negotiating the child-written archive can then come to be seen as a complex and difficult task; to even try to begin to represent and interpret it with equanimity let alone equality may be seen as an almost insurmountable problem. This chapter suggests ways of addressing some of these challenges.

17.4 Museums' Interpretation and Representation of Childhood: The Potential and Challenges of Digital Technologies

Taking advantage of the uniqueness of each museum visit (whether for adult or child audiences) and allowing the ambiguity of play, imagination and risk to be inherent in interpretation begins to negate some of the difficulties of the child-written archive (Light et al. 2018; Giles 2021). Andromache Gazi (2014, n.p.) evidences some of the profound difficulties faced by museums

[w]hen objects are put on public display some of the values associated with them are opted for over others and this often leads to heated debates among the various parties involved (museums, curators, citizens, indigenous peoples, governments or nations, collectors, art dealers and so on; cf. Warren 1999: 1). Secondly, exhibitions are very powerful representations and as such are responsible for shaping the public's perception in many, often unintended, ways.

Thus, when a child-created object is displayed it carries an epistemological weight. When that object is a collection of writing in a physical public display it can become a purely visual object; the possibility of engaging with the written content is reduced or eradicated. It is a disservice to both the child as creator and visitor if they cannot engage with each other across time and create their own narratives. However, we now have the additional advantage of technologies to facilitate a more comprehensive engagement between children through providing digital access to such writing.

Where previously there was less available space for counter or un-prescribed "readings" or interpretations of museum objects, the digital environment is one which aims ultimately not to be predicated on a person's physical space, place, role, and location. The child-created object is then not subject to an adult curator's physical interpretation and translation, for example in the case of choosing what page to display. Through play, imagination, and risk, the digital environment can be the place in which to create new forms of understanding. The child as a user can engage (play) with digital interfaces creating narratives (imagination) that come out of their own agentic individualism (risk). This process moves beyond Jacques Derrida and Prenowitz's notion that the power to interpret the archive lies with those who hold the archive (1995). Of course, adult curatorial decisions still have a defining influence on what is displayed and how it is displayed, but the subsequent options for engaging with the object are extended.

While the digital rendering of children's writings responds to issues around representation, the potential of such technologies has not yet been fully realized in current practice. Digitization, dissemination, and the subsequent opening up of multiple readings and interpretations that have been facilitated in cultural object engagement have subjected the object to issues similar to those incurred within the physical environment. To a large extent, popularity rules, whether that be funding allocation or choosing to digitize that which attracts the higher visitor numbers; this, combined with the need to justify the "value" of a digitized collection can re-enforce othering and marginalization of certain collections (De Meo 2014; Kelly 2014; Marsh et al. 2016). Michelle Moravec (2017, 187) notes that "the results of such decisions may have adverse consequences for the availability of sources about non-canonical historical subjects." The museum sector faces the recurrent problems of funding, digital acquisition, and appraisal, and facilitating hosting of digitized content. Yet, socio-culturally the public museum is no longer seriously in a position to partition the physical and the digital. The epistemological influence of both feeds into the "reading" of the cultural object in the museum space. How then does a museum display its collections when the digital has come to be expected, yet is still seen as a distraction from the actual material collection, and institutions often do not have the funds or capabilities to create this digital content? The weight of such responsibility often lies with the curator.

Public understanding of museum collections depends on the interpretation of them by curatorial staff and the individual visitor experience. A museum can have the ability to "control the representation of a community and its highest values and truths. It also has the power to define the relative standing of people in that community" (Duncan 1993, 8). The difference of opinion between two curators can determine what is and what is not a part of a collection. It is this ability, the "firm control over which knowledge" or object is made public (Colwell 2015, S268), that evidences the often unnoticed power at play in museal child-writing representation. This is pertinent in relation to the representation of childhood in museums; certain objects will have more value than others, depending on curatorial interest, conservation issues, storage space and whether the item is already represented in the collection, as we discuss in our interview later. Furthermore, competing understandings of what should be on display in a museum of childhood vary between visitors of different generational groups.

There is a dichotomy between what different visitors want and the perceived and actual role of a museum—holders of a fixed memory versus institutions that are in dialogue with their socio-cultural and temporal environment. Ben Light et al. (2018, 408) note that "[m]any critics have derided what they regard as the increasingly media and spectacle-dominated exhibitions, with their adaptation of digital technologies, conspicuous consumption and an emphasis on novelty." Yet, deriding variant forms of display and representation suggests objects can only be "read" in specific ways and actively negates museums' optimization of digital technologies in facilitating access, engagement, and collaboration in and with their collections.

Optimizing and future-proofing access to heritage collections might be synonymous with digitization, but not all museums can afford to implement digitization strategies to preserve their paper objects. Although digital museum elements are increasingly becoming expected by visitors and therefore are a primary consideration in exhibition design. And, studies have demonstrated that the implementation of digital technologies in exhibitions can improve visitors' overall experience (Bailey-Ross et al. 2017; Nisiotis and Alboul 2021; Varitimiadis et al. 2021). Given the steep developments in digital technology, touchscreen interactives and the use of apps, Artificial Intelligence (AI) and Virtual Reality (VR) are becoming more commonplace in larger museums.[1]

Exhibition through digital mediums has the potential to enhance visitor understandings of children's writings, particularly as they are not well-suited to traditional means of exhibition for several reasons. For example, displaying a child-made magazine or diary in a display case involves selecting one page or one double-page spread to represent the object as a whole. If the writing on one page is part of a longer piece, then the sense of the object cannot be ascertained. Moreover, issues in reading the child's handwriting can prevent visitors from understanding the object, and some objects might need to be seen in their entirety in order to be comprehended. There are also risks of light and environmental damage posed by long-term display of these objects. Although many of these factors also pose difficulties for the display of other manuscript and print materials, our interview with a Museum of Childhood curator, Lyn Stevens, presented in a later section of this chapter, explores the specific issues surrounding the display of children's writings. Digital remediation of these physical writings can provide readable and navigable transcriptions and a range of metadata which situates them in context. Utilizing social media tools might be another method of displaying children's cultures and facilitating engagement with youth and adult visitors alike (Kirschner and Bruyckere 2017).

There are potential connections still to be explored between young people's digital literacy and museum engagement. For example, digital tools can facilitate young people's engagement with historical cultures and practices that are not so different from their own. Arts Council England's "Every Child" report, written for and in conjunction with young people, identified that "Digital engagement was felt … to be a key area to focus on to enable engagement in arts and culture, especially amongst older boys" (2016, 6). The report goes on to state that "Digital access could lead to creative opportunities for children and young people, for making and sharing arts and culture, or for accessing collections and archives" (2016, 41). Connections between digital technology and collections and archives need to be put into practice to facilitate the modern child visitor's engagement.

17.5 Child-Written Texts and Connections to Digital Culture

Several historians of youth culture have examined how children's historical writing practices contain parallels to youth culture in the contemporary moment. For example, nineteenth-century children's circulated manuscript magazines can be meaningfully compared to cultures of today, especially online cultures. This similarity is acknowledged by scholars researching children's cultural histories around the world. Anna Gilderdale (2019, 64) writes: "In New Zealand, Keith Scott likens *Dot's Little Folk* to Facebook and, in her ground-breaking work on the American correspondence page of *Robert Merry's Museum*, Pat Pflieger dubs the page an 'online community' where young people contributed letters (predominantly under pen-names) from as early as the 1840s." Gilderdale's observation about the connectedness of children's writing cultures enables us to understand them as part of young people's networked lives more broadly, across historical periods.

The digital public space is potentially an ideal platform on which to develop the connections between past and present children's written cultures, and build novel, playful and meaningful connections between object and visitor. There have been past attempts to recreate the writing cultures of children in public exhibition spaces. Kate Douglas (2019, 196) summarizes them:

> The UK's Mass Observation Project completed the "Children's Millennium Diary Project" in which 600 children in the Brighton and Hove areas were asked to keep a diary for one week during the year 2000. The UK's "Great Diary Project" collaborated with the Museum of Childhood in London during 2014 on an exhibition of children's diaries. The United Nations Children's Fund (UNICEF)'s "Voices of Youth Digital Diaries" represent children's eyewitness accounts of events from their world, and stories about their personal lives in blog-style posts. These narratives are hosted on UNICEF's Voices of Youth website.

The latter initiative "Voices of Youth Digital Diaries" specifically recognizes the fact that young people today live their lives in networked and digital spaces. Yet the nature of these projects as subject to limited funding brings to mind the potentially short lifespan of digital projects which are not maintained. In the words of Douglas (2019, 193), "though young people are prolific life narrators and self-representors, much of this currently happens in online spaces and much of the life writing that is produced is ephemeral." This idea of ephemerality raises questions about the best methods of collecting, storing, and curating children's cultural heritage. Both digital and social media's use in interpretation and exhibition are a necessary consideration in curating and preserving a culture which is both marginal and ephemeral.

As young people today communicate through networked digital environments in public spaces, this type of engagement ought to be mirrored in exhibition spaces. As Wyman et al. (2011, 465) identify

> When we allow museum experiences to diverge from everyday reality, or prevent our visitors from engaging in content as they are accustomed, we create a false choice of either experiencing new technology everywhere or not at all. Instead, we should accept the future, be mindful of traditions, and seamlessly merge them in natural ways.

Museums must not present a "false choice" to their visitors, but rather integrate familiar technologies into visitors' exhibition experience. Therefore, familiar technologies which also foster networked connections between young people are an obvious choice for an exhibition. Touch-screen technologies such as mobile phones and tablets combined with a social media set-up is an ideal combination. Given the emerging research that highlights a direct link between children's engagement in social media today and children's historical engagement in collaborative and circulating writing communities (Gilderdale), incorporating digital technologies in exhibition spaces is strongly suited to interpreting children's written cultures. In the following section we present a case study of a museum and examine how these initiatives might be incorporated into exhibition programming.

17.6 Edinburgh's Museum of Childhood: Introduction to the Museum's Collections

The Museum of Childhood in Edinburgh was founded by a city councilor, Patrick Murray, in 1955. His position in the local council meant that he was granted premises to store and exhibit his private collections related to the history of childhood. Thus the Museum of Childhood was founded—the first in the world. The collections represent childhood in modern history, with the majority of collections dating from the eighteenth century to the present day. The museum is still actively collecting.

The collections hold a wide range of objects related to the experience of childhood. Children's clothes, games, toys, medicine, prams, and bikes are represented in the on-site stores. A separate store in Edinburgh contains an extensive collection of children's books including annuals, encyclopedias, fairy tales, religious texts, and primers. Many of these books have been inscribed by children, teachers, or family members, and thus offer an avenue to access the perspectives of the child subject. Various child-made objects are held by the Museum. For example, the Museum holds dolls made from a shoe and bone made by pauper children around 1905, which were collected by the English folklorist Edward Lovett (1852–1933). There are various examples of children's writings, which are the focus of this chapter. Children's letters, diaries, workbooks, scraps, and collaboratively written magazines are all represented in the collections. The writings in the Museum constitute a museum collection. The collection does not use a cataloging system and is categorized by theme, like education, sport, or hobbies. The collection is not publicly searchable on an online catalogue, but people can access it by appointment.

The Museum is currently in a rudimentary stage of engaging with digital technologies for interpretation and exhibition. The 2017 redevelopment of Gallery 1 for the permanent "Changing Childhood" exhibition incorporates three digital exhibition elements, designed by two curators in conjunction with the design company Studioarc. One of the authors of this chapter, Lois Burke, curated these digital elements while working as a doctoral intern, funded by the Scottish Graduate School of Arts and Humanities. One of the digital elements was a touch-screen digital photo album, which presented photographs of children from the Museum's collections and those submitted by staff of the City of Edinburgh Council. Many photographs that had never been exhibited before were included in this digital exhibit. Another digital element was an edited video that is played on repeat in the gallery. The creation of this video involved significant collaboration with the National Library of Scotland's Moving Image Archive. The third digital element was a series of oral history listening stations, based on interviews that had been conducted with Edinburgh residents of varying ages. In order to assess the current plans and provision for digital content in the Museum of Childhood we conducted an interview with a curator for the specific purposes of this chapter.

17.7 Valuing Child-Created Objects: Interview with a Curator

In November 2019 the authors conducted a semi-structured interview with Lyn Stevens, one of the part-time curators at the Museum of Childhood in Edinburgh. This conversational interview provided insights into the curatorial perspective of child-made objects, the realities of the Museum's resources, and the practicalities of digital engagement. Stevens' curatorial view of the child-created object is evidenced in her explanation of an unusual object that she acquired for the collection—a cupboard door from a child's bedroom that is covered in stickers. Stevens (2019) said:

> Someone rang us up about four or five years ago and said, I'm redecorating my bedroom, my son's old bedroom and there's a cupboard door full of stickers and we're replacing the doors ... So how many people would think to offer us a door covered in stickers?

The door was valued by Stevens as a child-made creation; it was even loaned to the Scottish National Gallery of Modern Art (Modern Two) for the "Cut and Paste: 400 years of Collage" exhibition in 2019. But it was equally valued by the parent of the child who created it, which signals the importance of collaboration in the preservation of child-made objects.

Stevens (2019) also praised the positive aspects of utilizing children's perspectives and lived experience for building exhibitions and also learning more about the collections:

> ...the more we find out about something, the more we can build an exhibition on it because you put something in a case and you can say, you know, Chatterbox Phone, 1972, made by Fisher-Price. Well, that's all right. But if you can say, this was bought for Peter for his Christmas and Peter lived in this place and he went to this school and he used to play with his friend with this and they used to pretend they were in a shop [...] it becomes, you know, it's the same with the creative writing.

She highlighted the importance of gathering rich and detailed information about children's lives that surround and are contained in some of the child-made objects in the collection. Importantly, she identified the value of the thickly descriptive contextualizing evidence in the representation of said objects. As the curator, Stevens clearly demonstrated that she works against an essentialist representation of childhood and is instead actively working to show the life behind the object and the child who initially imbued the object with meaning. Specifically, Stevens acknowledges the social and cultural conditions that produce children's objects and that can provide unique data about children's lives.

Stevens referred to a series of manuscript magazines that are part of the Museum's collections, as further evidence of the rich and detailed perspectives of children, specifically the *Pierrot* (1909–1914), which was edited by a girl, Ruth Dent (b. 1898) from Kirkcudbright and was populated with writings by various other children, often younger than Ruth.[2] Notably, objects such as the *Pierrot* can demonstrate the connectedness of children's peer groups, which we might mistakenly only associate with more recent technological developments. One of the *Pierrot* magazines from 1914 particularly demonstrates the children's perception of war and cultural differences. Stevens believes that these children were in military families and moving around the country. One example from the magazine from 1914 shows that the children visited an army encampment in the New Forest, Wiltshire (Stevens 2019):

> It was where the troops gathered before they went off to the front. And because they have done drawings of the soldiers, you can see they're in kilts. So, you know it's a Scottish Regiment. And … they say something about the next regiment … and they're obviously a Sikh regiment because they talk about them wearing turbans and they talk about how they're wearing these very light trousers and their ankles are bare. They say how cold they must be. So … you are thinking, so I wonder if somebody in Wiltshire, New Forest, had ever seen a Sikh before. Yeah. They took note of what they were wearing because it was unusual. They might not have seen a Scottish man before and that's why they drew him in his kilt.

This demonstrates how detailed the accounts of some children's writings can be and that they have the ability to provide insight into lived social and cultural experience and expectations. As Stevens (2019) notes about the above example:

> The article is amazing because, you know, they joke … the children brought them [the soldiers] apples and they described throwing the apples across the fence … and one of the apples hits one of the soldiers on the head. And they make a joke about ha ha ha won't just be apples hitting your head soon and … oh my God, they had no idea.

This moment of child's writing provides an insight into the build-up to the beginning of the First World War in Britain and provides visceral evidence of the children's limited understandings of the horrors of war. Stevens notes that, more broadly, these written artefacts can provide a great deal of information on their creators "if you can talk about the children that created it, what motivated them to create it, what was influencing their ideas, where they lived, what kind of class and income they were in, how that affected what they wrote about" (2019). Not all children have the materials, time, inclination, and privilege to write, and therefore it is vital to note that often such collections only give a limited insight into the experience of children's written cultures.

Stevens (2019) informed us that digital and other interactive displays were a key idea from the outset of the plans for the "Changing Childhood" gallery:

> [T]he plan was that we would redevelop the ground floor and ... there would be different types of display. There would be different kinds of interactives. There would be digital, there would be hands on. There would be, you know, dressing up ... the things people expect and things they might not.

Moreover, the digital interactives that were installed in the "Changing Childhood" gallery in 2017 are a pilot, ahead of redeveloping the rest of the Museum's galleries: "the idea was that we will see what interactives people like and how they work. And that would inform how we then redeveloped the rest of the building." It is important to highlight this iterative process of discovery and experimentation which is not based on perceived need but explicitly embedded in visitor behavior and engagement. Pamela Barnes and Gayle McPherson (2019) have argued, for example, that museum visitors challenge what they see in exhibitions, and thus museums become spaces of co-creation. Regarding the visitors in the Museum of Childhood, Stevens (2019) said:

> The idea was to ... get some digital in there, because it's what people expect when they come to museums. They want hands-on. They want to be able to play and interact with a screen. So, we have audio, we've got listening points, and we have visual. We have film, as well as the sort of swipey photo album.

Yet the curators have noticed that there are downsides to these digital interactives. Stevens highlighted that visitors are not gentle with digital interactives, and there is no dedicated digital team in the Museum of Childhood or the council-run Museums and Galleries Edinburgh more broadly. Stevens describes the introduction of digital interactives—the film and digital photo album—as "high risk" (2019) in terms of visitor damage that cannot be quickly and easily fixed, when she says

> We have a high level of visitors (over 250,000 per annum) and that's a lot for a local authority museum ... So we have to be careful that the more digital we use in the public galleries, the more we have to make sure we've got the backup ... It was something that was on display down at Museum of Edinburgh ... basically, we can't use the equipment anymore because we'd have to buy a whole new suite of stuff to show this film because it's out of date and you can't even buy replacements anymore ... So, in some ways the non-digital interactives are much easier to deal with from our perspective, rather than the visitor perspective, because you can get someone that can literally make another wooden block and put it in there because we do have three technicians, but they're not digital.

Yet, Stevens suggested that the addition of further interactives, alongside traditional display, could augment and enhance visitor understanding. One of Stevens' roles as a curator is to give public talks while using a handling collection. Although some items in the Museum's collections are well suited to a handling collection—for example the book collection, where duplicate or already damaged books intended for disposal make ideal candidates for public handling—this is not possible with children's writings. Stevens states (2019): "the handwritten stuff that we've got in this collection would be too fragile to do that. We haven't got enough of it … it's not sort of high-quality printed material … it's very fragile … And so you could only really share that physically digitally." She acknowledges inherent curatorial and conservation issues in sharing children's writings with the public, which do not need to be considered for other types of objects and that sharing these items digitally could be a solution:

> And then you could have the digital photo album in front of it. People go through the pages. I mean, that's perfect. Because they could read every single page if they wanted to and then see the real thing … So I think digital gives us extra layers.

The dual experience of the physical object and its digital remediation is suggested as the ideal combination, providing "layers" of visitor engagement. With specific reference to the child visitor, in seeking to verify the value of a combination of digital and physical engagement with the creative writings held at the Museum of Childhood, it should be remembered that "children combine digitally-enhanced and non-digitally-enhanced experiences to co-construct narratives, showing agency by claiming authorship of valid knowledge" (Scollan and Farini 2020, 37). This layered form of engagement is therefore the goal for exhibitions.

Providing diverse forms of representations of children's creative writing means that the curator does not have to give a focus for interaction, allowing children to choose. For children to socially interact without being guided by adults enables them to be masters of their own agency, allowing them to read, interact and interpret what they engage with, without having that interaction prescribed for them by adults. Presenting children's agency as sufficient and rational can create new kinds of knowledge. Scollan and Farini (2020, 46) suggest that the use of digital technology can enable "more cohesive and collaborative moments of storytelling" by children. We have evidenced similar behavior among both adults and children during interaction with digital technology, specifically a digital photo album, at the Museum of Childhood. On visiting the museum in November 2019 we noted the positive and persistent engagement with this form of digital interaction. Both adults and child visitors cooperatively engaged with the digital touch-screen photo album in particular. They created narratives which extended beyond the contextual digital information given about the images of the children, such as the activity they were engaging in, or related their own experience to the geographical location from which the image was taken (Burke and Simpson 2020).

Although there might be a wariness by some that the use of digital technologies and forms of presentation may primarily serve a desire for spectacular effects to the detriment of the primary object, that is not the case. Stevens (2019) observes that,

> Interestingly, people seem to like the non-digital and the digital, as much as each other. I see just as many people interacting with the magnetic tiles and the pairs game, as I do standing at the photo album or watching the film ... In the visitor survey and the feedback cards, you get people saying that they love the film, they love the photo album, but you also get them saying I love dressing up, I love playing with magnetic tiles. So I'm not sure if people are more for one than the other, but they expect both.

Unfortunately, the Museum's other existing digital tools and resources are limited. Stevens states that the Museum's "biggest digital resource" (their collections database hosted on the collections software KE EMu) "is not public-facing." Furthermore, in terms of social media engagement, it seems that the Museum does not have a wide reach. Followers of the Museum of Childhood, Edinburgh Facebook page are adults who are likely already familiar with the Museum. Stevens (2019) explains the purpose of the Facebook page:

> I just do a weekly post and it's a picture of an object ... People really like Transformers and Wombles ... He-Man is very popular ... I sometimes put historic things on like a sampler or one of the older books. They do get less response, but I try and mix it up a bit. I could just do seventies and eighties nostalgia the whole time. That'd be fine, but I try to show the breadth of the collection.

Although the social media page offers an opportunity to share curatorial insight and collections not on display, the engagement with these posts primarily comes from returning visitors who have an interest in specific collections.[3] Stevens recognizes that teenagers are the hardest age group to reach—an observation which has been confirmed by research (Arts Council England 2016). She explains further (Stevens 2019):

> If we're thinking about people we don't reach, it would be trying to see how digital would bring them in. I'm not sure that is a quick win or an easy fix ... If you had a fancy app that gave you a guided tour around the museum, you've still got to get them here to the museum.

Stevens maintains a sense of skepticism around utilizing digital tools to increase engagement among the least-active visitors.

The collections held at the Museum of Childhood show that the voices and experiences of children and young people are more accessible than ever before but the task of understanding how one locates, curates, interprets, and shares children's collections through digital means has only just begun. As the above interview demonstrates, the real-world implications of facilitating this digital action on the child-created cultural object are complex and inherently fiscally bound.

17.8 Conclusion

The use of digital environments for the presentation of child-created objects can enhance and complicate the unique visitor experience. In this chapter we have argued that the ongoing dissolution between the physical and digital object is part of this democratizing and individualizing boundary breaking. We have highlighted some of the potentials for digital media engagement with child-made objects and children's writings in particular. Building on existing scholarship, we have stressed that the connection between the museum and the object is not neutral. Neither is the creator an autonomous agent of production. Rather—drawing on Haraway's (1992) concepts—the social, political, technical, mythical, textual, intentional, and physical are all bound in the creation and interpretation of an object.

Utilizing digital representation alongside engagement with physical objects is, we argue, the only way to negotiate these various aspects successfully, and not, as has been suggested, "sensational," but a way to change understanding and read against the grain of hegemonic narratives of representation. Thus, we should reconceive the notion of the museum display and the constructed nature of knowledge creation, while acknowledging the inherent ambiguity and difficulty such renegotiation creates. In order to negotiate representations of child-writing in a museum setting, as well as the foundational ethical points raised earlier, we argue for a framework based on three critical elements:

- That discovery and experimentation, based on visitor behavior and engagement, are at the heart of curation of child-created cultural objects.
- It is the dual experience of physical and digital which best facilitates visitor engagement.
- Child agency in the role of creator or museum visitor must be regarded as sufficient and rational; new forms of knowledge creation do not have to be mediated by adults.

Through presenting objects digitally, museum exhibitions can stimulate children's epistemic agency and facilitate new knowledge and interpretations of historically adult-bound objects and their representations. This is especially important in relation to child-made written objects that are regarded as too fragile and which have therefore precluded more active engagement by children so far. Facilitating multiple ways of "reading" an object embraces disruption and creates new perspectives among visitors.

NOTES

1. In 2019 the Museums + AI network was established, and a toolkit was published which reflected the new issues that museum professionals face in incorporating AI into their practice. See https://themuseumsai.network/toolkit/.
2. The *Pierrot* is the subject of a forthcoming book chapter co-authored by Lois Burke and Charlotte Lauder, in *The Edinburgh History of Children's Periodicals*, edited by Kristine Moruzi, Beth Rodgers, and Michelle Smith.
3. The Facebook page for the Museum, which was exclusively run by Stevens, was retired in summer 2020 as individual council-run Museums merged into a collective Facebook page for Museums and Galleries Edinburgh.

REFERENCES

Arts Council England. 2016. "Every Child: Equality and Diversity in Arts and Culture with, by and for Children and Young People." https://www.artscouncil.org.uk/document/every-child-equality-and-diversity-arts-and-culture-and-children-and-young-people. Accessed 3 Dec 2020.

Baggerman, Arianne. 2002. "Autobiography and Family Memory in the Nineteenth Century." In *Egodocuments and History: Autobiographical Writing in Its Social Context Since the Middle Ages*, edited by Rudolf Dekker, 161–73. Hilversum: Verloren.

Bailey-Ross, Claire, Steven Gray, Jack Ashby, Melissa Terras, Andrew Hudson-Smith, and Claire Warwick. 2017. "Engaging the Museum Space: Mobilizing Visitor Engagement with Digital Content Creation." *Digital Scholarship in the Humanities* 32 (4): 689–708. https://doi.org/10.1093/llc/fqw041.

Barnes, Pamela, and Gayle McPherson. 2019. "Co-creating, Co-Producing and Connecting: Museum Practice Today." *Curator: The Museum Journal* 62 (2): 257–67.

Bennett, Tony. 2017. *Museums, Power, Knowledge: Selected Essays*. Abingdon: Routledge.

Birch, Jo. 2018. "Museum Spaces and Experiences for Children: Ambiguity and Uncertainty in Defining the Space, the Child and the Experience." *Children's Geographies* 16 (5): 516–28. https://doi.org/10.1080/14733285.2018.1447088.

Burke, Lois. 2019. "Meantime, it is quite well to write": Adolescent Writing and Victorian Literary Culture in Girls' Manuscript Magazines." *Victorian Periodicals Review* 52 (4): 719–748. https://doi.org/10.1353/vpr.2019.0052.

Burke, Lois, and Kathryn Simpson. 2020. "Neither Literature Nor Object: Children's Writings in the Digital Public Realm." *Magazén: International Journal for Digital and Public Humanities* 1 (2). https://edizionicafoscari.unive.it/riviste/magazen/2020/2/neither-literature-nor-object-childrens-writings-i/#!.

Clover, Darlene E., and Williamson, Sarah. 2019. "The Feminist Museum Hack as an aesthetic practice of possibility. *European Journal for Research on the Education and Learning of Adults*. 10 (2): 143–159. https://doi.org/10.3384/rela.2000-7426.RELA9142.

Colwell, Chip. 2015. "Curating Secrets." *Current Anthropology* 56 (S12): S263–S275. https://doi.org/10.1086/683429.

De Meo, Misty. 2014. "History, Archives and the Problem with Treating Every Problem as a Tech Problem." *Model View Culture* [blog]. https://modelviewculture.com/pieces/the-politics-of-digitization.

Derrida, Jacques, and Eric Prenowitz. 1995. "Archive Fever: A Freudian Impression." *Diacritics* 25 (2): 9–63.

Douglas, Kate. 2019. "'Share the Shame': Curating the Child's Voice in *Mortified Nation!*" In *Children's Voices from the Past: New Historical and Interdisciplinary Perspectives*, edited by Kristine Moruzi, Nell Musgrove, and Carla Pascoe Leahy, 191–207. Cham: Palgrave Macmillan.

Douglas, Kate, and Anna Poletti. 2016. *Life Narratives and Youth Culture*. London: Palgrave Macmillan.

Duncan, Carol. 1993/1995. *Civilizing Rituals: Inside the Public Art Museum*. Abingdon: Routledge.

Eklund, Lina. 2020. "A Shoe Is a Shoe Is a Shoe: Interpersonalization and Meaning-Making in Museums: Research Findings and Design Implications." *International Journal of Human–Computer Interaction* 36 (16): 1503–13. https://doi.org/10.1080/10447318.2020.1767982.

Fraser, Jemima W. 2004. *Museums, Drama, Ritual and Power: A Theory of the Museum Experience*. PhD thesis, University of Leicester.

Gazi, Andromache. 2014. "Exhibition Ethics: An Overview of Major Issues." *Journal of Conservation and Museum Studies* 12 (1). http://doi.org/10.5334/jcms.1021213.

Gilderdale, Anna. 2019. "Where 'Taniwha' Met 'Colonial Girl': The Social Uses of the *Nom de Plume* in New Zealand Youth Correspondence Pages, 1880–1920." In *Children's Voices from the Past: New Historical and Interdisciplinary Perspectives*, edited by Kristine Moruzi, Nell Musgrove, and Carla Pascoe Leahy, 53–84. Cham: Palgrave Macmillan.

Giles, Rebecca. 2021. "Playing with Print? An Investigation of Literacy Indicators in Children's Museums." *Literacy Practice and Research* 46 (1): Article 4. https://doi.org/10.25148/lpr.009340.

Gleadle, Kathryn. 2016. "The Juvenile Enlightenment: British Children and Youth During the French Revolution." *Past and Present: A Journal of Historical Studies* 233 (1): 143–83. https://doi.org/10.1093/pastj/gtw043.

Haas Dyson, Anne. 2013. *Rewriting the Basics: Literacy Learning in Children's Cultures*. New York and London: Teachers College Press.

Haraway, Donna. 1992. "The Promises of Monsters: A Regenerative Politics for Inappropriate/d Others." In *Cultural Studies*, edited by Lawrence Grossberg, Cary Nelson, and Paula Treichler, 295–337. London: Routledge.

Kelly, Elizabeth. 2014. "Assessment of Digitized Library and Archives Materials: A Literature Review." *Journal of Web Librarianship* 8 (4): 384–403.

Kirschner, Paul, and Pedro De Bruyckere. 2017. "The Myths of the Digital Native and the Multitasker." *Teaching and Teacher Education* 67: 135–42.

Light, Ben, Gaynor Crawford, Garry Crawford, and Victoria Gosling. 2018. "The Material Role of Digital Media in Connecting With, Within and Beyond Museums." *Convergence* 24 (4): 407–23.

Marsh, Diana E., Ricardo L. Punzalan, Robert Leopold, Brian Butler, and Massimo Petrozzi. 2016. "Stories of Impact: The Role of Narrative in Understanding the Value and Impact of Digital Collections." *Archival Science* 16 (4): 327–72.

Moravec, Michelle. 2017. "Feminist Research Practices and Digital Archives." *Australian Feminist Studies* 32 (91–92): 186–201. https://doi.org/10.1080/08164649.2017.1357006.

Museums Association. 2016. "Code of Ethics for Museums." https://www.museumsassociation.org/campaigns/ethics/code-of-ethics/. Accessed 4 Sept 2020.

Nisiotis, Louis, and Lyuba Alboul. 2021. "Initial Evaluation of an Intelligent Virtual Museum Prototype Powered by AI, XR and Robots." In *Augmented Reality, Virtual Reality, and Computer Graphics. AVR 2021. Lecture Notes in Computer Science*, vol. 12980, edited by L. T. De Paolis, P. Arpaia, and P. Bourdot. Cham: Springer. http://doi.org/10.1007/978-3-030-87595-4_21.

O'Connor, Molly, Kristen C. Nelson, Amit Pradhananga, and Megan E. Earnest. 2020. "Exploring How Awareness-Making Elicits Meaning-Making in Museum Visitors: A Mixed-methods Study." *Journal of Museum Education* 45 (2): 187–99. https://doi.org/10.1080/10598650.2020.1739466.

Scollan, Angela, and Federico Farini. 2020. "In, Out and Through Digital Worlds: Hybrid-Transitions as a Space for Children's Agency." *International Journal of Early Years Education* 28 (1): 36–49. https://doi.org/10.1080/09669760.2019.1695586

Seebach, Swen. 2018. "Creativity, Interactivity and the Hidden Structures of Power: A Reflection on the History and Current Reality of the Museum Through the Eyes of Foucault." *Digithum* 21: 11–20. https://core.ac.uk/download/pdf/159632378.pdf.

Shapin, Steve. 1994. *A Social History of Truth: Civility and Science in Seventeenth-Century England*. Chicago: University of Chicago Press.

Shildrick, M. 1996. "Posthumanism and the Monstrous Body." *Body & Society* 2 (1): 1–15. https://doi.org/10.1177/1357034X96002001001.

Silverman, Lois H. 1995. "Visitor Meaning-Making in Museums for a New Age." *Curator* 38 (3): 161–70. https://doi.org/10.1111/j.2151-6952.1995.tb01052.x.

Simpson, Kathryn. 2020. "The Digital Archive as Space and Place in the Constitution, Production and Circulation of Knowledge." In *Humanities of the Future: Perspectives from the Past and Present*. Glasgow: Bell & Bain.

Stevens, Lyn. 2019. "Interview by Lois Burke and Kathryn Simpson." Museum of Childhood, Edinburgh, November 17.

Varitimiadis, Savvas, Konstantinos Kotis, Dimitra Pittou, and Georgios Konstantakis. 2021. "Graph-Based Conversational AI: Towards a Distributed and Collaborative Multi-Chatbot Approach for Museums." *Applied Sciences* 11 (19): 9160. https://doi.org/10.3390/app11199160.

Wyman, Bruce, Scott Smith, Daniel Meyers, and Michael Godfrey. 2011. "Digital Storytelling in Museums: Observations and Best Practices." *Curator* 54 (4): 461–68. https://doi.org/10.1111/j.2151-6952.2011.00110.x.

CHAPTER 18

A Data-Driven Approach to Public-Focused Digital Narratives for Cultural Heritage

Nicole Basaraba, Jennifer Edmond, Owen Conlan, and Peter Arnds

18.1 INTRODUCTION

This chapter discusses how heritage narratives can be developed using "big data," digital media, and involve public participation which is becoming increasingly prevalent. History is often understood as portraying and understanding past events and as White (2000, 3) argues, if "there is no narrative, there is no distinctively historical discourse." Thus, narrativizing[1] cultural heritage content can aid the public's understanding of the past. For example, the process of museums curating artefacts and writing the descriptive labels involves narrative decisions in terms of what should be displayed, in what order, and with which historical notes. The concept of history as a "single unified story of the human past" emerged in the eighteenth century and as historiography[2] was modernized, it began to consider multi-perspectivity and layered meanings into a representation of factual content that extended beyond the specific situation (Fulda 2014, para. 13). White (1986, 485–86) discusses "historical pluralism" as a concept that recognizes the possibility of a number of plausible accounts of the past where history is made up of "*lived stories* that only await the historian capable of *discovering* them and

N. Basaraba (✉)
Coventry University, Coventry, UK
e-mail: nicole.basaraba@coventry.ac.uk

J. Edmond · O. Conlan · P. Arnds
Trinity College Dublin, Dublin, Ireland

© The Author(s), under exclusive license to Springer Nature Switzerland AG 2022
A. Schwan and T. Thomson (eds.), *The Palgrave Handbook of Digital and Public Humanities*, https://doi.org/10.1007/978-3-031-11886-9_18

then relating them in a *narrative*." Narrative is often viewed as "an impediment to history's transformation into a science, rather than as the 'natural' way of representing historical phenomena" (White 1986, 491), but history is not a science; it is a humanities discipline. History involves moments in time recorded by individuals who wrote from a specific historical context and cultural viewpoint. Therefore, adopting a "pluralist" or multi-perspective approach to narrativizing cultural heritage in digital formats helps to sidestep the issue of abiding by the conventions of historiography or constructing a top-down narrative from one perspective.

Heritage institutions and practitioners are using communication technologies and social media to encourage visitor interaction with cultural heritage. For instance, galleries, libraries, archives, and museums (GLAMs) are increasingly digitizing their materials (e.g., artefacts, books, photos, records, etc.), creating virtual tours, and personalized experiences for the public to experience history and culture (Ardissono et al. 2012). Some are enabling contemporary communities to digitally reproduce historical environments and create "collective narratives and geographical visualisations that cluster individual perspectives into shared forms and processes of remembering" (Silberman and Purser 2012, 14). However, GLAMs have, at times, used digital technologies to "merely enhance the dominance of the authorized, official narratives that have degraded and, in many cases, replaced the creative power of both individual and collective memory" (Silberman and Purser 2012, 17). The reason for this was that historically heritage interpreters found it easier to present a specific moment in time, but this has become a challenge in a rapidly changing society where multiple histories are being read, interpreted, and acted out at heritage sites (Aitchison et al. 2014, 109). Heritage can be presented in a myriad of ways through the curation of artefacts and narratives, the perspectives presented (e.g., marginalized groups), and the use of digital media. The challenge for GLAMs, who have not traditionally employed storytellers or creatives, is how to capitalize on digital media for the presentation of public-focused narratives? As digital projects for cultural heritage are increasingly interdisciplinary and collaborative, it presents new challenges for managing different perspectives and goals while considering public audiences. Therefore, this chapter provides a critical review of these collaborative methods and proposes a data-driven methodology that aims to help GLAMs, other cultural heritage organizations, scholars, other stakeholders engage with public participants and tailor digital narrative experiences to different audiences to achieve their desired communication goals, which may include displaying more digitized artefacts and sharing unknown histories, for example.

18.2 Digital Narratives for Cultural Heritage

The museum experience is moving towards audience-oriented exhibitions, which shifts focus from individual objects to a "whole gallery experience" where objects are rarely left to "speak for themselves" and meaning is made in collaboration with semiotic modalities, such as space, visual images, and language (Meng 2004, 31). Social historians are supplementing objects with maps, photographs, documents, and oral history taken from everyday experience to create a range of stories about an object and uncover hidden stories of disadvantaged social groups, such as the working classes, women, minority ethnic groups and children (Aitchison et al. 2014, 98). Heritage is socially constructed and the presentation of these narratives in digital forms allows for a more democratic process of creation, posing new opportunities for using digital narratives. Heritage "meanings and values are not attached to artefacts, buildings or sites. Neither are they frozen in time. They are the results of repeated and ongoing interactions in the lived world of ordinary people" (Byrne 2008, as cited in Giaccardi 2012, 2). Therefore, ordinary people should be considered and, better yet, involved in the construction of heritage, which expresses "constantly evolving values, beliefs, knowledge and traditions" (Giaccardi 2012, 2). Historians have used the concept of *shared authority* to describe the democratization of the knowledge-building process where audiences are not passively consuming knowledge produced by expert historians (Cauvin and O'Neill 2017, 5). Contributing to a move towards sharing authority; user-generated content (UGC) published using social media on the Internet has resulted in niche blogs and other documentation on heritage topics from personal, local, national, and global perspectives, as "ordinary people" are sharing their cultural customs and life experiences. This UGC should be considered by digital heritage narrative creators to further understand public audiences and engage them with expert-produced histories.

GLAMs are increasingly developing interactive digital products to engage the public, which is often referred to as a turn towards "immersive experiences" (Kidd 2018) and "participatory approaches" to digital heritage (Tammaro 2016). The current practices are varied in terms of the levels of success as measured through audience engagement and there are fewer instances of narrative-based productions. Participatory heritage in a European context has developed a series of initiatives that are undertaken by cultural and educational institutions to harness the affordance of information communication technologies to explore different types of partnerships with the public (Carletti 2016). Four typical models of public participation in heritage projects are: (1) contributory projects (e.g., citizen science) where visitors provide limited and specified objects, actions, or ideas to institutionally controlled processes; (2) collaborative projects where visitors serve as active partners in the creation of projects that are originated and controlled by the institution; (3) co-created projects (e.g., participatory action research) where community members work with the institutional staff from the beginning to define the project goals and participate in all stages of the process to generate the product based on community interests; and (4) hosted projects where the institution provides a portion of its facilities or resources to showcase programmes developed by public groups (Carletti 2016, 200). Contributory projects are conducted based on a primarily top-down approach. Collaborative and co-created projects often use a combination of top-down and bottom-up approaches. Finally, hosted projects use a bottom-up approach. These methods come with challenges, such as sourcing contributions from the public, managing a balance between expert-produced and user-produced content, and achieving "public engagement" or "immersive experiences." Many such participatory projects to date have focused on the digital preservation of intangible heritage using social media and crowdsourcing for specific tasks; developing co-created experiences for cultural content; examining user experiences with new media technologies, such as virtual and augmented reality for museums; using geographic information systems (GIS) and 3D modelling for archaeological sites for the development of mobile applications for educational contexts (Economou 2015). The following analysis highlights the current practices and the limitations or challenges in developing digital narratives for cultural heritage in the common formats of (1) co-created/crowdsourced digitization projects, (2) creating immersive and virtual museum experiences, and (3) serious and locative[3] games.

18.3 Crowdsourced Digitization Projects

Continually improving the methods of digitizing library and museum archives has led to an abundance of digital humanities projects and provided the public with access to an immense number of digitized artefacts—a big data corpus of expert-produced cultural heritage content. However, the challenge with these types of projects is that the public often do not use these databases after their initial launch and there can also be other limitations imposed by top-down funding requirements and lack of open-access. Alternative models according to tripartite research collaborations that engage researchers, cultural heritage institutions, and interested members of the general public have grown and developed over time. Many of the foundational projects, such as the Transcribe Bentham (Causer and Wallace 2012) or Letters of 1916 (Schreibman et al. 2017) projects, were based on the paradigm of crowdsourcing labour, inviting and incentivizing members, often from the public, to become contributors to the scholarly transcription efforts at the heart of the resource enhancement efforts. While these two projects each deployed a relatively straightforward approach to interface design and interaction, other projects, such as the Finnish Library's Digitalkoot use a visually stylized, gamified look and feel, where users are encouraged to grow flowers and remove garden moles by correcting messy optical character recognition results in the library's digitized collections (Chrons and Sundell 2011). Projects that involved crowdsourcing labour indicated that while engaging the general public as a resource was enriching in many ways (e.g., building its profile and diversifying its user base), the project overhead required to recruit and retain volunteers was high, and the additional labour force did not necessarily save labour overall because crowdsourced input needed to be checked and verified.

Perhaps more successful, therefore, have been models where the input of the crowd has been unique to each user and the motivation to contribute richer. A leading example of this kind of engagement has been the Europeana digital library collection days, in which members of the public are encouraged to contribute their personal stories and artifacts, via their local heritage institutions, to Europe-wide collections on themes such as the First World War, work, or migration (Europeana, n.d.). There are of course many smaller examples of the co-creation of digitally enabled interactions between institutions and their publics, such as those facilitated within public history or digital humanities training programmes via internships and projects. In addition to this, research infrastructures focusing on the intersection between the humanities and the digital are working to support this transition, such as the Digital Research Infrastructure for the Arts and Humanities (DARIAH) and the Common Language Resources and Technology Infrastructure (CLARIN). Example initiatives include the DARIAH call for "Public Humanities" (DARIAH EU 2016) and the two organizations' shared training module on "Citizen Science in the (digital) Arts and Humanities" (PARTHENOS Training Suite, n.d.). Ultimately, however, these projects remain largely institutionally controlled, top-down initiatives. While the ethos and growth of citizen science have certainly found their way into the arts and humanities as well as the hard sciences, the ethics of collection management and the professional practices of archives still tend to be protective of the sources and narratives these institutions have been historically bound to share and protect.

18.4 Immersive and Virtual Museums

In addition to digitization projects, significant developments and changes are also taking place in museum practices in relation to digital media. Digital experiences in the museums allow visitors to see and interact with more content that may not be available or suitable for physical display. Kidd (2018, 5) explains that as immersive museums continue to be developed, the modalities of aural, haptic, olfactory, and kinaesthetic are being explored as meaning-making moves towards becoming a "whole-body endeavour" in a physical sense. In addition to immersive in-museum digital exhibitions, GLAMs are developing *virtual museums*, commonly published as websites, which are broadly defined as "a logically related collection of digital objects composed in a variety of media" (Styliani et al. 2009, 521). It is important to note that some virtual museums can employ a variety of technologies, such as imaging technologies, Web3D, virtual reality (VR), augmented reality (AR), mixed reality, haptics, and handheld devices (e.g., cell phones, personal digital assistants, and tablets) (Styliani et al. 2009, 520–24). Since these technologies are expensive and take specialized skills to develop, many virtual museums at present function as content museums providing visitors with a digital database of their collections and some, especially due to the impacts of COVID-19, offer 360-degree virtual tours through the physical galleries. For example, visitors to the websites for the Louvre,[4] the Smithsonian,[5] or the Vatican Museums[6] can take a 360-degree virtual tour of past or current exhibitions.

The role of museums and curators is changing as society is increasingly becoming sceptical of experts. Nielsen (2017, 441–45) argues that due to this cultural shift museums need to re-evaluate their approaches to "interpretation, interaction and meaning making" and particularly as many exhibitions are becoming more storytelling oriented by allowing visitors to contribute. In this light, contemporary museums are exhibiting their materials across multiple media and using social media to communicate with their audiences. There is also an increasing shift to the dynamic of trust because the audience members are becoming authors through the production of user-generated content which museums are incorporating into some exhibitions through interactive digital displays present within the buildings and for online gaming aspects (Kidd 2014). For example, the UK-based storytelling project called *Culture Shock!* used museums and galleries to inspire members of the public to create their own stories through social media; the project garnered 550 participants whose digital stories were added to the relevant museum collections and broadcast online and at special events (Nielsen 2017, 449). Since museums are incorporating more storytelling and public participation, there are more team members involved in developing digital heritage projects and more complexities in terms of content management when a combination of a top-down and bottom-up approach is applied.

Creating virtual museums comes with many technical challenges. For example, there is the danger of visitors interpreting a graphic system's presentation of an image as being true/accurate, but reconstructed items are often the result of a personal and subjective interpretation (Styliani et al. 2009, 525). Similarly, computer reconstructions only offer one aspect of the subject rather than reflecting the many ways the past can be interpreted. Users without digital literacies may be excluded from the experience and the selected software may not be accessible to museologists (Styliani et al. 2009, 525). Museums may provide a fragmented experience with no obvious informational connections or context, and some museums lack clarity in their identified purpose so they need to identify target communities to better determine how content should be structured and delivered (Styliani et al. 2009, 525–26). Despite these challenges, digital cultural heritage narratives offer more opportunities to communicate alternative interpretations, offer a narratively cohesive experience, and the ability to personalize content for different users by eliciting their participation in narrative production.

18.5 Gamification and Serious Games

In addition to museum-based productions, GLAMs and other organizations are gamifying heritage experiences. These have most commonly been realized in the form of serious games, which is a term often used interchangeably with *game-based learning, gamification, pervasive games,* and *alternate reality games* (Xu et al. 2017). Gamification uses game design elements in digital applications to engage users and motivate desired behaviours, while serious games are often developed for training and educational purposes (Andreoli et al. 2017, 3). Game-like applications developed for cultural heritage have been classified into virtual museums—as discussed in the previous section; prototypes and demonstrators; commercial historical games; and mobile applications (Anderson et al. 2009, 3). Prototype and demonstrators often focus on digital visualizations of reconstructed archaeological sites like Rome in 320 AD, ancient Pompeii before the eruption of Mount Vesuvius in 79 AD, and the reconstruction of the sculptural decorations on the Parthenon in 437 BC (Anderson et al. 2009, 2–3). These prototypes and demonstrators provide little information beyond the visualization and little user agency to make narrative choices. Serious games exist as mobile applications (apps), web-based solutions, computer games, and mixed reality games, which combine real and virtual interactions (Anderson et al. 2009, 2). For example, *Viking Ghost Hunt* is a narrative-led location-aware game based in Dublin, Ireland that engages the player in local Viking history between the years 800 and 1169 through a ghost-hunting game (Paterson et al. 2013, 65). This project gamified and narrativized history related to specific locations and the players may, as a result of interaction, have learned something. In the tourism sector, gamification has been used as a method of marketing locations and brands to potential visitors to create awareness and enhance their on-site experiences at a destination (Xu et al. 2017). For example, *Musica Romana*, intended for use by tourists, is a website for mobile phones that allows users to experience classical music associated with and playable at specific churches located in Rome, Italy (Fagerjord 2017). *Musica Romana* has aspects of gamification as a "locative auditory" experience because it allows users to search for different churches to hear the associated music; however, it is not considered a serious game because it does not have a more cohesive plot/story with planned learning outcomes and targets for competition (e.g., completing different tasks or levels).

The advantages of location-based games are that they make use of multimodality, they are immersive, and they create a narrative experience. However, they often remediate the conventions of fictional narratives by focusing on characters in the storyworld, which downplays the history and prioritizes gameplay. Mobile apps also allow for personalization options, such as retrieving places, topics, or exhibits of interest, allowing users to book locations, create their own itinerary to better plan their experience, and share their experience through social media networks (Kourouthanassis et al. 2015, 71). That said, not all apps are created equal and some are more useful than others. In the current market, there is still a gap in delivering personalized user experiences. Ardissono et al. (2012, 86) noted that "while mobile guides are now a common sight in cultural heritage settings and social web technology is spreading fast, personalized services are not." For personalization to reach critical mass in cultural heritage systems, he suggests creating a "pathfinder" or "tour provider" approach to share personal views or individual navigation paths in collections; allowing users to reflect on their experiences with the system; and considering social interaction in groups based on group user modelling, which could be developed by soliciting user-generated content (Ardissono et al. 2012, 87–90). Some of the common challenges with existing digital cultural heritage systems were identified and summarized by Ardissono et al. (2012) who conducted a large-scale analysis of 37 personalized digital cultural heritage systems on desktop, mobile, and wearable devices. They found that in many cases, digital cultural heritage products are extensive web-based collections that are difficult to navigate, visitors are highly heterogeneous and require different types of information, and users are often first- and short-time visitors to an unknown place (Ardissono et al. 2012, 74). Therefore, in order to increase public participation in digital heritage beyond crowdsourcing content, creating personalized narratives can provide immersive and engaging experiences that users will remember and be more likely to share with their friends and family, as well as return to in order to learn more.

Overall, as can be seen through the formats of digitization projects, virtual museums and serious games, the current practices of narrativizing cultural heritage have largely been top-down where the users are in fact *end*-users, rather than being involved in the development process. This brief overview shows that a variety of scholars and creatives are experimenting with cultural heritage narrative content in the digital medium. However, with experimentation come the challenges of creating an intentional narrative, providing users with the agency to make choices to personalize their experience, and eliciting further user participation or action. As the number of digital products has increased in GLAMs and academia, there is a need for more methods of involving public participation, personalization options, and purposefully communicating an intended narrative. Therefore, a data-driven method for creating public-focused narratives is proposed as a way to further incorporate a bottom-up approach to a largely top-down process.

18.6 A Data-Driven Approach to Public-Focused Digital Heritage Narratives

18.6.1 *Personalizing Audiences' Narrative Experiences*

Existing practices for developing personalized content systems by computer scientists can be drawn upon for the creation of public-focused digital narratives for cultural heritage. The process of personalization in digital systems aims to tailor content and services to different users' preferences, goals, and context while making reuse of media easier (Lawless et al. 2016, 172). Adaptive hypermedia technologies are used to service each user's interests, prior experience, or location to provide personalized navigations of relevant digital resources or suggested recommendations based on similar users' behaviour and feedback (e.g., social recommendation) (Lawless et al. 2016, 172). Key steps in designing personalized systems are to model users, model content,

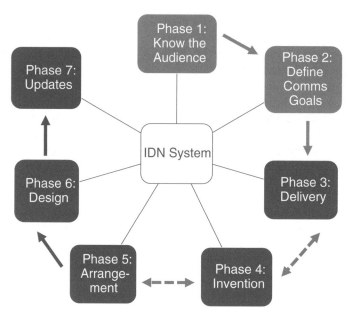

Fig. 18.1 Seven-phase theoretical framework for interactive digital narrative (IDN) creation

and then create an adaptive system (Lawless et al. 2016, 175–79). This overarching personalization process was previously adapted into a Theoretical Digital Narrative Creation Framework which was developed specifically for creative teams working in the cultural heritage sector (Basaraba 2018). The framework consists of seven phases, namely (1) Know the audience, (2) Define communication goals, (3) Select and consider digital delivery, (4) Invention including content curation, (5) Arrangement of narrative structure, (6) Design digital system, and (7) Revise after user testing (Basaraba 2018). These phases involve public input through the collection and analysis of big data, which includes user-generated content, technical needs, and subject-matter interests as well as later user testing of the digital narrative product. The following sections discuss how GLAMs can allow the public can be considered and included in the early phases through the process of modelling the audience(s), tailoring the communication goals and method of narrative delivery to the target audience(s), and incorporating UGC for the final narrative product (phases 1–4) (Fig. 18.1).

18.6.2 Identifying Target Audience(s): Multiple Publics and Digital Data Analysis

The first step in personalizing cultural heritage narrative content for different users is to "know the audience" by creating a user model. User models, often used by computer scientists, are commonly developed in one of three ways:

(1) by identifying user characteristics and interests in advance of building the systems; (2) through initialization where users fill in questionnaires to determine their preferences; or (3) through dynamic user modelling based on tracking user interactions with the system and adapting content delivery to their use patterns (e.g., artificial intelligence) (Ardissono et al. 2012, 83–84). The first two methods of user modelling are particularly useful for GLAMs, which can, with relative ease, track the visitors to the buildings through ticket sales, library cards, website analytics, and post-visit surveys. The collected data can provide insight into demographic details, total number of visitors, in some cases the duration of their visit, and feedback on the visitor's overall experience with any digital components included in the exhibition. In addition to gathering new demographic data, many previous studies have been published on visitor experiences and digital preferences for different publics, such as tourists (domestic and international) and students. Existing demographic information can provide a baseline for GLAMs who may not be aware of who commonly visits or who would be interested in digital narrative about cultural heritage.

Previous studies on museum visitors have shown that the majority are often domestic, have a high level of education, and there is often a higher proportion of women than men (Falk et al. 2006; Mokatren et al. 2019; Foster et al. 2020). For example, interviews with 576 visitors to the Ara Pacis museum in Italy showed that 89% were residents of Italy, 67% were highly educated, 59% were female, and 45% were return visitors (Trunfio et al. 2018, 667). Other studies have found that students visit museums in groups and are another major target audience for digital heritage learning-focused projects (Bossavit et al. 2018; Çil et al. 2016; Hillman et al. 2016; Rowan et al. 2016). Heritage tourists are one group that is most-commonly interested in cultural heritage experiences. Tourism scholars have divided heritage tourists into different sub-groups, such as educated visitors, professionals, families or groups, school children, and nostalgia-seekers (Nuryanti 1996, 253). Heritage tourists are between the ages of 30–55 years and educated to at least the level of a bachelor's degree (McKercher 2002; Ramires et al. 2018), which provides insight into their reading and comprehension levels and perhaps their expectations of historical depth, for example. It is acknowledged that in addition to these common public audiences discussed, other audiences interested in contributing to and consuming digital heritage narratives are professionals who work in cultural heritage and memory institutions including historians, museum curators, non-profit heritage organizations, librarians, academics, and other subject-matter experts who would have even higher abilities and/or expectations of the breadth and depth of the narrative information presented. Collecting visitor demographics and surveying visitor experiences and preferences can lead to user models that inform digital narrative content development. For example, students aged 18 years and younger would have different attention spans, interests, and digital literacy levels compared to highly educated heritage tourists aged 35–55 years. Some museums, in the past, have lacked clarity in their identified purpose so they need to identify target audiences to better determine how content should be structured and delivered (Styliani et al. 2009, 526). If GLAMs want to attract new types of visitors, for example, they can identify one or more target groups and research their needs, demographics, and preferences to model the potential audience(s). This audience information informs the decision-making process as to whether the digital narratives need to be presented in different ways or levels of detail for these audiences that have varying levels of education and digital literacies.

18.6.3 Defining Narrative Goals and Delivery Method

The results of the demographic data gathered can be analysed to inform decision-making on defining the communication goals of the digital narrative and the platform for narrative delivery. Considering the increased number of collaborators and contributors involved in creating digital heritage narrative experiences, it becomes more important to develop a project plan, according to the seven-phase Digital Narrative Creation Framework to ensure that the narrative communication goals are achieved (Basaraba 2018). Museum exhibition creators, designers, and curators are becoming more involved in storytelling by focusing on live interpretation, living history, and guided tours (Nielsen 2017, 448). Digital narrative formats offer opportunities to communicate many alternative cultural interpretations and narrative authoring tools (e.g., software) can be used to personalize content for different users by eliciting their participation in making choices to produce an emergent narrative. For example, based on the audience research, one digital narrative experience could include an option for school-aged children, one for the average GLAM visitor, and one for visitors with a higher level of expertise/education. Therefore, determining which narrative perspectives and levels of desired personalization the prospective audience desires informs the choice of delivery medium.

The audiences' abilities, access, and interest need to be considered by the narrative creation team members prior to selecting the delivery medium. For example, a mobile application may have accessibility limitations due to the operating system (Android vs. MacOS) and the availability of WiFi or data. Websites commonly have a hierarchical navigation, which limits narrative flexibility and video games may permit more choices for players, but they require a larger budget to produce effectively. The delivery method also needs to be carefully considered in regard to which modes would best carry the intended message. Cultural context shapes the method of communication and the current cultural context has moved towards multimodality (Kress 2003). With the continually developing technologies available such as VR, AR, mixed reality, etc., narrative producers increasingly need to know what type of content is best suited for each semiotic mode of communication (Sánchez-Mesa et al. 2016, 16). Therefore, data collection on the targeted audiences in terms of their demographics, interests, and digital delivery preferences can inform the decision-making processes for the narrative design choices and help ensure the narrative communication goals, whether they be informative, persuasive, or educational, are achieved.

18.6.4 Narrative Content Modelling: Digitized Archives and Social Media Content

As there is a growing abundance of digitized archives and associated historical data, these resources can be used for narrative content modelling. A bottom-up approach is suggested so that the narrative can also incorporate or allow for user-led co-creation of the narrative by drawing from social media data. Both the digital historical and user-generated data can be multimodal (e.g., text, image, video) and appear in different media (e.g., printed books, blogs, and photos) and thus, the data formats require different methods of analysis for the purpose of developing a content model. Content modelling involves trying to identify the characteristics that may be pertinent to the users' exploration of key related artefacts or topics (Lawless et al. 2016, 175). These types of complex data can be analysed using *distant reading* and *close reading* techniques to identify themes that are of interest to the previously modelled targeted audience(s). Distant reading helps generate an abstract view by shifting from the observation of individual textual content towards visualizing global features of multiple texts (Jänicke et al. 2017, 84). Distant reading is performed using a variety of computational tools where possible, but some datasets may require close reading techniques due to the quantity and nature of the data. Since the goal of analysing the data is to gain a bird's-eye view of content themes for narrative modelling, distant reading is recommended where possible and close reading when necessary. As Günther and Quandt (2016) explain, a deductive method for text analysis is based on a pre-defined codebook with a set of relevant categories and this allows for the inductive interpretation to emerge from the results of close readings. Most digital datasets should be large enough to warrant the use of software to analyse the collected texts and images. Distant reading can also be followed by a close reading to uncover further narrative details and in cases where the dataset is too small or complex (e.g., unreadable historical terminology, special characters) for computational processing. Data analysis can also help identify the most common modalities used across the collected datasets and which modalities could be used for which types of narrative content. For example, historical artworks and paintings could be used to show a depiction of the time period or the narrative setting, and text allows for the provision of more detailed information. Rather than a top-down approach of unsubstantiated, or in some cases heavily biased, impressions of what the content creator believes should be included in protostory development, distant reading allows for themes to be deduced from the datasets and the collected datasets, which can include user-generated narratives.

Topic modelling is a helpful method for finding meaning in a large volume of text and generating new ways of looking at content, materials, or qualitative data that emerge from the data rather than seeking to prove that a preconceived idea is correct (Graham et al. 2012, 119–20). Although topic models are frequency-based descriptions and visualizations are effective methods of getting to know big data, it is noted that they are only a starting point acting as a lens through which material can be examined through a closer reading (Graham et al. 2012, 120). Text analysis tools commonly used for topic modelling purposes have weak or non-existent semantic capabilities because "they count, compare, track and represent words, but they do not produce meaning—we do" (Sinclair and Rockwell 2015, 288). However, in order to

> understand the system in its entirety, we must accept losing something. We always pay a price for theoretical knowledge: reality is indefinitely rich; concepts are abstract, are poor. But it's precisely this "poverty" that makes it possible to handle them, and therefore to know. This is why less is actually more. (Moretti 2013, 48–49)

Frequently used text analysis software used to identify topics which can also be used to model cultural heritage narratives are MALLET, Voyant Tools, and Leximancer. MALLET is an open-source Java-based package for statistical natural language processing, document classification, and information extraction (McCallum 2002). Voyant Tools are open-source statistical and visualization tools that accumulate perspectives in order to generate questions for further investigation, they can be used for many forms of analysis, and they address a variety of research questions across disciplines (Sinclair and Rockwell 2016). Leximancer is a subscription-based text mining software that analyses collections of textual documents and visually displays the extracted information in a conceptual map that represents the main concepts contained within the text and how they are related (Leximancer Pty Ltd. 2020). Large-scale image analyses of user-generated photos and/or historical artwork collections for example, can be done using software, such as PixPlot which is an open-source code that visualizes thousands of images in a two-dimensional projection and clusters similar images together (YaleDHlab 2018). Similar images are grouped into as many clusters as needed to create meaningful differentiation and aesthetic patterns, motifs, and themes as identified by the researcher. Other image analysis software include the open-source ImageJ (written in Java) and those built by research groups, such as the Cultural Analytics Lab in the USA, or the Multimodal Analysis Group in Curtin University, Perth, Australia. While only a few examples are noted here, multiple software, both open-source and licenced, have been developed to analyse literary texts (e.g., Dunst et al. 2017), historical texts and newspapers (e.g., Jänicke et al. 2017), audiovisual media history and audiovisual data analyses (Aasman et al. 2018), and topics of sociocultural discourse (O'Halloran et al. 2019). These techniques can be applied to content modelling whereby the results of topic modelling approaches to text and image analyses help determine what themes could and/or should be included in digital heritage narrative productions. A combination of distant and close reading techniques is a general approach to analysing different accessible corpora, but more specific methods and frameworks were required to accommodate the selected datasets particular to each project and model the content to produce the desired digital narrative experience.

A content model can be developed by using the systematic methodology termed *multimodal discourse analysis* of the multiple collected datasets. Multimodal discourse analysis is a repeatable method of cultural data analysis developed by scholars in linguistics, semiotics, and multimodal studies. It extends the study of language to other phenomena "such as image, music, gesture, symbols and, increasingly, multimodal analysis annotation" (Krisjanous 2016, 342). This methodology is often used by scholars studying multimodal content as a form of distant reading. At present, "no techniques exist that truly combine multimodal analysis, data mining, and information visualization simultaneously, due to the inherent complexity and the challenges of disciplinary and theoretical integration" (O'Halloran et al. 2018, 23). To address this challenge, O'Halloran et al. (2018, 23) proposed a research method that integrates qualitative and quantitative methods for application to discourse-related research topics. O'Halloran et al.'s method (2018, 24) involves the process of (a) determining the multimodal dataset including metadata and contextual information, (b) automated data processing using algorithms and manual analysis to identify key systems, and (c) identifying discourse patterns in interactive visualizations that allow for the exploration of content and the tone of messages over time and space, which is useful for narrative development.

18.6.5 Exemplifying Data-Driven Heritage Narrative Development: A Case Study

To date, this described method of data-driven digital narrative creation for personalized cultural heritage experiences has been successfully tested on one case study and two other studies are currently in progress. An interactive web documentary (iDoc) titled *Sentenced to Transportation: A Virtual Tour of Australia's Convict Past* was developed by collecting multimodal datasets that were analysed using distant and close reading techniques as described. The user model was developed based on an analysis of existing tourism demographics drawn from Australian Government statistics, tourist attraction public reports, and user-generated social media data. Then a total of nine datasets, sourced from tourism marketing (brochures, travel guidebooks, websites), user-generated social media posts (TripAdvisor, Instagram, personal blogs), and digitized historical archives (databases on Australian history, such as digitalpanopticon.org and the State Library of NSW), were analysed to develop the content model that served as the thematic narrative outline for the iDoc. The digitized historical resources, user-generated narratives, and information sourced from site visits underwent topic modelling and further analyses so that a variety of narrative content could be curated and combined into a series of narrative paths based on the geo-locations of 11 UNESCO Australian Convict World Heritage Sites.

The different narratives that emerged from the bottom-up analysis of the datasets were: multinational perspectives on the transportation of convicts who were British, Welsh, Scottish, Irish, and female as well as social themes of forced labour, corporal punishment, and the impacts of colonization on Indigenous populations. These themes were used to develop multiple storylines for possible exploration to allow the iDoc users to choose their own digital adventure. The iDoc was tested on two user populations namely, potential heritage site visitors and professional/experts in Australian convict history. Overall, the user testing with the iDoc showed that it achieved the overall narrative goals of persuading tourists to engage in further participation after their interaction with the digital narrative as users expressed a desire to visit the locations featured in the iDoc and share their experiences through social media (Basaraba 2020). This case study demonstrates how the Digital Narrative Creation Framework (Basaraba 2018) can guide the data-driven development of digital cultural heritage narratives to (1) offer personalization options for public audiences based on the user model, (2) content model based on different emergent themes from the data, and (3) achieve the pre-determined communication goals (for more details on this case study, see Basaraba 2020).

18.7 Conclusion

As GLAMs and digital humanities projects are increasingly engaging in storytelling for public audiences, future creators are invited to apply and test this approach to determine whether it is feasible and leads to new ways of engaging audiences in a variety of cultural heritage narrative projects. For example, this data-driven method could be used in future development projects to create location-based mobile applications or serious games, digital installations within museums or virtual museums, and other emerging formats, such as re-creating historical landmarks or cities through narrativized virtual reality experiences. The resulting creative format for the digital narrative experience can vary and will be influenced by the history, available modalities of the existing data, and on the message(s) and experiences the creative team aims to achieve. This data-driven method presents a converged bottom-up and top-down approach to creating digital narratives that focus on public interests and engagement. The benefits of this approach are that the narrative creators now often have feasible access to existing digitized datasets, and it allows for personalization of the narrative experience for individual users with different interests and preferences. The process of getting to know the audience first and modelling the prospective users or identifying new audiences of the digital narrative informs which narrative delivery platform should be developed (e.g., handheld device, audio tour, etc.) and can result in new multi-perspective narratives that adapted to interests of different age groups and cultures. Modelling the narrative based on existing data also allows museologists, historians, archaeologists, scholars, and other heritage sector professionals who may not have experience with storytelling to draw new connections, uncover new histories, and participate in narrativizing heritage. While a data-driven approach to narrative may not be suitable for all projects, it opens up new opportunities for engaging the public in digital heritage experiences.

Notes

1. Narrativization is a constructive process that "enables readers to recognize as narrative those kinds of texts that appear to be non-narrative" (Fludernik 1996, 46).
2. Historiography is a research area that encompasses the forms and functions of narration and narrative in history (Fulda 2014, para. 1).
3. Locative media is a "mobile media movement in which location and time are considered essential to the work" (Tuters as cited in Nisi et al. 2008, 72), and require the user to physically move to progress in the game.
4. Louvre Museum virtual exhibition: https://www.louvre.fr/en/visites-en-ligne#tabs.
5. The Smithsonian Museum virtual tours: https://naturalhistory.si.edu/visit/virtual-tour.
6. Vatican Museums virtual tour: http://www.museivaticani.va/content/museivaticani/en/collezioni/musei/tour-virtuali-elenco.html.

References

Aasman, Susan, Tom Slootweg, L. M. Melgar Estrada, and Rob Wegter. 2018. "Tales of a Tool Encounter: Exploring Video Annotation for Doing Media History." *VIEW: Journal of European Television History and Culture/E-Journal* 7 (14): 73–87.

Aitchison, Cara, Nicola E. MacLeod, Nicola E. Macleod, and Stephen J. Shaw. 2014. *Leisure and Tourism Landscapes: Social and Cultural Geographies*. London: Routledge.

Anderson, Eike Falk, Leigh McLoughlin, Fotis Liarokapis, Christopher Peters, C. Petridis, and Sara de Freitas. 2009. "Serious Games in Cultural Heritage." In *The 10th International Symposium on Virtual Reality, Archaeology and Cultural Heritage VAST—State of the Art Reports*, edited by M. Ashley and F. Liarokapis, 29–84, 22–25 September, Valletta, Malta.

Andreoli, Roberto, Angela Corolla, Armando Faggiano, Delfina Malandrino, Donato Pirozzi, Mirta Ranaldi, Gianluca Santangelo, and Vittorio Scarano. 2017. "A Framework to Design, Develop, and Evaluate Immersive and Collaborative Serious Games in Cultural Heritage." *Journal on Computing and Cultural Heritage (JOCCH)* 11 (1): 1–22.

Ardissono, Liliana, Tsvi Kuflik, and Daniela Petrelli. 2012. "Personalization in Cultural Heritage: The Road Travelled and the One Ahead." *User Modeling and User-Adapted Interaction* 22 (1–2): 73–99.

Basaraba, Nicole. 2018. "A Framework for Creative Teams of Non-Fiction Interactive Digital Narratives." In *Interactive Storytelling: 11th International Conference on*

Interactive Digital Storytelling, ICIDS 2018, Dublin, Ireland, December 5–8, 2018, Proceedings, edited by Rebecca Rouse, Hartmut Koenitz, and Mads Haahr, 143–48. Springer, Cham.

Basaraba, Nicole. 2020. *Remixing Transmedia for Cultural Heritage Sites: The Rhetoric, Creative Practice, and Evaluation of Digital Narratives*. PhD thesis. http://www.tara.tcd.ie/bitstream/handle/2262/94133/Remixing_Transmedia_PhD%20Thesis_BASARABAnicole.pdf?sequence=8.

Bossavit, Benoît, Alfredo Pina, Isabel Sanchez-Gil, and Aitziber Urtasun. 2018. "Educational Games to Enhance Museum Visits for Schools." *Journal of Educational Technology & Society* 21 (4): 171–86.

Carletti, Laura. 2016. "Participatory Heritage: Scaffolding Citizen Scholarship." *International Information & Library Review* 48 (3): 196–203.

Causer, Tim, and Valerie Wallace. 2012. "Building a Volunteer Community: Results and Findings from *Transcribe Bentham*." *Digital Humanities Quarterly* 6 (2). http://digitalhumanities.org/dhq/vol/6/2/000125/000125.html.

Cauvin, Thomas, and Ciaran O'Neill. 2017. "Negotiating Public History in the Republic of Ireland: Collaborative, Applied and Usable Practices for the Profession." *Historical Research* 90 (250): 810–28.

Çil, Emine, Nihal Maccario, and Durmuş Yanmaz. 2016. "Design, Implementation and Evaluation of Innovative Science Teaching Strategies for Non-Formal Learning in a Natural History Museum." *Research in Science & Technological Education* 34 (3): 325–41.

Chrons, Otto, and Sundell, Sami. 2011. "Digitalkoot: Making Old Archives Accessible Using Crowdsourcing." http://www.aaai.org/ocs/index.php/WS/AAAIW11/paper/view/3813.

DARIAH EU. 2016. https://www.dariah.eu/activities/dariah-theme/dariah-theme-2016/.

Dunst, Alexander, Rita Hartel, and Jochen Laubrock. 2017. "The Graphic Narrative Corpus (GNC): Design, Annotation, and Analysis for the Digital Humanities." In *2017 14th IAPR International Conference on Document Analysis and Recognition (ICDAR)*, vol. 3, 15–20. https://www.computer.org/csdl/proceedings/icdar/2017/11gop0Hn9ni.

Economou, Maria. 2015. "Heritage in the Digital Age." *A Companion to Heritage Studies* 15: 215–28.

Europeana Collection Days. n.d. https://blog.europeana.eu/tag/europeana-collection-days/.

Fagerjord, Anders. 2017. "Toward a Rhetoric of the Place: Creating Locative Experiences." In *Rhetoric and Experience Architecture*, edited by Lisa Potts and Michael J. Salvo, 225–40. Anderson, SC: Parlor Press.

Falk, John H., Lynn D. Dierking, and Marianna Adams. 2006. "Living in a Learning Society: Museums and Free-Choice Learning." *A Companion to Museum Studies* 1: 323–39.

Fludernik, Monika. 1996. *Towards a "Natural" Narratology*. London: Routledge.

Foster, Scott, Ian Fillis, Kim Lehman, and Mark Wickham. 2020. "Investigating the Relationship Between Visitor Location and Motivations to Attend a Museum." *Cultural Trends*: 1–21.

Fulda, Daniel. 2014. "Historiographic Narration." *The Living Handbook of Narratology*, March 25. https://www.lhn.uni-hamburg.de/node/123.html.

Giaccardi, Elisa, ed. 2012. *Heritage and Social Media: Understanding Heritage in a Participatory Culture*. New York: Routledge.
Graham, Shawn, Scott Weingart, and Ian Milligan. 2012. *Getting Started with Topic Modeling and MALLET*. The Editorial Board of the Programming Historian. https://programminghistorian.org/en/lessons/topic-modeling-and-mallet.
Günther, Elisabeth, and Thorsten Quandt. 2016. "Word Counts and Topic Models: Automated Text Analysis Methods for Digital Journalism Research." *Digital Journalism* 4 (1): 75–88.
Hillman, Thomas, Alexandra Weilenmann, Beata Jungselius, and Tiina Leino Lindell. 2016. "Traces of Engagement: Narrative-Making Practices with Smartphones on a Museum Field Trip." *Learning, Media and Technology* 41 (2): 351–70.
Jänicke, Stefan, Greta Franzini, Muhammad Faisal Cheema, and Gerik Scheuermann. 2017. "Visual Text Analysis in Digital Humanities." In *Computer Graphics Forum* 36 (6): 226–50.
Kidd, Jenny. 2014. *Museums in the New Mediascape: Transmedia, Participation, Ethics*. Farnham: Ashgate.
Kidd, Jenny. 2018. "'Immersive' Heritage Encounters." *The Museum Review* 3 (1). https://www.themuseumreview.org/articles-1.
Kourouthanassis, Panos, Costas Boletsis, Cleopatra Bardaki, and Dimitra Chasanidou. 2015. "Tourists Responses to Mobile Augmented Reality Travel Guides: The Role of Emotions on Adoption Behavior." *Pervasive and Mobile Computing* 18: 71–87.
Kress, Gunther R. 2003. *Literacy in the New Media Age*. London: Routledge.
Krisjanous, Jayne. 2016. "An Exploratory Multimodal Discourse Analysis of Dark Tourism Websites: Communicating Issues Around Contested Sites." *Journal of Destination Marketing & Management* 5 (4): 341–50.
Lawless, Séamus, Owen Conlan, and Cormac Hampson. 2016. "Tailoring Access to Content." In *A New Companion to Digital Humanities*, edited by Susan Schreibman, Ray Siemens, and John Unsworth, 171–84. Chichester and Malden, MA: Wiley.
Leximancer Pty Ltd. 2020. Brisbane, Australia. https://info.leximancer.com/science.
McCallum, Andrew Kachites. 2002. "MALLET: A Machine Learning for Language Toolkit." http://mallet.cs.umass.edu.
McKercher, Bob. 2002. "Towards a Classification of Cultural Tourists." *International Journal of Tourism Research* 4 (1): 29–38.
Meng, Alfred Pang Kah. 2004. "Making History in From Colony to Nation: A Multimodal Analysis of a Museum Exhibition in Singapore." In *Multimodal Discourse Analysis: Systemic Functional Perspectives*, edited by Kay L. O'Halloran, 28–54. London: Continuum.
Mokatren, Moayad, Veronika Bogina, Alan Wecker, and Tsvi Kuflik. 2019. "A Museum Visitors Classification Based on Behavioral and Demographic Features." In *Adjunct Publication of the 27th Conference on User Modeling, Adaptation and Personalization*, 383–86. New York, NY: Association for Computing Machinery.
Moretti, Franco. 2013. *Distant Reading*. Verso Books.
Nielsen, Jane K. 2017. "Museum Communication and Storytelling: Articulating Understandings Within the Museum Structure." *Museum Management and Curatorship* 32 (5): 440–55.
Nisi, Valentina, Ian Oakley, and Mads Haahr. 2008. "Location-Aware Multimedia Stories: Turning Spaces into Places." *Universidade Católica Portuguesa*: 72–93.

Nuryanti, Wiendu. 1996. "Heritage and Postmodern Tourism." *Annals of Tourism Research* 23 (2): 249–60.

O'Halloran, Kay L., Sabine Tan, Duc-Son Pham, John Bateman, and Andrew Vande Moere. 2018. "A Digital Mixed Methods Research Design: Integrating Multimodal Analysis with Data Mining and Information Visualization for Big Data Analytics." *Journal of Mixed Methods Research* 12 (1): 11–30.

O'Halloran, Kay L., Sabine Tan, Peter Wignell, John A. Bateman, Duc-Son Pham, Michele Grossman, and Andrew Vande Moere. 2019. "Interpreting Text and Image Relations in Violent Extremist Discourse: A Mixed Methods Approach for Big Data Analytics." *Terrorism and Political Violence* 31 (3): 454–74.

PARTHENOS Training Suite. n.d. https://training.parthenos-project.eu/sample-page/citizen-science-in-the-digital-arts-and-humanities/.

Paterson, Natasa, Gavin Kearney, Katsiaryna Naliuka, Tara Carrigy, Mads Haahr, and Fionnuala Conway. 2013. "Viking Ghost Hunt: Creating Engaging Sound Design for Location–Aware Applications." *International Journal of Arts and Technology* 6 (1): 61–82.

Ramires, Ana, Filipa Brandao, and Ana Cristina Sousa. 2018. "Motivation-Based Cluster Analysis of International Tourists Visiting a World Heritage City: The Case of Porto, Portugal." *Journal of Destination Marketing & Management* 8: 49–60.

Rowan, Leonie, Geraldine Townend, Catherine Beavis, Lynda Kelly, and Jeffrey Fletcher. 2016. "Museums, Games, and Historical Imagination: Student Responses to a Games-Based Experience at the Australian National Maritime Museum." *Digital Culture and Education* 8 (3): 169–87.

Sánchez-Mesa, Domingo, Espen Aarseth, Robert Pratten, and Carlos A. Scolari. 2016. "Transmedia (Storytelling?): A Polyphonic Critical Review." *Artnodes* 18. https://doi.org/10.7238/a.v0i18.3064.

Schreibman, Susan, Vinayak Das Gupta, and Neale Rooney. 2017. "Notes from the Transcription Desk: Visualising Public Engagement." *English Studies* 98 (5): 506–25.

Silberman, Neil, and Margaret Purser. 2012. "Collective Memory as Affirmation: People-Centered Cultural Heritage in a Digital Age." In *Heritage and Social Media: Understanding Heritage in a Participatory Culture*, edited by Elisa Giaccardi, 13–39. New York: Routledge.

Sinclair, Stéfan, and Geoffrey Rockwell. 2015. "Text Analysis and Visualization: Making Meaning Count." In *A New Companion to Digital Humanities*, edited by Susan Schreibman, Ray Siemens, and John Unsworth, 274–90. Chichester and Malden, MA: Wiley.

Sinclair, Stéfan, and Geoffrey Rockwell. 2016. *Voyant Tools*. http://voyant-tools.org/.

Styliani, Sylaiou, Liarokapis Fotis, Kotsakis Kostas, and Patias Petros. 2009. "Virtual Museums, a Survey and Some Issues for Consideration." *Journal of Cultural Heritage* 10 (4): 520–28.

Tammaro, Anna Maria. 2016. "Participatory Approaches and Innovation in Galleries, Libraries, Archives, and Museums." *International Information & Library Review* 48 (1): 37–44.

Trunfio, Mariapina, Adele Magnelli, Maria Della Lucia, Giovanni Verreschi, and Salvatore Campana. 2018. "Augmented and Virtual Reality in Cultural Heritage: Enhancing the Visitor Experience and Satisfaction at the Area Pacis Museum in

Rome, Italy." In *8th Advances in Hospitality and Tourism Marketing and Management (AHTMM) Conference*, 662–74. http://www.ahtmm.com/wp-content/uploads/2018-8th_AHTMM_proceedings_2018_1.pdf.

White, Hayden. 1986. "Historical Pluralism." *Critical Inquiry* 12 (3): 480–93.

White, Hayden. 2000. *Figural Realism: Studies in the Mimesis Effect*. Baltimore, MD: Johns Hopkins University Press.

Xu, Feifei, Dimitrios Buhalis, and Jessika Weber. 2017. "Serious Games and the Gamification of Tourism." *Tourism Management* 60: 244–56.

YaleDHlab. 2018. *PixPlot*. Yale University. https://github.com/YaleDHLab/pixplot.

CHAPTER 19

"People Inside": Creating Digital Community Projects on the *YARN* Platform

Simon Popple and Jenna Ng

19.1 Introduction

We have taken inspiration from Imran Ali's characterization of the human element that was central to the process of co-producing our *YARN* platform: "As technology companies tout their inventions as having Intel inside, or being data-driven, we loved saying with confidence that *YARN* was story-driven with People Inside" (Ali 2021). The notion of "People Inside" drove our creative and intellectual processes, and built the conceptual foundations of two formative projects as delivered by a team of researchers at the Universities of Leeds and York, and led by the first author between 2013 and 2018. Both projects were funded by the Arts and Humanities Research Council (AHRC). The first project, *Pararchive: Open Access Community Storytelling and the Digital Archive* (2013–2015), explored digital tools, archives and storytelling. The second follow-on project, *Digital Community Workspaces: Delivering Impact Through Public Library and Archive Networks* (2017–2018), sought to apply the tools and develop impact directly in local communities through the local library and archival hubs. It particularly focussed on marginalized, isolated and underrepresented communities.

S. Popple
University of Leeds, Leeds, UK
e-mail: S.E.Popple@leeds.ac.uk

J. Ng (✉)
University of York, York, UK
e-mail: jenna.ng@york.ac.uk

The inspiration for both projects came from previous research with communities involved in the 1984–1985 Miners' Strike.[1] As part of that research, the first author worked with the BBC's news archive to produce counter-narratives that provided community perspectives and insights missing from the main corpus of the archive (Buchanan and Bastian 2015; Popple 2015). These stories were produced as a total of ten short self-directed films.[2] Everyone realized that these films represented an important set of practices which demonstrated both the desire and innate capacity of communities to take control of their own histories and challenge dominant narratives and media stereotypes (Flinn 2010; Ridge 2014). However, the opportunities to do so were limited and privileged as film-making was only available to a core number of participants. What was needed was a set of digital tools that could provide the whole community with similar opportunities. Such tools would afford them the opportunity to bring to bear ideas of local identity and democracy, community histories, and specific issues around gender and media practices. For instance, *We Are Women, We Are Strong* (2009) examined the experiences of women involved in the Women Against Pit Closures movement. The lacunae of such tools also represented the community's desire to respond to top-down depositories of narratives, such as the BBC news archive, and postulated a new counter-archive of digital stories and testimony. As Caswell notes, a move towards the community archive comes from the need to make archives "for the people, by the people, that often eliminate the traditional middlemen of the professional archivist and university or government repository" (Caswell 2014, 32).

The first *Pararchive* project (https://pararchive.com/) enabled the researchers to co-design and implement such a set of community digital storytelling tools. Through a series of iterative learning out of practice and co-production workshops, the research allowed project partners to co-design a digital resource for users to tell their stories and create new collaborative archives (Popple and Mutibwa 2016). This resource was launched as *YARN* (www.yarncommunity.org) in 2015 and further developed in the *Digital Community Workspaces* project in 2017. The *YARN* project partnered with four public library and archive organizations based in the Isle of Bute in Scotland, and York, Leeds and Wakefield in England to engage their local communities in digital projects with local cultural heritage resources. *YARN* has consequently also responded to a variety of community needs and institutional aspirations, including difficult self-identified issues such as local history work, genealogy, co-working, publishing, and working with disadvantaged and hard to reach audiences, as well as with "hidden" or degraded digital resources. The outputs manifested as a range of stories published on the *YARN* platform which reflect not only a community's ties, but also its cultural identity, histories and heritage. The platform has subsequently been adapted and adopted by a range of community projects and ongoing AHRC-funded research to provide bespoke resources for co-produced research.[3]

In this chapter, we will discuss and reflect on our engagement with and consideration of the communities with whom we worked across these projects. In particular, we will focus on the process and reflections of involving the community in research across two main thematic strands:

(i) engaging and working with the community as part of a research "public" to create a platform suited for them; and
(ii) creating a resource with and for the community that interweaves the logic of database and narratives to best meet their needs and support their unique modes of engagement and storytelling.

Through these reflections, we hope to add two corresponding strands to the conversation. The first is a demonstrated approach to community research and engagement with them. The second is to illustrate the vacillation of a digital tool between its functions of storytelling and repository, and thinking through what that ambiguity implies for communities with unique needs and means of engagement.[4] Weaving lessons from the two strands, we will also present an experience-based toolkit on researching with communities which reflects the lessons of our engagement, including problems and their solutions. We hope the toolkit will benefit other researchers on community-based projects.

19.2 Co-Creation and Engagement: Diverse Communities on the Research Projects

The first aim of the *Pararchive* project was to get a foundational sense of what communities wanted and needed for their research/storytelling practices, and to understand the best means of achieving a co-produced specification for the platform (Lambert 2013). We wanted to eschew established design studio approaches to client-led development and evaluation, and innovate honorific methods of working together (Kimbell 2011). As lead designer Imran Ali noted, co-production was about turning such principles on their head and designing for small and intimate sets of groups on a case-by-case basis. The resulting aggregation of models, principles and practices would then be used to orchestrate the final digital resource. As Ali (2021) noted:

> *YARN* was a step change for our company in how we'd usually conceive of a digital product. Though we're very familiar with co-design practices and creating architectures of participation, they're generally conducted at a scale of millions of users and usually remotely and as abstract personas.

In the course of our research, there was an implicit recognition of the varied and often contradictory needs and frameworks that needed to be addressed. Unlike a commercial approach to digital design, *YARN* users were putative clients and not excluded from most of the developmental stages of digital innovation. In the standard design studio model, the usability and iterative testing and evaluation phases come much later in the process, with the often-untested assumption that such tools are easily translated, scalable and operationalized for commercial contexts (Kerridge and Michael 2018). However, more recent critical commentaries suggest otherwise (Tsing 2004, 2015). Moreover, specific socio-cultural contexts need to be foregrounded and tested. One size does not fit all. The specificity of what we were going to produce together had to be reflective of all partners, and thus sensitive and reflexive in nature.

The rationale of our approach was based on a primary recognition that the idea of community is a complex and non-homogenous entity—a moving and unfolding set of "publics" who coalesce around contexts of location, affinity and challenge. No one community is alike, and we wanted to draw on a pluralistic range of contexts, traditions and expertise. Our sense here of the diversity of community or publics similarly resonates with others' views and definitions. For example, Warner (2002, 10) writes of how a public "is to be a certain kind of person, to inhabit a certain kind of social world, to have at one's disposal certain media and genres, to be motivated by a certain normative horizon, and to speak within a certain language ideology." He thus recommends adopting a strongly historical approach to understanding the public and the "preconditions of its intelligibility" (2002, 9). In more nuanced terms, Delanty (2010) highlights ambivalence in the idea of community between the local against the universal. In a more traditional sense, the community exists as the bonds which unite particular, immediate social relations (Tönnies 1963). Yet in "other and more post-traditional forms," community pushes "an expression of global humanity" (Tönnies 1963, 5). As such, our approach to our communities similarly took on these tensions in covering the diverse values and contradictory temperaments inherent in its concept. As a result, we were conscious that our engagement with and designs for them also as a whole has implicit ethical and operational consequences (Denison and Stillman 2012).

To incorporate a broad range of experience, digital literacies and practice traditions from each group, we adapted an Action Research-based methodology (Burns 2007; Hacker 2013). The resulting variant, Community Based Participatory Action Research (CBPAR), is founded on an iterative series of engagements with partners to undertake four steps (see also Popple and Mutibwa 2016). The first involves discussion of the research itself, inviting participants to identify what they want from the process (in terms of tools, functions and needs); frame the important questions and consider what they want to work on (see Fig. 19.1). The second involves making with developers and designers (modelling; specification writing; prototyping). The third is a reflective stage where what has been achieved in step two is considered. The fourth is a planning stage that leads into the next iteration of the cycle (Fig. 19.2). The cycle can be repeated a number of times to refine and develop ideas as well as build consensus about the value of the tool and its functionality. Hence, the core processes were aimed at involving all partners in ongoing iterations of research questions, ideas and practical explorations of storytelling, research traditions and possible digital models.

Fig. 19.1 Discussions with the Isle of Bute Rothesay library community group

Fig. 19.2 Collage of post-it notes, workshops and sketches of discussion, planning and reiteration

The process of listening and cycles of mutually beneficial exploration centred on action research models fostered a core process of learning through collective "doing." Being able to participate in the production of a specification for a digital platform developed skills and confidence. Its iterative process allowed for ideas and learning to run at a mutually defined rate. The CBPAR approach also established equanimity within and between participant groups, and allowed parallel paths to be followed (Kindon et al. 2007). At all stages, we were guided by the sense that we wanted to avoid the imposition of a hierarchy in working sessions in the collective research team (Janes 2015). Our developers noted how they stepped back rather than controlled or managed the process or dictated the output. They saw themselves as facilitators rather than instigators. As Ali (2021) noted:

> With *Yarn*, we had the privilege of working with just dozens of people, whom we could understand as whole people, not just personas and archetypes. Listening to and hearing their fears, hopes and aspirations, inhabiting their lives with them gave us a new and very human design material... people.

The CBPAR method also allowed us to reflect on the scale and dynamics of the groups with whom we were working. It enabled us to challenge a commercial "imaginary" with the multiple realities on the ground and in sync with the intent to evolve tools and approaches that were applicable across a range of contexts and could meet multiple needs. The action research-based approach meant that each of the partner communities was focussed explicitly on their own interests and needs. For example, one group based in and around Stoke-on-Trent had a strong interest in the pottery industry that had dominated their city. It had left a legacy of industrial pride, aesthetically beautiful artefacts, and ongoing pollution and health conditions. Calling themselves Ceramic City Stories, in participating in our projects they wanted to focus on these aspects of their history, drawing on their own knowledge and experiences. They possessed their own archives, but also wanted to link with national collections such as those curated by the Science Museum. As a result, we were able to apply for separate funding to follow this specific interest and work with the Science Museum to provide access and to build experimental digital models of the stores that communities could visit remotely.[5] That follow-on project, *Science Museum: Community-in-Residence*, thus allowed the group to address their specific concerns, follow their passions and build their own projects in parallel to our research (Mutibwa et al. 2020). In that respect, our CBPAR approach led to developing communities' confidence and spurred additional activities as the groups evolved and deepened their individual interests, and eventually enabled them to work outside the main strands of the projects.

Similarly, our partners on the Isle of Bute developed interests out of our projects in local heritage, as well as the broader economic regeneration of the island's tourist economy and the role of digital infrastructure to enable connectivity and foster online activities. To investigate more on the roles of digital infrastructure, adoption and literacies, we secured funding for a complementary project called *Island Stories* (2014) to explore perceptions of the island's digital infrastructure at that time and the central role of heritage as part of a regeneration strategy (Duffy and Popple 2017). The *Island Stories* project was also revealing in highlighting the difficulties of engaging every participant in common purpose projects. It showed the breadth of interests and personal motivations for taking part. As part of a survey conducted during the project, all 57 respondents said they were interested in local heritage—seemingly an indicator of common purpose. However, when further asked about their specific interests, the same sample identified a total of 31 unique foci. This breadth of interests clearly signalled the individuated investment in the locality as a source of inspiration, and further evidenced the capabilities of digital resources to resolve and allow individual as well as collective projects.

We further realized that participation was often contingent on specific needs related to the interests and expertise of partners. As Paul Duffy, our community organizer on the Isle of Bute, noted, "only half of the research topics studied as part of the project became digital *YARN*s, with the other participants choosing to disseminate their stories through traditional formats and forums" (Duffy 2020, 60). Many of these were digital platforms such as Facebook which was dominant on the island. This realization disrupted our sense of what the issues with digital inclusivity fully entailed, and that self-exclusion was a factor we had not considered. The lesson here was thus for us to listen and not presume that certain practices might be preferable.

What emerged from these experiences out of the two projects were a series of individuated foci and approaches, independent iterations and different models of doing things that were used to build and test the digital platform. The insights were so rich that we could not incorporate all of them into prototypes. Rather, there was a collective recognition that we needed to boil down the various features we felt important to develop. For example, while some participants were using other forms of digital platforms to distribute their research and stories, others keenly felt that they did not want the platform to resemble social media. The compromise was that stories could be tweeted following publication. Copyright was another important theme that permeated projects and played out through discussion and modelling. There was a strong feeling that people did not want to lose control of their own material, and simply give it away online. Similarly, they wanted to be able to use other people's content without fear of breaking copyright. We reconciled these two concerns by deciding not to build a repository as part of the platform. Instead, the platform would feature hyperlinks from other hosting sites to aggregate online content. In so doing, we also recognized a compromise that meant stories and research were ephemeral and subject to loss as they depended on the stabilities of the original hosting sites.

Moreover, on one hand, explorations allowed for multiple iterations of the research questions through a range of expanding projects—the more partners, the more input. On the other hand, we had to accept a competing plurality of opinions and recognition that user-centred design is honorific but risky. The range of opinions, different needs and conflicting positions on issues such as ownership and control certainly complicated the developmental process. However, in a community context, it is demonstrably a moral and ethical imperative to embrace complexity and recognize that not everyone can be satisfied (Banks et al. 2013).

Our experiences of working with partners in Stoke-on-Trent and on the Isle of Bute are emblematic of the many communities we worked with on the projects, and illustrate the specificities of each's context, tradition and set of needs and aspirations. They do not represent finite or definitive lessons in how to proceed, but add to the sum of knowledge on how to approach community-based digital projects. The underpinning platform was thus both the product of collaboration, and a resource for future collaborations crossing communities, individuals and organizations. Indeed, one of its ongoing aims is to continue to foster genuinely meaningful relationships between institutions of all scales and the general public, and engender a series of ongoing projects and dialogues.[6]

19.3 Storage and Narrative: "Publics" Globally Across the Digital Database

The *YARN* project's second major aim of engaging with the publics was to create a *grassroots database of narratives*. In this sense, the public become both producers and custodians, as reflected in its central tagline: "Make, share and connect stories with things on the web" (Fig. 19.3). Hence, the *YARN* resource is, firstly, a storytelling *tool* as a processual platform with prompts on its interface for the user to build their narrative, and which enables uploads of text and media onto the Web. At the same time, the resource is also an organized *database* that contains the community's collection of stories and digital media, searchable through query fields of projects, contributors, times and media assets.

YARN thus converges two key and competing forms of cultural expressions: *narrative* and *database*. On one hand, they stand across contrasting binaries: one ancient, the other relatively recent; one of the symbolic systems of writing and the image, the other of the computer; one ephemeral, the other for the futurity of reference and search. But they are also reconcilable: both are cultural forms with which to present models of each community's world; both give voice to their stories and lives. The idea of the "public" which the project serves thus interweaves between the community that tells, creates and leaves traces of their existence and belonging; and the community which refers to, searches, consults and retrieves the building blocks of the community's narratives, histories and memories as their collective stories. The illustrations through *YARN* and implications of such imbrication will be discussed throughout this section.

Fig. 19.3 YARN's landing page

This convergence of database and narrative in relation to new media is not new. The database features in much of new media, starting from CD-ROMs as storage media to webpages as collections of disparate elements, such as text, images, videos and hyperlinks. However, online databases, by being relatively more accessible, have also begun to adopt collective storytelling, aligning with other common digital practices such as remix, mashups and fan fiction. Recent examples of online storytelling databases include Cowbird (https://cowbird.com; still accessible, though now inactive and no longer accepting any more contributions), which holds a self-proclaimed "87,891 stories on 28,107 topics from 14,574 authors in 186 countries." Most are vignettes of text and images which the viewer selects and navigates at will. Another example is the Atlas of the Civic Imagination (https://www.ciatlas.org/). Its website invites the sharing of stories and experiences: "Our goal here is to *make the stories that inspire the imagination visible* and through this encourage conversation, creativity and action" [Emphasis added]. Both examples are not only databases in terms of structured and searchable collections. They are also collections formed by the public as internet users who subscribe to the collections' aims and contribute their labours to it—indeed, bringing it into existence—while at the same time used as a storytelling tool. The databases' aims tend to be noble and idealistic. Cowbird self-bills as a "public library of human experience"; the Atlas springboards off its mother project, the Civic Imagination Project, and asks for contributions to "[tap] the civic imagination," or "our collective vision for what a better tomorrow might look like" so as "to bridge perceived cultural gaps between diverse communities." Wrapped in this rhetoric of "public library" and "collective vision" is likewise the competing, yet paradoxically complementary, logics of narrative and database—of story and collection—which weave through their warp and weft.

Democratization of culture in the participatory nature of digital interactivity thus overarches the twin logics of narrative and database. Mainstream and mobile Internet access further extends interactivity to the wider Web-using public. What emerges is not only a user's unique formation of a story, but also potential for civic engagement and persuasion (Nash 2014). Interweaving between database and narrative is thus also the politics of participation which colours the notion of the public: they are not only creators and producers with agency, but also the complicit drivers of the ideology of interactivity as the politics for change.

Turning to *YARN*, we now describe two contrasting engagements with partner communities who worked with us on the project as illustrations of its competing logics of database and narrative. The first is the project team's engagement with the Chinese community in Leeds as a sub-project to build on existing local history resources held by the Leeds City Library and Archives. The aim was to develop new user communities within Leeds drawn from isolated or hard to reach groups. Leeds is home to one of the largest Chinese populations in the UK: 1.5% of all Chinese people in the UK live in Leeds, compared to 3.4% in Manchester as the city with the largest proportion (Gov.uk 2020, n.p.). However, by the Leeds City Library's own admission, the community is not very well represented in its archives. This is despite the UK registering high growth rates of different kinds of Chinese migrants. These range from students in UK higher education to "highly skilled migrants" who enter the UK under its points-based system of border control to high-net-worth, central-London-residing individuals (Knowles 2015). The motivation of engaging with this community via *YARN* was to give the community a space for representation, and for *YARN* to be a tool for its stories. Our primary community partner was the Leeds Chinese Community School (LCCS), where we held two *YARN* workshops for their members to share stories on living in Leeds or the UK.

Notably, the community did not extensively adopt *YARN* as a storytelling tool, so not many stories emerged from the community on the platform. Rather, *YARN* developed for this community in two other ways. Firstly, the Leeds City Library deposited onto *YARN* a number of media assets, such as scanned photographs of historic playbills which alluded to Chinese events and culture at Leeds. Examples include "Chinese Entertainment" consisting of juggling, acrobatic tricks, fire eating and advertisements of Chinese comic opera and magic shows. Scans of census records, some from 1911, were also uploaded with highlighted notes of Leeds Chinese residents' details, such as their occupations, birthplace and age. Historic photographs, particularly of Chinese businesses in the city, were also posted, alongside comments by Leeds residents relating their memories of those businesses, such as meals at restaurants. The logic of the resource as a depository here is clarion, particularly in terms of widening accessibility to these records out of the Leeds library, which are otherwise visible only on a physical visit to its archives.

Secondly, stories which we did succeed in soliciting from members of the LCCS proved to be fleeting. Brief accounts were given on how current community members stay in touch with their families in China; some concise stories were also offered on how members' families had arrived in the UK. Other stories took the form of brief comments and observations, such as this one by a resident: "My Dad's takeaway was closed on Sundays and the community used to get together. It feels like everyone knew each other back then" (http://yarncommunity.org/stories/585). Other comments noted how "Leeds's Chinese community lacked cohesion and a sense of shared identity when compared to other Northern cities such as Manchester and Liverpool." While these observations might not appear to be in the form of a conventional story, we also take for these purposes Georgakopoulou's (2017) argument of how "sharing stories out of the moment"—in terms of small, fragmented open-ended tellings—may become what she calls, albeit in the context of social media, the taking of a narrative stance. Nevertheless, even in these fragmented, stance-like instantiations, the stories were not formally documented or recorded on the *YARN* resource. Ultimately, their stories at the workshops were collected by the researchers and logged onto *YARN* as recollections related to them. Longer stories and accounts via interviews with a few individuals in connection to the LCCS were also collected, recorded and set to a film, directed by Leeds researcher Michael Schofield and posted onto *YARN*. In light of such use, *YARN* functioned more effectively as an archive than a tool, particularly as a live collection of small fleeting moments which proved difficult to pin down from the community, be that due to a reluctance to engage with the technology, or simply that migrants' stories, while rich and eventful, in themselves tend to be fleeting and ephemeral. After all, these are stories of journeys, and invariably about passing, transition, adaptation and assimilation.

The Leeds Chinese community's engagement with *YARN* may be contrasted against another sub-project: the 60th anniversary in 2017 of the twinning of York and Münster, cities in North East UK and North West Germany, respectively. The anniversary's timing fell fortuitously at the outset of the *YARN* project. The project partner was Explore York, an integrated library, archive and museum. Our common interest was in exploring the potential of creating narratives on a digital resource out of digitized materials from Explore York collections for York communities. At this point, the *YARN* resource was still operating along the logic of the database, with concern on the accessibility of archival resources for the community.

However, what emerged on *YARN* in relation to the York-Münster twinning anniversary were numerous stories and reminiscences out of the twinning, primarily from three associations: the York-Münster Association; Explore York Archives; and Rotary York-Ainsty (which was twinned with the Rotary Club of Münster St. Mauritz, and therefore host to a similar UK–Germany relationship). Stories from all three sources related visits to each other's cities, and reflections on the meaning of their associations' long international and intercultural friendships and relationships. The stories were usually recorded in written text, but there were also a number of voice-only recordings. One poignant example is by Dennis Miller, a long-time York Rotarian, who spoke of his first visit to Münster with his wife, during which they received news of the birth of their first grandchild on the morning after their arrival. That day also happened to be their host's birthday. Their hosts then sang a song for Dennis and his wife at a formal dinner that evening to celebrate their grandchild's birth. As Dennis recalled, "I have no idea what the words were!" (https://yarncommunity.org/stories/479). Another lengthy story was posted onto *YARN* by the secretary of the York-Münster Twinning Association relating how they had visited Münster for the first time in 2012. It was a story consisting of many memories, personal associations (such as family connections to Germany) and photographs taken of sights in the city, such as the Prinzipalmarkt, St. Paulus Dom, the townhall and the Stumble Stones to commemorate the residences of Jewish victims of the Nazi regime (https://yarncommunity. org/stories/447). Janet Robinson, another York Rotarian, described a school trip to Münster she had taken in 1960 to visit a pen-friend in Münster. Part of her story contained a remarkable photograph of the school group as assembled at York station in their school uniforms and alongside their teacher, Mrs. Jones, and their luggage trunks (https://yarncommunity.org/stories/484).

In this case, *YARN* was not only a site for hosting the stories, but also a resource tool for producing them. The logic of narrative is clearly deployed here through the formation and appearance of the story in accordance with *YARN*'s narrative-specific interface. This interface specifically prompts the user to relate their story through blocks of story "passages," including descriptions of events as well as the inclusion of media assets such as voice recording, personal photographs and text. Almost all of the *YARN* stories related on the twinning anniversary were of nostalgia and numerous personal memories, perhaps as a direct result of the occasion of its 60th anniversary. Only a couple of stories, such as those by Explore York Archives, were deposits of archival collections. One of these was scans of the first letter of invitation from Münster's *Oberbürgermeister* (mayor) through the UK Foreign Office inviting a civic delegation from York to visit Münster in May 1957. Another was the itinerary of the civic delegation from Münster to York in July 1957 (which included a visit to and tour of Rowntree's Cocoa and Chocolate Works!). Otherwise, the stories as told through *YARN* took on a narrative logic which reflected numerous personal voices, sometimes literally so in the form of audio recordings of a verbal account. The poignancy of these personal stories is resonant in conveying the sense of living memories, alive only with the people who had undergone and experienced them in their time, and which will also soon vanish with their passing. The personal voices of the narratives through *YARN* in this case thus take on an emotional heft that is larger than the story itself—the narrative here is also of life itself and the very passing of lived time in an accumulated form as accentuated by the database. These are stories with unmistakable personal resonance. Through the resources on which they were produced, these stories interweave both logics of narrative and database.

Database and narrative are thus two competing imaginations which shape and form the *YARN* resource. This contrast, in turn, reflects the encounters of the community with the digital resource in terms of how they take (or do not take) to it, as well as their engagement with their own stories as a whole. But engagement with the public humanities along these strands of logic also carries its own hazards. For instance, in terms of narrative, the resource becomes an open work (Eco 1989), whose interactive nature privileges the individual voice even as it mirrors the loss of narrative authority, such as from an institution. The result of such open-endedness is likely to be a cacophony of babel, if at least authentic in its chaos. By virtue of such engagement, the contingency and indeterminate nature of narrative might just have to be the language of the public humanities. Conversely, in terms of the database, a similar chaos appears as the vulnerabilities of a grassroots digital database are laid bare. For instance, all media assets have to be uploaded onto alternative platforms, such as YouTube or Vimeo (for videos); Flickr (for images) and Soundcloud (for sound files). This dependency also renders the assets extremely vulnerable, where links break or are taken down by the original owner or even the platform. Files are also constantly subject to copyright issues. The database of the public humanities thus also has to contend with the contingency of the ephemera that defines the digital—it is part of the nature of the beast.

19.4 Toolkit/Core Principles for Community-Based Research

Drawing together what we have learned from these and other strands of related research, we collate here a set of governing principles based on experience that may guide colleagues in their approach to digital co-production and collaborative working. These are by no means comprehensive; we continue to learn and evaluate what we do and refine approaches accordingly. Rather, we present them as a starting point from which to develop the specific parameters of future projects.

19.4.1 Recognize the Complexities of Managing Relationships with the Community

Firstly, engagement with the publics in research requires skill and understanding of managing relationships with communities. Such understanding comes through negotiation and jointly evolving strategies for managing research. Methods and approaches often emerged through working together, and we learnt to adapt and respond to ideas and concerns as part of our working relationships. For example, in the early stages of research, it is important to allow time for getting to know each other and hearing about the interests and traditions within partner communities. We also advocate and take responsibility for using languages of inclusion, and of parity of contribution and opinion. We use language that is open and accessible, mutually determined and non-specialist. For example, we decided against the standard term "tag" on the platform as there was a sense that people wanted to distance themselves from the modalities of social media. Instead, we used the alternatively agreed term of "people" as that felt more natural. We also feel it is important to begin all projects by discussing practices and traditions, and not assume what people want or need. Recognize iniquity and be open about how far you can adjust to the partner's participations, with equal value attached no matter how partial or limited.

It is also crucial to provide resources and skills building for participants. These skills may be in digital terms, such as the workshops held on the use of *YARN*. They may also be non-digital skills, such as accessing archives and reading resources together. At the same time, engagement with the community, as much as it is about providing for them, is also about letting them have a space. As mentioned, the biggest risk we faced was pre-judgement of what our participants might want and to model idealized communities that we were going to support through a digital design and evaluation process. We were constantly surprised and occasionally confounded by our partners, and quickly learnt to be guided by them. Our best engagements with the communities came about by simply listening to them and their concerns, and trusting their expertise. We stayed alert to not "governing" or imposing on them our ideas of what the project is or which directions it should take.

At the same time, it is also important to understand when to let go as communities develop in their own natural ways which may or may not be in alignment with the continued aims of the project. We learnt to worry increasingly less about the framework we had devised in the funding phase and plans of work. We certainly found this gradual release liberating, although difficult in the initial phases. Yet as we recognized and embraced the complexities of our groups, each with their own dynamics, we quickly rejected our preconceived ideas of community in favour of emergent ideas which began to coalesce around what was needed for the project.

In these respects, we feel it is easier to think of a complex range of constituencies or publics in terms of affinity (as based on the community's broad shared values) and interests, rather than a homogeneous notion of community. The distinction is important because it helps to better frame the motivations for engaging in projects, working together and then disengaging with them. These distinctions became apparent from the outset of the first project as the tensions between what were seen as broad community wants conflicted with individual or small group public needs, such as around political positioning or media frames (see also Bailey and Popple 2011). The means of engagement are often circumstantial, at best fortuitous and always organic.

19.4.2   Co-Produce Research Questions and Consult on Methods That Are Practicable

Much of the two projects was conducted by way of co-creating the digital resource with the partner communities through workshops, as well as more formal sessions such as project meetings and conferences. Trust is critical in this process. The communities should genuinely subscribe to the projects' aims and believe they have an integral stake in them and in the achievements of the projects, rather than feel they are mere participants in the work from whom the researchers draw data. The integrity in this regard of the *Pararchive* and *YARN* projects as "bottom-up" research work was thus paramount to the researchers. It was an issue that we always took care and time to explain. The communities' feedback was also always taken seriously, as was debriefing, usually by way of a project closing conference. This is so for the communities to see and understand their impact on the project and to reinforce trust and shared purpose.

Crucial to the success of this approach is the need for agreement on the objects of research. These discussions should then be turned into a series of core research questions that avoid isolating academic terms and that are clearly related to the methods to be used. For instance, do not talk about "data" in an abstracted research context. Rather, explain how you are going to explore the questions together, how you are going to work on the problems identified in the questions and how you are going to approach them through the activities you are doing together.

19.4.3   Allow Things to Go Wrong and Embrace Failures

Virtually all projects will go wrong in some way. Where engagement with communities are concerned, much of that engagement may be unpredictable and subject to going astray. Nevertheless, it is important to recognize that there is value in the dead ends of the project. Those dead ends will carry significance, if sometimes retrospectively. One example for us is our engagement with the Chinese community in Leeds. While not as engaged in the ways which we had hoped and anticipated, it nevertheless showed us new and illuminating aspects of the *YARN* resource. Back-up plans also help, as does a willingness to change perspective and review the results which emerge and the direction which the project has taken.

The key is to understand that working with publics always involves a degree of organic flexibility in terms of how and in what ways these groups engage with the research. Be open to the project's flux and flexes. The ability to commit time and sustain activities is often difficult for people, and flexibility is essential. Do appreciate that all participation is valuable.

19.4.4 Recognize the Limitations of Working with Large Institutions in a Community Context

A number of our partners for both projects were large institutions, such as the BBC and the Science Museum in London. The original collaboration had been to produce creative links to these institutions' archives, whose materials were otherwise relatively constrained on how they can be used. We were all intrigued and excited by the potential of unique stories to emerge from such institutional material.

However, what transpired were clear limitations under which these institutions operated, where decision-making was labyrinthine, staff was over-committed and action was difficult to drive. In the end, the collaboration was considerably different from what was originally intended, which in turn affected the scope of what we wanted to achieve on the projects. The lesson learnt, then, is to have a clear understanding of how a large partner institution works and to appreciate the limitations of working with them. Be prepared to adapt activities and the scale of the project. It is easy to get carried away with the opportunities and glamour of what can be achieved with such high-profile partnerships. Making them work practically on the ground is sometimes another matter.

19.4.5 Build Trust, Relationships and Legacy

Of critical importance was the project's relationships with its various stakeholders, such as project partner institutions and communities. Relationships within the research team, made up of members from different institutions, were also significant. Again, trust was paramount throughout the relationships in both projects. In trust also lay the belief that every member would make a valuable contribution to the project, even if it was not immediately apparent. At the end of the day, it was this virtuous cycle of trust, value and shared purpose which enabled both projects to operate smoothly and productively. The most important element in the process of building relationships is time. These were relationships which took time, effort and engagement to build and maintain. There is no shortcut. Through dialogue, workshops, constructive engagement, verbal and non-verbal appreciations of community input and continuing conversations about the project and its aims, the researchers built the relationships of trust, ownership and belief which turned out to be crucial in powering the project and enabling the work to be done.

What was also of huge benefit to the project teams were continuing relationships and legacies which came out of it. These benefits took various forms, such as continuing collaboration. Even as we write this, members of the research team are still working with the project partners by way of other research grants and grant applications. Again, such continuation of relationships takes work and time, but as important is the fundamental sharing of purpose and beliefs from the project. Research engagement with the public thus requires this genuine communality across the work, where participation is more than just the contributions to the project but takes the form of a wider sense of shared purpose and mission.

19.5 Conclusion

As we slowly emerge from the Covid-19 pandemic and resume face-to-face research work with communities, we hope that these reflections will allow researchers to develop genuinely consequential partnerships with communities at the heart of research and its outcomes. We want this approach to drive and facilitate community research, including campaigning, innovating and using digital resources in experimental and surprising manners. In our own research, we use these lessons of community design processes to rethink what potential *YARN* has for other communities and what iterations of the platform are now possible. This is particularly important as universities seek to develop their civic missions and demonstrate the value of public partnerships (Hart et al. 2013).

There are already signs that experiences of lockdown and dislocation have engendered a more questioning and collaborative response to the ways in which we conduct digital research and how we see our research as challenging and changing. It has certainly tested commonly held assumptions such as that research should be "digital by default" and technologically driven. When our collective experience of online communications, social and professional interactions is evaluated, perhaps we can re-set our quest for universalist and ubiquitous digital solutions, and roll back to the particular and specific. We can start to really build with "People Inside."

Notes

1. See the AHRC funded project Open Archive: The Miners' Strike: A Case Study in Regional Context—(AH/H500030/1).
2. Branded as Strike Stories, the films can be accessed at https://ahc.leeds.ac.uk/media/dir-record/research-projects/356/strike-stories-opening-the-archives-on-the-miners-strike-1984-85.
3. See, for example, Fabulous Femininities (https://fabulousfemininities.co.uk/) and Impacts of Covid-19 (https://www.culturalvalue.org.uk/the-team/covid-19-research-project/).

4. The platform acts as a repository of the text and links produced by the user but does not act as a formal archive for digital objects. It works on hyperlinks to content.
5. The prototype store is accessible at http://tomjackson.photography/interactive/blythehouse.html?html5=prefer. A permanent library record of the 3D prototype can be viewed at http://dx.doi.org/10.17639/nott.339.
6. Some of these projects have had global reach, for example being involved in hosting community research film-making from an ongoing participatory arts project around preparedness for earthquakes in Chile. For an account of the research undertaken as part of the NERC Seismic Cities (2018) project in Chile, see Popple (2019).

References

Ali, Imran. 2021. "Interview with the Authors." Personal Interview. Leeds, June 15.

Bailey, Michael, and Popple, Simon. 2011. "The 1984/85 Miners' Strike: Re-Claiming Cultural Heritage." In *Heritage, Labour and the Working Classes*, edited by Laurajane Smith, Paul Shackel, and Gary Campbell, 19–33. London: Routledge.

Banks, Sarah, Andrea Armstrong, Kathleen Carter, Helen Graham, Peter Hayward, Alex Henry, Tessa Holland, et al. 2013. "Everyday Ethics in Community-Based Participatory Research." *Contemporary Social Sciences* 8 (3): 263–27.

Buchanan, Alexandrina, and Michelle Bastian. 2015. "Activating the Archive: Rethinking the Role of Traditional Archives for Local Activist Projects." *Archival Science* 15 (4): 429–51.

Burns, Danny. 2007. *Systemic Action Research: A Strategy for Whole System Change*. Bristol: Policy Press.

Caswell, Michelle. 2014. "Seeing Yourself in History: Community Archives and the Fight Against Symbolic Annihilation." *The Public Historian* 36 (4): 26–37.

Delanty, Gerard. 2010. *Community*. 2nd ed. London and New York: Routledge.

Denison, Tom, and Larry Stillman. 2012. "Academic and Ethical Challenges in Participatory Models of Community Research." *Information, Communication & Society* 15 (7): 1037–54.

Duffy, Paul R. J. 2020. "New Island Stories: Heritage, Archives, the Digital Environment and Community Regeneration." In *Communities, Archives and New Collaborative Practices*, edited by Simon Popple, Andrew Prescott, and Daniel H. Mutibwa, 53–64. Bristol: Policy Press.

Duffy, Paul R. J., and Simon Popple. 2017. "*Pararchive* and *Island Stories*: Collaborative Co-Design and Community Digital Heritage on the Isle of Bute." *Internet Archaeology* 46. https://intarch.ac.uk/journal/issue46/4/index.html. Last accessed 12 July 2021.

Eco, Umberto. 1989. *The Open Work*. Translated by Anna Cancogni. Cambridge, MA: Harvard University Press.

Flinn, Andrew. 2010. "Independent Community Archives and Community-Generated Content." *Convergence: The International Journal of Research into New Media Technologies* 16 (1): 39–51.

Georgakopoulou, Alexandra. 2017. "Sharing the Moment as Small Stories: The Interplay Between Practices and Affordances in the Social Media-Curation of Lives." *Narrative Inquiry* 27 (2): 311–33.

Gov.uk. 2020. "Chinese Ethnic Group: Facts and Figures." https://www.ethnicity-facts-figures.service.gov.uk/summaries/chinese-ethnic-group#population. Last accessed 12 July 2021.

Hacker, Karen. 2013. *Community-Based Participatory Research*. Thousand Oaks, CA: Sage.

Hart, Angie, Ceri Davies, Kim Aumann, Etienne Wenger, Kay Aranda, Becky Heaver, and David Wolff. 2013. "Mobilising Knowledge in Community-University Partnerships: What Does a Community of Practice Approach Contribute?" *Contemporary Social Science: Special Issue* 8 (3): 278–91.

Janes, Julia E. 2015. "Democratic Encounters? Epistemic Privilege, Power, and Community-Based Participatory Action Research." *Action Research*: 1–16 [online]. https://doi.org/10.1177/1476750315579129.

Kerridge, Tobie, and Mike Michael. 2018. "'Engaging With' and 'Engaged By': Publics and Communities, Design and Sociology." In *Energy Babble*, edited by Andy Boucher, Bill Gaver, Tobie Kerridge, Mike Michael, Liliana Ovalle, Matthew Plummer-Fernandez, and Alex Wilkie, 103–9. Manchester: Mattering Press.

Kimbell, Lucy. 2011. "Rethinking Design Thinking: Part I." *Design and Culture* 3 (3): 285–306. https://doi.org/https://doi.org/10.2752/175470811X13071166525216.

Kindon, Sara, Rachel Pain, and Mike Kesby, eds. 2007. *Participatory Action Research Approaches and Methods: Connecting People, Participation and Place*. London: Routledge.

Knowles, Caroline. 2015. "Who Are the New Chinese Migrants in the UK." *Runnymede*, April 2. https://www.runnymedetrust.org/blog/who-are-the-new-chinese-migrants-in-the-uk. Last accessed 12 July 2021.

Lambert, Joe. 2013. *Digital Storytelling: Capturing Lives, Creating Community*. 4th ed. London: Routledge.

Mutibwa, Daniel H., Alison Hess, and Tom Jackson. 2020. "Strokes of Serendipity: Community Co-Curation and Engagement with Digital Heritage." *Convergence: The International Journal of Research into New Media Technologies* 26 (1): 1–12.

Nash, Kate. 2014. "What Is Interactivity For? The Social Dimension of Webdocumentary Participation." *Continuum* 28 (3): 383–95.

Popple, Simon. 2015. "The New Reithians: *Pararchive* and Citizen Animateurs in the BBC Digital Archive." *Convergence: The International Journal of Research into New Media Technologies* 21 (1): 132–44.

Popple, Simon. 2019. "When Elvis Dances: Activating Community Knowledge in Chile." In *Participatory Arts in Participatory Development*, edited by Paul Cooke and Inés Souria-Turner, 89–104. London: Routledge.

Popple, Simon, and D. H. Mutibwa. 2016. "Tools You Can Trust? Co-Design in Community Heritage Work." In *Cultural Heritage in a Changing World*, edited by Karol Jan Borowiecki, Neil Forbes, and Antonella Fresa, 197–214. Open Access: Springer Verlag. https://doi.org/10.1007/978-3-319-29544-2.

Ridge, M. 2014. "Introduction." In *Crowdsourcing Our Cultural Heritage*, edited by M. Ridge, 1–14. Farnham: Ashgate.

Tönnies, Ferdinand. [1957] 1963. *Community and Society*. Translated by Charles P. Loomis. New York: Harper and Row.

Tsing, Anna. 2004. *Friction: An Ethnography of Global Connection*. Princeton, NJ: Princeton University Press.

Tsing, Anna. 2015. *The Mushroom at the End of the World: On the Possibility of Life in Capitalist Ruins*. Princeton, NJ: Princeton University Press.
Warner, Michael. 2002. *Publics and Counterpublics*. New York: Zone Books.

CHAPTER 20

3D Modelling of Heritage Objects: Representation, Engagement and Performativity of the Virtual Realm

Visa Immonen

20.1 Introduction: 3D Technology as a Cultural Phenomenon

3D modelling means the usage of computer-based tools to record a mathematical representation of any or all surfaces of a physical object (Dey 2018, 5), and such digitization of heritage objects has become a booming area of activity. Heritage institutions are digitizing sites and artefact collections, partly for research and preservation, partly for public engagement (King et al. 2016). 3D modelling, in addition to being incorporated into curatorial practices, important for its growing popularity, has enabled objects to be made available online. Not surprisingly, elementary 3D modelling is becoming part of the established skillset of many heritage professions.

In pace with the 3D modelling of heritage objects, academic inquiry has also become increasingly developed concerning digital models and their applications. Scholarship on 3D modelling tends to focus on finding technical solutions and best practices for digitization, as well as for storing and using models at heritage institutions. Such technically oriented scrutiny is crucial for the efficient use of the technology. Equally important, however, is the analysis of the cultural and theoretical implications of 3D digitization for which the fundamental issue is the relationship between 3D models and heritage. Digital technologies are shaping the ways in which we interact with heritage objects,

V. Immonen (✉)
University of Bergen, Bergen, Finland
e-mail: visa.immonen@uib.no

© The Author(s), under exclusive license to Springer Nature Switzerland AG 2022
A. Schwan and T. Thomson (eds.), *The Palgrave Handbook of Digital and Public Humanities*, https://doi.org/10.1007/978-3-031-11886-9_20

and such a major change necessitates a response, a theoretically informed scrutiny of the production, distribution and effects of digitalization.

Approaching 3D models as a cultural phenomenon requires a conceptual framework, and in this chapter, I will present a survey of previous theoretical work on 3D modelling in museum environments. The review reveals three concepts through which these digital objects have been analysed: representation, mode of engagement and performativity. *Representation* refers to the distinction between real objects and their virtual counterparts or surrogates. These two entities, one imitating the other, are connected to each other by correspondence, which can be seen concretely in the striving for ever more accurate and life-like 3D models. The assumption that representation is the most important characteristic of 3D models has been criticized (Shanks and Webmoor 2013; Kenderdine 2016; King et al. 2016), in favour of the concept of the *mode of engagement*. This conceives the primary trait of the 3D models to be their ability to establish new relationships between humans, virtual and real objects, and other entities. Instead of representation, the focal point is thus on the effects that 3D models have. For example, it has been shown that the involvement of local communities in 3D modelling can transform and widen views on heritage (Jones et al. 2018; Magnani et al. 2018; Jeffrey et al. 2020).

Although the mode of engagement has induced new and productive ways to see 3D models as a cultural phenomenon, it remains a concept focused on the present. To acknowledge also the historical aspect of engagements with 3D models, I will introduce the third conceptualization of digital objects. This is based on *performativity*. Performativity refers to the situations in which the historically layered meanings of 3D models, their material effectivity and audiences become entangled and defined. When the concept is applied in heritage studies, it usually draws on Judith Butler's (1990, 1993) work, emphasizing the socio-cultural setting of 3D modelling, but I will also refer to Karen Barad's (2007) rethinking of performativity. She considers it as the process of materialization of human and non-human bodies through material-discursive practices. The concept of performativity moves the ways in which digital heritage is defined through a set of discourses and material practices into the limelight.

Consequently, instead of making an irreconcilable distinction between the real and the virtual, or exaggerating the significance of engagement here and now, performativity suggests a differentiated continuum between heritage objects, 3D models and the varied audiences. It allows scrutinizing ontological and epistemological dimensions of 3D modelling together. This leads me to analyse how 3D modelling of heritage objects frequently repeats deeply historical conceptions of knowledge, and the role of the visible in knowing. These conceptions hinge on the Western philosophical and scientific tradition in which seeing and knowing are intimately connected, and sight is privileged as the primary sense of experiencing reality (Jay 1993).

The historical connection with knowing and seeing is exemplified by the development of linear perspective, "an early form of virtual reality" (Tyler 2020, 1265), in the Renaissance arts, and its concomitant importance for the progress of natural sciences (Edgerton 2009). The use of 3D technology in museums continues this juxtaposition of truth and the visible and supports the primacy of sight in accessing heritage. Such a performative setting has implications for creating and using 3D models, especially as a form of engagement with indigenous communities and other minorities. I will argue that despite 3D digitization being a new technology, its applications in museums can be seen as reiterations of existing methods of valuing and representing heritage. These therefore conform to established forms of understanding and usage of heritage. 3D models as such do not necessarily alter heritage and engagement *per se*.

Before venturing into studies of 3D models as cultural phenomena, and describing the three conceptualizations of digital objects, however, I will start by providing a historical introduction to the 3D modelling of heritage. This already shows how the workflow of producing 3D models has gradually become adapted to heritage work, and how, performatively, 3D models partly enact traditional ways of using new technologies in heritage institutions. After this historical survey, I will proceed to a brief review of 3D technologies and their uses, and then proceed to engage with the conceptual framework.

20.2 The History of 3D Modelling Within a Heritage Context

Making models of three-dimensional heritage objects and projecting them on a two-dimensional plane, whether on paper or on a computer screen, has a long history that begins in the nineteenth century. Firstly, 3D modelling belongs to the repertoire of replication technologies that were developed to reproduce and disseminate heritage objects. These technologies include plaster casting, photography and other techniques of copying heritage objects (Aguerre and Cormier 2018, 21). Secondly, digital modelling is also embedded in the modern optical tradition of depicting three-dimensional objects on a two-dimensional plane (Schröter 2014), and ultimately the development of linear perspective in visual arts, and scientific illustrations in the early modern period.

Despite its suitability for heritage work, the technology of 3D modelling was not born in heritage institutions, and its technical development takes place largely outside museums. Presently such IT giants as Google and Apple, as well as the video game industry, invest huge sums in developing digital technology, which is gaining importance also in the construction, design, entertainment and health industries as well as visual arts. Subsequently, the technology has become commercially ingrained, from the basic tools of digitization to established online products. Through various forms of digitalization, therefore, the institutional set-up of cultural heritage, which is primarily national and public, has become tied to international, commercial platforms (Bonde Thylstrup 2018, 5–6).

The digital 3D documentation of archaeological and other heritage sites began in the 1990s, and the first 3D models of museum objects were created in the latter part of that decade. Among the earliest cases was the Digital Michelangelo Project in 1998–1999 (Levoy et al. 2000). This scanned ten sculptures made by the Renaissance master and produced such precise models that tool marks on their surfaces could be examined. By the same token, Michelangelo's famous sculpture, the Deposition, was the object of another early 3D digitization project (Bernardini et al. 2002).

These pioneering projects focused on individual or a small group of widely recognized works of Renaissance art, but large-scale projects, such as the 3D modelling of entire museum collections, took another decade to develop. In 2011, the Smithsonian Institution in Washington, DC launched a massive digitization of its collections (Lipowics 2012), with the first models released online a few years later. Meanwhile the Victoria and Albert Museum in London began a trial to 3D model its collections (Stevenson et al. 2012). A more recent development has been the 3D digitization of heritage objects of indigenous origins (Hollinger et al. 2013). Not only portable objects and works of art, but also pieces of architecture and entire heritage sites have become objects of 3D modelling. The Neolithic site of Çatalhöyük in Turkey in the early 2010s was among the earliest large-scale excavations where a 3D workflow was integrated into the fieldwork programme (Forte et al. 2012; Lercari 2017). However, 3D modelling only made its true breakthrough in museums in the latter part of the 2010s, once the technology gained further footholds in other areas of modern life and became less expensive.

Since the 3D modelling of heritage requires investments in terms of both equipment and skilled labour, large-scale digitizations have often required the support of international or governmental institutions. In Europe, 3D modelling is systematically pushed into heritage work by the European Commission, which produced the Declaration of Cooperation on Heritage Digitization in 2019. The document stressed the importance of 3D models and launched a pan-European initiative for the digitization of heritage artefacts and monuments (European Commission 2019). The European Union is currently investing in numerous projects which apply the technology or develop the 3D modelling of heritage.

As 3D modelling has gained a more substantial role in heritage work, motivations for undertaking digitization have become varied. Meanwhile, the aims still tend to fall into one of three major categories. Firstly, as an accurate and pervasive means of recording, 3D models help in the non-invasive documentation and preservation of physical artefacts and sites. Secondly, they allow new ways of conducting scholarly research. Digitization can place otherwise inaccessible objects within the reach of a larger community of scholars or enable objects hosted in different museums to be examined at the same time. In addition, fragments of the same object dispersed across different collections can be reunited, and partly destroyed objects reconstructed by digitally combining documentation from different periods (Dey 2018, 28–30).

The most exciting applications of 3D models in scholarly research, however, apply digital means to virtually enhance, manipulate and analyse objects and their properties and thus reveal details not visible to the naked eye (e.g. Jones et al. 2015). Thirdly, despite the growing research use of virtual models, most 3D digitization projects are justified as enhancing public engagement. They offer novel opportunities for presenting heritage in exhibitions, at heritage sites and online. While glass showcases in museums constrain the visitors' possibilities to examine the exhibited objects (Berns 2016), 3D models offer more freedom for manipulation, although without haptic sensation.

Selecting and setting up the appropriate technology and creating effective workflows for 3D modelling remain important concerns for heritage institutions. Besides these technical issues, the digital technology also raises concerns which are more specific to museums and heritage (Wellington and Oliver 2015). Such questions include which museum items are chosen for digitization, in which ways the results are made available for different audiences, and how 3D models affect the experience of museums objects and heritage in general (Immonen and Malinen 2021). Heritage institutions tend to answer them with well-worn solutions. In fact, as Diane Zorich (2018, 75) points out, museums tend to digitize in "a way that reflects the past". This reinforces the established approach to heritage, but the real aim, she argues, should be to digitize materials in a way that is oriented to the future and opens new ways of seeing and experiencing heritage.

20.3 Basics of 3D Modelling Technology

The devices and software for doing 3D modelling are quite diverse and are continually being developed. Nonetheless, in heritage work, there are three main techniques for creating 3D models: photogrammetry, laser scanning and structured light scanning, which I will describe below. While these all have different pros and cons from a heritage perspective, the quality of the 3D models produced depends also on the available equipment as well as the skills of those who do the digitization.

The first of the three techniques, 3D photogrammetry, is a relatively old method based on converting two-dimensional data obtained from digital photographs into three-dimensional measurements and a final product (Fig. 20.1). In the technique known as structure from motion (SfM), tens or hundreds of overlapping photographs of an object are taken from different angles, and then matched and compiled into a single, digital model. The photographs can be shot with any digital camera, but special software is needed to process the images and generate a dense point cloud. A point cloud is a large set of spatial coordinates sampled from the external surfaces of the physical object. In comparison to the two other techniques, SfM is easier, faster and cheaper, since digital imaging has evolved, as have the different software tools needed for creating the finished products (Historic England 2017). It is even possible to do 3D photogrammetry with the use of a smartphone (Obudho 2019).

The second technique, laser scanning, varies greatly in its operating principles, precision, accuracy and price (Artec3D 2019). The technology is based on active data collection where a laser beam is emitted and received from a dedicated device to determine its distance to the surface of the modelled object. The collection of data can be carried out from a stationary tripod, from a vehicle or from the air. Handheld and backpack systems are also available. Like photogrammetry, laser scanning has many applications. It is used in archaeological and architectural documentation (Dey 2018, 24) as well as for creating 3D models of portable artefacts. However, unlike photogrammetry, laser scanning cannot record the colour data or the texture of a surface, which must be added by other means. One solution is to integrate laser scanning data with point clouds created by means of 3D photogrammetry. This kind of hybrid approach to produce 3D models is considered optimal in terms of a model's resolution and texture (Historic England 2017).

Like laser scanning, the third technique, structured light scanning, requires specialized equipment (Dey 2018, 24; Historic England 2018). The device projects a structured light pattern of stripes and grids onto a surface that is

Fig. 20.1 Photogrammetry can be done with very simple equipment—here with two digital cameras on a tripod (*Photo* Annukka Debenjak-Ijäs)

then recorded by an infrared camera. By measuring how the pattern is transformed by the surface, the device calculates variations in depth. The measuring device is often accompanied by an integrated digital camera which records the colour data of the scanned surface, and coloured models are generated and visualized on a computer screen in real time.

After a 3D model has been finalized, another set of issues emerges regarding the distribution, use and archiving of the results. In fact, for heritage institutions, these are crucial concerns: Firstly, it should be decided how much of the raw material and related datasets are preserved alongside the actual model. The final 3D model comprises only a small part of the data collected during the digitizing process. Secondly, to enhance the transparency and usability of 3D models in heritage institutions, adequate *metadata* should be provided for these. The term refers to information which is affixed to the actual content to provide facts about the model, including the technical framework of the production process, but also the heritage context and content of the model (e.g. DPO 2018; Europeana Network Association Members Council 2020).

Thirdly, while some 3D models are intended to be used only by heritage professionals or in museums and heritage sites, many are put online for public use. There are several websites offering free services for publishing, sharing and viewing 3D models, like Sketchfab. In addition, public platforms for digital cultural heritage, such as the European Union's Europeana, are developed to provide both content management and sharing of 3D models. The distribution and use of 3D models are not only a technical exercise, but also require the solution of issues related to intellectual property and copyrights. Usually, heritage institutions resort to different public copyright licences, of which the Creative Commons licence is the most important.

20.4 Representation as the Basis of Heritage Analysis

The commercial and technical facets of 3D modelling are intertwined with the theoretical issue of how 3D models should be conceived and analysed. This conceptual framework affects the way in which 3D models and their relationship with users and heritage institutions is understood. An easily recognizable distinction can be made between the material or real and the virtual, where the former refers to the actual, physical heritage object, whereas the latter is the digital, non-physical *representation* of that object. Representation is a complex concept with a long history. It implies a relationship between two entities, one standing in for or corresponding with the other (Marin 2001; Schröter 2014, 378). This distinction is exemplified by the *reality–virtuality continuum*, a concept introduced in 1995 (Milgram et al. 1995). The continuum is a scale ranging between the completely real environment and the entirely digital virtual experience. It encompasses all possible variations and compositions of real and virtual objects. For instance, augmented reality, where digital objects or elements are superimposed on a real environment, is not entirely virtual or real, but it nonetheless can be positioned on the continuum.

In heritage digitalization, the idea of representation is evident from the term *digital surrogate*, which refers to the digital reproduction of a preexisting physical object. It can be a text, image, sound, portable object or site (Garstki 2017), which bears the "closest fidelity to the actual object that can be achieved digitally" (Arnold and Geser 2008, 63). The wording of "closest fidelity" is significant, because digital surrogates stand as representations of the original object. The idea can be further developed with closely related concepts. In contrast to the surrogate, the *digital proxy* is a digitization not intended to be of closest fidelity to the original, but merely sufficient for the use at hand (Lindner 1995), such as the dissemination of a 3D model online.

The fidelity of digital surrogates is not an unambiguous matter and remains a relative notion. Not only has the actual physical presence of the object become reduced to digital data concerning its surfaces and dimensions, but parts of the model are never based on measurements extracted from the physical object. Depending on the original artefact or site, and its level of complexity, the digitized dataset does not cover all aspects of the original object but remains always a representative sample. It must be completed by software (Cameron 2007). Furthermore, as an entity of the virtual realm, a 3D model is not subject to similar physical and temporal forces as its material counterpart, such as inhabiting only one location in the physical world (Kallinikos et al. 2013).

The creative element of 3D models complicates the relationship between originals and their surrogates. For instance, the London Charter for the Computer-based Visualisation of Cultural Heritage, created in 2006, underlines the importance of providing "sufficient information to enable their audiences to distinguish between fact and fiction" (Denard 2012). This echoes the 1964 Venice Charter, or the International Charter for the Conservation and Restoration of Monuments and Sites, which states that "[r]eplacements of missing parts must integrate harmoniously with the whole, but at the same time must be distinguishable from the original so that restoration does not falsify the artistic or historic evidence" (Venice Charter 1964). However, unlike in artefact and building conservation, 3D models are fundamentally based on the blending of fact with fiction, and therefore cannot be similarly distinguished.

The fidelity of representation is even more problematic when the users of the models are included in the analysis. Overly successful digital imitation of historic objects and the immersive quality of 3D models can raise questions regarding the authenticity of the original heritage object—it might appear plainer and more muted than the digital copy (Cameron 2007, 51). Thus, on the other hand, 3D modelling can be seen as misrepresenting heritage objects, but on the other hand, it also produces visually idealized or purified version of the physical counterparts, and subsequently models can be encountered and experienced as more true-to-life than their physical equivalents.

20.5 The Mode of Engagement

Representation and concepts closely related to it are frequently used in technically oriented publications on cultural heritage digitization, and they are indeed an efficient way of characterizing and developing answers to technical problems. Occasionally, however, this conceptual framework spills over into the analysis of other aspects of 3D modelling, including the cultural, heritage and social implications of digitization. This kind of transfer is problematic, and therefore scholars have presented alternatives to the concept of representation in the analysis of 3D visualization. The criticism of representation is part of a twentieth-century intellectual current in which, for instance, philosophy became suspicious of the strong link between seeing and knowing, and many thinkers explored other, holistically embodied ways of knowing (Jay 1993). Similarly modern art is critical of linear perspective and naturalism, and the avant-garde art often interrogated the limits of representation, breaking up physical objects and reassembling them visually in new ways (Brettell 1999).

Transforming collections into virtual objects offers much more than just digital copies of original artefacts. Michael Shanks and Timothy Webmoor (2013, 107) point out that rather than focusing on the representational function of digital objects, these media entities should be considered as events or situations in the sense that they create something. Instead of secondary representations, 3D models should be seen as achievements of engaging with heritage. It is not so much a matter of what is passively represented but how digital visualizations actively translate physical objects into something new. Following Shanks and Webmoor (2013, 98, 103), 3D models are to be seen as transformative; they translate between past and present, us and heritage, and this translation is not merely acknowledging the correspondence between the object and its digital counterpart. It is thus more productive to consider 3D models as a *mode of engagement*. They bring together digital and physical objects, people, heritage institutions and commercial actors, and allow something new to emerge through this encounter. Consequently, in lieu of distinctions, the mode of engagement suggests a continuum between heritage objects, 3D models and the varied audiences.

The mode of engagement emphasizes the importance of the encounter with digital objects and the ways in which heritage becomes operationalized in and through them. To develop further the new ideas brought by this framework, a new set of concepts become relevant. In recent discussions on 3D modelling, some of the most important ones have been *community* and *digital embodiment* (Hollinger et al. 2013; Kenderdine 2016). In the following, I will define these two concepts and trace their impact on both the theory and practice of 3D modelling.

20.6   3D DIGITIZATION AS A COMMUNITY EFFORT

While 3D modelling can be performed solely for the purposes of heritage management, with its need for accurate documentation, public engagement is also frequently mentioned as the main motivation for producing digital objects. In practical terms, this can be understood as the digitization of heritage objects that have significance for a certain community, and the provision of free access to 3D models of these online. However, the public engagement can take even more consequential forms, and include the selection of heritage objects to be digitized as well as the actual digitization process (Jones and Rapley 2018, 82). By engaging amateurs at each step and allowing them to participate in 3D modelling, communities could become more invested in heritage as a whole.

For greater public engagement, 3D technology has been applied in making museum collections accessible to indigenous communities. Matthew Magnani, Anni Guttorm and Natalia Magnani (2018) describe the visual repatriation of Saami artefacts, where objects related to craft production were digitized in 3D and made available online. Notably, case-by-case discussions were held with indigenous communities before digitization. The scholars also had to resolve ethical concerns related to intellectual property and appropriation: since 3D models are relatively easy to 3D print, this can lead to unscrupulous exploitation of indigenous crafts. On the other hand, 3D printing has been utilized to encourage community involvement as well. The Smithsonian Institution and the Tlingit community of southeast Alaska have digitized cultural objects for preservation and educational purposes (Hollinger et al. 2013). Although the 3D printed replicas were acknowledged as copies, some community members were apprehensive about 3D digitization, since the replicas—like the originals—evoked strong ancestral connections within the community. This is not an isolated case in which 3D digitization generates new forms of authenticity (Jones et al. 2018), or rather reveals that the conception of authenticity held by heritage management is not the only relevant version. Digital heritage can therefore help redefine the authenticity of heritage in general (Silberman 2008, 89).

While indigenous and local communities can be consulted as part of 3D digitization, their involvement can be particularly valuable when the technology is made available to amateurs to digitize heritage objects (Lowe 2018, 56), or made widely available through devices like smartphones as part of crowdsourcing campaigns. In the Glasgow-based ACCORD project, local communities were given an opportunity to 3D digitize heritage sites and objects of their own choosing. Instead of digital outcomes, the project emphasized the importance of getting the communities involved in the recording process both as a technical procedure and as a way of generating significance (Jeffrey et al. 2020, 885). When the participants chose heritage places important to them, the associated social and heritage values became part of 3D digitization and its products. In other words, 3D technology opened up a new mode of engagement.

As these examples show, and as Bruno Latour and Adam Lowe (2011) argue, digital technologies provide a fresh way to look at the original objects, altering the concept of original itself. Digital surrogates do not erode the power of the original, but some of the authenticity of the originals may migrate to them instead. The degree of this transfer is conditioned by technological sophistication and other physical and cultural factors. The value of heritage objects can also be accumulated and shaped by co-design as was concluded in the ACCORD project, where 3D models produced communally accrued values similar to the original objects and allowed the originals to be perceived differently (Jones et al. 2018, 344–45). Some digital objects can even establish their own authenticity, since they are artefacts with accumulated history (Cameron 2007, 67).

The idea of the mode of engagement carries the promise of making digital heritage available to different communities and concurrently supporting their ways of life. However, the concept does not address the intellectual background of 3D modelling—i.e. the modern Western epistemology—which links knowing with seeing at the expense of other senses and reinforces linear perspective and naturalism as the dominant modes of visual engagement. Other epistemological traditions, like indigenous ways of knowing, do not necessarily agree with such assumptions, and can even lead 3D modelling to become a neo-colonial practice (Christen 2015, 369–81). Kimberley Christen (2015) argues that it is not enough to give communities access to 3D technology. In community collaborations, instead of merely making the digital tools and items of heritage accessible, museum professionals need to contribute by exploiting and reshaping their own expertise and lending their authority to newly envisioned digital objects.

20.7 Digital Embodiment

Using 3D models, especially if one has not done so before, can be exciting and provoke feelings of surprise and enchantment (Cameron 2007, 61). Such experiences stem from the difference between the everyday and the virtual, even though the expressed aim of the digitization might be to bridge this very gap. In addition to the spectrum of emotions that the virtual models spark, their unlimited manipulability creates bodily experiences different to the ordinary situations. This bodily encounter with the 3D models can be described using the concept of *digital embodiment*, which refers to the capacity of the body to feel, perceive and act as part of digital interactions (Munster 2006). Digital embodiments are therefore sensual and material qualities that 3D models prompt.

Sarah Kenderdine (2016) argues that digital embodiment poses a challenge to the heritage context where visitors are expected to be passive receivers of information. Not surprisingly, most of the analyses on 3D models focus on describing how the model can be manipulated and what the model allows from the perspective of an ideal user, but pay less attention to how these interactions actually unfold as embodied experiences. Some studies on digital embodiment, nevertheless, have been published.

Although not discussing 3D models *per se*, Catherine Eberbach and Kevin Crowley's 2005 study concludes that learning differs depending on the mode of engagement. They analysed how families learned about pollination in a botanical garden by interacting either with living plants, physical models of plants or a virtual animation of plants. The results show that family discussions about model and virtual plants created more connections to substance learned at school, while the living plant inspired families to explain pollination in terms of their everyday experiences. In the context of 3D modelling, moreover, the ACCORD project discovered that rock climbers had pronounced embodied experiences when engaging with 3D models of the rocks they had previously climbed. In their responses, the climbers mixed old memories with new insights, induced by the 3D models, into the relationship between their physical bodies and rock surfaces (Jones et al. 2018, 345). In this way, therefore, digital objects have the power to generate new digital embodiments.

Digital embodiment can also be experienced in the sense of enjoyment that can appear as a side product of heritage applications. This can be exemplified with the "Turku Goes 1812" event that took place in Turku, Finland in spring 2019 (Fig. 20.2). Using VR devices in a dedicated space, the public stepped into a virtual reality model of the city centre in 1812. The digital visits were organized as guided museum tours given to small groups at a time. When I observed these visits, and interviewed the museum guides, it became apparent that while some visitors behaved as was expected of museum audience, many were not interested in the heritage aspect of the model. On the contrary, they were far more attracted by the delight created by the virtual technology, the particular digital embodiments that technology made possible. The guides of the virtual tour had the role of keeping up discipline, but the tours could become a kind of play activity, with guides in the role of schoolteachers trying to control unruly groups of pupils. The "school visit to museum" situation became the social pattern which structured the participants' behaviour and organized the ways in which they experienced heritage within the virtual world. Experiencing digital embodiment was, therefore, not only a matter of interaction between human and computer, but a complex situation in which technologies, people in distinct social roles, and heritage became mingled, affecting the mode of engagement.

20.8 Performativity and 3D Models

As the examples of community involvement and digital embodiment evince, 3D models represent both a novelty and something old, since they reinforce traditions surrounding the application of modern visual technologies and established patterns of social behaviour. If something new is to emerge

Fig. 20.2 The Turku Goes 1812 virtual model produced by the Turku Museum Centre and launched in 2019 was highly popular (*Photo* Tanja Ratilainen)

through 3D models, this requires not merely a technological feat, but changes in the conceptualization of heritage objects. Given the co-existence of old and new, it becomes evident that using the concept of *representation* has consequences which obfuscate the understanding of 3D models. For instance, representation does not fully acknowledge that 3D models are not just products, but that they also possess histories of production and relations to the individuals involved in making and using them. In addition, representation might not be the best approach to tackle the fact that users inhabit the real world while engaging with the virtual. However, an equally problematic notion is the *mode of engagement*. Although the concept disengages scholars from the rigid framework of originals and their surrogates, and enables the detection of emergent, novel phenomena, it rejects the notion of representation and downplays the importance of historicity regarding 3D models. Representation and historicity, nonetheless, remain important for the analysis of 3D models. To overcome these conceptual complications, I will next turn to the concept of *performativity*.

Performativity has been used to describe digital cultures (Bachmann-Medick 2016), and how they "condition and are shaped by techno-social processes and agencies, and … afford new possibilities for performative practices and interventions" (Leeker et al. 2017, 9). Performativity is a term used in different schools of thought; I base my approach on Butler's and Barad's work. Broadly speaking the concept of performativity is based on the conviction that "doing" and "thinking" coincide in a situation in which matter, actors, and meanings are structured by the situation and conditioned by the historicity of entities involved as well as by relations of power. The latter refers to the circumstances in which digital objects are formed and perceived and the contribution of various agents—e.g. technology, professionals and amateurs—to this process. Performativity brings together materials and social practices, the real and the virtual, without making a distinction between these—unless the distinction is significant for some particular situation. If the focus is on digital embodiment, performativity describes how bodily experiences and gestures are partly defined by the things outside the body. An example of this would be how a rock surface and its digital model affect the experience of climbers of themselves and their abilities.

Performativity has several implications for the analysis of 3D models. Firstly, digital objects contain information on the performative situation in which they were produced, and often also reproduce more than what is apparent or intended. In this manner, the framing of 3D models subtly imposes a certain understanding of them. For instance, the rhetoric regarding digital objects often speaks of *users* and *user experiences* as though referring to an undifferentiated group of people engaging with similar objects. As seen above, 3D models of heritage objects, however, entail communities to which the originals have belonged, or for whom they are heritage, and other groups of people with different ways of interacting with these objects.

Secondly, a digital object possesses its own history. For instance, the visual tradition of European art inform how 3D models are presented. They tend to isolate an artefact, displaying them in bright light on seemingly neutral backgrounds, and in this they follow the scientific ideals of consistency and clarity, as well as the aesthetics of modernism. Moreover, while earliest works of art to be 3D modelled were Renaissance masterpieces, other objects chosen for digitization are typically finished products and of high material value, indicating hierarchies of value in heritage. In some cases, 3D models of artefacts are presented within a context that simulates their assumed original environment, as with the buildings in the "Turku Goes 1812" virtual space. This links the appreciation of virtual houses to some moment in their past which is considered historically authentic by the digitizers. On the other hand, in applications of augmented reality, heritage objects can be transported into entirely alien spaces, like present-day street views, emphasizing their distinctness and difference from our life.

Thirdly, in addition to heritage, performativity also reveals other processes in which 3D models participate. The museum settings in which 3D models are displayed, or the applications within which the digital heritage objects are experienced, frequently reiterate the visual and textual conventions of identifying certain categories of items as heritage objects which deserve our attention. Yet a certain flexibility to manipulate the digital object, to look at it from all angles or to freely destroy it, not available in the case of material museum objects, can also place 3D models with the context of consumerism, as merchandise available for inspection (Geismar 2018, 30). In these multiple ways, the historicity of performativity draws attention to the repetition of material and cultural patterns in encounters with 3D models—whether these are displayed as products of digitization and IT industry, or entice regressive behaviours (e.g. of acting like a pupil at school) or follow the epistemological conventions of representing objects in two dimensions.

20.9 Conclusion: 3D Models as New Heritage?

Because they potentially realign the relations between objects, humans and heritage, 3D models offer pathways to new forms of cognition and practice. The introduction of 3D models into a heritage context, nonetheless, comes with a plethora of technical and practical problems and imposes infrastructural demands. Importantly, the digitization of heritage objects is also accompanied by issues of a more conceptual character. Based on the concepts of *representation*, *mode of engagement* and *performativity*, I have identified three areas of particular interest which should be taken into consideration when analysing 3D models within a heritage context. The first is the relationship between museum objects and their digital surrogates, the second being the varied engagements with 3D models and the third is the functioning of heritage institutions as digitizing institutions. Although I have distinguished them for the sake of convenience, from the perspective of performativity, they are actually inseparable.

Technically speaking, the relationship between museum objects and their digital surrogates is defined by the 3D model's accuracy and precision in representing its physical original. The situation is more complicated, however, if this relationship is seen as affecting our culturally and materially conditioned relationship with objects, where the distinction between the real and virtual becomes performatively defined. The technology based on the primacy of sight reflects modern Western philosophical and artistic traditions. Culturally saturated spaces such as museum environments should be sensitive to the materializations of these epistemological assumptions. Like the artefacts in museum exhibitions, 3D models are encountered and seen in a historical framework which mixes our real and virtual encounters with artefacts and, as a result, produces knowledge. In fact, 3D models bring together very disparate kinds of audiences to experience heritage objects, with not all of them being typical museum visitors.

Besides the object-centred approach, the second area of interest in 3D modelling is the users (Li et al. 2018). It is slightly misleading, however, to adopt the terms *user* and *user experience* from a commercial context into the analysis of 3D models in a heritage environment. The terms problematically imply an abstract notion of a uniform user and associated stereotypical actions. This complies well with museums' traditional aim to control their visitors' behaviour and create homogenized experiences. However, 3D modelling potentially challenges these ideas of a passive, obedient body, and offers fresh means for "mapping and remediating the tangible and intangible heritage encompassing embodiment" (Kenderdine 2016, 23). The effects of heritage digitization are thus manifold, covering institutional, emotional as well as individual aspects. Thirdly, 3D modelling, along with other forms of digital technology, may cause changes in heritage institutions. It allows new forms of community involvement and fundamentally calls into question the separation between institutions and audiences. Yet, although 3D modelling can relatively easily be made available and heritage objects accessible to different communities, it is museum experts who are in the prime position to address the ontological and epistemological concerns and related visual traditions with which the digital technology resonates.

As digital and cultural phenomena, 3D models are flexible and multifaceted objects. However, unleashing their full potential requires both technological know-how and an historically and socially sensitive attitude. If these are successfully combined, it is possible to break new ground for heritage institutions and public engagement. Unlike representation, or mode of engagement, the concept of performativity suggests that heritage and digital objects belong to the same, although differentiated, sphere of historically embedded encounters. Understanding heritage objects and experiences performatively requires the analysis of a multitude of elements entangled within a performative situation. The emergence of novel forms of heritage is as much about something technologically new appearing as it is about creating concepts for identifying and naming this emergent form. This reveals the precarious, potentially fluid character of 3D models and other heritage objects.

References

Aguerre, Anaïs, and Brendan Cormier. 2018. "Introduction." In *Copy Culture: Sharing in the Age of Digital Reproduction*, edited by Brendan Cormier, 19–26. London: V&A Publishing.

Arnold, David, and Guntram Geser. 2008. *EPOCH Research Agenda for the Applications of ICT to Cultural Heritage*. Budapest: EPCOH and ARCHAEOLINGUA.

Artec3D. 2019. *Artec 3D Scanning Applications in Art and Design*. Accessed November 21, 2020. https://www.artec3d.com/cases/design.

Bachmann-Medick, Doris. 2016. *Cultural Turns: New Orientations in the Study of Culture*. Berlin: De Gruyter.

Barad, Karen. 2007. *Meeting the Universe Halfway: Quantum Physics and the Entanglement of Matter and Meaning*. Durham, NC: Duke University Press.

Bernardini, Fausto, Holly Rushmeier, Ioana M. Martin, Joshua Mittleman, and Gabriel Taubin. 2002. "Building a digital model of Michelangelo's Florentine Pietà." *IEEE Computer Graphics and Applications* 22 (1): 1–9.

Berns, Steph. 2016. "Considering the Glass Case: Material Encounters Between Museums, Visitors and Religious Objects." *Journal of Material Culture* 21 (2): 153–68.

Bonde Thylstrup, Nanna. 2018. *The Politics of Mass Digitization*. Cambridge, MA and London: The MIT Press.

Brettell, Richard R. 1999. *Modern Art 1851–1929: Capitalism and Representation*. Oxford: Oxford University Press.

Butler, Judith. 1990. *Gender Trouble: Feminism and the Subversion of Identity*. New York and London: Routledge.

Butler, Judith. 1993. *Bodies That Matter: On the Discursive Limits of "Sex."* New York and London: Routledge.

Cameron, Fiona. 2007. "Beyond the Cult of the Replicant: Museums and Historical Digital Objects: Traditional Concerns, New Discourses." In *Theorizing Digital Cultural Heritage: A Critical Discourse*, edited by Fiona Cameron and Sarah Kenderdine, 49–75. Cambridge, MA: MIT Press.

Christen, Kimberly. 2015. "On Not Looking: Economies of Visuality in Digital Museums." In *The International Handbooks of Museum Studies: Museum Transformations*, edited by Annie E. Coombes and Ruth B. Phillips, 365–86. Chichester: Wiley Blackwell.

Denard, Hugh. 2012. "A New Introduction to the London Charter." In *Paradata and Transparency in Virtual Heritage*, edited by Anna Bentkowska-Kafel, Hugh Denard, and Drew Baker, 57–71. New York: Routledge.

Dey, Steven. 2018. "Potential and Limitations of 3D Digital Methods Applied to Ancient Cultural Heritage: Insights from a Professional 3D Practitioner." In *Digital Imagining of Artefacts: Developments in Methods and Aims*, edited by Kate Kelley and Rachel K. L. Wood, 5–35. Oxford: Archaeopress.

DPO. 2018. Smithsonian 3D Metadata Model. *SI Digi Blog*, January 11. Accessed November 21, 2020. https://dpo.si.edu/blog/smithsonian-3d-metadata-model.

Eberbach, Catherine, and Kevin Crowley. 2005. "From Living to Virtual: Learning from Museum Objects." *Curator* 48 (3): 317–38.

Edgerton, Samuel Y. 2009. *The Mirror, the Window, and the Telescope: How Renaissance Linear Perspective Changed Our Vision of the Universe*. Ithaca, NY: Cornell University Press.

European Commission. 2019. *EU Member States Sign Up to Cooperate on Digitising Cultural Heritage*, April 9. Accessed November 21, 2020. https://ec.europa.eu/digital-single-market/en/news/eu-member-states-sign-cooperate-digitising-cultural-heritage.

Europeana Network Association Members Council. 2020. *3D content in Europeana task force*. The Hague Europeana Network Association Members Council, March

26. Accessed November 21, 2020. https://pro.europeana.eu/project/3d-content-in-europeana.
Forte, Maurizio, Nicoló Dell'Unto, Justine Issavi, Llonel Onsurez, and Nicola Lercari. 2012. "3D archaeology at Çatalhöyük." *International Journal of Heritage in the Digital Era* 1 (3): 351–78.
Garstki, Kevin. 2017. "Virtual Representation: The Production of 3D Digital Artefacts." *Journal of Archaeological Theory and Method* 24 (3): 726–50.
Geismar, Haidy. 2018. *Museum Object Lessons for the Digital Age*. London: UCL Press.
Historic England. 2017. *Photogrammetric Applications for Cultural Heritage: Guidance for Good Practice*. Swindon: Historic England. https://historicengland.org.uk/images-books/publications/photogrammetric-applications-for-cultural-heritage/.
Historic England. 2018. *3D Laser Scanning for Heritage: Advice and Guidance on the Use of Laser Scanning in Archaeology and Architecture*. Swindon: Historic England. https://historicengland.org.uk/images-books/publications/3d-laser-scanning-heritage/.
Hollinger, R. Eric, John Edwell Jr., Harold Jacobs, Lora Moran-Collins, Carolyn Thome, Jonathan Zastrow, Adam Metallo, Günter Waibel, and Vince Rossi. 2013. "Tlingit-Smithsonian Collaborations with 3D Digitization of Cultural Objects." *Museum Anthropology Review* 7 (1–2): 201–53.
Immonen, Visa, and Ismo Malinen. 2021. "3D Imaging in Museums." In *Museum Studies: Bridging Theory and Practice*, edited by Nina Robbins, Suzie Thomas, Minna Tuominen, and Anna Wessman, 253–70. Paris and Jyväskylä: ICOFOM and University of Jyväskylä.
Jay, Martin. 1993. *Downcast Eyes: The Denigration of Vision in Twentieth-Century French Thought*. Berkeley, Los Angeles and London: University of California Press.
Jeffrey, Stuart, Siân Jones, Mhairi Maxwell, Alex Hale, and Cara Jones. 2020. "3D Visualisation, Communities and the Production of Significance." *International Journal of Heritage Studies* 26 (9): 885–900.
Jones, Andrew Merion, Andrew Cochrane, Chris Carter, Ian Dawson, Marta Díaz-Guardamino, Eleni Kotoula, and Louisa Minkin. 2015. "Digital Imaging and Prehistoric Imagery: A New Analysis of the Folkton Drums." *Antiquity* 89 (347): 1083–95.
Jones, Laura, and Vernon Rapley. 2018. "Connecting Cultures: An Interview with Laura Jones and Vernon Rapley." In *Copy Culture: Sharing in the Age of Digital Reproduction*, edited by Brendan Cormier, 79–85. London: V&A Publishing.
Jones, Siân, Stuart Jeffrey, Mhairi Maxwell, Alex Hale, and Cara Jones. 2018. "3D Heritage Visualisation and the Negotiation of Authenticity: The ACCORD Project." *International Journal of Heritage Studies* 24 (4): 333–53.
Kallinikos, Jannis, Aleksi Aaltonen, and Attila Marton. 2013. "The Ambivalent Ontology of Digital Artifacts." *MIS Quarterly* 37 (2): 357–70.
Kenderdine, Sarah. 2016. "Embodiment, Entanglement and Immersion in Digital Cultural Heritage." In *A New Companion to Digital Humanities*, edited by Susan Schreibman, Ray Siemens, and John Unsworth, 22–41. Hoboken, NJ: Wiley.
King, Laura, James F. Stark, and Paul Cooke. 2016. "Experiencing the Digital World: The Cultural Value of Digital Engagement with Heritage." *Heritage and Society* 9 (1): 76–101.
Latour, Bruno, and Lowe, Adam. 2011. "The Migration of the Aura or How to Explore the Original Through Its Facsimiles." In *Switching Codes: Thinking Through*

Digital Technology in the Humanities and the Arts, edited by Thomas Bartscherer, 275–98. Chicago, IL: University of Chicago Press.

Leeker, Martina, Imanuel Schipper, and Timon Beyes 2017. "Performativity, Performance Studies and Digital Cultures." In *Performing the Digital: Performativity and Performance Studies in Digital Cultures*, edited by Martina Leeker, Imanuel Schipper, and Timon Beyes, 9–18. Bielefeld: transcript.

Lercari, Nicola. 2017. "3D Visualization and Reflexive Archaeology: A Virtual Reconstruction of Çatalhöyük History Houses." *Digital Applications in Archaeology and Cultural Heritage* 6: 10–17.

Levoy, Marc, Kari Pulli, Brian Curless, Szymon Rusinkiewicz, David Koller, Lucas Pereira, Matt Ginzton, et al. 2000. "The Digital Michelangelo Project: 3D Scanning of Large Statues." *SIGGRAPH '00: Proceedings of the 27th Annual Conference on Computer Graphics and Interactive Techniques*, 131–44.

Li, Yue, Eugene Ch'ng, Shengdan Cai, and Simon See. 2018. "Multiuser Interaction with Hybrid VR and AR for Cultural Heritage Objects." *Digital Heritage 2018, 3rd International Congress & Expo*, 26–30 October 2018, San Francisco, USA. http://eprints.nottingham.ac.uk/56156/.

Lindner, Jim. 1995. "Digitization Reconsidered: A Video Guru Takes on the Technocrats." *SAA Business Archives Newsletter* 12 (1): 1, 12–14.

Lipowics, Alice. 2012. "Smithsonian Gets Dedicated Funds for Digitization and New Media." *FCW: The Business of Federal Technology*, January 2. https://fcw.com/articles/2012/01/12/smithsonian-to-spend-8.7m-on-digitization-and-new-media-in-fy2012.aspx.

Lowe, Adam. 2018. "Changing Attitudes to Preservation and Non-contact Recording." In *Copy Culture: Sharing in the Age of Digital Reproduction*, edited by Brendan Cormier, 51–65. London: V&A Publishing.

Magnani, Matthew, Anni Guttorm, and Natalia Magnani. 2018. "Three-Dimensional, Community-Based Heritage Management of Indigenous Museum Collections: Archaeological Ethnography, Revitalization and Repatriation at the Sámi Museum Siida." *Journal of Cultural Heritage* 31: 162–69.

Marin, Louis. 2001. *On Representation*. Stanford: Stanford University Press.

Milgram, Paul, Haruo Takemura, Akira Utsumi, and Fumio Kishino. 1995. "Augmented Reality: A Class of Displays on the Reality-Virtuality Continuum." *Proceedings SPIE Volume 2351, Telemanipulator and Telepresence Technologies*, 282–92.

Munster, Anna. 2006. *Materializing New Media: Embodiment in Information Aesthetics*. Hanover, NH and London: Dartmouth College Press and University Press of New England.

Obudho, Brian. 2019. "Best 3D Scanner Apps for Android & iPhone." *All3DP*, April 7. Accessed November 21, 2020. https://all3dp.com/2/5-best-3d-scanner-apps-for-your-smartphone/.

Schröter, Jens. 2014. *3D: History, Theory and Aesthetics of the Transplane Image*. New York: Bloomsbury.

Shanks, Michael, and Timothy Webmoor. 2013. "A Political Economy of Visual Media in Archaeology." In *Re-presenting the Past: Archaeology Through Text and Image*, edited by Sheila Bonde and Stephen Houston, 85–108. Oxford and Oakville: Oxbow Books and Brown University.

Silberman, Neil. 2008. "Chasing the Unicorn? The Quest for 'Essence' in Digital Heritage." In *New Heritage: New Media and Cultural Heritage*, edited by Yehuda E. Kalay, Thomas Kvan, and Janice Afflek, 81–91. London: Routledge.

Stevenson, James, Carlos Jimenez, Peter Kelleher, and Una Knox. 2012. "3D Modelling of Cultural Objects in the V&A Museum: Tools and Workflow Developments." *Archiving Conference, Archiving 2012 Final Program and Proceedings*: 168–73.

Tyler, Christopher W. 2020. "The Intersection of Visual Science and Art in Renaissance Italy." *Perception* 49 (12): 1265–82.

Venice Charter. 1964. *International Charter for the Conservation and Restoration of Monuments and Sites (The Venice Charter 1964)*. Paris: ICOMOS. Accessed November 21, 2020. http://www.international.icomos.org/charters/venice_e.pdf.

Wellington, Shannon, and Gillian Oliver. 2015. "Reviewing the Digital Heritage Landscape: The Intersection of Digital Media and Museum Practice." In *The International Handbooks of Museum Studies: Museum Practice*, edited by Conal McCarthy, 577–98. Chichester: Wiley Blackwell.

Zorich, Diane. 2018. "Scanning on an Industrial Scale: An Interview with Diane Zorich." In *Copy Culture: Sharing in the Age of Digital Reproduction*, edited by Brendan Cormier, 67–77. London: V&A Publishing.

CHAPTER 21

Making Museum Global Impacts Visible: Advancing Digital Public Humanities from Data Aggregation to Data Intelligence

Natalia Grincheva

21.1 Introduction

This chapter has two important goals. First, it aims to situate big data analysis within the growing field of digital humanities. Second, it employs an empirical exploration of the project "Deep Mapping: Creating a Dynamic Web Application Museum Soft Power Map" to discuss and demonstrate challenges and opportunities of the recent advancements in the big data digital humanities, specifically in the field of cultural geo-visualization. The chapter offers an empirical example of a close interconnection between current digital humanities scholarship and the professional world of contemporary museology, or, in other words, with public humanities. As Hsu (2016, 280) points out, public humanities include both widening the readership of humanities scholarship and collaborating with cultural heritage institutions, such as museums, archives, galleries, and libraries. The chapter shares important insights from the practice-based cultural mapping and data visualization project to further theorize and conceptualize big data digital humanities as an area of research that entails a strong engagement with wider publics beyond academia.

Since 2011, the term "big data" has been exponentially spreading in academic scholarship and the media. The *Oxford English Dictionary* (2003)

N. Grincheva (✉)
School of Creative Industries, LASALLE College of the Arts, Singapore, Singapore
e-mail: natalia.grincheva@lasalle.edu.sg; natalia.grincheva@unimelb.edu.au

School of Culture and Communication, Digital Studio, The University of Melbourne, Melbourne, VIC, Australia

© The Author(s), under exclusive license to Springer Nature Switzerland AG 2022
A. Schwan and T. Thomson (eds.), *The Palgrave Handbook of Digital and Public Humanities*, https://doi.org/10.1007/978-3-031-11886-9_21

defines it as "data of a very large size, typically to the extent that its manipulation and management present significant logistical challenges." However, it is not the volume of information that transforms data into "big data," but rather it is its "relationality" to other data. Big data is "fundamentally networked" and challenges in its analysis are primarily associated with its interconnected nature. Ward and Barker (2013) define big data as a twofold framework. On the one hand, it includes a large volume of data, reaching in some cases hundreds and thousands of terabytes generated per week. On the other hand, from the methodological perspective, big data draws on quantitative analysis and visualization to identify meaningful patterns in order to create new knowledge.

Research in big data digital humanities focuses "on large or dense cultural datasets, which call for new processing and interpretation methods" (Kaplan 2015, 1). While digital humanities, as a dynamic and constantly evolving academic discipline, is undergoing non-stop transformations by applying different quantitative methodologies, it has also actively employed "computational approaches of humanities research problems and critical reflections of the effects of digital technologies on culture and knowledge" (Schreibman et al. 2008, xvii). To cope with data explosion, digital humanities has long supplemented historical analysis, archival research, and qualitative research methods with computer-based methodologies "that allow bird's eye views at large data collections, thereby allowing the scholars to explore novel means of knowledge generation" (Salah et al. 2013, 409). Manovich (2016, 1) defines this intersection between data science and humanities research as cultural analytics, "the analysis of massive cultural datasets and flows using computational and visualization techniques."

This approach converts a mere data collection into a focused data analysis based on visual pattern recognition. This visualization and scalable interaction with the visualized material allows researchers to gain new insights about regularities and disruptions that create new knowledge about various cultural phenomena. While traditional digital humanities scholars use computing to analyze mostly historical artifacts and digitized data sets of large corpora of cultural materials, the use of quantitative computational analysis in humanities outside of the historical framework has been steadily growing (Manovich 2016). This chapter specifically focuses on a practice-based research project that stands outside of the historically oriented digital humanities. Instead, it finds its inspiration in cultural analytics, in the sense that it is based on aggregating, exploring, analyzing, and visualizing big data generated by contemporary museums to ask and answer critical questions about their current and future audiences, institutional relationships, and most importantly, cultural, social, and even economic impacts at home and abroad.

Exploring how big data relates to digital humanities, Kaplan (2015) suggested a three-dimension research framework that includes the following components: (1) big cultural data, (2) digital culture, and (3) digital experience. The first trajectory deals with the research of large cultural datasets as well as new knowledge that they generate. The second focuses on new digital phenomena that emerge within digital humanities discourses, concerning digital communities, and mediating software. Finally, the digital experience is based on the analysis of actualization of big cultural datasets or their manifestations in specific software interfaces that enable new cultural practices (Kaplan 2015). While this framework is helpful to organize multifaceted big data digital humanities research in theoretical terms, it is quite problematic to apply it to the field of public humanities without some adaptations.

This chapter reconfigures Kaplan's (2015) framework to explore the challenges and opportunities that big data digital humanities research brings to the world of professional museology. Specifically, the chapter identifies and examines three foundational levels of digital humanities research practices within the framework of the project "Deep Mapping: Creating a Dynamic Web Application Museum Soft Power Map" (Grincheva 2020a). These levels include (1) Data Aggregation, (2) Data Visualization, and (3) Data Intelligence. Each of these levels forms a progression of the digital public humanities research from mere capture of cultural data to its strategic employment for generating new insights to forecast the development of a specific digital phenomenon, object, or a process. While this classification across three levels is based on the specific empirical example, it is important to note that this work can be further generalized and theorized to apply to a broader field of digital public humanities.

Following this framework, the chapter consists of three key sections, respectively, devoted to these levels of data curation within the digital humanities research agenda. The first section "Data aggregation" exposes a wide diversity of various data sets across urban and institutional domains to discuss several challenges of their consistent collection to benefit the growing research field in digital public humanities. The second part "Data visualization" not only demonstrates how data visualization becomes the main method of analysis and research of cultural phenomena; more importantly, it identifies the implications of data visualization techniques for overcoming different challenges and growing research demands dictated by the public agenda beyond academia. Finally, the section "Data intelligence" shares preliminary results of exploiting machine learning and algorithmic modeling to advance digital humanities research and bring it to the next level of its methodological capacities to generate new knowledge and critical insights.

Before the chapter moves on, though, to explore these three levels of research, it is important to provide more details about the project and explain its value and importance for the public humanities. The next section "Playing with museum data" addresses these tasks and shares important details about the project "Deep Mapping: Creating a Dynamic Web Application Museum Soft Power Map," developed at the Digital Studio at the University of Melbourne in 2018.

21.2 Playing with Museum Data: How and Why "Deep Mapping" Came About

The project "Deep Mapping" trialed a pilot version of the dynamic web application Museum Soft Power Map[1] to enable museums to strategically use their cultural resources to assess, predict, and leverage their attraction power at home and abroad (Grincheva 2020a). It intended to address existing needs in the museum sector in cultural impact assessments by utilizing deep mapping to geo-visualize multiple quantitative museum data and tell stories about museums' institutional networks, communities, and global audiences. This creative practice-based research project was developed in partnership with the Australian Centre for the Moving Image (ACMI) in Melbourne.

Having its roots in the State Film Centre, first established in 1946, ACMI was founded in 2002 to house the nation's largest collection of moving image documents including films, web content, gaming, digital art objects as well as other hybrid forms of digital media. A young, dynamic, and ambitious institution, ACMI in the past two decades managed to develop a large audience reaching in 2018–2019 up to 2.5 million visitors to its local programs and touring international exhibitions (ACMI 2019). As a partner in the project, ACMI provided access to its historical institutional records, including multiple data sets across its collections, visitation, programming, and exhibitions for the last 15 years. More importantly, it offered a stimulating infrastructure and institutional support for the industry engagement project that stemmed primarily from the academic context but aimed to make impacts beyond academia.

Specifically, this project contributed to research activities unfolded in the framework of ACMI X museum incubator, an innovative research hub for Melbourne's creative practitioners, digital artists, producers, designers, web developers, and creative start-uppers. ACMI X connects its residents and a thriving membership community to cross-disciplinary partnerships and programs that foster a creative culture enabling discovery, learning, innovation, and sustainability in Melbourne (ACMI 2016). In 2016 ACMI partnered with the University of Melbourne to support academics, doctoral students, and early career researchers to join the ACMI X incubator space to work on their digital practice-based research projects. The project on geo-visualization of museum soft power has become one of the exemplar models that emerged out of this cross-disciplinary collaboration that was designed, on the one hand, to address industry needs and, on the other hand, to contribute to the development of the theoretical field of digital humanities.

From the practical perspective, the research partnership with ACMI and the development of the pilot demo attempted to offer innovative digital tools for the use among museums to measure and map their local and global contributions to the creative economy and urban development. It employed Joseph Nye's concept of soft power, defined as an actor's ability to exercise influence through persuasion and attraction. Soft power refers to intangible forms of power such as culture, ideology, and institutions. In the context of the knowledge-based global economy, soft power is a more sophisticated tool to influence international politics, in contrast to military or economic coercion (Nye 2004). A country generates soft power if it can exploit culture, information, and technology to shape and inhabit the mind space of another country (Chitty et al. 2017; Watanabe and McConnell 2015). In the past decade, a nation's soft power has increasingly become a subject to measurement, with the Portland Soft Power 30[2] or Global Power City Index[3] reports, providing a convincing evidence of this growing trend.

However, for many nation-states measurement of their soft power has remained an unresolved challenge. For example, in the context of Australia, in 2018 the Department of Foreign Affairs and Trade (DFAT) conducted a Soft Power Review and solicited contributions from civil society to explore ways of how Australia can better leverage its assets and build effective partnerships to advance national reputation, security, and prosperity (DFAT 2018). In the past decade Australia strived to overcome misperceptions of its global image, mostly known for the country's rich natural resources, environment, and agriculture, while its international reputation for cultural and scientific achievements suffered from underexposure (Mar 2014). The 2014–2016 Public Diplomacy Strategy developed by DFAT specifically emphasized an urgent need to advertise Australia's competitive investment environment, excellence in culture, science, and technology to make the country globally known as "an attractive place to study, visit, live and invest" (DFAT 2016).

Considering this cultural-political agenda, the project offered innovative digital solutions to measure soft power by focusing on key players in creative urban economies, such as museums. Historically, museums have been important vehicles of soft power, building cultural bridges across borders whether by developing cultural tourism or by organizing traveling exhibitions and international programming overseas (Krenn 2005; Sylvester 2009; Grincheva 2019a). In recent decades, museums have advanced their place in urban creative economies. They have proven to work well to accelerate tourism, generate economic activity in urban neighborhoods, and attract international investments (Pearce 2000; Heilbrun and Gray 2001; Guasch and Zulaika 2005). Museums transformed into key centers of soft power because they elevate the global visibility of cities, shape and even define their urban identities. They do this by hosting international cultural festivals and mega-events, facilitating urban regeneration, and developing diplomatic connections with cultural institutions abroad (Lord and Blakenberg 2015).

For example, evaluations conducted by the Australian Council of the Arts in late 2018 revealed that almost 50% of tourists visit Australia seeking cultural experiences, while 43% directly engage with the arts during their stay. More importantly, visiting museums and galleries has been the most popular activity for arts tourists (ACA 2018b). Specifically, Melbourne, which was originally conceived as a museum city (Bonyhady 1985, 12), is home to Australia's busiest arts galleries and the national urban center for cultural tourism, bringing $2 billion per year to Victoria. Since 2004 Creative Victoria facilitated 23 major international art exhibitions through its highly successful Melbourne Winter Masterpieces program attracting more than 5 million attendances. In 2017 alone, the National Gallery of Victoria's *Van Gogh and the Seasons* exhibition generated almost $56 million for the local economy by attracting almost half a million visitors (CV 2018). Making a direct reference to the geo-visualization project "Deep Mapping," the 2018 Australian Council for the Arts report submitted to the DFAT Soft Power Review stressed the key role of museums to facilitate cultural tourism and contribute to social cohesion, international cooperation, and security (ACA 2018a).

Within this national cultural context, the research project "Deep Mapping" attempted to develop innovative computational methods that can visualize and assess the soft power of museums. Contributing to the growing scholarship on cultural mapping (Bodenhamer et al. 2015; Duxbury et al. 2015), the project employed geo-visualization, data mining, and digital storytelling to develop a deep mapping application that can demonstrate museum global influence across five key layers of soft power from mere resources to social outputs to economic outcomes (Grincheva 2019b). This system correlates multiple sets of museum collections, visitation, programming, and revenue data with demographic statistics and cultural analytics of specific locations, viewing them as politically, culturally, and economically defined locales. While addressing practical tasks in contemporary museology, the application also offered a promising tool for a more rigorous and in-depth analysis of theoretical and conceptual questions.

Specifically, the web application Museum Soft Power Map enables an exploration of fundamental questions of political geography advancing research on soft power and its urban and institutional actors. Running multiple queries through the mapping system exposes correlation of and interrogates multiple datasets pertaining to wider overarching themes. For example, the pilot application has been instrumental to reveal the rapidly changing nature of museum power shifting from hard, material power resources of historical artifacts to the digital post-industrial economy of creative content (Grincheva 2019b). This is evident when one compares (1) the multicultural geography of museum collections with a potential to appeal to global publics and (2) the social geography of audience engagement limited to a few countries of developed economies with stronger global connectivity and access.

This simple geospatial comparison prompts multiple questions, including but not limited to such themes as digital inequalities and digital imperialism, economic power of creative industries, political and cultural implications of protectionist media policies concerning digital access, censorship, and freedom of expression. Posing, validating, and exploring these questions of global cultural, social, and political geography through data-intense research significantly advances the field of digital humanities and broadens its research horizons. The next three sections discuss further what challenges and opportunities these advancements bring to digital public humanities research and practice.

21.3 Data Aggregation

Data aggregation is a premier fundamental level of digital humanities research that deals with collecting a large-scale corpus of different types of data. This data ranges from digitized artifacts or born-digital objects in possession of museums, libraries, or cultural archives to text, image, audio, or even geospatial data generated by users who interact with these objects either online, in closed digital environments or on-site through different mobile applications. Kaplan (2015) indicates that these interconnected digital data could be extremely diverse, big, and even "fuzzy" and "likely to be in continuous expansion" that challenges digital humanities research (3). The confrontations with these "massive" data calls for important questions: "What can really be extracted from these huge datasets and what interpretations can be drawn based on these extractions?" (Kaplan 2015, 3). The project "Deep Mapping," developed in collaboration with ACMI, started exactly from the point of identifying, categorizing, exploring, and collecting different institutional data sets that could be further analyzed and visualized.

The multilayered mapping project aimed to produce a system that allows users to assess and visualize the influence of ACMI on several interconnected levels. First, the Soft Power Map application maps the ACMI Film Collection and calculates its potential appeal to national audiences in different countries around the world. The application also offers a way to explore ACMI audiences, ranging from onsite local visitors to online guests to the institutional website and to dedicated followers of its social media channels like Facebook and YouTube. It also exposes ACMI's international network of institutional connections and partnerships through Global Connectivity Power layer that maps organizational ecosystems in the global context. Finally, the application enables an exploration of local impacts of ACMI blockbuster exhibitions, such as Dreamwork Animation and Game Masters, touring around the world, and assesses their local attraction power in different cities in Asia–Pacific, Europe, and the Americas.

These multilayered geo-visualization tasks required focused work with a large amount of different sets of data, collected not only from the institution itself through various databases, like digital collection catalogue, google analytics, ticket sales system or even annual institutional reports, but also contextual data generated outside the organization. For example, one of the key layers of the soft power mapping system is Melbourne Engagement Power Layer (see Fig. 12.1). This layer allows users to explore ACMI's power to attract local audiences in Melbourne. On the one hand, it draws on ticket sales data provided by ACMI from 2011 till 2017 inclusive. This data combines quantitative information on ticket sales with geospatial data collected from

ACMI visitors by soliciting postcodes of their home locations. On the other hand, the layer geo-visualizes social demographic and cultural analytics data of urban neighborhoods across two hundred postcodes in Melbourne. Not only does this overlaying of data help identify where the majority of ACMI audiences or ticket purchasers come from; but it also illuminates who these people are, what languages they speak or what religion they practice among other characteristics.

To explore a profile for each of the local communities of ACMI visitors the web application aggregates and geo-visualizes multiple sets of Australian Census data. This data includes social demographic and immigration statistics, cultural, linguistic, and religious diversity data, family and household information, professional affiliations, and income data, among other data sets. For example, as the Fig. 21.1 demonstrates, one of the most "involved" ACMI neighborhoods with up to 65% of Local Engagement Power index is Little Italy or the "Italian Precinct," located on famous Lygon Street in Melbourne and mostly known as the Italian community. It is situated in the suburb of Carlton with a postcode 3057. According to the 2016 census data, apart from English, Italian is the most spoken language in the neighborhood, and the local population composition includes 11% of families with Italian ancestry and 4% of first-generation Italians with many having arrived in Melbourne in 2006–2015. According to the social demographic profile, the Italian community is home to quite a wealthy younger population (up to 39) with higher educational degrees and professional affiliations.

These demographic insights partially explain why ACMI welcomed so many Little Italy residents to its doors in the past decade. The museum is known for its dynamic and young audiences-oriented programming coming to visitors at

Fig. 21.1 Melbourne Engagement Power layer

a cost of $ AU 10–35 for a single ticket depending on the event, ranging from film screenings to special exhibits. However, as the application convincingly demonstrates, the dedicated programming implemented by ACMI in the past several years to celebrate Italian culture and heritage proved to be quite productive in terms of increasing ticket sales from the neighborhood. For instance, in 2016 ACMI co-organized the Melbourne International Film Festival to celebrate Italian screen culture featuring their vast collection of Italian feature films. The same year it convened a special event "An Italian voyage through Melbourne," bringing together Melbourne's famous writers, politicians, and cultural practitioners of Italian ancestry to discuss the history of Italian migration and its cultural impacts in Australia (ACMI 2017). This example is a good illustration that the correlation between the institutional information and urban context data reveals meaningful insights that can help museums explain and understand their audience development patterns.

The capacity of the Local Engagement Power layer to expose this cultural and linguistic diversity information of actual and potential ACMI onsite visitors can advance institutional capacities in audience engagements as well as inform cultural programming, fundraising, and economic development. However, applying a finer grained data with such a level of demographic detail for calculating local engagement power across two hundred neighborhoods in Melbourne is not an easy task. It required an aggregation of reliable and consistent census data, provided to the project by the Australian Urban Research Infrastructure Network (AURIN). This is a collaborative network of researchers and data providers across the academic, government, and commercial sectors, established in 2010 by the Australian Government under the National Collaborative Research Infrastructure Strategy. It offers access to thousands of multi-disciplinary datasets, from multiple sources and analytical tools covering spatial and statistical modeling, planning, and visualization enhancing innovative urban research (AURIN 2010).

AURIN supported the project through data access and focused consultations on the intricacies of statistical geographic hierarchies, naming conventions, and algorithms of data aggregation that helped to organize the census statistics and apply the data for calculating of the local engagement index. The result was the application's functionality to accurately map where ACMI visitors live and link this information to important demographic and cultural diversity data. The experience of the "Deep Mapping" project demonstrates the importance of reliable and comprehensive data aggregation. This remains a challenging task for researchers who in many cases deal with non-consistent, non-complete urban and state or even federal level data collected through multiple methodological approaches and are dispersed across different sources (Swafford 2016). There is a growing need for comprehensive models and dynamic data aggregation tools that can collect and integrate reliable social demographic, economic, and cultural data into open databases with API access for more accurate digital humanities research.

For example, the Smarter London Together Strategy stresses the importance of mapping the city's cultural infrastructure across all boroughs by benchmarking cultural venues and their supporting ecosystems to facilitate strategic economic and cultural planning. The Culture Team of the Smart City division developed an open-source Cultural Infrastructure Map that is available for public use and crowdsourcing contributions (GLA 2019). It geovisualizes the cultural assets of London alongside useful contextual data, like transport networks and population growth to offer a detailed snapshot of information (MOL 2020). The map makes it possible to correlate different sets of data across transport, planning, audience, and demographic, that is specific to a various geographic area. Such systems significantly enhance digital public humanities research by making data aggregation stage a realistic and achievable endeavor.

This is especially critical for implementing big data digital humanities research projects similar to "Deep Mapping." While this pilot project offered a robust solution for data integration and analysis across multiple levels of soft power (Grincheva 2019b, c), it also exposed those results of the mapping exercise lose their relevance in time, as museums continue to generate new data across all layers of soft power. Moreover, social demographics, cultural analytics, and census statistics are dynamic data, constantly changing over time. It is important to find ways for a more automated and continuous data aggregation that cannot only constantly update data from online open data sources, but also automatically retrieve new data from institutional sources as well as provide an interface for manual data integration allowing users to monitor and control data accuracy.

In future, adding a timeline to the mapping software interface can make it possible to explore soft power as a changing continuum. It will allow the system to accumulate and preserve historical data of institutional and soft power development in time and space, exposing dynamic changes of organizational and urban impacts on the global map and pushing soft power research to a new exploratory level. While the data aggregation stage is the foundation for a successful development and implementation of big data digital humanities research, the data visualization level is crucial to transform a vast amount of different data sets into a platform for knowledge generation.

21.4 Data Visualization

Data analysis through computational visualization is an important level of digital humanities research that can help produce new knowledge. This happens through strategic data processing and targeted interpretation in a specific context driven by a project's key research goals and objectives (Kaplan 2015). A key challenge in analyzing large data sets has been to transform the raw data into dynamically curated data, contextualized data, and deep knowledge (Beheshti et al. 2019). Big data visualization models and methodologies are quite diverse and complex and range from network visualizations to word clouds to mapping solutions that can be applied accordingly to generate the most critical insights and highlight important findings. The project "Deep Mapping" tested the soft power measurement framework (Grincheva 2019b) and was predominantly based on geo-visualization of multiple sets of data to assess museum soft power. This approach applied Geographic Information Systems (GIS) or digital systems for handling, processing, analyzing, and visualizing a complex set of data that has a geographic dimension (Dorling and Fairbairn 1997).

Deep Mapping is an interdisciplinary methodology empowered by GIS that facilitates the integration of different types of data through a cartographic display that aims to visualize and evaluate interrelationships, coexistence, and processes of complex phenomena (Bodenhamer et al. 2015). As Blloom (2016, 1) defined it, deep mapping "is a way to be conscious of a place in such a manner as to hold multiple layers of understanding of the present moment in a non-reductive and robust manner." In the project of developing the Museum Soft Power Map application, the methodology of deep mapping provided an effective tool for the accurate integration of different sets of research data across museum resources, outputs, networks, and impacts to expose correlations of data and processes happening on different levels of soft power analysis (Grincheva 2019b).

Such a multilayered mapping aimed to address several major challenges that contemporary museums and cultural or heritage institutions face in the age of growing datafication and digitalization. First, it attempted to design a new platform for museums to systematize, organize, analyze and use their data not only for a more sustainable and strategic institutional development; it also aimed to build a new impact evaluation and demonstration tool to justify their existence for their stakeholders to increase funding and development opportunities. In the last decade, government policies in Australia, as everywhere else across countries, reinforced the instrumental value of culture as a tool for local development. They urged cultural organizations and museums to look for comprehensive and reliable means to prove that they are worthy of public support (Lee and Gilmore 2012). In a time of reduced public funding and increased competition for existing resources, museums must offer convincing arguments in support of their case (Scott 2006).

However, a proper evaluation framework needs to offer a reliable interface between government policies encouraging measurable outputs and deeper assessments which acknowledge complex institutional ecosystems. In the project, the geo-visualization methodology, in fact, allowed the identification of measurable sources of museums' soft power. At the same time, it helped reveal how these indicators relate to local factors which shape social and economic contexts of museum influence. Such a multilayered mapping redirected the focus from simplistic quantitative assessments, so favored by governments, to the geography of museums' outreach and influence. Moreover, it allowed a visualization of museum global ecosystems, exposing rich connections, complex networks, and diverse areas of impacts. This mapping exercise helped expose important connections and ties developed by museums with their local communities, at the same time tracing their "embeddedness" in larger international networks. Finally, with the growing agenda of museums to "create meaningful experiences for peoples of all origins and backgrounds" and to serve as agents of change to address challenges of inclusion and diversity (ICOM 2020), the system offered valuable tools for museums to understand and diversify their audiences at home and abroad.

Furthermore, each of the layers in the geo-visualization system not only maps a certain dimension of the institutional soft power, but also measures this power in different countries by calculating a power index. This index is a weighted sum of several key normalized indicators based on specific collection, visitation, or online engagement data in correlation to social demographic variables for each country or city. The scale from 0 to 100 for each of these indices progresses in a linear fashion, not logarithmically. For each layer of soft power geo-visualization, the score allows a comparison of different countries in terms of the potential appeal of the collections to people living in this geographic area, its actual engagement with ACMI activities as well as its direct impacts. In this way, the score for each country in combination with color coding reveals geographic areas of missed opportunities and identifies zones of maximum influence.

Such a geo-visualization model intends to create a collegial professional environment among institutions, encouraging cooperation and eliminating a competitive framework. In a growing competition for funding, audiences and investment opportunities, museums have been searching for a more efficient ways of data assessments and results demonstration without disclosure of sensitive data of institutional performance. The Museum Soft Power Map application addresses these concerns by offering new ways of data visualization through indexes that do not disclose institutional data on their audiences or economic gains. The system also stresses and highlights institutional interdependencies by capturing complexities generated by connections and relationships among institutions and their stakeholders, currently not well reflected in traditional museum reports and white papers.

For example, the first layer Collection Appeal Power Index demonstrates the global cultural and linguistic diversity and scope of ACMI collections, highlighting the geographic areas of their origins. With around 200,000 items in its collection, 70% of ACMI's holdings come from outside Australia and feature content in 49 different languages, spoken in more than 230 countries around the globe. For each country, the Collection Appeal Power Index calculates the potential of the ACMI Collection to attract and engage national audiences from different countries by correlating two types of key data, such as basic characteristics of films (country of production, language, and cultural content) and social demographic indicators, including immigration and tourism statistics from this country to Melbourne.

The intensity of the green color on the global map, allows the Collection Appeal Power Layer to visually highlight countries and geographic areas, where the Collection has the strongest appeal. Digital hyperlinked stories attached to the most important content suppliers help to explore further the ACMI film archives, telling illuminating stories about how the collections' items connect the museum to many communities and organizations across the world.

The second layer, the Online Engagement Power Index, geo-visualizes the geographic diversity of ACMI global online audiences (see Fig. 21.2). It shows the size and density of online website visitors as well as followers and subscribers to ACMI social networking spaces. The layer draws on the museum website visitation records and social media statistics collected from Facebook, two YouTube channels, and TripAdvisor, a website where international tourists rate cultural institutions based on their experience. The intensity of the blue color, highlighting countries with the most engaged ACMI online audiences, enables a quick snapshot of institutional digital influence on the world map demonstrating the unequal distribution of power across geographic areas. The layer helps quickly reveal where the museum's online visitors come from, while posing challenging questions about why audiences coming from certain countries are more engaged than others.

For example, as Fig. 21.2 illustrates, Colombia with a very low Collection Appeal Power Index (only 12) stands out on the global map for its Online Engagement Power Index reaching 58, outperforming France (31), Germany (41), and even the UK (52). Historically, ACMI established stronger connections with these countries as its main collection suppliers, who have Collection Appeal Power Index 84, 72, and 100, respectively. These figures suggest that ACMI holds enormous culturally and linguistically appealing content with which it can attract people from these countries through online activities.

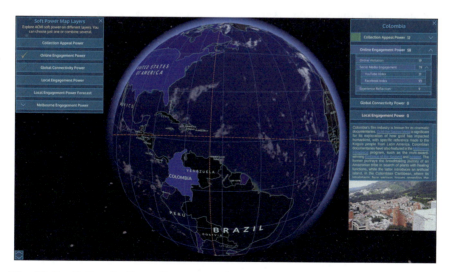

Fig. 21.2 Online Audience Engagement layer

Colombia in this case, with a very high Facebook Engagement Index (93), convincingly demonstrates that it is not enough for a museum to have culturally diverse collections featured through its digital catalogue. These soft power resources need to be activated through social engagement strategies and dedicated online activities in order to "win hearts and minds" of targeted online audiences (Grincheva 2020b).

The third layer, Global Connectivity Power Index, maps ACMI's international networks of partners, collaborators, and contacts, that in the past decade worked with the museum on various cross-cultural projects, curatorial and artistic exchanges. The layer geo-visualizes links between ACMI and its 185 institutional partners in about 80 cities around the world on all continents. It not only exposes the global ecosystem of ACMI in terms of its institutional network connectivity, but the layer also helps measure the strength and durability of these links, progressing from mere one-time collection exchanges, marked as the weakest links, to organizational collaborations and, finally, to long-term partnerships, known as the strongest connections. The digital storytelling component, accompanying this layer, helps illuminate details about ACMI's historic collaborations across the globe through digital hyperlinked annotations.

Revealing interesting patterns, drawing meaningful insights, and generating new knowledge about the institutional performance across several layers of soft power works even more productively through a focused simultaneous correlation of data from different layers. This overlaying of multiple data sets allows for a more accurate and in-depth insight generation offering a more comprehensive picture. For example, enabling all three layers of soft power mapping, such as Collection Appeal Power, Online Engagement Power, and Global Connectivity Power allows users to analyze complex information in a single snapshot that highlights important details in correlation to each other.

For example, in the case of the USA one can observe an impressive level of international cooperation between ACMI and almost 80 cultural organizations in the USA, located in 25 different cities. This is not surprising considering that the Collection Appeal Power Index in the country reaches 98, demonstrating that ACMI film archives possess a high percentage of items originating from the USA. This index also indicates that the national physical and digital mobility of the US population significantly increases the probability of ACMI content consumption by Americans either online or onsite. Considering these enormous power resources, the online engagement of US audiences with ACMI digital and social media activities remains quite low, demonstrating unrealized potentials and missed opportunities in global audience development. This quick snapshot poses important questions about institutional international priorities and programming, offering a platform for designing more productive development strategies.

Sullivan and Wendrich (2015) indicate that GIS is frequently criticized in academic research, because it presents information in a "distinctly positivist way," by emphasizing the importance of quantitative (rather than qualitative) data (191). They indicate that these platforms are not equipped to display the critical approach that characterizes the humanities. To address these concerns, this project employed GIS to visualize, relate, and evaluate different types of data on multiple layers to enrich interpretations. The multilayered visual design provided a more accurate picture of how soft power of museums accumulates from its multicultural resources and transforms through international outputs to global connections and relations and finally impacts local audiences.

As Bodenhamer et al. (2015) argue, it is important to shift "from GIS as system to GIS as science" (170). The Museum Soft Power Map application employs GIS not simply as a set of tools to display data on museum cultural assets, international activities, audiences, and networks, but primarily as an inductive exploratory research platform that helps to articulate important questions and hypotheses requiring further research and analysis. It offers a knowledge system not to build a one-time argument but primarily to provide an avenue for a long-term research endeavor to finally reach data intelligence.

21.5 Data Intelligence

Data intelligence is a more advanced model of strategic data curation that enables organizations to explore, analyze, and organize large amounts of complex data not only to assess their previous performance, but more importantly to forecast and predict their future development. Scalable algorithms that employ data to extract insights and further build on recognized patterns significantly harness data curation architecture and improve the quality of generated knowledge compared to more traditional data visualization methods (Beheshti et al. 2019). While digital public humanities have been concerned with understanding and exploring cultural phenomena in the past, with the development of machine learning algorithms, big data digital humanities might reach a new level of data intelligence to envision future developments of cultures, societies, and organizations.

Specifically, most recently the "Deep Mapping" project employed algorithmic models of soft power evaluations going beyond mere assessments of results accomplished by museums in the past. The project developed a prototype solution for predicting the soft power of museum traveling exhibitions in specific geographic areas by predicting how local variables of different locales affect and correlate with existing museum resources and targeted outputs to achieve desirable outcomes. This forecast system builds on data first collected and analyzed through the Local Engagement Power Layer that maps ACMI's traveling blockbusters at different hosting museums and cities around the world (see Fig. 21.3). Since 2012, two ACMI blockbusters, Game Masters and Dream Works Animation, have been hosted by sixteen museums in a dozen countries.

This layer draws on a large amount of data describing local contexts of hosting cities and museums, including three types of key indicators: Urban context, Museum context, and Attraction power. Urban context data includes

Fig. 21.3 Local Engagement Power layer

multiple variables that reflect the level of the city's global exposure and cultural infrastructure correlated with the total urban population, migration, and tourist visitation rates. Museum context data shows quantitative characteristics of a hosting institution, demonstrating its international visibility, and online representation and power. The Attraction Power data mostly consist of the statistics on visitors to this exhibition during the hosting period (usually around twelve to sixteen weeks).

In May 2019, the Museum Soft Power Map application launched a new layer, the Local Engagement Power Forecast. It predicts the soft power of the most recent ACMI blockbuster exhibition Wonderland, that was exceptionally well received in Melbourne in 2018, hosting almost two hundred thousand onsite visitors (ACMI 2019). This layer forecasts the attraction power of this traveling exhibition in potential hosting cities across continents. Employing algorithmic modeling and drawing on the results of measuring the soft power of previous traveling exhibitions in different places, the mapping system calculates potential local impacts of the traveling blockbuster, taking into account multiple factors. Beyond the Urban and Museum contexts variables, this layer also draws on Online engagement power and Cultural relevance indexes adding more factors to predict the local attraction power. This allows a more accurate forecast of the attendance numbers of this exhibition to calculate its potential outcomes in different geographic locations.

The Local Engagement Power Forecast is based on the prediction model of linear regression that combines a specific set of numeric input values to predict outputs. The forecast index draws on the supervised machine learning algorithm as a subset of artificial intelligence. This algorithm is closely related to computational statistics that make predictions employing computing. It builds a mathematical model of a set of data that contains both the inputs and forecasted outputs that consist of training examples, refined and upgraded each time when the actual outputs are received (Russell and Norvig 2021). In this way, this machine learning algorithm trains a model that dynamically processes newly available data to make more accurate predictions.

For example, among 17 potential cities where Wonderland might travel in the next decade, from Los Angeles to Taipei, the prediction model of linear regression forecasted Singapore and Wellington in New Zealand to be among the leading receiving cities in the Asia–Pacific with the Local Engagement Power Forecast indexes reaching 59 and 78, respectively. This forecast is based on the first iteration of input data collected from a series of DreamWorks Animation blockbuster exhibitions that proved to be highly successful among Asia–Pacific audiences. This exhibition traveled in the region in 2015–2017 and was hosted by a number of museums, such as the ArtScience Museum in Singapore, the Te Papa Museum in New Zealand, the Seoul Museum of Art in South Korea, and the National Taiwan Science Education Center.

When compared across four cities it was revealed that the DreamWorks Animation blockbuster was received exceptionally well in Singapore and Wellington, with the Local Attraction Power Index reaching 55 in the former case and 100 in the latter case. During 15 weeks of DreamWorks Animation visiting Wellington, Te Papa Museum received as many visitors as ArtScience Museum did while hosting the exhibition for 16 weeks. The fact that the local attraction power of the exhibition in Wellington is almost twice as high could be explained by many factors. However, it is important to stress that Wellington's population is almost ten times lower than the population of such a cosmopolitan megapolis as Singapore, and its international tourism operates at a much more modest scale. Nevertheless, despite its small urban size, Wellington's cultural infrastructure (75) and global exposure (67) indexes, in comparison to Singapore's (81 and 79, respectively), point out that the city offers an exceptionally favorable cultural environment for the exhibition to attract local and international audiences.

Furthermore, Te Papa Museum in Wellington outperforms ArtScience Museum in its global visibility and popularity as evidenced in the Museum Context indexes (92 versus 26). For example, Te Papa's annual online visitors and social media followers are several times larger than ArtScience Museum's digital audiences. Most importantly, due to geographic and cultural proximity, ACMI has established more durable and stronger connections with cultural institutions in Wellington and has a much higher popularity among New Zealand audiences, as the Global Connectivity Power Indexes demonstrate (91 in New Zealand and only 43 in Singapore). Based on these input data, collected through the first iteration, the prediction model calculated Local Engagement Power Forecast indexes in the case of Wonderland, that recently traveled to Singapore and Wellington.

Wonderland's actual visitation numbers, recently collected from ArtScience and Te Papa museums, in fact, proved the forecast calculations to be quite accurate. The exhibition started its global tour in April 2019 in Singapore and was hosted by the ArtScience Museum until September. Then it moved to Te Papa Museum in December 2019 and stayed in Wellington until March 2020. As the forecast model predicted, in total Te Papa Museum generated only 2.5 times lower visitation in 13 weeks than ArtScience Museum did during 24 weeks of hosting the exhibition. In fact, Te Papa Museum, located in a city with a population of only half a million people, invited up to 67% of the ArtScience Museum's daily visitors in Singapore, the megapolis with more than 5 million residents. This explains Te Papa Museum's higher local attraction power index, predicted through the forecast model.

The second iteration of input information provided valuable data to feed the local attraction forecast machine learning algorithm that will obtain a higher degree of precision once Wonderland and other future exhibitions of ACMI will travel to other cities across the globe, generating different attraction power in different locations to supply more input data. In the case of Wellington and Singapore, the first results of the forecast algorithm, though, convincingly proved Urban and Museum contexts data as well as Online engagement factors to be important and useful variables that affect traveling exhibitions' visitation and attraction power making the forecast algorithmic modeling possible.

This model of soft power prediction not only significantly enhances the international exchange opportunities and traveling exhibition management of contemporary museum, but it also can be employed through digital humanities research to reveal important patterns of cultural consumption across countries exposing new insights about different societies and cultures. While such data intelligence systems are in their infancy at the moment, they pave the way for a development of the big data digital humanities in the years to come. This chapter aimed to demonstrate that with emerging projects like "Deep Mapping" public digital humanities research acquires a new area of exploration, expanding the historical enquiry of cultural phenomena of the past to new horizons of envisioning the future.

21.6 Conclusion

This chapter shared the research results of the project on geo-visualization of museum soft power to demonstrate its implications for public humanities, as well as to outline its challenges and opportunities in relation to three key levels of research development in the area of the big data digital humanities from data aggregation to intelligence. In relation to the first task, this chapter was instrumental to reveal strong relationships between practice-based digital humanities research and growing demands in the contemporary cultural and museum sector for data-intense research support to address impact assessments and audience development tasks.

These reflections have been supported by the results of the project's evaluation activities, conducted upon completion of the pilot to assess its direct impact on the industry and exploring its future development opportunities in conversation with potential stakeholders. For example, in 2018–2020 the pilot web application Museum Soft Power Map was shown to professional museum audiences and government agencies in different cities. They included invited demonstrations in Melbourne, Sydney, New York, Washington, DC, London, Brighton, Singapore, Moscow, and online through a global webinar, facilitated by the international Cultural Research Network. Online survey evaluations, conducted during these engagements indicated that more than 90% of museum and cultural management professionals among almost two hundred respondents from around the world favorably assessed the museum soft power map application, its functionality, design, usability, and applicability to museum needs.

More importantly, many respondents reported that the project strongly resonated with urgent professional issues and needs, indicating that the project generated new knowledge that can enhance the work of contemporary museums. These international survey results were further confirmed and deepened with more qualitative data collected during the business accelerator program at the University of Melbourne in the Melbourne Entrepreneurial Centre, Translating Research at Melbourne (TRaM) in 2019. The business accelerator provided a platform to closely engage with and interview museum professionals representing different cultural institutions in Melbourne and Australia, including major museums and government organizations such as Creative Victoria, City of Melbourne, and City of Melbourne Open Data, as well as cultural associations like the Australian Council for the Arts or Cultural Development Network, among others. All interviews proved that capturing, understanding, and analyzing data in museums and arts organizations for their strategic development was crucial to remain relevant in the twenty-first century.

The interviews also revealed that in most cases museums do not have a comprehensive well-developed framework or model that would allow to strategically use the data to capture the institutional impacts on the local or international levels or to engage more closely with institutional big data at all stages of their accumulation to enhance strategic organizational development. These insights proved the project "Deep Mapping" to be relevant, important, and timely. These close industry engagements, supported by the direct focused collaboration with ACMI, ensured that the project developed to benefit the public sector to adhere to its main principle of a professional "community-driven technology," allowing main stakeholders "to participate in the design and development of a project from its very beginning" (Hsu 2016, 280). At the same time, these professional consultation practices invited further research development of the project to move it further from a focused single museum soft power evaluation pilot into a new platform of cross-institutional analysis. On the next iterations of its development the system will develop new means to measure soft power in correlation to much bigger and more diverse sets of data generated among institutions and urban contexts.

Furthermore, the chapter identified and discussed three stages of public digital humanities research from the perspective of big data curation progressing from mere data collection to data intelligence. The level of data aggregation is an important stage of the digital humanities research requiring careful consideration of many factors of data collection, ranging from identifying specific data sets, and locating their sources to understanding their important characteristics. For instance, data consistency, reliability, access, and its temporality significantly impact research development and, in many cases, challenge the implementation of promising digital humanities projects that might face unresolved issues of data availability or accuracy.

The data visualization stage is the next important step in big data digital humanities research during which collected data sets transform into knowledge. Data visualization through different methods, including digital mapping that was explored in the chapter, is something more than mere data demonstration. It is increasingly considered to constitute the very analysis of data, generating important insights. Enhancing data visualization through different computational means, for instance GIS enabled deep mapping, significantly increases analytical capacities of data systems to reveal complex patterns or highlight important details moving forward the research development to effectively address public humanities needs and concerns.

Finally, data intelligence is the next step in big data digital humanities research that is based on a complex manipulation of data through artificial intelligence and machine learning algorithms. These innovative ways of data analysis allow a more advanced level of critical insight and understanding of various phenomena, objects or processes going beyond the historical analysis of their behavior or characteristics. Instead, data intelligence promises digital humanities scholars to envision or even forecast the future and look into the next stages of development of different phenomena.

This chapter used a single empirical example of the research project "Deep Mapping" to illustrate these three foundational levels or components of digital humanities research. Further enquiries can draw on this chapter's insights but should also consider other projects rapidly developing within the field of big data digital humanities (Castro 2017; Kaplan 2015) or Cultural Analytics (Manovich 2016). Specifically, the level of data intelligence requires a more focused and dedicated theoretical conceptualization to better understand how it challenges and advances digital humanities research practices within and beyond academia. Future practice-based projects that closely engage with wider publics can supply more empirical data to allow for a more accurate and valid generalization and theorization of knowledge generated through big data digital humanities research.

NOTES

1. Museum Soft Power Map: http://victoriasoftware.com/demo/.
2. Portland Soft Power 30: https://softpower30.com/.
3. Global Power City Index: http://mori-m-foundation.or.jp/english/ius2/gpci2/index.shtml.

REFERENCES

Australian Council for the Arts (ACA). 2018a. "Submission to the DFAT Soft Power Review." Accessed January 2019. https://bit.ly/2DsbJRJ.

ACA. 2018b. "International Arts Tourism." Accessed January 2019. https://bit.ly/2VRdCzN.

Australian Center for the Moving Image (ACMI). 2019. "Annual Report 2018/19." Accessed June 3, 2020. https://bit.ly/3gG3x1X.

ACMI. 2016. "ACMI Xcel Accelerator." Accessed June 3, 2020. https://bit.ly/2YR37zv.

ACMI. 2017. "Annual Report 2016/17." Accessed June 3, 2020. https://bit.ly/3lAGXLx.

Australian Urban Research Network (AURIN). 2010. "About." Accessed August 15, 2020. https://bit.ly/3lvsaSu.

Beheshti, Amin, Boualem Benatallah, Alireza Tabebordbar, Hamid Motahari-Nezhad, Moshe Barukh and Reza Nouri. 2019. "DataSynapse: A Social Data Curation Foundry." *Distributed and Parallel Databases* 37 (1): 351–84.

Blloom, Brett. 2016. "Deep Maps–Breakdown Break Down." Accessed June 3, 2020. https://bit.ly/3gG8M1D.

Bodenhamer, David, John Corrigan, and Trevor Harris, eds. 2015. *Deep Maps and Spatial Narratives*. Bloomington: Indiana University Press.

Bonyhady, Tim. 1985. *Images in Opposition: Australian Landscape Painting 1801–1890*. Oxford: Oxford University Press.

Castro, Antonio. 2017. "Big Data in the Digital Humanities. New Conversations in the Global Academic Context." *Humanities Commons*. https://doi.org/10.17613/M6434X

Chitty, Naren, Li Ji, Gary Rawnsley, and Craig Hayden, eds. 2017. *Routledge Handbook of Soft Power*. London: Routledge.

Creative Victoria (CV). 2018. "Data." Accessed January 2019. https://creative.vic.gov.au/research/data.

Department of Foreign Affairs and Trade, Australian Government (DFAT). 2016. "Public Diplomacy Strategy 2014–2016." Accessed January 2019. https://bit.ly/3jresOL.

DFAT. 2018. "Soft Power Review." Accessed January 2019. https://bit.ly/2MjFjLv.

Dorling, Daniel, and David Fairbairn. 1997. *Mapping: Ways of Representing the World*. New York: Taylor and Francis.

Duxbury, Nancy, William F. Garrett-Petts, and David MacLennan. 2015. *Cultural Mapping as Cultural Inquiry*. London: Routledge.

Greater London Authority (GLA). 2019. "Smarter London Together." Accessed June 3, 2020. https://bit.ly/2MmYIOl.

Grincheva, Natalia. 2019a. *Global Trends in Museum Diplomacy*. London: Routledge.

Grincheva, Natalia. 2019b. "Mapping Museum Soft Power: Adding Geo-visualization to the Methodological Framework." *Digital Scholarship in the Humanities* 34 (4): 730–51.

Grincheva, Natalia. 2019c. "The Form and Content of 'Digital Spatiality': Mapping Soft Power of DreamWorks Animation in Asia." *Asiascape: Digital Asia* 6 (1): 58–83.

Grincheva, Natalia. 2020a. "Deep Mapping: Creating a Dynamic Web Application Museum Soft Power Map." In *Visualizing Objects, Places, and Spaces: A Digital Project Handbook*, edited by H. Jacobs and B. Fischer. https://doi.org/10.21428/51bee781.3856e5cb.

Grincheva, Natalia. 2020b. "Museums as Actors of City Diplomacy: From 'Hardware' Resources to 'Soft' Power Strategies." In *City Diplomacy: Current Trends and Future Prospects*, edited by E. Sevin and A. Sohaela, 111–36. Cham: Palgrave Macmillan.

Guasch, Anna, and Joseba Zulaika. 2005. *Learning from the Bilbao Guggenheim*. Reno: Center for Basque Studies, University of Nevada.

Heilbrun, James, and Charles Gray. 2001. *The Economics of Art and Culture*. Cambridge: Cambridge University Press.

Hsu, Wendy. 2016. "Lessons on Public Humanities from the Civic Sphere." In *Debates in the Digital Humanities*, edited by M. Gold and L. Klein. Minneapolis, MN: University of Minnesota Press.

International Council of Museums (ICOM). 2020. "Museums for Equality: Diversity and Inclusion." Accessed August 15, 2020. http://imd.icom.museum/2020-museums-for-equality-diversity-and-inclusion/.

Kaplan, Frederic. 2015. "A Map for Big Data Research in Digital Humanities." *Frontiers in Digital Humanities* 2 (1): 1–7.

Krenn, Michael. 2005. *Fall-Out Shelters for the Human Spirit*. Chapel Hill, NC: The University of Northern California Press.

Lee, David, and Abigail Gilmore. 2012. "Mapping Cultural Assets and Evaluating Significance: Theory, Methodology and Practice." *Cultural Trends* 21 (1): 3–28.

Lord, Gail, and Ngaire Blankenberg. 2015. *Museums, Cities and Soft Power*. Lanham, MD: Rowman & Littlefield.

Manovich, Lev. 2016. "The Science of Culture? Social Computing, Digital Humanities and Cultural Analytics." *Journal of Cultural Analytics* 1 (1): 1–14.

Mar, Phillip. 2014. "Australia's Approaches to Cultural Diplomacy With/in Asia: An Overview." *Report: Australian Council of Learned Academies*. Accessed January 2019. www.acola.org.au.

Mayor of London (MOL). 2020. "Cultural Infrastructure Map." Accessed June 3, 2020. https://bit.ly/32bduRd.

Nye, Joseph. 2004. *Soft Power: The Means to Success in World Politics*. New York: Public Affairs.

Oxford English Dictionary (*OED*). 2003. "Big Data." Accessed August 15, 2020. https://bit.ly/31HKH61.

Pearce, Susan. 2000. *Museum Economics and the Community*. London: A&C Black.

Russell, Stuart, and Peter Norvig. 2021. *Artificial Intelligence: A Modern Approach*. London: Pearson education limited.

Salah, Almila, Lev Manovich, Albert Ali Salah, and Jay Chow. 2013. "Combining Cultural Analytics and Networks Analysis: Studying a Social Network Site with User-Generated Content." *Journal of Broadcasting & Electronic Media* 57 (3): 409–26.

Scott, Carol. 2006. "Museums: Impact and value." *Cultural Trends* 15 (1): 45–75.

Schreibman, Susan, Ray Siemens, and John Unsworth. 2008. *A Companion to Digital Humanities*. Malden, MA: Wiley-Blackwell.

Sullivan, Elaine, and Willeke Wendrich. 2015. "Time, Aggregation, and Analysis Designing Effective Digital Cultural Mapping Projects." In *Cultural Mapping as Cultural Inquiry*, edited by W. F. Garrett-Petts, N. Duxbury, and D. MacLennan. London: Taylor & Francis.

Swafford, Joanna. 2016. "Messy Data and Faulty Tools." In *Debates in the Digital Humanities*, edited by M. Gold and L. Klein. Minneapolis, MN: University of Minnesota Press.

Sylvester, Christine. 2009. *Art/Museums: International Relations Where We Least Expect It*. London: Paradigm Publishers.

Ward, Jonathan, and Adam Barker. 2013. "Undefined by Data: A Survey of Big Data Definitions. Cornell University." Accessed August 15, 2020. https://arxiv.org/abs/1309.5821.

Watanabe, Yasushi, and David McConnell. 2015. *Soft Power Superpowers*. London: Routledge.

PART V

Engaging Space and Place

CHAPTER 22

Maps, Music, and Culture: Representing Historical Soundscapes Through Digital Mapping

Sara Belotti and Angela Fiore

22.1 Introduction

Cartography is one of the main sources for the analysis of landscape and territorial structures, as well as for the reproduction of the way in which past populations perceived them. Although no map is a true and irrefutable representation of the territory, but only a visualization of a particular constructed narrative, this tool helps us see the interventions associated with the history of a territory, its population, as well as with the political, economic, and social sphere. In this sense, a map helps define the values followed by a community to interpret the surrounding world (Federzoni 2006). A society acts on space and creates its own territory, while maps are the instruments used to represent the territory and, consequently, the culture of a society.

Map making has been an integral part of human history since its origins,[1] but it is certainly starting from the Renaissance that the race towards modern cartography begins with the development of mathematical cartography. Nowadays the use of digital technologies has completely changed how we make a map, as well as the study of historical cartography. Among digital tools, cartographic support can contribute to new data visualizations, thanks to the development of numerous mapping tools and of Geographical Information

S. Belotti (✉)
University of Bergamo, Bergamo, Italy
e-mail: sara.belotti@unibg.it

A. Fiore
University of Messina, Messina, Italy
e-mail: angela.fiore@unime.it

© The Author(s), under exclusive license to Springer Nature Switzerland AG 2022
A. Schwan and T. Thomson (eds.), *The Palgrave Handbook of Digital and Public Humanities*, https://doi.org/10.1007/978-3-031-11886-9_22

Systems (GIS). The structure of these systems based on a database is associated with geographic information (coordinates) for the georeferencing of the data. A GIS uses a logical model that subdivides the elements into superimposed layers, with numerous technical and data management benefits, allowing simultaneous queries on the various information levels and extraction of information based on their positioning (Fea and Loret 2010). The use of GIS, which began in the 1960s mainly in public administration or in the field of earth sciences, has progressively spread to numerous sectors, including archaeology, cultural heritage, and marketing. Considerable success can also be found in the application of GIS to historical analysis. In fact, GIS tools are useful not only for the creation of maps but also for the extrapolation and reworking of information relating to the territory in various historical phases, allowing to detect its dynamics in the act (Vagnini 2010).

Digital cartography, with the support of the latest software, enables the observation of changes in the local area, for example by superimposing historical maps on satellite images. The territorial information systems allow acquiring, storing, organizing, cataloguing, modifying, re-elaborating, integrating, and returning data concerning phenomena that take place in the territory. These tools can also be used in various disciplinary fields interested in urban history, such as musicology. Cartographic tools, facilitating the visualization of places, institutions, urban areas, and paths affected by the musical activities of a city, allow us to investigate, through a wide-ranging perspective, the soundscape and the identity of cities. Cartography and mapping tools permit musicological research to pinpoint centres of musical production in urban contexts, to improve knowledge of spaces and modalities of cultural production and to understand the interaction and the reciprocal influence between music and social events. Applied to cartography and musicology, digital mapping allows for putting to use synergies of different disciplines (musicology, urban history, cartography, geography, and computer sciences) which are oriented to the reconstruction of territories as cultural identities and soundscapes.

For musicological research purposes, cartography is very useful for locating music production centres within the urban context, improving knowledge of places[2] and music production, dissemination methods and above all understanding how geographical areas and musical expression have interacted with and influenced each other. Currently, the historical disciplines and especially musicology are showing great interest in the study of music production in relation to the urban context. Starting from this assumption, this chapter takes into consideration the cartographic collection of the Biblioteca Estense Universitaria of Modena in order to propose new forms of enhancement through the digital humanities. The use of web and digital cartography, in fact, allows us to show how members of the Este Court lived in the spaces of the city, how central a part music played in the urban culture, and the ways in which it contributed to the construction of the cultural identity of the city itself. Innovative paths will offer the chance to have new points of view to study a city and its historical and cultural development, passing from the inventory and cataloguing of documents to the creation of multimedia.

22.2 Maps of the Estense Library: An Overview

The Biblioteca Estense Universitaria (Estense Library) in Modena is one of the most important European dynastic libraries. Today, it preserves numerous noteworthy manuscripts, illuminated codices, precious printed editions, and incunabola, ancient maps, and musical sources The Estense Library was established in the fifteenth century in Ferrara and was subsequently transferred to Modena in the seventeenth century. It moved to its current location at the Palazzo dei Musei in 1882 and became part of the new Gallerie Estensi Museum in 2016. In 2018, an important digitization project of the Estense Library's heritage began. The project is the result of a collaboration between Gallerie Estensi, the Fondazione di Modena and the University of Modena and Reggio Emilia. Today the digital library is available at https://edl.beniculturali.it and lets us benefit from an important documentary resource.[3]

Among the collections preserved today at the Estense Library we will focus here on the cartographic one. This collection consists of documents produced between the fifteenth and early twentieth centuries, characterized by the presence of some precious handwritten documents of ancient copper engravings and more modern prints. The current collection had a slow constitution: born from the Estes' interest in geography,[4] it continued to grow, in more recent years, with donations from private libraries of some important Modenese families. After the transfer of the court in Modena,[5] the collection of ancient maps was kept in the Ducal Palace until 1859, when Francesco V left Modena due to the arrival of the army of King Vittorio Emanuele II of Sardinia. The riots unleashed by the situation also involved the library, with the theft and disappearance of numerous geographical maps. Some documents, including the precious fifteenth-century *Mappamondo catalano estense* were found only eleven years later by Giuseppe Boni, a Modenese collector of geographical relics, who donated them to the Estense Library.

The annexation of the Este Duchy to the Kingdom of Sardinia in 1860 marked a new phase for the Library thanks to numerous donations from several Modenese noble families. Due to these events, the maps of the Estense Library are now included in various catalogues. The main one is the *Inventario dei portolani, delle carte nautiche e geografiche della R. Biblioteca Estense*, transcribed in 1892 by Clemente Lazzarini: a single list relating to all the maps owned by the library up to the unification of Italy.[6] In addition, there are catalogues of the collections donated, acquired, or purchased by the Library. Among them, the most notable is the maps collection of the Modenese nobleman Giuseppe Campori. Deposited in the Library in 1893, the collection contains some handwritten atlases and nautical charts of the seventeenth century. In 1920, the Este map collection increased with the collection of maps donated by Chiaffredo Hugues, a Modenese intellectual. The Hugues collection preserves over one hundred topographic maps and city plans, mainly from the nineteenth century. Between 1945 and 1946, the collection of Antonio Bertacchini-Mattioli enriched the Estense Library: it is based on eighteen maps produced in the second half of the nineteenth century. In 2007 the collection of the Forni family was added to the Estense Library. The Forni's collection consists of four albums with over two hundred maps produced between the eighteenth and nineteenth centuries[7] and a nucleus of topographic maps, plans, and city views made in the nineteenth century.[8] Over time, the donations were also accompanied by important purchases, including the Pio Falcò di Savoia collection, containing a dozen maps produced between the end of the seventeenth century and the end of the nineteenth century.[9] Another excellent purchase is the *Planisfero Castiglioni*,[10] created in 1525; it is an example of the so-called *Padrones Reales*, a secret Spanish master map.[11] Finally, two series of maps are also part of the Estense cartographic heritage: the *Piante di Modena e dello Stato* in which about thirty maps of the city and province have been grouped; and the *Serie Atlantica*, containing about sixty maps from different parts of the world, created between the eighteenth and nineteenth centuries by various authors, including Guillaume De L'Isle.

Overall, the collection now includes about a thousand maps in loose sheets and numerous atlases, including those of Gerhard Kremer and the Blaeu family.[12] Considering the richness and heterogeneity of the material present in the Estense Library, the cataloguing project focused in particular on cartography in loose sheets. The aim was to prepare a unique inventory of the maps owned by the Estense Library with a descriptive entry for each map. A unique, digital catalogue allows the user (primarily academics and students) today a better knowledge and usability of this important heritage.

22.3 The Sound of Modena

The Estense Library also preserves an important music collection which is now considered one of the most prestigious European musical collections. Today, the Estense collection is an indispensable resource for studying some musical genres such as madrigal, oratorio, cantata, and instrumental music. The Estense music collection owes a lot to Francesco II. The tenth duke of Modena and Reggio Emilia from 1674 to 1694, Francesco II was a patron of the art of music. Francesco II promoted extensive cultural initiatives in the city, including the renewal of the university, the activities of literary academies, the continuation of artistic and architectural works in the Palazzo Ducale, and the reorganization of the ducal library. The duke felt compelled to collect and commission music for his own leisure and practice, as well as for entertainment at court. The ducal court welcomed new genres and forms under the cultural stimulus of Francesco II: oratorios, dramas, and cantatas by the leading composers of the time such as Alessandro Stradella, Alessandro Scarlatti, Giovanni Bononcini, Bernardo Pasquini, Alessandro Melani are today preserved in the music collection. Towards the mid-seventeenth century, thanks to the Este dukes, Modena effectively became one of the music capitals of Italy. The city turned into a repository of innovations and artistic trends supported by an enlightened court that was surprisingly sensitive to the musical ferment of the Baroque period. Social life in Modena gradually became entwined with art music. The city's physical locations participated in the evolution of musical language, influencing the ways in which music was produced, performed, and listened to.

The city of Modena has often been studied from various points of view. In the field of musicology, a plethora of studies concern different aspects of the Este musical heritage. The most important studies concern: musical sources of the house of Este (Luin 1936; Chiarelli 1987; Seifert 2002); and musical activity of some city institutions (Martinelli Braglia 1985; Crowther 1990). A group of essays focuses on musical genres of the House of Este (Jander 1975); on court musicians (Roncaglia 1952; Suess 1999; Wilk 2004), and their individual music production (Gianturco 1974). However, an organic reconstruction of the different types of musical activities in the city and especially a music-oriented investigation of the relationship between court and city is lacking to date. At the same time, geographers and historians have always paid more attention to the study of some maps of the Estense collection for their historical value (Campbell 1987; Milano 1991, 2001; Milano and Battini 1995; Rombai 2007; Woodward 1987) or to the cultural environment of the Este court, including the geographical culture of the Este family (Donattini 2000; Federzoni 2001; Gambi 1982; Rossi 2006), but a study on the soundscape of Modena is still missing.

The study and cataloguing that we have conducted on these collections have permitted us to read these sources from a different perspective. Comparing musical manuscripts, historical maps, and archival sources is particularly useful to grasp the multiform connections between court, city, and territory, offering many details in the complex relationships between sound and space within the urban context. Therefore, our idea has been to fully exploit the potential of digital humanities and to go beyond the simple digitization of sources. Musical sources can be interpreted as the product of an interaction between court and city. The Este collection of musical sources shows us the city's musical identity: certain sources bear witness to the various sonic experiences in which the court and the city participated. Reading and interpreting places and spaces through the sound production that took place in them, constitutes a point of confluence between musicology and geography (Giuriati 2015, 115). In fact, sound has been one of the essential components in the development of city spaces. Even in the course of history, musical production has been conditioned by the place for which and in which it was performed. At the same time, the music itself has helped to define the identity of a place, influencing in some cases its architecture (Dell'Agnese and Tabusi 2016; Rocca 2013). The city represents a privileged environment for musical creation, showing through its history, the complex network of institutional relationships that made it possible; the methods of circulation of music, sources, and genres; and the social status and mobility of musicians (Bombi et al. 2005, 18).

Unlike other Italian cities in which cultural affairs were governed by the state, Modena was entirely managed by the court, including all artistic and cultural activities. The presence of a court probably improved its citizens' quality of life and favoured the creation of a lively cultural and musical scene that could converse with the most prestigious European courts. While under Francesco I's rule Modena underwent numerous architectural transformations and new spaces were created for lavish celebrations to extol the glory of the House of Este, under Francesco II music "left" the court to engage in dialogue with the city. It was during the two decades of Francesco II d'Este's reign that the city's musical splendour reached its peak. Francesco II understood the need to provide many more opportunities to create music through cooperation with some of the city's institutions: the Oratorio di San Carlo Rotondo, certain theatres in the city, and the Accademia de' Dissonanti (Crowther 1992; Jander 1975).

Moreover, during the seventeenth century, the city's spaces often provided a stage for spectacular events involving different civil and religious institutions and featuring music and renowned musicians. Modena's squares and streets were often settings for special events organized by the court such as masquerades, tournaments, and jousting. Already in the late sixteenth century, masquerades and quintains were held in the city's open spaces, featuring floats and theatrical performances. These occasions were not only intended as a means of celebrating an anniversary, entertaining the court and the people, or organizing cultural events; they were also excellent opportunities for dukes to demonstrate the magnificence of the court. The music of the Este family in Modena in the late seventeenth century thus became a social art designed to be displayed and used as a tool for building consensus and publicly affirming the prince's power. The different occasions of music present in the ducal city had resulted in a varied "soundscape" comprised of both ostentatious aspects and a more intimate musical tradition restricted to the everyday life of the court.

22.4 The Este Soundscape Project

Our project intends to turn its gaze towards urban musicology and soundscape studies to consider music as a social and cultural activity, not just as something artistic. With their social and cultural resources, cities have been a prerequisite for the growth of music production. The work carried out has not only led to the study of the two Estense collections but has also stimulated reflection on the enhancement of this heritage, leading to the launch of a multidisciplinary project which, taking advantage of the possibilities offered, once again, by digital humanities, wants to go beyond cataloguing. In fact, in recent years, the evolution of this field of study has opened new research opportunities, allowing not only the digitization of documents, but also the preparation of catalogues, virtual spaces, collaborative research, and in-depth paths. In particular, the comparison and cross-referencing of data through new display modes offers the opportunity to highlight the existence of networks and relationships that cannot otherwise be analysed. Thus, the idea of a digital platform dedicated to the results obtained from the study of the musical and cartographic heritage of the Este House was born.

The Este soundscape project intends to create a digital platform through which to reconstruct and explore sounds, places, events, and people who contributed to the creation of a city's musical identity.[13] The online platform, which is currently under construction, will enable the user to explore and see the urban landscape of early modern Modena, to hear the sounds and music of this city, to access resources dedicated to different sonic events, to read musical sources, and to have data instantly about the context of their production.[14] Thanks to the use of state-of-the-art web development tools and GIS, the platform will feature an interactive search and navigation environment, plus an interactive map with geo-localized objects and events. The chronological period considered by the project is the seventeenth century: it is in fact in this century that Modena becomes a first-rate cultural centre and creates its "sound identity".

22.4.1 The Cartographic System

The fulcrum of the Este soundscape project is an interactive map within the platform. The map, as we will see in the following pages, will allow the identification of the musical centres of early modern Modena, to carry out advanced searches to filter the data and view the insights through *pop-ups* and hypertext links. For the creation of the digital map, the Google Satellite Web mapping service was used as a basis, on which two historical maps of the collection of the Estense Library were superimposed. The map enables the user to compare the structure of the city in two different historical moments: the end of the seventeenth century and the beginning of the nineteenth century.

The first map chosen is an eighteenth-century reproduction of the famous 1684 map by Gian Battista Boccabadati,[15] made by Domenico Vandelli.[16] The representation shows both the above-ground Modena, with a plan drawing of buildings and streets, and the underground Modena, with the canals and drains already partially buried. This detailed document points out the *forma urbis* of the city after changes that occurred in the sixteenth and seventeenth centuries: the Herculean Addition, the Citadel of Castellamonte, and the Palazzo Ducale.[17] Modena would maintain this structure until the end of the eighteenth century, when various interventions, promoted by both Francesco III and his son Ercole III, would completely modify the urban aspect (Bertuzzi 2001). Therefore, Vandelli's map that wants to describe the city in detail, is particularly suitable for our project, because it is possible to identify buildings, streets, squares, and the main infrastructures on it thanks to the numerous labels. Finally, the Vandelli's map constitutes a significant testimony for the city of Modena, created to pay homage to the city itself. The map, commissioned by the Community of Modena in 1684, was displayed in the Council Room "in the service of the city", with the order that it never be removed from that place (Quaderni dell'Archivio Storico di Modena 2009, 4).

The second map is probably dated to the beginning of the nineteenth century. On this map it is possible to appreciate the interventions implemented by Francesco III and Ercole III during the eighteenth century. In 1760 Francesco III started the renewal of the city from the expansion of the Via Emilia. This renewal was based on an urban plan inspired by the ideals of rationality and regularity typical of the age of Enlightenment. The main aim was to demolish unhealthy houses and improve the city's services, transforming it into a modern European capital.[18] Looking at this map we can identify different urban nuclei which, having developed over time, constitute today's city. The southern part, from the current Viale delle Rimembranze, near the ancient Porta S. Francesco, to the Via Emilia, represents the medieval core that still characterized the city before the sixteenth century, articulated in curvilinear and often narrow paths. The northern part, from the Via Emilia to what is now Viale Crispi and Piazzale Natale Bruni, has a more "modern" structure. Here the so-called "Addizione Erculea" was created, promoted by Ercole II in the sixteenth: an "addition" to the ancient city with an orthogonal grid and wide streets. The ducal palace, built in 1634, is also located in this area (Bertuzzi 2001). Finally, in the north-western part, where today the Novisad Park is located, the military Citadel was built, between 1635 and 1642, by Francesco I, subsequently demolished in the twentieth century. The two historical maps are the basis of the digital system. On them are icons which, as we will see below, testify to the centre of music production in Modena and allow interaction with a database in which the sheets of the archival sources are stored.

22.4.2 *The Database*

The platform is based on a *relational database system*, containing data derived from the analysis and study of musical, cartographic, historical, and archival sources. The *database* created in *Django Framework* is divided into interrelated entities called *Sources, People, Genres, Events, and Institutions*. The database offers various possibilities for accessing the data: the traditional search and browse resources; a free text search; a search index; and a time slider.

The *Sources* entity represents the main core of the database and holds records of musical sources examined. The *Persons* entity stores data related to musicians and composers. In *Genres* entity musical sources are divided according to their musical form. In *Events*, one can find all spectacular and musical events realized in the public spaces of the city. Finally, the *Institution* entity contains records related to the centre of music production in Modena.

The *Institutions* are the connecting element between the relational database system and the virtual map called EsteWebGis: each institution is georeferenced through the OpenStreetMap plug-in present in the database, showing the location of each institution on the map. The virtual map provides an interactive city navigation environment through the Google Satellite Web mapping service. Thanks to the features of the QGIS software, the historical map of Domenico Vandelli and the nineteenth-century map of Modena were georeferenced, matching them with the satellite image of modern Modena. By simply ticking or deselecting the layer of the historical maps, this overlap enables a comparison of the historic city structure to the present day, and a study of the evolution of the urban landscape over the centuries (Fig. 22.1). Moreover, using queries, it will be possible to filter and to cross-reference data to obtain re-elaborations of the base map according to specific criteria.

Furthermore, centres of music production in the city can be identified on the map using polygons. They have been divided into four categories: *Theatres, Squares, Palaces, and Churches*.

Thanks to the web layers, the EsteWebGis proposes different views: it is possible to select a specific category or view all categories from the menu. For example, theatres can be highlighted rather than churches or squares. Informative pop-ups display information regarding institutions and their musical activities and give direct access to the related musical sources (Fig. 22.2).

During the seventeenth century, several theatres in the city began to host opera performances, offering a busy, high-quality calendar of events supported by the various dukes. The city's first theatrical activity was carried out at the Teatro della Spelta, built at the behest of duke Francesco I, who was keen to provide the duchy's new capital with a theatre that met the needs of the court. Instead, the first court theatre, housed in the Palazzo Ducale, dates back to 1669. It was a small theatre exclusively intended for the court's private use. Among them, the most interesting theatre, which managed to

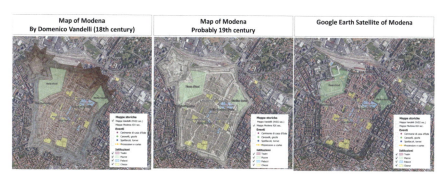

Fig. 22.1 Este WebGis: comparison of the historical map of Domenico Vandelli, the nineteenth-century map of Modena, and the satellite image of modern Modena (Authors' elaboration. Use of historical maps by the courtesy of Ministero della Cultura—Gallerie Estensi, Biblioteca Estense Universitaria)

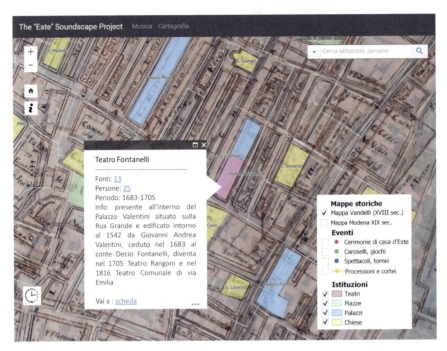

Fig. 22.2 Este WebGis: Teatro Fontanelli (Authors' elaboration. Use of historical maps by the courtesy of Ministero della Cultura—Gallerie Estensi, Biblioteca Estense Universitaria)

combine the needs of the court with those of the city, was the Teatro Fontanelli, the most important theatre in the Este States, directly linked to the duke's cultural policy (Fig. 22.3). The theatre, renamed Teatro Fontanelli, was chosen by Francesco II as the place to host theatrical performances that were sponsored by the court, but open to a paying audience. The Estense Library now preserves nine opera scores and the Fontanelli family's collection of librettos.[19] The presence and correspondence of archival documentation, musical sources, and libretti allows us to reconstruct the whole operatic activity of the Fontanelli Theatre, providing at the same time, an accurate portrait of the court opera in Modena.

The Fontanelli Theatre does not exist today. Its location remains visible only in some historical maps of Modena, like the Vandelli one. A pop-up displays brief explanatory notes, the number of sources and people associated with the theatre, and a hypertext link to the corresponding institution record (Fig. 22.3).

The record contains data about the history of the institution, bibliographic, and archival sources connected to it. It is possible to visualize the musical sources linked to the institution and present in the database, and to access the specific entry.

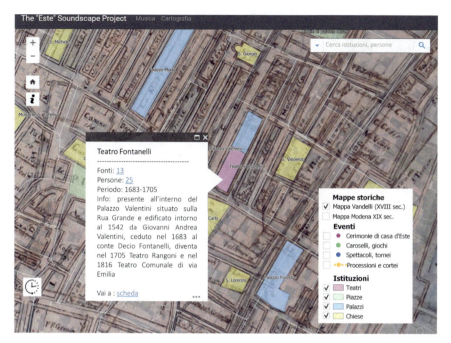

Fig. 22.3 Institution record: Teatro Fontanelli (Authors' elaboration)

The map will also be able to display a series of external events (*carousel, shows, ceremonies, processions*) through which the court interacted with the city (Fig. 22.4). The map shows the performance spaces in the city and in case of itinerant events, such as civic and religious parades and processions, the path can be displayed.

For example, throughout the sixteenth century, Piazza Grande was one of the city's key locations. The main buildings of civic and religious power stood on either side of the square: the cathedral with its bell tower known as the "Ghirlandina", the Palazzo Comunale, and the Palazzo della Ragione. The main religious ceremonies were also held in this square in the seventeenth century, especially liturgies related to the liturgical year, the cathedral and the rites of San Geminiano, patron saint of Modena. The chronicler Giovan Battista Spaccini (1999, 105–6) describes an impressive "masquerade" that took place in Piazza Grande for the Carnival in 1604: several Modenese noblemen took part and a "very cheerful show" was organized featuring "French-style ballets with very pleasant and lively music" that continued during the night. The music was "arranged by Mr. Orazio Vecchi". The masquerade, according to Spaccini, had passed along the city's streets preceded by "many players of different instruments, dressed in delicate colours to ward off melancholy".[20]

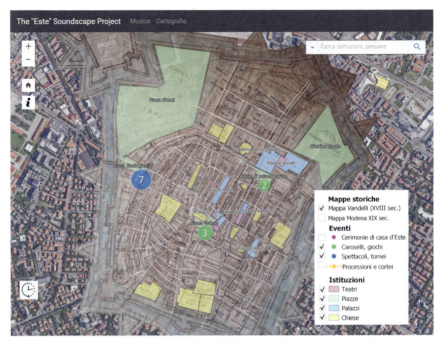

Fig. 22.4 Este WebGis Screenshot: Events (Authors' elaboration. Use of historical maps by the courtesy of Ministero della Cultura—Gallerie Estensi, Biblioteca Estense Universitaria)

The musical source of this event has been lost. However, the map shows the place and space of performance. A concise pop-up links to a specific record describing the event; it offers access to related historical and bibliographic sources and image galleries. Furthermore, if several events have been carried out in the same places, a cluster will indicate the total number. Through the search function, it will be possible to filter results. A time slider will allow the user to discover the chronological evolution of the spectacular events. The slider will also be useful for obtaining information on the period of activity of an institution present on the map or for knowing the number of musical activities present in the city in a specific period.

22.5 Potential of the Platform for Teaching

This platform can also be a teaching tool for scholars dealing with early modern cities in several respects. It offers new opportunities to animate academic teaching about the cultural history of Modena and more generally about the urban musical culture. According to teaching methodologies related to "action research", the Este soundscape interactive map can be useful for the realization of projects by students. Specifically, this didactic method has been developed to understand the problems existing in specific contexts by sharing theoretical and practical knowledge. Action research is structured in several phases: (1) identification of the problem; (2) diagnosis, to be corroborated through data research, thanks to which intervention hypotheses can emerge; and (3) verification and revision of the diagnosis through the documentation of the perception of the different actors involved in the same action. It is in the last phase that the student fully enters as a protagonist who offers a different contribution to understand the problem and reformulate it (Elliott et al. 1993, 22). Through the analysis of documents and spaces of the city, students can realize some specific projects to understand in a deeper way how the daily life of the court unfolded. For instance, the action research path can, therefore, begin with the presentation of a case study, proposed by the teacher to the students, divided into small working groups. The working groups will then be able to proceed independently, collecting data through the web platform and deepening them through a bibliographic search. Finally, each group will be able to present their work to the class by proposing their reflections and ideas that emerged during the diagnosis phase, also having the opportunity to compare their work with that of their colleagues and to discuss the topic at hand (Pasquinelli d'Allegra 2010). The flexibility and potential of the platform permit adding other layers, in addition to geographic and musicological information, linked for example to the history of art, urban history, etc. The realization of projects dedicated to urban history can actively involve students and allow for connections with other didactic areas, favouring interdisciplinary connections.

22.6 Conclusion

The development of a digital project dedicated to city soundscape can open a discussion in geographical fields on music and landscape in the early modern era, also providing a useful tool for the representation of the city. The innovative approach will allow users to study the musical heritage in an urban context using an online interactive map with digital resources. The possibility of cross-references between several types of documents through digital tools not only enables access to musical sources but also allows users to gain insight into the multi-faceted network of musicians and musical activities realized both in and by the Este court. Moreover, the map enables the user to have new points of view to study a city and its historical and spectacular development. In this sense, the Este WebGIS can be a valid tool for analysing the artistic and spatial context of a city in a more general sense. Thanks to digital technology, the platform will feature an interactive search and navigation environment. Above all the project wants to propose a collaborative and multidisciplinary model for historical research and provide new ideas for the enhancement of cultural heritage. In this regard, one of the aims of the project is that of building a common platform which can be further employed in different geographical and historical contexts. To foster re-use, reproducibility, and further adoption by other scholars, the source code of the platform will be made publicly available.

NOTES

1. Historians of cartography identified some examples of prehistoric maps in different forms of picture art and rock art. Some examples are the picture map from Çatal Hiiyiik, a Neolithic site in central Turkey, or the petroglyph maps around Mont Bégo (France) and Valcamonica (Italy), dated from the Bronze and Iron Age (Delano Smith 1987).
2. In this context it is important to emphasize that a map is not regarded as a technical tool. The map is understood in its double role: as social product that shows us the ways in which a given society builds its own items of territorial knowledge and as a means of communication, whereby these knowledge items are circulated. Maps are therefore considered as tokens of the intellectual appropriation humans pursue as they endeavour to master the world (Casti 2015). Using a map to study the territory, therefore, provides a deeper understanding of the society that produced it.
3. The library offers the possibility of comparing and annotating over 700 thousand pages of manuscripts preserved at the Estense Library. The platform is based on the *International Image Interoperability Framework* (IIIF), a protocol for standardized image retrieval created by a community of the world's leading research libraries and image repositories. Through this technological tool, a high-definition image becomes comparable with others, editable and freely annotated. Rare manuscripts, maps, and musical sources in the Estense Digital Library are now browsable, comparable with other images, and shareable.
4. This interest in geography and cartography on the part of the Este family represents a particularly important means of facing the challenge of Ferrara's spatial and political marginality, as the maps "summarize" the information brought to Europe by explorers, navigators, and markets (Salomons and Moretti 1984).
5. Entrusted to the Este dynasty in the late thirteenth century, Modena became the capital of the Este state at the end of the sixteenth century. In 1598, following the "Conventions of Faenza", the Este were forced to quickly move from Ferrara to Modena, the duchy's second most important city.
6. No previous catalogs are present today in the Estense Library, only some sporadic lists of the maps can be found. This situation does not make it easy to reconstruct the original nucleus of the collection.
7. The history of this collection begins with the Modenese cleric Matteo Pagliaroli (1716–77) who in the first half of the eighteenth century formed a rich library; later it passed to the Forni counts by inheritance and over time expanded with new accessions.
8. This part of the collection is currently being catalogued and has only been partially digitized.
9. The Pio Falcò di Savoia collection was purchased by the Italian Ministry for Cultural Heritage and Activities (Ministero per i Beni e le Attività Culturali—MiBAC) and then donated to the Estense Library in 2001.

10. According to tradition, the Planisphere was donated as a sign of benevolence by the Emperor Charles V to Baldassare Castiglioni, a talented military man and man of letters and the *apostolic nuncio* to Spain.
11. *Padrones Reales* maps were constantly updated based on the news that came from exploration trips. They were jealously guarded by the Spanish crown to avoid commercial espionage.
12. Gerhard Kremer (Gerardus Mercator) was a geographer and a cartographer who introduced the term atlas for a collection of maps. The Blaeu family ran a famous workshop of maps and globes in Flanders.
13. The platform is currently under construction.
14. Initially conceived at the Interdepartmental Center on Digital Humanities, University of Modena and Reggio Emilia, the project is currently being developed independently by the authors.
15. Giovan Battista Boccabadati (Modena 1635–96) was a lawyer, also involved in mathematical and scientific studies. In 1671 he was appointed court librarian by Duke Francesco II and in 1681 the Duke appointed him court engineer. In 1684 he was commissioned by the Municipality of Modena to create a map of the city. The original map of Giovan Battista Boccabadati is today preserved in the Modena Municipal Archive.
16. Domenico Vandelli (Levizzano Rangone 1691—Modena 1754) studied with the Jesuits, following an ecclesiastical career, later becoming Abbot, and at the University of Modena applying himself in philosophy, mathematics, and theology. Thanks to his studies he became professor of mathematics and engineering at the University of Modena. He was also a geographer of the Este court and antiquarian and then inspector of rivers and drainage.
17. With the investiture of Modena as the capital of the Este duchy, a process of urban renewal began to give it an aspect more suited to its new function. In the second half of the sixteenth century, the Herculean Addition had expanded the urban area to the north, although the city still preserved a medieval-type layout. During the seventeenth century, numerous construction sites were opened (for the construction of churches and the embellishment of noble palaces). The most important projects carried out in this period were the construction of the military Citadel, between 1635 and 1642, and the Ducal Palace to replace the old castle.
18. When the Este court moved its capital to Modena, it was a provincial town, with low houses with dark arcades, narrow winding streets, and where even the buildings of the most important families were modest (Bertuzzi 2001).
19. The Fontanelli Family's collection consists of 1352 music librettos, all printed and dated from the early seventeenth century to around 1760. Many of them relate to Modenese performances of musical dramas that took place at the Teatro Fontanelli during the reign of Francesco II.
20. Spaccini's chronicle is a valuable account that offers a vivid insight into the most important events in the city of Modena. Spaccini produced nine volumes of chronicles: the first two rework the diaries of Iacopino and Tommasino Lancellotti, while the rest report the episodes that Spaccini witnessed between 1588 and 1636.

References

Bertuzzi, Giordano. 2001. "Rinnovamento edilizio di una capitale." In *Lo Stato di Modena. Una capitale, una dinastia, una civiltà nella storia d'Europa. Atti del convegno, Modena, 25–28 marzo 1998*, edited by Angelo Spaggiari and Giuseppe Trenti, 93–104. Roma: Ministero per i beni e le attività culturali. Direzione generale per gli archivi.

Bombi, Andrea, Juan José Carreras, and Miguel Ángel Marín. 2005. *Música y cultura urbana en la edad moderna*. Valencia: Universitat de Valencia.

Campbell, Tony. 1987. "Portolan Charts from the Late Thirteenth Century to 1500." In *The History of Cartography, vol. I, Cartography in Prehistoric, Ancient, and Medieval Europe and the Mediterranean*, edited by J. B. Harley and David Woodward, 371–463. Chicago and London: University of Chicago Press.

Casti, Emanuela. 2015. *Reflexive Cartography: A New Perspective on Mapping*. Amsterdam: Elsevier.

Chiarelli, Alessandra. 1987. *I codici di musica della raccolta estense: ricostruzione dall'inventario settecentesco*. Firenze: Olschki.

Crowther, Victor. 1990. "A Case-Study in the Power of the Purse: The Management of the Ducal 'Cappella' in Modena in the Reign of Francesco II d'Este." *Journal of the Royal Musical Association* 115, no. 2: 207–19.

Crowther, Victor. 1992. *The Oratorio in Modena*. Oxford: Clarendon Press.

Delano Smith, Catherine. 1987. "Cartography in the Prehistoric Period in the Old World: Europe, the Middle East, and North Africa." In *The History of Cartography, vol. I, Cartography in Prehistoric, Ancient, and Medieval Europe and the Mediterranean*, edited by J. B. Harley and David Woodward, 54–101. Chicago and London: University of Chicago Press.

Dell'Agnese, Elena, and Massimiliano Tabusi. 2016. "Introduzione." In *La musica come Geografia: suoni, luoghi, territori*, edited by Elena Dell'Agnese and Massimiliano Tabusi, 5–12. Roma: SGI.

Donattini, Massimo. 2000. "Cultura geografica ferrarese del Rinascimento." In *Storia di Ferrara, vol. VI: Il Rinascimento. Situazioni e personaggi*, edited by Adriano Prosperi, 407–58. Ferrara: Corbo.

Elliott, John, André Giordan, and Cesare Scurati. 1993. *La ricerca-azione. Metodiche, strumenti, casi*. Torino: Bollati Boringhieri.

Fea, Maurizio, and Emanuele Loret. 2010. "Che cos'è un GIS. Esempi di applicazioni scientifiche." In *GIS tra natura e tecnologia. Strumento per la didattica e la diffusione della cultura scientifica*, edited by Simone Bozzato, 53–76. Roma: Carocci.

Federzoni, Laura. 2001. "Gli Stati di casa d'Este nella cartografia." In *Lo Stato di Modena. Una capitale, una dinastia, una civiltà nella storia d'Europa*, vol. 1, edited by Angelo Spaggiari and Giuseppe Trenti, 451–80. Roma: Ministero per i beni e le attività culturali. Direzione generale per gli archivi.

Federzoni, Laura. 2006. *Marco Antonio Pasi a Ferrara. Cartografia e governo del territorio al crepuscolo del Rinascimento*. Firenze: Istituto geografico militare.

Gambi, Lucio. 1982. "Stato degli studi sulla produzione cartografica presso la corte degli Estensi." In *La corte e lo spazio: Ferrara Estense*, edited by Giuseppe Papagno and Amedeo Quondam, 223–32. Roma: Bulzoni Editore.

Gianturco, Carolyn. 1974. "The Oratorios of Alessandro Stradella." *Proceedings of the Royal Musical Association* 101, no. 1: 45–57.

Giuriati, Giovanni. 2015. "Il suono come forma di conoscenza dello spazio che ci circonda. Una prospettiva musicologica." *Semestrale di studi e ricerche di geografia* 27, no. 2: 115–28.

Jander, Owen. 1975. "The Cantata in Accademia: Music for the Accademia de' Dissonanti and their Duke Francesco II d'Este." *Rivista Italiana di Musicologia* 10: 519–44.

Luin, Elizabeth J. 1936. "Repertorio dei Libri musicali di S. A. S. Francesco II d'Este nell'Archivio di Stato di Modena." *La Bibliofilía* 38, no. 11/12: 418–45.

Martinelli Braglia, Graziella. 1985. "Il Teatro Fontanelli: Note su impresari e artisti nella Modena di Francesco II e Rinaldo I." In *Alessandro Stradella e Modena. Atti del Convegno internazionale di studi Modena 15–17 dicembre 1983*, edited by Carolyn Gianturco, 107–15. Modena: Teatro comunale di Modena.

Milano, Ernesto. 1991. *La carta del Cantino e la rappresentazione della terra nei codici e nei libri a stampa della Biblioteca Estense Universitaria*. Modena: Il Bulino.

Milano, Ernesto, ed. 2001. *Planisfero Castiglioni: Carta del navegare universalissima et diligentissima, 1525: C.G.A.12 Modena, Biblioteca Estense universitaria. Commentario all'edizione in facsimile*. Modena: Il Bulino.

Milano, Ernesto, and Annalisa Battini, eds. 1995. *Il mappamondo catalano estense*. Zurigo: Urs Graf Verlag.

Pasquinelli d'Allegra, Daniela. 2010. "I GIS nella didattica della geografia." In *GIS tra natura e tecnologia. Strumento per la didattica e la diffusione della cultura scientifica*, edited by Simone Bozzato, 77–84. Roma: Carocci.

Quaderni dell'Archivio Storico di Modena. 2009. *La "Rappresentazione" della Città di Modena. Gian Battista Boccabadati Poeta, Letterato, Cartografo*, XXIV. Modena: Archivio Storico di Modena.

Rocca, Lorena. 2013. "Le impronte del paesaggio sonoro: un'opportunità per la didattica della storia e della geografia." *Ri-Vista ricerche per la progettazione del paesaggio* 11, no. 1: 17–25. Accessed 31 Aug 2020. https://oaj.fupress.net/index.php/rivista/issue/view/215.

Rombai, Leonardo. 2007. "Cartography in the Central Italian States from 1480 to 1680." In *The History of Cartography, vol. III (Part I), Cartography in the European Renaissance*, edited by David Woodward, 909–39. Chicago and London: University of Chicago Press.

Roncaglia, Gino. 1952. "Giuseppe Colombi e la vita musicale modenese durante il regno di Francesco II d'Este." *Atti e Memorie dell'Accademia di Scienze, Lettere e Arti di Modena* 5, no. 10: 31–52.

Rossi, Massimo. 2006. "La geografia del Furioso, sul sapere geo-cartografico alla corte estense." In *Lucrezia Borgia. Storia e mito*, edited by Michele Bordin and Paolo Trovato, 97–138. Firenze: Olschki.

Salmson, June, and Walter Moretti, eds. 1984. *The Renaissance in Ferrara and its European Horizons. Rinascimento a Ferrara e i suoi orizzonti europei*. Ravenna: Edizioni del Girasole.

Seifert, Herbert. 2002. "Die 'Estensische Musikalien' der Österreichischen Nationalbibliothek." *Studien zur Musikwissenschaft. Festschrift Leopold M. Kantner zum 70. Geburtstag* 49: 413–23.

Spaccini, Giovan Battista. 1993–2008. *Cronaca di Modena (1588–1636)*, edited by Albano Biondi, Rolando Bussi and Carlo Giovannini. 6 vols. Modena: Panini.

Suess, John. 1999. "Giuseppe Colombi's Dance Music for the Estense Court of Duke Francesco II of Modena." In *Marco Uccellini: atti del convegno "Marco Uccellini da Forlimpopoli e la sua musica,*" edited by Maria Caraci Vela and Marina Toffetti, 141–62. Lucca: LIM.

Vagnini, Alessandro. 2010. "Il GIS come strumento dell'analisi storica." In *GIS tra natura e tecnologia. Strumento per la didattica e la diffusione della cultura scientifica*, edited by Simone Bozzato, 217–29. Roma: Carocci.

Wilk, Piotr. 2004. "Carl'Ambrogio Lonati and Giuseppe Colombi: A New Attribution of the Biblioteca Estense Violin Sonatas." *Musica Iagellonica* 3:171–95.

Woodward, David. 1987. "Medieval Mappaemundi." In *The History of Cartography, vol. I, Cartography in Prehistoric, Ancient, and Medieval Europe and the Mediterranean*, edited by J. B. Harley and David Woodward, 286–370. Chicago and London: University of Chicago Press.

CHAPTER 23

Civic Interaction, Urban Memory, and the Istanbul International Film Festival

Sarah Jilani

23.1 Introduction

Destruction is done in the name of progress, a concept that today still holds the status of a supreme authority, sparing people the responsibility for their destructive actions and making them believe that their actions were guided by an authority higher than human interests. (Ariella Aïsha Azoulay 2019)

The socio-political stakes of the Istanbul International Film Festival (IIFF) exceed its temporal and spatial limits. Existing as it does at the charged intersection between urban development, collective memory, and freedom of assembly, the festival has survived thirty-eight years of the Turkish state's (once secular-authoritarian, now Islamist-authoritarian) censorious attitude toward the arts—thanks in various parts to civic stewardship, activist journalism, state appeasement, and private capital. However, 2010–2013 saw a culture of urban resistance flourish with every April iteration of the film festival; its immediate cause was the impending destruction of the IIFF's flagship cinema, Emek, but its long-fomenting context was the encroachment of the Turkish state, in collusion with the private construction sector, on the urban fabric, collective memory, and spatio-civic life of Istanbul. Holding space as it does—physically and discursively—for civic interaction, urban history, and public art, the

S. Jilani (✉)
University of London, London, UK
e-mail: Sarah.Jilani@city.ac.uk

© The Author(s), under exclusive license to Springer Nature Switzerland AG 2022
A. Schwan and T. Thomson (eds.), *The Palgrave Handbook of Digital and Public Humanities*, https://doi.org/10.1007/978-3-031-11886-9_23

IIFF was politicized through direct action that together constituted the Emek Cinema Resistance. This grassroots movement turned the content and form of the IIFF into a public matter and a public undertaking for three years—that is to say, it initiated a culture of urban resistance that in many ways became a precursor to the millions-strong Gezi Park Protests of May–August 2013, fostering ideas of urban memory and street-based civic interaction during and beyond the official two-week run of the IIFF.

While the temporal specificity of the movement yields important understandings of the relationship between Istanbul's urban fabric, the associations of film-going for one section of its population, and recent forms of social organizing against the privatization of space in Istanbul, this localized movement also attempted a more expansive confrontation. As the Turkish government, the Istanbul Metropolitan Municipality (also helmed by the governing party at the time), and their cronies in various sectors like construction and transport persistently sought to justify their urban interventions, they resorted to an ambiguous terminology of "progress." Enshrining the concept as a kind of "supreme authority" (Azoulay 2019, 69), their implication was that to challenge these interventions meant risking the economic well-being of one's own society. In a neoliberalizing and atomizing city, however, this was not the idea of progress shared by some Istanbulites. They temporarily formed, in Michael Warner's definition, what had "the content and differentiated belonging of a group" (2002, 76), but in seeking to extend the circulation of their political discourse to all the inhabitants of the city, became a "public."

In this chapter, I will argue that two considerations make my above reading possible. The first hinges on historical-social context: namely, how cinemagoing, as an art form that cut across various segments of Turkish society since its popularization in the mid-twentieth century, still carries political import in its ability to blur some of the divides in contemporary Istanbul. The second focuses on the festival's urban locality, Beyoğlu: a space of overlapping social, political, and economic tensions that render the centuries-old district the closest thing this sprawling metropolis has to a city center. Taksim Square, located at the end (or beginning) of Beyoğlu's bustling and pedestrianized Istiklâl Avenue, has long been a site of political life. Its place in Istanbul's collective urban memory ranges across different groups: from a place of memoriam and mourning for the aging left (who recall their 1970s May Days spent marching in Taksim), to a place of daily struggle against marginalization for the Syrian refugees looking for casual work in its cheap eateries. This discussion will conjoin these two foci—the social history of cinema in Istanbul and the collective spatial experience/memory of Beyoğlu—through an exploration of the public response to the destruction of Emek Cinema. In Turkey's (still ongoing) period of overlapping Islamist and neoliberal pressures, these two factors and their socio-spatial effects situated the IIFF squarely within civic concerns around who gets to shape urban space.

23.2 Historical Context and Key Theoretical Concepts

As book after book has attested to (Freely 1974; Ortaylı 1987; Mansel 1998; Hughes 2017), it would not be hyperbole to acknowledge that Istanbul is a unique city in terms of history, patterns of migration, geopolitical position, and religious significance. Its six millennia of urban life have yielded a veritable sedimentation of pasts that are still discernible in the present-day metropolis of well over 15 million (World Population Review 2020). The politics of managing its "too much history," in Elif Batuman's apt words (2015, n.p.), often quite literally reveals the priorities, policies, ideologies, and vested interests of those in power. That power itself is transient, not only in the political sense (Istanbul has had elected mayors with constitutionally limited terms since 1930) but also in a spatio-temporal sense. The 2004–2013 Yenikapı Harbor Excavation, for instance, revealed a Byzantine harbor dating back to the fifth to eleventh century CE, delaying the construction of a high-speed underwater railway. Archeologists were about to call it a day, having unearthed thirty-seven shipwrecks, when a final check of the seabed revealed the remains of a Neolithic dwelling from around 6000 BCE (Kocabaş 2015, 6). An exasperated President Erdoğan decried that a few "pots and pans" were standing in the way of prosperity for the living (Bora 2016).

The city has thrown up such obstacles to centralizing power for centuries; its topography in some ways "lives outside time" (Hughes 2017, 6), thwarting the streamlining of urban transport and construction in accordance with twenty-first-century expectations, while still being "connected to many worlds" (Hughes 2017, 6) as a vital transit point for shipping oil, gas, and grain (Reuters 2016). However analytically rich it could be to approach historic cities through the contradictions revealed by the above and other examples, the temporal siloing this can imply is untenable. I find it theoretically fruitful to instead focus here on one aspect of Istanbul's urban fabric and publics, taking my cue from Andreas Huyssen's suggestion that no real city can ever be grasped in its present or past totality, but can certainly be approached through the prismatic vocabulary of the notion of urban imaginaries (2008). The notion of urban imaginaries allows for the multitude of perspectives and subject positions that make sense of urban-spatial practices. "In some deep dimension all cities remain invisible," Huyssen proposes (2008, 3), which resonates both with the sedimented nature of Istanbul so vivid in the example above, and with the variously classed, gendered, and raced experiences of this urban space for its inhabitants.

To approach the economic and political dimensions of the Emek Resistance in the contentious district of Beyoğlu, I will also work with David Harvey's (2012) and Mark Purcell's (2002) treatments of Henri Lefebvre's notion of "the right to the city" ([1968] 1996). When Lefebvre argues that "the urban fabric, with its multiple networks of communication and exchange, is likewise part of the means of production … the division of labour affects the whole of space – not just the 'space of work'" ([1974] 1991, 347), he draws attention to the necessity of a politics of space that can encompass the affective and interpersonal aspects of being urban dwellers—which together may be defined as seeking "the right not to be alienated from the spaces of everyday life" (Mitchell and Villanueva 2010, 667). Harvey's expansion upon this Lefebvrian "right to the city" ([1968] 1996) as a "collective rather than individual right, since reinventing the city inevitably depends upon the exercise of a collective power over the processes of urbanization" (Harvey 2012, 4) highlights how the former occurs alongside and through collective demands of a material nature, including social, political, and economic rights and the right to education, work, health, leisure, safety, and accommodation. While I will take into account the affective nuances of Beyoğlu's urban imaginary, I therefore seek to keep in sight that "urbanization [as]... a class phenomenon" (Harvey 2012, 5) plays out in Istanbul via the dual-pronged material forces of neoliberal-Islamist and neoliberal-Western capital. The spontaneous civil disobedience of 2010–2013 was a case where people attempted to (re)claim their shaping power over some of these material processes of spatial control. Particularly helpful for reading some of their actions will be Purcell's stress on the "right to participation" and "right to appropriation" (2002, 102–3) in Lefebvre's thought.

23.3 Urbanization and Spatial Amnesia

Since 2002, Turkey has been ruled by the democratically elected, pro-Islamic authoritarian government of Recep Tayyip Erdoğan's Justice and Development Party (abbreviated to AKP in Turkish). It has a pro-free market bent that has boosted Turkey's economy, which grew on average at a rate of 7.2% between 2002 and 2007 and remained relatively prosperous for the duration of the 2008 global financial crisis. This success has been attributed to IMF loans, low inflation, and an increase in private investments, labor productivity, and exports, alongside "maintaining strong macroeconomic and fiscal policy frameworks and opening to foreign trade and finance," in the approving words of the World Bank (2019). This made it the darling of international investors, and the West's poster child for a pro-capitalist, constitutionally secular, but demographically majority-Muslim, country. That said, the "Turkish model" was also taken seriously in other majority-Muslim countries, with much discussion around the time of the Arab Spring about whether Turkey's social and economic practices could be replicated elsewhere (Akyol 2012).

Even though the rapid urbanization that accompanied Turkey's economically strong decade is noted, less frequently is it analyzed as a mechanism for the absorption of capital surpluses. That is precisely the nature of much of the accelerated construction and privatization that characterizes the 2010s in Istanbul. So successful was government-sanctioned urbanization that the subsequent chronic urban space shortage in Istanbul birthed a series of promised construction endeavors of gigantic proportions. Dubbed *Çılgın*

Projeler (Crazy Projects) by supporters and critics alike, these environmentally detrimental undertakings opened new peri-urban locations to the construction sector.[1] The "new ruling class fortified with construction" (Kentel 2016, 140) consists of leading figures in the AKP government and a strata of *yandaş* (follower, adherent) contractors and developers with financially lucrative loyalties to the ruling party. Harvey points to how capital surplus absorption drives (and indeed necessitates) such a situation; urbanization allows accumulation to continue, which creates outlets to absorb the surplus and thereby avoid systemic crises (2012, 18). In this sense, during its two-decade rule, "AKP has primarily fulfilled the requirements of a modern capitalist economy despite its 'New Turkey' rhetoric and 'conservative' and religious discourse" (Kentel 2016, 143). The AKP paints the familiar surplus–absorption–urbanization model as a kind of Turkish nationalism ("New Turkey") rather than capitalism's imperative. The historic neighborhoods of Istanbul, seen through the lens of market logic, were thus "developed" in ways that "entailed repeated bouts of urban restructuring through 'creative destruction'" (Harvey 2012, 17). Sulukule, Istanbul's historically Roma neighborhood, and Karaköy, a waterfront working-class district that specialized in ship maintenance, are examples that underwent what Harvey describes as the "new 'urbanism' movement that touts the sale of community and a boutique lifestyle as a developer product to fulfill urban dreams" (2012, 14).[2]

By 2013, the neoliberal economic motivations of capital surplus absorption had been well consolidated, and the government's ideological and political preferences as to how urban space should be used became more overt. Socially authoritarian ideas were floated by the state, even if they were never heard of again (for instance, restrictions around the consumption of alcohol and on street-side seating), in a barely veiled warning to the secular demographic of Istanbul. In the midst of such interventions, the IIFF became an unexpected facilitator—physically and discursively—of a period of civic interaction that grew out of the district of Beyoğlu, where the first film screening in Turkey took place in 1896.

23.4 "Beyoğlu is a tough nut. Those who enter it mindlessly with their axes should beware"

Once a neighborhood of *levantens* (the European population of the Ottoman Empire's late decades), Beyoğlu grew more ethnically Turkish after the violence on September 6–7, 1955 Istanbul Pogroms, where the district's Greek and Jewish businesses and populations were driven out.[3] Today, because of the relatively cheap accommodation to be found in the area's aging buildings, as well as the availability of informal work in the district's many retail units, Beyoğlu attracts foreign migrants, representing "a nexus of active agents from different ethnic and cultural backgrounds, working with different languages" (Demirkol-Ertürk and Paker 2014). As Ozan Karaman notes in the preface to his study on urban renewal and resistance Istanbul, there is "no single predominant factor that determines the trajectories of grassroots mobilizations and urban renewal in general" (2014, 291). These are determined by a multitude of local and extra-local dynamics, alliances, and discourses. However, in Istanbul the public sphere of street and square situates, as it does in many cities, collective life, thereby inscribing "potential for political interchange that in turn recomposes the metropolis" (Cuff et al. 2020, 2). Taksim Square, which leads into Beyoğlu's main thoroughfare, Istiklâl Avenue, together forms the route of most demonstrations in Istanbul, past and present. Throughout the 1950s, '60s, and '70s, Istiklâl Avenue was also the locus of Istanbul's cinema-going culture and the heart of Turkey's *Yeşilçam* film industry. Atilla Dorsay, Turkey's veteran film journalist, paints an at times seedy, at times glamorous, and always socio-culturally vibrant urban locale in his 2013 memoir *Emek Yoksa Ben De Yokum!* (If Emek Goes, So Do I!). There, all manner of people deemed by mainstream Turkish society as "bohemians" (journalists, actors, writers, artists) and "misfits" (drag performers, cis and trans sex workers) felt at home (Dorsay 2013, 97).[4]

Dorsay further speaks of this district as inscribed with a certain resistant or dissenting texture that is both topographical and social: "Beyoğlu is a tough nut. Those who enter it mindlessly with their axes should beware" (2013, 112). This speaks both to the ideal of spatial justice—that which "gives orientation" to the "transformative potential" of complex "hyperobjects" like cities (Cuff et al. 2020, 5)—as well as to how Beyoğlu's architectural and spatial configurations render it difficult for state power to permanently penetrate and transform it (whether through ostensibly legal routes like building permits, renovation plans, and public works, or through shadowy means, like state-sanctioned arson).[5] Dorsay wrote the above in the national daily *Cumhuriyet* in 1990 and clarifies upon rereading his own material that "[he] probably wrote this in response to yet another bungled urban intervention on the part of the local municipality" (2013, 112). There is a degree to which Beyoğlu's history, demographics, and urban texture lend the district the reputation of being "a tough nut," in Dorsay's turn of phrase. That is, its social history, current demographic, and its subterranean "too much history" (Batuman 2015, n.p.) seem to partially block state authority from penetrating the district; steep hills and narrow streets thwart the bulldozer; and its heterogeneous inhabitants cannot all be appealed to through AKP's ideology. This heterogeneity is, however, conducive to the forging of dialogues between spatial concerns and other social goals. Ayşe Deniz Ünan (2015) discusses how Istanbul's LGBTQ+ groups mapped their ongoing struggle for rights onto spatial justice demands during the 2013 Gezi Park protests, in doing so increasing their own interactions with other identity groups—including conservative ones like Turkey's self-identifying "anti-capitalist Muslims" (Başcı 2017). Such new alliances amplified LGBTQ+ voices, drawing attention to the intersections of homophobia, police brutality, and privatization.

The Emek Resistance was born into this socio-spatial push–pull. While valuable studies of political subjectivity (Tascón and Wils 2016); activist cultures

(Iordanova and Torchin 2012); and social change (Sharpe 2008) have begun to take account of the relationship between film festivals and political activism, scholarship has less often discussed urban space in intersection with this relationship. On the other hand, although Murat Akser brings the municipal politics behind Turkey's film festivals to the fore (2014, 141), he glosses over the IIFF on the grounds that it is insulated from the politics of its local space on account of being funded by private enterprise. In attending to the characteristics of the urban locality within which the Emek Resistance took place, and examining how it was harnessed by protestors from 2010 to 2013, I hope this chapter will begin to address these two omissions, while stressing that the picture I arrive at is only one example of how this relationship transpired at a particular time and place.

23.5 Emek, Space, and Power

A historic movie theater seating 875, Emek was founded in 1924 by Jewish partners Arditi and Saltiel inside the Cercle d'Orient, a neoclassical 1882 building that was built by the Armenian Abraham Pasha (SALT 2011). Purchased by a Turkish family in 1932, the then-called Melek (Angel) Cinema got a second lease on life when it was bought in 1957 by the state pension fund and reopened under public ownership as Emek (Labor) Cinema. The main venue of the IIFF since its inception in 1982, Emek's flagging for demolition in 2010 to make way for what was rumored to be yet another shopping center—Istanbul had nearly 100 at the time (Habertürk 2018)—sparked collective civic action that reached a peak in terms of participation, media attention, and politicization around every April edition of the annual two-week festival.

Even this cursory summary begins to suggest the multiple temporal and social layers embedded in Emek the building and the cinema. Dorsay and many of his generation recall Emek and the other cinema salons of Beyoğlu as the "sites of [their] coming-of-age milestones, in imagination and in reality" (2013, 14), as well as a rare depository of both working-class and middle- to upper-class urban memories. As working-class entertainment, cinemas flourished in open-air settings in semi-urban and rural Turkey throughout the mid-twentieth century. These experiences often involved live audience reactions, the excitement of attending an "acceptable" space of transgression (in the sense of close opposite-sex socializing), and the fascination of adolescents seeing heterosexual romantic acts in plain (on-screen) sight for the first time. Although Istanbul's cinema-going crowds included upper-class audiences, matinée, and weekend screenings were within the reach of working salaries. Cinema-going grew to have associations of being the "people's art form" (Hayır 2014). This was the result of a combination of factors that brought about changes in people's attitudes to leisure and socialization in Istanbul (Hayır 2014, 184), with money and time often set aside for film-going relative to one's earning power. Factors contributing to these changes included rural to urban migration in the 1960s, the rarity of televisions in homes, the rise of "star" fandoms, which involved actors typecast into a macho-yet-honorable male protagonist trope that held especial cultural appeal, and the relatively politically liberal atmosphere in Turkey in that decade. As such, the state kept a close eye on this popular pastime, using censorship often.[6]

However, this relative class diversity amongst audiences during the golden age (1960s) of *Yeşilçam* (Green Pine), the Turkish film industry, intersected with what was a comparatively ethnically and religiously homogenous time in the locality. In both its built environment and social history, Emek Cinema was a reminder of the pre-1955 cosmopolitanism of Beyoğlu. The first film screening in Turkey that took place in 1896 on Istiklâl Avenue had the participation of a mainly Christian demographic (Arslan 2011, 25), with cinema coming to the city's predominantly Muslim districts like Fatih around the same time. This segregated start is not so much a result of differing receptions of film by religious affiliation, but because all aspects of life were concentrated in particular districts for particular demographics: a remnant of organic Ottoman-era urban-spatial proximities by ethnicity. However much Istanbul's *gayrimüslim* (non-Muslim) communities have since been decimated in numbers, Beyoğlu is marked by visual reminders of its cosmopolitan past in ways that recall Dolores Hayden's idea of "body memory" in relation to urban place, wherein body memory "connects into places because shared experience of dwellings, public spaces, give body memory to its social component, modified by gender, class, race" (1995, 48).

An example of such "body memory" resurfacing was in 2012, when the İnci (Pearl) Bakery, by then a veritable institution in its 68th year of operation, went bust. Located at street level within the Cercle D'Orient building and established in 1944 by Albanian Greek migrant Lucas Zigoridi, "it always represented the last public emblem of Beyoğlu's non-Muslim community, a culture long on life support," wrote one elegy for the shop (Culinary Backstreets 2012, n.p). The area grew more religiously homogenous (Muslim Turkish, in this case) from the 1960s, but body memories that complicated this homogeneity lived on. One such memory is Dorsay's, of the 1988 IIFF's closing ceremony he spent on a protest walk against censorship with the celebrated Greek-American director Elia Kazan (Jilani 2011, n.p.). A sexagenarian IIFF attendee, meanwhile, recounted to me how "a film at Emek, then a pudding at İnci" lives on in memory as her quintessential festival experience. Lefebvre's reference to space as "inscriptions in the simultaneity of the external world of a series of times, the rhythms of the city, the rhythms of the urban population" ([1970] 2003, 224) is thus especially applicable to the loaded cultural and social meanings of this cinema, in this particular building, in this district. During 2013s converging neoliberal pressures, this spatial inscription of time was poised to succumb to the consequences of space being fundamental in any exercise of power (Gregory et al. 2015).

23.6 "Hands off Our Labor"

The Emek Resistance occurred largely from April 2010 to April 2013, after the state shut Emek's doors for the last time in October 2009 following the end of that year's *Film Ekimi* (Film October) festival, a smaller off-shoot of the IIFF. As works on the Cercle D'Orient building began, defending this space became defending "a series of times" (Lefebvre [1968] 1996, 10) embodied in Beyoğlu. The movement, which consisted of demonstrations that took various forms on Istiklâl Avenue and Yeşilçam Street, closely embedded the aesthetic into the political and the urban-spatial. It used forms of civic assembly and action including marches, protests, demos, talks, outdoor film screenings, impromptu musical performances, and collective mnemonic engagement in the absence of Emek. This latter entailed the spontaneous and informal exchange of memories and anecdotes between strangers. Having a "favorite row" in Emek, for example, was a frequently discussed quirk amongst the participants (*Audience Emancipated* 2016), speaking to the powerful body memory (Hayden 1995) that the architecture of the Art Nouveau movie theater—with its "troublesome" seats in terms of screen visibility—had fostered in its audiences. These interactions began to draw connections between the encroachment of neoliberal capital on urban space, memories of cinema-going, and "art action" as acts of reclaiming space.[7]

The demonstrations involved participants of all ages, with a large representation of students and arts sector workers, blocking pedestrian and vehicle usage of Istiklâl Avenue in non-violent gatherings. Despite the high representation of students of diverse backgrounds, and of educated but financially precarious "misfits" (in Dorsay's tongue-in-cheek shorthand for dissident writers, artists, and activists), the relatively broad concerns of the movement's demands actually revived, to an extent, Istanbul's aforementioned historic cross-class affiliations with cinema. Conservative-leaning small shopkeepers, increasingly stretched by the effects rapid development was having on their place of business, LGBTQ+ communities, for whom Beyoğlu was a relative safe haven, and sex workers, who felt policed all the more by the proliferation of private security in the new shopping centers and construction sites, were some of the groups who also participated in demonstrations in smaller numbers. Actions included speeches delivered non-hierarchically, from both organizers and participants, tying hundreds of film tickets to the railings of Emek's shuttered entrance, hanging large banners down the length of the Cercle D'Orient building's façade, and chanting slogans about rights to art, rights to space, affordable renting, anti-consumerism, and the reclamation of Beyoğlu from state securitization. Slogans and chants markedly articulated both a defense of Emek Cinema, and resistance to its demolition's root causes. The "shopping-mall-ification" (Ateşman 2015) of Istanbul was a key refrain here, addressing the state's "destruction in the name of progress" (Azoulay 2019, 69). Banners explicitly linking the destruction of Emek with "shopping-mall-ification" pointed to the mutually exclusive notions of urbanization that each embodied: the former, Emek, standing for a vision of public space as an affordable place of art, entertainment, and community within a building that spoke to its inhabitants of Istanbul's living history, the latter, the mall, a vision of public space as a tightly controlled, sterile environment of cosmetic brilliance and constant surveillance, where taking up space without consuming is loitering. The slogan *"Emek'ten çıkın, Demirören'i yıkın"* ("Quit Emek, demolish Demirören"), for instance, referred to the Demirören shopping center that one section of the Cercle D'Orient building had already been transformed into by 2011.

This language bespeaks a refusal of the state's attempts at appeasement, which included assurances that a "new and improved Emek" would be accessible through Demirören. The words of a participant interviewed in 2014 illustrate how the demonstrators were able to see through the state's claims by drawing from their own spatial experiences of Beyoğlu:

> Rather than 'actual' movie theaters which stand in their own right, I am forced to be in places where I cannot breathe, [where] I cannot reach the street easily. They promote [multiplex movie theaters inside shopping malls] in order to prohibit people's habits and activities on the streets, and make them consume more. (Ateşman 2015, 693)

In addition to the refusal of the shopping center as an acceptable alternative to public urban space, the vocabulary of dissent throughout the demonstrations also expressed a more broadly anti-capitalist demand by punning on the meaning of the word "emek." Emek, used in the cinema's case as a proper noun, is its name; however, as a noun, it translates from the Turkish as "labor." The slogan "Hands off our Emek(/labor)" and similar others associated the collective place and body memories evoked by the movie theater with the participants themselves as productive classes, as opposed to *yandaş* developers and corporate entities reliant on privatization, speculation, and embezzling public funds. Building identification around the concept of "labor," this allowed the participants—in their shared but varied situations of disenfranchisement within Istanbul's urban spaces—to feel like "addressees" rather than "bystanders" during the demonstrations, in Warner's definition of publics (2002, 77). "I think a certain segment of society, which was not on the streets before, was mobilized against the demolishing of the movie theatre," one co-organizer of the Emek Resistance said (Ateşman 2015, 693) during the 2014 IIFF. Ateşman's interviewee points out that the issue of public urban space brought into the Emek movement's remit people who would not have necessarily identified with, or come out onto the streets for, "arts and culture" issues. My personal observations during the IIFF's iterations (2010–2016), as well as the audience ethnographies of Ayşe N. Erek and Ayşe H. Köksal (2014) and Ateşman (2015), suggest that the movement did, to an extent, therefore bring together people with different income levels and backgrounds. They ranged from students and intellectuals who were responsive to arts issues; to old-timers who were keenly feeling the destruction of their place memories in and around Beyoğlu's film scene; to those whose situations were foremost materially rather than affectively tied to the survival of Beyoğlu's urban fabric itself, such as those with precarious work in the district, or for whom Beyoğlu was a relative refuge from exclusion.

Participation could thus broadly be called cross-class, in that the above range of socio-economic backgrounds were represented, but it should be noted that this also derived from the two "sides" I sketched above in this particular situation. The two larger categories of affiliation, which put working and middle-class participants on the same "side" even if everyone's reasons for coming out to the street differed somewhat, were delineated along the fault lines indicated by the participants' appropriation of the word "labor." The recurring slogans, signs, and chants included: "Hey you – put down our Emek/labor"; "Hands off our Emek/labor, AKP"; "Emek/labor and capital will never reconcile"; "Wake up Istanbul, defend your Emek/labor"; and "Don't touch my Emek/labor, my culture, my history."[8] This vocabulary of relations between public place, neoliberal capital, and labor rights fostered collective identification about being of the vast majority in the city—in the sense that all, whether unemployed or in working or middle-class jobs, reproduced their urban existence through their labors. The "them" that participants could define themselves against, and in doing so perhaps minimize some of the class differences amongst themselves, was in this case the *yandaş* developer class, who grew capital through access to capital in the first place, not through labor. Although strategically binaristic, this broad "us" and "them" made possible a "side" that could make its demands from a place of commonality.

Also accompanying the demonstrations were "guerrilla" film screenings on Yeşilçam street, outside the boarded-up entrance to Emek. The screenings, carried out with little more than a projector and whatever chairs could be gathered from local businesses, turned the street into "an active street again," in one participant's words (Ateşman 2015, 692). To make sense of it as a form of civil disobedience and a demand for spatial justice, rather than "merely" an outdoor film screening, we can consider the specific situation that it generates. "What arises when moving images are encountered in public spaces are specific situations," scholar Annie Dell'Aria describes: "The content, context and structure of the work, in addition to the specificity of the spectator, construct each situation. The meaning of the work of public art is thus embedded within that particular configuration of space, place, image, sound, and spectator" (2016, 18). In these semi-spontaneous screenings on Yeşilçam street, the line between audiences and co-organizers became blurred as troubleshooting technical issues, curating the film selection, and crowd control became collective tasks fulfilled by all present. "Unlike the predetermined architecture and seating arrangements of the cinema and domestic television, the body's relationship to the screen in public space is ever-changing and fluid" (Dell'Aria 2016, 19), and in this case, to recreate the architecture and seating arrangements of the cinema in light of the attack on the space of the said cinema itself became a mode of civic interaction in which embodied cinema-going was one in a series of actions that created a public out of a group. Warner points out that "the idea of a public, unlike a concrete audience or the public of any polity, is text-based – even though publics are increasingly organized around visual or audio texts" (2002, 51). The observation maps remarkably well on to this collective appropriation of Yeşilçam street, which turned, mediated by the audiovisual text, an audience into a public. Embodying "the world-making and creativity of publicness" (Warner 2002, 54) in its usage of space, these guerrilla street screenings "spilled" the IIFF out of the multiplexes it was forced to utilize after 2009 following Emek's closure—a move which festival-goers understood to be a neoliberalizing tactic (Ateşman 2015, 693). The guerrilla screenings even challenged the structures of a private film festival itself, by delivering a parallel kind of "service" through voluntary, collective labor—thus also highlighting how "externally organized frameworks of activity" prove "a poor substitute" to self-organized discourse, in the context of a public "produc[ing] a sense of belonging and activity" (Warner 2005, 52).

In a self-reflexive move, participants in the Emek Resistance also chronicled the period through their own eyes. *Audience Emancipated: The Struggle for Emek Movie Theater* was created by a collective called *Emek Bizim İstanbul Bizim* (Emek is Ours, Istanbul is Ours), an initiative formed in 2010 whose members remain anonymous. This 48-minute collage documentary was released in 2016, and consists of footage collected by all involved. Featuring scenes from the demonstrations, impromptu interviews, musical performances, and inserts from other audiovisual material, it forms a record of three years of activism. *Audience Emancipated* retells the Emek Resistance as a series of interwoven narratives both borne of, and constantly bearing upon, the city as a site of concrete social connections.

An attitude of shared ridicule directed toward the powers encroaching upon Beyoğlu is one such register of social connection captured by the documentary. This collective tone or mood did significant affective and political work throughout the Emek Resistance. Perhaps best described as a mixture of sarcastic humor about the everyday ineptitudes of the authorities, world-weariness toward the city's pace and chaos, and a defensive affection toward these latter elements, this shared attitudinal register was recreated in the documentary using Dadaist influences and montage. A sequence, for example, overlays the intro tune of Twentieth-Century Fox onto a clip of magnificent skyscrapers glinting at sunset. The dramatic soundtrack peters out as we cut to a Turkish contractor giving a press tour of the partially demolished Cercle D'Orient building. The contractor's vague arm gestures and words— "the new Emek will begin roughly here. There'll be an exit out to Yeşilçam street here"—form a deliberate contrast with the pompous grandeur of the music, mocking the government contractors' self-image as magnanimous businessmen. Ridicule is also deployed in segments that depict police use of water cannon on crowds on Istiklâl Avenue on April 7, 2013 in an attempt to disperse protestors outside Demirören Mall. As the crowd backs off reluctantly, booing the police, the documentary cuts to a clip from *State of Siege* (1975) by Costa-Gavras, which depicts police officers comically running to-and-fro in a deserted courtyard. The montage leaves us with the impression of a cornered state apparatus that fears the creative humor of its own populace. Humor was something that the Gezi protests later harnessed spectacularly for its subversive power.[9]

23.7 Conclusion

The *Emek is Ours, Istanbul is Ours* collective highlight that their documentary "aims to reflect the common imagination of the people who defended their right to the city. It carries the idea of a new publicness" (*Audience Emancipated* 2016). The idea of a new "publicness" does important political and conceptual work in the context at hand: one where those "spatial embodiments of histories, collective lives, intimacies, contestations, power relations, and social distinctions" together form "the cultural artifacts of urban space and the micro-settings of everyday life" in Istanbul (Cuff et al. 2020, 12). I propose that the idea of a "new publicness" gestures to, and provides an illustration of, Lefebvre's "right to the city" ([1968] 1996) in ways that highlight the concept's "more radical, more problematic, and more indeterminate" aspects (Purcell 2002, 99). These are aspects that Purcell dubs a new "urban politics of the inhabitant," which I believe maps closely onto the vision that the *Emek is Ours, Istanbul is Ours* collective sought to pin down with the phrase "new publicness." Purcell highlights that we lack a comprehensive explanation of what the "right to the city" (Lefebvre [1968] 1996) is or how it would challenge, compliment, or replace current rights. The case of the IIFF and the Emek Resistance can enrich our understanding of those elements that collectively form the demand of the "right to the city" (Lefebvre [1968] 1996) in a situation where, ostensibly, the state *appears* to be delivering services and "destruction in the name of progress" (Azoulay 2019, 69). The power relations that currently underlie the production of urban space are ones that disenfranchise people with respect to decisions that produce urban space. Purcell singles out the "right to participation" and the "right to appropriation" (Purcell 2002, 102–3) from Lefebvre's thinking in order to sketch out what enfranchisement could look like. Briefly, urban inhabitants would have a direct and central role in decisions that produce urban space such as policy and investment. The right to appropriate, meanwhile, would entail the ability to physically access, occupy, and use urban space.

There is a close alignment here with this concretizing reading of Lefebvre's concept and the primary grievances of the movement that is the case study of this chapter. The transformation of Beyoğlu took place amidst state contempt, opacity, and authoritarianism, where urban inhabitants were neither consulted nor informed (the denial of the right to participation), and its results further restricted physical access to urban space for any purpose other than being an individual consumer (the denial of the right to appropriation). This resistance period in Istanbul articulated desires that are at once intangible—subjective and concrete—economic: complementary and intersecting desires that, as Lefebvre suggested, converge upon how much people feel they have physical access to, and decision-making power over, the production of their urban space and its social relations. The *Emek Is Ours, Istanbul Is Ours* collective describe their activist approach in terms that make these connections, historicizing the on-again, off-again three-year period of civic disobedience within Istanbul's longer-term transformations, while explicitly reminding the viewer of the movement's political goals: "Should we search for the story of Emek in encyclopedias, or in what its curtain and screen witnessed over the years? Or in its layered history, [which] overlaps with historical turning points in Turkey? We didn't do any of these; instead, we searched for Emek's story in the streets" (*Audience Emancipated* 2016). The term "the streets" abstracts the events they recorded by designating as a storyteller urban space itself, which is the political base from which public pressure can be—and was, in Beyoğlu's case—exerted upon those seeking to reserve the power to produce urban space. It also, at one and the same time, refers specifically to the hundreds who were physically occupying Istiklâl Street and, in doing so, continuing to write "Emek's story" in the building's hour of peril.

That *Emek Is Ours, Istanbul Is Ours* dubs this state of being "a new publicness" suggests not only the political but also the intersubjective potential experienced by participants throughout the three years: the potential to be *in/of* Istanbul, and (re)produce its urban space in ways that exercise a "right to participation" and "right to appropriation" (Purcell 2002, 102–3). A period where urban memory was activated, the Emek Resistance holds lessons for those of us concerned with what the fight for the "right to the city" (Lefebvre [1968] 1996) can look like today, in how it attempted to call into being a new publicness that was about socio-spatial laboring: that is, the labor of refusing, contesting, resisting, subverting, mocking, and where possible outright challenging those processes, actors and institutions that have no investment in the production of urban space except whatever enables the absorption and re-generation of capital. Whether or not the Emek Resistance succeeded in wresting some of these rights away from the state is a question without a definite answer, but the attempt itself briefly created a public—and that public continues to remember.

Notes

1. See also Baba (2020) on these projects, like Canal Istanbul.
2. See also Karaman (2014) and van Dobben Schoon (2014) on Sulukule.
3. See also Güven (2011) on these pogroms.
4. All subsequent quotes from Dorsay (2013) and other Turkish sources cited are my translations.
5. Emine Uşaklıgil's study (2014) details some of these tactics.

6. On Turkish state politics and censorship in the '60s and '70s, see Mutlu and Koçer (2012).
7. I borrow the term from Altuğ Yalçıntaş to mean activism with creativity and humor that "turns the joyful rhetoric of action into a series of serious threats for political authority" (2015, 118).
8. Sources for these slogans and posters include press coverage by bianet.org, sendika.org, the @EmekBizim Twitter handle, and diken.com.tr; personal observations; and visuals shared on social media by attendees from 2010 to 2013.
9. See also Yalçıntaş (2015) on humor in Gezi.

References

Akser, Murat. 2014. "Turkish Film Festivals: Political Populism, Rival Programming and Imploding Activities." In *Film Festival Yearbook 6: Film Festivals And The Middle East*, edited by Dina Iordanova and Stefanie Van de Peer, 141–55. St. Andrews: St. Andrews Film Studies.
Akyol, Mustafa. 2012. "The Turkish Model." *The Cairo Review of Global Affairs*. 2012. Accessed August 3, 2020. https://www.thecairoreview.com/essays/the-turkish-model/.
Arslan, Savaş. 2011. *Cinema in Turkey*. Oxford: Oxford University Press.
Ateşman, Özge Özdüzen. 2015. "The Politicization and 'Occupy'sation of the Istanbul Film Festival Audience." *Participations: Journal of Audience and Reception Studies* 12, no. 1: 679–702.
Audience Emancipated: The Struggle for the Emek Movie Theater. 2016. Directed by Emek Bizim İstanbul Bizim.
Azoulay, Ariella Aïsha. 2019. *Potential History: Unlearning Imperialism*. London: Verso.
Baba, Ece Ceylan. 2020. "The Risks of Mega Urban Projects Creating a Dystopia: Canal Istanbul." *City and Environment Interactions* 6. Accessed August 26, 2020. https://www.sciencedirect.com/science/article/pii/S2590252020300209.
Başcı, Emre. 2017. "Türkiye'de Anti-kapitalist Müslümanlar: Politik Dönüşümleri, Amaçları ve Tüketim Davranışları Üzerine Nitel Bir Model." *The Journal of Turk-Islam World Social Studies* 13, no. 13: 113–28.
Batuman, Elif. 2015. "The Big Dig." *The New Yorker*. August 24, 2015. Accessed August 20, 2020. https://www.newyorker.com/magazine/2015/08/31/the-big-dig.
Bora, T. 2016. *İnşaat Ya Resulullah*. Istanbul: İletişim Yayınları.
Cuff, Dana, Anastasia Loukaitou-Sideris, Todd Presner, Maite Zubiaurre, and Jonathan Jae-an Crisman, eds. 2020. *Urban Humanities: New Practices for Reimagining the City*. Cambridge, MA: MIT Press.
Culinary Backstreets. 2012. "Elegy for Istanbul's İnci Pastanesi." Accessed August 16, 2021 https://culinarybackstreets.com/cities-category/istanbul/2012/inci-pastanesi/.
Dell'Aria, Annie. 2016. "Spectatorship in Public Space: The Moving Image in Public Art." In *Making Sense of Cinema: Empirical Studies into Film Spectators and Spectatorship*, edited by CarrieLynn D. Reinhard, 17–36. London: Bloomsbury.
Demirkol-Ertürk, Şule, and Saliha Paker. 2014. "Beyoğlu/Pera as a Translating Site in Istanbul." *Translation Studies* 7, no. 2: 170–85.

Dorsay, Atilla. 2013. *Emek Yoksa Ben De Yokum!*. Istanbul: Kırmızı Kedi.
Erek, Ayşe N., and Ayşe H. Köksal. 2014. "Relocating the Arts in the New Istanbul: Urban Imaginary as a Contested Zone." *Visual Resources* 30, no. 4: 301–18.
Freely, John. 1974. *Stamboul Sketches*. Istanbul: Redhouse Press.
Gregory, Derek, Peter Meusburger, and Laura Suarsana. 2015. *Power, Knowledge, and Space: A Geographical Introduction*. New York: Springer.
Güven, Dilek. 2011. "Riots against the Non-Muslims of Turkey: 6/7 September 1955 in the Context of Demographic Engineering." *European Journal of Turkish Studies* 12. Accessed August 26, 2020. https://journals.openedition.org/ejts/4538.
Habertürk. 2018. "İstanbul'daki AVM sayısı 2020 yılında 136 olacak." March 3, 2018. Accessed July 18, 2020. https://www.haberturk.com/istanbul-da-avm-sayisi-2020-yilinda-136-olacak-1861200-ekonomi.
Harvey, David. 2012. *Rebel Cities: From the Right to the City to the Urban Revolution*. London: Verso.
Hayden, Dolores. 1995. *The Power of Place: Urban Landscapes as Public History*. Cambridge, MA: MIT Press.
Hayır, Celal. 2014. "The Turkish Cinema Between Its Inception And Downfall: A Historical Overview." *The Journal of International Social Research* 7, no. 35. Accessed August 16, 2021. http://www.sosyalarastirmalar.com/cilt7/sayi35_pdf/9digersosyalbilimler/hayir_celal.pdf.
Hughes, Bettany. 2017. *Istanbul: A Tale of Three Cities*. London: Weidenfeld & Nicolson.
Huyssen, Andreas, ed. 2008. *Other Cities, Other Worlds: Urban Imaginaries in a Globalizing Age*. Durham, NC: Duke University Press, 2008.
Iordanova, Dina, and Leshu Torchin, eds. 2012. *Film Festivals and Activism*. St. Andrews: St. Andrews Film Studies.
Jilani, Sarah. 2011. "Cinema and the City." *Nouse*. May 12, 2011. Accessed August 28, 2021. https://nouse.co.uk/2011/05/12/cinema-and-the-city.
Karaman, Ozan. 2014. "Resisting Urban Renewal in Istanbul." *Urban Geography* 35, no. 2: 290–310.
Kentel, Ferhat. 2016. "The Right to the City during AK Party's Thermidor." In *The Turkish AK Party and its Leader: Criticism, Opposition and Dissent*, edited by Umit Cizre, 132–65. London: Routledge.
Kocabaş, Ufuk. 2015. "The Yenikapı Byzantine-Era Shipwrecks, Istanbul, Turkey: a Preliminary Report and Inventory of the 27 Wrecks Studied." *The International Journal of Nautical Archaeology* 44, no. 1: 5–38.
Lefebvre, Henri. [1968] 1996. "The Right to the City." In *Writings on Cities*, translated and edited by Eleonore Kofman and Elizabeth Lebas, 63–177. Oxford: Blackwell.
Lefebvre, Henri. [1970] 2003. *The Urban Revolution*, translated by Robert Bononno. Minneapolis: University of Minnesota Press.
Lefebvre, Henri. [1974] 1991. *The Production of Space*, translated by Donald Nicholson-Smith. Oxford: Blackwell.
Mansel, Philip. 1998. *Constantinople: City of the World's Desire, 1453-1924*. New York: St. Martin's Press.
Mitchell, Don, and Villanueva, Joaquin. 2010. "Right to the City." In *Encyclopedia of Urban Studies 2*, edited by R. Hutchinson, 667–671. Los Angeles: Sage.

Mutlu, D. K., and Z. Koçer. 2012. "A Different Story of Secularism: The Censorship of Religion in Turkish Films of the 1960s and Early 1970s." *European Journal of Cultural Studies* 15, no. 1: 70–88.
Ortaylı, Ilber. 1987. *İstanbul'dan Sayfalar.* Istanbul: Hil Yayın.
Özdüzen, Özge. 2018. "Cinema-Going during the Gezi Protests: Claiming the Right to the Emek Movie Theatre and Gezi Park." *Social & Cultural Geography* 19, no. 8: 1028–52.
Purcell, Mark. 2002. "Excavating Lefebvre: The Right to the City and its Urban Politics of the Inhabitant." *GeoJournal* 58: 99–108.
Reuters. 2016. "Turkey's Huge and Rising Role in World Trade of Oil, Gas, Grains." Accessed August 8, 2020. https://www.reuters.com/article/turkey-security-commodities/factbox-turkeys-huge-and-rising-role-in-world-trade-of-oil-gas-grains-idUSL8N1A215Q.
SALT. 2011. "The Making of: Emek Cinema." Accessed July 8, 2020. https://saltonline.org/en/76/the-making-of-emek-cinema.
Sharpe, Erin K. 2008. "Festivals and Social Change: Intersections of Pleasure and Politics at a Community Music Festival." *Leisure Sciences* 30, no. 3: 217–34.
Tascón, Sonia, and Tyson Wils, eds. 2016. *Activist Film Festivals: Towards a Political Subject.* Chicago: University of Chicago Press.
The World Bank. 2019. "Overview – Turkey." Accessed August 3, 2020. https://www.worldbank.org/en/country/turkey/overview.
Ünan, Ayşe Deniz. 2015. "Gezi Protests and the LGBT Rights Movement: A Relation in Motion." In *Creativity and Humour in Occupy Movements: Intellectual Disobedience in Turkey and Beyond*, edited by A. Yalcintas, 76–94. London: Palgrave Macmillan.
Uşaklıgil, Emine. 2014. *Bir Şehri Yok Etmek: İstanbul'da Kazanmak ya da Kaybetmek.* Istanbul: Can Yayınları.
Van Dobben Schoon, Danielle. 2014. "'Sulukule is the Gun and We Are Its Bullets': Urban Renewal and Romani Identity in Istanbul." *City: Analysis of Urban Trends* 18, no. 6: 655–66.
Warner, Michael. 2002. "Publics and Counterpublics." *Public Culture* 14, no. 1: 49–90.
Warner, Michael. 2005. *Publics and Counterpublics.* New York: Zone Books.
World Population Review. 2020. "Istanbul Population 2020." Accessed August 20, 2020. https://worldpopulationreview.com/world-cities/istanbul-population.
Yalçıntaş, Altuğ. 2015. "Epilogue: Joy is the Laughter of the Resistance." In *Creativity and Humour in Occupy Movements*, edited by Altuğ Yalçıntaş, 116–9. London: Palgrave.

CHAPTER 24

Look at the Graves!: Cemeteries as Guided Tourism Destinations in Latvia

Solvita Burr, Anna Elizabete Griķe, and Karīna Krieviņa

24.1 INTRODUCTION

Cemeteries as places with specific social functionality, architectonics, and individuals' personal data as a peculiar public information dataset can be perceived, conceptualized, and experienced at various spatial levels, from personal space to community space, to regional space, and to national space, depending on scales of interests and actions.

Latvia has about two thousand cemeteries (Neogeo 2021), and many are designated as protected sites of national cultural significance (e.g., Riga Great Cemetery). This status indicates one possible function of cemeteries, but at different times cemeteries in Latvia have been considered differently, based on historical events, beliefs, and politics. Other labeling includes cemetery groups by affiliation with (1) municipality (city, town, or village), (2) religion and congregation (Catholic, Lutheran, Orthodox, Old Believers, or Muslims), or (3) military operations: war, battle, military unit, or representing power (e.g., World War I, The Christmas Battles, Latvian Riflemen, Soviet and German soldiers). Nowadays, some of these groups tend to be less segregated in practice.

S. Burr (✉) · A. E. Griķe
Latvian Language Institute, University of Latvia, Riga, Latvia
e-mail: solvita.burr@gmail.com

K. Krieviņa
Kurzeme Institute of Humanities, University of Liepāja, Liepāja, Latvia

© The Author(s), under exclusive license to Springer Nature Switzerland AG 2022
A. Schwan and T. Thomson (eds.), *The Palgrave Handbook of Digital and Public Humanities*, https://doi.org/10.1007/978-3-031-11886-9_24

Moreover, due to cemetery visits and cultural activities practiced in these sites, cemeteries in Latvia can be seen as locally shared spaces in which various religious, ethnic, and linguistic communities form their own cemetery culture through regular practices, customs, and traditions. Two typical examples of social and cultural practices are the Celebration of the Cemetery (*Kapusvētki* in Latvian) in summer and the Candlelight Evening (*Svecīšu vakars* in Latvian) in autumn. In this light, cemeteries represent an inclusive local culture combining various identities, practices, and beliefs.

However, although, cemeteries are open spaces for the public and anyone interested can enter these sites, this openness must be viewed critically. Accessibility to outsiders, or people outside a cemetery's community (including tourists), does not automatically guarantee the social acceptance of these outsiders by relatives of buried people and local communities.

Combining these interrelated understandings of cemeteries as socio-spatial platforms (i.e., marked, practiced, explored; see Lefebvre 1991), the aim of the article is to discuss guided tourism practices in cemeteries in Latvia as being either observational or participatory. We ask the following research questions to achieve this goal:

- What do cemetery tourism and its management look like today in Latvia?
- How are cemetery tours in Latvia discussed by guides, and how do they share their knowledge?

The answers to these questions will help us to better understand the place of guided cemetery tourism—one of audience-oriented humanistic activities and of ways of sharing knowledge, practices, and experiences—in the public humanities.

The structure of the article consists of seven parts. After the introduction, the article reviews multidisciplinary cemetery studies, with more attention being paid to research on cemeteries as touristic sites. Then the research methodology is described. The article continues with an overview of cemeteries in Latvia. This is followed by an analysis of interviews with five cemetery tour guides as mediators between local individuals/local communities and the public, highlighting their and visitors' experiences in individual cemeteries. Lastly, the article discusses current tourism practices in Latvia's cemeteries and proposes ideas for improving guided tourism there.

24.2 Theoretical Overview

At the end of the twentieth century, the phenomena of space became more important in describing the relationship between space and place, people's social practices in space, and socio-spatial dialectics (e.g., Taun 1977; Lefebvre 1991; Tilley 1994). Lefebvre (1991) defines space as a (social) product and on-going process of social practices, spatial knowledge, and perceptions. More specifically, social space is seen as physical space with human (inter)actions: habits of space-filling, functional use, and social relationships (Lefebvre 1991, 26–27). The following conceptual triad is important in understanding space: (1) representational space, or *conceived space*, conceptualized by technocrats, planners, scientists, politicians, and policymakers; (2) *perceived space*, observed and passively experienced by visitors and learners, and (3) *lived space*, intimately experienced and known by locals (Lefebvre 1991, 33–48).

The framework of social spaces can be applied to cemetery tourism. Research on cemetery tourism, tourist routes in cemeteries, and tourism materials (such as booklets and information on the internet) show how cemeteries are contextualized and presented to the public. Blog posts about individual or collective activities and observations in a cemetery depict the perceived space and, through personal stories, supplement associations with and knowledge of conceived space. But social and cultural practices, beliefs, and attitudes of local communities help to expose lived space and can bring tourism services closer to these local experiences.

24.2.1 Why Do Cemeteries Matter in Tourism?

As the tourism industry develops, tourism service providers are looking for new ways to attract tourists and to offer them fresh emotions, experiences, and knowledge. Special interest tourism (hereinafter SIT) is one of the ways to do such: to narrow the focus of tourism to specialize in the identities, interests, and habits of target tourist groups. In this way, types of SIT such as bird-watching tourism, gambling tourism, LGBTQ tourism, slum tourism, soccer tourism, and cemetery tourism (or tombstone tourism, grave-hunting tourism) have been pinpointed and practiced all around the world (e.g., George 2019).

When viewed via SIC alone, cemeteries and cemetery tourism represent one of many tourism niches; a cemetery itself, though, is a complex phenomenon. This is reflected in its being seen, utilized, and described by individuals and groups as:

- a form of physical citation in the landscape and a valuable historic resource, which can tell visitors about religion, historic events, architecture, genealogy, social status, and the lives of the individuals who are buried there (e.g., Semple and Brookes 2020),
- a touristic site with significant heritage value, distinctive architecture, monuments, and statuary for heritage attractions and potentially educational purposes (e.g., Odgers 2011),
- a therapeutic place for mental relaxation and contemplation of nature's temporal rhythms (e.g., Nordh et al. 2017),

- a green space for such leisure activities as recreational walking, dog-walking, jogging, sunbathing, and having a picnic (e.g., Swensen et al. 2016),
- a setting for a range of anti-social behavior and a site for "dark" (or deviant) leisure activities including drug-taking, drinking, and sexual encounters (e.g., Deering 2010).

The list of interpretations shows the potential use of cemeteries and highlights their social importance. In this vein, it also points to a potential two-pronged view of cemetery visitors. On the one hand, visitors go to a cemetery to get to know such place (including masterpieces of artifacts) and locals' traditions. On the other hand, visitors with their own embodied presence and practices in a cemetery create unique cemetery experiences, thus expanding lived space's dimensions of cemetery, social functionality, and meanings.

However, the main function—a burial place and commemoration site for the dead—instills in visitors the idea (and importance) of *death*; this is an essential denotative and connotative part of a cemetery. In turn, cemetery tourism should be primarily seen in the context of the depiction of death and the dead in modern society and culture (e.g., movies, art exhibitions, video games, and death cafés); taphophilia, or passion for cemeteries, including an interest in their art, tombstone inscriptions, and (famous) graves (Zenith 2021); and such emerging interdisciplinary research areas as *Deathscape Studies*, *Necrogeography*, and *Dark Tourism*.

Topographic and symbolic sites related to death and the dead have been intensively studied in necrogeography and deathscapes studies since the second half of the twentieth century. Both fields are united by a multidisciplinary view of the cemetery as a local phenomenon, a genealogical record, and a reflection of associations, attitudes, established practices and cultural values (e.g., Maddrell and Sidaway 2010; Semple and Brookes 2020).

Dark tourism was first proposed to an academic audience in a 1996 paper in a themed edition of the *International Journal of Heritage Studies* (Foley and Lennon 1996). For Foley and Lennon, dark (or "tragic") tourism was defined as "the presentation and consumption (by visitors) of real and commodified death and disaster sites" (Foley and Lennon 1996, 198). Later work on dark tourism deepened the view of deathscapes as gathering sites, as information sources proposing stories about tragic human experiences, horrors, and suffering, and as emotionally charged places which create a catharsis for tourists (see more in Light 2017). Such tourism, due to a deathscape's history and its authenticity in terms of its death horrors and the tourist experiences involved, is even characterized by different degrees of darkness: "dark," "darker," and "darkest" tourism (Miles 2002; Strange and Kempa 2003). Tours in cemeteries (excluding war cemeteries) are usually classified among the "lightest" forms of dark tourism practices (e.g., Seaton et al. 2015).

According to Light (2017, 286), the main motives for visiting deathscapes are:

- desire or opportunity for learning about what happened at the site
- connecting with one's personal or family heritage
- leisure
- pilgrimage
- remembrance
- sense of moral obligation.

However, there is a small quantity of research on "lightest" forms of dark tourism practices so far, more focusing on cognitive and emotional experiences and rituals in "darkest" tourism (see more in Light 2017, 287). This opens new opportunities in places with an already established research tradition in deathscapes and dark tourism and provides direction in places where cemetery research is still in its infancy. Latvia is somewhere in the middle, because a fair amount of research in cemetery studies has been conducted in Latvian (including the dissertation-in-progress of one of our authors, Karīna Krieviņa, examining cemeteries from a linguistic perspective). The next subsection expands on topics on which researchers have focused when analyzing Latvian cemeteries.

24.2.2 Cemetery Studies in Latvia

The study of Latvian cemeteries thus far has been associated mainly with socio-semiotics, paying attention to cemetery architectonics (sculptures, material objects, and symbols) in the context of religious denominations, art, and cultural practices (e.g., Campe 2014; Kruks 2015). Latvian researchers have paid close attention to tombstone inscriptions, considering the social identities of buried people (ethnic, linguistic, and professional) and these texts' linguo-cultural characteristics: multilingualism, typical linguistic features, and textual units such as poems and farewell words (e.g., Treija 2006; Spārītis 2008).

In Latvia, there is no academic research on cemeteries as tourism sites, but, at various times, stakeholders, journalists, and visitors have published informative and promotional texts on cemetery tourism and its possible development. For instance, in the 1930s there were two periodicals dedicated to tourism: *Ekskursants*, "The Tourist" (1933–1937), and *Tūrisma apskats*, "A Tourism Overview" (1936–1940). Both provide examples of cemeteries as individual/guided tourism destinations in Latvia and include stories from different cemetery excursions. An overview of Soviet periodicals produces similar observations; the periodicals mainly include visits to memorials or soldiers' cemeteries, chronicled in articles linking tourism and cemeteries. The articles are marked strongly by the epoch's political background. Nowadays, there are individual visitor's notes on the internet, which reflect on the visual condition of tombstones and graves, provide encouragement to visit cemeteries, and share somatic and emotional experiences and information learned of being in such a place (e.g., Treibergs 2020; Berra 2020).

In sum, the descriptions of cemetery and cemetery tourism in Latvia show three trends: (1) the decorative, or visually perceivable, dimension of cemeteries is the dominant research topic in theoretical literature; (2) the periodicals depict perceived and perceivable cemeteries by locals; and (3) individual reflections/personal stories share more immersive experiences and feelings in a cemetery.

24.3 Methodology

This research is based on qualitative approaches. First, desk studies were carried out, identifying the global tradition of cemetery research and research trends in Latvia and learning about cemeteries in Latvia. Then the information available in print/digital publications about the locals' cemetery culture, management of cemetery tourism, and tourism opportunities in Latvian cemeteries was examined. Moreover, to get a true picture of cemetery tourism in Latvia, semi-structured interviews with five practicing guides who organize tours in several cemeteries in Riga, the capital of Latvia, and regional cities (Liepāja, Rēzekne, and Aizpute) were conducted. The questions posed to the guides relate to the three interrelated thematic blocks: (1) professional experience in cemetery tourism and description of individual tours, (2) forecasts for future perspectives in cemetery tourism, and (3) personal feelings and attitudes toward cemetery tourism, individual cemeteries, and tourist groups. The completed interviews were then viewed as individual guides' narratives; the interviews also revealed tourists' motivations, wishes, and feedback about their experiences visiting cemeteries. Bearing in mind the subjectivity factor, the interviews were analyzed and compiled according to the more frequently repeated and emphasized topics, problems, and professional experiences.

Finally, the case of Latvia was considered in the context of theoretical literature and the results of other practical research, critically evaluating the potential of cemetery tourism in Latvia in connection with spatiality (Lefebvre 1991), dark tourism, and innovative tours as opportunities to promote living history, cultural heritage, and regional studies.

24.4 Context: Cemeteries in Latvia

Latvia is one of the Baltic States, which has experienced Christianization, Livonian Confederation, Swedish rule, a tsarist Russian empire, World War I and II, and Soviet rule. Latvia declared independence only in 1991. These historical events have determined that the territory of Latvia has been characterized by multiculturalism and multilingualism. For instance, Latvians, Russians, Belarusians, Ukrainians, Germans, Jews, Poles, Lithuanians, and Roma all are traditional ethnic communities in Latvia (Zvidriņš 2021). Cemeteries reflect these historical events and the diversity of society. Examples include cemeteries created for soldiers of specific wars, ideological symbols, and inscriptions on tombstones in different languages (e.g., Latvian, Russian, German, Yiddish, Polish, and Latgalian).

On one hand, cemeteries in Latvia combine visually perceptible cultural signs and testimonies about the social structures of the population living in the territory of Latvia during various periods. For example: Tombstones with engraved names, coats of arms, and memorials have survived from the fifteenth century at some of the oldest burial sites. Cemetery memorials, monuments, sculptures, and symbols represent different styles of architecture and art (e.g., classicism, baroque, and modernism). Arrangements of graves in cemeteries show the social differentiation of the dead by wealth, ethnicity, and/or religion, which has been practiced in many cemeteries since at least the sixteenth century (Gross 2022). Today, Latvia has 49 cemeteries of German soldiers from both World Wars; these have survived the wholesale demolition of German-linked cemeteries during the Soviet era (Vācu kapi 2021).

On the other hand, cemeteries in Latvia are associated with care and gathering. Cemeteries have been decorated with flowers, special wood carvings, ribbons, and garters as far as the Latvian written tradition carries. These decorations were later supplemented with candles and crosses. The tradition of grave care is included in the Latvian cultural canon. Prominent examples of gatherings include Candlelight Evening, the torchlight procession on Lāčplēsis Day (*Lāčplēša diena* in Latvian), Memorial Day for soldiers who fought for the independence of Latvia (in late autumn), and the Celebration of the Cemetery in summer. Thus, cemeteries are experienced individually and collectively through memories, care, pilgrimages, and rituals.

24.4.1 Typical Features of Cemeteries in Latvia

The first similarity among many cemeteries is location: Most cemeteries are located on the outskirts of a city, town, or village. The second similarity is the density of graves of renowned people in central city cemeteries. In Riga cemeteries, more than in regional cemeteries, cemeteries have graves of internationally and nationally recognized persons and graves of Baltic Germans. For instance, *Rīgas Lielie kapi* ("Riga Great Cemetery") includes the graves of German sculptor August Franz Leberecht Volz, Baltic-German chemist and Nobel laureate Wilhelm Ostwald, and Latvian folklorist and active representative of the Latvian national awakening Krišjānis Barons. It is also the main burial site of Baltic Germans in present-day Latvia. Similarly, *Rīgas Meža kapi* ("Riga Forest Cemetery") has many graves of renowned persons, e.g., the first president of Latvia Jānis Čakste, academic Pauls Stradiņš, film director Gunārs Cilinskis, and a savior of Jews during World War II, Žanis Lipke.

The third similarity is a history of vandalism and disrespect, notably during Soviet times, when bronze and metal elements of graves and granite and marble monuments were stolen and many chapels demolished. For example, a street was built across the burial land and through Riga Great Cemetery, removing tombstones and monuments in the process (Juškēvičs 1936). The

Old Cemetery in Liepāja was desecrated with the permission of the city's local authorities: a new thermal power plant was built, and a steam pipeline was laid through the cemetery (Driķe 1999).

The main differences between cemeteries are related to size, layout, and architectonics. Three cemeteries serve as examples:

Riga Forest Cemetery consists of two parts—the First Forest Cemetery and the Second Forest Cemetery—together comprising an area of around 85.5 hectares. It was built as and remains an open, park-like cemetery, with low grave sites without fences around them. It includes many artistic sculptures, chapels (including unique rows of chapels with inscriptions and coats of arms), great monuments, memorials (e.g., one for the people of Latvia's national awakening and two for those deported to Siberia), and decorative fences, together depicting various art and architectonic styles.

Riga Great Cemetery comprises 36.7 hectares and more than 10 thousand graves, representing several church congregations and ethnic and social groups (mostly elite Riga society); its layout is based in classicism. The cemetery houses different political ideologies, masterpieces made by Latvian sculptors (e.g., Kārlis Zāle and Teodors Zaļkalns), and poetic epigraphs on tombstones and memorials. The well-kept condition of the cemetery is the basis for the high artistic and cultural appreciation of the cemetery by experts and random visitors (e.g., Kruks 2015).

Liepājas Līvas kapi ("Līva's Cemetery") covers an area of 5.5 hectares. It consists of three separated and socially segregated parts: the Central section, the Jewish graveyard, and the Cross cemetery. The Central section contains luxurious graves and monuments to the area's elite (including many locals of German descent); burial elements of Jewish graves also testify to wealth. There are almost no memorials in the Cross cemetery, because from the cemetery's early years, victims of diseases and warfare and those dead without relatives were buried there. The cemetery relates to the city's main architect of German origin, Paul Max Bertschy, whose projects span Liepāja (Liepāja Travel 2019). Bertschy designed Līva's Cemetery's Byzantine-style chapel, its pavilion for funeral ceremonies, and individual tombstones depicting Gothic and Neo-Gothic art trends.

Various narratives about unnatural death and personal tragedy reveal cemeteries as dark tourism sites. For instance, Līva's Cemetery in Liepāja is famous among locals for its own tragic version of Romeo and Juliet: two young people, Nikolai and Elza, committed suicide in 1907 due to their parents' prohibition of their marriage (Jākabsone 2021). In *Miera ielas kapi* ("Miera Street Cemetery"), a Catholic-origin cemetery in Rēzekne, the tombstone of Francis Trasuns (1864–1926) was illegally placed in 1975, with an inscription in Latgalian, the regional language. Trasuns was a priest, a politician, and an active defender of Latgalian culture and language who was criticized for his public activities and excommunicated. He died of a heart attack when he was not allowed to observe Holy Mass in the church on Easter. Furthermore, the Roman Catholic Church prohibited him from being buried in a Catholic cemetery; therefore, his grave lies in Brothers' Cemetery in Rēzekne. Later, in 1998, the excommunication of Trasuns was reversed (Malahovskis 2021). Many people visit Miera Street Cemetery each summer to remember Trasuns during the Celebration of the Cemetery.

24.4.2 Annual Celebration of the Cemetery

The term *Kapusvētki* combines two words: *kapi*, or "cemetery," and *svētki*, or "holiday/festivity"; it was first mentioned in church archives and Latvian newspapers in the eighteenth century. Today, the Celebration of the Cemetery (hereinafter the Celebration) is organized by various denominations and takes place every summer from June to September (the specific day depends on the tradition of each cemetery).

The Celebration combines several parts, which differ in their openness to outsiders (private, semipublic, or public), formality (formal or informal), and functionality (site cleaning, religious practice, commemoration, family reunification, maintenance of local identity, socialization, and entertainment). For instance, Catholics (mainly in the eastern part of Latvia, Latgale) perform various rituals that are practiced today with a more flexible adherence to tradition. The Celebration, in Catholic tradition, starts with pre-celebration activities such as cemetery cleaning works; decorating the central cross of the cemetery and altar tables in the corners of the cemetery; weather prediction; and preparing a meal for guests. The religious part of the Celebration usually begins with a liturgy of the intercession of the dead in church. The main part is a procession of the cross, two flags, and symbolic mourning mats and singing chants around the entire cemetery, with stops and special prayers at the altars in each corner. The procession continues to the middle of the cemetery, where closing prayers take place at the central cross. The social function of the Celebration is manifested in the greeting of people known and new; conversations at tombstones (including sharing family's achievements, comparing recently lain tombstones and flower arrangements); the joint remembrance of those dead and buried; photography; and a joint meal at a tombstone, in the parking lot, and/or at the home of a relative/friend. Strong commercialization of the Celebration is visible in many places (especially cities and towns): outdoor markets sell religious and cemetery-culture-related souvenirs (e.g., icons, candles, and flowers) and secular items (e.g., clothing, accessories, toys, food, and drinks). Some secular traditions related to the Celebration are associated with entertainment: going to a ball with live music at a local culture house or open-air stage in the evening; viewing a concert, a play, or dance performance (this was especially true in Soviet times).

The Celebration is a complex cemetery event with different functions. Some of them involve personal relationships, some relate to the cemetery community and/or the local community—and some parts of the event open a space for outsiders (including tourists), too. In this sense, the Celebration opens an opportunity for the public to experience a cemetery as lived space.

In sum, Latvian cemeteries, like cemeteries elsewhere in the world, can be seen from different perspectives: culture and art, architecture, linguistics, social relations, individual identities, published human data, power, and ideology. However, unlike other parts of the world, the cemetery in Latvia is also an active space of human culture and social practices, which as a unique tradition can attract the attention of tourists who seek immersive experiences.

24.5 Organized Tours to Cemeteries: Guides' Perspective

On the Official Latvian Tourism Portal online, writing the key word "cemetery" only produces a search result for the Salaspils Memorial (a prison and labor camp near Riga from 1941 to 1945). Another rich tourism portal for visitors to the capital city, *Cita Rīga* ("A Different Riga") covers almost all the city's cemeteries, but the information is only in Latvian and Russian. The Investment and Tourism Agency of Riga, broadly known as *Live Riga*, has included Riga Great Cemetery in its Cycling Tour, which is a rare example.

Finding guides and information about guided tours in cemeteries in Latvia for this study was challenging, as there is no one who works exclusively in cemetery tours. Fortunately, five guides were found and interviewed. None of them works as a guide full-time—each described it as one of their side-jobs or as a hobby: Dace, a former Latvian language teacher, works mainly as a guide in Riga; Rihards, who has linked his Japanese language knowledge with tourism, offers tours to foreign groups in Riga; Dzintra, Raivis, and Arnis work in regional cities (Rēzekne, Liepāja, and Aizpute).[1]

These interviews reveal the positions and roles of the guides and tourists during the tour, each group's knowledge and expectations, the experiences gained, and the prospects of the SIT niche.

24.5.1 Guiding Observational Tourism Practices

The motivation to host guided tours in cemeteries was each guide's individual decision rooted in the conviction that the niche has not been properly included in general tourism practices in Latvia. Dace notes that it is easier to conduct tours in larger cemeteries, as it is more difficult to create tours in small cemeteries due to the lack of narrative material.

24.5.1.1 Guides' Mission, Challenges, and Perspectives
According to the guides, an organized tour guide must provide a well-grounded explanation for visiting such tourism sites and give opportunities to discuss many cultural and social issues related to cemeteries.

The cultural richness of cemeteries is one of the primary factors motivating outsiders to visit cemeteries. For instance, both Līva's and the Old Cemetery in Liepāja have high architectonic value, while the Forest Cemetery in

Riga tends to be "[Latvia's] open-air sculpture exhibition" (Dace), providing "an overview of the local history of art" (Rihards). Raivis emphasizes that his aim in preparing and conducting a guided tour is "to cause people to look differently at the graves that they would otherwise just pass by." However, the guides express concern regarding the maintenance of the cultural heritage of cemeteries and implore public authorities to take more responsibility in the matter.

Dace is convinced that learning about the life stories of buried people is more important than accidental visual inspection of cemeteries. In this vein, visiting a cemetery is a pre-planned educational experience. In Rihards's words: "Everyone — from different origins, languages, denominations — can lie next to one another, even share the same gravestone. A cemetery is like a micro-painting of a land's inhabitants, and you can learn a lot about the peoples' various cultures just by taking a walk through a cemetery."

In addition, all guides agree that nowadays cemeteries are not objects of political fancy but instead are witnesses and tacit teachers of history. Raivis states: "The memorial to Soviet pilots in Liepāja Central Cemetery is infinitely interesting and tragic. There is an extended list of people who died on May 8, 1945; they all were just boys, the eldest being 26 years old. When you see it and discuss the war, then you forget whether these were Russians, Latvians, or Germans: you rethink individual tragedies caused by the war." Likewise, Dace is critical toward the idea of removing monuments: "All epochs have their own prints left in the form of monuments, and it helps us in talking about history. How will we discuss history with younger generations? The Soviets let Čakste's [the first president of Latvia] grave grow over with weeds, but we will destroy the Monument of Victory [in Riga]? We don't have to rewrite history!" Both examples reveal personal and collective tragedies behind the war, repressions, and political attitudes expressed in cemeteries. It is toward a more humane and down-to-earth understanding of the fragility of human lives that dominates in the narratives of the guides.

In all cases, guided tours are a learning experience allowing the visitor to absorb information and to explore both the architecture and art of the cemetery. Thus, a guide must possess the abilities to specify different historic, cultural, and social ideas, to comply with social norms in different cemeteries, and to provide information about individual traditions and personalities. The preparation of these tours has demanded a lot of effort. Guides rely on their own innovation to create itineraries and collect relevant information. The initial work on the preparation of the tours is characterized by struggle at a basic level: the unavailability of maps, e.g., requiring guides to make their own. This could partly explain why most guides have neither switched to digital presentation tools nor created an audio guide.

Guides have been directly affected by their own present-day tragedy—the Covid-19 pandemic. Not being able to work in the field, Dace is considering requalification. Interviewed in May, however, guides preserve hope that tourism will relaunch in summer 2021. A question remains about the organization of guided tours and the requirements of such. Dzintra mused about the change of perception of cemeteries during and after the pandemic, when these spaces have become marked by another tragic stage of history.

24.5.1.2 Tourist Groups and Their Expectations

Tourists have different motivations to take a guided tour in a cemetery. The tour can be included as a part of a larger visit of an area and last less than an hour, or it can constitute a separate event covering an entire day. Visitors range from kindergarten children taken to Riga Brothers' Cemetery to learn the history of Latvian independence to emigrated Latvians returning to search for the graves of their ancestors.

Groups of children and adolescents are taken to Brothers' cemeteries during commemoration days. Dace has found her own ways of switching the excursion into question-and-answer session, thus creating vivid interaction: "For instance, on the front wall of the Brothers' Cemetery there are soldiers leaving for war and soldiers coming home — why? The walls are telling a story they learn to capture." Dzintra, who also runs tours for youth, notes that schoolchildren in Rēzekne enjoy the opportunity to get to know their native city; her tours emphasize distinct personalities and their life stories. Questions mainly concern the visual markers on the graves, such as signs or crosses. Dzintra notes that regional tours in cemeteries are more suitable for locals and less relevant for outsiders.

All guides work with various adult groups, including families and colleagues. Dace recalls two tours, both presented as gifts: the first one from colleagues on a sixtieth anniversary, the other a surprise from the family of a young man turning eighteen, both offering a guided story tour through Riga Great Cemetery. Such personal initiatives indicate the limits of people's—including locals'—capacity to perceive cemeteries in their entirety without the help of competent guides.

Raivis sometimes includes unplanned stops at cemeteries in some of his city tours. When asked about what sorts of questions he receives, his answer as to the most common is straightforward: "What are we going to do in a cemetery?" However, once visited, some even mention the cemetery as the best part of the tour. Groups of pensioners are among the more common of cemetery visitors. Compared to other tourist groups, seniors are keen to ask specific questions, which can challenge guides. Foreign tourists are said to have a lack of knowledge necessary to decide to visit cemeteries in Latvia; for this, Dace blames the unattractive image kept by public tourism authorities who do not provide accessible information about guides' different specialties and omit cemeteries from their lists of tourism offerings.

24.5.2 Participatory Tourism Practices

The active participation of tourists in cemetery tourism often occurs in two manners. The first is that they imitate the cultural practices of local people in cemeteries, simulating locals' behavior and activities in cemeteries and delving deep into local experiences. Special mention should be made of Japanese tourist groups. According to Rihards, Japanese tourists want to experience the cemetery tour in a ritual way, following a certain sequence of activities (including the direction of the route) and considering the meanings of different symbols. They are particularly well-prepared for the tours, bringing flowers and candles, and always wear appropriate clothing.

The second is that tourists look for ancestors' graves. People of different nationalities and denominations have such a desire. In Rēzekne, mainly those of Jewish origin search for their deceased family members. Dzintra mentions, too, that in Rēzekne, there is a guide knowledgeable in local Jewish cultural heritage. While such root-seeking fits less in the category of organized tours, Dace has experienced on several occasions people booking an excursion and indicating at its outset that their motivation is to find an individual grave, which she is then expected to find. This can lead to disappointment, if she is unable to find the grave, and indicates another way guided excursions in cemeteries still might alter their mission and format.

24.6 Discussion

24.6.1 Present Tourism Practices

The description of cemeteries shows that Latvia's cemeteries are a valuable resource of individuals', local communities', and nation's knowledge, experiences, and cultural practices if there is someone who knows how to "read" them and skillfully transfer the knowledge acquired to individuals and tourist groups. At the same time, it is not possible to say that all cemeteries are equally suitable and interesting for different groups of tourists. Thus, for example, according to the guides, cemeteries in smaller towns and villages are more suitable for local tourists (including students), to learn about the cultural history of the region or to study family heritage. In this vein, cemetery tourism has a mission to keep the conception of cemetery as lived space alive. In contrast, organized tours in the largest cemeteries in Riga are better suited—and more often offered—to foreign tourist groups. Thus, these cemeteries function more as explorable spaces. As the interview data show, different age groups of tourists go to cemeteries, so it can be concluded that tours of this "lightest" form of dark tourism are equally available to tourists of different ages.

The above-mentioned functions of cemetery tourism (respectively, education, interest in history/culture, connection with one's family heritage, and finding concrete graves) are the most frequently mentioned motives for why tourist groups in Latvia choose to go to cemeteries accompanied by a guide.

These are the main reasons for cemetery tourism in other parts of the world, too (see Light 2017).

A guide oversees creating and telling stories about cemeteries (layout, history, architecture, religious/ethnic/linguistic communities) and the people buried in them, and shows how to multimodally "read" and interpret cemeteries (e.g., the objects, symbols, and inscriptions on tombstones), or perceive such places. This is shown in the example where the guide analyzed the sculptures together with pupils in the Brothers' Cemetery in Riga (see above).

However, it is absurd, with today's technology, that helping visitors find individual graves should be the guide's main task on a tour. Accurate and easy-to-use digital maps should replace this task. Moreover, cemetery plans are an essential tool that helps both locals and outsiders navigate a particular cemetery more easily. An audit carried out in 2018 in 170 local government cemeteries (out of 1757) shows that only 50 cemeteries have developed burial plans (LR Valsts kontrole 2018). Even though the audit covers only a small percentage of Latvia's cemeteries, it uncovers one of the main problems in the current cemetery-management practices: insufficient information for relatives of the deceased, for researchers, for tourists, etc. This situation has gradually improved in recent years. For instance, cemetery plans for all seven cities' cemeteries of Liepāja are digitized (TV Kurzeme 2020), and sporadic information about more than 400 cemeteries is available on websites created by private and academic initiatives (e.g., Cemety 2021; Garamantas 2021). Some historical information about Riga Great Cemetery and notable people buried there is included in the global, virtual, and sociohistorical encyclopedia "Time Note" (Time Note 2021). There are only a few examples of booklets with routes in cemeteries (e.g., the "Multicultural Rēzekne" booklet, which includes a tourist route with stops in the city's cemeteries).

Current tourism practices in Latvia show that organized cemetery tourism is not focused on separate thematic niches (e.g., horror stories, crime, tombstone inscriptions), instead combining different points of view and educational entertainment stories related to the visited cemetery. Therefore, it can be assumed that not all tourists are aware of the value and benefits of visiting cemeteries, but if they are visiting the cemeteries, they see those spaces as useful, unusual, even an alternative tourism option.

Another significant obstacle to the development of guided cemetery tourism in Latvia is related to the previous challenge, namely, the availability of information in foreign languages (sometimes also in Latvian), which does not promote an increase in the number of highly motivated visitors to Latvian cemeteries. However, the information placed in cemeteries must be seen in the context of funding and vandalism. A decade ago, the Riga Cemetery Board planned to place audiovisual points in five languages at Riga cemeteries and to create a special website with virtual walks through Riga cemeteries, but the project did not receive funding and the idea has not been implemented so far (Tiļļa 2011). In 2004, the artist Aigars Bikše and his team created and placed the installation *Zemes mātes birojs* ("Mother Earth's Office") in the Riga Great

Cemetery. It was a partially buried glass room with a desk and a computer displaying information about people buried in the cemetery. Unfortunately, vandals have ruined it. This example raises the question not only about the placement of information, but also about its security.

24.6.2 Future Perspectives on Organized Tourism in Latvia

The prospects of cemetery tourism can be viewed from at least two points of view. One is related to the improvement of cemetery tourism management and infrastructure by developing a strategy and management model for the development of such tourism with clearly defined goals, tasks, and responsibilities for the involved actors (including the promotion of cemetery tourism locally and globally). Registration and digitization of graves is one of the tasks.

The second point of view is related to offering organized cemetery tourism to local and foreign tourists. These can be specialized tours depending on target audience, thematic topic, and interactivity. Here are some examples: In addition to the life stories of national heroes, guides can focus on the life stories of celebrities or people of unusual professions from recent history, supplementing a tour with illustrative materials (e.g., photographs, songs, objects). Tours of the most heinous crimes would be among the "darker" of dark tourism options. Biologists can see cemeteries as islands of biodiversity, which maintain the viability of species as varied as birds, moths, and plants (see Barrett and Barrett 2002; Tryjanowski et al. 2017). There are many places in Latvia that would be suitable for this—for instance, Lāčupe's Cemetery in Riga, which has been described as a "cemetery and dendrological park in one place, with a variety of decorative shrubs and plants" (Treibergs 2020). Similarly, linguists or language students can view cemeteries as a set of visually perceptible languages and texts, a part of various linguistic landscapes (see Malinowski et al. 2020), to learn more about multilingualism, language development, the most frequently used personal names and their spellings across different places and times, figurative language in farewell words, wishes, and poems published on tombstones.

Interactivity can be viewed in two ways. On the one hand, this could mean that tourists perform specific tasks on a cemetery tour, such as exchanging places with the guide and acting as detectives or geocachers, finding specific cemetery objects (e.g., graves, sculptures, symbols, trees), obtaining additional information on the internet (e.g., song, painting, the description of an event or place), complete an online express test, or answer the guide's spontaneous questions on their mobile phone.

On the other hand, interactivity facilitates immersion into an authentic cemetery cultural event. Previously, the chapter discussed the Celebration of the Cemetery—a unique, integrative, community-based ritual with religious, philosophical (existential), folkloristic, social, and emotional dimensions, which can be interesting for tourists who want to experience the symbiosis of the spiritual and the secular (e.g., Getz 2011). Such events can attract tourists to lesser-known places, create a positive image for those places, and encourage sharing of locals' knowledge, traditions, and values (e.g., Getz and Page 2016). According to Interaction Ritual Theory (Collins 2004, 48), the Celebration of the Cemetery can be seen as a collective ritual in which participants practice group assembly, mutual focus of attention, and a shared mood, the outcomes of which can be group solidarity, individual emotional energy, stronger social relationship, and standards of morality. As mentioned above, the Celebration of the Cemetery can provide an authentic experience (or sense of lived space, see Lefebvre 1991) for an observer and for a pre-negotiated group member. Both interactivities show the transition from passive tourists' experience to active participation.

24.7 Conclusions

Cemetery tourism is a prospective niche in the tourism industry and thus in public humanities worldwide; research of this niche has supplemented cemetery studies by widening the understanding of these public spaces and social activities practiced there. The present study focused on the analysis of touristic groups' experiences. In Latvia, guided cemetery tourism is mainly practiced by locals. Educational visits are offered to pupils, and adult groups visit to deepen their general knowledge or to supplement their knowledge of genealogies. The understanding of cemeteries as representative in social and cultural terms has motivated guides to offer cemetery tours also to foreign tourists; such tours are based on the assiduous work done by guides themselves in creating itineraries, collecting stories, and promoting such tourism opportunities. Cemetery tourism in Latvia has poor visibility, and precaution was heard in the voices of guides when discussing the potential of different Latvian cemeteries as tourist sites.

Such a tardy and cautious development of the niche could be partly explained by the thriving cemetery culture in Latvia. As a social space, the cemetery is actively maintained by local caretaking traditions and supplemented by various annual commemorative events. If in larger cemeteries interaction between locals and visitors can be minimized, then in smaller cemeteries such encounters can be distracting for locals and can lead to conflict. The latter could be due to locals' will to preserve their cemeteries: Unfortunately, cemetery vandalism still takes place, especially in rural areas. In brief, in Latvia the perception of cemeteries as lived spaces tends to predominate over that of conceived and/or perceived spaces; that becomes particularly clear when discussing cemeteries in the context of guided tourism practices.

Although this chapter has several limitations due to the number of cemeteries considered and the few tourism participants interviewed, it shows that Latvia's cemeteries are a rich resource for various thematic tours for local and foreign tourists to spread the word about living history, culture, traditions, and social practices in local communities. However, to consider Latvia's cemetery tourism as an independent tourism sub-sector, responsible representatives of tourism should fulfill several preconditions. First, the management of cemetery tourism needs to be organized by agreeing on forms of cooperation between the main stakeholders—tourism information centers, tourism companies (including guides), and cemetery keepers. Useful information must be published for tourists—for instance, general information about guided tours in cemeteries (advertisements) and guides' contact information, in foreign languages, too. A no less important precondition is the professional education of guides on the specifics of cemetery tourism (including ethics issues), thematic choices for tours, and various strategies to offer tourists valuable, strong, and memorable experiences. Research into cemetery culture, history, semiotics, and language would help guides in their professional development. The creation or modification of digital maps with marked stops or express tasks (e.g., finding something, answering questions, or uploading photos) could be included among the desired interactive techniques and skills for guides to acquire in attracting the attention of tourists.

Note

1. All names have been changed for privacy.

References

Barrett, Gary W., and Terry L. Barrett. 2002. "Cemeteries as Repositories of Natural and Cultural Diversity." *Conservation Biology* 15 (6) (January): 1820–24. https://doi.org/10.1046/j.1523-1739.2001.00410.x.

Berra (Burr), Solvita. 2020. "Epitāfija kā sapresēta liecība par cilvēku un viņa dzīvi." Blog, April 12. https://pilsetuteksti.blogspot.com/2020/05/epitafija-ka-sapreseta-lieciba-par.html.

Campe, Paul. 2014. "Mauzoleji Rīgas, Jelgavas un Liepājas pilsētas kapsētās." *Mākslas Vēsture un Teorija* 17: 52–59.

Cemety. "Kapsētas." Kapsētu informācijas digitalizācija un datu pārvaldības sistēma. Accessed April 20, 2021. https://cemety.lv/public/cemeteries.

Collins, Randall. 2004. *Interaction Ritual Chains*. Princeton: Princeton University Press.

Deering, Bel. 2010. "From Anti-social Behaviour to X-Rated: Exploring Social Diversity and Conflict in the Cemetery." In *Deathscapes: Spaces for Death, Dying, Mourning and Remembrance*, edited by James D. Sidaway and Avril Maddrell, 75–93. Aldershot: Ashgate.

Driķe Nora. 1999. "Vecie kapi bez svētkiem." *Diena*. Written September 21. Accessed June 9, 2021. https://www.diena.lv/raksts/pasaule/krievija/vecie-kapi-bez-svetkiem-10525324.

Foley, Malcolm, and John J. Lennon. 1996. "JFK and Dark Tourism: A Fascination with Assassination." *International Journal of Heritage Studies* 2 (4): 198–211.

Garamantas. "Latviešu folkloras krātuves digitālais arhīvs." Accessed May 3, 2021. http://garamantas.lv/.

George, Richard. 2019. *Marketing Tourism in South Africa*. 6th edition. Oxford: Oxford University Press.

Getz, Donald. 2011. "The Nature and Scope of Festival Studies." *International Journal of Event Management Research* 5 (1) (January): 1–47.

Getz, Donald, and Stephen J. Page. 2016. "Progress and Prospects for Event Tourism Research." *Tourism Management* 52 (February): 593–631. https://doi.org/10.1016/j.tourman.2015.03.007.

Gross, Daina. 2022. "Cemetery Culture." https://kulturaskanons.lv/en/archive/kapu-kopsanas-tradicija/.

Jākabsone, Kristīne. "Par interesanto mums apkārt." Accessed May 10, 2021. https://www.liepajniekiem.lv/viedokli/kristine-jakabsone-par-interesanto-mums-apkart/

Juškēvičs, Jānis. 1936. *Vecā Rīga*. Rīga: Zinātne.

Kruks, Sergejs. 2015. "Piemiņas zīmju semiotika Latvijas kapsētās." *Letonica* 29: 27–42.

Lefebvre, Henry. 1991. *The Production of Space*. Oxford: Blackwell.

Liepāja Travel. "Berči arhitektūra Liepājā." Last modified May 7, 2019. https://liepaja.travel/app/uploads/2019/02/liepaja_karte_berci_lv.pdf.

Light, Duncan. 2017. "Progress in Dark Tourism and Thanatourism Research: An Uneasy Relationship with Heritage Tourism." *Tourism Management* 61 (August): 275–301. https://doi.org/10.1016/j.tourman.2017.01.011.

LR Valsts kontrole. "Kapsētu saimniecība Latvijā." Written February 7, 2018. https://www.lrvk.gov.lv.

Maddrell, Avril, and James D. Sidaway. 2010. *Deathscapes: Spaces for Death, Dying, Mourning and Remembrance*. Farnham: Ashgate.

Malahovskis, Vladislavs. 2021. "Francis Trasūns." Nacionālā enciklopēdija. March 10. https://enciklopedija.lv/skirklis/95851-Francis-Trasuns.

Malinowski, David, Hiram H. Maxim, and Sébastien Dubreil, eds. 2020. *Language Teaching in the Linguistic Landscape Mobilizing Pedagogy in Public Space*. New York, NY: Springer.

Mantojums. "Pieminekļi." Modified 2016. https://is.mantojums.lv/.

Miles, William F. S. 2002. "Auschwitz: Museum Interpretation and Darker Tourism." *Annals of Tourism Research* 29 (4) (April): 1175–78. https://doi.org/10.1016/S0160-7383(02)00054-3.

Neogeo. "Latvijas kapi." Accessed July 3, 2021. http://neogeo.lv/ekartes/latvijas-kapi.html.

Nordh, Helena, Katinka Horgen Evensen, and Margrete Skår. 2017. "A Peaceful Place in the City: A Qualitative Study of Restorative Components of the Cemetery." *Landscape and Planning* 80 (June): 108–11. https://doi.org/10.1016/j.landurbplan.2017.06.004.

Odgers, David, ed. *Caring for Historic Graveyard and Cemetery Monuments*. London: English Heritage, 2011.

Seaton, Tony, Magda North, and Gabriela Gajda. 2015. "Last Resting Places? Recreational Spaces or Thanatourism Attractions: The Future of Historic Cemeteries and Churchyards in Europe." In *Landscapes of Leisure: Space, Place and Identities*, edited by Sean Gammon and Sam Elkington, 71–95. London: Palgrave Macmillan.

Semple, Sarah, and Stuart Brookes. 2020. "Necrogeography and Necroscapes: Living with the Dead." *World Archaeology* 52 (1) (July): 1–15. https://doi.org/10.1080/00438243.2020.1779434.

Spārītis, Ojārs. 2008. "Mākslas vēsturnieka skats uz Latvijas epigrāfiju." *Linguistica Lettica* 18: 103–24.

Strange, Carolyn, and Michael Kempa. 2003. "Shades of Dark Tourism: Alcatraz and Robben Island." *Annals of Tourism Research* 30 (2) (April): 386–405. https://doi.org/10.1016/S0160-7383(02)00102-0.

Swensen, Grete, Helena Nordh, and Jan Brendalsmo. 2016. "A Green Space Between Life and Death: A Case Study of Activities in Gambebyen Cemetery in Oslo, Norway." *Norsk Geografisk Tidsskrift-Norwegian Journal of Geography* 70 (March): 41–53. https://doi.org/10.1080/00291951.2015.1102169.

Taun, Yi-Fun. 1977. *Space and Place: The Perspective of Experience*. London: Arnold.

Tiļļa, Andris. 2011. "Notīrīt eņģelim spārnu." *Mājas Viesis*, September 30.

Tilley, Christopher. 1994. *A Phenomenology of Landscape: Places, Paths and Monuments*. Oxford: Berg.

Time Note. "Kapsētu saraksts." Accessed July 7, 2021. https://timenote.info.

Treibergs, Toms. 2020. "Miera salas meklējot. Rīgas kapu recenzija." November 6. https://satori.lv/article/miera-salas-meklejot-rigas-kapu-recenzija?fbclid=IwAR0_rRDM81S43aM5qtqLoDQDpj6oet-7klYhglDKmdCoRLLAv6xcuu_0_So.

Treija, Rita. 2006. "Latviešu kapsētu epitāfiju tekstu struktūra: Galvenās apprises." *Letonica* 14: 259–84.

Tryjanowski, Piotr et al. 2017. "Bird Diversity in Urban Green Space: A Large-Scale Analysis of Differences Between Parks and Cemeteries in Central Europe." *Urban Forestry & Urban Greening* 27: 264–71. https://doi.org/10.1016/j.ufug.2017.08.014.

TV Kurzeme. "Liepājā digitalizētas visas septiņas pilsētas kapsētas." Accessed September 16, 2020.

Vācu kapi. "Saldus Vācu karavīru kapi." Militärerbe Tourismus. Accessed May 6, 2021. https://militaryheritagetourism.info/de/military/sites/view/90?0.

Zenith, Autumn. "What Is Taphophilia? Exploring the Fascinating Subject of Grave Hunting." Accessed July 24, 2021. https://witchcraftedlife.com/what-is-taphophilia-exploring-the-fascinating-subject-of-grave-hunting/.

Zvidriņš, Pēteris. 2021. "Iedzīvotāju etniskais sastāvs Latvijā." Nacionālā enciklopēdija, May 25. https://enciklopedija.lv/skirklis/5186-iedz%C4%ABvot%C4%81ju-etniskais-sast%C4%81vs-Latvij%C4%81.

PART VI

Public Discourse, Public Art and Activism

CHAPTER 25

Public Historians, Social Media, and Hate Speech: The French Case

Deborah Paci

25.1 Introduction

The rise of social media is providing an unprecedented amount of data about the social relations and behaviors of very large groups of people around the world. Social media is having a relevant impact on political and social processes. Hate speech in the form of anti-Semitic remarks is a common occurrence on social media. Twitter and Facebook have been seeking to oppose hate speech while taking into account the right to freedom of speech. Social media are leading to rapid polarization in public debates and accelerate the spreading of hate speech. For public historians, social media offers interesting opportunities and promises. The interest in a social media platform is a meaningful avenue for public-historical engagement. Nevertheless, social media reflects the limitations of sharing authority on these platforms. They are a remarkable mechanism for exchanging ideas but also for spreading hate speech. On these

---

This project has received funding from the European Union's Horizon 2020 research and innovation programme under grant agreement No. 732942 and was written in the context of the ODYCCEUS H2020 Research Project (https://www.odycceus.eu/).

D. Paci (✉)
University of Corsica, UMR LISA, Corte, France
e-mail: deborah.paci4@unibo.it

University of Bologna, Department of History and Cultures, Bologna, Italy

---

© The Author(s), under exclusive license to Springer Nature Switzerland AG 2022
A. Schwan and T. Thomson (eds.), *The Palgrave Handbook of Digital and Public Humanities*, https://doi.org/10.1007/978-3-031-11886-9_25

platforms, we can find an abuse of history and a significant amount of hate speech referring to ethnic or religious categories of people. Hate speech—or the degeneration of historical discussions in social media—plays a role in shaping public opinion and, in some cases, forms its backbone.

This chapter aims to examine the potential and the limitations of shared authority for preventing the abuse of history and hate speech. I will focus on the French context in particular by analyzing, on the one hand, how anti-Semitic hate speech is propagated online, diffusing its ideas in an uncontrolled and pervasive manner, and, on the other hand, how public historians can face this phenomenon. The main argument of the essay is that contemporary modes of communication, which have substantially shifted online and to social media, greatly increase the size of potential and actual audiences for hate speech and anti-Semitic agitation. Jürgen Habermas's concept of the public sphere (1991) is an influential model for our understanding of public communication on social media. The public sphere "requires unlimited access to information, equal and protected participation, and the absence of institutional influence, particularly regarding the economy" (Kruse et al. 2018, 63). Social media have not led to the re-emergence of this space: "the Internet and social media sites have not promoted unlimited access to information, equal access and participation, nor have these spaces – particularly social media site – been free of institutional influence" (Kruse et al. 2018, 64). The information produced on social media is no longer being edited and conveyed by an intellectual élite, as was the case in the nineteenth century, but is now produced by the readers themselves—who are also authors—moving along dispersive trajectories. In the 2000s, anti-Semitic hate speech is no longer exclusively being diffused in the press, but online: its platform is now the Infosphere alluded to by philosopher Luciano Floridi (2014), and instead of uniquely polarizing society, it spreads pernicious ideas, avoiding a face-to-face open encounter. Many of these messages are written anonymously and it is this anonymity that has led to a radicalization on a scale never seen before.

25.2 Shaping Public Opinion Online

The celebrated formula of Marshall McLuhan—"the medium is the message" (1964)—expresses the distinct relationship of the interdependence between the author and the means through which the author who holds authority communicates. The medium can contribute to and give substance to the message making it more clear. According to McLuhan the means of communication has the ability to give meaning to interpersonal relations and to be agent and motor of history. In this way the media is key to reading history and interpreting society. New digital technology and the Internet shape the ways in which people perceive space and time. As a consequence the same social boundaries undergo a redefinition that influences the manner in which society talks about itself. Certainly the media acts like social glue; it is a mediator between people and groups, thus functioning as a vehicle of ideas and contributing to the shape of the public sphere. However it also represents a "barrier" and a "message of separation." When we connect to the net we do it with a physical instrument, a computer, on which we are dependent, and this can present an obstacle (Ortoleva 2011, 212). Those who use social media do so in the knowledge of dominating the means and of having the power to use this instrument as a platform for their own ideas. Apparently social relations grow thanks to the absence of boundaries and the possibility of exponentially increasing opportunities for social dialogue, yet in reality the computer screen acts as an obstacle to knowledge: it works like a mirror in which we reflect that part of ourselves imbued with cliché and falsehoods.

The hyper-medium represented by the Internet is marked by a particularly relevant feature: the speed of access and diffusion of the information and above all its disintermediation. It has however become fertile terrain for the proliferation of fake news and inaccuracy propagated in a context in which the figure of an intermediary is absent. The users of the net have in reality "eroded the space of the traditional elite, which has in the meantime lost credibility and social representativeness" (Quattrociocchi and Vicini 2018, 27). Despite the premise that the most enthusiastic users of the web have prefigured a world in which the Internet favors a plurality of viewpoints, in reality the contrary has occurred: the formation of so-called echo-chambers, characterized by a substantial homogeneity of viewpoints and by the consequent lack of consideration of dissenting opinions. It concerns a widespread phenomenon, in which there is a convergence of primal instincts to be part of a reassuring community and the role of algorithms in the selection of news to which we are exposed (Di Piazza et al. 2018, 187). In reality, though, it would be reductive to consider the impact of media by recourse to the theory of echo-chambers and the hypodermic needle model. The theory of echo-chambers discerns the origins of the radicalization of offline life and assigns to social media simply the role of amplifier of a reality that exists in the real world. On the contrary, the hypodermic needle model holds that the massive spillover effect of social media is the cause of the ease with which users allow themselves to be influenced by radical events. According to the scholars who developed this model, it is more productive to consider the relationship between social media and the subjects radicalized (Alava et al. 2017). That which takes shape in social media is then public opinion in real time: users of social media deal with historical themes with extreme disregard and flippancy making rash comparisons between dictators of the past and the governments of today, glorifying totalitarian regimes, retrieving racist and anti-Semitic rhetoric.

"Social media is restructuring notions of the past and present … historical knowledge, reduced to a sum of disintermediated opinion, has been removed from the memory of the past, lending itself to instant application to the emotional experience of the interconnected public" (Noiret et al. 2021, 134). Social media inserts itself within the impermanence of "updatism," a digital reality in which archived data is constantly updated by the flow of ongoing events in the present (Pereira and Araujo 2019). In this context of disintermediation social media becomes "an intermediary of information (*gatekeeper* between publishers and users) and search engines, based upon pre-selection of the content that can be seen (*filter bubble*), tending to organize the results of the search by (pre-) conceptions of the visitors, deluding them – with an effect defined '*disruptive*', 'misleading'– on the soundness and indisputability of their own evaluation (*echo chamber*)" (Luceri and Ribezzo 2020).

25.3 Social Media and Anti-Semitic Hate Speech

The digital turn has produced a recrudescence of several historical phenomena, including anti-Semitism, and manifestations of primal hatred based on entrenched anti-Semitic themes, such as the idea that there is an international project to achieve Jewish global hegemony in all sectors of society, from culture to the economy, and political institutions. These conspiracy theories have seen an exponential rise with the advent of the Internet, a space without filters that serves as a propagator of hate speech. A search on Google permits rapid access to the information sought but at the same time does not favor the development of critical reflection: that which is promoted, more or less consciously, is a nullification of the process of interpretation and maturing of thought.

If, for example, we hit upon an anti-Semitic website, Google continues to propose content similar to that sought; Shoshana Zuboff (2019) has spoken in terms of "extraction of behavioural surplus" on the part of colossi like Google to predict our desires as consumers, cultural desires included. Thinking along the same lines is Safiya Noble (2018) who observed how the algorithms that determine the architecture of a Google search do not return neutral results, but, on the contrary, reproduce and amplify narratives, stereotypes, and systems of discrimination, including those regarding gender and skin color. This condition ensures that the same information that one can find by a simple Google search is strongly conditioned by the bias of the algorithm. We see therefore how algorithms can contribute to the formation of public opinion in sharp contrast to the historical method which insists on the need for interpretation and seeks to foster critical thinking.

Anti-Semitic hate speech reveals the "porous" borders established between the digital and the real world. As Floridi (2014) suggests the digital era is characterized by "onlife": we are in the presence of a permanent connectivity between offline and online. Hate speech draws its symbolic power from the totality of representations within society and is based on divisive and binary polarity (bad/good, inside/outside, us/other) reproducing a distinct vision of social disorder. Through the invocation of injustice the haters appeal to the ethos of their interlocutors. Therefore it is not possible to fully understand hate speech without questioning "the narrative models that structure the narrative of hate, likewise with the stereotypes that construct its semantic perimeter.

These reflect the operation of framing and naming that pre-exist the act of hateful enunciation" (Monnier et al. 2021, 10).

Twitter is a form of mixed public sphere and at the same time a net of information. "Retweeting can be understood both as a form of information diffusion and as a means of participating in a diffuse conversation. Spreading tweets is not simply to get messages out to new audiences, but also to validate and engage with others" (Boyd et al. 2010). Twitter presents itself as an ideal place for self-affirmation and social mobilization: users deploy social media as a means to personally attack political adversaries, manifesting their indignation toward wrongs suffered or denouncing presumed conspiracies. Social media can act as a platform for manifestations of anti-Semitism that occur in real life (Albertini and Doucet 2016). On 19 February 2019, Emmanuel Macron, the President of the French Republic, visited a desecrated Jewish cemetery in Quatzenheim. The regional television channel France 3 filmed the event but was forced to cut the live feed on Facebook because the channel's page was flooded by hate messages targeting Macron and the representatives of the Jewish community. According to a report by the Observatoire de l'antisémitisme en ligne (2020), 9% of online anti-Semitic content for 2019 is linked to the desecration of the Jewish cemetery in Quatzenheim.

25.4 Social Media and Freedom of Speech

In social media the propagators of hate who have made anti-Semitic hate speech their trademark oppose liberty of expression for their detractors. In the digital era the principle of free speech must inevitably face up to the concept of Post-truth, which according to the *Oxford English Dictionary* means a condition in which in the transmission of arguments it is not the verified facts that form public opinion but recourse to emotions and personal conviction. According to Maurizio Ferraris (2017, 11), the proliferation of information within the Post-truth rubric is a direct consequence of postmodernism. Although there is no direct connection between postmodernism and Post-truth, we can highlight how Post-truth claims have taken up, and misrepresented, the two theses attributed to postmodern thought—namely that there are no facts but only interpretations and that truth as such is a statement of authority, as Michel Foucault argued. The questioning of the notion of truth comes from the idea that facts do not exist, only interpretations and the presumption to know (Di Piazza et al. 2018, 189–90).

Post-truth claims making is not some dangerous projection of postmodernist theorizing. As outlined by Bert Spector "it involves a particular kind of pact between claims maker and intended audience in which the leader lies by asserting inaccurate claims, expecting the intended audience to put aside that acknowledged inaccuracy in support of a belief in some shared goal" (2020, 9). Post-truth claims create fertile ground for the spread of hate speech. A relevant aspect in the investigation of hate speech is really the nexus that arises between expressions of hate and the liberty of expression. In this respect we have to take into account the bad management of social media platforms; the greater part of them do not worry about identifying content containing hate speech but ask this of their users via spontaneous reporting that permits administrators to intervene and possibly remove illicit content. In the case of Facebook algorithms are in place that process reports of hate speech and on the basis of the evidence pass on, where the terms warrant it, the messages for examination by administrators. This type of control is effective for pictures, such as those that are nude, pornographic, or violent, but the same cannot be said for reported text—in this case—hate speech. This occurs because the algorithms are trained and consequently only look for patterns taught by the developers.

Hate speech spreads on the net and proliferates particularly on social media due to several conditions that facilitate its diffusion: the anonymity of the authors of the content; the "itineracy" of these messages, that is the condition in which the content spreads to platforms different to those on which it was first published; and the absence of a supranational authority appointed to coordinate all the measures taken by individual states. In an attempt to counter this legislative vacuum in May 2006 a code of conduct was adopted by important Internet Service Providers (Facebook, Twitter), sharing platforms (YouTube), and multinational companies (Microsoft), to block online hate speech which envisaged the removal of this content within 24 hours of its publication (Luceri and Ribezzo 2020). On 10 October 2012, the hashtag #UnBonJuif—an abbreviation of "the only good Jew is a dead Jew"—was the third most tweeted hashtag in France. Although it was soon followed by #UnBonMusulman and #UnBonRaciste, these hashtags did not enjoy the same success in the Twitter community. Far from wishing to appear racist or anti-Semitic, the authors of these tweets with the hashtag #UnBonJuif claimed to be exercising freedom of expression and freedom of speech as well as the right to use forms of humor. By way of example, I quote a tweet attacking the behavior of those who believe that it is morally unacceptable to express hate against Jews and Israelis. User EM writes on 6 January: "#un BonJuif is a matter that should be taken to court #Un BonMusulman is freedom of expression. That's what we need to hurry up and understand …."

Following a ruling on 24 January 2013 the Paris Court Orders asked Twitter to provide to the five antiracist organizations who had filed the lawsuit data it held on the accounts of people who had published hate speech: "The plaintiff associations claimed they were alerted to various clearly illegal tweets grouped under the hashtag #unbonjuif and #unjuifmort containing messages violently anti-Semitic, contrary to French public order" (Legalis 2013). In March 2019 white suprematist content was found on certain Facebook pages (Cox and Koebler 2019). In this way a distinction was made between forms of national identity, such as Basque, Breton, or Corsican nationalism, and white supremacy, which instead presupposed a whole raft of racist practices and the submission of African-Americans. Whoever published posts with racist insults or search terms seeking white supremacy came to the web page "Life

After Hate" (https://www.lifeafterhate.org) run by a non-profit organization founded by former white supremacists, who offer educational resources, support, and sensitization, to put a brake on racist behavior. With these countermeasures Mark Zuckerberg, co-founder of Facebook, showed his desire to stem the widespread phenomenon of hate speech, their terms of reference made explicit in the community standards section. In reality, as was revealed in an enquiry conducted in September 2017 by the online magazine ProPublica, Facebook permitted its subscribers to sell Nazi memorabilia or recruit protesters for a rally of the extreme right. Facebook consented to the publication of ads aimed at 2300 people who had expressed interest in topics including "Jew hater," "How to burn Jews," or, "History of why Jews ruin the world" (Angwin et al. 2017).

One month before on 12 August 2017 at Charlottesville, Virginia, a protest took place which degenerated into violence that cost the lives of three people and saw several others wounded. The protagonists were white supremacists, who were protesting against the decision to remove the statue of Confederate General Lee, and people opposed to their racist ideology (Stolberg and Rosenthal 2017). Following this serious incident, Zuckerberg published a long post distancing himself from what happened, reiterating that Facebook was a place that abstained from hate speech, foregrounding how his own Jewishness made him all the more sensitive to expressions of anti-Semitic hate (2017).

The social networks are in fact a place in which the expression of hate multiplies, becoming viral: one statistical study by the site The Verge analyzed 4.6 million comments that appeared on Reddit to evaluate the incident in terms of the number of times terms such as "Hitler" or "Nazi" appeared, taking care to not take into account discussion of an historical nature. The results of the study revealed that there is a 78% probability that in a discussion with more than 1000 comments a user will use one of the two terms (Vincent 2016). Previously in 1990 Mike Godwin developed the Law of Godwin, which states that to the extent that an online discussion develops, regardless of its content, the probability that a user will make a comparison with Nazis or Hitler rises exponentially. This law is coupled with "reductio ad Hitlerum," an expression referring to a rhetorical device which aims to discredit an interlocutor by comparing him to Adolf Hitler (Godwin 1994). Social media has thus become the chosen place for the so-called Chanterculture "that exists not just in opposition to racial diversity in politics and culture, but in order to advance its own agenda, which across a variety of fronts seeks to preserve and promote the cultural and political preeminence of white guys. This new movement, and it is a movement, combines age-old racist and sexist rhetoric with bleeding-edge meme culture and technology" (Bernstein 2015).

25.5 ANTI-SEMITISM AND SOCIAL MEDIA: THE FRENCH CASE

In the anti-Semitic rhetoric expressed on the Internet and in social media all the evils of modern society are embodied in the Jew. The anti-Semitic argumentation rests on a representation that sees Jews as the fifth column in the service of foreign powers, artifact of a world conspiracy hatched together with the State of Israel and the United States and responsible for threatening the secularism of the French state with their religious sectarianism (Taguieff 2007). This line of argument is not an invention of the twenty-first century: "the last three decades of the 19th century are the moment in which modern political anti-Semitism in the strict sense was founded. ... anti-Semitism is associated above all with the societies in which it emerges and manifests itself, with Jews becoming the symbolic object of the tensions, contradictions, and clashes taking place in these societies" (Levis Sullam 2008, 30). The debate around anti-Semitism identifies several factors that were at the origin of anti-Semitism in France in the 1880s–90s (Kalman 2010). The defeat of Sedan in the Franco-Prussian war of 1870 with the consequent ceding of the provinces of Alsace and Lorraine stoked the fires of revanchist patriotism while weakening the republican nationalism of the Jacobite matrix. There prevailed a faith in the armed forces which was seen as the bedrock upon which the nation would redeem itself. This nationalism aimed to call into question the postulates on which the republic was founded, starting with consideration of the decadence of modern times and the fall of the Third Republic. As Stephen Wilson observed, the reasons for resentment toward Jews can be attributed to the fears of the period (1982). Attributing blame to Jews for being at the root of all evil furnished a justification for all the changes that assaulted modern society (Kreis 2017). In this context, the famous court case involving the French officer of Jewish origin Alfred Dreyfus from 1894 onwards—unjustly accused of treason for supplying secret military documents to the Germans—can be fully understood.

Anti-Semitic hate speech and francophone Holocaust deniers made their first appearance in the summer of 1995, preceded by a series of basically chauvinist comments about Belgians: both were published in a humor forum fr.rec.humour (Karmasyn et al. 2000, 18). From that moment the deniers started to participate in several generalist francophone forums such as fr.soc.divers, soc.culture.french, and fr.soc.politique, visited also by non-French users, in particular, Belgian, Canadian, and Danish. The French active in the discussion forum took care to make themselves anonymous to get around the Gayssot law adopted in 1990 to punish those who denied the genocide of Jews. This law together with an analogous one in Germany was unprecedented in Europe (Canopé, n.d., 2), passed against the backdrop of a wave of anti-Semitism: two months previously, on the night between the 8th and 9th of May 1990, the cemetery of Carpentras was profaned (Schneider 2006). The enacting of the Gayssot law gave rise to much controversy in the

Assemblée Nationale and the Sénat as well as among intellectuals and historians: the party of the extreme right, Front National, under the presidency of Jean-Marie Le Pen, called openly for the abrogation of the law in the name of freedom of expression. The historian Pierre Vidal-Naquet rallied against what he considered an intrusion of the law into history: "Negationists make me throw up. But I have always been against the Gayssot Law. The state should not tell us how to teach history" (cited in Rosello 2010, 207).

In December 2005, the Association d'historiens Liberté pour l'Histoire launched a petition backed by 19 academics and signed by 1000 historians, for the abrogation of the suite of memorial laws, the Gayssot law among them (Vie publique 2021). What animated this association was condemnation of any form of political and judicial interference in the arena of competence of the historian. The forum fr.soc.politique featured at the time a considerable amount of anti-Semitic content, and content of racist character generally, but starting from the 1990s the French deniers made their presence felt by creating ad hoc websites on which they published anti-Semitic texts, exploiting hypertextuality and hypermediality which enabled cross-linking between the various web portals. By way of example we can mention the Association des anciens amateurs de récits de guerre et d'holocauste (AAARGH) created in 1996 at the initiative of the sociologist and denialist Serge Thion who claimed the right of anonymity of his contributors (Karmasyn et al. 2000, 43–49). Ahmed Rami was one of the first on the Internet to spread the denialist articles of Robert Faurisson (the noted denialist and then professor of French literature at the University of Lyon II). Rami is a Moroccan Islamist refugee in Sweden, noted for having created a mix of pan-Arabism, religious fanaticism, and visceral anti-Semitism (Igounet 2012). In 1987 Rami founded together with David Janzoon, spokesman of the extreme right Swedish party Sveriges Nationella Förbund (National League of Sweden), the radio station Radio Islam, from which he broadcast anti-Semitic and denialist propaganda. In 1990 Rami had to serve a prison term of six months; Radio Islam went off air from 1993 to 1995 and in 1996 the website Radio Islam was created, which was multilingual and managed autonomously by the person in charge of each language service (http://islam-radio.net/islam/french/french.htm). Radio Islam re-directed to anti-Semitic websites, including the extremist Catholic and anti-Semitic website holywar.org (now blocked).[1] It showed how "the link between denialist propaganda and that of fundamentalist anti-Zionism is representative. The base rhetoric of Ahmed Rami, the new hero of this protest, integrates ultra-radical islamic ideas impregnated with anti-Zionism and anti-Semitism" (Igounet 1999, 581).

Following the Six-Day War the anti-Jewish discourse began to overlap with more ideological attacks on Israel as a Jewish state. Anti-Zionism emerged mainly in intellectual circles to the extent that people began to refer to— new anti-Semitism based on a paradigm comparing Israeli actions to American imperialism (Poliakov 1969). As pointed out by Marie-Anne Matard Bonucci, anti-Semitism has become a system of representation based on opposition to what is "other" to ourselves (2005, 11–12), namely the so-called "generation Dieudonné." The website Jewpop.com dedicated an article to "anti-Semitism 2.0," expressed by the "Dieudonné generation": "a generation immersed in extreme mental confusion using the right to mock everyone, with the pretext of being humorous, to display a sickening anti-Semitism that finds its common denominator in a real feeling of an unfair political, social, and financial 'Jewish domination'" (L'OBS 2012). A prominent role was played in this context by Dieudonné M'bala M'bala, a French comedian and actor with Cameroonian origins who is also known for having invented the gesture known as "glisser la quenelle" (literally "sliding a quenelle," the gesture evokes the practice of fisting). The gesture involves pointing one arm downwards while resting the palm of the other hand on the opposite shoulder. Evoking an inverted Nazi salute, the gesture appeared on election campaign posters when Dieudonné ran in the 2009 European Parliamentary elections as one of the candidates of the Île-de-France region on an anti-Zionist list—Liste antisionniste—together with Yahia Gouasmi, a Shiite religious figure, and the writer Alain Soral, obtaining 1.30% of votes (L'OBS 2009). In 2007, Soral founded the Egalité et Réconciliation website, which provided a platform for his extremist opinions and for purveyors of anti-Semitic hate in general (Bruneteau 2015, 226–33).

According to the study conducted by Caterina Froio of the four websites that occupy a central position in the network of the extreme right in France pre-eminent is Égalité et Réconciliation with a very high relative score of betweenness centrality (937.7), since it measures the extent to which a vertex lies on paths between other vertices, the greater the betweenness, the greater the power possessed by the node represented. Égalité et Réconciliation is in a strategic position in the network (Froio 2017, 52). As Robin D'Angelo and Mathieu Molard (2015) have noted, Soral has created a sort of "facho business," becoming hugely popular among young people from the banlieues thanks to his pseudo-analyses and videos posted on YouTube. In February 2020, the Conseil Représentatif des Institutions juives de France (CRIF), the organization representing French Jews, published the first study on online anti-Semitism in France carried out by the Observatoire de l'antisémitisme en ligne (2020). The Observatory found 51,816 examples of anti-Semitic content published in 2019: this figure is limited to public profiles on social media platforms and those published after being vetted by moderators. According to the report drawn up by the Observatoire de l'antisémitisme en ligne (2020, 16), 63% of anti-Semitic content is published on Twitter, followed by Facebook (17%), reseau international (3%), YouTube (2%), and forum.hardware.fr (2%).

25.6 Social Media and Public-Historical Engagement

The recrudescence of hate speech is the product, to a certain extent, of an environment in which a self-reliant movement of users has established itself.

Charles Leadbeater and Paul Miller (2004) have spoken of the so-called "Pro-Am Revolution," that is, the phenomenon represented by professional amateurs who pursue their own leisure activities in cultural environments with all the hallmarks of professionalism. The user-generated content (UGC) with an historic imprint are those products generated by amateur users that are loaded onto shared platforms. Some are realized with intellectual honesty and imitate the work of professional historians; others contain evident distortions stretching the truth.

The amateur enterprise which is at the foundation of UGC is based on the reciprocity of sharing: the logic of the division of work which instead involves the recognition of specific competence is extraneous. For example in Wikipedia anyone can write and revise an entry and nobody can claim special authority on the basis of the competence they possess. The division of work is not established straight off on the basis of the competence of each one, but grows from the activity itself and can be susceptible to modification over time (Flichy 2011, 267). The creation of UGC occurs within a collective process: these productions are published on the web and are the object of comment by users. The authority of the professional is inevitably undermined by the proliferation of UGC. And it is here that the public historian intervenes, who—loyal to the principle of shared authority (Frisch 2011)—inserts himself or herself within a process of division of work, acting like a *passeur* of history (Noiret 2009, 295).

The discipline of history, as noted, requires rigorous methodology: the historian confronts and dialogues constantly with the sources, calling for a bibliography as exhaustive as possible and recourse to bibliographic references is essential to allow other researchers to verify the information (Bloch 1949 [1963]). The vocation of the historian is the result of years of training that is superfluous to pro-am and to content carried on social media, the non-place in which there is a proliferation of information and historical content intentionally simplified that answers to a logic that favors simplification and refuses complexity. Therefore the public historian is called to restore the complexity of historical understanding adopting clear language, suited to a non-specialist public, and turning to techniques of digital storytelling that can be integrated in social media. The historian can thus adopt an "alternative narrative" that can prove itself effective in countering hate speech: "it is not only about deconstructing a perspective, but to offer one completely different, and hence – in the case of hate speech – not oppositional (us versus them) but inclusive (us + them) and based on new ideas" (Faloppa 2020, chap. 10).

Public historians act therefore as digital storytellers entering into public debate that takes place in social media. To counter arguments bearing signs of anti-Semitism they can intervene in the comments referring to projects of digital storytelling: such products in virtue of the hypermedial nature of the product, that is the co-presence of various elements including video, audio, and text, allows to gain the attention of the user. Furthermore they can start a virtuous circle that, as per the logic of shared authority, induces the commentators of the anti-Semitic post or tweet to begin to think in historic terms over a longer timeframe. However, this is probably an overly optimistic assumption. The risk of this operation is that the attempts of the public historian are rendered futile by the community of haters. The public historian might also become himself or herself the target of hate. Nevertheless, the hypermediality establishes favorable conditions in which to recount history, and social media represents a place suited to promulgating the products of digital storytelling. Public history has called upon academia to move away from over-specialization and open itself up to external demands. The public historian is invested with a civic duty to combat the abuse of history that social media contributes to and feeds: they must not only communicate history by connecting it to the problems of the day being debated in the public arena, specifically in social media, but also "bring history in direct contact with the evolution of the mentality and of the sense of collective belonging of diverse communities that live together in the national space and global village and promote the study of their identity" (Noiret 2009, 275).

The History Manifesto (2014) by Jo Guldi and David Armitage is an invitation to historians to take note and come to terms with the processes of political, social, and cultural transformation of the present age. This work contains a denunciation of the crisis of authority and of the social role of the historian, whose capacity to intervene and influence contemporary debate in virtue of their knowledge of the past and their interpretative competence with respect to sources is not recognized. In the face of the "spectre of the short term," *The History Manifesto* "is a call to arms to historians and everyone interested in the role of history in contemporary society" (Guldi and Armitage 2014). This contains a forceful attack on micro-history and at the same time it exhorts historians to recall the Braudelian lesson of the *longue durée*, an approach seen as antidote to the redrafting of the role of history in society. Moreover the development of the concept of *longue durée* was born of the need perceived by Fernand Braudel (1949 [1975]) in the aftermath of World War II to provide a methodological perspective in contrast to presentism that placed history in the service of a future in which his contemporaries had renewed confidence. Thanks to the *longue durée* it would have been possible to understand the dynamics of the present since they were the result of a series of choices over the long term. The Braudelian lesson viewed history as a tool with which to understand the past in order to plan the future (Baritono et al. 2015). Historians in the current era are thus not asked to contrast a vision that is too flatly focused on the present, but to stimulate a critical sense in a society that is invested by the phenomenon of updatism. "The inter-reality of social media, which is configured like a hybrid social space, in which the digital has a direct impact on the processes of construction of social identity" (Riva 2017, 211) is not "the fruit of presentism, nor of traditionalism … but is the realisation of *updatism*" (Noiret et al. 2021, 134). Therefore the public historian is called upon to deal with not so much presentism as updatism: the objective is that of making understandable how knowledge of the past, namely "lighthouse of humanity" (Borghi 2016) and "common good" (Giardina et al. 2019), is determinant in acquiring an awareness of the problems posed by the present in constant update, countering the abuse of history and putting the brakes on the rapid spread of hate speech.

New technology and in particular the study of big data offers, from the point of view of Guldi and Armitage, a further opportunity for the discipline of history to attain a renewed role within the hierarchy of knowledge. The authors of *The History Manifesto* highlight the urgency of shaking up the halls of academic historians so that they will descend from their ivory towers and put themselves at the service of the community, furthering their studies by exploiting the opportunity given by digital communication and that they do it proposing a reflection of *longue durée*. The abuse of history on social media, that happens when anti-Semitic arguments are put forward, is the fruit of a vision of history understood via short-termism: hate speech finds fertile terrain in an environment in which the idea that history is made up of single events prevails. If in the public discourse anti-Semitism is confused with anti-Zionism, it is because the *longue durée* of anti-Semitism is ignored. Already by the 1880s, anti-Semitic messages were being widely diffused both in the press and as a consequence of a hugely successful tract entitled *La France juive: Essai d'histoire contemporaine* by Édouard Drumont (1886). The Drumontian work saw a certain revival in the 1930s and 40s and particularly during the Vichy collaboration. But not only then: we can easily ascertain the *longue durée* of Drumontian messages in the twenty-first century. Their diffusion is not on printed paper but on the net.

In January 2013, Soral (2013) announced that his publishing house KontreKulture would republish *La France juive* in its "Les InfréKentables" collection, referring to Drumontin's laudatory terms. In the French language section of Radio Islam entitled "Pouvoir juif" we can find the transcription of the article published on the site "Égalité et Réconciliation" as well as a link to two volumes of *La France juive*. We can see therefore a continuity in the arguments between Drumont and Soral or Dieudonné. Drumont's Rothschilds and Pereiras are the precursors or "founders" of the financial lobby that Dieudonné considers to be responsible for all of the world's evils (Paci, 2022). The confusion between anti-Semitism and anti-Zionism is aggravated by a false interpretation—created for political ends—in the public debate as evidenced in the press release issued by Macron in 2017. During the commemoration of the Vélodrome d'Hiver roundup—which took place in July 1942, during the collaborationist Vichy regime, when there were mass arrests of Jews in greater Paris—Macron gave a speech before Israeli Prime Minister Benjamin Netanyahu in which he stated: "We will cede no ground to messages of hate, and we will cede no ground to anti-Zionism, for it is a mere reinvention of anti-Semitism" (France 24, 2019). In spite of what Macron says, anti-Semitic hate speech has a long history. However, we observe how the UGC reproduce narratives that most of the time, as Guldi and Armitage put it, are the fruit of short-termism. The users of the net and social media in particular give life to a "montage of the past, without specifying sources nor historical contextualization, presented as an opportunity to integrate, and often contrast, the little histories of the local community with the official narrations of professional historians" (Noiret et al. 2021, 135).

Although *The History Manifesto* has attracted criticism (Clavert 2014), I believe that the mere adoption of the concept of *longue durée* by the public historian could make an effective contribution to countering hate speech and abuses of history. The public historian, adhering to the principle of shared authority, could adopt the concept of *longue durée* to counter the widespread opinion that history is a succession of events and at the same time introduce the idea that this could be studied using big data as a source (Tripodi et al. 2019). The practice of shared authority will demonstrate how the collective memory is "the totality of social representations regarding the past that every group produces, institutionalizes, safeguards, and transmits through the interaction of its members among themselves" (Jedlowski 2001, 375). In this context a renewed role for the public historian will thus be essential in which they will be called upon to function as an intermediary in a position to propose a reflection on conflict between the different memories that animate the public sphere. By way of example, I quote the Turulpata Facebook page, a satirical page that has over 8000 followers and was considered good practice by the Congress of Local and Regional Authorities of the Council of Europe. The public historian could learn from this counter-narrative campaign on social media carried out by Political Capital—an independent policy research, analysis, and consulting institute founded in 2001 in Budapest. Turulpata is a fictitious Hungarian settlement inhabited and governed by far-right-leaning individuals in Hungary. Posts on the Turulpata Facebook page deal with satirical reflections on current issues of Hungarian domestic politics, popular beliefs and, in general, topics used by the extreme right to spread hate speech. The Turulpata Facebook page does not produce counter-narrative as a direct response to specific online hate speech. The counter-narrative campaign aims at stimulating online users to perform the following actions: (1) Become a follower; (2) Spread the counter-narrative content through sharing; (3) increase the popularity of the content by liking it; (4) Become financial supporters of the project to enable the maintenance of the page. This is a practical example of how to contrast hate speech by sharing authority with online users. In this way, the authors of the Turulpata Facebook page and online users work together in order to counter and prevent radicalization "by reducing both the attractiveness of extreme right ideology and the receptivity of youngsters to ideas of the extreme right" (Richter 2009, 25).

25.7 Conclusion

Shared authority could therefore be a response to the attention-seeking of individuals and the community who feel the need to talk about themselves.

The net, instead of cultivating a familiarity with history, contributes to the foment of a narcissistic attitude: social media, a place of not only private but also public discourse, becomes the space in which one can give vent to one's own expectations, disappointments, and fears. Public historians do not need to bother reaching those who express hate, but it is their task to educate the wider public. The narrative of the enemy (Fotia 2021) is produced in these containers, without spatial or temporal borders, and it is there that, without a physical counterbalance but only with the reflection on the screen of ourselves, one nourishes the abuses of history. Worth noting are the actions undertaken to counter hate speech on the net of the Délégation interministérielle à la lute contre le racisme, l'antisémitisme et la haine anti-LGBT (Dilcrah). Created in 2012 Dilcrah offers support to civil society initiatives. The struggle against hate on the Internet in France is one of the priorities of the Plan national de lute contre le racisme et l'antisémitisme 2018–2020. Dilcrah, in concert with other ministerial actors and French parliamentarians, is engaged in deliberation leading to legislative revision to provide a serious counter to hate speech on the Internet and, in particular, in social media. Day to day Dilcrah monitors platforms for illicit videos and posts so they can be removed and above all, and this is what most interests me, sustains the production of counter-narratives or alternative conversations that can foster a critical spirit (Poinsot 2019, 133). In this context the figure of the public historian can be of great utility in favoring a joint engagement between civil society and political institutions. According to Thomas Cauvin, Public History should be understood not only and simply as a history *for*, i.e., addressed *to*, the public, but also as a history *with*: this means that in addition to the importance given to communication, equal importance is given to public participation. Cauvin invites historians to assume a civic responsibility: "Historians have a role to play, but this role comes with a set of obligations. Historians should accept that they do not work for the sake of history only, to advance historical research, but also for and with others" (2016, 2).

The public historian is not detached from the social context since they live in the deep interconnections that they establish with the very society with which they communicate (Paci 2021). It is not a given that anti-Semitic hate speech, as observed by Michael Marrus (1990, 8), will define the agenda of the historians of anti-Semitism, just as flat earth theories do not influence the activities of astronauts; however the public historian has the civic responsibility to talk not with the haters but about the haters. To the extent that people contravene all the rules of the practice of history, there cannot be any exchange with them in the field of history. The mediation of the historian to counter the abuse of history can thus provide an antidote to oppose the proliferation of hate speech. As pointed out by Massimo Leone (2016, 188), even systematic condemnation risks providing the spreaders of hatred with a platform: "opinion leaders like Dieudonné openly utter these statements. They are well aware of the legal consequences that they will have to face as a result. Indeed, for as punitive as these consequences might be, they inevitably turn into the most effective megaphone that the opinion leaders might have. That is one of the dilemmas with which Western societies must deal in the present time: on the one side, limiting the diffusion of hate speech and on the other side, facing the risk that any limitation becomes involuntary propaganda."

Note

1. Following the attacks in Toulouse and Montauban in March 2012 that led to the death of three soldiers and four Jewish civilians, an alphabetical register appeared outright on holywar.org, of "intellectuals friendly to Israel": writers, university professors, politicians, journalists, philosophers, and scholars defined as "very dangerous."

References

Alava, Séraphin, Noha Najjar, and Hasna Hussein. 2017. "Étude des processus de radicalisation au sein des réseaux sociaux: place des arguments complotistes et des discours de rupture." *Quaderni*. Accessed June 25, 2021. http://journals.openedition.org/quaderni/1106.

Albertini, Dominique, and David Doucet. 2016. *La Fachosphère. Comment l'extrême droite remporte la bataille du Net*. Paris: Flammarion.

Angwin, Julia, Madeleine Varner, and Ariana Tobin. 2017. "Facebook Enabled Advertisers to Reach 'Jews Haters.'" *ProPublica*. Accessed June 25, 2021. https://tinyurl.com/2heryrth.

Baritono, Raffaella, Paolo Capuzzo, Mario Del Pero, Giovanni Gozzini, and Giovanni Orsina. 2015. "Historians of the world, unite! Tavola rotonda su 'The History Manifesto,' di Jo Guldi e David Armitage." *Ricerche di Storia politica*. Accessed June 25, 2021. https://tinyurl.com/474wr8z5.

Braudel, Fernand. (1949 [1975]). *The Mediterranean and the Mediterranean world in the age of Philip II*. 2 vol. London: Fontana.

Bernstein, Joseph. 2015. "In 2015, The Dark Forces of the Internet Became a Counterculture." *BuzzFeed.News*. Accessed June 25, 2021. https://tinyurl.com/kt82hvr4.

Bloch, Mark. (1949 [1963]). *The Historian's Craft*. New York: Knopf.

Borghi, Beatrice. 2016. *Il faro dell'umanità. Jacques le Goff e la storia*. Bologna: Patron.

Boyd, Danah, Scott Golder, and Gilad Lotan. 2010. "Tweet, Tweet, Retweet: Conversational Aspects of Retweeting on Twitter." Accessed June 25, 2021. https://tinyurl.com/yvxhcky9.

Bruneteau, Bernard. 2015. "Les permanences de l'antisémitisme antimondialiste (fin XIX e -début XXI e siècle)." *Revue d'histoire moderne et contemporaine* 62 (2–3): 226–33.

Canopé. n.d. "Législation et négationnisme: une spécificité française?" Accessed June 25, 2021. https://tinyurl.com/akjn57n4.

Cauvin, Thomas. 2016. *Public History: A Textbook of Practice*. New York and London: Routledge.

Clavert, Frédéric. 2014. "Jo Guldi, David Armitage, the History Manifesto." *Lectures*. Accessed June 26, 2021. https://tinyurl.com/4335746s.

Cox, Joseph, and Jason Koebler. 2019. "Facebook Bans White Nationalism and White Separatism." *Motherboard Tech by Vice*. Accessed June 25, 2021. https://tinyurl.com/zfb5rpa9.

D'Angelo, Robin, and Mathieu Molard. 2015. *Le Système Soral, enquête sur un facho business*. Paris: Calmann-Lévy.

Di Piazza, Salvatore, Francesca Piazza, and Mauro Serra. 2018. "Retorica e post-verità: una tesi controcorrente." *Siculorum Gymnasium* 71 (4): 183–205.

Faloppa, Federico. 2020. *#ODIO Manuale di resistenza alla violenza delle parole*. Torino: UTET.

Ferraris, Maurizio. 2017. *Postverità e altri enigmi*. Bologna: Il Mulino.

Flichy, Patrice. 2011. "Internet, il medium dei dilettanti?" *Problemi dell'informazione* 26 (2–3): 263–75.

Floridi, Luciano. 2014. *The Fourth Revolution: How the Infosphere Is Reshaping Human Reality*. Oxford: Oxford University Press.

Fotia, Laura. 2021. "On Hate and the Enemy, from the 20th Century to Today: A Global View." *Diacronie. Studi di Storia Contemporanea* 45 (1): 1–13. Accessed June 26, 2021. http://www.studistorici.com/2021/03/29/fotia_01_numero_45.

France 24. 2019. "Macron Announces Measures to Combat Anti-Semitism in France." Accessed June 26, 2021. https://tinyurl.com/5thns4pd.

Frisch, Michael H. 2011. *A Shared Authority: Essays on the Craft and Meaning of Oral and Public History*. Albany: State University of New York Press.

Froio, Caterina. 2017. "Nous et les autres L'altérité sur les sites web des extrêmes droites en France." *Réseaux* 2–3 (202–203): 39–78.

Giardina, Andrea, Liliana Segre, and Andrea Camilleri. 2019. "L'appello: la storia è un bene comune, salviamola." *la Repubblica*. Accessed June 26, 2021. https://bit.ly/33zULiP.

Godwin, Mike. 1994. "Meme, Counter-meme." *Wired*. Accessed June 25, 2021. https://www.wired.com/1994/10/godwin-if-2/.

Guldi, Jo, and David Armitage. 2014. *The History Manifesto*. Accessed December 6, 2021. https://www.cambridge.org/core/services/aop-file-manager/file/57594fd0fab864a459dc7785/historymanifesto-2Oct2014.pdf.

Habermas, Jürgen. 1991. *The Structural Transformation of the Public Sphere: An Inquiry into a Category of Bourgeois Society*. Cambridge, MA: MIT Press.

Igounet, Valérie. 1999. *Histoire du négationnisme en France*. Paris: Seuil.

Igounet, Valérie. 2012. *Robert Faurisson: portrait d'un négationniste*. Paris: Denoël.

Jedlowski, Paolo. 2001. "Memorie. Temi e problemi della sociologia della memoria nel XX secolo." *Rassegna Italiana di Sociologia* 3: 373–92.

Kalman, Julie. 2010. *Rethinking Antisemitism in Nineteenth-Century France*. Cambridge: Cambridge University Press.

Karmasyn, Gilles, Gérard Panczer, and Michel Fingerhut. 2000. "Le négationnisme sur Internet – Genèse, stratégies." *Revue d'Histoire de la Shoah* 3 (170): 7–67.

Kreis, Emmanuel. 2017. *Quis ut Deus? Antijudéo-maçonnisme et occultisme en France sous la IIIe République*. Paris: Société d'édition Les Belles Lettres.

Kruse, Lisa M., Dawn R. Norris, and Jonathan R. Flinchum. "Social Media as a Public Sphere? Politics on Social Media." *The Sociological Quarterly* 59 (1): 62–84.

Leadbeater, Charles, and Paul Miller. 2004. *The Pro-am Revolution: How Enthusiasts are Changing our Society and Economy*. London: Demos.

L'OBS. 2009. "1,30 % pour laliste 'anti-sioniste' de Dieudonné." *L'OBS*. Accessed June 25, 2021. https://tinyurl.com/3b5k4j9w.

L'OBS. 2012. "Record de tweets antisémites, selon l'UEJF, qui veut rencontrer Twitter." *L'OBS*. Accessed June 25, 2021. https://tinyurl.com/46j3xbyc.

Legalis. 2013. *Tribunal de grande instance de Paris Ordonnance de référé 24 janvier 2013*. Accessed June 25, 2021. https://tinyurl.com/49t3pwsw.

Leone, Massimo. 2016. "Il bastian contrario nella rete: Pattern rituali di formazione dell'opinione nella semiosfera dei social networks." *Lexia. Rivista di semiotica* 25–26: 173–210.

Levis Sullam, Simon. 2008. *L'archivio antiebraico. Il linguaggio dell'antisemitismo modern*. Bari: Laterza.

Luceri, Caterina, and Francesco Ribezzo. 2020. "La libertà di espressione: aspetti problematici nell'era di internet." *Ius in Itinere*. Accessed June 25, 2021. https://tinyurl.com/uax6wayv.

Marrus, Michael Robert. 1990. *L'Holocauste dans l'Histoire*. Paris: Éditions Eshel.

Matard-Bonucci, Marie-Anne. 2005. *AntiséMythes: l'image des juifs entre culture et politique (1848–1939)*. Paris: PUF.

McLuhan, Marshall. 1964. *Understanding Media: The Extensions of Man*. New York: McGraw-Hill.

Monnier, Angeliki, Annabelle Seoane, Nicolas Hubé, and Pierre Leroux. 2021. "Discours de haine dans les réseaux socionumériques." *Mots. Les langages du politique* 125 (1): 9–14.

Noble, Safiya Umoja. 2018. *Algorithms of Oppression: How Search Engines Reinforce Racism*. New York: New York University Press.

Noiret, Serge. 2009. "'Public History' e 'storia pubblica' nella rete." *Ricerche Storiche* 39 (2–3): 275–327.

Noiret, Serge, Deborah Paci, Marcello Ravveduto, and Manfredi Scanagatta. 2021. "La storia come bene comune: le nuove frontiere della public history digitale." *Passato e Presente* 113: 119–134.

Observatoire de l'antisémitisme en ligne. 2020. Accessed June 25, 2021. https://tinyurl.com/eyecuy.

Ortoleva, Peppino. 2011. "Media. Riflessioni intorno a un concetto." *Problemi dell'informazione* 36 (2–3): 193–216.

Paci, Deborah. 2021. "Conoscere è partecipare: digital public history, wiki e citizen humanities." *Umanistica digitale* 10: 235–49.

Paci, Deborah. 2022. "Hate Speech in France: From Drumont to Dieudonné." *Antisemitism*.

Poinsot, Marie. 2019. "Lutte contre le racisme, l'antisémitisme et les discriminations: actualité et collaboration avec le Musée national de l'histoire de l'immigration." *Hommes & Migrations* 1324: 132–39. https://doi.org/10.4000/hommesmigrations.8795.

Pereira, Mateus, and Valdei Araujo. 2019. "Updatism. Comparsa e diffusione della parola update come fenomeno rivelatore della nostra era digitale." In *La storia in digitale. Teorie e metodologie*, edited by Deborah Paci, 27–46. Milano: Unicopli.

Poliakov, Léon. 1969. *De l'Antisionisme à l'antisémitisme*. Paris: Calmann-Lévy.

Quattrociocchi, Walter, and Antonella Vicini. 2018. *Liberi di credere. Informazione, internet e post-verità*. Torino: Codice.

Rosello, Mireille. 2010. *The Reparative in Narratives: Works of Mourning in Progress*. Liverpool: Liverpool University Press.

Richter, Hannah. 2009. "Research Report." Accessed November 6, 2021. https://www.rnw.org/wp-content/uploads/2020/12/GC-State-of-the-Art-Analysis-Full-Report.pdf.

Riva, Giuseppe. 2017. "Interrealtà. Reti fisiche e digitali e post-verità." *Il Mulino* 2: 210–17.

Schneider, Floriane. 2006. "Carpentras, 10-15 mai 1990, polysémie d'une profanation." *Temps des médias* 6 (1): 175–87.

Soral, Alain. 2013. "Sortie de La France juive, d'Édouard Drumont." *Egalité et Réconciliation*. Accessed June 27, 2021. https://tinyurl.com/yyvupnb8.

Spector, Bert. 2020. "Post-Truth Claims and the Wishing Away of Brute Facts." *Leadership* 16 (1): 9–24.

Stolberg, Sheryl Gay, and Brian M. Rosenthal. 2017. "Man Charged After White Nationalist Rally in Charlottesville Ends in Deadly Violence." *The New York Times*. Accessed June 25, 2021. https://tinyurl.com/mh99xz7b.

Taguieff, Pierre-André. 2007. *L'imaginaire du complot mondial. Aspects d'un mythe moderne*. Paris: Fayard/Mille et une nuits.

Tripodi, Rocco, Massimo Warglien, Simon Levis Sullam, and Deborah Paci. 2019. "Tracing Antisemitic Language Through Diachronic Embedding Projections: France 1789–1914." *Proceedings of the 1st International Workshop on Computational Approaches to Historical Language Change*, 115–25. Firenze: Association for Computational Linguistics.

Vie publique. 2021. *Lois mémorielles: la loi, le politique et l'Histoire*. Accessed June 25, 2021. https://tinyurl.com/4ez5ff6m.

Vincent, J. 2016. "Nearly 80 Percent of Reddit Threads with More Than a Thousand Comments Mention Hitler." *The Verge*. Accessed June 25, 2021. https://tinyurl.com/6spwk73.

Wilson, Stephen. 1982. *Ideology and Experience: Anti-Semitism in France at the time of the Dreyfus affair*. London and Toronto: Associated University Presses.

Zuboff, Shoshana. 2019. *The Age of Surveillance Capitalism: The Fight for Human Future at the New Frontier of Power*. New York: Public Affairs.

Zuckerberg, Mark. 2017. Post on Facebook. Accessed November 6, 2021. https://www.facebook.com/zuck/posts/10103969849282011?pnref=story.

CHAPTER 26

The Public Artist as a Fringe Agent for Sustainability: Practices of Environmentalist Driven Art-Activism and Their Digital Perspectives

Diego Mantoan

26.1 INTRODUCTION: INVESTIGATING ENGAGED ART PRACTICES

Christening hills made of industrial debris, planting trees in urban areas, cleaning laundry water through a homegrown wetland, signaling waterways in cityscapes, or liberating squids from a fish market are some public artworks produced over the last decades that address environmental issues. Since the beginning of the millennium, the climate crisis further heightened the public artist's role as civic agent in society, thus working at the margins of the art field. Ever since practitioners like Barbara Steveni, John Latham, Nancy Holt, and Joseph Beuys called in the 1970s for public art to widen the scope and audience of visual arts, growing numbers of artists directed their intervention at society in order to foster the debate on the conditions for sustainable development (Braddock and Ater 2014, 2–8). Early on, the theories and practices developed by public artists focused on the complex interactions between gender politics, racial discrimination, and environmental issues (Lippard 1976, 338). In recent years, public art has moved decidedly toward a wider definition of sustainability to overcome attitudes grounded in patriarchy, colonialism, capitalism, and extractivism (Boettger 2008, 154–61). Public art thus operates on the fringe, placing itself between the global and the local, between the art world and society at large.

D. Mantoan (✉)
University of Palermo, Palermo, Italy
e-mail: diego.mantoan@unipa.it

Faced with the immense challenges connected with the ongoing ecological crisis, it seems necessary to assess the contributions the visual arts have offered to the debate on sustainability thanks to the civic agency of public artists concerned with environmental issues, especially over the last two decades. While these artists unleashed their actions in the public sphere, the scholarly community tried to come to terms with the concepts and strategies underlying the connection between art and sustainability (Pröpper 2017). However, the difficulties encountered by current research are limited either by the inability to go beyond the bland description of artists working on sustainability or the hubris with which art is envisioned by many academics as simply another means to communicate scientific outcomes (Miles 2015). To the contrary, public artists demonstrated that art should be employed to its maximum aesthetic, participatory, and immersive potential for a radical shift in our individual and collective environmental paradigms (Mantoan 2021, 17). It seems relevant to tackle the subject from a theoretical and historical perspective, thus appreciating the trajectory commencing with environmentalist and feminist stances in the 1970s (Bois et al. 2016, 654–60). Such historical examples clearly prove that art is far from an "emotional" language that can be naively adopted for empathetic immediacy (Thomsen 2015). Nor should art be taken as a neutral instrument, which might be exploited at will to instrumentally convey scientific outcomes (Bendor et al. 2017). Moving toward the new millennium, public artists addressed climate change, global warming, and the Anthropocene with artistic means to offer creative solutions, both within and outside the art world, such as with group exhibitions like *Beyond Green* (2006) in Chicago and *Melting Ice/A Hot Topic* (2007) in San Francisco. Several artist groups, networks, and consortia emerged to create a network of experiences and practices—for instance Julie's Bicycle and COAL—which also benefitted from digital tools to propagate their action into society. Simultaneously, scholars increasingly paid attention to the appearance of artworks, projects and even entire exhibitions connected to the topics of global warming (Dunaway 2009, 9–31). In this regard, Sacha Kagan (2011), Nathalie Blanc, and Barbara Benish (2018), T. J. Demos et al. (2021) went a step further, superseding the merely descriptive approach and interrogating engaged art practices to find how they could assist societal progress toward a sustainable future.

Pondering on theoretical stances and suggesting a few analytical categories, this chapter argues that since its very inception public art operated on the fringe of two domains—the art world and society at large—thus framing a space for new artistic practices to be employed, as well as for a wider and diverse audience to be involved. Drawing on an interdisciplinary approach that resorts to public humanities and art history, it is possible to explore key concepts, practices, debates, and projects that define the evolution of public art as a form of activism addressing environmental concerns. First, I shall investigate the origins of earnest ecological attitudes in public art, further trying to categorize the kind of civic agency that practitioners embraced to involve a non-art-related audience. Subsequently, I turn to the examination of a much more recent period, roughly spanning over the last two decades, when the term sustainability firmly entered the creative vocabulary and daily practice of public artists operating at local and global level. Eventually, the last section presents two case studies that allow to understand how public artists shaped their response to community engagement and digital presence. The first case is the seminal group show *Weather Report* (2007) organized by feminist activist Lucy Lippard in Boulder, Colorado. I will consider it as a public manifesto for art's intervention into the climate crisis that opens a distinct field from the elite art world. The second case explores the activities of *gala* Green Art Lab Alliance, an international network of practitioners employing art projects and digital tools to disseminate their practices, as well as to strengthen the public range of environmentalist artworks produced in different parts of the world. These case studies shall help determine how artists proceed from the fringe to engage with non-art-related audiences in the public sphere, as well as to what extent the digital dimension can help create a niche, which is autonomous from the elite art world. Finally, this analysis might provide a much-needed reflection on the effectiveness of participatory art projects for the sake of sustainability, stressing the relevance of public strategies firmly grounded in the grammar of contemporary art and enhanced by a growing ecological ethos in younger generations of public artists.

26.2 Turning to Environmentalist Practices

First, a common misconception about art and the environment must be discussed, one that frequently deceives those who are not well versed in art historical developments. In the past, terms like "Environmental Art" or "Land Art" were applied to a specific kind of artworks and projects informed by Minimalism, Conceptualism and Anti-Form that emerged during the 1960s and 1970s, highlighting the connection with a given place, be it natural or urban (Pancotto 2010, 35). However, this does not necessarily mean they had a genuinely ecological root; rather they made an aesthetic reference to the natural features of a site and were thus largely displayed as photographic documentation, like with the interventions of Claes Oldenburg, Richard Long, Günther Uecker, and Hans Haacke presented at Dwan Gallery, New York, in the 1968 *Earthworks* exhibition (Pesapane 2005, 406–34). Land Art artists began to use or shape environmental elements taken as core material of their projects, though often unconcerned about the invasiveness of their creative proposition, such as with the land excavations of Michael Heizer's *Double Negative* (1969–1970) or Walter De Maria's *Las Vegas Piece* (1969).

If seen from the perspective of today's environmental sensibility, hardly any of these artworks would be considered ecologist. Environmental or Land Art simply does not equal contemporary environmentalist stances, as can be decidedly seen in works like *Asphalt Rundown* in Rome (1969) or *Glue Pour* in Vancouver (1970) by Robert Smithson, who literally discarded an entire truck-trunk of concrete and gallons of sticky liquid in a natural setting. From an aesthetic point of view these artworks are formally impeccable, though in the eyes of ecological activism they are but a punch in the stomach due to their intrusiveness, a true affront to nature more typically associated with construction business and industry (Carlson 1986, 638–39). In recent years, although armed with genuine environmental concerns, artists like Ralf Schmerberg still missed the point with his public installation *Der Stromfresser* (2010), which was supposed to address the squandering of electricity through everyday appliances in domestic households (Haderer 2010, 50–51). On the Gänsemarkt in Hamburg he built an igloo-shaped construction made of 322 fridges with their back turned inwards, while the unnecessary power consumption was instantly measured on an electric calculator to admonish the public, but eventually the artwork participated in the very electrical waste it addressed.

Although Land Art appears to stray from ecological standards, it was helpful in preparing the art world for earnest environmentalist art practices. After the 1973 oil crisis a growing number of practitioners embarked on public art projects that decidedly turned toward an ecologist approach (Braddock and Ater 2014, 6). Historically, the aims and scope of artworks referring to this new sensibility can roughly be divided into two principal kinds. On the one hand, there are awareness-raising projects meant to foster a shift in the public mindset on environmental topics, as in the case of Holt and Latham, although they did not really denounce the current situation. On the other hand, one can identify radical interventions and action-taking projects in the works of Beuys, Nicolás García Uriburu, and Betsy Damon, which intended to involve the public and promote behavioral change.

Concerning the first typology, it is interesting that Holt developed her gentle attitude toward nature, while working alongside her husband Smithson. Truly, he introduced the art world to a radical rethinking of landscape, but she developed an earnest ecologist attitude intervening on discarded environments for the purpose of their regeneration (Mantoan 2018, 7–9). In *Dark Star Park* (1979–1984) for a highway crossroad in Roslyn, Virginia, as well as in *Sky Mound* (1988) for a landfill in New Jersey, Holt rescued two derelict pieces of land by building megalithic structures aligned with the stars, thus creating public parks for astrological observation that connect people with their planet (Lippard 2011, 59–60). A clear analogy can be drawn to the public projects *Niddrie Woman* and *Five Sisters* (1975–1976) by Latham, founder of the Artist Placement Group with his wife Steveni, who lyrically turned a group of mining bings in the Scottish landscape into admonishing monuments through the act of christening them (Richardson 2012). Addressing the toxic and indelible residue of industrial development, Latham confronted society with the scars inflicted upon the landscape by providing a scientific and lyrical analysis of the dump hills, giving them names to ensure the human deeds and greed that had caused them would not be forgotten.

The second kind of historical examples, those characterized by action-taking, can be identified in the participatory projects of Beuys, such as his paramount *7000 Eichen* (1982–1987). On the world-renowned documenta exhibition, the German artist attempted to afforest the city of Kassel by unloading a hoard of basalt monoliths in front of the Museum Fridericianum, each one to be removed only for a new oak tree planted in the urban area. Directly involving the public in the action, Beuys succeeded in mobilizing an entire community, restarting their relationship with nature, instead of building monuments (Schwarze 2012, 122–24). A similar intervention was the *Coloration of the Grand Canal* (1968/1980) undertaken by Uriburu during the Venice Biennale, when he dyed the waters of the lagoon with harmless Fluorescein to promote consciousness about water pollution (Bayon 1972, 349). A particular strain of eco-activism developed over the 1980s from feminist art practitioners such as Damon, who created *A Memory of Clean Water* (1988) by means of an elongated paper cast taken from a dried-out riverbed along Castle Creek, Utah. Through performances and projects implying land reclamation or nature emendation, ecofeminism showed a particular ability in joining hands with Mother Earth, as if womanhood had a privileged access to the environment and thus could collaborate with nature itself (Stein 1994, 243–45). In this regard, patriarchy was targeted as the root of the kind of extractivist attitude that brought the world to the brink of collapse. By the end of the twentieth century, denouncing the Anthropocene was not enough, because the real quest was by then overcoming the economic, social, and political paradigms of late capitalism, which had allowed the ruthless exploitation of natural resources (Wallen 2012, 234–42).

26.3 Civic Agency Is for the Public Artist

According to a broad definition of public art, all the above-mentioned projects—be they truly significant for ecology or not—would have been labelled public artworks, since they comply with three main characteristics that are deemed necessary by most scholars (Cartiere and Zebracki 2015; Krause Knight and Senie 2016). In the first instance, they lie outside of an institutional setting, such as an art gallery or a museum. Furthermore, they are installed or take place in a site that is publicly accessible, which means that they can be experienced from non-art-related audiences or even unaware spectators. Eventually, they are meant to be site-specific, thus responding to the elements of a given place—be they geographic, historical, natural, or artificial (Baker 1976, 75). For the second half of the twentieth century, "site" or "place" at first became terms of radical opposition with the Modernist idea of the artwork, which was conceived as an ontologically independent object existing for itself (Crimp 1993, 17). Earth Works, Land Art, and Environmental Art thus disrupted Modernist paradigms by trying to either harmonically integrate with a site or categorically react to a given place's spatiotemporal dimension (Deutsche 1992, 22–27). In both cases, the possibility of a "disembodied eye" recognizing the artwork's independence was vehemently denied and substituted by the embodied encounter of a spectator present with an artwork in a defined time, place, and cultural setting (Kwon 1997, 34–35).

While addressing a specific site or responding to a given context were radical acts against Modernism, for early practitioners of public art they were hardly drastic enough. The debate taking place among socially engaged artists and critics tended to specify the aims and scope of public art even further by introducing other elements, such as the focus on social relevance, the open-endedness of the creative process, and audience involvement in the creative process (Crickmay 2003, 119–33). In the 1980s Lippard, Caroline Tisdall, and Su Braden maintained that, in order to have public art, it was not sufficient to move artistic practices from an institutional setting to the public space, but rather the role and mindset of the artists needed to change with regard to the places and communities that were involved (Braden 1978, 1–15). Artists working in the public sphere understood early on that they needed to abandon the elite art world to engage directly with prospective audiences and resort to the practice of negotiation—both of means and meanings (Harding 1995). As seen through the lens of Howard Becker's multiple "art worlds" theory, public artists started their own grassroots experiences and founded separate networks of organizations—artist-run galleries, alternative spaces, group exhibitions with a distinctive anti-elite character (Becker 2008, 38). Practitioners envisaged a more distinct definition of public art, one that considered audience involvement and civic agency essential parts of such transformative activities (Roth et al. 2001, 61). Still today, public artists find themselves working at the fringe of the elite art world, operating as a catalyst of societal change (Baker et al. 2002, 202–3).

Another relevant development emerging from such a specific attitude toward public art was direct audience participation, which led artists to engage with "emancipated" spectators. It became paramount to supersede the traditional classroom paradigm that had dominated cultural production—the artist as a teacher patronizing the pupils—and let the public fully participate with their own stances in the cultural debate unleashed by the artworks (Rancière 2009, 10–15). Grant Kester referred to the term "dialogic" to describe public art's intimate nature, as well as the peculiar aesthetic experience granted by participatory and socially engaged practices that offer a space for an egalitarian type of critical thinking and meaning making (Kester 1999, 155–57). This discursive character implies the necessity of dialogue to create provisional consent, abandoning the illusion of universal truths, and allowing the coexistence of different stances in the public sphere (Habermas 1989, 47). Public artists intended as civic agents agree to let people into a collective artistic process that creates a shared and often unforeseen outcome of which artists are simply the catalysts (Kester 1999, 158–59). The "dialogic" principle in public art implements forms of "connected knowing" and empathetic relationships that allow the spectators to interact with the artistic project and close the circle of meaning—or open it up even more (Schweickart 1996, 317) (Fig. 26.1).

Fig. 26.1 Tega Brain, *Coin Operated Wetland* (2012), courtesy of the artist

26.4 Inception of Sustainable Art

A curious fact about public art intended as civic agency, or perhaps a necessary side-effect, is that over the decades practitioners usually took the lead on theorizing the motives, methods, and outcomes of their interventions (Braden 1978). Public artists often exercise the role of critics in the peculiar field they have chosen, frequently arguing about the environmentalist, social, political, and ideological reasons that lie behind their work (Heinich 1999, 27–28). Usually, they are also teachers at art schools, where they try to instill their novel approach into students (Crickmay 2003). It is true, though, that they often resort to teaching as their principal source of income, exactly because they are at the fringe of the art world and cannot—or would not—make their money through the art market (Throsby 1996, 345). Indeed, very few artists reached celebrity status working on public art projects, Beuys being one of the few, while the majority never really made it into the artist elite or only found posthumous acknowledgment. On the one hand, these dynamics offer public artists the benefit of freedom from market rules, although on the other hand it makes it harder for them to find resources for their projects, thus going public is a convenient strategy to involve people and share expenses. In any case, public artists are committed to explicitly activist agendas, their art projects being vocational endeavors, as for example in eco-art where it is their mission to combine art with science to "reawaken embodied relationships and innovative response" (Wallen 2012, 239).

As described so far, public art appears capable of immersing participants in a different vision and thus serves as a cultural innovator for behavioral patterns. Not by chance, over the years environmentalist-driven art tried to carve a role for itself in encouraging dialogue and offering visions of desirable sustainable futures, which tended toward forms of "ecological ethic" or shaped the concept of "ecological justice" (Braddock and Ater 2014, 5). Public artists immediately recognized that the overwhelming size of sustainability issues was paralleled by the indeterminateness of the term itself and its multi-faceted nature, which often falls prey to contrasting views (Lang et al. 2012, 25–43). Furthermore, the concept of sustainability, as coined by the Bruntland Commission in the report *Our common future* in 1987, was dominated by a rather technical, social, and economic interpretation, leaving little space for the cultural aspects that shape our understanding of sustainable development (Kagan 2011, 15). Even before the relevance of a fourth cornerstone for sustainability was recognized, the so-called cultural pillar, artists and scholars tried to explore the transformative role of art (Pröpper 2017). Until the beginning of the new millennium, the humanities hesitated to adopt the term sustainability, although in practice they were already researching what their role was in shaping society's mindset and behavior toward it (Lemenager and Foote 2012, 573). The relationship between art and sustainability was made explicit with the *Tutzinger Manifest* in 2001, elaborated at a conference near Munich, Germany, which was perhaps the earliest call for the recognition of culture as a fundamental basis for sustainable development.[1] One of its key contributors, the artist Hildegard Kurt, insisted that the success of sustainability depended on its reconciliation with humanist education and the arts, in particular, given the importance of symbolic and aesthetic creative practice in framing our understanding of the world (Kurt 2004, 238). The role of the arts should become paramount, because only if sustainability is seen as a cultural challenge may one hope to accomplish global justice, ecological ethics, and the final humanization of industrialism (Wallen 2012, 239–40).

Once the term was finally introduced in the cultural sector, public artists consciously started practices and generated reflections that could prompt society to imagine a sustainable world (Lemenager and Foote 2012, 575). The processual and participatory approach of public art seemed to offer solutions in both art and life, but so far gained little acknowledgment from the elite art world (Kagan 2011, 348). Hardly a surprise, it is the planned outcome of an artistic endeavor that is poignantly developed as fringe activism, whose principal aim is not building individual careers, but sensitizing society—from communities at the bottom to policymakers at the top. Curators Maja and Reuben Fowkes openly claimed that sustainable art practices were increasingly turning artists into alternative knowledge producers, addressing issues marginalized in mainstream culture and drawing society away from the anthropocentric model (Fowkes and Fowkes 2006). In 2015, on the occasion of the Paris Climate Accords, one of the first organizations to produce and assess sustainable art projects, Julie's Bicycle, published a truly political manifesto

Fig. 26.2 Tiziana Pers, *Vucciria* (2018), photograph by Isabelle Pers, courtesy of the artist

that addressed society and its ruling bodies at large, not only the small art elite, stating what public art would do on its own: "speak out to our audiences and customers, using our creative voices to affect the public narrative and create social consensus for action on climate change and environmental degradation; … take a leadership role with a cultural mandate for action, which exceeds the commitments of governments" (Julie's Bicycle 2016, 27) (Fig. 26.2).

26.5 Categories of Sustainable Art

Since the inception of the new millennium public artists, curators, critics, and organizations devoted to sustainability projected themselves into a range of practices and topics that span much wider than sole environmental concerns (Demos et al. 2021). They did so simultaneously in many different parts of the world, not just in developed countries, covering all five continents and addressing both global and local issues (Moore and Tickell 2014, 12–25). Furthermore, public artists independently interpreted their role in the framework of sustainability, employing postmodern artistic strategies in a way that can be divided conveniently into four categories according to the principal artistic means deployed: ecological interventions, community engagement, radical action, and digital presence.[2] In doing so, practitioners resorted to the consolidated grammar of contemporary art, as well as to the particular knowledge and sensibility of past public artworks and environmentalist practices, though operating firmly at the fringe of society and innovating artistic means and strategies for the sake of sustainability (Mahony 2021).

Browsing through some examples, the first category is perhaps the most obvious and directly linked to environmentalist practices emerging from the past century, although recent practitioners demonstrate a heightened competence regarding ecological issues. This can be seen in profoundly researched projects such as *Coin Operated Wetland* (2012) by artist and engineer Tega Brain, displayed at Firstdraft Gallery in Sydney. For this project Brain secured a domestic arrangement for a filtering wetland within a typical metropolitan laundry system in order to reuse its sewage ad libitum (Garrett-Jones 2012). A similar use of environmental knowledge is evident in *Pushing up Daisies* (2018) by eco-artist Ruth Wallen, created for the Public Address exhibition *DesEscondido: No Longer Hidden* at the California Center for the Arts. Wallen employed the principle of Hugelkultur and covered a portion of soil with branches and leaves of trees that had died as a consequence of climate change, which in turn would provide moisture and nutrients for a new generation of plants (Wallen 2019).

Secondly, community engagement derives from socially engaged art practices, though several public artists recently showed how fostering audience participation in a process of reflection and exploration of sustainability issues becomes itself a moment of reckoning with our societal malfunctioning, far beyond the mere demand of democratizing the art world. Gayle Chong Kwan confronted the participating public of *At the Crossroads* (2018), a pleasurable banquet held at the British Library, with the practical consequences of our food habits in connection to the politics of transportation, energy consumption, and food waste (Mantoan 2021, 24). Likewise, Mary Miss developed a series of projects that aim at catalyzing continuous societal engagement on topics such as natural resources and immigration. For *Stream/Lines* (2015–2016) in Indianapolis she positioned a cluster of mirrors and red beams conceived as pedestals to activate citizens through their gaze on the waterways that support urban life (Sheridan 2015).

Thirdly, as far as radical actions are concerned, protest initiatives were common in early public art, though an increasing number of younger practitioners have decidedly devoted their entire practice to a particular cause pursuing solutions with artistic means. Sisters Isabella and Tiziana Pers, for example, are on a quest for animal freedom that led them to host animals liberated from the slaughterhouse at their farm in North-East Italy. On the occasion of the itinerary biennial Manifesta, Tiziana Pers performed *Art History/Vucciria* (2018) at the fish market in Palermo, where she offered her paintings for the life of crabs and squids to be liberated in the sea (Tribò 2018). Again, in Sicily, resorting to the ancient tradition of sewing flower garments, Sasha Vinci covered in a flower mantlepiece organized *Mutabis* (2016), a community procession that saved a historical landmark from being turned into a landfill (Mantoan 2018, 8).

In contrast to the previous three categories, the exploration of the digital realm by public artists developed simultaneously with the inception of sustainable art. Thus, practitioners could test digital media both for actions and networking purposes as they emerged. Amplified through social media, websites, and blogs, the artist collective *Aravani Art Project* for instance built a safe platform for transgender awareness in India's caste society fostering the creation of social interventions and mural paintings into local communities and neighborhoods (Ottaviano 2020). Exploiting digital business models is the core of *Innobiliare Sud-Ovest* (2019–2020) by Giovanni Scotti, who founded a fake online agency selling former American army barracks in Naples, Italy, in order to address the speculation of real estate markets affecting public spaces (Vertaldi 2020). Digital experimentation provided the possibility to engage in environmental sustainability even for celebrity artist Olafur Eliasson who prompted the interactive application *Earth Speakr* (2019–2020), consisting of a digital platform for kids and teenagers to post short video messages on environmental issues with their faces tarnished in natural elements. Employing augmented reality, the artist intended to mediate the experience of nature for younger people, although in the light of the digital divide the chosen means are problematic in terms of economic accessibility (Giannitelli 2021). Thanks to the high standing of Eliasson, the project was well-orchestrated, with the involvement of the German government and the Goethe Institut, but it rather spoke to an elite—of teenagers and art world specialists—tending toward a well-meant vanity project. Nevertheless, it demonstrates that sustainability gained prominence in public discourse up to a point that even star-artists are trying to operate beyond the art world, although perhaps missing to grasp the alternative character and deep commitment of public artists that are used to working on the fringe (Fig. 26.3).

26.6 Creative Responses on the Fringe and Through the Digital: Two Case Studies

Drawing toward the end of this journey, it appears necessary to explore two realities that emerged as historical reference points in the field. In this section the group exhibition *Weather Report* curated by Lippard in 2007 and the worldwide network of cultural organizations *gala* Green Art Lab Alliance founded by Yasmine Ostendorf in 2012 shall serve as case studies. Indeed, they set the benchmark, on the one hand, for the public art practices to be employed, both with regard to artistic means and participatory strategies, and, on the other hand, for the kind of networking activities and digital perspectives that can foster civic agency.

After Sumatra Tsunami in 2004 and Hurricane Katrina in 2005 wrought havoc, and following Al Gore's catastrophic documentary, *An Inconvenient Truth* (2006), which led him to win the 2007 Nobel Peace Prize with the Intergovernmental Panel on Climate Change, the time was ripe for a reckoning in contemporary art (Scott 2013, 1–2). Thereafter, a spate of exhibitions

Fig. 26.3 Giovanni Scotti, Innobiliare Sud-Ovest (2020), courtesy of the artist

devoted to environmental issues took place in several museums around the world, though not in the main venues of the elite art world (Boettger 2008, 154–55). Among the most prominent count the group shows *Beyond Green: Toward a Sustainable Art* (2006) at Chicago's Smart Museum of Art, *Melting Ice/A Hot Topic: Envisioning Change* (2007) at San Francisco's Natural World Museum, *Still Life: Art, Ecology, and the Politics of Change* (2007) at the eighth Sharjah Biennial, *Green-washing: Environment, Perils, Promises and Perplexities* (2008) at Turin's Fondazione Sandretto Re Rebaudengo, *Sound the Alarm: Landscapes in Distress* (2008) at Wave Hill in the Bronx, and *Radical Nature: Art and Architecture for a Changing Planet 1969–2009* (2009) in London's Barbican Art Gallery. In retrospect, however, the most relevant was perhaps *Weather Report: Art and Climate Change* (2007) at the Boulder Museum of Contemporary Art, Colorado. There are several reasons that make this exhibition stand out, particularly because it suited the aforementioned principles of socially engaged public art and the categories of visionary-driven sustainable practices. It featured an interconnected group of local artists working on environmental projects that were created in an open dialogue between art and sustainability sciences (Demos 2013, 18).

Another striking fact was the commitment of Lippard as guest curator, who coordinated the various contributions displayed in the museum and in numerous public venues (Boettger 2008, 156). The participation of a pioneer of Art Feminism concerned with fringe activism helped to reinforce the alternative character that sustainable art must possess, in its aims and methods. The conceptual transition from feminism toward environmentalism was a natural one for Lippard, since she always advocated for a shift in the value system of socially engaged art, which should insist upon cultural workers supporting and responding to their constituencies (Lippard 1980, 362). Lippard gathered works that responded to the three models of interaction already established for feminist public art to produce an assertive overview of sustainable art practices (Boettger 2008, 154–61). The projects comprised "group and/or public ritual; public consciousness-raising and interaction through visual images, environments, and performances; cooperative/collaborative/collective or anonymous artmaking" (Lippard 1980, 364).

The *Carbon Portraits* (2007) of Sherry Wiggin were exemplary works trying to scold the public's responsibility by involving participants to measure their individual carbon footprint, display the results on the wall as text pieces, and reflect upon it in an interview with the artist. Miss created the site-specific urban installation *Connect the Dots: Mapping the High Water, Hazards and History of Boulder Creek* (2007). For the occasion, she affixed circular blue signs across the town to allow the public to visualize the likely water level of floods caused by climate change, while walking on their own through the urban space. Resorting to digital technology, the computerized video *The Mountain in the Greenhouse* (2001) by Helen Mayer and Newton Harrison employed the data provided by a study on biodiversity loss to show how flora will climb up an imaginary mountain until disappearing forever due to rising temperatures. Again, through the digitally processed images of the series *Running the Numbers: An American Self-Portrait* (2007), Chris Jordan confronted the public with the huge size of waste from Western living standards. For instance, he produced a digital collage of the quantity of plastic bottles used by Americans every five minutes—an astonishing 2 million.

As with Art Feminism decades earlier, Lippard's selection in Boulder sent a clear message, tackling the very notion of progress that informs our patriarchal, extractivist, and capitalist world (Lippard 1980, 362). To some extent the disparate works on show may have seemed ambiguous content-wise and professionally inconsistent, but their greatest contribution to a sustainable future was precisely the lack of contribution to established art dynamics, so that *Weather Report* offered a socially concerned alternative for society at large (Boettger 2008, 159). Lippard thus proved that public artists are more willing to accept that art can be aesthetically and socially effective, as they truly aspire to change the character of art for the benefit of sustainable development (Scott 2013, 10) (Fig. 26.4).

While exhibitions devoted to sustainability popped up around the world, the number of organizations openly working on sustainable art projects also soared across the globe. Many of these endeavors intended to provide platforms for artistic inquiry, imagination, and experimentation, challenging participants in the search for a radical shift in their individual and collective behavior (Kagan 2015, 32). Among the earliest initiatives count Julie's

Fig. 26.4 Mary Miss, Stream/Lines (2015–2016), courtesy of the artist

Bicycle in the United Kingdom, DutchCulture|TransArtists in The Netherlands, and COAL Coalition for Art and Sustainable Development in France. Their aim was to mobilize artists and cultural operators on social and environmental issues, supporting the creation of artworks and implementing concrete solutions through exhibitions, events, prizes, and online resources such as ressource0.com and the *Creative Green Tools* to measure organizational carbon footprints (Van Den Bergh 2015, 3–5). In 2012 Ostendorf created a collaboration between the Dutch and British ventures to start the *gala* Green Art Lab Alliance at an experimental level for a period of two years, trying to create a pan-European network of likeminded cultural organizations. Initially the project activated a partnership between nineteen organizations, mainly in Europe, conceived as a pilot that would test different approaches and exchange practices to promote environmental sustainability through cultural work (Staines 2015, 2–3). The strategy to achieve these results was twofold, on the one hand delivering sustainability workshops for all partner organizations, on the other hand supporting artists to offer creative solutions.

Over the decade the alliance grew at an exponential rate, soon involving organizations from three continents—Asia, Europe, and Latin America—to exchange good practices on how to advocate on environmental sustainability and constantly encourage the use of digital calculators made available online to assess the carbon impact of their activities (Ostendorf 2015, 33). The alliance developed into one of the most comprehensive networks of fringe activism in the cultural sector, promoting practical workshops and artistic activities, putting resources and events online, supporting local initiatives and connecting knowledge at a global level. The strategy of establishing horizontal networks of local projects complemented by transnational links turned out to be a catalyst for promoting global civic agency by means of solidarity, co-funding, and co-learning (Paker 2021, 94). In just a couple of years the alliance reunited forty-five partners from across the globe, making members feel less alone on their mission, and finally rose to a true pressure group on funding bodies, policymakers, and the wider creative industries to abide by high environmental standards. To promote sustainable behavior *gala* concentrated on offering three main outcomes: sustainability tools, guidance protocols, and certifications (Barea 2021, 38).

As regards the tools, *gala* partners developed special online carbon footprint calculators, as well as databases offering automated information and resources for the wider cultural sector, such as carbon auditing and footprint results. It was indeed one of the earliest commitments of the *gala* program to agree that the carbon emissions of the workshops, labs, and events would be quantified accurately assessing the impact in terms of energy, water, waste, travel, and other resources (Staines 2015, 17). Particularly the *Creative Green Tools* of Julie's Bicycle are now used by over 3000 organizations across 50 countries, including the mentioned *Earth Speakr* project by Eliasson.[3]

Concerning guidance, *gala* and its individual partners produced a number of publicly available publications, websites, and apps that gather information and advice on best practices, worksheets, templates, and case studies to inspire creative responses and improve environmental performance. They comprise the *Future Materials Bank*, a database to advise on materials for artists that propose sustainable, biodegradable, or non-toxic alternatives, and the *Country Guides* exploring local peculiarities in the quest to connect contemporary art and sustainability.[4] The kind of transnational knowledge acquired through partner relationships made the network understand that sustainable development must be translated locally to speak to specific audiences and environments, thus highlighting the different challenges, resources, and languages that inform successful creative responses (Ostendorf 2015, 34).

Eventually, certifications include several standards and awards developed by individual *gala* partners to assess, reward, and assure that a cultural activity meets predetermined environmental criteria, thus functioning as incentives for incorporating environmental sustainability (Barea 2021, 39). Although digital tools for artistic creation, exchange, assessment, and dissemination proved instrumental for the success of the network, the alliance is aware of the impact information technology has on CO_2 emissions, thus indicating the urgency for more research into renewable energy opportunities and efficient management solutions for the digital industry (Forrest et al. 2008, 10–11). The organizational ability, local adaptability, digital availability, and strong commitment demonstrated turned *gala* into a paramount example for delivering and promoting sustainable art practices, which are situated at the fringe of the art world, enabling artists to deploy their role as transnational civic agents in local communities and global society—both offline and online.

26.7 Conclusion: An Artistic Calling for a Sustainable Society

Not just the evident consequences of climate change, but also the difficulty of inspiring sustainable behavior by means of rigorous scientific communication motivated public artists to pursue a relationship between art and sustainability (Connelly et al. 2016). Sustainable art thus experimented with forms of knowledge production and sharing within and beyond various disciplinary fields, in order to complement academic research and policy development (Van Poeck et al. 2017). While for artists it is a straightforward fact that art can influence knowledge building and our empathetic capability, sustainability sciences tended to position art at the end of the research process to instrumentally convey science by exploiting artistic means (Rathwell and Armitage 2016; Bendor et al. 2017). The development of fringe activism for sustainability by public artists across the globe demonstrates that cultural operators found their own role in the quest for sustainable development—that of civic agents choosing to do much more than blandly commenting on environmental topics or naively transferring scientific outcomes (Miles 2015; Thomsen 2015). This overview, as well as the case studies, conveys the mindset of public artists engaged in sustainability who truly act on the premise of a vocation. Indeed, it is this artistic calling toward civic agency that explains why public artists hardly seek to build a career in the art world, but rather devote themselves to a lifelong mission on the brink of institutions to foster debate on wider societal issues.

Be it through ecological interventions, community engagement, radical actions, or digital sharing, public artists and a growing number of cultural organizations have efficiently addressed environmental concerns. They did so by working as civic agents on the fringe of the art world, placed in local communities, and connected to the global society, in order to involve ever-growing audiences far beyond mere art-related spectators. Considering the spate of environmentalist exhibitions and the soaring number of art-ecological organizations initiated in the past twenty years, it is obvious that the climate crisis has enhanced art-activism related to sustainable development. However, activism did not rest alone with protest actions or awareness-raising initiatives; it enabled a decidedly pragmatic and transformative approach to find creative solutions and societal strategies for fostering behavioral change. Digital technologies proved paramount not just in the production of public artworks, but even more in offering a concrete platform for campaigning practices, exchanging experiences, sharing resources, defining best practices, and building bridges across local perspectives around the globe. The digital domain allowed these practitioners to carve a niche for themselves that dwells independently and perhaps even unconcerned from the elite art world. In doing so, they started a new domain in the sense of Howard Becker, with its own canons, practices, players, methods, and legitimacy (Becker 2008, 39). Since the art world is still dominated by capitalist, extractivist, and patriarchal paradigms, public artists de facto created their own sector characterized by a transformative potential. It became what Lippard would call a "separatist" domain, one that shall reunite with the elite art world only when the latter will have fully assimilated sustainability among its paradigms (Lippard 1976, 339). By means of participatory projects and public strategies firmly grounded in the grammar of contemporary art springing from 1970s environmentalist and other activist movements, a new generation of public artists and cultural organizations was able to disseminate its growing ecological ethos at the intersection of art and society, thus inspiring a much-needed change in vision and behavior toward a—hopefully—sustainable future.

Notes

1. The conference was titled *Aesthetics of Sustainability* and took place at the Evangelical Academy of Tutzing, Germany.
2. Parts of the public art projects presented were researched together with a team of BA and MA graduates at Ca' Foscari University of Venice, Italy, who engaged in the programme of Sustainable Ca' Foscari and in classes of public art. Among them were Francesca Barea, Silvia Ballarin, Fabiola Chiericato, Letizia Rossi, and Asja Lazzari.
3. See: https://juliesbicycle.com/resource_hub/introducing-the-creative-green-tools/.
4. See: https://www.futurematerialsbank.com/. https://greenartlaballiance.com/creative-responses-to-sustainability/.

References

Baker, Elizabeth C. (1976 [1983]). "Artworks on the Land" in *Art in America* 64; reprinted in *Art in the Land: A Critical Anthology of Environmental Art*, edited by Alan Sonfist, 73–84. New York: Dutton.

Baker, George, Rosaline Krauss, Benjamin Buchloh, Andrea Fraser, David Joselit, James Meyer, Robert Storr, Hal Foster, John Miller, and Helen Molesworth. 2002. "Round Table: The Present Conditions of Art Criticism." *October* 100, Issue: Obsolescence (Spring): 200–28.

Barea, Francesca. 2021. "Half-Way Between Public and Sustainable." In *Waste Matters*, edited by Francesca Barea, Anna Bonfante, and Diego Mantoan. Venice: Edizioni Ca' Foscari: 31–44.

Bayon, Damian. 1972. "Les arts plastique." *La Nouvelle Revue Des Deux Mondes* (Regards sur l'Amérique Latin I): 346–50.

Becker, Howard. 2008. *Art Worlds*. London: University of California Press.

Bendor, Roy, David Maggs, Rachel Peake, John Robinson, and Steve Williams. 2017. "The Imaginary Worlds of Sustainability." *Ecology and Society* 22 (2). https://doi.org/10.5751/ES-09240-220217.

Blanc, Nathalie, and Barbara L. Benish. 2018. *Form, Art and the Environment*. London: Routledge.

Boettger, Suzanne. 2008. "Global Warnings." *Art in America* (June/July): 154–61.

Bois, Yve-Alain, Benjamin H. D. Buchloh, David Joselit, Hal Foster, and Rosalind Krauss. 2016. *Art Since 1900: Modernism Antimodernism Postmodernism*. London: Thames & Hudson.

Braddock, Alan C., and Renée Ater. 2014. "Art in the Anthropocene." *American Art* 28 (3) (Fall): 2–8.

Braden, Sue. 1978. *Artists and People*. London: Routledge & Kegan Paul.

Carlson, Allen 1986. "Is Environmental Art an Aesthetic Affront to Nature?" *Canadian Journal of Philosophy* 16 (4) (December): 635–50.

Cartiere, Cameron, and Martin Zebracki, eds. 2015. *The Everyday Practice of Public Art*. London: Routledge.

Connelly, Angela, Simon C. Guy, Edward Wainwright, Wolfgang Weileder, and Marianne Wilde. 2016. "Catalyst Reimagining Sustainability with and Through Fine Art." *Ecology and Society* 21 (4). https://doi.org/10.5751/ES-08717-210421.

Crickmay, Chris. 2003. "Art and Social Context." *Journal of Visual Art Practice* 2 (3): 119–33.

Crimp, Douglas. 1993. *On the Museum's Ruins*. Cambridge: MIT Press.

Demos, T. J. 2013. "Contemporary Art and the Politics of Ecology." *Third Text* 27 (120): 1–9.

Demos, T. J., Emily Eliza Scott, and Subhankar Banerjee, eds. 2021. *The Routledge Companion to Contemporary Art, Visual Culture, and Climate Change*. London: Routledge.

Deutsche, Rosalyn. 1992. "Tilted Arc and the Uses of Public Spaces." *Design Book Review* 23 (Winter): 22–27.

Dunaway, Finis. 2009. "Seeing Global Warming." *Environmental History* 14 (1): 9–31.

Forrest, William, James M.Kaplan, and Noah Kindler. 2008. "Data Centers: How to Cut Carbon Emissions and Costs." *POV McKinsey Report*, 1–10. McKinsey & Company.

Fowkes, Reuben, and Maja Fowkes. 2006. "The Principles of Sustainabilty in Contemporary Art." *Praesens: Contemporary Central European Art Review* 1: 5–11.

Garrett-Jones, Megan. 2012. "Slow Cycle, The Evolution of Coin Operated Wetland." *Runway* 21 (March): 20–25.

Giannitelli, Tiziana. 2021. "Earth Speakr, l'App che dà voce ai più piccoli contro i cambiamenti climatici." *Matis Magazine* (April 2). Accessed July 14, 2021. https://metismagazine.com/2021/04/02/earth-speakr-lapp-che-da-voce-ai-piu-giovani-contro-i-cambiamenti-climatici/.

Haderer, Karoline. 2010. "Der Treibhauseffekt." *Denkanstösse Magazin* 3: 50–56.

Habermas, Jürgen. 1989. "Justice and Solidarity: On the Discussion Concerning 'Stage 6'." *Philosophical Forum* 21 (1–2): 32–48.

Harding, David. 1995. "Another History: Memories and Vagaries." In *Art with People*, edited by M. Dickson, 26–30. Sunderland: Artist Information.

Heinich, Nathalie. 1999. "Objets, Problematique, Terrains, Methodes." In *Sociologie de l'art*, edited by Raymonde Moulin, 11–28. Paris: L'Harmattan.

Julie's Bicycle. 2016. "COP21 MANIFESTO." *CSPA Quarterly* 14 (August): 27–29.
Kagan, Sacha. 2011. *Art and Sustainability*. Bielefeld: Transcript.
Kagan, Sacha. 2015. "Prefiguring Sustainability." In *Art for the Planet's Sake*, edited by Hannah Van Den Bergh, 29–32. Brussels: IETM.
Kester, Grant. (1999) 2015. "Conversation Pieces: The Role of Dialogue in Socially-Engaged Art." In *Theory in Contemporary Art since 1985*, edited by Zoya Kocur and Simon Leung, 153–65. Malden: Wiley-Blackwell.
Krause Knight, Cher, and Herriet F. Senie, eds. 2016. *A Companion to Public Art*. Chichester: Wiley.
Kurt, Hildegard. 2004. "Aesthetics of Sustainability." In *Ecological Aesthetics*, edited by Hermann Prigan, Heike Strelow, and Vera David, 238–41. Basel: Birkhäuser.
Kwon, Miwon. (1997 [2015]). "One Place After Another: Notes on Site Specificity (1997)." In *Theory in Contemporary Art since 1985*, edited by Zoya Kocur, and Simon Leung, 34–55. Malden: Wiley-Blackwell.
Lang, Daniel J., Arnim Wiek, Matthias Bergmann, Michael Stauffacher, Pim Martens, Peter Moll, Mark Swilling, and Christopher J. Thomas. 2012. "Transdisciplinary Research in Sustainability Science." *Sustainability Science* 7 (1): 25–43.
Lemenager, Stephanie, and Stephanie Foote. 2012. "The Sustainable Humanities." *PMLA* 127 (3) (May): 572–78.
Lippard, Lucy R. 1976. "Projecting a Feminist Criticism." *Art Journal* 35 (4) (Summer): 337–39.
Lippard, Lucy R. 1980. "The Contribution of Feminism to the Art of the 1970s." *Art Journal* 40 (1–2) (Autumn–Winter): 362–65.
Lippard, Lucy R. 2011. "Tunnel Visions: Nancy Holt's Art in the Public Eye." In *Nancy Holt: Sightlines*, edited by Alena J. Williams, 59–72. Berkeley: University of California Press.
Mahony, Emma. 2021. "From Institutional to Interstitial Critique: The Resistant Force that is Liberating the Neoliberal Museum from Below." In *The Routledge Companion to Contemporary Art, Visual Culture, and Climate Change*, edited by T. J. Demos, Emily Eliza Scott, and Subhankar Banerjee. London: Routledge.
Mantoan, Diego. 2018. "Carezze e pugni: Vinci/Galesi alle radici dell'arte ambientale e partecipativa." In *La Repubblica delle Meraviglie*, edited by Diego Mantoan, and Paola Tognon, 7–9. Caserta: aA29 Project Room.
Mantoan, D. 2021. "Sustainability Way Beyond Academia." In *Waste Matters*, edited by Francesca Barea, Anna Bonfante, and Diego Mantoan, 15–30. Venice: Edizioni Ca' Foscari.
Miles, Malcolm. 2015. *Limits to Culture: Urban Regeneration vs. Dissident Art*. London: Pluto Press.
Moore, Sadhbh, and Alison Tickell. 2014. "The Arts and Environmental Sustainability." *D'Art Report* 34(b), IFACCA and Julie's Bicycle.
Ostendorf, Yasmine. 2015. "The S-word." In *Art for the Planet's Sake*, edited by Hannah Van Den Bergh, 33–34. Brussels: IETM.
Ottaviano, Giulia. 2020. "Aravani Art Project: street art e murales per dare voce alla comunità transgender indiana." *Artribune* (26 May). Accessed July 10, 2021. https://www.artribune.com/arti-visive/street-urban-art/2020/05/aravani-art-project-india-transgender/.
Paker, Hande. 2021. "Arts and Culture for Ecological transformation." *Report Istanbul Foundation for Culture and Arts* (February). Accessed June 28, 2021. https://www.iksv.org/en/reports/arts-and-culture-for-ecological-transformation.

Pancotto, Pier Paolo. 2010. *Arte contemporanea: dal minimalismo alle ultime tendenze*. Rome: Carocci.

Pesapane, Lucia. 2005. "Land Art." In *Arte contemporanea*, edited by Francesco Poli, 406–34. Milan: Mondadori Electa.

Pröpper, Michael H. 2017. "Sustainability Science as if the World Mattered: Sketching an Art Contribution by Comparison." *Ecology and Society* 22 (3). https://doi.org/10.5751/ES-09359-220331.

Rancière, Jacques. 2009. *The Emancipated Spectator*. London: Verso.

Rathwell, Kaitlyn J., and Derek Armitage. 2016. "Art and Artistic Processes Bridge Knowledge Systems About Social-Ecological Change." *Ecology and Society* 21 (2). https://doi.org/10.5751/ES-08369-210221.

Richardson, Craig. 2012. "Waste to Monument: John Latham's Niddrie Woman." *Tate Papers* 17 (Spring). Accessed June 15, 2021. https://www.tate.org.uk/research/publications/tate-papers/17/waste-to-monument-john-lathams-niddrie-woman.

Roth, Moira, Suzanne Lacy, Julio Morales, and Unique Holland. 2001. "Making & Performing 'Code 33'." *PAJ—A Journal of Performance and Art* 23 (3) (September): 47–62.

Schwarze, Dirk. 2012. *Meilensteine: Die documenta 1 bis 13*. Berlin: Siebenhaar.

Schweickart, Patrocinio P. 1996. "Speech Is Silver, Silence Is Gold: The Asymmetrial Intersubjectivity of Communicative Action." In *Knowledge, Difference and Power*, edited by Nancy Rule Goldberger, Jill Mattuck Tarule, Blythe McViker Clinchy, and Mary Field Belenky, 305–31. New York: Basic Books.

Scott, Emily Eliza. 2013. "Artists' Platforms for New Ecologies." *Third Text* 27 (120) (January). Accessed June 25, 2021. http://www.thirdtext.org/artists-platforms-for-new-ecologies-arc.

Sheridan, Jill. 2015. "StreamLines Mixes Art and Science to Connect People with Local Waterways." *wfyi Indianapolis* (8 September). Accessed June 28, 2021. http://www.wfyi.org/news/articles/streamlines-mixes-art-and-science.

Staines, Judith. 2015. "An Evaluation/Reflection on the GALA Project." *GALA Green Art Lab Alliance* 6. Accessed June 11, 2021. https://greenartlaballiance.files.wordpress.com/2020/06/gala-report-final.pdf.

Stein, Judith E. 1994. "Collaboration." In *The Power of Feminist Art*, edited by Norma Broude and Mary D. Garrard, 228–45. New York: Harry N. Abrams Publishers.

Thomsen, Dana C. 2015. "Seeing Is Questioning: Prompting Sustainability diScourses Through an Evocative Visual Agenda." *Ecology and Society* 20 (4). https://doi.org/10.5751/ES-07925-200409.

Throsby, David. 1996. "Disaggregated Functions for Artists." In *Economics of the Arts. Selected Essays*, edited by Victor Ginsburgh and Pierre-Michel Menger, 331–46. Amsterdam: Elsevier.

Tribò, Francesca. 2018. "Art History/Vucciria, la performance di Tiziana Pers per MEMORIA COLLETTIVA." *Art for Breakfast* (22 October). Accessed June 29, 2021. https://artforbreakfast.it/2018/10/22/art-history-vucciria-tiziana-pers/.

Van Den Bergh, Hannah, ed. 2015. *Art for the Planet's Sake*. Brussels: IETM.

Van Poeck, Katrien, Jeppe Læssøe, and Thomas Block. 2017. "An Exploration of Sustainability Change Agents as Facilitators of Nonformal Learning: Mapping a Moving and Intertwined Landscape." *Ecology and Society* 22 (2). https://doi.org/10.5751/ES-09308-220233.

Vertaldi, Raffaele. 2020. "L'agenzia che rivende ai cittadini proprietà pubbliche non utilizzate." *Domus* (24 July). Accessed July 5, 2021. https://www.domusweb.it/it/arte/gallery/2020/07/21/bene-pubblico-vendesi-o-meglio-offresi-ai-legittimi-proprietari.html.

Wallen, Ruth. 2012. "Ecological Art: A Call for Visionary Intervention in a Time of Crisis." *Leonardo* 45 (3): 234–42.

Wallen, Ruth. 2019. "Walking with Trees." *Dark Matter: Women Witnessing* 9, Issue: Extinction Illness: Grave Affliction and Possibility. Accessed June 26, 2021. https://darkmatterwomenwitnessing.com/issues/Oct2019/articles/Ruth-Wallen_Walking-with-Trees.html.

Correction to: The Role of Digital and Public Humanities in Confronting the Past: Survivors' of Ireland's Magdalene Laundries Truth Telling

Jennifer O'Mahoney

Correction to:
Chapter 9 in: A. Schwan and T. Thomson (eds.), *The Palgrave Handbook of Digital and Public Humanities*, https://doi.org/10.1007/978-3-031-11886-9_9

The original version of Chapter 9 was inadvertently published as non-open access, which has now been changed to open access under a CC BY 4.0 license, and the copyright holder has been updated to 'The Author(s)'. The correction to the chapter has been updated with the changes.

The updated original version of this chapter can be found at https://doi.org/10.1007/978-3-031-11886-9_9

© The Author(s) 2023
A. Schwan and T. Thomson (eds.), *The Palgrave Handbook of Digital and Public Humanities*, https://doi.org/10.1007/978-3-031-11886-9_27

Open Access This chapter is licensed under the terms of the Creative Commons Attribution 4.0 International License (http://creativecommons.org/licenses/by/4.0/), which permits use, sharing, adaptation, distribution and reproduction in any medium or format, as long as you give appropriate credit to the original author(s) and the source, provide a link to the Creative Commons license and indicate if changes were made.

The images or other third party material in this chapter are included in the chapter's Creative Commons license, unless indicated otherwise in a credit line to the material. If material is not included in the chapter's Creative Commons license and your intended use is not permitted by statutory regulation or exceeds the permitted use, you will need to obtain permission directly from the copyright holder.

Index

A
Academic citizenship, 23
Academy, 2, 4, 20, 31–35, 43–45, 70, 165, 239, 243, 307, 426
Access, 1, 5, 41, 49, 52, 56, 61, 62, 71, 72, 75, 79, 90, 109, 120, 132, 149, 157–159, 162, 163, 165, 166, 176, 185, 188, 200, 209–211, 224, 227, 240, 250, 257, 275, 283, 286, 288, 303, 317, 318, 322–324, 326, 340, 347, 351, 362, 366, 386, 387, 400, 402, 405, 416, 429, 431, 432, 434, 435, 451, 453, 482–484, 505
Achebe, Chinua, 195, 197, 198, 200, 202, 204, 205, 209–212
Action Research-based methodology, 360
Activism, 39, 89, 95–97, 99, 101, 133, 154, 155, 159, 172, 173, 176, 177, 190, 191, 240, 303, 447, 452, 455, 501, 502, 504, 508, 512, 514, 516
Adventures in Time and Gender, 72, 80–83
Affect, 5, 37, 60, 132, 166, 173, 177, 178, 217, 229, 381, 383, 390, 411, 414, 443, 509
African, 195, 197, 200, 203, 205, 206, 208, 209, 211, 212, 298
Agency, 20, 23, 24, 114, 117, 134, 143, 152, 178, 240–243, 248, 252, 276, 288, 318, 319, 321, 330, 332, 343, 344, 366, 511

Anonymity, 114, 125, 173, 482, 486, 489
Anthropocene, 502, 505
Anti-Semitism, 484, 485, 488–491, 493, 495
Anti-Zionism, 489, 493
Applied humanities, 32, 39
Approach, 3, 5, 12, 16–19, 22–25, 32, 33, 36, 37, 39, 41, 44, 56, 70, 72, 76, 77, 80, 83, 100, 106, 110, 112, 113, 133, 138, 140, 142, 152, 155, 157, 160, 162, 163, 172–174, 176, 178, 179, 182, 188, 196, 198–202, 210, 216, 223, 227, 238, 239, 241–244, 247, 249, 250, 252, 260, 261, 285, 286, 338–340, 342–344, 348, 349, 351, 352, 359, 360, 362–364, 369–371, 373, 381, 382, 389, 390, 392, 398, 405, 407, 411, 435, 443, 454, 464, 492, 502, 504, 507, 508, 514, 516
Archival pedagogy, 240
Archive(s), 5, 21, 49, 52, 55, 62, 71, 75, 93, 97, 98, 149, 151, 153, 157, 161, 164–166, 216–218, 220, 224, 227, 238–241, 243, 244, 258, 260–264, 267, 270, 272, 276–279, 282–284, 286, 287, 289, 290, 292, 298, 309, 318, 319, 321, 322, 324, 340, 341, 350, 357, 358, 362, 366, 367, 370, 372, 374, 403, 409, 410, 467

© The Editor(s) (if applicable) and The Author(s), under exclusive license to Springer Nature Switzerland AG 2022
A. Schwan and T. Thomson (eds.), *The Palgrave Handbook of Digital and Public Humanities*, https://doi.org/10.1007/978-3-031-11886-9

524   INDEX

Arendt, Hannah, 131–134, 137, 140, 141, 143
Art
  art action, 449
  art feminism, 512, 513
  art history, 502
  art world, 501–504, 506–508, 510–512, 516, 517
Artificial intelligence (AI), 215, 216, 218, 231, 323, 346, 412, 416
Artistic, 21, 72, 78, 134, 142, 195, 228, 384, 391, 410, 426–428, 435, 466, 502, 506, 508–511, 513, 515, 516
Arts and humanities, 1, 2, 12, 17, 18, 26, 34, 105, 165, 341
Assessment, 15, 18, 26, 36, 37, 42, 44, 61, 70, 109, 116, 137, 172, 407, 408, 411, 515
Attachment, 132–134, 140, 141, 144
Audiences, 19, 22–24, 34, 35, 38, 39, 41–44, 69, 71, 72, 78, 80–82, 110, 111, 113, 117, 119, 120, 135, 137, 142, 143, 172, 196–200, 207, 210–212, 217, 218, 229, 239, 243, 245, 247, 251, 264, 290, 299, 306, 307, 310, 318, 320, 321, 338, 339, 342, 345–348, 351, 358, 378, 381, 384, 385, 388, 392, 398, 400, 402–406, 408–411, 413–415, 432, 447–452, 460, 462, 473, 482, 485, 501–503, 505, 506, 509, 510, 515, 516
Australian Center for the Moving Image, 400, 403–405, 408–415
Authentic, 15, 16, 37, 108, 111, 117, 184, 251, 369, 391, 473, 474
  authentic assessment, 19, 20, 26, 37, 46, 242
  authentic assignments, 13, 25, 26
Authenticity, 26, 72, 79, 83, 106, 116, 135, 242, 243, 384, 386, 387, 462
Authority, 55, 69, 71, 73, 78–80, 95, 106, 111, 112, 117, 133, 136, 141, 143, 179, 207, 282, 283, 300, 319, 329, 339, 369, 387, 442, 446, 481, 482, 485, 486, 491, 494

B

Beliefs, 34, 70, 106, 137, 155, 197, 203, 245, 276, 292, 339, 372, 373, 459–461, 485, 494
Bias, 3, 60, 61, 216, 220, 221, 277, 282, 284, 285, 292, 318, 484
Big data, 172, 189, 337, 340, 345, 349, 397, 398, 406, 415, 416, 493, 494
  big data analysis, 397
  big data digital humanities, 397–399, 406, 411, 414, 416
Black Lives Matter, 36, 132
Body memory, 448, 449
Book inscriptions, 276–280, 282–286, 288, 289, 291, 292
Brighton-Fuse, 21
Brothers' Cemeteries, 467, 470, 472
Budapest, 49, 136, 138, 494
Bute, Isle of, 358, 361–364

C

Canada, 57, 89, 93, 96, 97, 99, 101, 102, 149, 283, 297, 306, 310
Canadian Writing Research Collaboratory (CWRC), 97–101
Capital surplus absorption, 445
Carbon footprint, 513–515
Carceral, 105, 106, 108, 111, 113–115, 117
Cartesian dualism, 34
Cartography, 423, 424, 426, 436
Celebration of the Cemetery, 460, 465, 467, 473, 474
Cemetery(ies)
  cemetery plan, 472
  cemetery tourism, 5, 460–464, 471–475
  cemetery tours, 460, 468, 474
Ceramic City Stories, 362
Challenge-based learning, 23
Chanterculture, 487
Children's, 159, 160, 210, 244, 275, 282, 286, 291, 299, 303–305, 311, 318–322, 324–328, 330–332, 339, 346, 347, 470
  children's cultures, 319, 320, 324
  children's writing, 317–320, 322–324, 326, 328, 330, 332

INDEX 525

Chinese community, 366, 367, 371
Cinema, 52, 107, 135, 138, 145, 441, 442, 447–451
Cisgender people, 82
Citizen humanities, 4
Civic agency, 502, 506, 507, 511, 515, 516
Civil disobedience, 444, 451
Civilization, 195, 197, 200, 207, 208, 212
Clash, 198, 202–204, 206–209, 488
Class, 276
Classroom, 12, 15, 18, 33–39, 41–45, 199, 211, 241, 246, 309, 506
Climate change, 251, 502, 509, 510, 513, 516
Close, 31–33, 39–42, 56, 60, 62, 74, 117, 136–139, 197, 199, 202, 204, 211, 212, 225, 226, 302, 305, 348, 350, 397, 415, 447, 448, 453, 463, 506
Close reading, 31, 32, 39–42, 56, 197, 199, 202, 204, 211, 212, 348, 350
Co-authorship, 114, 120
Co-creation, 3, 18, 22–24, 39, 62, 119, 135, 142, 329, 341, 348
Co-creational learning design, 242
Co-design, 23, 51, 62, 155, 358, 387
Collaboration, 4, 16, 22, 44, 52, 56, 62, 73, 80, 83, 98, 105, 106, 112, 116, 119, 124, 154, 160, 163, 238, 240, 251, 278, 287, 292, 323, 326, 327, 339, 340, 364, 372, 373, 387, 400, 403, 410, 415, 425, 429, 493, 514
Colonial, 145, 179, 195–197, 207, 297, 300, 311
Colonialists, 195–198, 202–204, 207
Commune, 138–140
Community(ies), 195, 197, 198, 200, 203, 207–209, 212
   community archive, 4, 258, 260, 261, 267, 358
   Community Based Participatory Action Research (CBPAR), 360, 362
   community building, 72, 74
   community engagement, 503, 509, 510, 516
   community resource, 80

Computational, 53, 61, 91, 92, 98, 160, 196, 199–202, 207, 209, 212, 246, 348, 398, 402, 406, 412, 416
Computer, 53, 60, 91, 92, 98, 176, 200, 202, 219, 245, 342–345, 364, 379, 383, 388, 424, 473, 483
Computing, 152, 245, 398, 412
Conflicts, 100, 136, 143, 145, 195–198, 202, 203, 207–212, 474, 494
Consciousness-raising (C-R), 171, 173–176, 181–183, 185–187, 191, 513
Construct, 35, 117, 153, 165, 182, 240, 261, 292, 317, 451, 484
Construction, 125, 176, 181, 210, 240, 288, 303, 319, 320, 339, 379, 424, 429, 437, 441–444, 449, 504
Consumerism, 391, 449
Contemporary art, 503, 509, 511, 512, 515, 517
Content analysis, 292
Contextual markup, 248, 249
Contingent belonging, 135
Co-ownership, 2
Co-production, 3, 58, 70, 71, 78, 155, 358, 359, 369
   co-production of knowledge, 5
Corpus, 58, 202–204, 206, 212, 247, 248, 250, 292, 340, 358, 403
Correspondence, 217, 229, 239, 244–247, 324, 378, 385, 432
Cosmopolitanism, 448
Counter public, 72
Covid-19
   Covid-19 lockdown, 12, 24
   Covid-19 pandemic, 5, 6, 132, 188, 260, 263, 267, 269, 373, 469
Cowbird, 365, 366
Creative processes, 140, 506
Creativity, 21–23, 80, 83
Critical practice, 318
Critical race studies, 4
Cross-disciplinary, 3, 22, 400
Crowdsourcing, 19, 217, 220, 223, 227, 260, 340, 344, 386, 406
Cultural
   Cultural and Creative Industries (CCI), 21, 22
   cultural capital, 114, 320

cultural heritage, 1, 4, 5, 21, 49, 154, 162, 198, 212, 240, 292, 325, 337, 338, 340, 342–346, 349, 351, 358, 380, 383–385, 397, 424, 435, 464, 469, 471
cultural impacts, 405
cultural mapping, 397, 402
cultural memory, 131
Culture(s), 195–199, 202–204, 206–212
  clash of, 198, 202
Curator, 71, 263, 317, 318, 321–324, 326, 327, 329, 330, 342, 346, 347, 509, 512
Cyberbullying, 186, 188
Cyrillic alphabet, 218

D

#dariahTeach, 12, 13, 17–22, 24–26
#dariahTeach YouTube channel, 19, 26
Dark tourism, 462–464, 466, 471, 473
Data
  data aggregation, 399, 403, 405, 406, 414, 416
  database, 41, 50–53, 56, 57, 60, 61, 92, 93, 95, 97, 98, 102, 224, 284, 307, 309, 331, 340, 341, 350, 359, 365, 366, 368, 369, 403, 405, 424, 430–432, 515
  data curation, 399, 411
  data intelligence, 399, 411, 414, 416
  data-intense research, 402, 414
  data visualization, 53, 56–60, 62, 397, 399, 406, 408, 411, 416, 423
Day of DH, 11
Deathscape, 462, 463
Decolonization, 4, 297
Deep Mapping, 400, 402, 403, 405–407, 411, 414–416
Democratization, 33, 70
  democratization of culture, 366
  democratization of knowledge, 339
Design thinking, 17, 20, 22–24
Developers, 18, 25, 58, 102, 247, 360, 362, 400, 445, 450, 451, 486
DH pedagogy, 15, 16, 21, 25, 238
Dialogical approaches, 77
Digital
  digital activism, 176, 177, 180

digital archive; and cataloguing, 286; and provenance, 286
digital citizenship, 12, 24
digital community, 173, 189, 399
digital editing, 5, 241
digital environments, 164, 176, 187, 244, 318, 322, 325, 332, 403
digital ethnography, 172, 183, 186, 191
digital humanities, 1–4, 6, 11, 13–15, 17–20, 22–26, 50–52, 93, 98–100, 151–157, 160, 162, 163, 165, 171, 196, 198–200, 212, 237–242, 245, 249, 252, 258, 277, 278, 288, 292, 301, 306, 308, 340, 341, 351, 397–400, 402, 403, 405, 406, 411, 414, 416, 424, 427, 428; digital humanities pedagogy, 15, 16, 21, 25, 238
digital literary discourse, 199
digital mapping, 5, 71, 416, 424
digital public history, 72, 258, 263, 267
digital public humanities, 4, 83, 171, 173, 258, 260, 263, 270, 272, 399, 403, 406, 411
digital representation, 89, 100, 332
digital scholarly editing, 242, 250, 252
digital spaces, 71, 72, 183, 186, 187, 306, 317, 325
digital storytelling, 22, 402, 410, 491, 492; digital storytelling tools, 358
digital technology, 21, 156, 178, 181, 196, 199, 211, 278, 317, 320, 321, 323–326, 330, 331, 338, 377, 379, 381, 387, 392, 398, 423, 435, 482, 513, 516
digital tools, 16, 155, 157, 160, 196, 198, 199, 202–204, 206, 210, 211, 238, 288, 320, 324, 331, 357, 358, 387, 400, 423, 435, 502, 503, 515
Digitization, 155–157, 165, 219, 278, 322, 323, 340, 341, 344, 377, 379–381, 384–387, 390–392, 425, 427, 429, 473
Digitized archives, 348

Discourse, 2, 33, 34, 36, 37, 42, 45, 52, 75, 135, 150, 166, 177, 180, 199, 200, 202, 210, 237, 310, 337, 349, 350, 378, 399, 442, 445, 446, 452, 489, 495, 511
discourse analysis, 350
Disintermediation, 483, 484
Distant reading, 53, 57–60, 348, 350
Diversity, 19, 21–23, 60, 71, 73, 74, 82, 90, 92, 95, 96, 98, 142, 176, 195, 237, 277, 278, 360, 399, 404, 405, 408, 409, 448, 464, 487
Documentary, 107–110, 112, 118, 136, 140, 239, 244, 251, 318, 425, 452, 453, 511

E
Earth Works, 505
Eco-art, 507
Ecology, 4, 178, 278, 505
Ecosystem, 14, 18, 20, 24, 62, 200, 204, 403, 406, 407, 410
Edinburgh, 124, 319, 326, 327, 329, 331
Educational design patterns, 15
Edwardian, 276, 278, 279, 283–286, 288, 291, 292
 Edwardian Britain, 276, 279, 281, 284, 285, 290, 291
 Edwardian digital archive, 276, 279, 282, 286, 288, 291, 292
Ego-documents, 264, 268, 270, 271
Embodiment, 133, 166, 321, 387, 388, 390, 392, 453
Engaged research, 18, 70, 76
Engagement, 1, 2, 13–16, 23, 24, 32, 35, 40, 41, 44, 62, 70, 71, 78, 81, 92, 111, 113, 115, 120, 124, 141, 155, 157, 164–166, 178, 184, 185, 187, 238, 241, 242, 288, 291, 292, 317, 320–325, 327, 329–332, 339, 341, 351, 359, 360, 366, 367, 369–373, 378, 379, 385, 387, 388, 391, 392, 397, 400, 402, 405, 408, 410, 412, 414, 415, 449, 481, 495, 510
English studies, 31, 33–36, 40, 43, 44, 199

Entangled practices, 16
Environmental art, 503, 505
Environmentalism, 513
Este, 424, 425, 427–429, 431, 432, 434–437
Ethics, 4, 32, 73, 96, 105, 106, 112, 155, 183, 318, 341, 475, 508
Eurocentric, 195, 204
Exhibition, 13, 25, 78, 125, 240, 260, 271, 288, 290, 317–320, 322, 323, 325–327, 329, 330, 332, 338, 341, 342, 346, 347, 352, 381, 391, 400–403, 411–414, 462, 502, 503, 505, 506, 510–514, 516
Experiences, 3, 15, 22, 26, 36–38, 41, 71, 72, 75, 80, 81, 106, 108, 110, 111, 114–118, 133, 140, 144, 149, 151–155, 161, 165, 166, 174, 175, 177, 181, 196, 229, 238, 241, 242, 244, 246, 275, 277, 279, 291, 299, 305, 311, 318, 320, 325, 330, 331, 338–344, 346, 347, 350–352, 358, 362–365, 373, 387, 388, 390, 392, 401, 408, 427, 443, 447, 450, 460–464, 468, 471, 474, 475, 502, 506, 516
Experiential, 131–133, 137, 140, 242
 experiential education, 37–43, 45
 experiential learning, 31, 32, 37–42, 45, 46, 244, 247
Expertise, 3, 26, 43, 53, 70, 73, 78, 79, 83, 152, 163, 164, 300, 306, 347, 360, 363, 370, 387
Experts, 2, 60, 73, 78, 82, 155, 161, 164, 185, 227, 230, 289, 339, 340, 342, 346, 351, 392, 466
Extensible markup language (XML), 93, 95, 97, 101, 246–248, 250

F
Facebook, 181, 183–185, 187–189, 191, 192, 217, 218, 309, 324, 363, 403, 409, 481, 485–487, 490
 Facebook Groups, 173, 179, 183, 185, 187–192
 Facebook Pages, 173, 185, 190, 191, 331, 333, 494

Failure, 36, 40, 41, 110, 172, 189, 204, 208, 271, 284
Family, 75, 109, 116, 121, 123, 183, 207, 216–218, 231, 266, 284, 289, 297, 299, 319, 326, 344, 368, 388, 404, 426–428, 432, 436, 437, 447, 467, 470, 471
  family heritage, 463, 471
  family history, 218, 276, 288, 289, 304, 308, 311
Feminist, 33, 76, 100, 171, 172, 174–177, 179–186, 189–191, 278, 318, 503, 505
  feminist digital collectivity, 171–173, 176, 177, 179, 180, 186, 191
Fieldification, 3
Film festival, 5, 120, 405, 441, 447, 452
Film-making, 105, 106, 111, 113, 134, 135, 358, 374
Flipped
  flipped classroom, 18, 241
Forecast algorithm, 414
Foreign, 195, 203, 209, 444, 445, 468, 472, 475, 488
  foreign tourists, 470, 471, 473, 474
France, 57, 244, 409, 436, 486, 488, 490, 493, 495, 514
Francophone activism, 90
Freedom of speech, 481, 485, 486
Frontier Nursing Service, 243, 249

G

Galleries, libraries, archives, and museums (GLAMs), 22, 338, 339, 341, 342, 344–347, 351, 397
Gamification, 343
Gay, 77, 192
  gay liberation, 89, 90, 93, 95–99, 101
Gender, 23, 73, 74, 77, 82, 105, 175, 205, 216, 278–280, 283, 290, 358, 448, 484, 501
  gender democracy, 4
  gender norms, 73
Gendered Intelligence (GI), 73, 83, 84
Geographic Information System (GIS), 340, 407, 410, 411, 416, 424, 429
Geo-visualisation, 402

German, 58, 197, 215, 217–222, 224, 260, 261, 459, 464–466, 469, 488, 505, 511
Graph databases, 95
Grave care, 465
Guide, 6, 52, 165, 210, 351, 369, 468, 469, 471–473

H

Handwritten text recognition (HTR), 215, 216, 218, 219, 224–227, 229–231
Hate speech, 2, 5, 481, 482, 484–488, 490, 491, 493–496
Heritage, 11, 22, 26, 55, 73, 152, 161, 163, 218, 227, 299, 323, 337–339, 342, 346, 347, 350–352, 358, 362, 377–381, 385–388, 390, 405, 425–428, 435, 461
  heritage institutions, 23, 338, 340, 341, 377, 379, 381, 383, 385, 391, 392, 397, 407
  heritage objects, 377–380, 383–387, 389–392
Heteronormativity, 72
Hidden histories, 277
Higher education, 2, 11–18, 24, 25, 41, 69, 120, 243, 251, 366
Historical
  historical bias; in digital humanities, 284; in library collections, 279
  historical manuscripts, 218, 225
  historical methodologies, 77
  historical soundscape, 5
Historiography, 337, 338, 352
History, 31, 32, 51, 54, 55, 70, 71, 75–78, 81–83, 89, 92, 96–98, 109, 136, 138, 143, 144, 149, 153–155, 157, 161, 163, 166, 179, 183, 203, 209, 231, 244, 257, 264, 267, 268, 270, 271, 275–278, 282, 283, 285–287, 289, 291, 292, 298, 301, 305, 337, 338, 343, 347, 349–352, 358, 362, 366, 379, 383, 387, 390, 405, 423, 424, 427, 428, 432, 434–436, 441–443, 446, 448, 450, 454, 462, 464, 465, 469–475, 482, 491–495

history from below, 69, 276, 277
history of childhood, 318, 326
Homophobia, 446
Humanistic, 4, 31, 43, 199, 258, 460
  humanistic study, 31, 32, 34, 35, 40, 43–45, 309
Humanity(ies), 2–5, 11–16, 22–25, 31, 34, 36, 38, 40–43, 45, 50, 53, 89, 92, 95, 97, 100, 120, 131, 133, 152, 155, 156, 160, 161, 165, 196, 198–201, 208, 210, 212, 226, 237–239, 241, 245, 251, 257, 258, 264, 270–272, 277, 278, 306, 310, 338, 360, 369, 397–399, 403, 411, 416, 493, 508
Hungarian Uprising, 136
Hybrid
  hybrid education, 11, 12, 14–16, 24, 25
  hybrid environment, 11, 15, 16, 24, 26
  hybrid learning, 11, 13–16, 24, 26
Hybridity, 11, 14, 15, 24, 178
Hyperobjects, 446

I
Identity categories, 77
Igbo, 195–198, 200, 202, 204, 205, 207–211
IGNITE, 13, 17–19, 22–26
Image analysis, 349
Imaginaries of publicness, 132, 135, 141–144
Impact, 2, 6, 17, 23, 42, 50, 62, 72, 74–76, 83, 98, 120, 125, 132, 152, 155, 160, 166, 172, 180, 181, 197–200, 210, 226, 241, 243, 268, 285, 288, 291, 292, 301, 304, 341, 351, 357, 371, 373, 385, 398, 400, 403, 406–408, 411, 412, 414–416, 481, 483, 492, 514, 515
  impact assessments, 400, 414
Imprisoned, 106, 107, 110–116, 118, 120
Imprisonment on screen, 109, 117
Incarcerated, 2, 106–108, 111–114, 119, 120, 150

Inclusion, 14, 71, 95, 141, 161, 171, 200, 368, 370, 408
Indigenous, 5, 209, 211, 212, 300, 322, 351, 379, 380, 386, 387
Indigenous languages and cultures, 297
Institute of Sexology (2014–15), 73
Institutionalization, 3, 32, 33, 166, 239
Interactive, 17, 18, 37, 49, 60, 100, 160, 161, 163, 323, 329, 330, 339, 342, 350, 369, 429, 431, 434, 435, 475, 511
  interactive documentary (iDoc), 350, 351
Interdisciplinary, 1, 32, 56, 133, 163, 165, 279, 338, 407, 435, 462, 502
Intersectional feminism, 4
Intersectionality, 12, 175
Island Stories, 363
Istanbul, 441–454

J
Jail, 114, 115
Jews, 464, 465, 486–488, 490, 493

K
Kurrent, 217–220, 224

L
Ladder of participation, 78
Land Art, 503–505
Landscape, 50, 55, 138, 139, 267, 309, 423, 429, 431, 435, 461, 473, 504
Laser scanning, 381, 382
Latin alphabet, 218, 229
Latvia, 459, 460, 463–474
Learning platform, 18
Leeds, 357, 358, 366, 367, 371
Lefebvre, Henri, 443, 444, 448, 449, 453, 454, 460, 461, 464, 474
Left-wing melancholy, 140
Lesbian and Gay Liberation in Canada (LGLC), 89–98, 100, 102
LGBTQ+ history, 277
Linguistics, 201, 350, 468
Linked data, 55, 61, 89–92, 95, 97, 98, 100, 101

Linked Infrastructure for Networked Cultural Scholarship (LINCS), 97–100
Linked open data, 53–56
Literary, 1, 33–37, 39, 40, 42, 44, 74, 76, 79, 124, 153, 195–201, 205, 207, 209, 211, 212, 227–229, 244, 248, 272, 287, 298, 319, 349, 426
  literary studies, 31, 33–36, 42, 44, 298, 306
Literature, 4, 33, 35–42, 44, 46, 49, 54, 72, 78, 155, 182, 198, 199, 211, 228, 231, 238, 257, 272, 275, 288, 289, 292, 297, 301, 306, 464, 489
Līva's Cemetery, 466
Lived space, 461, 462, 467, 471, 474
Local tourists, 471

M

Machine learning, 215, 216, 218, 399, 411–414, 416
Magdalene Laundry, 155, 161, 163
Maker culture, 15, 17, 22
Manuscripts, 216, 217, 219–221, 223, 225, 227, 230, 231, 425, 427
Maps, 100, 260, 339, 403, 408, 410, 411, 423–426, 427, 429–432, 434, 452, 453, 469, 472, 475
Media studies, 50–54, 56, 61
Medicine, 81, 83, 326
Memorials, 463, 465, 466
Memory, 5, 131–133, 137, 144, 153, 165, 240, 264, 267–269, 271, 277, 283, 291, 317, 323, 338, 346, 441, 442, 448, 483, 494
Metadata, 52, 53, 55, 56, 92, 159, 164–166, 240, 247, 248, 260, 279, 318, 324, 350
Methodology(ies), 14, 33, 50, 51, 53, 54, 56, 70, 73, 152, 154, 157, 160, 162, 163, 178, 196, 198, 199, 202, 207, 209, 238–240, 338, 350, 398, 406, 407, 434, 460, 491
Methods, 17–20, 23, 26, 36, 38, 45, 51, 52, 61, 72, 107, 157, 160, 161, 172, 178, 199, 201, 202, 204, 212, 219, 238, 241, 244, 251, 275, 284, 303, 318, 325, 338, 340, 344, 346, 348–350, 359, 370, 371, 379, 398, 402, 411, 416, 424, 428, 507, 512, 517
Micropublic, 173, 183, 184, 191
Migration, 217, 289, 341, 405, 412, 443, 448
  migration languages, 215, 217
Minority groups, 75
Mobile applications, 340, 343, 347, 351, 403
Modena, 424–434, 436, 437
Modern, 71, 72, 74, 77, 106, 133, 136, 137, 139, 207, 209, 212, 218, 220, 223, 225, 226, 230, 237, 239, 248, 251, 277, 285, 306, 317, 324, 326, 327, 379, 380, 385, 387, 388, 391, 423, 425, 429–431, 434, 435, 445, 462, 488
Monoform, 139, 144
Montage of attractions, 137
Multi-stakeholder model, 24
Museum(s)
  museum interpretation, 322
  museum objects, 322, 380, 391
  museum soft power map, 397, 399, 400, 402, 407, 408, 411, 412, 415
  museum visitors, 317, 320, 329, 346, 392
Music, 21, 22, 43, 80, 109, 112, 161, 343, 350, 424, 426–429, 433, 435, 452, 467
  music production, 424, 427, 428, 430, 431
Musical, 78, 424, 426–431, 434, 435, 449, 452
  musical sources, 425, 427, 429–433, 435, 436
Musicology, 424, 427, 428

N

Narrative, 18, 19, 72, 81, 106, 109, 110, 112, 114, 116–118, 131, 137–139, 150, 151, 154, 175, 182, 191, 195, 197, 200, 203–206, 208, 244, 248, 305, 337–339, 342–348, 350–352, 364–369, 423, 468, 484, 494, 495, 509

National Co-ordinating Centre for Public Engagement (NCCPE), 70
Neoliberal, 142, 442, 445, 448, 449, 451
  neoliberal Islam, 444
  neoliberal politics, 5
Neural networks, 200, 215, 216
New criticism, 33, 45
New history from below, 277
New York, 223, 298, 299, 301–304, 415, 503
Nigeria, 195–197
1984–85 Miners' Strike, 358
Non-binary people, 72, 73, 81, 83
Novel, 13, 75, 83, 133, 196–198, 202–207, 209–212, 241, 245, 317, 325, 381, 390, 392, 398, 507

O

Official institutions, 282, 283, 285–287, 292
Okonkwo, 196–198, 202–211
Online communities, 181, 186, 190, 324
On the Outside, 106, 108, 112–114, 116–118, 120, 124, 125
Ontologies, 55, 90–92, 97–101, 133
Open access, 56, 158, 238, 243
Open education resources, 243
Open innovation, 24
Open pedagogy, 239, 243, 247, 252
Open-source teaching, 13
Oral history, 69, 75, 79, 150–154, 156, 157, 161, 162, 326, 339
Orature, 199
Ordinary writing, 282, 283, 288, 291, 292
Ottoman Turkish (OT), 216, 218, 226–231
Ownership, 1, 114, 149, 275, 276, 280, 282, 284, 285, 291, 292, 364, 373, 447

P

Pararchive, 357–359, 371
Paris, 139, 486, 493
  Paris Climate Accords, 508
Participation processes, 15
Participatory, 4, 17, 19, 21, 23, 24, 51, 52, 60–62, 73, 78, 113, 131, 134, 339, 340, 366, 374, 460, 502–504, 506, 508, 511, 517
  participatory film-making, 106, 113
  participatory storytelling, 113
Pathos, 137, 138
Pedagogy, 62, 138, 237, 238, 240–243, 245, 251, 306
Penal, 107, 108, 110, 112, 115, 117
  penal apparatus, 106, 109
  penal settings, 105, 117
Perceived space, 461, 474
Performance, 18, 78, 105, 116, 153, 217, 221, 222, 226, 229, 230, 279, 408, 410, 411, 433, 434, 467, 515
Performativity, 378, 388–391, 392
Persona, 140, 141, 143
Personalization, 175, 181, 191, 343–345, 347, 351
Philology, 32, 33
Photogrammetry, 381, 382
Play, 2, 42, 43, 52, 74, 76, 82, 111, 115, 116, 162, 176, 196, 198, 202, 219, 220, 225, 240, 292, 321–323, 327, 329, 388, 444, 467, 482, 495
Plurality, 18, 131, 133, 363, 483
Podcasts, 70, 72, 76, 78, 79, 81–83, 96, 107, 161
Political movements, 276, 277
Possibility models, 77
Power
  power dynamics, 2, 81, 106
  power hierarchies, 120
Practical criticism, 33
Practitioner networks, 16
Praxis, 3, 31, 37, 41, 43
Precarious, 172, 186, 190, 191, 392, 449, 451
Prison, 105–115, 117–120, 124, 468, 489
  prison abolitionism, 106
  prison documentary, 107
Privatization, 61, 442, 444, 446, 450
Privilege, 3, 35, 120, 134, 191, 227, 321, 329, 362, 369
Productive failure, 242, 243
Professional practice, 13, 341

Project, 3, 4, 13, 17, 19, 20, 22, 39, 41, 42, 44, 50, 51, 53–56, 60–62, 71–73, 75–81, 83, 89–93, 95, 97–100, 105, 106, 112–114, 116–120, 124, 138–141, 150–153, 155–166, 171, 185, 198, 200, 202, 205, 215–221, 223, 227, 230, 231, 238–243, 247, 248, 250, 251, 258, 260–262, 264, 266, 270, 271, 278, 286, 287, 291, 292, 298, 299, 301, 306–310, 325, 339–344, 346, 350–352, 357–359, 362–364, 366, 367, 369–373, 380, 382, 386, 388, 397–403, 405–407, 410, 411, 414–416, 426, 428, 429, 435, 466, 472, 491, 502–507, 510, 511, 513, 517

Protest, 97, 132, 133, 174, 203, 442, 448, 449, 453, 487, 489, 510, 516

Public
  public art, 105, 441, 451, 501, 502, 504–513, 517
  public digital humanities, 4, 24, 100, 200, 239, 307, 414, 416
  public engagement, 4, 32, 36, 42, 70, 71, 73, 84, 200, 251, 340, 377, 381, 386, 392
  public freedom, 131
  public history, 69, 70, 72, 83, 92, 95, 100, 257, 258, 263, 267, 341, 492
  public humanities, 1–5, 31, 32, 36–38, 41–45, 51, 61, 83, 92, 105, 106, 119, 131, 133, 134, 141, 144, 152, 156, 171, 173, 198, 199, 201, 243, 257, 258, 260, 262–264, 270–272, 306, 369, 397, 399, 403, 406, 411, 414, 416, 460, 474, 502
  public opinion, 184, 482–485
  public scholarship, 2, 31, 42, 44, 155, 159, 163, 238, 241, 248, 251
  public space, 15, 41, 43, 133, 134, 142, 325, 430, 448, 450, 451, 474, 506, 511
  public sphere theory, 132

Publicness, 131, 133–137, 141, 143, 452–454

Publics, 1, 2, 4, 5, 31, 32, 34, 35, 37, 39–41, 43, 44, 70, 100, 131, 132, 134, 135, 138, 139, 142–144, 173, 178, 238, 341, 346, 360, 364, 370, 372, 397, 402, 416, 443, 450, 452

Q
Queer history, 71, 93

R
Radicalization, 482, 483, 494
Reading, 33, 34, 36, 42, 76, 77, 105, 134, 142, 157, 202, 209, 210, 216, 218, 227, 228, 230, 241, 244, 248, 322–324, 332, 346, 348, 349, 370, 427, 442, 444, 453, 482
Reality–virtuality continuum, 383
Real-life cases, 24
Reconstruct, 136, 198, 429, 432, 436
Re-enactment, 114, 115, 136, 138, 141, 143
Rehabilitation, 106, 124
Rehabilitative, 108, 114, 115, 119
Remediation, 136–138, 324, 330
Representation, 1, 49, 71, 111, 114, 116, 117, 139, 156, 195, 201, 237, 238, 245, 277, 278, 284, 286, 291, 292, 318–323, 327, 337, 366, 377, 378, 383–385, 389, 390, 392, 412, 423, 429, 435, 449, 488, 489
Research, 4, 11, 12, 14, 15, 17, 19, 20, 25, 32, 35, 36, 38, 39, 49–56, 59–62, 70, 73, 75–77, 79, 80, 89, 90, 92, 93, 95, 97, 98, 100, 113, 120, 133, 138, 152, 155, 157, 160, 162–166, 172, 173, 177, 178, 196, 199–202, 212, 220, 227, 230, 238–241, 243, 244, 248, 250, 258, 264, 268, 271, 277, 279, 284, 287, 289, 292, 318, 320, 325, 331, 339–341, 347, 349, 350, 358–360, 362, 363, 369–373, 377, 380, 381, 397–400, 402, 403, 405–407, 410, 411, 414–416, 424, 429, 435, 460–464, 474, 475, 494, 495, 502, 515, 516

Rhetoric, 32, 33, 35, 36, 76, 109, 173, 178, 179, 238, 239, 278, 366, 390, 445, 455, 483, 487–489
Riga Great Cemetery, 459, 465, 468, 470, 472, 473
Right
  right to appropriation, 444, 453, 454
  right to participation, 444, 453, 454
  right to the city, 443, 444, 453, 454
Russian, 19, 101, 183, 215, 217, 218, 223–225, 230, 464, 465, 468, 469

S
Scholarship of engagement, 43, 45, 155
Science, 3, 21, 23, 32, 53, 55, 73, 81, 83, 91, 101, 199, 271, 272, 338, 339, 341, 379, 398, 401, 411, 424, 507, 512, 516
Science Museum: Community-in-Residence, 362
Scotland, 106, 112, 113, 119, 326, 358
Second-hand bookshops, 284
Second-wave, 173–175, 182, 186
Self-reflexive, 3, 452
Semantic Web, 53, 89–92, 95, 97–99
Seneca language, 299, 307, 309
Serbian, 215, 217, 218, 225, 226
Serious games, 342–344, 351
Service learning, 38, 39, 41, 42, 45, 46, 105, 124, 141
Sexology, 74
Sexual, 74, 77, 82, 83, 99, 111, 118, 150, 152, 173, 180, 187, 188, 190, 216, 462
  sexual assault, 118, 149, 172, 173, 181, 186, 188–190
  sexual harassment, 172, 176, 177, 180, 186, 188
Shared authority, 70, 98, 339, 482, 491, 492, 494
Shopping-mall-ification, 449
Situated knowledges, 22
Slavic, 231
Social
  social action, 34, 39
  social change, 99, 101, 113, 119, 152, 155, 161, 166, 179, 447

social justice, 2, 71, 99, 105, 106, 119, 154, 175, 278
social media, 13, 19, 52, 70, 72, 79, 173, 178, 181, 184–186, 188, 191, 217, 218, 223, 226, 230, 237, 290, 309, 324, 325, 331, 338–340, 342, 343, 348, 350, 351, 363, 367, 370, 403, 409, 410, 413, 455, 481–488, 490–492, 494, 495, 511
social movement, 106, 171, 173–175, 177, 179, 182
social movement studies, 171
social transformation, 106, 119
Society, 12–14, 16, 24, 34–36, 40, 42, 44, 76, 82, 132, 138, 150, 151, 156, 163, 176, 196, 198, 201, 205, 206, 208, 211, 267, 268, 275–277, 279, 284, 291, 305, 318, 338, 342, 401, 423, 436, 442, 446, 450, 462, 464, 466, 482, 484, 488, 492, 495, 501, 502, 504, 508–511, 513, 516, 517
Socio-cultural, 197, 204, 210, 318–320, 323, 349, 360, 378
Socio-political, 195, 207, 211, 298, 441
Soft power, 400–403, 406–408, 410–412, 414, 415
Solidarity-building, 191
Soundscape, 424, 427–429, 434, 435
Space of appearances, 132, 137
Spatial justice, 446, 451
Spectator, 451, 505, 506, 516
Stereotypes, 107, 195, 288, 292, 358, 484
Storytelling, 69, 74, 113, 134, 175, 178, 330, 342, 347, 351, 352, 357, 359, 360, 364–366
Students, 5, 12–20, 23, 25, 26, 31–46, 96, 100, 124, 136, 153, 161, 238–252, 261, 264, 267, 268, 271, 288, 289, 292, 299, 304–307, 346, 366, 400, 426, 434, 435, 449, 450, 471, 473, 507
Stylistics, 200–202
Stylometry, 200
Survivors, 151–157, 159–161, 163, 166, 172, 173, 186, 188–190

Sustainability, 53, 61, 240, 250, 251, 400, 501–503, 508–517
Sustainable development, 501, 508, 513, 515, 516
Sütterlin, 217–219

T

Teaching, 12, 13, 15, 17–20, 22–26, 33–35, 39, 44, 46, 70, 76, 77, 83, 211, 238, 245, 248, 251, 276, 282, 305, 306, 434, 507
Technology(ies), 1, 5, 16, 18, 21–23, 53, 72, 95, 101, 107, 152, 156, 157, 160, 163, 165, 176, 178, 196–201, 206, 207, 209–212, 216, 218, 220, 230, 231, 246, 278, 319, 322, 325, 338–341, 343, 344, 347, 357, 367, 377, 379–382, 386–388, 390, 391, 401, 415, 472, 487, 493, 515
Text, 195, 197, 199–202, 204–207, 210–212
  text analysis, 250, 348, 349
  text encoding, 245, 247, 248, 250, 252
  Text Encoding Initiative (TEI), 19, 93, 95, 101, 246–248, 250
Textual, 32, 33, 52, 153, 163, 166, 200, 204, 205, 210, 247, 250, 317, 319, 332, 348, 349, 391, 463
Thematic, 5, 134, 138, 195, 202–204, 206, 210, 211, 350, 359, 464, 472–475
Theme(s), 3, 73, 78, 111, 138, 140, 153, 160, 161, 198, 199, 204, 207, 210, 211, 246, 326, 341, 348–351, 363, 402, 483, 484
They Them Studios, 78
Things Fall Apart (TFA), 195–197, 202–205, 207, 209–212
3D modelling, 22, 340, 377–381, 383–388, 392
Tombstones, 463, 465–467, 472, 473
Topic modelling, 200, 349, 351
Tourism management, 473
Traditional, 3, 12, 15–17, 20, 21, 23, 26, 35, 36, 42, 43, 51, 98, 100, 152, 166, 179, 195–200, 202–205, 207, 209, 212, 216, 227, 241, 282, 283, 285, 298–300, 303–305, 310, 323, 330, 358, 360, 363, 379, 392, 398, 408, 411, 430, 464, 483, 506
Tradition(s), 32, 33, 107, 113, 137, 164, 197, 198, 208, 210, 211, 364, 378, 379, 390, 428, 437, 463–465, 467, 468, 510
Trans
  trans history, 71, 72, 76–79, 81, 83
  trans people, 71–75, 80–82
  trans studies, 71
Transcriptional markup, 248, 249
Transformations, 72, 73, 83
Transitional objects, 133
Transkribus, 216–221, 223, 224, 227, 228, 231
Transvengers, 73, 84
Trauma, 2, 5, 108, 109, 111, 166, 173, 188
Traumatic, 108, 111, 118, 189
Tropes, 107–110, 117, 448
Turkey, 57, 110, 227, 380, 436, 442, 444–448
Turkish, 217, 218, 226, 227, 229, 441, 442, 444–448, 450, 452, 454, 455
Turkish nationalism, 445

U

Universities, 2, 12, 14, 15, 17, 18, 20, 21, 24, 26, 32, 35, 36, 39–41, 44–46, 52, 70, 71, 73, 83, 84, 114, 120, 124, 260, 264, 266, 271, 272, 284, 309, 358, 373, 426, 496
University-prison partnerships, 105, 106
Updatism, 483, 492
Urban
  urban imaginaries, 443
  urban memory, 5, 442, 454
  urban resistance, 441, 442
  urban restructuring, 445
  urban space, 442–445, 447, 449, 450, 453, 454, 513
Urbanization, 444, 445, 449
User-generated content (UGC), 342, 344, 345, 491

V

Value, 2, 6, 12, 14, 18, 19, 21–23, 31, 32, 34–36, 40, 42, 45, 52, 53, 70, 72, 75, 83, 91, 106, 112, 141, 155, 156, 161, 164, 165, 172, 176, 183, 184, 189, 196–198, 203, 207, 209, 219, 230, 243, 245, 248, 250, 270–272, 276, 278–280, 287, 289, 290, 292, 301, 306, 319, 322, 323, 327, 330, 339, 360, 370–373, 386, 387, 390, 399, 407, 412, 423, 427, 461, 462, 468, 472, 474, 513
Vernacular, 116
Versailles, 139
Virtual museums, 341–344, 351
Visitor, 71, 95, 150, 157, 164, 289–291, 305–308, 311, 317, 320–325, 329–331, 338, 339, 341–344, 346, 347, 351, 381, 387, 388, 392, 400, 402–405, 409, 412–414, 460–463, 466, 468–470, 472, 474, 484
   visitor engagement, 330, 332
   visitor experience, 323, 332, 346
Voice-over, 108–110, 112, 117
Voices, 18, 19, 41, 45, 74, 79–83, 108, 112–114, 139, 152, 153, 155, 175, 204, 276, 282–284, 288, 291, 292, 309, 331, 369, 446, 474, 509
Vox pop, 139, 143
Voyeurism, 111, 112

W

Watkins, Peter, 132, 134–145
WebGis, 431, 432, 435
Wellcome Trust, 72, 73, 84

Western, 32, 34, 60, 71, 72, 74, 83, 110, 175, 176, 195, 198, 200, 203, 207–209, 211, 212, 304, 378, 387, 391, 496, 513
Wikidata, 50, 52–62
Women, 76, 77, 90, 95–99, 101, 106–120, 149–155, 159–162, 164, 166, 174–176, 179–181, 185, 186, 188, 189, 208, 244, 276–278, 288–291, 319, 321, 339, 346, 358
Women-in-prison genre, 107–110, 117, 118
Women's activism, 97
Working classes, 276
   and education, 275
   and literacy, 285, 286, 288
   and political mobilization, 275, 285
Works, 14, 36, 41, 71–73, 76, 78, 110, 114, 135, 142, 164, 187, 189, 195–197, 199–201, 205, 206, 211, 212, 241, 260, 303, 319, 320, 327, 372, 374, 380, 390, 410, 426, 446, 449, 467, 468, 483, 503, 504, 513
World War I, 459, 464
Writing, 35, 36, 40, 41, 43, 51, 69, 72, 75, 106–108, 114, 115, 135, 183, 199, 201, 210, 216, 219, 220, 223, 225–228, 239, 245, 246, 248, 251, 278, 279, 282, 286, 287, 289, 292, 300, 308, 309, 318–320, 322, 324–328, 330, 337, 360, 364, 468

Y

YARN, 357–359, 363, 364, 366–371, 373
York-Münster, 368

Printed in the United States
by Baker & Taylor Publisher Services